HELP: 1980

The Indispensable Almanac of Consumer Information

Arthur E. Rowse, Editor

Ruth C. Fort
Joel Makower
Merrill Rose

Assistant Editors

EVEREST HOUSE
Publishers   *New York*

The editors are grateful for help beyond the call from many people, especially: Kurt Bacci, Rajni Bakshi, Valerie Cerrone, Betty Clemmer, Billie Cook, Katherine Grayson, Rose Haspadora, Patrice Hill, Bryan Howell, Thomas O'Day, Louise Franklin-Ramirez, Bettyann Rowse, Mary Elaine Rowse, Ruth Simon, Lydia Tucker and Meryl Vinitsky.

ISBN: 0-89696-071-4
Published simultaneously in Canada by Beaverbooks, Pickering, Ontario
PRINTED IN THE UNITED STATES OF AMERICA
2RRDI80

TABLE OF CONTENTS

HELP: 1980

**The Indispensable Almanac
of Consumer Information**

What's Happening To Americans

Worry and frustration amid plenty.

Those are the words most often used by pollsters and personal counselors to describe the condition of most Americans on the brink of the 1980s.

Much of the worry is about how to meet the cost of living with incomes that never seem to quite catch up. Inflationary stresses are forcing many people to alter their ways of living faster than they expect or want to. Skyrocketing prices are leading people to eat less well, entertain less, keep homes chillier in winter and warmer in summer than comfort requires and to do without many other things that used to be taken for granted. Fuel shortages are cutting vacation plans and sending people to bus stops and train stations in droves.

Life is growing more complicated also in other ways. People living near nuclear plants and working in hazardous occupations are worrying more as a result of the frightening nuclear accident at Three Mile Island and almost daily discoveries of new carcinogens and toxic waste dumps. Workers are becoming more discontented with their jobs in general and consumers are becoming more dissatisfied with the quality of products.

CHANGES COMING TOO FAST FOR MANY

Compared to people in almost all other countries, Americans still appear to be materially better off. Almost every household has at least one car and television set, plus other mechanical marvels of convenience and pleasure enjoyed by relatively few people in the world. But even those who "never had it so good" in economic terms are running into a bewildering array of problems in their daily lives. Success in the business or professional world and widespread affluence have brought malaise rather than happiness to many Americans.

Marriages are breaking up at a record pace, crime is invading the suites as well as the streets, personal relationships of all kinds seem more fragmented and bizarre actions of one kind or another more frequent. High incomes are proving no barrier to personal problems.

Particularly disconcerting is the growing realization that nobody—from top government leaders to the so-called experts on any subject—knows how to reverse the most disturbing trends. While appearing to have a plan to steer the nation back on course, successive administrations in Washington have demonstrated that they could not find the rudder. The only permanent thing seems to be change itself . . . and at an increasing pace.

Despite high incomes, abundant conveniences and limitless forms of entertainment, many Americans seem to be growing bored and unhappy with life.

A Citibank poll of 1,400 adults with incomes over $20,000 showed in early 1979 that almost 35 per cent felt they were worse off than they were 12 months earlier, while only 25 per cent thought they were better off. More than three out of four also felt the economy would get even worse in the next six months. Their forecasts proved accurate.

On the other hand, there appears to be considerable acceptance and stoicism in the face of these changes. While people seem to complain more frequently and loudly, many seem to be drawing on their own resourcefulness to keep financial and personal problems from destroying their lives. Many are making do with less and finding new pride and enjoyment in doing so. Simpler lifestyles are drawing more and more adherents in a quest for security and happiness.

POLLUTION AND COMMERCIALISM EVERYWHERE

Those who try to escape or drop out eventually find that there are no hiding places left. While it is still possible to slow down the pace of life by moving to the country, it is no longer possible to escape pollution or commercialism or crime or uncertain mail service.

People also have become more dependent on each other. The pesticide a farmer uses in Iowa turns up on dinner plates a thousand miles away, and the acid fumes from Midwest factories kill fish in mountain lakes of New York State. Carbon dioxide emitted from factories and other sources threatens to warm the world's atmosphere eventually enough to melt the ice caps and destroy coastlines everywhere with flooding oceans.

At a time when social problems are becoming more universal and more pervasive in nature, there is a growing cry for less government and more dispersal of government functions to the states and smaller units. Demands for less regulation drown out calls for cleaner air and water, leaving the problems to grow ever bigger for future generations.

NEED FOR MORE INFORMATION

Information has become a major problem. Despite an ever-increasing flood of words and pictures from the commercial media, most people remain confused. They grope for information that will help them ease their own problems, and they tend to distrust the news media when the answers are not readily available. When people find out how much they were not told about the Vietnam War, about nuclear hazards and about White House crimes before President Nixon's re-election, distrust of the media and government spreads further.

Free flow of information, of course, is the life blood of a democratic society. Voters need to know about candidates for public office before entering the polling booth. Information has also become more essential than ever to personal health and financial security. It is the quality, not the quantity, of information that can make the difference to each individual.

As the pace of life continues to quicken, people have an increasing need to know how changes will affect them. Only with this kind of information can they determine what to do for their own good. And only by learning what is happening to themselves can people determine what must be done on a larger scale by their elected leaders.

Where are we headed? With only four more years to 1984, will George Orwell's already prophetic book provide the blueprint for American life? There are growing signs that it will at least come close, unless some strong trends are reversed.

David Goodman, a research scientist, identified 137 forecasts in Orwell's work and concluded that more than 100 have already come true. Writing in the December, 1978, issue of *The Futurist* magazine Goodman said every scientific and technological development foreseen by Orwell—from the stationing of giant "lenses in space" to the military use of manufactured germs—has either already occurred or could occur in the near future with present technology.

Goodman himself invented a way to measure an animal's heartbeat from a distance, similar to the device used by Big Brother in *1984* to spy on the feelings of people and watch for suspicious physiological reactions to certain events. While scientists in the book tried to find, in Orwell's words, "how to kill several hundred million people in a few seconds without giving warning beforehand," Goodman points out that this goal is well within human capabilities at the present time.

Goodman cited the present proliferation of thought-control methods and behavior modification therapies foreseen by Orwell. "The result of all this scientific progress," said Goodman, "is a phychocivilized society—a world where people achieve better living through surgery, electrical currents, drugs . . . structural integration, bioenergetics, hypnosis and control of body language." Few, if any, of the things Orwell foresaw go beyond what is being done or can be done today, in Goodman's view, although he admits what present trends are not rapid enough to create a real *1984* in four more years.

ECONOMIC CONDITIONS

Americans are being hit hard by inflation. The average family must now earn twice what it earned in 1970 to maintain the same standard of living, according to figures of the Conference Board. A family of four earning $13,200 in 1970 would require more than $25,000 in June, 1979, to equal its 1970 purchasing power. Median family income actually rose from $9,900 to $18,800 during that time, leaving purchasing power unimproved. By July, purchasing power stood 3.9 per cent below what it was a year earlier.

Federal income taxes have dropped steadily for more than nine years, but increases in Social Security taxes have more than made up the difference. Some 35 million older people, however, narrowed their losses somewhat in July, 1979, when Social Security benefits automatically rose 9.9 per cent to match increased living costs. It was the largest single increase in the program's history.

PRICE OF NECESSITIES SOARS

Prices of necessary items went up at an annual rate of 16.4 per cent in the first quarter of 1979, according to the National Center for Economic Alternatives. These items included food, energy, housing and health care, as measured by the government index. That was more than twice the 7.8 per cent annual-rate increase for all other items in the index. Energy prices alone went up at an annual rate of 24.9 per cent at the same time, while food went up 21.6 per cent, housing rose 13.3 per cent, and medical costs increased 11.1 per cent. These items account for about 70 per cent of the budget for four of five American households. By July, the government's Consumer Price Index was 13.1 per cent higher (at an annual rate) than on January 1, 1979.

In April, 1979, the government raised its official poverty level to reflect the increase in living costs. For a non-farm family of four, the income level indicating poverty was raised to $6,700 from $6,200, the level 12 months earlier. For a farm family of four, the level was raised from $5,270 to $5,700 in the same period. Following are poverty income levels for various family sizes compared to a year earlier:

Family Size	April 1979 Continental U.S.		April 1978 Continental U.S.	
	Nonfarm	Farm	Nonfarm	Farm
1	$3,400	$2,910	$3,140	$2,690
2	4,500	3,840	4,160	3,550
3	5,600	4,770	5,180	4,410
4	6,700	5,700	6,200	5,270
5	7,800	6,630	7,220	6,130
6	8,900	7,560	8,240	6,990

Poverty levels can be important to many people, for they determine eligibility for various federal, state and local programs, including employment and training programs, housing programs, Medicare and other benefits.

CONSUMER BORROWING ESCALATES RAPIDLY

Americans are withdrawing savings and borrowing more to keep up with inflation. Spurred largely by increased use of credit cards, total consumer debt rose a record 17 per cent in 1978 to $1.2 trillion. By the end of the year, the average person owed $5,512.

Mortgage lenders are finding no shortage of customers at 11.5 per cent interest despite the fact that many borrowers wind up paying two to three times the price of the house in interest during the life of the loan.

The rapid rise in consumer debt is worrying economists and government officials more than consumers. Their main concern is that debts will become too much for many people to handle and will push the country further into an economic downturn. But the delinquency rate (failure to meet payment dates) has remained close to 2.5 per cent, well below the 3 per cent rate of the last recession.

However, bankruptcies, both commercial and individual, are rising, and so is the number of people seeking help in managing their debts. The National Foundation for Consumer Credit reported in mid-1979 that its 219 credit counselling centers were being inundated by people seeking help. (See Banking and Borrowing chapter for details on the Foundation program.)

Most advisers recommend that a family put no more than 20 per cent of its take-home pay into credit payments other than mortgage obligations. Obviously, many Americans are exceeding this guideline.

SOME PEOPLE PROFITING FROM INFLATION

Not everyone is being hurt by rising living costs. People who have money invested in tangible property increasing in value faster than living costs are in a position to profit greatly upon sale of that property. In recent years, many people have cashed in stocks, bonds, low-yield savings certificates and annuities and purchased gold, jewelry, antiques, art objects and other so-called collectibles.

Buyers of real estate generally stand to profit during inflationary times, particularly those who took out mortgages a few years ago before the latest spurt in prices and interest rates. But even at 11.5 per cent, the borrower has the advantage of deducting interest payments from income tax obligations. Then there is the new, one-time tax exemption of $100,000 for older people who profit from the sale of a family income.

THE 'RIPOFF' SOCIETY

Many may be suffering more from unjustified price increases than from passed-on cost increases. There is growing evidence that inflation is being used as an excuse for unwarranted price boosts by businesses, professionals and almost anyone who sells anything. In August, 1979, the White House went so far as to accuse food retailers and "middlemen" of failing to pass on reductions in farm prices.

After-tax profits of corporations zoomed upward in the last quarter of 1978 and first quarter of 1979, at annual rates of 44.5 and 35.1 per cent. George Meaney, president of the AFL-CIO, promptly labeled them "the grossest demonstration of profit-gouging since the opening days of the Korean War." A House subcommittee estimated oil and gas overcharges amounted to $2 billion in three years. In the second quarter of 1979, corporate profits after taxes dipped 2.4 per cent, according to the Commerce Department, largely because of a sharp decline in automobile sales.

Profits in the petroleum industry continued high, however, fueling a new wave of public resentment at the oil companies. Gasoline retailers were added to the public's hate list as prices at the pump soared throughout the spring and summer while service stations cut down on operating hours and accompanying services. Ironically, many retailers protested to the government that their profit margins were being squeezed unfairly by regulations of the Department of Energy. The Department promptly relaxed them.

BUSINESS PUTS BLAME ON GOVERNMENT POLICIES

The main reason for inflation, in the eyes of most business representatives, is the federal government. The blame has been placed at various times on increases in minimum wages, environmental regulations, product safety rules, "red tape," government waste, excessive taxation, rising budget deficits and unwise monetary and fiscal policies. When Chrysler Corporation verged on bankruptcy in late August, 1979, company officials sought to blame government regulations.

Some government policies and actions indeed raise consumer costs and prices. Regulations restricting airlines, truckers, farmers and ocean shipping firms especially have raised consumer prices and helped spark the campaign for "regulatory reform." But when efforts were launched to eliminate some of the uneconomic rules, many firms in the affected industries rose up in opposition. Large firms in regulated industries, despite their loud complaints, generally favor government regulations because they tend to make it harder for small firms to compete. Farmers also tend to favor government subsidies and marketing restrictions that raise consumer prices.

Thanks greatly to the business-oriented campaign for regulatory reform, "Washington" has become a dirty word in many parts of the nation. It has become fashionable for political candidates—from Presidents on down—to campaign against "big government," "government spending" and other popular symbols of contempt for the national government. The rash of ethical and crimincal complaints against members of Congress has added to the disdain.

PROBLEMS OF SOCIETY MORE PERVASIVE

When major consumer problems arise, the usual attitude of business representatives is to leave it to the states, where legislators can more easily be controlled.

One example is state policing of automobile insurance, health insurance, life insurance and almost all other types of insurance despite their interstate characteristics. Few states have taken effective action to contain major abuses in these fields.

While business interests continue to fight federal regulations on a broad front and encourage state regulation as the only alternative, many of the consumer problems become more pervasive and more national in scope. Insurance is but one example.

Others are the problems of water and air pollution, industrial and municipal disposal, transportation of hazardous products, consumer fraud and deception and production of potentially hazardous products such as nuclear power. Businesses that used to be only local in nature now have the potential of affecting people in all states and nations.

INCREASING CONCENTRATION OF BUSINESS

Not only are such problems broader in scope but so are the business firms associated with them. What happens in American society is determined by fewer and fewer large corporations and wealthy individuals. One per cent of the population now owns more than 14 per cent of all bank deposits and real estate, half of all stocks and bonds and one-fourth of the value of everything owned in the United States, according to *U.S. News & World Report.*

In the business world, only 100 of the 1.5 million corporations get half of all profits in manufacturing, and 200 firms get 70 per cent, according to a 1978 study by the Senate Subcommittee on Reports headed by the late Lee Metcalf of Montana. Large firms are also tied together with others through joint membership on boards of directors (joint directorships). Although competitors are prohibited by law from sitting on the same board of directors, they often sit together on other boards. These links tend to discourage competition and encourage similar policies.

Industry after industry has been taken over by a few large firms. The number of industries controlled by four or fewer companies has increased steadily through horizontal mergers (purchase of competitors). Vertical mergers have also increased corporate concentration. The oil industry is a prime example of vertical integration, the ownership of all major marketing operations from production to retailing.

With few firms still available for merger, the desire for further acquisition has become channeled into conglomerate mergers, the take-over of unrelated firms by one large firm. The merger movement reached a high point in early 1979, according to the Federal Trade Commission, more than double the rate in 1978 when the value of 2,000 mergers reached $34 billion.

The growing power of corporations has begun to worry some public officials. FTC Chairman Michael Pertschuk expressed concern in 1979 that "these huge private enterprises, which are among the most tightly controlled organizations in our society, will increase their power at the expense of smaller and less organized groups and the individual." He said the principal danger "is encroachment upon the viability of bedrock institutions: a free market, a responsive political system, a pluralistic society."

BUSINESS TIPS BALANCE IN WASHINGTON

There is growing evidence that corporations already swing the balance of power in the Nation's Capital. When the FTC proposed some restrictions on television commercials aimed at inducing children to eat sugary products, it ran into a concerted campaign of opposition including not only cereal and candy industries but advertising agencies, broadcasters and general business interests.

Before the FTC proposal was decided, an internal memorandum of the Association of National Advertisers privately proclaimed that the combined power of the business groups had effectively "neutralized" the federal agency's public hearing as well as the press itself. For other examples of business influence on national events, see the chapter on "Making Your Voice Count."

Numerous state legislatures have gained the reputation of being subservient to large corporate interests. Yet few of the news media maintain effective surveillance over such things. In Texas, the situation reached the point where a state legislator who became a judge called the legislature "a wholly owned subsidiary of big business and special interest groups."

GOVERNMENT INCREASES ANTITRUST ACTIVITY

Until a few years ago, there was little effort by either state or federal governments to pursue price fixers. During the late 1960s and early 1970s, an average of only 30 people and 55 corporations were indicted on federal charges. Since 1977, the number of individuals and corporations indicted has risen to 103 and 153 respectively.

Penalties have increased, from virtually none 10 years ago to nearly $2 million in individual fines, $11 million in corporate fines and prison for 29 individuals in 1978. But those are not large figures for the size of the problem. State attorneys general also have stepped up their antitrust activity.

In late 1978 and early 1979, the Justice Department filed antitrust suits against producers of copper wire, electric fuses, gas meters, water heaters, packaged meat, milk and lead additives, among other items. And it agreed to settle cases involving manufacturers of electrical wiring devices; wholesalers of plastics, adhesives and cigarettes; the New York Coffee and Sugar Exchange; and marine construction firms.

In June, 1979, the largest criminal fine ever imposed under the Sherman Antitrust Act was levied against seven large shipping firms and 13 executives. Penalties totaled $6.1 million. They were charged with conspiring to fix prices on container freight shipments between U.S. and Europe between 1971 and 1975. No jail sentences were imposed, but each executive was fined $50,000 on misdemeanor charges.

This increased activity of state and federal agencies has had no noticeable effect, however. Economic interests continue to become more concentrated and more powerful economically and politically over the lives of individual Americans.

LIVING CONDITIONS

The United States is undergoing some sweeping social changes, many of which are not readily visible. One is the steady aging of the population.

This is occurring because of continuing declines in the birthrate and continuing increases in the life span. Back in 1900, the average lifetime was 50 years; in 1976, the average had grown to 73 years, according to the National Center for Health Statistics.

Women have greatly widened their edge in longevity, now outliving men by nearly eight years. A white baby boy born in 1976 had a life expectancy of 69.7 years, compared to 77.3 years for a white female baby. Lives are about five years shorter for non-whites of both sexes. People in a number of other countries, however, outlive Americans.

DROP IN INFANT MORTALITY

One of the reasons for increased ages is the steady drop in infant mortality. In 1976, says NCHS, 11 infants out of 1,000 were likely to die within a month of birth, compared to 20 in 1950, a drop in the rate of almost 50 per cent.

The birth rate has been dropping almost as fast, from 23.6 per 1,000 people to 14.8 in the same period. For many years, the population increased more than 1 per cent a year, but since 1972, the rate has fallen below that figure.

Birth rates have been dropping largely because marriage rates have been falling. From a high of 12.2 marriages per 1,000 people in 1945, the rate dropped to 8.5 in 1960, then spurted upward to 11.0 in 1972 and went back down steadily to 10.0 in 1976, the latest year for which NCHS has data. Divorces have steadily increased from 1.2 per 1,000 in 1930 and 3.5 in 1945 to 5.0 in 1976. That meant a ratio of marriages to divorces of 2 to 1, compared to a ratio of 6 to 1 in the 1930s and 1940s.

Death rates are also dropping. From 1945 to 1976, they went from 10.9 to 8.9 per 1,000 people. If present trends continue, more than one in eight Americans will be 65 years of age or more by the year 2000.

Causes of death are also changing. In 1900, the leading causes were influenza and pneumonia; next in order were heart and cerebrovascular diseases. In 1976, the latest year for such data, the leading cause was heart disease, followed by cancer, cerebrovascular diseases and accidents.

POPULATION MOVING WEST AND SOUTH

People are still moving geographically to the south and west as well as away from the big cities. But there are signs that this latter trend may be reversing. Moves back to the city are being speeded up by the influx of many city problems in the suburbs, including crime, traffic and noise. Shortages and high prices of gasoline may also hasten this shift.

People moving in and out of the city tend to be well above the poverty level, while those who remain are often below. Large numbers of legal and illegal aliens are taking over menial jobs and buying up small businesses in the inner cities. The result is more demand for public services and less ability of cities to pay for them.

These changes are putting unprecedented pressures on urban budgets, forcing some cities to the brink of bankruptcy and sending mayors to Washington for federal assistance. At the request of the Carter Administration, Congress raised money for this purpose but far less than the amounts likely to be needed.

Efforts to revive central cities by enticing large companies to locate there have had only limited success. A survey of 352 firms by Rep. Henry Reuss (D-WI) in 1978 showed many reluctant to move into these areas because of crime, high land prices, pollution, high taxes and lack of decent schools.

EFFORTS TO PRESERVE NEIGHBORHOODS

President Carter took note of these problems in 1978 when he announced a National Urban Policy to conserve communities and neighborhoods. He called for 160 "improvements" to make federal programs more sensitive to urban problems. He announced more low-cost loans for housing rehabilitation, more revenue sharing and a national development bank to encourage business expansion in distressed areas. (See Housing and Land chapter for further details.)

In 1979, a massive study by the National Commission on Neighborhoods issued 200 recommendations. Rather than seeking new programs, it urged a realignment of existing programs, plus "a united effort to reorganize our society—away from the stranglehold of a relative few with a near monopoly of power and money in political, social and economic institutions to a new democratic system of grass-roots involvement that allows individuals to have control over their own lives."

Among the recommendations were calls for revision of tax laws to encourage neighborhood rebirth and a shift of federal funds to older areas, plus a program to create jobs and an end to discrimination in lending practices against inner-city areas.

NUMBER OF HOUSEHOLDS SOARING

Households have also been changing rapidly. New ones are now forming three times as fast as the population is growing. Households are also becoming smaller, largely because of the breakup of family units. As a result, the demand for housing has pushed real estate prices up faster than construction costs.

To help pay the increased housing costs, more people from each household are working. Women are moving out of the kitchen and into the job market in large numbers. From 1965 to 1975, the average number of hours spent at home by women dropped from 50 to 44, according to the U.S. Department of Commerce. This has meant less time for the traditional role of caring for children and more demand for child-care services than ever before.

Men also are spending less time at home and in family activities, although many men have swapped homemaking chores with working wives. Leisure time is taking bigger portions of life for both men and women, with the average number of hours in such activities increasing from 35 to 39 per week in the 10-year period studied by Commerce.

Most leisure time is spent watching television. From 1960 to 1974, the percentage of people claiming that TV-watching was their favorite leisure activity rose from 28 to 46, according to a Gallup Poll. But surveys since then have indicated that the television viewing is dropping in favor of more active, spare-time pursuits.

INFLATION ADDS TO PERSONAL PROBLEMS

Inflation is adding to problems of nervous tension caused by overcrowded living conditions, jammed shopping centers, highway traffic, financial pressures and personal conflicts. In place of the more direct, physical hazards of earlier times are more subtle, hidden ones, such as carcinogens and pollution.

The impact of emotional strain on the human body is well known. Some studies indicate a direct link between economic anxiety and suicide rates, divorces, admissions to mental hospitals, death from alcoholism and crime. A chain reaction often occurs. Financial reverses cause stress among family members, causing separations and splitups, which in turn make financial problems worse for those involved. Many Americans know this chain reaction all too well.

Inflation is also affecting health care, according to a survey for General Mills in 1979. Sixteen per cent of families reported cutting back on dental work because of inflation, while 13 per cent were reducing annual checkups, 11 per cent cutting back on eyeglass exams and 19 per cent serving lower quality meals than a year earlier.

MENTAL HEALTH PROBLEMS INCREASE

Increasing stresses of life are having a devastating effect on the mental and emotional stability of Americans. In 1978, the President's Commission on Mental Health concluded that between 20 and 32 million Americans "need some kind of mental health care at any one time" in addition to the estimated 6 million people considered mentally retarded. According to some members of the Commission, the total of mentally ill people in the U.S. is closer to 40 million.

One of the main reasons for such high figures, said the report, was the continuing stigma attached to mental illness. It cited "negative public attitudes" toward getting treatment for these ailments. By 1979, much of the stigma was beginning to wear off, as more and more people were seeking help with mental problems.

On the other hand, psychiatry itself may be entering what *Time* magazine calls a "depression." Many of its methods and practices are being questioned as to their effectiveness. Drug and diet therapies are replacing other forms of treatment.

But, according to former HEW Secretary Joseph Califano, physical health is improving. "We have made considerable progress in improving the health status of Americans," he said in a detailed report to President Carter in December, 1978.

As evidence, he pointed to increased life expectancy, record low death rates and a decline in the toll from acute respiratory diseases. He also noted a decrease in heart disease. But he acknowledged that "serious problems remain."

WHERE IS THE BEST PLACE TO LIVE?
Urban Areas Compared for Quality of Life

Which are the better metropolitan areas for overall living conditions?

The answer would vary for each individual, depending on the importance given to various factors, such as being near one's family or friends or to cultural or recreation sources. There is no widely accepted set of statistics to determine the overall quality of living conditions. But it is possible to compare metropolitan areas on the basis of some health, environmental and social characteristics using statistics from public and private sources.

According to the latest revision in 1979, the San Francisco-Oakland metropolitan area once again scored the highest among 50 places, with Minneapolis-St. Paul and Rochester, N.Y., again in second and third place. However, the rankings changed substantially for many other cities because of new information factored into the comparison.

WESTERN AREAS IMPROVE STANDINGS

Moving up to fourth place, from 11th place, was San Diego, Calif., while Sacramento rose from seventh to fifth place. Also moving up were Washington and Honolulu, from eighth and ninth place to a tie for sixth place. Milwaukee improved its position, from 10th to 8th and Los Angeles-Long Beach rose from 13th to ninth. On the East Coast, Boston went from 15th to 11th, and New York rose all the way from 25th to 12th place. Also jumping substantially in the standings were Miami, from 28th to 14th; Newark, N.J., from 29th to 13th; and Buffalo, from 30th to 19th. Baltimore rose from 45th to 22nd place.

On the other hand, some metropolitan areas dropped in the rankings. Indianapolis was perhaps the biggest loser, falling from fifth place to 21st, with Denver-Boulder, Colo., dropping from sixth to 18th, and Seattle-Everett, Wash., down from fourth to 10th place.

Each area was compared in 16 categories rather than the 14 used previously. Air pollution and weather factors were given extra weight by counting each of the two types of pollution and each of the two weather factors separately rather than as one combined score. Overall rankings are based on the sum of each city's ranking in each category. (See table.)

COMPARISON OF STATE QUALITIES

Following is a comparison of all 50 states and the District of Columbia on 15 controversial issues selected to reflect governmental concern for human values.

The issues include whether a state has laws requiring registration of charities TV/radio repair shops and automobile repair shops. Registration itself does not guarantee integrity, but studies indicate that it fosters more responsible operations than would otherwise exist.

Two issues involve landlord-tenant relations. Both indicate an effort by a state to improve tenant rights, which traditionally have been ignored by state and local laws.

Other issues include whether a state has a law allowing lower cost generic drugs to be substituted by pharmacists for higher-priced branded items; whether a state has federally approved regulations governing the quality of mobile homes; whether a state has a law allowing motorists to collect for accidental losses regardless of fault; whether open dating of foods is required in order to help shoppers avoid stale and spoiled products; whether there is a law to control hazardous substances; whether private trade schools are regulated; whether a state's public utility laws and regulations are consumer-oriented, according to a study done by Common Cause, a public interest group; whether a state has any tax incentives for installation of solar energy in the home; and whether a state has a law allowing terminally ill patients to be allowed to die rather than kept alive against their will or that of close relatives.

Total scores indicate that the leading states in these areas are California and Connecticut, followed closely by Florida, Massachusetts Michigan and Oregon. The worst state, with a score of only 1, is Wyoming.

THE QUALITY OF LIFE IN 50 METROPOLITAN AREAS

HELP: The Indispensable Almanac—1980

Metropolitan Area	Overall rank	Previous rank	16 Per capita income	15 Unemployment rate (pct.)	14 Per capita gov't. expenditure on health, welfare	13 Per capita gov't expenditure on education	12 Voting participation (% over 18 voting)	11 Crime rate (crimes/100,000 persons)	10 High school grads (% of adults over 25)	9 Average days above 90°, below 32°	8 Rainy and snowy days per year	7 Particles in air (µg/m³)	6 Sulfur dioxide in air (µg/m³)	5 Infant mortality per 1,000 births	4 Doctors per 100,000 population	3 Poverty rate (percent)	2 Budget, urban family of four	1 Income disparity index (city/suburb)
San Francisco	1	1	9260	5.7	230.12	418.32	58.1	8052.2	66.1	7	62	62.2	10.2	12.5	290.0	11.9	27,421	.84
Minneapolis	2	2	8021	3.5	158.18	379.17	70.6	5687.8	65.1	172	127	76.0	30.1	13.1	189.6	6.7	23,186	.92
Rochester	3	3	7751	5.7	188.64	436.96	59.4	4846.8	56.3	146	184	93.6	35.0	12.4	229.9	7.4	23,186	.80
San Diego	4	11	7070	6.1	149.80	403.45	49.4	6547.8	65.3	3	41	78.1	10.0	13.7	221.9	10.9	21,848	1.08
Sacramento	5	7	7119	8.3	145.34	441.52	57.4	8026.4	65.1	94	58	66.2	0.0	13.4	201.8	11.3	22,071	1.03
Washington	6	8	9306	5.0	183.51	419.96	43.0	6277.2	68.3	111	117	92.6	65.1	18.7	236.8	8.3	24,078	.84
Honolulu	6	9	7950	7.0	4.64	NA	49.1	6231.6	66.0	9	102	46.5	6.8	13.7	175.4	8.8	27,421	NA
Milwaukee	8	10	7908	3.9	176.08	426.64	61.7	4691.2	56.8	155	136	118.6	27.4	13.9	167.6	7.9	23,409	.82
Los Angeles	9	13	8429	6.2	220.11	389.32	49.3	7201.5	62.0	5	35	127.5	24.0	13.8	229.1	10.9	22,294	1.03
Seattle	10	4	8457	6.1	32.55	312.58	58.5	6746.6	67.8	35	166	65.3	26.3	14.3	233.1	7.5	22,071	1.07
Boston	11	15	7590	6.1	54.74	347.25	57.0	6445.2	62.6	109	139	92.7	95.8	13.3	293.6	8.5	26,350	.79
New York City	12	25	8105	7.8	531.32	380.42	57.9	6967.3	50.1	97	129	108.9	48.0	17.3	370.9	11.9	27,421	.84
Newark	13	29	8632	7.4	138.23	377.40	34.2	5421.6	55.9	104	130	101.0	70.0	18.4	205.5	9.1	23,855	.56
Miami	14	28	7755	5.8	90.88	333.56	47.7	9482.1	51.9	32	129	68.7	7.0	16.6	295.9	14.2	20,733	.77
Syracuse	15	12	6514	NA	179.64	421.51	56.9	4443.9	57.8	145	199	101.7	26.3	13.1	198.7	9.5	22,294	.96
Cleveland	16	24	8315	5.4	110.89	343.86	52.4	5378.4	54.6	126	138	120.2	76.4	16.6	218.2	9.0	22,294	.66
Portland	17	14	7875	NA	11.80	391.27	60.6	7776.0	62.9	53	155	85.5	26.0	15.7	218.6	9.7	21,406	.93
Denver	18	6	8050	4.6	96.27	391.43	64.0	6806.5	67.4	196	106	141.4	13.5	13.5	149.1	10.0	21,179	1.02
Buffalo	19	30	6980	7.5	203.84	389.81	55.7	4798.3	50.4	138	194	108.3	20.2	18.0	197.0	9.1	23,855	.85
Richmond	20	16	7897	4.2	86.58	269.58	54.5	6461.5	46.3	126	118	63.4	28.5	15.3	243.0	12.1	20,288	.90
Indianapolis	21	5	7563	5.4	139.81	278.48	57.9	6452.4	56.0	135	130	96.8	27.3	13.8	184.9	8.8	21,402	1.04
Baltimore	22	45	7155	6.9	107.61	374.12	43.7	6473.4	44.6	130	121	113.4	26.3	18.1	250.4	11.3	22,517	.79
Houston	23	20	8247	3.5	36.99	310.03	52.3	6143.1	51.7	105	109	92.4	9.0	16.0	181.6	12.6	19,842	1.05

(Omaha)	1.10	21,400	9.3	199.2	13.5	63.5	49.7	110	1/4	62.7	2837.1	51.2	304.88	82.08	3.8	6986	19	24
Phoenix	1.00	20,956	10.9	202.6	14.4	9.4	146.0	34	178	60.1	9482.2	53.5	220.60	55.73	5.2	7174	17	24
Salt Lake City	1.20	20,288	9.5	195.9	12.5	16.0	98.0	106	192	67.6	6578.8	69.5	347.58	20.67	4.3	6466	18	26
Kansas City	.92	21,848	9.6	169.9	15.2	13.0	99.4	110	140	59.9	7099.4	51.0	299.02	67.16	4.0	7883	26	27
Tulsa	1.35	20,288	12.7	117.1	16.0	5.3	61.1	94	154	56.2	5781.6	59.8	268.12	42.21	3.6	7383	32	28
Chicago	.80	22,740	9.3	195.2	19.5	105.8	121.4	135	139	53.9	6142.7	55.0	387.31	35.72	5.1	8522	34	29
Atlanta	.84	20,288	11.7	165.4	16.4	22.6	83.3	117	77	50.4	6225.2	46.2	292.84	105.84	5.7	7352	27	30
Cincinnati	.93	20,510	10.6	183.2	13.3	25.4	93.3	168	134	48.4	5145.1	42.5	370.64	89.58	6.0	7272	21	30
Philadelphia	.83	22,963	10.9	213.1	17.8	68.2	110.2	117	120	50.6	4289.8	44.1	328.67	67.20	7.5	7436	40	30
Columbus	.81	21,625	9.7	170.7	17.6	32.0	90.9	174	132	59.9	6588.3	57.2	330.99	71.43	5.7	6798	33	33
New Orleans	.93	19,619	14.5	225.2	19.6	8.3	79.8	114	80	45.8	5453.4	52.2	228.35	47.77	5.3	6801	36	34
San Antonio	.65	19,173	20.1	167.2	12.8	6.8	55.6	80	135	46.5	6631.5	44.2	310.69	43.96	5.8	6007	45	34
Dallas	1.03	20,065	16.5	149.1	16.6	5.9	81.8	80	127	53.6	7530.4	53.2	302.72	42.34	3.7	7704	22	36
Detroit	.80	22,740	8.5	152.6	17.3	43.3	120.9	137	158	52.2	7915.8	54.9	372.02	100.55	7.8	8535	43	36
Oklahoma City	1.04	20,288	12.5	176.5	17.6	3.7	71.8	85	144	59.6	6838.4	54.7	232.78	33.88	4.0	6932	34	36
Charlotte	1.22	20,288	13.0	117.8	14.6	14.4	48.7	114	103	44.9	6473.9	43.7	312.21	75.36	3.2	7050	45	39
Louisville	.91	20,065	11.3	174.9	13.2	51.7	73.7	130	116	46.5	5615.3	51.0	242.49	52.72	5.7	7300	31	40
Nashville	.95	20,065	14.3	203.0	13.6	11.3	60.9	123	112	47.3	5418.3	30.3	225.42	46.58	NA	6647	23	41
Toledo	.86	21,625	9.2	140.3	14.7	22.4	100.6	148	148	51.9	6191.8	45.1	324.53	53.12	NA	7312	37	42
Pittsburgh	.91	21,402	9.5	168.6	15.9	64.4	156.5	156	113	53.4	3289.6	52.6	305.68	36.51	6.7	7487	38	43
Memphis	.91	20,065	11.3	197.6	17.7	13.8	78.4	123	112	48.2	7055.4	48.8	228.12	67.92	5.3	6465	47	44
Providence	.97	22,294	10.2	198.8	15.7	49.2	85.5	135	131	44.4	5572.3	56.8	262.26	21.37	7.9	6850	41	45
Birmingham	.84	19,396	19.5	188.6	14.1	11.2	141.5	118	100	44.9	5229.8	42.5	220.60	55.73	6.5	6812	39	46
Tampa	.93	19,619	14.5	150.4	16.2	NA	NA	107	89	50.7	7488.3	52.9	279.55	37.63	5.4	6406	48	47
St. Louis	.78	21,406	10.9	173.5	16.7	49.3	121.2	116	143	47.8	7103.0	36.8	309.04	43.63	5.4	7524	50	48
Jacksonville	NA	19,619	17.6	142.0	19.0	NA	NA	116	95	50.8	7362.6	45.0	313.59	111.21	5.9	6536	49	49
Norfolk	.92	19,619	16.6	125.8	21.1	42.0	61.7	118	83	46.9	6041.9	39.6	247.40	91.64	7.1	6111	42	50

SOURCES: Data for above are the latest available from the following sources, with dates, listed by column from left to right: (1) Advisory Commission on Intergovernment Relations, 1973; (2) For high-budget urban family of four, U.S. Department of Health, Education and Welfare; (3) Census of population, 1970, Department of Commerce; (4) Bureau of Census, 1974-5; (5) Number of deaths of infants under one year divided by number of live births, HEW, 1975; (6 & 7) Council on Municipal Performance, N.Y., and Environmental Protection Agency, 1968-73; (8 & 9) National Oceanic and Atmospheric Administration, 1976; (10) Bureau of Census, 1974-5; (11) Federal Bureau of Investigation, 1975; (12) Percentage of eligible voters casting ballots in 1976 Presidential election; (13 & 14) Bureau of Economic Analysis, Department of Commerce, 1975-6; (15) Department of Labor, March, 1979; (16) Bureau of Economic Analysis, Department of Commerce for 1977. Metropolitan areas are standard Metropolitan Statistical Areas.

STATES WITH PRO-CONSUMER LAWS
See text for explanation of laws

	Alabama	Alaska	Arizona	Arkansas	California	Colorado	Connecticut	Delaware	Dist. of Col.	Florida	Georgia	Hawaii	Idaho	Illinois	Indiana	Iowa	Kansas	Kentucky	Louisiana	Maine	Maryland	Massachusetts	Michigan
Number of positive scores	3	6	5	6	13	7	13	7	6	12	6	7	3	9	4	6	7	7	8	7	10	12	12
Death with dignity laws				×	×								×										
Unit pricing of foods required							×			×				×						×	×	×	
TV/radio repair registration required					×		×		×	×					×				×			×	
Tax incentives for solar energy		×	×	×	×	×	×	×			×	×	×	×	×		×		×	×	×	×	×
Effective utilities regulations	×				×		×		×	×		×					×		×			×	×
Private trade schools regulated	×	×	×		×	×		×	×	×		×		×		×	×		×			×	×
Hazardous substances act			×		×	×	×			×				×	×		×	×		×	×	×	×
Registration of charities required				×	×		×		×	×	×	×		×		×	×	×		×	×	×	×
Open dating of foods required					×		×			×				×									×
No-fault auto insurance in effect				×		×	×	×		×	×	×					×	×			×	×	×
Mobile home rules approved by U.S.	×	×	×	×	×	×	×	×		×	×		×	×	×	×	×	×	×	×	×	×	×
Rent deposits must be put into escrow		×			×	×	×	×		×	×	×		×		×		×	×	×	×	×	×
Landlord-tenant rights established		×	×		×		×	×		×		×				×		×		×	×	×	×
Generic drug substitution allowed		×		×	×	×	×	×	×	×	×					×		×		×	×	×	×
Auto repair shop registration required					×		×		×					×					×		×		×

State	1	2	3	4	5	6	7	8	9	10	11	12	13	14	15	Total
Minnesota	–	×	×	×	×	×	×	–	×	×	–	×	–	–	–	9
Mississippi	–	–	–	–	×	–	–	×	–	×	–	–	–	–	–	3
Missouri	–	–	–	–	×	–	–	–.	–	–	×	–	–	–	–	2
Montana	–	×	×	–	×	–	–	–	×	×	–	×	–	–	–	6
Nebraska	–	–	×	–	×	–	–	×	–	×	–	–	–	–	–	4
Nevada	–	–	×	×	×	–	–	–	–	×	–	×	–	×	×	7
New Hampshire	×	×	×	×	×	–	–	×	×	×	–	×	–	–	–	9
New Jersey	–	–	–	×	×	×	×	×	×	–	×	×	–	×	–	9
New Mexico	–	×	–	×	×	–	–	–	×	×	–	×	–	–	×	7
New York	×	–	–	×	×	×	–	×	–	–	×	×	–	×	–	8
North Carolina	–	–	×	×	×	–	–	×	×	×	–	×	–	–	×	8
North Dakota	–	–	×	×	×	×	–	–	×	×	×	×	–	–	–	8
Ohio	–	×	×	×	×	–	–	×	×	×	×	–	–	–	–	8
Oklahoma	–	×	–	×	×	–	–	×	×	×	×	×	–	–	–	8
Oregon	–	×	×	–	×	×	×	×	×	×	–	×	×	×	×	12
Pennsylvania	–	×	×	×	×	×	–	×	–	×	–	×	–	–	–	7
Rhode Island	×	×	×	×	×	–	×	×	×	×	–	×	–	×	–	10
South Carolina	–	–	–	–	×	×	–	×	×	×	–	–	–	–	–	5
South Dakota	–	–	×	–	×	×	–	×	–	–	×	×	–	–	–	6
Tennessee	×	×	×	–	×	–	×	×	×	×	×	×	–	–	–	11
Texas	–	–	–	×	×	×	–	–	×	–	×	×	–	–	×	7
Utah	–	×	–	–	×	×	–	–	–	–	–	×	–	–	4
Vermont	–	–	×	×	–	–	–	–	×	×	–	×	×	×	–	7
Virginia	–	×	×	×	×	×	×	×	×	×	–	×	–	–	–	10
Washington	–	–	×	×	×	–	×	×	–	–	×	×	–	–	×	8
West Virginia	×	–	–	–	×	–	–	×	–	×	–	–	–	–	–	4
Wisconsin	–	×	×	×	×	–	–	×	×	×	–	×	–	–	–	8
Wyoming	–	–	–	–	×	–	–	–	–	–	–	–	–	–	–	1

Sources: Council of State Governments, *Book of the States 1978-79* (auto repair registration, generic drugs, landlord-tenant rights, rent in escrow, mobile homes, open-dating of foods, private trade schools, TV/radio repair, unit pricing, death with dignity); Common Cause (effective utilities regulation); American Association of Fund-Raising Counsel (registration of charities); Consumer Product Safety Commission (hazardous substances); National Bureau of Standards (solar incentives); and American Mutual Insurance Alliance (no-fault insurance).

Individual Rights

In This Chapter

- **Rights of Women**
- **Rights of the Disabled**
- **Marketplace Rights**
- **Rights of the Elderly**
- **Right to Privacy**
- **Marriage and Divorce Laws**

Americans are proud of their rights, and they keep asking for more. But their success rate is extremely spotty. A Supreme Court with four appointees of President Nixon continues to chip away at decisions of the Earl Warren court, which touched off the explosion of new rights with its school desegregation decision of 1954. And lower courts continue to behave erratically, allowing special interests to shop around for judges friendly to their points of view.

Many new voices have been raised in pursuit of rights. Indians have become more insistent on obtaining vast land areas allegedly taken from them illegally, and in some cases, they have gained ground. Then there are the elderly, the handicapped, the women, the "pro-life" groups, the taxpayers, the homosexuals, even the Nazis, all demanding more rights.

Society has never been so splintered by diverse groups pressing for changes in traditional relationships and institutions. Groups tend to feed on each other, with one group's methods and manners copied by another, while others spawn opposition groups. All compete for public attention and support, mainly through the news media, which have grown more wary and cautious of pressure groups over the years. Essentially, each group represents individuals who feel that they are being denied rights which they should have as American citizens.

DEMANDS NOT CONFINED TO FRINGE GROUPS

The rights movement is beginning to encompass all of society, including those who are supposed to be in the driver's seat. In 1979, for example, the Nation's Capital saw the spectacle of hundreds of farmers tying up traffic with $30,000 tractors to demonstrate for higher prices for their crops at a time when overall farm income was at record heights. The farmers were followed a few months later by dozens of independent truckers using their own $50,000 tractor-trailers to press their right to more diesel fuel at a time when ordinary motorists were waiting in line for hours at a time to get gasoline at nearly $1 per gallon.

Business executives are complaining more than ever about alleged losses of rights to hire whom they please and generally conduct their businesses as they wish. They see the government itself as an ominous threat to the "right of free enterprise."

The U.S. Chamber of Commerce set up a "grassroots lobby" called Citizens Choice to keep individual freedoms from eroding further. And the National Association of Manufacturers began calling more members to Washington to demonstrate—behind the scenes with personal contacts—against or for various government actions deemed to threaten business freedom.

INDIVIDUAL RIGHTS WEAKENED IN MANY CASES

Many individual rights have been weakened in recent years if one looks at key court decisions. The Supreme Court headed by Warren Burger has wavered on some issues but has generally done little to protect the average person from unfairness or injustice.

The court has narrowed the scope of desegregation by ruling that evidence of discrimination itself is not enough to warrent corrective action; there must also be proof that discrimination is the basic purpose as well as the result. The court has also put new roadblocks in the way of group suits—sometimes called "class actions"—by people with a common grievance.

Earlier court decisions leaning toward awarding attorney fees to public interest groups that win court cases were overturned in a case brought by the Wilderness Society against the Alaskan pipeline company. In effect, the court denied court access to citizens who cannot afford legal counsel to represent their interests.

Later, in the Illinois Brick Company case, the court ruled that only the direct purchaser of goods can collect treble damages when the seller is found guilty of antitrust violations. Thus, the state of Illinois could not collect from the Company for overcharges passed on to consumers; only builders who bought the cinder blocks could.

On the other hand, the Supreme Court ruled in June, 1979, that purchasers of items for their personal use have the right to file suit for triple damages against violators of antitrust laws. The decision restored a suit by a hearing aid buyer against five manufacturers charged with fixing prices.

CONSUMER GROUPS LOSE STANDING

Meanwhile, the right of citizen groups to bring suit as public representatives ran into trouble with the Justice Department and lower courts. Ralph Nader's stock in trade, the lawsuit to block a certain action or policy deemed harmful to the public, hit a legal stumbling block in March, 1979, when a federal judge said Nader had no legal right to file such a suit against the Food and Drug Administration.

The suit sought to overturn regulations allowing drug manufacturers to continue selling products containing ingredients that had not been proven effective. Judge John J. Sirica, who became known for his Watergate decisions, turned down the suit because Nader's Public Citizen group had no dues-paying members and no elected officers. Sirica said neither Nader nor his group could claim to represent all consumers and therefore did not have what lawyers call "standing" before the federal courts. Sirica later relaxed his ruling.

The Justice Department doubled the shock two months later when it said Consumers Union lacked standing in a suit it brought against the Federal Reserve Board. The consumer organization, which has members and elected officers, was seeking to overturn the Fed's decision to weaken the three-day cooling off period in which a consumer can cancel certain credit transactions.

In a memorandum submitted to the D.C. District Court, Justice argued that CU lacked standing because it did not demonstrate that the issue was "germane to the organization's purpose." Relying on Sirica's decision, Justice said CU's suit was not "the product of pressure brought to bear by individual members who wish CU to advocate and protect their interests." Many citizen groups may suffer because of these cases.

FIRST AMENDMENT RIGHTS KNOCKED DOWN

First amendment rights also have lost ground. Although press protection from libel suits has generally been broadened, rights of individual journalists and their oganizations have suffered in other ways.

The Supreme Court has ruled in favor of police searches of a newspaper office without a warrant or advance notice and has approved secret government seizure of personal telephone records of reporters. It also has implicitly approved of the jailing of numerous reporters who refuse to submit their notes to courts when subpoenaed to do so. And it has approved of barring the press and public from pre-trial hearings.

A 1979 case involving alleged libel may indicate a change of view by the Supreme Court on libel matters. The court decided in favor of forcing reporters to reveal their "thought processes" in order to help complainants determine whether any malice was involved. The case involved a claim by Lt. Col. Anthony Herbert that CBS' *Sixty Minutes* had falsely portrayed him as a liar when questioning him about war crimes in Vietnam.

The first case of a news organization being legally prohibited in advance from publishing something also occurred in 1979 when the Justice Department sought to block the *Progressive* magazine from printing an article about how to make an atomic bomb.

SOME INDIVIDUAL RIGHTS STRENGTHENED

On the other hand, the Supreme Court has strengthened individual rights in some cases. One was the so-called Bakke case, in which a white applicant for medical school charged that he was discriminated against because he was not black. The court decided that he should be admitted because the school's policy was too rigid but that more flexible affirmative action programs based on race were constitutional.

In another case, the court ruled that a person cannot be unwillingly committed to a mental hospital without "clear and convincing" evidence of being mentally ill and likely to be dangerous. The court in effect raised the levels of proof required for commitment by many states.

And the court helped the cause of "whistleblowers" in government when it decided that a public employee does not forfeit his or her freedom to speak under the First Amendment by submitting complaints privately to a superior rather than publicly. Previously the court had indicated that a whistleblower might give up his or her rights if public disclosure causes undue interference with the organization involved. The case involved the firing of a teacher because of allegedly hostile attitudes toward school policies. In other words, said the court, a person cannot be fired for merely expressing criticism privately. There has to be other grounds for a firing to be justified.

THE BILL OF RIGHTS
From the U.S. Constitution

AMENDMENT I—Congress shall make no law respecting an establishment of religion, or prohibiting the free exercise thereof; or abridging the freedom of speech, or of the press; or the right of the people peaceably to assemble, and to petition the Government for a redress of grievances.

AMENDMENT II—A well-regulated militia, being necessary to the security of a free State, the right of the people to keep and bear arms, shall not be infringed.

AMENDMENT III—No soldier shall, in time of peace be quartered in any house, without the consent of the owner, nor in time of war, but in a manner to be prescribed by law.

AMENDMENT IV—The right of the people to be secure in their persons, houses, papers, and effects, against unreasonable searches and seizures, shall not be violated, and no warrants shall issue, but upon probable cause, supported by oath or affirmation, and particularly describing the place to be searched, and the persons or things to be seized.

AMENDMENT V—No person shall be held to answer for a capital, or otherwise infamous crime, unless on a presentment or indictment of a Grand Jury, except in cases arising in the land or naval forces, or in the militia, when in actual service in time of war of public danger; nor shall any person be subject for the same offense to be twice put in jeopardy of life or limb; nor shall be compelled in any criminal case to be a witness against himself, nor be deprived of life, liberty, or property, without due process of law; nor shall private property be taken for public use without just compensation.

AMENDMENT VI—In all criminal prosecutions, the accused shall enjoy the right to a speedy and public trial, by an impartial jury of the State and distrist wherein the crime shall have been committed, which district shall have been previously ascertained by law, and to be informed of the nature and cause of the accusation; to be confronted with the witnesses against him; to have compulsory process for obtaining witnesses in his favor, and to have the assistance of counsel for his defense.

AMENDMENT VII—In suits at common law, where the value in controversy shall exceed twenty dollars, the right of trial by jury shall be preserved, and no fact tried by a jury shall be otherwise reexamined in any court of the United States, than according to the rules of the common law.

AMENDMENT VIII—Excessive bail shall not be required, no excessive fines imposed, nor cruel and unusual punishments inflicted.

AMENDMENT IX—The enumeration in the Constitution, of certain rights, shall not be construed to deny or disparage others retained by the people.

AMENDMENT X—The powers not delegated to the United States by the Constitution, nor prohibited by it to the States, are reserved to the States respectively, or to the people.

OTHER AMENDMENTS ON INDIVIDUAL RIGHTS

AMENDMENT XIV—All persons born or naturalized in the United States, and subject to the jurisdiction thereof, are citizens of the United States and of the State wherein they reside. No State shall make or enforce any law which shall abridge the privileges or immunities of citizens of the United States; nor shall any State deprive any person of life, liberty, or property, without due process of law; nor deny to any person within its jurisdiction the equal protection of the laws. . . .

AMENDMENT XV—The right of citizens of the United States to vote shall not be denied or abridged by the United States or by any State on account of race, color, or previous condition of servitude . . .

AMENDMENT XIX—The right of citizens of the United States to vote shall not be denied or abridged by the United States or by any State on account of sex . . .

AMENDMENT XXIV—The right of citizens of the United States to vote in any primary or other election for President or Vice President, for electors for President or Vice President, or for Senator or Representative in Congress, shall not be denied or abridged by the United States or any State by reason of failure to pay any poll tax or other tax . . .

AMENDMENT XXVI—The right of citizens of the United States, who are 18 years of age or older, to vote shall not be denied or abridged by the United States or any State on account of age . . .

RIGHTS OF WOMEN
Progress But Little Equality

Although women have made significant gains both legally and socially, a 1978 report by the U.S. Commission on Civil Rights showed their overall status had improved little since the 1960s.

The report found many women overqualified and overeducated for their jobs and said they still earn only half as much as white males. A Department of Labor study the same year confirmed the Commission's findings. It said women in full-time jobs earned about 60 per cent as much as males, and although earnings for blacks and other minorities had risen 22 per cent since 1967, women's earnings remain virtually the same.

Meanwhile, more women have become involved in state and local politics, according to the National Women's Political Caucus. But involvement at the federal level is still weak. Elections for the 96th Congress brought a net loss of three women but also saw the election of the first woman to the Senate in 12 years.

The defeat of several liberal Congressmen was partially attributed to the active lobbying of anti-abortion groups. Despite the 1973 Supreme Court decision legalizing abortion, such groups have been effective in keeping the issue alive.

ERA DEADLINE EXTENDED

A major victory for women's rights was the extension of the March 22, 1979, deadline for ratification of the Equal Rights Amendment (ERA) to June 30, 1982. A pro-extension rally and march brought 100,000 participants to Washington in July, 1978 to display support.

The proposed 27th amendment to the Constitution would set a uniform standard of equality for both men and women. It would also preclude the need for a case-by-case definition of equality. The amendment reads: "Equality of rights under the law shall not be denied or abridged . . . on account of sex. Congress shall have the power to enforce the amendment and it shall take effect two years after ratification."

The ERA would require every state and the federal government to change all laws, regulations and government practices that do not provide equal treatment for men and women. Changes would eliminate all differences in jury service laws, educational opportunities, minimum wage laws, unemployment insurance laws, Social Security, age laws for marriage, conditions for divorce, alimony standards, penalties for crime, state protective labor laws and many other areas.

MARRIAGE LAWS, BY STATE

State	Age marriage can be contracted without parental consent		Age marriage can be contracted with parental consent(1)		Max. period bet. exam & issuance of license (days)	Common law marriage	
						May be contracted but not valid if attempted after date shown	Recognized if valid at time & place where contracted
	Male	Female	Male	Female			
Alabama	18	18	17	14	30	Yes	Yes
Alaska	18	18	16	16	30	1/1/64	Yes
Arizona	18	18	16	16	30	No	Yes
Arkansas	18	18	17	16	30	No	Yes
California........	18	18	18	16	30	1895	Yes
Colorado	18	18	16	16	30	Yes	Yes
Connecticut	18	18	16	16	35	No	(2)
Delaware.........	18	18	18	16	30	No	Yes
Dist. of Col.	18	18	16	16	30	Yes	Yes
Florida	18	18	18	16	30	1/1/68	Yes
Georgia	18	18	16	16	30	Yes	Yes
Hawaii..........	18	18	16	16	30	No	Yes
Idaho	18	18	16	16	30	Yes	Yes
Illinois..........	18	18	16	16	15	6/30/05	(2)
Indiana	18	18	17	17	30	1/1/58	(2)
Iowa	18	18	16	16	20	Yes	Yes
Kansas..........	18	18	18	18	30	Yes	Yes
Kentucky........	18	18	none	none	15	No	Yes
Louisiana	18	18	18	16	10	No	Yes
Maine	18	18	16	16	60	(2)	(2)
Maryland	18	18	16	16	—	No	Yes
Massachusetts	18	18	18	18	30	No	Yes
Michigan	18	18	16	16	30	1/1/57	Yes
Minnesota	18	18	18	16	—	4/26/41	(2)
Mississippi	21	21	17	15	30	4/5/56	(2)
Missouri	18	18	15	15	15	3/31/21	(2)
Montana	18	18	18	18	20	Yes	Yes
Nebraska	19	19	18	16	30	1923	Yes
Nevada	18	18	16	16	—	3/29/43	Yes
New Hampshire ...	18	18	14	13	30	No	Yes
New Jersey	18	18	18	16	30	1/12/39	Yes
New Mexico	18	18	16	16	30	No	Yes
New York	18	18	16	14	30	4/29/33	Yes
North Carolina	18	18	16	16	30	No	Yes
North Dakota	18	18	16	16	30	No	Yes
Ohio	18	18	18	16	30	Yes	Yes
Oklahoma	18	18	16	16	30	Yes	Yes
Oregon	18	18	17	17	30	No	Yes
Pennsylvania	18	18	16	16	30	Yes	Yes
Rhode Island	18	18	18	16	40	Yes	(2)
South Carolina	18	18	16	16	—	Yes	Yes
South Dakota	18	18	16	16	20	7/1/59	(2)
Tennessee	18	18	16	16	30	No	Yes
Texas	18	18	14	14	21	Yes	Yes
Utah	18	18	16	14	30	No	Yes
Vermont	18	18	16	16	30	No	(2)
Virginia	18	18	16	16	30	No	Yes
Washington	18	18	17	17	—	No	Yes
West Virginia	18	18	none	none	30	No	Yes
Wisconsin	18	18	16	16	20	1913	(2)
Wyoming	19	19	17	16	20	No	Yes

(1)Younger persons may obtain license through legal proceedings. (2)Legal status unclear.
Source: Department of Labor, Women's Bureau.

ERA THREE STATES SHORT OF RATIFICATION

Thirty-five states have approved the ERA, but three of those (Idaho, Nebraska and Tennessee) voted to rescind earlier actions. While the U.S. Department of Justice has called the rescisions invalid, the ultimate decision is up to Congress. Congress does not have to decide the issue, however, until the 38 states necessary for ratification have voted approval.

Opponents of the ERA have been led by Phyllis Schlafly and her organization, Stop ERA. Schlafly contends that ERA would actually take away from women many rights they now enjoy, such as exemption from the draft.

She also sees ERA as shifting to the federal government "the last remaining aspects of our lives that it does not already control, including marriage, divorce, child custody, prison regulations, protective labor legislation and insurance rates."

*   *   *

Following is a summary of women's rights, including recent changes. Other rights afforded women as well as minorities in housing, employment, credit, and other areas are detailed in this chapter under "Civil Rights."

*   *   *

ABORTION: In recent years, Congress has taken steps to limit a woman's right to choose abortion. Anti-abortion riders were added to a bill outlawing pregnancy discrimination (see below) and to the bill extending the life of the U.S. Commission on Civil Rights. The Commission is now prohibited from researching and reporting on abortion issues.

Federal funds for abortion were also limited for Defense Department programs and for the Peace Corps.

Laws now prevent government-funded legal services from handling abortion rights cases; hospitals receiving public funds from performing abortions—even if the hospital is the only health facility in an area; and the U.S. Agency for International Development from developing or distributing birth control methods that promote or encourage abortion.

A compromise reached between the House and Senate in late 1977 provides that federal funds will not be used to pay for abortions except when the life of the mother is at stake; where medical procedures are necessary for victims of rape or incest; when such rape or incest has been reported promptly (within 60 days) to a law enforcement agency or public health service; or when two physicians have determined that carrying a pregnancy to term would have severe and long-lasting physical effects on the mother.

The National Abortion Rights Action League found that Medicaid abortions dropped 98 per cent after January, 1978, as a result of the Congressional action.

PREGNANCY: Other Congressional actions have significantly improved the rights of child-bearing women.

Two Supreme Court decisions considered unfavorable to pregnant women were invalidated by a 1978 law requiring employers to treat pregnant women the same as other employees on the basis of their ability or inability to work. Discrimination based on pregnancy is now considered unlawful sex discrimination. Although the law allows pregnant women to receive coverage under a company's disability insurance program, it does not require employers to offer benefits for abortions.

DIVORCE LAWS, BY STATE

State	Residence Before Filing Suit	"No-fault" Divorce* Break-down	Separa-tion	Adul-tery	Cru-elty	Deser-tion	Alco-hol/ Drugs	Non-Sup-port	Insa-nity
AL	6 mos.	X	2 yrs.	X		1 yr.	X	X	5 yrs.
AK		X		X	X	1 yr.	X	X	18 mos.
AZ	90 days	X							
AR	60 days		3 yrs.	X	X	1 yr.	X	X	3 yrs.
CA		X							X
CO	90 days	X							
CT	1 yr.	X	18 mos.	X	X	1 yr.	X		5 yrs.
DE	3 mos.	X							
DC	6 mos.		6 mos.						
FL	6 mos.	X							3 yrs.
GA	6 mos.	X		X	X	1 yr.	X		2 yrs.
HI	3 mos.	X	2 yrs.						
ID	6 wks.	X	5 yrs.	X	X	X	X	X	3 yrs.
IL	90 days			X	X	1 yr.	2 yrs.		
IN	6 mos.	X							2 yrs.
IA	1 yr.	X							
KS	60 days	X		X	X	1 yr.	X	X	3 yrs.
KY	180 days	X							
LA			2 yrs.						
ME	6 mos.	X		X	X	3 yrs.	X	X	
MD	1-2 yrs.		1-3 yrs.			1 yr.			3 yrs.
MA	30 days	X		X	X	1 yr.	X	X	
MI	180 days	X							
MN	1 yr.								
MS	1 yr.	X		X	X	1 yr.	X		3 yrs.
MO	90 days	X							
MT	90 days								
NB	1 yr.	X							
NV	6 wks.	X	1 yr.						2 yrs.
NH	1 yr.	X		X	X	2 yrs.	X	X	
NJ	1 yr.		18 mos.	X	X	1 yr.	X		2 yrs.
NM	6 mos.	X		X	X	X			
NY	1 yr.		1 yr.	X	X	1 yr.		X	5 yrs.
NC	6 mos.		1 yr.	X					3 yrs.
ND	1 yr.	X		X	X	1 yr.	X	X	5 yrs.
OH	6 mos.	X	2 yrs.	X	X	1 yr.	X	X	4 yrs.
OK	6 mos.	X		X	X	1 yr.	X	X	5 yrs.
OR	6 mos.	X							
PA	1 yr.			X	X	2 yrs.			3 yrs.
RI	2 yrs.		5 yrs.	X	X	5 yrs.	X	X	
SC	3 mos.		3 yrs.	X	X	1 yr.	X		
SD				X	X	1 yr.	X	X	5 yrs.
TN	6 mos.			X	X	1 yr.	X	X	
TX	6 mos.	X	2 yrs.	X	X	1 yr.			3 yrs.
UT	3 mos.		3 yrs.	X	X	1 yr.	X	X	X
VT	6 mos.		6 mos.	X	X	X		X	3 yrs.
VA	6 mos.	X	1 yr.	X	X	1 yr.			
WA		X							
WV	1 yr.		2 yrs.	X	X	1 yr.	X		3 yrs.
WI	6 mos.		1 yr.	X	X	1 yr.	X	X	1 yr.
WY	60 days		2 yrs.	X	X	1 yr.	X	X	2 yrs.

*"No-fault" includes all proceedings where no proof for divorce is needed. Not called "no-fault" in all states.

Source: U.S. Department of Labor, Women's Bureau.

To file a complaint concerning alleged pregnancy discrimination contact the appropriate Equal Employment Opportunity Commission (EEOC) regional office. Federal employees should file with the EEO counselor at the agency involved. (For more information see "How to Report Employment Discrimination" in the section of this chapter called "Civil Rights.")

DISPLACED HOMEMAKERS: More and more middle-aged women, either through their husband's death or through divorce, are finding themselves displaced from both a social role and economic support. Many of these women do not qualify for pensions or Social Security because of age and have little or no work experience.

Legislation passed in 1978 reauthorizing the **Comprehensive Employment and Training Act** (CETA) recognized displaced homemakers as disadvantaged in the labor market. The U.S. Department of Labor set aside $5 million for special programs and activities to aid such women.

Pressure on Congress has resulted in other provisions for training displaced homemakers. **Amendments to the Vocational Education Act** recognize that half of the 6.4 million women in public vocational education are in "nongainful" homemaking courses, 30 per cent are in secretarial or other office work and only 8 per cent are in fields traditionally dominated by men. With the amendments, the law now requires that states participating in the Vocational Education Program must draw up five-year plans for equal vocational education opportunities for men and women. States must provide money and full-time staff to reduce sex stereotyping in vocational education. The law also provides for the inclusion of women familiar with sex discrimination on state and national vocational advisory councils.

For more information on programs and funding for displaced homemakers write the Displaced Homemakers Network, 2012 Massachusetts Ave. NW, Washington, DC, 20036.

EDUCATION: Title IX of the Education Amendment of 1972 prohibits schools receiving federal funds from discriminating on the basis of sex. Discrimination is prohibited in sports, course enrollment, tests, admissions and all aspects of school employment such as recruitment, hiring, promotion, sick leave, vacation and medical benefits. Regulations provide that pregnancy, childbirth and abortion be treated the same as any temporary disability.

Perhaps the most controversial issue involving Title IX is funding for women's athletics. The U.S. Department of Health, Education and Welfare, which enforces Title IX, issued its proposed regulations in this area in late 1978.

The regulations would require the average per capita expenditures for men's and women's athletics to be "substantially equal" in financially-measurable areas (scholarships, equipment, etc.). They would also require that men and women be provided "comparable benefits and opportunities" in non-financially measurable areas (facilities, practice time, etc.).

The National College Athletic Association has opposed the regulations and is seeking an exemption for college athletics.

Complaints must be filed within 180 days after discrimination occurs. However, as with the Equal Pay Act, if the discrimination is ongoing, complaints may be filed anytime. To file a complaint, a letter should be sent to HEW, Office for Civil Rights, Washington, DC, 20201, or any HEW regional office.

A Supreme Court decision in May, 1979, significantly strengthened women's rights under Title IX by ruling that individuals could bring sex discrimination suits against schools and colleges. The only means of redress prior to the ruling was a lengthy administrative procedure.

EQUAL PAY: The Equal Pay Act of 1963 protects employees subject to the federal minimum wage law from discrimination in salaries, overtime, sick pay, vacation pay, pension benefits and hospital and health insurance benefits. The Act requires that men and women performing under similar working conditions receive the same wages, overtime pay and benefits when their jobs require "substantially" equal (not "identical") skill, effort and responsibility under similar working conditions. The standard is determined by job requirements and performance, not by job classifications or titles.

Wage differences based on seniority or merit systems are permitted as long as sex is not a factor. Employers are prohibited from lowering an employee's wage in order to equalize pay between the sexes.

The Department of Labor found a 27 per cent increase in Equal Pay violations during the first half of 1978 over the same period in 1977. The responsibility for enforcing the Equal Pay Act was transferred from the Department of Labor to the Equal Employment Opportunity Commission in July, 1979.

To file a complaint based on Equal Pay, contact the nearest area or distrist office of the Equal Employment Opportunity Commission (EEOC). Complaints must be kept confidential.

CIVIL RIGHTS
Affirmative Action Drawing Negative Response

During the past 30 years, virtually every federal department, agency and commission has had the responsibility of enforcing one or more of the nearly 90 laws and executive orders prohibiting discrimination on the basis of race, color, religion, sex, age, national origin and mental or physical handicap.

Yet none of these agencies has come close to eliminating discrimination. In fact, recent actions indicate that much of society is beginning to question the value of some equal opportunity and affirmative action programs. The 1978 Bakke decision, in which the Supreme Court decided in favor of a white male who claimed he was a victim of reverse discrimination in being rejected by medical school, stirred new debate. Subsequent cases have made enforcement of civil rights laws more difficult.

SEARS CALLS EMPLOYMENT LAWS UNFAIR

In January, 1979, Sears Roebuck, facing federal discrimination charges, filed suit against 10 federal agencies, charging that improper and deficient enforcement of the eight major laws affecting employment discrimination were hindering the company's efforts to promote a "balanced workforce." The suit asked the courts to require the agencies "to coordinate the enforcement of the anti-discrimination statutes and issue uniform guidelines which instruct employers how to resolve existing conflicts between affirmative action requirements based on race and sex and those based on veteran's status, age and mental or physical handicaps."

A federal judge dismissed the suit in May, however, saying that while equal employment was a "formidable task" it was "not beyond the notable skill and competence of Sears." Although Sears was unable to show that its complaint was justified, the company's documentation of agency ineptitude focused more attention on what had already become an increasing area of controversy.

SEGREGATED SCHOOLS STILL COMMONPLACE

In 1979, 25 years after the Supreme Court decision prohibiting racial segregation in school, fully-integrated education is still a dream in many areas. In the North, one out of every four children attends a racially segregated public school and in the South, one in ten. Congress has not passed a law to support desegregation since 1972 and has made repeated attacks on the use of busing to achieve such a goal.

New defiance of progressive civil rights measures has also appeared. In May, 1979, the University of North Carolina went to court to fight a desegregation plan outlined for it by HEW. The University charged that the requirements were unrealistic and would be detrimental to the overall university system.

MANY DENIED DECENT HOUSING

Segregated education and segregated housing tend to reinforce each other, according to a 1979 report by the U.S. Commission on Civil Rights. It claimed that unlawful discrimination still exists 11 years after the passage of a law prohibiting it and said many people are "denied a decent home and a suitable living environment." The report blamed the federal government, saying that such conditions were due to a weak fair housing law, the failure of federal agencies to carry out their responsibilities and inadequate funds for enforcement.

There was an attempt to eliminate at least one discriminatory practice in housing, however, by the Federal Home Loan Bank Board. It issued regulations in 1978 barring savings and loans from "redlining"—refusing to make loans for properties in neighborhoods that are old or have a high proportion of minorities.

Extension of the ratification deadline for the Equal Rights Amendment was cited by the American Civil Liberties Union (ACLU) as the lone bright spot in the actions of the 95th Congress. The ACLU accused Congress of being more interested in limiting civil rights than extending them. Among issues arousing new debate were busing, affirmative action, tuition tax credits and criminal code reform.

MAJOR CIVIL RIGHTS LAWS

Following are major civil rights laws prohibiting discrimination on the basis of race, sex, color, national origin and religion. Specific laws affecting only women, handicapped people and the elderly are described in separate sections of this chapter. Each listing is followed by the name of the law and the agency which administers it. Abbreviations are as follows: EEOC, Equal Employment Opportunity Commission; HEW, U.S. Department of Health, Education and Welfare; HUD, U.S. Department of Housing and Urban Development.

CREDIT

No creditor may discriminate against any applicant with respect to any aspect of a credit transaction. (Equal Credit Opportunity Act—see Banking and Borrowing chapter)

EDUCATION

No person shall be denied admission to a public college on the basis of race, color, religion, sex or national origin. Federal funds are available for elementary, secondary and state and local government-assisted public colleges for implementing desegregation plans. (Title VII, Civil Rights Act of 1964—HEW, Justice)

State and local governments must provide equal educational opportunity. (Equal Educational Opportunity Act of 1974—HEW)

Government-insured lenders may not discriminate against applicants for student loans. (Title IV of the Higher Education Act of 1965—HEW)

Colleges and universities may not receive federal funds for any project which states that certain groups be barred from performing such a project. (Title XII, Higher Education Act of 1965—HEW)

EMPLOYMENT

All employers with 15 or more employees (including unions and state and local governments) are prohibited from discriminating in classification, selection, hiring, upgrading, benefits, layoffs or any other condition of employment. (Title VII of the Civil Rights Act of 1964—EEOC, Justice)

Federal employers may not discriminate and must develop affirmative action programs in each department and agency. (Executive Order 11478—EEOC)

Contractors and subcontractors with federal government contracts exceeding $10,000 may not discriminate in hiring of employees and apprentices. Those with more than 50 employees or $50,000 in contracts must develop affirmative action plans with goals and time tables for advertising, recruiting, hiring and training women and minorities. (Executive orders 11246 and 11375—Labor)

All grants, contracts and agreements under the Comprehensive Employment and Training Act (CETA) must contain a provision prohibiting discrimination. CETA provides federal funds for the creation of public service jobs and for employment training.

HOUSING

Discrimination in the sale or rental of residential property is prohibited, as is discrimination in advertising such a sale, financing and providing brokerage services. (Title VIII of the Civil Rights Act of 1968—HUD)

Recipients of housing grants, government-insured loans, and other federal financial assistance may not discriminate. (Executive Order 11063—Departments of Agriculture, Commerce, Interior, Justice, Transportation, HUD and HEW)

Discrimination is prohibited in any program funded by the Housing and Community Development Act of 1974. This act provides federal funds for decent housing, a suitable living environment and expanding economic opportunities for low and moderate income families. (HUD, Justice)

PUBLIC ACCOMMODATIONS

Discrimination or segregation is prohibited in places of public accommodation. (Title II, Civil Rights Act of 1964—Justice)

TRIAL BY JURY

All people entitled to a trial by jury have the right to juries selected at random from a cross section of the community where the court convenes. No person may be excluded from jury service on account of race, color, religion, sex, national origin or economic status. (Jury Selection and Services Act of 1968—Justice)

VOTING

No person shall be denied the right to vote on account of race, color, age or because a person is a member of a language minority. No state may impose a voting qualification, standard, practice or procedure or prerequisite which is discriminatory. (Voting Rights Act of 1965—Justice, Commerce)

FILING A CIVIL RIGHTS COMPLAINT

People who suspect that they are victims of discrimination on the basis of sex, race, color, religion or national origin, and desire to file a complaint, have a number of agencies to contact.

Below are agencies and their specialties:

VOTING: For problems in trying to register, vote or take part in any political party activity, campaigning for office or serving as an election official, contact the Civil Rights Division, U.S. Department of Justice, Washington, DC, 20530.

PUBLIC ACCOMMODATIONS: For discrimination by a hotel, restaurant, theatre, sports arena or similar place of public use, contact the Civil Rights Division, U.S. Department of Justice, Washington, DC, 20530.

POLICE BRUTALITY OR LACK OF POLICE PROTECTION: Contact the Civil Rights Division, U.S. Department of Justice, Washington, DC, 20530.

PUBLIC SCHOOLS AND COLLEGES: For discrimination or segregation, contact the Office for Civil Rights, U.S. Department of Health, Education and Welfare, Washington, DC, 20201.

FARM: For complaints concerning federal farm programs, contact the Assistant to the Secretary for Civil Rights, Department of Agriculture, Washington, DC, 20250.

HOUSING: For discrimination while trying to buy or rent a house or apartment, or segregation in housing financed or insured by the federal government, contact the Fair Housing and Equal Employment Division, Department of Housing and Urban Development, Washington, DC, 20410.

ANTIPOVERTY: For complaints about discrimination in federal anti-poverty programs, contact the Assistant Director for Civil Rights, Office of Economic Opportunity, Washington, DC, 20506.

NON-FEDERAL EMPLOYMENT: For discrimination by a private employer in job testing, promotion, dismissal, work opportunities or work conditions, or by an employment agency or labor union, contact the Equal Employment Opportunity Commission, Washington, DC, 20506. Complaints must be filed on a standard EEOC form which can be obtained from the Washington office or from regional offices.

FEDERAL EMPLOYMENT: Complaints about a federal employer should first be directed to the equal employment opportunity officer for the individual agency. Complaints not solved promptly may be directed to EEOC.

WAGES: Contact EEOC, Washington, DC, 20506.

EMPLOYMENT BY A COMPANY WITH FEDERAL CONTRACTS: Complaints concerning the employment practices of any employer who has a contract with a federal agency or who does any construction work paid for by the federal government should go to the Office of Federal Contract Compliance, U.S. Department of Labor, Washington, DC, 20210.

The U.S. Commission on Civil Rights will also refer complaints to the appropriate agency. Write: Complaint Referral, U.S. Commission on Civil Rights, Washington, DC, 20425. Regional Offices are located at: 75 Piedmont Ave. NE, Atlanta, GA, 30306; 106 Broadway, San Antonio, TX, 78205; 312 N Spring St., Los Angeles, CA, 90012; 915 2nd Ave., Seattle, WA, 98174; 26 Federal Plaza, New York, NY, 10007; 230 S Dearborn St., Chicago, IL, 60604; 1405 Curtis St., Denver, CO, 80202; 2120 L St. NW, Washington, DC, 20037; and 911 Walnut, Kansas City, MO, 64106.

RIGHTS OF DISABLED PERSONS
Moving Into The Main Stream

Some of the most effective civil rights battles in recent years are being waged by disabled people. They are organizing into an aggressive force to shape public policy affecting their lifestyles.

Since September, 1973, federal law has prohibited discrimination on the basis of physical or mental handicap in every program or activity involving federal funds. Not until April, 1977, however, did the U.S. Department of Health, Education and Welfare (HEW) respond to demands of handicapped citizen groups by issuing regulations to enforce the 1973 law.

ESTIMATED COSTS HIGH

Estimates of the cost of providing disabled people with full access have ranged from $400 million for public schools to $2 to $8 billion for transportation. And while disabled advocacy groups have become more vocal, many of their demands have been squelched by the roar of inflation.

Disabled advocates argue that the social costs of segregation and institutionalization are excessively high and could be substantially reduced by providing access which will lead to independence and employment.

Some of the major setbacks have been in the area of transportation. U.S. Department of Transportation (DOT) plans to require the use of "Transbus," a fully accessible low-floored vehicle, were stalled in 1979 by American bus manufacturers who refused to produce it due to alleged heavy financial risks.

And DOT rules, proposed in April, 1979, weakened earlier ones by limiting the number of buses, subway, train and trolley stations which have to be modified to accommodate disabled people.

But federal activity has awakened some members of private industry to the needs of disabled citizens. Three television networks, PBS, NBC and ABC, agreed to provide up to 10 hours a week of programming captioned for deaf people beginning in 1980. People who have a special decoder on their sets will be able to see the captions.

The first major Supreme Court ruling on the 1973 law, which was passed down in June, 1979, was considered a major blow to the rights of disabled people. The court ruled that colleges receiving federal aid did not have to open all programs to disabled people; it said "legitimate physical requirements" could be imposed on those seeking admission. The case was brought by a deaf woman who was denied admission to a professional nursing program because she relied on lip reading and a hearing aid.

Twenty-eight federal agencies have now developed anti-discrimination regulations, but progressive measures have been thwarted in many cases by complaints about the high cost of implementation.

The following is a summary of Federal regulations affecting disabled people

PRE-COLLEGE EDUCATION

The basic requirements of the HEW regulations are:

● That no handicapped child be excluded from a public education because of disability;

● That every handicapped child is entitled to a free appropriate education regardless of the nature or severity of handicap;

● That handicapped students must not be segregated in public schools but must be educated with nonhandicapped students to the maximum extent appropriate to their needs;

● That state or local educational agencies locate and identify unserved handicapped children.

The regulations provide that school systems bear special responsibilities in some instances, for transportation of handicapped people to and from education programs. Where placement in a public or private residential program is necessary, the school district has the responsibility for costs of the program, nonmedical care, room, board and transportation.

COLLEGE EDUCATION

Quotas for admission of handicapped persons are ruled out, as are preadmission inquiries as to whether an applicant is handicapped. However, voluntary postadmission inquiries may be made in advance of enrollment to enable an institution to provide necessary services.

Higher education institutions must make programs and activities accessible to handicapped students and employees. Architectural barriers must be removed if the program is not made accessible by other means. A university is not expected to make all its classroom buildings accessible but it may have to undertake some alterations or reschedule classes to accessible buildings.

Other obligations of these institutions include:

● Tests which a college or university uses or relies upon, including standardized admissions tests, must be selected and administered so that the

---

UNCLE SAM CAN NOW SPEAK WITH DEAF PEOPLE

HEW's Office of Civil Rights (OCR) has installed teletype systems for communicating with deaf persons in 10 regional offices. Deaf persons who own or have access to such equipment (TTYs) can now call OCR for information or explanations about their rights.

The new equipment consists of a phone dial, a TV screen for reading incoming messages, and a special tape recorder. Deaf persons may call the OCR and type a message on the keyboard. The typed message is displayed on a screen at the other end and can be recorded on request.

For regional teletype numbers, deaf persons may call the Washington headquarters, (202) 472-2916.

test results of students with impaired sensory, manual or speaking skills measure the student's aptitude or achievement level and not his disability.

● Students with impaired sensory, manual or speaking skills must be provided auxiliary aids although this may be done by informing them of resources provided by government or charitable organizations.

● Colleges and universities must also make reasonable modifications in academic requirements, where necessary, to ensure full educational opportunity for handicapped students.

HEALTH, WELFARE AND SOCIAL SERVICES

Health and welfare providers must ensure that persons with impaired sensory or speaking skills are provided effective notice concerning the provision of benefits, waivers of rights and consent to treatment.

Health, welfare and social services for handicapped people must be equal in quality to those in the institution's overall program, and equitable standards of eligibility are required.

TRANSPORTATION

In 1979, DOT required that all new transportation facilities utilizing federal funds be made accessible and that the following modifications be made in existing facilities:

● One-half of buses used during peak hours must be made accessible within 10 years; if accessibility cannot be provided within three years, cities must provide interim service comparable to mass transit service in operation.

● "Key" subway stations, including end-of-line and transfer points and those serving health care facilities, universities, major employment and government centers, must be made accessible within 30 years. At least one car per train must be accessible.

● Airports must be accessible within three years. Those which do not have ramps linking terminal buildings with aircraft must use lifts to assist boarding disabled passengers. At least one telephone with sound control and one teletypewriter must be provided for the hearing impaired. (Federal Aviation Administration regulations cover individual airlines—see below.)

● At least one Amtrak station in each metropolitan area and any station not within 50 miles of another accessible station must be made accessible within five years and all others within 10 years. Teletypewriters and sound-controlled telephones must be provided. One coach car and one food service car per train must be accessible within three years or food service provided disabled people in their seats.

● Highway rest stops must be made accessible within three years, and new pedestrian crossings must include curb cuts.

Communities may request a waiver of requirements in certain cases but only after full hearings are held and comments received from the disabled and other interested persons.

DOT's Federal Aviation Administration (FAA) issued guidelines for transporting disabled passengers by air in 1977. Although guidelines allow individual airlines to develop procedures of their own, FAA said it is trying to "ensure that as many physically handicapped persons as possible enjoy the benefits of air travel."

The Civil Aeronautics Board (CAB) is also in the process of developing its regulations to insure access.

GENERAL EMPLOYMENT REGULATIONS

Employers may not refuse to hire or promote disabled persons solely because of their disability. Reasonable accommodation, such as providing a cassette recorder for a blind employee or changing the physical location of the task to be performed, may have to be made.

Failure to employ or promote an employee who is unqualified or who cannot be helped by reasonable accommodation is not discrimination. However, an employer may not reject an applicant simply because reasonable accommodation is necessary.

Pre-employment physical examinations must not be required, and pre-employment inquiry cannot be made about a person's disabling condition. Employers may make an offer of employment conditional on a medical examination as long as the examination is required of all employees and no one is disqualified on the basis of a physical condition that is not job-related.

Employment discrimination complaints against federal agencies must be brought to the attention of the agency within 30 days after the discrimination occurred. Complaints should be made to the Equal Employment Opportunity counselor, the administrator of the agency, the personnel officer or another official.

Complainants may file civil action in federal court within 30 days of notice of final action by the agency or by the Equal Employment Opportunity Commission (EEOC). Court action may also be taken if the EEOC or the agency has not taken final action after 180 days of the original filing.

Complaints against companies which have contracts with the federal government should be mailed to the Office of Federal Contract Compliance, Department of Labor, Washington, DC.

Recent legislation allows any disabled individual who wins a discrimination case to collect attorney's fees from the other side if the court so rules. This provision means lawyers may be more willing to take such a case on a contingency basis and recover a fee at the end of the case only if the case is won.

OTHER FEDERAL PROGRAMS

HOUSING: The U.S. Department of Housing and Urban Development (HUD) announced in 1977 that 5 per cent of new family units constructed under public housing programs would be designed for use by the disabled. Other programs provide housing loans and rent subsidies to low-income disabled persons. For more information contact HUD's Office for Independent Living for the Disabled, 7th and D Sts. SW, Washington, DC, 20410.

TAXES: Persons who have expenses for employment-related household services, child care, disabled dependent care or disabled spouse care may be eligible for a 20 per cent tax credit. Contact the Commissioner of Internal Revenue, 1111 Constitution Ave., NW, Washington, DC, 20224.

BUSINESS: The U.S. Small Business Administration (SBA) will loan up to $350,000 for 15 years at 3 per cent interest to disabled persons who can demonstrate that they have the ability to own and operate a business successfully. Applicants must have experienced difficulty getting financing from other sources. Write the SBA, 1030 15th St., NW, Washington, DC, 20416.

MAJOR MARKETPLACE RIGHTS
New Rules To Protect Buyers

In the old days, retailers would claim proudly that "the customer is always right." Today's sellers of goods and services to the general public have other phrases meaning the same thing. But the advent of packaging, sophisticated technology and national advertising has made it difficult, if not impossible, for the retailer to protect the buyer's rights. The result has been a resurgence of consumer activism and a growing body of government rules and laws to help protect the rights of buyers in an increasingly impersonal marketplace.

President John F. Kennedy provided the impetus to the most recent wave of consumer interest by setting up the first consumer advisory council and consumer staff at the White House. In a formal announcement, he cited four basic consumer rights:

- The right to choose from a variety of alternatives;
- The right to information about products and services;
- The right to safe products; and
- The right to be heard in government and industry.

Those rights have led to increased efforts of private groups and government officials (local, state and federal) to enforce antitrust laws to assure adequate choice of products and services; various "truth" laws requiring disclosure of information; numerous laws to provide protection from unsafe products and conditions; and a new array of consumer representatives in both government and the business world.

In addition, many firms have adopted policies to improve customer relations and demonstrate respect for buyer's rights. Most retailers now offer some form of "satisfaction or your money back," to use a phrase in common usage. Food and department stores generally will refund the purchase price or replace a product that proves to be unsatisfactory, except for items sold at special sales or "as is." Other merchants will provide credit in such cases, but credit is less satisfactory to many buyers, especially those who paid cash in the first place.

GOVERNMENT LOOKS FOR PATTERNS

While government agencies administer marketplace laws and regulations, they do not ordinarily act on the basis of one complaint or one apparent violation. Agencies collect complaints and inquiries until they find a pattern indicating unlawful conduct on the part of an individual or organization. Thus, a person who reports a suspected violation to a government agency may eventually be helped if the agency takes action and obtains refunds or replacements for all victims.

In successful cases, however, the government usually collects fines or imposes jail terms. Most cases are settled by a consent order which requires the accused party to stop certain practices without admitting any violation. Victimized buyers rarely get anything more than the satisfaction of knowing that a measure of justice prevailed.

Actually, government officials take formal action in relatively few matters, and their success rate in punishing violators and stopping undesirable practices is extremely spotty. Time lags stretch some cases over many years and effectively defeat sincere efforts to bring justice.

In recent years, however, government agencies have been getting involved increasingly in individual cases. Among the federal agencies that try to get recourse for-consumers with legitimate complaints are the Interstate Commerce Commission, in cases involving rail, bus and truck transport; the Civil Aeronautics Board, in cases involving airlines; and the U.S. Office of Consumer Affairs, in cases involving matters not under other agency jurisdictions.

SUMMARY OF MAJOR CONSUMER RIGHTS

Following are summaries of major consumer rights under federal laws and regulations. Other consumer rights are discussed throughout this almanac. The agency with chief responsibility for administering the law or regulation is listed after each summary. Initials of the federal agencies are: DOT—Department of Transportation; FDA—Food and Drug Administration; FRB—Federal Reserve Board; FTC—Federal Trade Commission; HUD—Department of Housing and Urban Development; USPS—U.S. Postal Service.

ADVERTISING: Ads must not be false or unfair and must disclose all facts material to the purchase of the product advertised. (FTC) Advertising which falsely represents any product sold through the mails is also prohibited. (USPS) See Communications chapter for more details.

BALLOON PAYMENTS: Additional charges at the end of a lease, "balloon payments," are limited to no more than three times the average monthly payment, unless a person agrees to make a higher payment or has used the item more than average. Extra payments are based on the value of the property when it is returned to the lender. A buyer has the right to obtain an independent appraiser's estimate of worth which both parties must abide by. (Consumer Leasing Act—FTC, FRB)

BILLING ERRORS: If a seller fails to resolve a billing dispute within a set time, he may be sued for actual damages plus twice any finance charge (but no less than $100 or more than $1,000). A creditor who does not follow the procedure may lose the right to collect the amount, up to $50, even if there is no error. (FTC—see Banking and Borrowing chapter for further details)

CARE LABELING: All clothing, except hats, gloves and shoes, must be labeled with instructions for proper care and cleaning. Leather, suede, fur, plastic and most vinyl garments are exempted. (FTC)

CREDIT COSTS: Creditors must disclose the annual percentage rate and total finance charges. A periodic statement of transactions must be provided for credit cards, revolving charge accounts and overdraft checking accounts. If such information is not provided, a person can sue for actual damages plus twice the amount of any finance charge (but not less than $100 or more than $1,000). (Truth-in-Lending Act—FTC)

CREDIT DISCRIMINATION: A lender may not discriminate on the basis of sex, marital status, race, color, age, national origin or religion. Child support and alimony payments must be considered as income if disclosed by the applicant, but applicants have the right to withhold such information. A person who proves discrimination may be able to collect out-of-pocket expenses and punitive damages. (FTC, and others—see Banking and Borrowing chapter)

CREDIT FILES: Credit bureaus and credit reporting firms must tell people what is in their file (other than medical information) and reinvestigate any disputed statements on request. Any information which is inaccurate or not verified must be removed. Such firms and the merchants who use them may be sued for actual damages, plus punitive damages, if the violation is intentional. (FTC—see Banking and Borrowing chapter)

CREDIT PURCHASE CANCELLATION: A person who uses his home as security in a credit transaction has three business days to cancel at no obligation. The creditor must give written notice of the right to cancel and cancellation must be made in writing. (Truth-in-Lending Act—FTC, see Banking and Borrowing chapter

DEBT COLLECTION: Debt collectors are prohibited from using abusive, deceptive or unfair collection techniques. Debtors can sue for actual damages plus additional damages up to $1,000 if a collector harasses them. But those who sue in bad faith or who harass may be forced to pay the collector's legal fees. (FTC—See Banking and Borrowing chapter)

DOOR-TO-DOOR SALES: A person has three days to cancel purchases of $25 or more made away from the seller's business address, such as in the buyer's home, at private parties, or in rented hotel rooms. Upon cancellation, the seller has 10 days to refund money paid and an additional 10 days to pick up the product or arrange for the intended buyer to return it. This "cooling-off" rule does not apply to sales of real estate, insurance, securities or emergency home repairs. (FTC)

EYEGLASSES: A 1978 rule requires eye doctors to give patients a copy of their prescription so they can shop for the best buy in contact lenses or eyeglasses. It also allows such professionals to advertise prices of products and services. despite professional association bans on such advertising. (FTC)

FABRIC LABELS: Fur and fabric manufacturers must label the fiber content of their products. Either the name of the manufacturer or its code number (registered with the FTC) must appear as well. Fur manufacturers must disclose if the product is dyed and whether it is composed of paws, bellies, scrap pieces or waste furs. (FTC)

FRANCHISES: A 1978 rule prohibits franchisors from misrepresenting potential sales, income or profits to prospective investors. At least 10 days before final agreement, the franchisor must disclose financial information, business experience, number of franchises and number terminated in the past year. Investors must also be told initial and long-term costs, operating restrictions and training available. (FTC)

HEARING AIDS: Merchants are prohibited from selling hearing aids to anyone who has not had an examination by an independent medical specialist or audiologist. The examination may be waived by buyers, but sellers are prohibited from encouraging them to do so. (FDA)

HOBBIES: Imitation political items must be marked with date of manufacture and imitation coins must be marked "copy." In case of deception, a person can sue for damages and seek an injunction. (Hobby Protection Act—FTC)

INSTALLMENT PURCHASES: If a merchant sells a credit sales contract to a financial institution for collection, the institution (holder) must honor all terms originally laid out by the contract. In cases where a product is defective and the merchant and the holder refuse to resolve the problem, a person can sue either or both parties for the amount paid on the contract to date. (FTC)

JUNK MAIL: A person has a right to refuse any mail which is sent to his address by crossing out the name and address, writing "refused" on the envelope and signing his/her name below that. (USPS)

LAND SALES: A person must have 48 hours to review a property report before signing a sales contract and can revoke a contract 48 hours after signing if no report is provided. The report must disclose detailed characteristics of the development including utilities, roads, homes completed, accessibility and whether or not it is under water. It must also disclose provisions for recourse if the buyer or seller defaults on the mortgage. (HUD)

LEASING: Companies that lease personal property (cars, furniture, appliances, etc.) must disclose the cost and terms of the leases, including penalties for late payment, insurance required, and cancellation procedures. Property leased for less than four months is exempted. A person can sue for 25 per cent of the monthly payments (not less than $100 or more than $1,000) plus actual damages, court and attorney fees. (FTC)

MAIL ORDER: A person can cancel any mail-order purchase not shipped in 30 days with no obligation. The seller must notify the buyer of any delay and give the buyer the option to agree to a new shipping date or cancel. Although the seller has to provide a free means of reply (a postage-paid card, for example), failure to answer indicates the delay is all right with the buyer. Not covered are photo finishing, seeds and plants, magazines, credit and COD orders. (FTC—see Communications chapter)

ODOMETERS: Sellers of used cars must disclose the number of miles a car has been driven and sign a statement that the odometer has not been altered in any way. A person who finds an odometer has been tampered with can sue for $1,500 or three times the amount of damages suffered, plus court and attorney's fees. (DOT—see Automobiles chapter)

PORNOGRAPHY: Mailers are prohibited from sending sexually oriented materials or advertisements to people who file a Form PS 2201 with the post office. (USPS)

POST OFFICE BOXES: A person has the right to find out from the postal service the name and street address of any business using a post office box to receive mail. (USPS)

RECORD AND BOOK CLUBS: The negative option rule gives people the right to cancel such agreements any time. A negative option is an agreement between a seller and a subscriber in which a description of merchandise is forwarded periodically and, unless the subscriber tells the seller not to ship it, the merchandise is sent and the subscriber billed. Sellers are required to disclose any minimum purchase requirement, whether postage and handling is included and the frequency of notices. If the description of merchandise is not sent at least 10 days before shipment, the subscriber has the right to return the merchandise and receive full credit including postage. (FTC)

UNORDERED MERCHANDISE: Unordered merchandise received through the mail may be considered a gift. Only free samples clearly marked as such, and merchandise mailed by a charitable organization to ask for a contribution can be sent without prior consent. (FTC)

VOCATIONAL SCHOOLS: Students can drop out of vocational schools within 14 days and receive a full refund as of January, 1980. People who drop out after 14 days are entitled to a refund for unused courses minus a maximum registration fee of $75. Schools must disclose drop-out rates and substantiate any placement and earnings claims. In recent cases, schools have been forced to give refunds. (FTC)

WARRANTIES: Companies which offer warranties must disclose whether they are "full" or "limited" and state the terms in simple language. A person may sue if a company does not live up to warranty promises and collect damages as well as court and attorney's fees. Unless otherwise stated, warranty rights include the right to "consequential damages." In such cases, the company must

---

WARRANTY RIGHTS

Companies are not required to offer written warranties for products, but every product comes with an unwritten, implied warranty except when it is marked "as is."

Under the 1977 Magnuson-Moss Warranty Act, a warranty must be designated either "full" or "limited." It also must be disclosed clearly before purchase. A product, however may have a full warranty on a certain part and a limited warranty on the rest.

A FULL WARRANTY means:
- Free replacement or repair, including removal and reinstallation;
- Repair within a reasonable time;
- No unreasonable requirements for service, such as requiring shipping to the factory or requiring mailing of warranty card in advance; and
- Coverage for all owners during the warranty period.

A LIMITED WARRANTY means anything less, such as:
- Coverage for parts but not labor;
- Credit or pro-rated refunds instead of full refunds;
- Charges for handling; and
- Coverage for the first owner only.

IMPLIED WARRANTIES vary state by state. Even products with written warranties have implied ones. Two of the most common are:
- **WARRANTY OF MERCHANTABILITY:** the product must be fit and safe for its ordinary uses, i.e. a toaster must toast, a reclining chair must recline.
- **WARRANTY OF FITNESS FOR A PARTICULAR PURPOSE:** the product must live up to the claims relied on by the buyer. For example, a seller who says a sleeping bag is adequate for zero-degree weather warrants the bag for such conditions.

---

not only fix the defective product but pay for any damage the product caused as well. (FTC—see box)

RIGHTS OF THE ELDERLY
Making the Most of Seniority

By the year 2000, when the children of the baby boom begin to contribute to the geriatric boom, one in eight Americans will be "senior citizens." Today, elderly people represent the most rapidly growing and perhaps most neglected segment of the population.

Elderly activist groups have begun complaining loudly about discrimination in government and industry, and their opinions are being widely solicited by policy makers. The Gray Panthers, the American Association of Retired Persons, the National Council of Senior Citizens and other groups have testified before Congress and regulatory agencies on subjects including savings account interest rates, nuclear power and supplementary Medicare insurance.

And they have been getting some results. When interest rates for small savings accounts were lifted one-quarter per cent in May, 1979, the Gray Panthers, which had raised the issue initially, received most of the credit for the change. And a coalition of senior organizations which protested proposed budget cutbacks in the Social Security program in 1979 was able to insure that most of those cutbacks died on the Senate floor.

Although their voices are being heard more, there is still evidence that abuse of elderly people is widespread. A 1978 study by the U.S. Commission on Civil Rights of 10 federal programs providing health, education and legal services found that age discrimination existed in each of them. It said that although various age groups were affected, the most frequent victims of discrimination were aged 65 and older.

The results confirmed suspicions that the Age Discrimination Act of 1975 had not eliminated discrimination in federally assisted programs as it was designed to do.

CONGRESS APPROVES MORE SERVICES

In response to evidence that elderly people were not getting a fair shake, Congress in 1978 enacted several amendments to the Older Americans Act, the major vehicle for research, community services, employment and nutrition programs for the elderly.

The amendments strengthened programs providing "meals on wheels" for homebound elderly, legal services, and nursing home ombudsmen, and created a new program to provide elderly people with long term health care.

They also made it easier for persons who are victims of discrimination in federally-assisted programs to get relief. In addition to the administrative complaint procedures outlined by individual agencies, elderly people now have the right to sue if discriminated against and may collect attorney's fees.

Another significant victory in 1978 occurred when Congress abolished the mandatory retirement age for federal employees and raised it from 65 to 70 in private industry. The action amended the Age Discrimination in Employment Act which prohibits discrimination in public and private employment.

ELDERLY CONSUMERS STILL NEGLECTED

While government agencies have begun to pay increasing attention to the need for special services for the elderly, they have yet to acknowledge many of the unique problems of elderly consumers.

A 1978 study by the Federal Trade Commission found that the elderly are highly vulnerable and likely to experience a myriad of problems not encountered by other consumers. The report said elderly consumers were victimized in several areas including nursing home and other health care services, insurance, home repair and loneliness frauds.

The Commission claimed its own track record protecting elderly consumers was good and cited recent trade regulations concerning hearing aids, eyeglasses and funeral services (see index for further details). But it added that there was a definite need for continuing examination of such problems and an extensive consumer education program.

Much of the progress in elderly rights has taken place on the local level. Many communities now provide senior citizen discounts for public transportation, recreational and educational facilities and housing.

Congress has also passed a law requiring that all older people be given "reasonable access" to information about opportunities and services in the community. Nearly 5,000 multipurpose senior citizen centers have been established to provide such services.

HOW TO FILE A COMPLAINT
To file a complaint alleging age discrimination in federally assisted programs, contact the agency involved or the Office of the General Counsel, U.S. Department of Health, Education and Welfare, 330 Independence Ave. SW, Washington, DC, 20201. For discrimination in federal or non-federal employment contact a regional office of the Equal Employment Opportunity Commission or EEOC headquarters, 2401 E St. NW, Washington, DC, 20506.

FOR MORE INFORMATION
See *The Rights of Older Persons, an American Civil Liberties Union Handbook*, with sections entitled "The Right to An Adequate Income," "The Right to Health Care," and "The Right to Freedom from Restraints on Life, Liberty and Property." This comprehensive guide explains specific government programs in a question and answer format. It is available for $2.50 from Avon Books, 250 E 55 St., New York, NY, 10019.

THE RIGHT TO PRIVACY
'Big Brother' Getting Closer to Home

As new technology sends America racing into the 1980s, people are beginning to fear that progress may trample what was once an inalienable right—the right to privacy. A closed door or a wall between two rooms no longer protects people from being watched or overheard by microminiaturized bugs, hidden television monitors or other devices capable of penetrating physical barriers.

It is virtually impossible to obtain a loan, buy insurance, or apply for a job without disclosing one's Social Security number or other information collected and processed by electronic computers and then stored for potential future reference. Polygraph devices (lie tests) are used increasingly to determine if an employee is honest or a job applicant is mentally balanced. In short, Americans are rapidly approaching the state described by George Orwell's 1984 in which "virtually all personal privacy had been lost and the government knew almost everything that everyone was doing."

But the government is not the only "Big Brother" in today's society. A 1979 Harris poll revealed that people felt the biggest non-government invaders of privacy were finance companies (45 per cent), credit bureaus (44 per cent), insurance companies (38 per cent), credit card companies (37 per cent) and the media (31 per cent). Government agencies most cited were Internal Revenue Service (38 per cent), Central Intelligence Agency (34 per cent), Federal Bureau of Investigations (33 per cent), government welfare agencies (32 per cent) and the Census Bureau (24 per cent).

Of those surveyed by Harris, three out of four believed that the right to privacy should be akin to the right to life, liberty and the pursuit of happiness.

GOVERNMENT PROTECTION CRITICIZED
While federal laws have protected personal privacy in certain circumstances for a number of years, most cover relatively narrow areas and regulate government rather than the private sector. In 1977, the Privacy Protection Study Commission (which was established in the wake of Watergate to examine the

problem) proposed major rules for banking, credit, insurance, employment, health care, credit-cards, mailing lists, research and other areas. Congress has acted on few of those proposals, however.

In March, 1979, the Carter Administration called for legislation to protect privacy of medical records and federally-funded research, to limit the use of lie detectors and to reverse a Supreme Court ruling permitting police searches of reporter's materials without a court order.

In the meantime, private organizations are re-examining their record-keeping policies and formulating voluntary privacy codes in order to avoid federal intervention. One group which has been especially concerned is the Direct Mail Marketing Association (DMMA), which represents major mail-order firms. The DMMA strongly urged members at a 1978 meeting to remove names from mailing lists on request in order to cut down on the criticism of "junk mail."

Although federal action has been sparse, private citizens have gained some specific privacy rights as well as rights of access to certain information. Following are examples:

BANK RECORDS: In 1978, Congress reversed a Supreme Court ruling which said a depositor had no right to expect bank records to remain private. The Financial Right to Privacy Act prohibits government access to depositor's records except when there is a possible violation of the law. A depositor may copy bank records revealing which agencies requested or received information.

EDUCATIONAL RECORDS: Parents and students over 18 have a right to see most student records. Such information may not be released to outside sources without a parent's consent, and names of those who have asked for or been given access to records must be recorded. Records can be challenged and amended if inaccurate.

GOVERNMENT FILES: The Privacy Act of 1974 allows people to see personal government records and to dispute the contents. Agencies are prohibited from keeping any information which is irrelevant or not necessary for the function of the agency. Disclosure is permitted in certain cases without written consent, but names and addresses of those requesting access must be recorded.

TAX RETURNS: Federal tax returns and other tax information may not be disclosed to anyone other than the taxpayer except in certain cases.

FREEDOM OF INFORMATION
Your Right to Obtain Government Data

The 1966 Freedom of Information Act gives any person access to information in federal government files without having to say why it is needed or what it will be used for. Many states have similar laws. If a request is denied, the government must show why the information cannot be released; only certain exemptions are allowed.

Among the files available are civil rights compliance reports, state and federal meat inspection reports, government product testing reports and occupational health and safety inspection manuals.

To make a FOA request, write to the Freedom of Information Unit of the appropriate government agency. You must "reasonably describe" the records you seek. The agency has 10 working days to act.

A booklet with more details is available for 10 cents from the Freedom of Information Clearinghouse, P.O. Box 19367, Washington, DC, 20036.

Making Your Voice Count

In theory, American voters are represented in government by the people they elect. Every citizen is supposed to have an equal voice in the nation's decisions, at least to have his or her voice heard and heeded in the workings of a democracy.

In practice, however, the system does not work that way. In the Nation's Capital and in state capitals, the average person—the public at large—is often ignored or forgotten. The real wielders of power and influence are those with money to offer, with favors to give or with close personal ties that bind. This is especially true in Congress, which is supposed to be closer to the people than the other two branches of the federal government, the executive and judiciary. Congress is the main target more because of its power to obstruct than for its power to pass important proposals. All it takes in many cases is to reach one person in a key position to preserve the status quo from the threats of new ideas and changing conditions.

Yet the real workings of Congress have been largely hidden from view. Only in recent years have many of the details become known, thanks largely to procedural reforms and new laws requiring disclosure of most income. Although not everything has become visible, revelations so far depict a scene swarming with lobbyists offering large contributions on behalf of all interests except that of the general public. Although most legislators may still vote their conscience, many others appear to be vulnerable to pressures from special interests.

NEW LAWS AFFECT CONTRIBUTIONS

Federal election laws, applicable for the first time in 1976, changed the complexion of campaign financing. The free flow of massive sums, which played a big role in the 1972 Presidential election, was slowed down in 1976 by limitations on private contributions, mandatory public disclosure of contributions and large scale public funding by the U.S. Treasury.

The type of unrestrained financial activity conducted by Nixon's 1972 campaign committee, which raised almost $63 million, twice as much as had ever been recorded in behalf of a Presidential candidate, is now prohibited. During Nixon's campaign, 75 people contributed more than $100,000. His biggest backer was W. Clement Stone, chairman of the Combined Insurance Company of America, who gave more than $2 million.

Under the federal election laws, private citizens now may contribute no more than $1,000 to a candidate for any series of primary elections and up to another $1,000 for general elections. And a person's total contributions may not exceed $25,000 in a calendar year. As a result, just over half of the contributions by private citizens to Republican and Democratic candidates in the 1976 Presidential primaries were in amounts of $100 or less.

SOURCES MUST BE DISCLOSED
Candidates for federal office must now disclose where they get their campaign money and how they spend it. The name, address, occupation and principal place of business of every contributor of over $100 must be reported to the Federal Elections Commission, the governmental agency which administers the laws. Aggregate contributions which exceed $100 from a particular contributor must also be identified.

In addition, candidates must disclose all contributions from Political Action Committees (PACs) as well as proceeds from the sale of tickets to dinners, luncheons, rallies and other fundraising events, mass collections made at these events and profits from the sale of items such as campaign buttons, badges, flags, emblems, hats, banners, literature and jewelry. They also must report contributions in the form of gifts, loans, advances, facilities, equipment, personnel, services, advertising and membership lists.

REFORMS APPEAR TO HAVE BACKFIRED
These disclosure requirements and contribution limits, however, have not reduced the influence of special interests on political candidates or officeholders. Corporations are still prohibited by law from making direct contributions to candidates in federal elections. But the new laws allow them to set up political action committees (PACs), similar to those run by labor unions, in support of one or more candidates. A PAC is allowed to give as much as $5,000 to any candidate for any series of primary elections and the same amount in the general election.

But there is no limit on the number of candidates a PAC can contribute to in an election year. And there is no limit on the number of PACs that can be established by members of a corporation or other group. So the net effect has been to open new doors of influence for wealthy financial interests. Disclosure requirements also have encouraged contributions from such sources by allowing more open solicitation and removing the psychological restraints of making contributions secretly.

DISCLOSURE FAR LESS THAN FULL
In practice, disclosure requirements have not been observed or enforced the way reformers expected. The Federal Election Commission (FEC), which was set up to administer the new rules, has been hampered by relatively small funds and inadequate personnel to handle the massive task.

One of the biggest loopholes is the exemption for contributions of $100 or less and for those who buy tickets to fund-raising dinners of that amount. Edward Roeder, a Washington specialist on election matters, estimated that 22 per cent of the money contributed to Senators who ran for re-election in 1978 came from undisclosed sources because of these loopholes. He said another 12 per cent of funds collected in the last two weeks of the campaign were not disclosed until after election day. In addition, debts incurred before election were carried over without disclosing who paid them off until it was too late to affect the election.

Candidates themselves have not always been following the rules by disclosing full names, address, occupations and places of business of contributors. Roeder found that from 35 to 84 per cent of contributors to various Senatorial candidates were improperly identified.

CONSERVATIVE FORCES DOMINATE

There is no way to determine whether more money is flowing from special interests to members of Congress under the new laws, because there was no official tabulation of figures before. But the amounts are extremely large, and they pour in constantly, regardless of election dates or candidates' re-election plans or lack of them. There are more organized efforts, more pressure for money through formal solicitation campaigns and more careful selection of recipients than before. Raising money to influence Congress has become big business.

As a result, conservative political interests have become more powerful politically than other interests. Of the $60.4 million raised by non-party political committees from January 1, 1977, through September 30, 1978, almost all was from conservative groups. The list included $14.2 million from business corporations, $21.8 million from trade/membership/health groups mostly representing business, $1.8 million from producer cooperatives, $12.9 million from PACs not affiliated with other organizations and 16.8 from organized labor.

The dominance of conservative interests is indicated by the names of PACs with the largest amounts. They were, in order, Ronald Reagan's Citizens for the Republic, $2,662,746; National Conservative PAC, $2,579,283; Committee for the Survival of a Free Congress, $1,742,770; American Medical PAC, $1,589,831; Realtors PAC, $1,507,125; AFL-CIO COPE PAC, $1,389,842; Gun Owners of America Campaign Committee, $1,301,223; Automobile and Truck Dealers Election Action Committee, $1,248,082; UAW Voluntary Community Action Program, $925,999; and the National Committee for an Effective Congress, $827,477.

The biggest corporate cash bundles belonged, in order, to: Standard Oil of Indiana, American Family Corp. (insurance), International Paper, Winn Dixie Stores, LTV/Vought Corporation, General Motors, Boeing, Dart Industries and Grumman. Large funds among trade/membership/health groups included those of the California Medical PAC, Texas Medical PAC, Attorneys Congressional Campaign Trust (American Association of Trial Lawyers), National Rifle Association, Conservative Victory Fund (American Conservative Union) and National Association of Life Underwriters.

NARROW INTERESTS GET BROAD RESULTS

Political conservatives and business interests appear to have tightened their grip on Congress in the past few years despite the influx of liberal Democrats in 1976 and few changes in 1978. Victory of the Jarvis amendment in California to slash state taxes, the drive for a Constitutional amendment to require a balanced budget in Washington and the business-sponsored campaign against government regulators have tended to frighten liberals and encourage conservative votes on Capitol Hill. Money from special interests has sped up these drives.

The money has been quite productive. The defeat of no-fault auto insurance in 1978 was largely due to the efforts of the American Association of Trial Lawyers; passage of a gas deregulation bill, called "the worst scandal since Teapot Dome" by the Citizens Labor Energy Coalition, was aided by oil companies and other big business representatives; a Senate-passed bill to exempt many real estate firms from disclosure requirements on land sales was helped by realtor groups and others; medical groups combined to help defeat efforts of the Carter Administration to slow down hospital costs; life insurance lobbyists got a House Appropriations Committee to warn the Federal Trade Commission against favoring any type of cost disclosure not approved by the industry; and numerous business and political conservative groups were influential in getting Congress to defeat the perennial proposal for a new consumer agency in the federal government and defeat other measures advocated by citizen groups.

ENVIRONMENTAL GROUPS WIN SOME POINTS

A possible exception to the pattern on Capitol Hill is the environmental movement. In contrast to the consumer movement, this coalition of public interest organizations has gained strength in recent years. It scored a major victory in May, 1979, with House passage of the Alaska lands bill, despite well financed lobbying from oil, timber and mining interests, as well as the National Rifle Association, Chamber of Commerce, AFL-CIO and the state of Alaska itself. What was expected to be a close vote turned out to be a walkaway, 268 to 157.

However, the bill was not a clearcut victory. In the words of one environmentalist, "What came out was highly favorable to industry. They got 95 per cent of what they wanted. We stopped them from getting 100 per cent."

A decade ago, environmentalists got Congress to pass fairly strong legislation to control air and water pollution. But since then, the Environmental Protection Agency, pushed by industry and White House officials, has postponed and watered down numerous regulations. Environmentalists also have generally failed to get Congress to reduce expensive water projects even with President Carter's help.

NEWCOMERS TO CONGRESS BACKED BY PACs

Special interests are bound to dominate Congress for a long time if only because of the way they put newcomers into their debt. A survey of contribution records by Common Cause, a public interest group advocating political reform, showed that special interest groups played a big role in the election of 77 new members of the House in 1978. The winning candidates received $3.3 million from PACs, an average of $45,000 each. That was more than double the average two years earlier.

Most of the beneficiaries were people with conservative views. The bulk of the PAC money went to incumbents and those with voting records most favorable to PAC donors. Of the $27.7 million given to House candidates in 1978 by PACs, all but $7.7 million went to those running for re-election.

Common Cause official Fred Wertheimer saw cause for alarm. "The new FEC figures and our study," he said, "show a continuation of the dangerous trend toward PAC domination of our elected officials in Congress. We are facing government of, by and for the PACs of America, unless this fundamental flaw in our political system is corrected."

CONGRESSIONAL LEADERS DEEPLY INDEBTED TO PACs

Special interests have also become special friends of the most influential members of Congress, according to election data. In 1978, the eight Congressional leaders who won re-election divided up nearly $1 million from PACs despite the fact that none faced any significant opposition. They included Republican Senators Howard Baker of Tennessee and Tad Stevens of Alaska. Baker received the largest amount, $336,000, and Stevens the second largest, $177,000. Next largest amount went to Republican House Minority Leader John Rhodes of Arizona, who received $123,000. Democratic Majority Leader Thomas P. (Tip) O'Neill of Massachusetts received only $23,000 from PACs, but that was more than enough to pay the $14,000 campaign costs he incurred.

Many of today's familiar faces in Congress may no longer be there in January, 1981, as a result of campaigns 20 months in advance by conservative groups to defeat them. The National Conservative Political Action Committee (NCPAC) has picked a number of notable liberals as targets of early advertising and solicitation drives. Among the main targets are Senators George McGovern and John Culver, Democrats of South Dakota and Iowa.

VOTING PATTERNS APPEAR TO SWITCH

One aim of the early campaigns is to influence the legislators to change their ways immediately. There were indications early in 1979 that the ploy was working on many issues. On votes involving school prayers and balancing the budget, several Senators chose to take stands they never would have taken otherwise.

Eighteen of the 23 Democratic Senators who are up for re-election in 1980 have been members of the liberal wing of the Democratic Party. Two who would have run but decided not to in 1979 are Adlai Stevenson, Illinois Democrat, and Abraham Ribicoff, Connecticut Democrat.

1980 PRESIDENTIAL RACE STARTS EARLY
With Heavy Funding From Special Interests

Politicians with ambitions to become President in 1981 have begun campaigning and raising funds earlier than at any other time in history. By April, 1979, 18 months before the election, Republican candidates had already raised more than $4 million, mostly from special interests, according to the Washington Post.

John Connally, former Treasury Secretary, had $1.2 million in the bank, largely from oil and gas industry sources from his native Texas, while fellow Texan and Republican George Bush, had raised $663,000, much from the same interests. The one with the biggest bundle at that point was Republican Congressman Philip Crane of Illinois, with $1.7 million. Former California Republican Governor Ronald Reagan had collected $527,000. Two other Republicans, Senators Howard Baker of Tennessee and Robert Dole of Kansas, also had sizeable amounts before they had formally announced their plans.

But these figures are merely part of the picture. Reagan had the use of mailing lists and travel money from Citizens for the Republic, with a budget of $2.5 million. And Dole used money from Campaign America, a group backing Republican candidates, to travel to New Hampshire eight times before even announcing his candidacy.

By April, President Carter had raised $305,000 in only two weeks of fund raising, much of which came from special interests. He also had the advantage of holding office and having the government pay for many expenses not directly attributable to campaigning. Senator Edward Kennedy, who seemed to be running for President, also had the benefit of a large staff and expense money as well as considerable family wealth.

JUDGES BLOCK OWN FINANCIAL DISCLOSURE

The Ethics in Government Act of 1978 calls for disclosure of personal finances by high government officials with salaries above $44,599 and declared candidates for federal office. The law was designed to expose conflicts of interest or potential ones.

But on May 15, 1979, the day when disclosure statements were to be filed, a group of federal judges in four southern states obtained a restraining order blocking the law on the grounds that it was unconstitutional. Supreme Court Chief Justice Warren Burger was one of the judges who did not file on time but did file later.

His statement showed assets of about $600,000, mostly in two companies, Minnesota Mining and Manufacturing and Honeywell, plus real estate holdings and large debts to two banks. Potter Stewart reported the largest estate, with at least $1.3 million in assets, including substantial holdings in oil companies and other large firms, perhaps explaining his frequent abstention from cases involving the oil industry. Associate Justice Harry Blackmun also listed numerous corporate securities.

It may have been indicative that the most liberal of the Supreme Court justices, Thurgood Marshall, listed no assets and a personal debt of $5,000 to $15,000.

The reason for the imprecise figures is that the law asks for details only within certain ranges.

BIG BUSINESS SWINGS ITS WEIGHT
Steps Up Efforts to Influence Public Opinion

Business interests are becoming increasingly militant and determined to influence public opinion on political issues. They are putting more advertising dollars into arguing their points of view in the media, getting special programs into the schools, counteracting unfavorable news stories through letters to editors and pressuring employees and stockholders to write, visit and telephone public officials to act the way business wants.

Such activity has increased since the Supreme Court ruled in April, 1978, against a Massachusetts law that prohibited banks and other corporations from financing propaganda for or against issues that do not directly affect their interests. In effect, the court said corporations have the same right as individuals to freedom of speech. The decision negated similar laws in 17 other states.

The laws had sought to prevent the type of situation that occurred in California in 1976 when energy corporations succeeded in defeating a referendum to restrict construction of nuclear power plants. Business interests raised $2.5 million, nearly $1 million more than proponents of the measure could raise. In Montana, a similar referendum was defeated when corporations raised $144,-000, while proponents could raise only $450.

BUSINESS TRYING TO OFFSET NEGATIVE IMAGE

For many years, it has been standard operating procedure in the business world to launch a public relations program to counteract negative public views caused by business abuses or other unfavorable developments. Thus, when many business interests are accused of gouging the public with unjustified price increases or when profit rates take a big jump, many firms and associations turn to issue advertising in an attempt to offset unfavorable opinions.

One example of this type of response occurred in May, 1979, after the Department of Transportation had released a survey showing that automobile owners had only about a 50-50 chance of getting proper repairs done. Associations representing the auto repair industry immediately sprung into action—not to admit that there were serious problems or announce voluntary measures to improve practices—but to go on the offensive with a publicity ploy. Three national groups issued a news release saying they had sent a letter to President Carter asking him to demand that DOT Secretary Brock Adams "publicly apologize to the 137 million motorists and to the entire automotive industry." No apology resulted, but Adams later was fired for other reasons.

MANY PROBLEMS BLAMED ON GOVERNMENT REGULATIONS

No issue has caused more discussion or had more effect on the public in recent years than government regulation of business. With few exceptions, business leaders are convinced that all their problems are caused at least indirectly by government involvement of one kind or another. Rules are too strict or too picayune, paperwork is overwhelming, taxes are too high, and the government is too nosey, in their view. Even Chrysler blamed its financial woes on Washington in August, 1979.

So successful has been the anti-regulation campaign that counter-arguments are rarely heard or seen. A few cases where government rules are indeed silly or unintelligible have received more currency than one-dollar bills. Politicians sensitive to where large contributions come from, have willingly echoed the business views so much that many victims of business abuse are convinced that all government regulation is wrong. Yet when these same people are asked whether specific rules regarding product safety or the environment should be repealed or cut back, they tend to support regulations, according to numerous polls on the subject.

TARGETS OF GOVERNMENT ACTION FIGHT BACK

Many leaders of the anti-government, anti-regulation drive are companies and executives accused of breaking rules designed to protect both consumers and competing businesses from unfair and deceptive practices.

One of the leaders has been Richard DeVos, president of Amway Corporation, a large door-to-door seller of household wares. DeVos also has been chairman of the Communications Advisory Committee of the National Association of Manufacturers (NAM). In the May, 1979, issue of *Enterprise*, the NAM's monthly journal, DeVos called on his fellow business executives to "wake up" and fight to save the free enterprise system. DeVos said they have been surrendering their freedoms to the federal government "without much more than a whimper." He urged businesses to do more "communicating" with stockholders, customers, employees and suppliers on a regular basis "about the merits of the system which produced the highest standard of living ever achieved by mankind." He told of his own firm's construction of a $3 million Center of Free Enterprise, which offers "educational" workshops to train school teachers in economics. He told also how his company emphasizes "the good news" to its employees.

Two months later, the Federal Trade Commission sent out a press release announcing final action on a case involving Amway. "Amway Corporation," said the FTC, "has been ordered to stop fixing retail and wholesale prices and misrepresenting the profitability of Amway distributorships . . ." A simultaneous release by the company to all recipients of the FTC release started out: "Finally, after more than four years of legal proceedings . . . the FTC has found that Amway is 'a vigorous new competitive presence into (a) highly concentrated market' and upheld the Amway sales and marketing plan."

BUSINESS AIMING TO MOLD YOUNGSTERS

Amway is one of many firms and business groups that have found school administrators and teachers receptive to their views and free materials. Amway has even added a Ph.D program at its Center of Free Enterprise and is participating in establishing a free enterprise economics course for 74,000 regional students of a national educational association that could eventually reach 520,000 per year, according to DeVos.

Other companies have donated sums to set up chairs at universities for the teaching of business economics. Goodyear Tire & Rubber Company gave $250,000 to Kent State and the University of Akron for such chairs, and Standard Oil of Ohio set aside nearly as much for similar purposes. These programs are part of a growing effort to offset what many executives feel are anti-business viewpoints being taught at all educational levels. According to the Council for Financial Aid to Education Inc., there are more than 100 programs linking companies and college campuses.

In addition, the National Association of Manufacturers has been campaigning for two years to "improve" the quality of business news reporting. Through seminars for journalists, scholarship programs, grants to schools and other means, the NAM has succeeded in spreading a viewpoint that business has been victimized more by bad journalism than by its own bad practices.

DOES CONGRESS REPRESENT YOU?
Special Interests Take Control of Capitol Hill

Do your Representative and Senators vote the way you want them to on important issues affecting you?

What a legislator says in letters, bulletins and news releases does not always coincide with the way he or she actually votes. In fact, when a series of votes are taken on the same measure, legislators often will be found voting on both sides of some issues. It is not easy to keep tabs on such performers and to report their activities accurately to the people who elected them to Congress.

One of the best ways to check up on elected representatives is to check the official tally of their action or non-action on topics of particular interest to people as consumers, taxpayers, workers and citizens. Among the more significant studies of Congressional voting records are the ones done each year by Ralph Nader's Congress Watch and by the Consumer Federation of America, a group of some 200 citizen organizations. They each rated the 95th Congress and found it wanting. The percentage of legislators voting the way these groups preferred has dropped steadily in recent years, apparently reflecting a turn to the right among the electorate despite heavy Democratic majorities in both the House and Senate.

BIG BUSINESS GETS ITS WAY

The 95th was tagged "the Corporate Congress" by Mark Green, head of Congress Watch, after reviewing the record on several dozen issues. Big business gained success on almost every area of interest, according to Green, because of large contributions, an anti-bureaucracy mood and cohesive Republican voting. "When this iron triangle of big business money, an anti-government sentiment and Republican unity link together," he added, "Congress seems to be incapable of responding to consumer proposals." Among causes that fell through cracks were an independent consumer protection agency at the federal level, expansion of public participation funding, public financing of Congressional campaigns and lobbying disclosure. Approved were a national cooperative bank, bank reform, civil service reform and an improved bankruptcy system.

The Senators with the best pro-consumer scores were Edward Kennedy (D-MA), Paul Sarbanes (D-MD) and Dick Clark (D-IA) with 98, 93 and 90 per cent respectively. For two years in a row, Elizabeth Holtzman (D-NY) tied for the highest score in the House with 98 per cent with Robert Drinan (D-MA). The lowest score in the Senate belonged to Milton Young (R-ND) with only 10 per cent of his votes considered correct. Sharing 13 per cent scores were Senators Stevens, McClure, Curtis, Hensen, Helms and Tower. The lowest score in the House was that of Arlan Strangeland (R-MN), with 3 per cent, only one correct vote in 40.

VOTING RECORDS COMPILED ON 39 ISSUES

Following are voting records for both the Senate and House for the 94th Congress and each year of the 95th Congress, as compiled by the Consumer Federation of America, which used almost the same issues used by Congress Watch. Nineteen issues are listed for the Senate and 20 for the House in 1978. Each issue is summarized by number, including final action and whether the "correct" position was "yes" or "no," as determined by the CFA.

Footnotes are explained at the end of each tally, and a list of legislators who were defeated or did not run in 1978 is also given. The letter "R" means

---

HOW TO INFLUENCE CONGRESS

Individual citizens can have an impact on Congress if they really want to and have some luck along the way. Letters are useful, even though most of them get routine treatment complete with automated signatures, and the legislator does not see either the incoming or outgoing correspondence.

Every legislator has aides to keep records of subjects covered and the number of letters received. Telegrams, telephone calls and personal visits can also make an impact.

If you wish to call the office of your Senator or Representative in Washington, the number of the U.S. Capitol is 202-224-3121. When the operator answers, ask for the legislator by name. Getting through to him or her personally may be too difficult to try. Leaving a message with an aide is the next best thing and usually counts much more than a letter or telegram. Most Congressmen and Senators maintain local offices which are less expensive to call than Washington.

If you are writing to a Senator, the address is Senate Office Building, Washington, DC, 20510. If you are addressing a Representative, the address is House Office Building, Washington, DC 20515.

a correct (right) vote for consumer interests; "W" is a wrong vote; "A" means absent; "P" means a vote of "present" and an italic "A" means absence due to illness requiring hospitalization. An asterisk designates a person who was not in the 94th Congress. "% 94" means the proportion of correct votes in the 94th Congress; "% 77" means the rating for the first session of the 95th Congress; "%78" refers to the second session of the 95th.

Ratings are determined by dividing the number of right votes by the total number of votes considered. A right vote for the consumer agency bill in 1978 (House vote 7) and natural gas deregulation (House vote 5) was counted double because of their importance to consumers. More details on the CFA Voting Record may be obtained from the CFA, 1012 14th St. NW, Washington, DC, 20005. Congress Watch's voting record can be had by writing to the group at 133 C St. SE, Washington, DC, 20003.

HOW YOUR SENATORS VOTED
On Key Issues Affecting You

1. Sugar Stabilization Act. Long (D-LA) motion to table Metzenbaum's (D-OH) proposal to establish 15¢/pound import price without an inflationary escalator clause. The Senate Finance Committee bill would double sugar prices by 1982. Motion agreed to. NO.
2. National Consumer Cooperative Bank. Creates bank with $300 million federal seed money plus technical and financial assistance to eligible cooperatives. Money is to be gradually repaid by participating co-ops. Bill passed. YES.
3. Natural Gas Pricing. Metzenbaum (D-OH) motion to recommit (kill) Natural Gas Conference Report, deleting all pricing provisions except those relating to Alaskan gas. Motion would have killed Conference Report's compromise on natural gas pricing, which would lead to deregulation by 1985 and thereby increase gas prices greatly. Motion rejected. YES.
4. Natural Gas Pricing. Senate voted adoption of Natural Gas Conference Report (see above). NO.
5. Coleman Nomination. Metzenbaum (D-OH) motion to recommit (kill) nomination of Lynn R. Coleman as general counsel to Department of Energy. Coleman had represented many major oil and gas producers in private practice. Motion rejected. YES.
6. Housing and Community Development. Schmitt (R-NM) amendment to allow one branch of Congress to veto by voice vote proposed regulations of Department of Housing and Urban Development (HUD). Motion rejected. NO.
7. Department of Defense Procurement Authorization. Proxmire (D-WI) amendment to delete $209 million of $541 million payment to two shipbuilding contractors who experienced large cost overruns due to mismanagement. Amendment rejected. YES.
8. Health Planning Reauthorization. Kennedy (D-MA) motion to table Huddleston (D-KY) amendment, Part I (known as "American Medical Association Amendment") to allow states to be more restrictive toward Health Maintenance Organizations than for other providers of outpatient health care. Motion agreed to. YES.

9. Health Planning Reauthorization. Kennedy (D-MA) motion to prevent reconsideration of Huddleston (D-KY) amendment, Part II, eliminating requirement that medical equipment over $150,000 could not be purchased without obtaining certificate-of-need. Amendment would have encouraged unnecessary purchase of expensive equipment by physicians. Motion agreed to. YES.

10. Hospital Cost Containment. Talmadge (D-GA) motion to table the Kennedy bill limiting hospital revenue increases to 9 per cent a year. Motion agreed to. NO.

11. Hospital Cost Containment. Talmadge (D-GA) motion to table Nelson (D-WI) amendment, which was a compromise measure to Kennedy amendment (see above). Nelson amendment provided for mandatory cutbacks when voluntary cost control efforts fail. Motion defeated. NO.

12. Labor-HEW Appropriations, Fiscal 1979. Byrd (D-WV) motion to table consideration of Bartlett (R-OK) amendment exempting workplaces with ten or fewer full-time employees from coverage under Occupational Safety and Health Act. Motion passed. YES.

13. Agriculture Appropriations, Fiscal 1979. Lugar (R-IN) amendment to delete $250 million for Food Stamp Program. Defeated. NO.

14. Housing and Community Development. Griffin (R-MI) amendment to broaden the term, "expected to reside," in the Community Development Act of 1974 and discourage community plans for housing low-income residents. Amendment rejected. NO.

15. HUD, Independent Agencies Appropriations, Fiscal 1979. Long (D-LA) motion to reconsider Proxmire (D-WI) amendment (initially defeated) to cut public housing by 2 per cent. Motion agreed to; Proxmire amendment subsequently adopted. NO.

16. United States-United Kingdom Tax Treaty. Church (D-ID) reservation to nullify part of Treaty encouraging foreign investment in U.S. farm lands and preventing states from restricting tax avoidance by U.K.-based multinational corporations. Reservation rejected. YES.

17. Revenue Act. Packwood (R-OR) amendment to repeal special tax treatment for Domestic International Sales Corporation (DISC), a program designed to create jobs by stimulating exports of American goods manufactured by

---

COMPUTER LOBBYING COMES OF AGE

During the past two years, Congress has been subjected to unprecedented "grass-roots" lobbying pressures. Large organizations are now using computerized mailing lists to urge members to write about a particular bill or issue.

The process started with anti-war groups in the 1960s, was later used effectively by environmental groups, but has now become primarily a tool of wealthy business groups.

Computerized mailings have been credited for the defeat of major legislation, including a cargo preference bill, a bill that would have expanded construction-site picketing and a bill to establish a federal consumer protection agency.

Among the large users are the National Association of Manufacturers, the U.S. Chamber of Commerce, the National Rifle Association, Common Cause, the AFL-CIO, the National Action Committee on Labor Law Reform, the Business Roundtable and the pro-Israel lobby.

small business firms. DISC has been ineffectual. Amendment rejected. YES.
18. Revenue Act. Danforth (D-MO) amendment to reduce maximum corporate income tax to 45% in 1980, 44% in 1981. Amendment adopted. NO.
19. Revenue Act. Adoption of Conference Report on the Revenue Act of 1978. Act contains virtually no reforms for low and middle income taxpayer; increases allowable tax-exempt capital gains and grants tax relief to special industry groups. Report adopted. NO.

The following Senators in the voting list are no longer in office: Abourezk, Allen, Bartlett, Case, Curtis, Eastland, Hansen, Hathaway, Humphrey, McClellan, Metcalf, Pearson, Scott and Sparkman.

SENATE VOTING RECORD

	1	2	3	4	5	6	7	8	9	10	11	12	13	14	15	16	17	18	19	%94	%77	%78
ALABAMA																						
Allen, M. (D)[1]	A	W	W	W	—	W	A	W	W	W	W	A	W	W	R	R	A	A	A	*	—	11
Sparkman (D)	A	R	W	W	W	R	A	R	W	W	R	R	R	R	R	A	A	W	W	26	16	40
ALASKA																						
Gravel (D)	W	R	W	W	W	R	W	W	R	A	R	R	R	A	R	R	W	W	W	26	32	40
Stevens (R)	A	R	W	W	W	W	W	W	A	W	W	W	W	R	R	R	W	W	W	29	12	20
ARIZONA																						
DeConcini (D)	W	R	W	W	R	R	R	W	W	W	W	W	R	W	R	W	W	W	W	*	52	30
Goldwater (R)	A	W	R	R	W	W	A	W	W	W	W	W	W	W	W	W	W	W	A	0	12	15
ARKANSAS																						
Bumpers (D)	W	W	W	W	W	R	W	R	R	W	R	W	W	R	W	W	R	R	W	68	56	35
Hodges (D)	W	W	W	W	W	R	W	W	W	W	R	W	W	W	W	R	R	W	W	*	—	20
CALIFORNIA																						
Cranston (D)	W	R	W	W	W	R	W	R	R	R	R	R	R	R	R	W	W	R	W	83	64	55
Hayakawa (R)	W	R	R	R	W	W	W	W	W	W	W	W	W	R	W	A	W	W	*	0	25	
COLORADO																						
Hart (D)	W	R	W	W	W	R	W	R	R	W	R	R	R	R	R	R	R	W	W	84	76	55
Haskell (D)	A	R	R	R	W	W	A	R	R	A	A	A	R	R	W	A	A	A	A	93	72	40
CONNECTICUT																						
Ribicoff (D)	A	R	W	R	W	W	R	R	R	R	R	R	R	R	R	R	W	W	W	90	64	50
Weicker (R)	A	R	R	R	W	R	W	R	R	A	A	R	R	R	W	W	W	W	W	55	48	55
DELAWARE																						
Biden (D)	A	R	R	R	R	R	R	R	R	W	R	W	R	A	W	W	R	W	W	83	68	60
Roth (R)	R	W	R	R	W	W	W	W	W	W	W	W	W	W	W	W	W	W	W	41	32	20
FLORIDA																						
Chiles (D)	W	W	W	W	W	R	W	W	R	W	R	W	R	W	W	W	W	W	W	52	40	25
Stone (D)	W	R	W	W	R	R	W	R	R	W	R	W	R	W	R	W	W	W	W	41	32	40
GEORGIA																						
Nunn (D)	R	W	W	W	W	W	R	W	R	W	W	W	W	R	W	W	W	W	W	28	24	20
Talmadge (D)	A	R	W	W	W	R	W	R	R	W	W	W	R	R	W	W	W	R	W	20	24	35
HAWAII																						
Inouye (D)	W	R	W	W	W	R	W	R	R	W	W	R	A	A	A	A	W	W	W	56	40	25
Matsunaga (D)	W	R	W	W	W	R	W	R	R	R	W	R	R	R	R	R	A	W	R	W	*	44	50
IDAHO																						
Church (D)	W	R	W	W	W	R	W	R	W	W	W	W	R	R	W	R	R	R	W	63	64	40
McClure (R)	A	A	W	W	W	W	W	W	W	W	A	A	W	W	W	A	R	W	A	A	0	4	5

	1	2	3	4	5	6	7	8	9	10	11	12	13	14	15	16	17	18	19	%94	%77	%78
ILLINOIS																						
Stevenson (D)	A	R	W	W	W	R	W	R	R	W	R	R	R	R	W	W	R	W		81	60	50
Percy (R)	R	R	W	W	W	R	W	R	R	W	W	W	W	R	R	W	W	W	W	58	52	35
INDIANA																						
Bayh (D)	R	R	R	R	W	R	R	R	R	W	R	R	R	R	R	W	R	R	W	46	88	80
Lugar (R)	R	W	R	R	W	W	W	R	W	W	W	W	W	W	W	W	W	W	W	*	20	25
IOWA																						
Clark (D)	W	R	W	W	R	R	R	R	R	A	A	R	R	R	R	R	R	R	A	90	88	65
Culver (D)	W	R	W	W	W	R	W	R	R	R	R	R	R	R	R	R	R	R	W	77	88	65
KANSAS																						
Dole (R)	W	R	R	R	W	W	W	W	W	W	W	W	R	W	W	W	W	W	W	16	28	25
Pearson (R)	A	R	W	W	W	R	W	R	R	W	W	W	W	W	W	W	A	W	A	36	32	20
KENTUCKY																						
Ford (D)	W	R	W	W	W	R	W	W	W	W	W	W	R	R	W	A	W	W	W	56	20	25
Huddleston (D)	W	W	W	W	W	A	W	W	W	W	W	A	R	A	W	A	R	A	R	60	28	10
LOUISIANA																						
Johnston (D)	W	A	R	R	W	R	W	W	W	W	W	A	W	W	W	A	A	W	W	26	32	15
Long (D)	W	R	R	R	W	R	W	W	W	W	W	R	W	W	W	A	W	R	W	10	8	35
MAINE																						
Hathaway (D)	R	R	W	W	R	A	R	R	A	A	R	R	R	R	A	R	A	A		97	88	55
Muskie (D)	R	R	W	W	W	R	R	R	R	R	R	R	R	R	R	R	R	R	W	90	48	80
MARYLAND																						
Sarbanes (D)	R	R	R	R	W	R	R	R	R	W	R	R	R	R	R	R	A	R	W	*	84	80
Mathias (R)	R	R	W	W	W	A	W	R	R	A	A	R	R	A	W	A	W	W	A	59	52	30
MASSACHUSETTS																						
Kennedy (D)	R	R	R	R	W	R	W	R	W	R	R	R	R	R	R	R	R	R	A	85	84	80
Brooke (R)	R	A	A	R	W	A	W	A	A	W	R	R	R	A	A	A	W	W	A	79	80	25
MICHIGAN																						
Riegle (D)	W	R	R	R	R	R	R	R	W	R	R	R	R	A	R	A	W	W		*	76	70
Griffin (R)	A	R	W	W	W	W	A	W	W	A	A	W	W	W	A	A	W	W	W	17	4	10
MINNESOTA																						
Anderson (D)	W	A	R	R	A	A	A	A	R	R	R	R	A	A	A	A	W	A		*	64	35
Humphrey, M. (D)[2]	A	R	R	R	R	R	W	A	A	R	R	R	A	R	A	R	A	R	W	*	—	60
MISSISSIPPI																						
Eastland (D)	A	W	W	R	W	R	W	W	A	W	W	W	W	W	W	W	A	R	A	0	12	15
Stennis (D)	A	W	W	W	W	R	W	W	W	W	W	W	W	A	W	A	W	R	A	13	20	10
MISSOURI																						
Eagleton (D)	A	R	W	W	W	R	W	R	R	W	R	R	R	A	R	W	R	W	W	81	56	45
Danforth (R)	W	W	W	W	W	R	W	R	R	W	W	W	R	R	W	W	W	W	W	*	24	25
MONTANA																						
Melcher (D)	W	R	W	W	R	R	R	W	W	W	W	R	R	W	W	R	R	A	W	*	44	40
Hatfield, P.[3] (D)	W	R	W	W	A	A	W	R	W	W	R	R	R	A	R	R	W	A	W	*	—	35
NEBRASKA																						
Zorinsky (D)	W	W	W	R	R	R	W	R	R	W	R	W	R	R	R	R	R	W	W	*	36	45
Curtis (R)	W	W	R	R	W	W	W	W	W	W	W	W	W	W	A	W	W	W	A	0	8	15
NEVADA																						
Cannon (D)	W	R	W	W	W	R	W	R	W	R	W	R	R	R	R	R	W	W	W	67	36	45
Laxalt (R)	A	W	R	R	A	W	W	W	W	W	W	W	W	W	R	R	W	W	W	0	20	20
NEW HAMPSHIRE																						
Durkin (D)	R	R	W	R	R	R	W	R	R	R	R	R	R	R	R	W	W	W		100	76	70
McIntyre (D)	A	R	W	W	R	R	A	R	R	A	A	R	R	R	A	A	R	R	R	89	76	50
NEW JERSEY																						
Williams (D)	R	R	W	W	W	R	W	R	R	R	R	R	R	R	R	W	W	W	W	89	68	55
Case (R)	A	R	W	W	W	W	R	W	R	R	R	R	R	R	R	W	W	W	A	97	68	50

	1	2	3	4	5	6	7	8	9	10	11	12	13	14	15	16	17	18	19	%94	%77	%78
NEW MEXICO																						
Domenici (R)	A	W	W	W	R	W	R	R	W	A	A	W	R	W	A	R	A	A	A	15	4	25
Schmitt (R)	W	W	R	R	R	W	W	W	W	W	W	W	W	W	W	R	W	W	W	*	8	25
NEW YORK																						
Moynihan (D)	A	R	W	W	W	R	W	R	R	W	R	R	R	R	R	W	W	W	W	*	48	45
Javits (R)	R	R	W	W	W	R	W	R	R	R	R	R	R	A	R	R	W	W	W	68	72	50
NORTH CAROLINA																						
Morgan (D)	W	R	W	W	W	R	W	W	W	W	W	R	R	R	R	A	R	R	W	51	44	40
Helms (R)	W	W	A	A	W	W	A	W	W	W	W	A	W	W	W	R	W	W	A	0	8	5
NORTH DAKOTA																						
Burdick (D)	W	R	W	W	W	R	R	R	R	W	R	R	R	A	R	A	R	R	W	72	48	55
Young (R)	W	W	W	W	W	W	W	W	W	W	W	W	W	W	A	A	W	A	A	4	0	0
OHIO																						
Glenn (D)	R	W	W	W	W	R	W	W	W	R	R	R	R	R	R	W	W	R	W	75	60	45
Metzenbaum (D)	R	R	R	R	R	R	R	R	A	R	R	R	R	R	R	R	R	R	W	*	84	90
OKLAHOMA																						
Bartlett (R)	W	W	R	R	W	R	W	W	W	W	W	W	W	W	W	W	W	W	W	0	8	20
Bellmon (R)	W	W	R	R	W	R	W	R	W	R	W	W	R	A	W	A	W	W	A	4	20	35
OREGON																						
Hatfield, M. (R)	W	R	W	W	W	A	R	R	W	W	W	A	R	A	R	R	W	W	R	48	24	35
Packwood (R)	A	W	R	W	A	W	W	W	W	W	W	W	W	W	W	R	R	W	W	47	28	20
PENNSYLVANIA																						
Heinz (R)	R	R	W	W	R	R	W	R	R	W	W	W	A	R	R	W	W	W	W	*	64	40
Schweiker (R)	R	R	R	W	W	W	R	R	W	W	W	W	W	W	W	W	W	W	W	97	52	35
RHODE ISLAND																						
Pell (D)	R	R	W	R	W	R	W	R	R	R	R	R	R	R	R	W	R	W	W	86	80	70
Chafee (R)	R	W	W	W	W	R	W	R	R	W	R	W	R	R	W	W	W	W	W	*	48	35
SOUTH CAROLINA																						
Hollings (D)	R	R	R	R	R	R	W	R	W	W	W	R	W	W	W	R	R	R	R	71	48	60
Thurmond (R)	W	R	R	W	W	W	W	W	W	W	W	W	R	W	W	W	W	W	W	0	24	20
SOUTH DAKOTA																						
Abourezk (D)	A	R	R	R	R	R	R	R	R	R	R	A	A	A	A	R	A	R	R	94	84	65
McGovern (D)	A	A	R	R	W	R	W	R	A	R	R	R	R	R	R	R	R	R	A	86	76	70
TENNESSEE																						
Sasser (D)	R	W	R	W	R	W	W	W	R	W	R	R	R	W	W	W	W	W	W	*	72	30
Baker (R)	R	A	R	R	W	W	W	W	W	W	W	W	W	A	W	A	W	W	W	20	8	20
TEXAS																						
Bentsen (D)	W	W	R	R	W	R	W	W	W	W	W	W	R	R	W	A	W	W	W	15	24	30
Tower (R)	A	A	R	R	W	W	W	W	W	A	A	W	W	W	A	W	A	A	A	3	4	15
UTAH																						
Garn (R)	W	W	R	R	W	W	W	W	W	W	W	W	W	W	W	R	W	W	W	0	12	20
Hatch (R)	W	W	R	R	W	W	W	W	W	W	W	W	W	W	W	A	W	W		*	12	15
VERMONT																						
Leahy (D)	W	R	W	W	W	R	W	R	R	W	R	R	R	R	R	R	W	W		87	68	55
Stafford (R)	A	R	W	W	W	R	W	R	A	W	R	R	R	R	W	W	W	W	A	76	48	35
VIRGINIA																						
Byrd, H. (I)	W	W	R	R	W	W	W	W	W	W	A	W	W	W	W	W	R	W	W	7	12	20
Scott (R)	A	W	R	R	W	W	W	W	W	A	A	W	W	W	W	R	A	W	A	6	16	20
WASHINGTON																						
Jackson (D)	W	R	W	W	W	R	W	R	W	W	R	R	R	R	R	W	W	R	W	76	68	45
Magnuson (D)	W	R	W	W	R	R	W	R	R	W	R	R	R	R	W	R	W	R	W	73	60	55
WEST VIRGINIA																						
Byrd, R. (D)	W	R	W	W	W	R	W	W	W	R	R	R	R	W	W	A	R	R	W	60	40	40
Randolph (D)	W	R	W	W	A	R	W	R	R	R	R	R	R	W	R	W	A	R	W	50	36	50

	1	2	3	4	5	6	7	8	9	10	11	12	13	14	15	16	17	18	19	%94	%77	%78
WISCONSIN																						
Nelson (D)	R	R	R	W	R	A	R	R	R	R	R	R	R	W	R	R	W			94	84	80
Proxmire (D)	R	W	R	R	R	R	R	R	W	R	R	W	R	W	R	W	W			91	88	70
WYOMING																						
Hansen (R)	W	W	R	R	W	W	W	W	W	W	W	W	W	W	W	W	W			0	8	15
Wallop (R)	W	W	R	R	W	W	W	W	W	W	W	W	W	W	A	W	A	W		*	8	15

Senate Footnotes

[1] Maryon Allen was appointed on June 1, 1978 following the death of her husband James Allen.

[2] Muriel Humphrey was appointed on January 25, 1978 to fill the vacancy created by the death of Hubert Humphrey.

[3] Paul Hatfield was appointed on January 22, 1978 to fill the vacancy created by the death of Lee Metcalf.

HOW YOUR REPRESENTATIVE VOTED
On Key Issues Affecting You

1. Farmer-to-Consumer Direct Marketing Act. Foley (D-WV) motion to suspend rules, pass bill authorizing $1.5 million for direct marketing demonstration projects. Motion rejected. YES.
2. Sugar Stabilization Act of 1978. Steiger (R-WI) amendment would add cost-of-production escalator clause, raising prices to consumers. (See Senate vote #1.) Amendment adopted. NO.
3. Outer Continental Shelf. Breaux (D-LA) substitute would have diluted most important provisions of bill, stifling competition, diluting governmental power to assess resources accurately and restricting use of alternative bidding systems. Substitute rejected. NO.
4. Outer Continental Shelf. Brown (R-OH) substitute would have applied alternative bidding systems to no more than 30 per cent of lease sales, thereby ensuring continuation of present practice of large, up-front cash payments before recovery of gas and oil. This practice eliminates smaller companies. Rejected. NO.
5. Consideration of Conference Reports (Natural Gas). Bolling (D-MO) motion to help consumers by preventing separate consideration of natural gas bill. Motion agreed to. NO.
6. National Energy Act. Adoption of Conference Report. Anti-consumer effects of the natural gas pricing provisions outweigh positive aspects. NO.
7. Office of Consumer Representation. Non-regulatory Office would have served as advocate for consumers before federal regulatory agencies for safe and effective products and reasonable rates. Defeated. YES.
8. Interior, Energy Appropriations, Fiscal 1979. Moffett (D-CT) amendment to delete language from bill prohibiting use of appropriated funds to pay citizens' expenses when intervening in regulatory proceedings before Economic Regulatory Administration. Amendment rejected. YES.
9. Office of Rail Public Counsel. Rooney (D-PA) motion to suspend rules, pass bill authorizing $2.2 million for operation of Office at ICC. Office has been effective consumer advocate since establishment in 1976, especially in rail abandonment cases. Motion rejected. YES.
10. Housing and Community Development Act. Brown (R-MI) amendment to allow either house of Congress to veto rules and regulations promulgated by HUD. (See Senate vote #6.) Amendment adopted. NO.

11. Federal Trade Commission Authorization, Fiscal 1979. Adoption of conference report authorizing funding for FTC, an agency promoting consumer protection. Report defeated. (Agency is operating under a continuing resolution.) YES.

12. Federal Election Commission Authorization, Fiscal 1979. Sisk (D-CA) motion to block public financing of Congressional candidates. Motion adopted. NO.

13. Department of Defense Procurement Authorization. Downey (D-NY) amendment to delete $209 million from naval vessels procurement authorization to be used for settlement of shipbuilding claims. (See Senate vote #7.) Amendment rejected. YES.

14. Airport and Aircraft Noise Reduction Act. Bill to tax passengers $4 billion to help airlines comply with FAA requirement to use quieter aircraft by 1985. Bill adopted. NO.

15. Transportation Appropriations, Fiscal 1979. Shuster (R-PA) amendment to prevent funds appropriated to National Highway Traffic Safety Administration from being used to enforce passive restraints in motor vehicles. Amendment adopted. NO.

16. Toxic Substances Control Act. Eckhardt (D-TX) motion to suspend rules and pass appropriations for controlling contaminants injected into environment. Motion rejected. YES.

17. Tris Indemnity Bill. Bill passed to pay $50 million to companies for losses incurred as result of government ban on children's sleepwear treated with cancer-causing Tris. NO.

18. Agriculture Appropriations, Fiscal 1979. Symms (R-ID) amendment to reduce appropriation for the Food Stamp Program by $290 million. (See Senate vote #13.) Amendment rejected. NO.

19. Revenue Act. Corman (D-CA) and Fisher (D-VA) amendment to provide $18.1 billion tax cut, benefiting chiefly those earning under $15,000. Amendment rejected. YES.

20. Revenue Act. Adoption of the Conference Report on the Revenue Act of 1978. (See Senate vote #19.) NO.

The following Representatives in the voting list are no longer in office: Allen, Badillo, Breckinridge, J.A. Burke, Burlison, Clawson, Delaney, Dent, F.E. Evans, Flowers, Flynt, Fraser, Frey, Harrington, Jordan, Kasten, Ketchum, Koch, LeFante, Leggett, Mahon, Mann, Meeds, Metcalfe, Milford, Moss, G. Myers, Nix, Pettis, Pike, Poage, Risenhoover, Rogers, Roncalio, Ruppe, Shipley, Sikes, Sisk, Skubitz, Teague, Thornton, Tonry, Tucker, Waggonner, Walsh, Whalen, Wiggins and J. Young.

HOUSE OF REPRESENTATIVES VOTING RECORD

	1	2	3	4	5	6	7	8	9	10	11	12	13	14	15	16	17	18	19	20	%94	%77	%78
ALABAMA																							
1 Edwards (R)	W	W	W	W	R	R	W	W	W	W	W	W	A	W	W	W	W	W	W	W	5	15	14
2 Dickinson (R)	A	W	W	W	A	A	W	W	W	W	W	W	A	R	W	W	W	W	W	A	5	5	5
3 Nichols (D)	W	W	A	W	W	R	W	W	W	W	A	W	A	R	W	W	W	A	W	W	25	15	9
4 Bevill (D)	W	W	R	R	W	W	W	W	W	A	W	W	W	R	R	W	W	W	W	W	34	40	18
5 Flippo (D)	W	W	W	W	W	W	W	W	W	W	R	W	W	W	R	W	W	W	W	W	*	10	9

	1	2	3	4	5	6	7	8	9	10	11	12	13	14	15	16	17	18	19	20	%94	%77	%78
6 Buchanan (R)	W	W	W	W	W	W	W	W	W	W	W	W	W	W	W	R	W	R	W	W	9	50	9
7 Flowers (D)	A	W	W	W	W	W	W	A	A	A	W	A	W	A	A	A	W	A	W	W	30	15	0
ALASKA																							
AL Young (R)	W	W	W	W	W	W	W	W	W	R	W	A	W	A	W	W	W	W	A	W	W	0	5	5
ARIZONA																							
1 Rhodes (R)	W	A	W	W	R	R	W	W	R	A	W	W	A	W	A	A	W	W	W	A	5	10	18
2 Udall (D)	R	R	R	R	W	W	R	R	R	R	R	R	A	A	R	R	R	R	R	A	48	70	73
3 Stump (D)	W	W	W	W	W	R	W	W	W	W	W	W	W	R	A	A	W	W	W	W	*	10	9
4 Rudd (R)	W	A	W	W	A	A	W	W	A	W	W	W	W	R	W	W	A	W	A	A	*	10	5
ARKANSAS																							
1 Alexander (D)	R	A	W	R	W	W	W	W	R	W	W	W	W	W	W	R	W	R	W	W	42	35	23
2 Tucker (D)	R	W	A	W	W	W	R	A	R	W	R	W	A	W	A	A	W	A	R	W	*	55	27
3 Hammerschmidt (R)	W	W	W	W	R	R	W	W	W	W	W	W	W	A	W	W	W	W	W	W	12	5	14
4 Thornton (D)	R	W	A	W	W	W	R	A	R	W	R	W	W	W	W	R	W	A	W	W	34	30	27
CALIFORNIA																							
1 Johnson (D)	R	W	R	W	W	R	W	R	W	R	W	R	W	W	R	W	W	R	R	W	83	55	50
2 Clausen (R)	W	W	W	W	R	W	W	W	W	W	W	W	A	W	W	R	W	W	W	W	5	5	14
3 Moss (D)	R	A	R	A	R	A	R	A	A	R	R	R	W	A	R	R	A	R	R	A	91	70	59
4 Leggett (D)	R	W	R	R	W	R	W	R	A	W	W	W	W	W	R	A	R	R	R	W	75	75	46
5 Burton, J. (D)	R	W	R	R	R	R	R	R	A	R	R	R	A	R	R	R	R	A	R	A	91	75	77
6 Burton, P. (D)	R	W	R	R	R	R	R	R	R	R	R	R	R	R	R	W	R	W	R	A	81	80	86
7 Miller (D)	A	W	R	R	R	R	R	A	R	A	R	A	A	R	R	A	R	A	R	A	96	65	59
8 Deliums (D)	R	W	R	R	R	R	R	R	R	R	R	R	R	R	R	R	R	R	R	R	96	95	96
9 Stark (D)	R	R	R	R	R	R	R	R	R	R	R	R	R	R	R	R	A	R	R	R	83	90	96
10 Edwards (D)	R	R	R	R	W	R	R	R	R	R	R	W	R	R	A	R	R	R	R	R	100	70	73
11 Ryan (D)	R	W	A	R	W	A	W	W	R	W	R	W	R	W	R	R	W	R	R	W	88	50	41
12 McCloskey (R)	W	W	R	W	R	W	R	R	W	A	R	R	A	W	W	W	W	W	W	W	29	35	36
13 Mineta (D)	R	W	R	A	W	W	R	R	R	R	W	R	R	W	R	R	W	R	R	W	87	65	59
14 McFall (D)	A	W	R	W	R	W	A	A	W	R	R	R	W	W	R	W	R	W	R	A	88	65	41
15 Sisk (D)	R	A	W	R	W	A	W	W	R	W	W	A	W	W	W	W	R	A	A		35	35	18
16 Panetta (D)	R	A	R	R	W	W	W	R	W	W	R	R	A	W	A	A	R	W	R	W	*	45	36
17 Krebs (D)	R	W	R	R	W	W	R	W	W	W	R	R	W	W	W	R	R	R	R	W	79	60	46
18 Vacancy[1]	—	—	—	—	—	—	—	—	—	—	—	—	—	—	—	—	—	—	—	—	—	—	—
19 Lagomarsino (R)	W	W	W	W	R	R	W	W	W	R	R	W	W	W	W	W	W	W	W	W	5	10	14
20 Goldwater (R)	W	W	W	W	R	R	W	R	W	W	W	W	W	W	W	W	W	W	W	W	5	10	14
21 Corman (D)	R	R	R	R	W	W	R	R	R	R	R	R	W	W	R	R	W	R	R	W	88	65	68
22 Moorhead (R)	W	W	W	A	R	R	W	W	W	W	W	W	W	W	W	W	W	W	W	W	9	15	14
23 Beilenson (D)	R	R	R	R	W	W	R	R	R	R	R	R	W	R	A	A	R	R	R	W	*	90	68
24 Waxman (D)	R	W	R	A	R	R	R	A	R	R	R	R	R	R	R	A	A	R	A	R	91	80	73
25 Roybal (D)	R	W	R	W	R	R	W	R	R	R	R	R	W	R	R	R	W	R	R	R	96	70	68
26 Rousselot (R)	W	W	W	W	R	R	W	W	W	W	W	W	W	W	W	W	W	W	W	W	0	10	14
27 Dornan (R)	W	W	W	A	R	W	W	W	W	W	W	W	W	W	W	W	W	W	W	W	*	0	9
28 Burke (D)	A	A	A	A	A	A	A	R	A	R	A	R	W	A	A	A	A	R	A	A	96	75	18
29 Hawkins (D)	R	W	R	R	W	R	R	R	R	R	W	A	W	R	R	A	A	R	R		96	60	59
30 Danielson (D)	R	R	R	R	W	W	R	R	R	R	R	R	W	W	R	R	W	R	R	W	79	60	68
31 Wilson, C.H. (D)	R	R	A	R	W	A	R	A	W	R	W	W	W	W	W	W	W	A	R	A	50	35	32
32 Anderson (D)	R	R	R	R	W	W	R	R	R	A	R	W	R	W	R	W	R	R	R	W	75	50	55
33 Clawson (R)	W	W	W	W	R	R	A	W	W	W	A	W	A	A	A	W	W	W	W	W	9	15	14
34 Hannaford (D)	R	R	W	R	W	W	R	R	R	W	R	R	W	W	W	R	W	W	R	W	75	35	50
35 Lloyd (D)	R	R	R	R	W	R	W	R	R	W	R	W	R	R	W	W	R	W	R	W	73	50	55
36 Brown (D)	R	W	R	A	W	W	R	R	R	R	R	R	W	W	R	R	R	R	R	W	75	75	64
37 Pettis (R)	W	A	A	W	A	A	W	W	W	A	A	W	A	W	W	W	A	W	W	A	9	20	0
38 Patterson (D)	R	R	R	R	W	W	R	R	R	R	R	R	W	R	R	W	R	R	R	W	79	65	64
39 Wiggins (R)	W	A	W	W	R	W	W	R	W	W	W	W	W	A	W	W	W	W	W	A	13	30	9

	1	2	3	4	5	6	7	8	9	10	11	12	13	14	15	16	17	18	19	20	%94	%77	%78
40 Badham (R)	W	W	W	W	A	A	W	W	W	W	W	W	A	W	W	W	A	W	W	A	*	10	0
41 Wilson, B. (R)	W	W	A	W	R	W	W	W	R	A	W	W	W	W	W	W	W	W	W	W	0	10	14
42 Van Deerlin (D)	R	R	R	R	W	W	R	W	R	R	R	R	A	W	A	A	W	R	R	W	78	75	55
43 Burgener (R)	W	W	W	W	R	W	W	W	W	W	W	W	W	W	W	W	W	W	W	W	0	5	9
COLORADO																							
1 Schroeder (D)	R	W	W	R	R	R	W	R	R	W	W	R	A	W	R	R	W	R	R	W	75	60	55
2 Wirth (D)	R	W	R	W	W	W	R	R	A	R	R	R	A	W	R	R	W	R	R	W	79	55	55
3 Evans (D)	R	W	R	W	A	R	W	R	R	R	R	R	W	R	A	A	R	W	A		67	50	50
4 Johnson (R)	W	W	W	W	R	R	W	W	A	W	R	P	W	W	W	W	W	W			13	0	18
5 Armstrong (R)	A	A	A	A	R	A	W	W	A	A	A	W	A	A	A	A	W	W	A		0	10	9
CONNECTICUT																							
1 Cotter (D)	A	A	R	R	W	W	R	W	W	R	W	W	A	A	W	W	R	R	W	W	91	70	32
2 Dodd (D)	R	W	R	R	W	W	R	R	R	W	W	R	W	W	R	R	W	R	R	R	96	50	59
3 Giaimo (D)	R	A	A	R	W	W	R	R	W	R	W	W	W	W	W	W	R	W	W		61	40	27
4 McKinney (R)	W	R	W	W	R	W	R	W	R	W	W	R	A	R	W	R	W	R	W	W	41	10	41
5 Sarasin (R)	R	A	W	W	A	R	W	W	A	W	A	W	A	A	A	W	W	W			25	50	9
6 Moffett (D)	R	R	R	R	R	R	R	R	R	R	R	W	W	R	W	R	W	R	R	W	100	75	82
DELAWARE																							
AL Evans (R)	W	R	W	W	W	W	W	W	R	W	A	R	W	R	W	W	R	W	W	W	*	30	23
FLORIDA																							
1 Sikes (D)	R	W	A	W	W	W	W	W	W	W	A	W	W	W	W	W	W	W	W		9	30	5
2 Fuqua (D)	W	A	W	W	W	W	W	W	W	W	A	W	W	R	R	W	W	A			34	20	9
3 Bennett (D)	W	R	R	R	W	W	W	W	W	W	W	W	R	W	W	R	W	W	R		48	25	27
4 Chappell (D)	W	A	W	W	W	W	W	W	W	W	A	W	W	A	W	W	A	W	W		4	10	9
5 Kelly (R)	W	W	W	W	R	R	W	W	W	W	W	A	R	R	A	A	W	W	W	W	5	5	23
6 Young (R)	W	W	W	W	W	W	W	W	W	W	W	R	W	W	W	W	W	W	W		12	10	23
7 Gibbons (D)	W	R	A	W	W	W	W	W	W	R	R	A	A	R	R	R	W	W	W		38	45	27
8 Ireland (D)	W	W	A	W	W	W	W	A	W	W	R	A	W	W	A	W	W	W			*	15	5
9 Frey (R)	A	W	W	A	A	W	W	W	W	A	A	A	A	A	A	W	W	A			0	15	0
10 Bafalis (R)	W	W	W	W	R	W	W	W	W	W	W	W	R	W	W	W	R	W	W	W	12	5	18
11 Rogers (D)	R	A	R	R	W	W	R	W	W	W	R	R	W	A	R	R	R	A	R	W	82	40	50
12 Burke (R)	W	W	W	W	R	A	W	W	R	W	W	W	A	W	W	W	W	W	A		16	25	14
13 Lehman (D)	W	R	R	A	W	A	R	W	R	R	R	R	A	A	P	R	R	R	R	A	71	55	55
14 Pepper (D)	A	R	A	R	W	R	R	A	R	A	W	A	W	A	A	W	R	R	W		60	40	36
15 Fascell (D)	R	R	R	R	W	R	R	R	R	R	R	W	W	R	R	W	R	R	R	W	83	60	68
GEORGIA																							
1 Ginn (D)	R	R	R	R	W	W	W	W	W	W	W	W	W	W	W	R	W	W	W	W	20	25	23
2 Mathis (D)	R	W	W	R	W	W	W	W	W	A	W	W	A	R	W	W	W	W	W	W	21	10	14
3 Brinkley (D)	R	W	W	W	W	W	W	W	A	W	R	W	R	W	W	W	W	W	W		17	25	14
4 Levitas (D)	R	R	R	R	W	W	R	R	W	R	W	R	W	W	W	R	R	W	R	W	54	35	46
5 Fowler (D)	R	R	R	R	W	W	R	A	W	R	R	R	W	R	R	W	R	W	W		*	55	55
6 Flynt (D)	W	W	W	W	A	W	W	W	W	W	A	W	W	W	W	W	W	A			12	0	0
7 McDonald (D)	W	W	W	A	R	R	A	W	W	W	W	W	R	W	W	W	W	A	W		9	15	18
8 Evans (D)	W	W	R	R	W	W	W	W	W	W	A	W	W	W	W	W	W	W			*	20	9
9 Jenkins D)	R	R	W	R	W	W	W	W	A	W	R	R	W	W	W	W	W	W			*	30	23
10 Barnard (D)	R	W	W	W	W	W	W	W	W	W	W	A	W	W	W	R	W	W	W		*	20	9
HAWAII																							
1 Heftel (D)	W	W	W	R	W	W	R	W	W	W	R	A	W	W	R	R	R	R	W	W	*	50	36
2 Akaka (D)	R	W	R	R	W	W	R	W	R	R	R	R	W	W	W	R	W	R	W	W	*	55	50
IDAHO																							
1 Symms (R)	W	W	A	W	R	R	W	W	W	W	W	W	R	R	W	W	W	W	W	W	0	10	23
2 Hansen (R)	W	W	W	W	R	R	W	W	W	W	W	W	W	R	W	W	R	W	W	W	0	10	23
ILLINOIS																							
1 Vacancy[2]	—	—	—	—	—	—	—	—	—	—	—	—	—	—	—	—	—	—	—	—	—	—	—

	1	2	3	4	5	6	7	8	9	10	11	12	13	14	15	16	17	18	19	20	%94	%77	%78
2 Murphy (D)	W	A	R	R	W	W	R	W	R	R	W	W	A	W	A	A	W	R	R	W	96	65	36
3 Russo (D)	W	R	R	W	W	W	R	W	R	W	W	R	A	W	W	R	W	R	W	W	88	50	36
4 Derwinski (R)	W	W	W	W	R	R	W	W	W	W	W	W	W	W	W	W	W	W	W	W	21	25	14
5 Fary (D)	R	W	R	W	W	W	R	W	R	R	W	W	W	R	R	W	R	R	R	W	54	60	55
6 Hyde (R)	W	R	W	W	R	R	W	W	W	W	W	W	W	W	W	W	W	W	W	W	12	35	18
7 Collins (D)	R	A	R	R	R	W	A	R	R	R	A	W	A	W	R	R	R	R	R	W	79	65	59
8 Rostenkowski (D)	W	R	R	R	W	W	A	W	R	R	R	A	W	W	R	W	R	R	R	W	78	55	41
9 Yates (D)	R	R	R	R	R	W	R	R	R	R	R	R	A	R	R	R	R	R	R	R	100	85	91
10 Mikva (D)	R	A	A	R	R	A	R	R	R	R	R	R	A	W	R	R	W	R	R	A	93	75	68
11 Annunzio (D)	R	W	R	R	W	W	R	W	R	R	R	W	W	W	A	W	R	R	R	W	76	70	46
12 Crane (R)	A	A	W	A	R	W	W	W	W	W	A	R	A	W	W	A	W	W	A	A	5	15	9
13 McClory (R)	W	R	W	W	R	W	W	A	W	W	W	A	W	W	W	W	W	W	W	W	13	20	18
14 Erlenborn (R)	W	R	W	W	R	W	W	W	W	W	A	W	W	W	W	W	W	W	W	W	17	15	18
15 Corcoran (R)	W	A	W	W	W	W	W	W	A	A	A	R	W	W	R	W	W	W	W	W	*	15	23
16 Anderson (R)	W	R	W	W	R	W	W	A	A	R	R	A	R	W	A	W	W	W	W	W	34	25	32
17 O'Brien (R)	W	W	W	R	R	W	R	W	R	W	W	W	W	W	W	W	W	W	W	W	9	10	23
18 Michel (R)	W	W	W	W	R	W	W	W	W	W	W	W	W	W	W	W	W	W	W	W	4	10	14
19 Railsback (R)	W	A	W	W	W	W	R	W	R	R	A	W	W	W	W	W	W	W	W	A	13	20	27
20 Findley (R)	W	R	A	W	R	R	W	W	W	A	W	W	W	R	W	W	R	W	W	R	5	35	32
21 Madigan (R)	W	W	W	W	R	W	W	R	W	A	W	W	W	R	W	W	W	W	W	W	12	30	23
22 Shipley (D)	A	A	R	R	A	A	A	A	A	A	A	A	A	W	A	R	A	A	W	A	35	20	14
23 Price (D)	R	W	R	R	W	W	R	R	R	R	R	R	W	W	R	R	R	W	R	W	96	60	64
24 Simon (D)	R	R	R	R	W	W	R	A	R	R	R	R	W	R	R	R	R	A	R	R	89	65	73
INDIANA																							
1 Benjamin (D)	R	W	R	R	R	R	W	R	W	W	W	W	R	W	R	R	R	R	R	W	*	70	59
2 Fithian (D)	R	W	R	R	W	W	W	W	R	W	W	W	W	W	W	W	W	R	R	W	53	40	32
3 Brademas (D)	R	R	R	R	W	W	R	R	R	A	R	R	W	R	R	R	R	R	R	W	96	55	68
4 Quayle (R)	R	R	W	W	R	W	W	W	W	W	W	W	R	W	W	W	W	W	W	W	*	15	27
5 Hillis (R)	W	A	A	W	R	W	W	W	W	W	W	W	W	W	W	W	A	W	W	W	20	20	14
6 Evans (D)	R	W	R	W	W	W	W	R	W	W	R	W	W	W	W	W	W	W	R	W	36	35	32
7 Myers, J. (R)	W	W	W	W	R	R	W	W	W	W	W	W	R	W	W	W	W	W	W	W	0	10	18
8 Cornwell (D)	R	R	W	W	W	W	W	R	R	A	R	R	R	W	R	R	W	R	W	W	*	30	46
9 Hamilton (D)	R	R	R	R	W	W	W	R	R	W	W	R	R	W	R	R	R	R	R	W	63	35	55
10 Sharp (D)	R	R	R	R	W	W	R	R	R	W	R	W	W	R	W	R	R	R	R	W	75	60	64
11 Jacobs (D)	W	R	R	R	W	R	W	W	R	W	W	R	R	W	W	W	R	W	R	R	71	55	46
IOWA																							
1 Leach (R)	A	W	W	W	W	W	W	W	W	W	R	R	A	W	W	W	W	W	W	W	*	30	18
2 Blouin (D)	R	W	R	R	W	W	R	W	W	W	W	W	R	A	R	R	W	R	R	W	87	55	50
3 Grassley (R)	W	W	W	W	W	R	R	W	W	W	A	W	W	W	W	W	R	W	W	W	13	15	18
4 Smith (D)	R	W	R	R	W	W	R	W	W	W	R	A	W	R	W	R	W	R	W	W	68	60	46
5 Harkin (D)	R	W	R	R	R	R	R	R	R	W	R	R	A	W	R	R	R	R	R	W	96	50	77
6 Bedell (D)	R	W	R	R	R	W	W	R	W	R	R	R	R	R	R	R	R	R	R	R	71	50	77
KANSAS																							
1 Sebelius (R)	R	A	A	W	R	R	W	W	W	W	W	W	W	W	W	W	W	W	W	W	4	0	18
2 Keys (D)	R	R	R	R	W	W	W	R	R	W	W	R	A	W	W	R	R	R	R	W	88	60	50
3 Winn (R)	W	W	W	W	R	R	W	W	W	A	W	W	W	W	W	W	W	W	W	W	0	15	14
4 Glickman (D)	R	W	W	W	W	W	R	W	W	R	R	R	W	W	W	R	W	R	W	W	*	40	32
5 Skubitz (R)	R	A	R	A	W	W	W	R	W	R	W	W	W	W	W	R	W	A	W	W	4	15	18
KENTUCKY																							
1 Hubbard (D)	W	W	W	W	W	R	W	W	R	W	W	R	W	R	W	W	R	W	R	W	36	30	27
2 Natcher (D)	R	W	R	R	W	W	W	W	W	R	R	R	W	W	R	W	W	R	W	W	58	45	41
3 Mazzoli (D)	W	R	R	R	W	W	W	W	W	W	W	R	A	R	R	W	W	R	W	W	76	65	32
4 Snyder (R)	W	R	W	W	R	W	W	W	W	W	W	W	R	R	W	W	R	W	W	W	28	15	27

	1	2	3	4	5	6	7	8	9	10	11	12	13	14	15	16	17	18	19	20	%94	%77	%78
5 Carter (R)	W	R	R	W	R	R	W	W	R	W	W	W	W	W	W	R	W	R	W	W	21	25	36
6 Breckinridge (D)	R	A	R	W	R	W	R	R	R	R	W	W	R	R	R	W	W	W	W	R	W	63	55	55
7 Perkins (D)	R	R	R	R	R	W	W	W	W	R	R	W	W	R	R	R	R	W	W		88	60	59
LOUISIANA																							
1 Livingston (R)	W	W	W	W	R	R	W	W	W	W	W	W	W	W	W	W	R	R	W	W	*	0	23
2 Boggs (D)	R	W	W	W	R	R	R	W	R	R	W	W	W	W	R	R	W	R	W	W	41	45	50
3 Treen (R)	W	W	W	W	R	R	W	W	W	W	W	W	W	W	W	W	R	R	W	W	0	0	27
4 Waggonner (D)	W	W	W	W	R	W	W	W	W	W	W	W	W	W	W	W	W	A	W	W	4	0	14
5 Huckaby (D)	R	W	W	W	R	R	W	W	W	W	W	W	A	A	A	A	W	R	W	W	*	15	23
6 Moore (R)	R	W	W	W	R	R	W	W	W	W	W	W	W	R	W	W	W	W	W	W	0	5	23
7 Breaux (D)	R	W	W	W	R	W	W	W	W	W	W	W	A	A	W	W	W	W	W	W	4	10	18
8 Long (D)	R	W	W	W	R	R	R	W	W	R	R	W	W	W	W	R	W	R	W	W	50	35	46
MAINE																							
1 Emery (R)	R	R	R	W	R	W	W	W	W	W	W	W	R	W	R	W	A	W	W	W	49	60	32
2 Cohen (R)	R	A	R	W	R	W	R	W	A	W	W	R	A	R	W	R	W	W	W	W	62	65	41
MARYLAND																							
1 Bauman (R)	W	W	W	W	R	R	W	W	W	W	W	W	W	R	W	W	W	W	W	W	0	10	23
2 Long (D)	R	R	W	R	W	W	R	W	R	W	R	R	R	W	W	R	R	R	W	W	63	65	55
3 Mikulski (D)	R	R	R	R	R	R	R	R	R	R	R	R	R	R	R	R	R	W	R	W	*	70	91
4 Holt (R)	W	W	W	W	R	R	W	W	W	W	W	W	W	W	W	W	W	W	W	W	0	15	14
5 Spellman (D)	R	R	R	R	R	R	R	R	W	W	W	W	R	W	A	W	R	W	R	W	96	70	64
6 Vacancy[3]	—	—	—	—	—	—	—	—	—	—	—	—	—	—	—	—	—	—	—	—	—	—	—
7 Mitchell (D)	R	W	R	R	R	R	R	R	R	R	R	R	A	R	R	R	R	R	R	R	100	75	91
8 Steers (R)	A	R	R	W	R	R	R	R	R	W	R	R	R	R	R	R	W	R	R	W	*	60	77
MASSACHUSETTS																							
1 Conte (R)	W	R	R	W	W	W	R	W	R	R	R	R	R	R	R	R	W	W	W	W	83	75	50
2 Boland (D)	R	A	R	R	W	R	R	R	R	R	R	A	R	W	R	W	R	W	R	W	91	65	73
3 Early (D)	A	R	R	W	W	R	R	R	R	W	R	W	R	W	R	R	R	R	R	W	96	70	68
4 Drinan (D)	R	R	R	R	R	R	R	R	R	R	R	R	R	R	R	R	R	R	R	W	100	100	96
5 Tsongas (D)	A	A	R	R	W	W	R	R	R	A	A	A	A	A	A	A	A	R	W		96	85	32
6 Harrington (D)	A	A	R	A	W	W	R	R	A	A	R	R	A	W	R	R	A	R	R	A	92	80	46
7 Markey (D)	R	R	R	R	R	R	R	R	R	R	R	R	R	W	R	R	R	R	R		*	95	96
8 O'Neill (D)[4]																					83	—	
9 Moakley (D)	R	R	R	W	W	R	R	R	R	R	R	R	A	R	W	R	R	R	W		100	75	68
10 Heckler (R)	R	R	R	W	R	W	R	W	R	R	R	R	A	W	W	R	W	R	R	W	70	80	64
11 Burke (D)	R	R	R	R	R	R	W	R	R	R	W	W	W	W	R	W	R	R	R		100	30	73
12 Studds (D)	R	R	R	R	W	R	R	R	R	R	R	W	R	R	R	W	R	R	R		100	90	86
MICHIGAN																							
1 Conyers (D)	R	A	R	R	R	R	R	A	R	A	R	R	A	A	R	A	A	A	R	R	66	85	64
2 Pursell (R)	R	W	R	W	R	W	R	W	R	W	W	R	W	R	W	R	W	W	W	W	*	35	46
3 Brown (R)	W	R	W	W	R	W	W	W	R	W	W	W	W	W	R	W	R	W	W	W	14	0	23
4 Stockman (R)	W	R	W	W	R	R	W	W	A	W	R	W	R	W	W	W	W	W	W	W	*	20	27
5 Sawyer (R)	W	R	W	W	R	W	W	W	W	W	A	W	A	W	W	W	W	A	A	W	*	15	14
6 Carr (D)	R	W	R	R	W	W	R	R	R	W	R	W	R	W	R	W	R	R	R	W	100	65	55
7 Kildee (D)	R	W	R	R	R	R	R	R	R	W	W	R	R	R	W	R	R	R	R	W	*	80	77
8 Traxler (D)	R	W	R	R	W	W	R	A	R	R	W	R	A	R	W	R	W	A	R	W	75	65	50
9 Vander Jagt (R)	W	W	W	W	R	A	W	W	W	W	W	W	W	W	W	W	A	A	W	W	13	15	9
10 Cederberg (R)	A	W	W	W	R	R	W	W	W	W	W	W	W	W	W	W	R	W	W	W	9	5	18
11 Ruppe (R)	W	R	A	W	R	A	A	W	A	A	W	R	W	W	W	W	W	W	W	A	20	20	18
12 Bonior (D)	R	W	R	R	R	R	R	R	R	R	R	R	R	R	A	W	R	R	R		*	90	86
13 Diggs (D)	A	A	R	R	A	A	R	R	A	R	A	W	A	W	W	R	A	R	R	A	61	70	41
14 Nedzi (D)	A	W	R	R	W	W	R	W	R	W	W	W	R	A	A	W	R	R	W		79	65	36
15 Ford (D)	R	R	R	R	W	W	R	A	R	W	A	R	W	W	W	R	W	R	R	W	96	60	50
16 Dingell (D)	R	R	R	R	W	W	R	R	R	W	R	W	A	W	W	R	W	R	R	W	80	70	55

	1 2 3 4 5 6 7 8 9 10 11 12 13 14 15 16 17 18 19 20	°₀94	°₀77	°₀78
17 Brodhead (D)	R R R R W W R R R R R R R R R W R R R	88	85	82
18 Blanchard (D)	R R R R W W R R R W W R W R W R W R R W	92	65	59
19 Broomfield (R)	W R A W R W W W W W W W R A W W W W W W	17	20	18
MINNESOTA				
1 Quie (R)	A A W W A A W A A A A A A A A A A A W A	13	35	0
2 Hagedorn (R)	W A W W R R W W W W W A W W W W W W W	4	5	14
3 Frenzel (R)	W W W W R W W W W W W W W R W W W W W A	26	15	14
4 Vento (D)	R A R R R R R R R R R R A R R R W R R W	*	90	82
5 Fraser (D)	R W R R R R R R R R R R R W A R R W R A R	70	60	77
6 Nolan (D)	R W R R W R R R R A R R R W A A W R R R	100	70	64
7 Stangeland (R)	W W W W R W W W W W W W W W W W W W W	*	20	9
8 Oberstar (D)	R W R R W R R R R W R R W R R W R R W	100	80	68
MISSISSIPPI				
1 Whitten (D)	R W W W A W W W W W W R W W W R R W	25	20	18
2 Bowen (D)	R W W W W A W W W W W W W W W A W W	17	25	5
3 Montgomery (D)	R W W W W W W W W W W W A R W A W W W	4	10	9
4 Cochran (R)	R A W W A R W W A W A R A A R W A W W	13	10	18
5 Lott (R)	W W W W R R W W W W W W W W W A W W W	9	5	14
MISSOURI				
1 Clay (D)	R W R R R R R R R R R W R W R R W R R R	78	55	82
2 Young (D)	R R W R R R W W W W W W W W R W R R W	*	55	41
3 Gephardt (D)	R W R R W W W W W R R W R R R W R W R W	*	70	41
4 Skelton (D)	R A W R W W W W W W W A W W W W R W	*	40	14
5 Bolling (D)	R A R R W W R W A R R R W R R W R R W	71	65	55
6 Coleman (R)	R W W R W W W W W W W W W W R W W W	*	20	18
7 Taylor (R)	W W W W R R W W W W W W W W W R W W W	0	0	18
8 Ichord (D)	W W W W A W W W W W W W R W R W R W A	18	0	9
9 Volkmer (D)	W W W R W W R W W R R A W W W R W W	*	50	36
10 Burlison (D)	R W R R W W W W R R R W W W R W R R W	88	60	41
MONTANA				
1 Baucus (D)	R W R R W W R R A W W R A W R W R R R W	75	45	50
2 Marlenee (R)	R W W W R A W W R W W W R W W W R W W A	*	10	27
NEBRASKA				
1 Thone (R)	W A W W R W W W A W A W A W W W W W W A	4	10	9
2 Cavanaugh (D)	R W R R W W W R W W R R W R W A R R R W	*	60	46
3 Smith (R)	W W W W R W W W W W W W A W W W W W W A	0	10	9
NEVADA				
AL Santini (D)	W R W R R W W W W W W R A W A W W W R A	83	35	27
NEW HAMPSHIRE				
1 D'Amours (D)	R R R R W W R R R W A R A W W W W R R W	92	90	50
2 Cleveland (R)	W A W W R R W W W W W W R A R W W W W W	34	35	23
NEW JERSEY				
1 Florio (D)	R R R R R R R W R A R R A W R R R R W	92	55	77
2 Hughes (D)	R R R R W W R W R W W R R W R R R W R W	87	60	59
3 Howard (D)	R R R R W W R R R R R A W R R W R R R W	100	80	68
4 Thompson (D)	R A A R W W R W A W R R W R W R W R W	75	60	46
5 Fenwick (R)	W R R R P W R W W W W R W R W R W W W W	50	75	36
6 Forsythe (R)	W R W W R R W W W W W A W W W W W W W	9	30	18
7 Maguire (D)	R R R R R R R R R R R R R R R R R R R W	86	100	96
8 Roe (D)	R A A R R W W R W R W R W R W R W R R W	86	60	50
9 Hollenbeck (R)	W A R R W W R W R R W R R R A R R R R W	*	55	50
10 Rodino (D)	R A A R W R R A A A R A A W A A W A A W	80	85	27
11 Minish (D)	R R R R W W R R R R R R R W R R R R R W	100	80	77
12 Rinaldo (R)	R R R R R W R W R W R R R W W R R R R W	87	70	73

	1	2	3	4	5	6	7	8	9	10	11	12	13	14	15	16	17	18	19	20	%94	%77	%78
13 Meyner (D)	R	R	R	R	R	W	R	R	R	A	A	R	W	W	A	A	W	R	R	W	92	85	59
14 Le Fante (D)	R	R	R	A	W	W	R	W	R	A	R	A	W	W	A	A	W	A	A	W	*	85	32
15 Patten (D)	W	R	R	R	W	R	W	R	R	R	A	R	W	R	R	W	R	R	R	W	83	75	59
NEW MEXICO																							
1 Lujan (R)	W	A	W	W	A	A	W	W	W	W	W	W	R	W	W	W	W	W	W	A	4	25	5
2 Runnels (D)	W	W	W	W	R	R	W	A	W	A	A	W	A	W	A	A	W	A	W	W	0	10	14
NEW YORK																							
1 Pike (D)	W	R	R	R	W	W	W	W	W	W	A	R	A	R	W	W	W	W	W	R	82	40	27
2 Downey (D)	R	R	R	A	W	W	R	R	R	R	R	R	R	W	R	R	W	R	R	W	100	60	68
3 Ambro (D)	R	R	R	R	W	W	R	R	W	W	R	R	R	W	W	R	R	R	W	R	96	80	59
4 Lent (R)	W	R	R	A	R	R	W	W	R	W	W	W	A	W	R	R	W	W	W	W	16	35	36
5 Wydler (R)	W	R	R	W	R	R	W	W	W	W	W	W	A	W	R	R	W	W	W	W	21	40	32
6 Wolff (D)	W	R	R	R	W	R	W	R	W	R	R	W	A	A	W	R	R	W	R	W	92	60	46
7 Addabbo (D)	R	R	R	R	W	R	W	R	R	R	R	A	W	R	R	W	R	R	R	W	100	75	64
8 Rosenthal (D)	R	R	R	R	R	W	R	R	R	R	R	A	R	R	R	R	R	R	R	A	91	65	86
9 Delaney (D)	W	R	R	R	W	W	W	W	W	W	A	R	W	R	W	R	R	R	W	W	75	65	41
10 Biaggi (D)	R	R	R	W	A	R	W	R	R	R	W	A	W	R	R	W	R	R	R	W	79	80	59
11 Scheuer (D)	R	R	R	R	W	R	R	R	R	R	R	R	R	W	R	R	W	R	R	A	100	85	73
12 Chisholm (D)	R	W	R	R	R	R	R	R	A	R	R	R	A	W	R	R	W	R	R	R	96	70	77
13 Solarz (D)	R	R	R	R	W	R	R	R	R	R	R	R	R	R	A	A	A	W	R	R	93	90	68
14 Richmond (D)	R	R	R	R	W	W	R	R	R	R	A	W	R	R	R	R	R	R	R	R	87	75	77
15 Zeferetti (D)	R	A	R	R	R	W	R	W	R	W	W	W	A	W	W	W	W	R	R	W	83	55	36
16 Holtzman, (D)	R	R	R	R	R	R	R	R	R	R	R	R	R	R	R	R	R	R	R	R	100	100	100
17 Murphy (D)	R	R	R	R	W	W	R	W	A	R	A	W	W	W	R	R	W	R	R	W	46	60	50
18 Green (R)[5]	R	R	—	—	W	W	—	R	R	W	R	R	W	W	R	R	W	R	W	W	—	—	50
19 Rangel (D)	R	R	R	R	W	W	R	R	R	R	R	R	R	R	R	R	R	R	R	W	93	85	82
20 Weiss (D)	R	R	R	R	R	R	R	R	R	R	R	R	R	R	R	W	R	R	R	R	*	95	96
21 Garcia (D)[6]	R	A	—	—	W	W	—	R	R	A	R	R	A	W	R	R	W	A	R	R	—	—	50
22 Bingham (D)	R	R	R	A	W	W	A	R	R	A	R	R	R	R	R	R	R	R	R	R	92	90	68
23 Caputo (R)	R	A	W	W	R	A	W	W	A	W	A	A	A	W	A	A	W	R	R	W	*	75	23
24 Ottinger (D)	R	R	R	R	R	R	R	R	R	R	R	R	R	R	R	W	R	R	R	W	92	100	91
25 Fish (R)	W	R	W	W	R	R	W	W	A	W	W	W	A	A	W	R	W	W	W	W	30	40	23
26 Gilman (R)	R	R	R	R	R	R	W	W	W	R	R	A	W	R	W	R	W	W	W	W	71	70	68
27 McHugh (D)	R	R	R	W	W	R	R	R	R	R	R	R	R	W	R	R	R	R	W	W	96	70	77
28 Stratton (D)	W	R	R	R	W	W	W	W	W	R	R	W	R	W	W	R	W	W	W	W	50	60	36
29 Pattison (D)	R	R	R	A	R	W	R	R	R	R	R	R	W	R	W	R	R	R	R	W	75	70	77
30 McEwen (R)	W	W	W	W	R	R	W	W	W	W	W	W	A	W	W	W	W	W	W	A	13	15	14
31 Mitchell (R)	R	W	W	W	W	W	R	W	R	W	W	W	R	W	W	R	W	W	W	W	26	20	27
32 Hanley (D)	R	R	R	R	W	W	W	W	W	R	R	R	W	W	W	W	R	R	R	W	83	55	46
33 Walsh (R)	W	A	A	W	R	R	W	R	W	W	A	W	A	W	W	R	W	W	W	W	39	30	18
34 Horton (R)	W	A	W	A	R	R	R	W	R	R	W	W	R	W	R	R	W	R	W	A	41	25	32
35 Conable (R)	W	A	W	A	R	R	W	W	W	W	W	W	R	W	W	W	W	W	W	W	13	20	18
36 LaFalce (D)	R	R	R	R	W	W	R	R	R	R	R	R	W	R	R	R	R	R	R	W	87	65	77
37 Nowak (D)	R	R	R	W	W	R	R	W	R	W	R	R	W	W	W	W	R	R	R	W	96	60	59
38 Kemp (R)	W	R	W	W	R	R	W	W	W	W	W	W	A	W	W	W	W	W	W	W	9	15	18
39 Lundine (D)	R	R	W	R	W	W	R	R	A	R	R	A	R	A	W	R	W	R	R	A	80	45	50
NORTH CAROLINA																							
1 Jones (D)	R	W	W	W	W	W	W	W	W	W	W	W	A	R	W	W	W	W	W	W	30	15	9
2 Fountain (D)	W	W	W	W	W	W	W	W	W	W	W	W	W	R	W	W	W	W	W	W	16	25	5
3 Whitley (D)	W	W	W	W	W	W	W	W	W	W	W	W	R	R	W	W	W	W	W	W	*	30	9
4 Andrews (D)	W	W	R	W	W	R	W	W	W	W	R	W	W	W	W	W	R	W	W	A	28	30	14
5 Neal (D)	R	W	R	R	W	W	W	W	W	W	W	R	W	W	R	W	W	R	W	W	57	40	23
6 Preyer (D)	W	W	R	R	W	W	W	R	W	R	W	R	R	W	W	W	R	W	W	W	54	35	41
7 Rose (D)	R	W	R	W	W	W	W	W	W	R	W	A	W	R	W	W	R	R	W	W	39	50	27

	1	2	3	4	5	6	7	8	9	10	11	12	13	14	15	16	17	18	19	20	%94	%77	%78
8 Hefnsr (D)	W	W	R	W	W	W	W	W	W	W	W	W	R	R	W	R	W	W	W	W	29	30	18
9 Martin (R)	W	A	W	A	R	W	W	W	W	W	W	W	W	W	W	W	W	W	W	W	9	15	9
10 Broyhill (R)	W	A	W	W	R	W	W	W	W	W	W	W	W	R	W	R	W	W	W	W	0	10	18
11 Gudger (D)	R	W	W	R	W	W	W	W	A	A	R	A	R	W	W	W	W	W	W	W	*	25	18
NORTH DAKOTA																							
AL Andrews (R)	W	W	W	W	R	W	W	W	R	W	W	W	W	W	W	W	W	W	W	W	29	20	14
OHIO																							
1 Gradison (R)	W	R	W	W	R	W	W	W	W	W	W	W	R	W	R	R	W	W	W		25	20	27
2 Luken (D)	A	R	W	R	R	R	W	W	W	W	R	R	W	W	W	R	W	R	W	R	*	60	46
3 Whalen (R)	R	R	R	R	R	R	R	A	R	A	A	R	R	R	A	A	R	A	R	W	87	65	68
4 Guyer (R)	W	W	A	A	R	R	W	W	W	W	W	W	W	R	W	W	W	A	W	W	5	20	18
5 Latta (R)	W	W	W	W	R	W	W	W	W	W	A	R	W	W	W	W	W	W	W	W	9	20	18
6 Harsha (R)	W	R	W	W	R	W	W	W	W	W	W	W	R	W	W	W	A	W	W	W	32	35	18
7 Brown (R)	W	R	W	W	R	R	W	W	R	A	W	W	A	A	W	W	W	W	W	W	0	30	23
8 Kindness (R)	W	W	W	W	R	W	W	W	W	W	W	W	A	W	W	W	W	W	W	W	9	15	14
9 Ashley (D)	R	A	R	R	W	W	R	W	R	R	R	W	W	R	W	W	R	R	W		70	60	55
10 Miller (R)	W	W	W	W	R	W	W	W	W	W	W	R	R	A	A	R	W	W	W		4	20	27
11 Stanton (R)	W	R	W	W	R	W	R	W	W	R	W	W	W	R	W	W	W	W	W		17	35	27
12 Devine (R)	W	W	W	W	R	W	W	W	W	W	W	W	W	W	W	W	W	A	W		0	10	23
13 Pease (D)	W	A	R	R	W	R	W	R	R	R	R	R	R	W	R	R	R	W			*	70	64
14 Seiberling (D)	R	R	R	R	W	R	R	R	R	R	R	A	R	R	R	W	R	R	R		88	75	86
15 Wylie (R)	W	R	W	W	R	R	W	W	W	W	W	A	R	R	R	W	W	W	W		9	45	41
16 Regula (R)	W	R	W	W	R	W	W	W	W	W	W	W	R	R	W	W	W	W	W		13	25	23
17 Ashbrook (R)	W	W	A	W	R	R	W	A	W	W	A	A	R	R	W	W	R	A	W	W	0	5	27
18 Applegate (D)	R	R	W	W	R	A	R	W	A	W	W	W	W	W	W	R	R	A			*	45	41
19 Carney (D)	R	A	R	R	W	A	R	R	R	R	R	R	W	W	R	W	R	R	A		100	60	55
20 Oakar (D)	R	W	R	R	R	R	R	R	A	R	R	R	A	W	R	R	R	R	W		*	75	77
21 Stokes (D)	R	W	R	R	R	R	R	R	R	R	A	R	A	W	R	R	W	R	R	R	100	80	77
22 Vanik (D)	R	R	R	R	R	R	R	R	R	R	R	R	R	R	R	R	R	R	R	W	79	80	96
23 Mottl (D)	W	R	R	A	W	R	R	R	W	W	W	R	A	W	R	W	R	W	R	A	87	65	46
OKLAHOMA																							
1 Jones (D)	W	R	W	W	R	R	W	W	A	R	W	W	W	W	W	W	W	W	W	W	9	5	23
2 Risenhoover (D)	A	A	W	W	W	W	W	A	W	A	W	W	W	W	W	W	W	W	W	W	14	25	0
3 Watkins (D)	W	W	A	W	R	R	W	W	W	W	W	W	W	W	W	W	W	W	W	W	*	20	14
4 Steed (D)	A	W	W	W	R	W	W	W	W	R	W	W	R	W	W	R	W	W	R	A	26	30	27
5 Edwards (R)	W	W	W	W	R	R	W	W	W	W	A	W	R	W	W	W	W	W	W		*	5	18
6 English (D)	W	W	W	W	R	W	W	W	W	W	W	R	W	W	W	W	W	W	W		21	20	9
OREGON																							
1 AuCoin (D)	R	R	R	W	W	R	R	A	W	W	R	R	W	A	A	W	W	W	W		50	65	41
2 Ullman (D)	R	R	R	R	W	W	W	W	R	W	W	W	W	R	W	W	R	W	W		63	45	32
3 Duncan (D)	A	R	R	W	W	W	W	W	W	W	W	W	R	W	R	W	R	W	R		46	40	27
4 Weaver (D)	R	A	R	R	W	W	R	R	W	A	R	R	R	W	R	W	W	R	A		91	70	55
PENNSYLVANIA																							
1 Myers, M. (D)	R	R	R	W	R	R	R	R	R	W	A	W	R	W	R	R	W				*	65	59
2 Nix (D)	R	R	R	W	W	R	A	R	A	A	A	A	A	A	W	R	R	W			83	75	41
3 Lederer (D)	R	R	R	W	W	R	R	R	R	W	W	W	R	W	R	W					*	80	59
4 Eilberg (D)	R	R	R	R	R	R	W	A	W	R	A	W	R	W	R	W					92	75	68
5 Schulze (R)	W	R	W	W	R	R	W	W	W	W	W	R	W	W	A	W	A	W			9	15	23
6 Yatron (D)	R	W	R	R	W	W	R	W	R	W	R	W	A	W	W	W	R	R	W		75	45	41
7 Edgar (D)	R	R	R	R	W	R	R	R	R	R	R	R	R	R	R	R	R	R	R	W	100	95	91
8 Kostmayer (D)	R	R	R	R	R	R	R	R	R	R	R	R	R	R	R	R	R	R	R	W	*	90	96
9 Shuster (R)	W	W	W	W	R	R	W	W	W	W	W	W	R	W	W	W	W	W	W		0	10	18
10 McDade (R)	W	R	W	W	R	R	W	W	R	W	W	W	A	W	R	R	A	W	W		61	60	32

	1 2 3 4 5 6 7 8 9 10 11 12 13 14 15 16 17 18 19 20	%94	%77	%7
11 Flood (D)	R W R A W W R W A R R W A W R R W R R W	83	65	46
12 Murtha (D)	W R R R W W W W R W R W W W W W R W W	46	30	27
13 Coughlin (R)	W R W W R R W W W W W A W W R W W W W	44	35	23
14 Moorhead (D)	R R R R W W R W R R A R A W R R W R R W	71	60	59
15 Rooney (D)	R W R R W W R W R R R R W W W R W R R W	87	55	55
16 Walker (R)	W R W W R R W W W W W W W R W W W A W W	*	40	23
17 Ertel (D)	R R R R W W P W W W R W W W W W R W	*	45	32
18 Walgren (D)	W R R R W R R W R R R A W R W W R R W	*	75	55
19 Goodling, (R)	W R W W R R W W W W W A R A A W W W W	5	30	23
20 Gaydos (D)	R R R R W R R W W W R W A W W W R R W	79	60	46
21 Dent (D)	R R A A W R A W W A R W A W A A W R R W	54	10	27
22 Murphy (D)	R R R R W W R W R W R R R W W R W R R W	*	65	59
23 Ammerman (D)	A A R R A A R R A W A R A A R W A R R A	*	60	41
24 Marks (R)	W R R W W W W W R W R R R W R W W W W	*	55	50
25 Myers, G (R)	W R W W W W R W R R R R W W R R W W W	29	20	46
RHODE ISLAND				
1 St. Germain (D)	R R R R W R R R R R R R W W A A W R R W	96	75	68
2 Beard (D)	R R R R W R A R R R R R W W W W R R W	83	65	55
SOUTH CAROLINA				
1 Davis (D)	R A W R R R R R R W R W W A A W W W W	49	25	46
2 Spence (R)	R W W R W W W W W W W W W W W W W W W	8	15	14
3 Derrick (D)	R W R R W W W R R R R W W W R A W R W	43	55	46
4 Mann (D)	W A W R W W W W W W R W A R A A W R W W	16	15	18
5 Holland (D)	R W W W W R W W R W A W R A A W W W W	29	20	18
6 Jenrette (D)	R W R R W W R A W R R R W R A A W A A A	53	30	41
SOUTH DAKOTA				
1 Pressler (R)	R W R W R R W R A W W A A W W W R W W	50	25	32
2 Abdnor (R)	R W W W R R W W W W W W W W W W W W W	16	5	18
TENNESSEE				
1 Quillen (R)	A R W W R W W W R W W W W W A A W W W W	0	15	18
2 Duncan (R)	W R W W R W W R W W W W W W W W W W W W	16	25	23
3 Lloyd (D)	R R W W W W W W W W W W W W W W A W	41	35	9
4 Gore (D)	R W R R R R R R W R R R R A A W R R R	*	60	77
5 Vacancy[7]	— — — — — — — — — — — — — — — — — — — —	—	—	—
6 Beard (R)	W W W W R W W W W W W W W W A W W W W	0	10	9
7 Jones (D)	R W W A W W A W R W W W W W W W W W W	29	50	9
8 Ford (D)	R W R R W W R A R R R R W A A W A R W	79	75	46
TEXAS				
1 Hall (D)	W W W W R R W W W W W R R W W R W W W	20	15	27
2 Wilson, C. (D)	R A W W W W W A W R W W W W W W W W W	38	25	9
3 Collins (R)	W W W W R R W W W W W W R R W W W W W W	4	15	23
4 Roberts (D)	W A W W R R W W W W W W A W W W W W W A	13	10	14
5 Mattox (D)	R R W W W R R R W W R R A W W R W W R A	*	45	46
6 Teague (D)	A A A A A A W A A A W A A A A A A A A	12	0	0
7 Archer (R)	W W W R W W W W W W W W W W W W W W W	0	15	14
8 Eckhardt (D)	R R R R W W R R A A R R W W R R W R R W	87	75	59
9 Brooks (D)	R R A W W R W W R R W A W W R R W W W	34	50	36
10 Pickle (D)	R R W W W R R W R W W W W W R W W W W	30	15	32
11 Poage (D)	W W W A W W W W W A W A R W W R W W A	13	0	9
12 Wright (D)	R W W R W A W A R W R A W R R W R R W	39	45	36
13 Hightower (D)	R W W A R R W W W R R W A W W W W W W	14	20	32
14 Young (D)	R W W W W R A W A A A W W A W A W R W W	26	25	18
15 de la Garza (D)	R W A W R R W W W W W W W R A A W R W W	18	40	27
16 White (D)	R W W W R R W W W W W W W W R A W W W	21	15	23

	1 2 3 4 5 6 7 8 9 10 11 12 13 14 15 16 17 18 19 20	%94	%77	%78
17 Burleson (D)	W W W W R R W W W W A W A W W W W W W W	4	5	14
18 Jordan (D)	R W W R R W R R R R R R R W R R R W	79	55	77
19 Mahon (D)	R W W W R R W W W R R W A R W W R R W W	13	20	41
20 Gonzalez (D)	R R W R A R R W R R R W W R R W W R R R	47	50	64
21 Krueger (D)	A A W W R R W W A A A W A A W R A A W A	14	25	18
22 Gammage (D)	A A W W R R W A W W A W W W W W W W	*	25	14
23 Kazen (D)	R W W W W R W W W W W W R W W R W W	22	25	18
24 Milford (D)	A R W W W R W A W A W A W W A W A W A	4	5	9
UTAH				
1 McKay (D)	R A W W W R W W W W W W W W R W A W W W	37	15	14
2 Marriott (R)	W W W W R R W W W W W W A W W W W W W W	*	10	14
VERMONT				
AL Jeffords (R)	R R R W R W R R R W A W R W R W R W W	54	65	64
VIRGINIA				
1 Trible (R)	W W W W R R W W W W W W R W W W W W	*	5	18
2 Whitehurst (R)	W A W W R R W W W W W W A W W W W W W W	8	10	14
3 Satterfield (D)	W W W W R R W W W W W W R W W W W W W W	0	5	18
4 Daniel (R)	W W W W R R W W W W W W W R W W W W W W	0	10	18
5 Daniel (D)	R W W W W W W W W W W R W W W W W W	0	10	9
6 Butler (R)	W W W W R W A W A W W W W W R A W W	0	10	14
7 Robinson (R)	W W W W R R W W W W R W W R W W W W W	0	5	18
8 Harris (D)	R R R R R R R A R W R R W W R R W R R W	91	75	73
9 Wampler (R)	R W A W R W W W R W W W W R W W W W W W	0	15	23
10 Fisher (D)	R R R R W W R W R R R R R W R R W W R W	92	70	64
WASHINGTON				
1 Pritchard (R)	A W W W R W R W R R R W R A W R R W A W W	25	35	36
2 Meeds (D)	A A R R W W R W A R R R W W R R A R R W	79	60	50
3 Bonker (D)	R W A R W W W W A R R R R W R R W R R W	87	70	46
4 McCormack (D)	R W R W R W W W W R A R W A R W R W R W W	65	30	32
5 Foley (D)	R W R W W W W W W R R R R W A W R W R W W	59	50	41
6 Dicks (D)	R A R R W W R R R A R W W R R W R W R W	*	55	59
7 Cunningham (R)	W W W W R W W W W W W W R W W W W W W W	*	17	18
WEST VIRGINIA				
1 Mollohan (D)	W R W W W W W W R W R W W R W W R R W W	44	40	27
2 Staggers (D)	R A R R W W R R R R R W A W R R R R R W	65	60	64
3 Slack (D)	W W W R W W W W W W R W A W W W W W W W	45	40	9
4 Rahall (d)	R A R R W W W R W R W A W R R W R W W	*	65	36
WISCONSIN				
1 Aspin (D)	R R R R W W R R R R R R A W R W R R R W	76	70	68
2 Kastenmeier (D)	R R R R R R R R R R R R R R R R R R R W	84	90	96
3 Baldus (D)	R W R R W W R R R R R R R R R W R R R W	96	80	73
4 Zablocki (D)	R W R R R W R W R R W W W R W R R R R W	100	70	50
5 Reuss (D)	R R R R R W R R R R R R A W R R R R R R	100	90	82
6 Steiger (R)	W W W W R R A W W A R W W R A R W W W W	9	50	27
7 Obey (D)	R W R W R W R W R R R R R R R R R R R W	96	70	73
8 Cornell (D)	R W R R R R R R R R R R R R R R R R R W	100	90	91
9 Kasten (R)	W A A W R R W W W W W A R W W R W A W W	0	30	23
WYOMING				
AL Roncalio (D)	R W W A W W R W A R A R W W A A W R R W	48	55	32

House Footnotes
[1]William Ketchum died on June 24, 1978.
[2]Ralph Metcalf died on October 10, 1978.

³Goodloe Gyron died on October 11, 1978.
⁴Thomas P. O'Neill is Speaker of the House and only casts votes to cause or break a tie.
⁵William Green was sworn in on February 21, 1978.
⁶Robert Garcia was sworn in on February 21, 1978.
⁷Clifford Allen died on June 18, 1978.

$1 MILLION PAYS OFF FOR REALTORS
Stronger Curbs on Land Sales Go Down Drain

The National Association of Realtors (NAR) knows how to get the most for its money on Capitol Hill. The leading organization of real estate agents was the second largest interest group in contributions in the 1978 Congressional elections. The following year, it won an important victory when the House voted, 245 to 145, to block new enforcement provisions for the federal Interestate Land Sales Full Disclosure Act. The motion to defeat such provisions was offered by Rep. Carroll Campbell (R-SC), who received $3,000 from NAR in 1978.

A study of votes on the measure by Common Cause, a Washington public interest group, showed that more than 300 Representatives received NAR contributions in their 1978 campaigns. (In the Senate, 32 of 35 Senators who won in 1978 also received NAR money.) Common Cause found that 203 of the 245 members who voted with the NAR had received contributions from the organization, with an average contribution of $3,665. All but two of the 56 members receiving the largest amounts voted the way the NAR wanted. (See table.)

Of the 145 who voted against the NAR position, 74 received no money from NAR and the remaining 71 received an average of only $1,440, less than half the average of those voting in favor. The NAR had opposed stronger enforcement measures in order to, in its words, "curb regulatory abuses and remove the regulatory burden from the back of small businessmen."

Following is a list of the 56 biggest beneficiaries of money from NAR with the amounts and votes (Y–yes; N–no):

OIL LOBBYIST OPENS THE LID
On Who Got What on Capitol Hill

A deposition filed in court by a lobbyist for Gulf Oil Corporation in April, 1978, provided a glimpse of how much money flows to how many office holders from one company intimately involved in public affairs.

Ordered to compile a list of recipients of nearly $4 million in cash over a decade of activity in Washington, Claude C. Wild Jr. listed 117 Senators and Senatorial candidates. He avoided naming members of the House by claiming that they were too numerous to list.

Although recipients could have been prosecuted by the government and censured by Congressional ethic panels, only one was penalized. James Jones, Democratic Congressman from Oklahoma, pleaded guilty in 1976 to failing to report a Gulf gift.

It was not campaign laws that ended the cash flow, however. It was the Securities and Exchange Commission which accused Wild and the company of violating security regulations. Both Wild and Gulf accepted consent judgments in which they admitted no violations of law.

REPRESENTATIVE	STATE	AMOUNT	VOTE
Henry J. Hyde	(R) Ill.	11,200	Y
George Hansen	(R)Id.	11,000	Y
Larry P. McDonald	(D) Ga.	11,000	Y
Tom Corcoran	(R) Ill.	10,500	Y
Steven D. Symms	(R) Id.	9,000	Y
John J. Rhodes	(R) Az.	8,400	Y
Robert K. Dornan	(R) Cal.	8,000	Y
Phillip Gramm	(D) Tex.	8,000	Y
Norman D. Shumway	(R) Cal.	8,000	Y
Ray Roberts	(D) Tex.	7,700	Y
Edward J. Derwinsky	(R) Ill.	7,500	Y
Richard C. White	(D) Tex.	7,500	Y
Thomas B. Evans, Jr.	(R) Del.	7,150	Y
Jim Wright*	(D) Tex.	7,100	Y
George M. O'Brien	(R) Ill.	7,000	Y
Tobias A. Roth	(R) Wis.	7,000	Y
Fernand J. St. Germain*	(D) R.I.	7,000	Y
Robert E. Bauman	(R) Md.	6,500	Y
Samuel L. Devine	(R) Oh.	6,500	Y
John J. Duncan	(R) Tn.	6,366	Y
Ike Skelton	(D) Mo.	6,300	Y
Richard Kelley	(R) Fla.	6,200	Y
Robin L. Beard, Jr.	(R) Tn.	6,166	Y
Douglas K. Bereuter	(R) Neb.	6,100	Y
Beryl Anthony	(D) Ark.	6,000	Y
Bill Boner	(D) Tn.	6,000	Y
Richard Cheney	(R) Wy.	6,000	Y
William E. Dannemeyer	(R) Cal.	6,000	Y
E. (Kika) De la Garza	(D) Tex.	6,000	Y
Wayne Grisham	(R) Cal.	6,000	Y
S. William Green*	(R) N.Y.	6,000	N
Jack Hightower	(D) Tex.	6,000	Y
Marjorie S. Holt	(R) Md.	6,000	Y
J. Marvin Leath	(D) Tex.	6,000	Y
Jerry Lewis	(R) Cal.	6,000	Y
Dan Lungren	(R) Cal.	6,000	Y
Ron Marlenee	(R) Mont.	6,000	Y
Robert McClory	(R) Ill.	6,000	Y
Charles Stenholm	(D) Tex.	6,000	Y
William C. Wampler	(R) Va.	6,000	Y
C.W. Bill Young	(R) Fla.	6,000	Y
William J. Hughes*	(D) N.J.	5,500	Y
Ed Jenkins	(D) Ga.	5,500	Y
Douglas Applegate	(D) Oh.	5,275	Y
Dan Marriott	(R) Ut.	5,100	Y
Daniel B. Crane	(R) Ill.	5,000	Y
Charles F. Dougherty*	(R) Pa.	5,000	Y
Newt Gingrich	(R) Ga.	5,000	Y
Sam B. Hall, Jr.	(D) Tex.	5,000	Y
Margaret Heckler	(R) Mass.	5,000	N
Ron Paul	(R) Tex.	5,000	Y
Floyd Spence	(R) S.C.	5,000	Y
Olympia J. Snowe	(R) Me.	5,000	Y
Dave Stockman	(R) Mich.	5,000	Y
Robert Whittaker	(R) Kans.	5,000	Y
Lyle Williams	(R) Oh.	5,000	Y

DOCTORS VS. CONSUMERS
How AMA Money Defeated Cost Control Bill

The financial clout of doctors is an important factor when the votes are counted on many issues in Congress and in state legislatures. It apparently was especially influential in killing President Carter's efforts to force hospitals to reduce their costs in 1978.

When the issue came up for a vote in the House Interstate Commerce Committee on July 18, the hospital cost containment measure was defeated, 22 to 21. The one-vote defeat came when Rep. Jim Broyhill (D-NC) successfully offered a substitute proposal described by Rep. Paul Rogers (D-FL), the bill's sponsor, as "just a gutting of the bill."

Since 1975, the American Medical Association has given more than $100,-000 to members of the committee in political contributions, according to a tally by Common Cause, a public interest group in Washington.

Nineteen of the 22 members voting to kill the cost control bill received $85,150 from various AMA committees. Their average was $4,482; the average for supporters of hospital cost controls was only $1,007. Members of the Committee and amounts received from the AMA were as follows:

*   *   *   *

Members Voting Against Administration's Health Cost Containment Legislation		Members Voting for Administration's Health Cost Containment Legislation	
Representative	**AMA**	**Representative**	**AMA**
James Broyhill (R-N.C.)	$ 1,200	Charles Carney (D-Ohio)	$ 400
Clarence Brown (R-Ohio)	2,300	Bob Eckhardt (D-Tex.)	100
Tim Lee Carter (R-Ky.)	10,000	James Florio (D-N.J.)	1,550
James Collins (R-Tex.)	7,500	Albert Gore, Jr. (D-Tenn.)	0
Samuel Devine (R-Ohio)	10,100	Andrew Maguire (D-N.J.)	300
John Dingell (D) Mich.)	200	Edward Markey (D-Mass.)	1,500
Louis Frey (R-Fla.)*	2,000	Ralph Metcalfe (D-Ill.)	2,500
Bob Gammage (D-Tex.)	0	Barbara Mikulski (D-Md.)	100
Bob Krueger (D-Tex.)	17,050	Toby Moffett (D-Conn.)	0
Norman Lent (R-N.Y.)	5,100	John Moss (D-Ca.)	3,109
Thomas Luken (D-Ohio)	0	John Murphy (D-N.Y.)	350
Edward Madigan (R-Ill.)	2,700	Richard Ottinger (D-N.Y.)	0
Marc Marks (R-Pa.)	5,000	Richardson Preyer (D-N.C.)	500
W. Henson Moore (R-La.)	5,000	Matthew Rinaldo (R-N.J.)	2,250
Carlos Moorhead (R-Ca.)	3,500	Paul Rogers (D-Fla.)	0
Fred Rooney (D-Pa.)	3,200	James Scheuer (D-N.Y.)	250
Martin Russo (D-Ill.)	2,800	Harley Staggers (D-W.V.)	0
James Santini (D-Nev.)	1,700	Lionel Van Deerlin (D-Ca.)	2,000
David Satterfield (D-Va.)	0	Douglas Walgren (D-Pa.)	100
Phil Sharp (D-Ind.)	200	Henry Waxman (D-Ca.)	1,000
Joe Skubitz (R-Kan.)	100	Tim Wirth (D-Colo.)	100
David Stockman (R-Mich.)	5,500		
		TOTAL	$16,109
TOTAL	$85,150		

*Rep. Louis Frey was absent for the vote.   Source: Common Cause

MARITIME MONEY AND VOTES
Loading the Docks of Congress

Since the early 1970s, the maritime industry has been trying to enact a "cargo preference" law that would require a larger amount of oil imported to the U.S. to be carried on American ships. Presently, only about 4 per cent of imported oil arrives on U.S. ships.

In 1974, both houses of Congress passed the "Energy Transportation Act," which would have required 30 per cent of imported oil to arrive on American tankers. But President Ford vetoed the bill. In 1977, the "Oil Cargo Equity" bill was introduced in Congress, setting the minimum at 9.5 per cent.

Lobbying efforts by maritime unions and companies in 1977 were extremely heavy. According to Common Cause, political contributions from maritime interests totaled about $1.3 million, not including a $1-million public relations and advertising campaign financed by shipping interests.

Shipbuilders and their suppliers, as well as shipping companies and U.S. seamen, benefit from direct taxpayer subsidies for construction and operating expenses to the tune of $1.1 billion annually. In addition, the government guarantees $800 million a year in the financing of construction and repairs, and a 1954 law requires that at least half of all government-generated cargo be shipped on privately owned U.S. flag ships when available. One Congressman estimated that the average American merchant sailor earns $18,000 for six to eight months at sea. Of that amount, $13,320 comes from federal subsidies.

$2 MILLION IN CONTRIBUTIONS

With such a stake in subsidies—and a chance of doubling business resulting from the bill's passage—maritime unions and industries pressed hard for the cargo preference bills. During 1975-77, the unions alone contributed nearly $2 million to Congressional candidates, almost half going to 1976 races. Maritime executives also contributed heavily to candidates, but their total gifts as individuals were not easy to identify from Federal Election Commission records.

Maritime unions contributed $969,441 to 1976 Congressional races, according to the Commission. Of this amount, $449,410 went to the campaigns of 214 successful candidates for House elections. A large share of the contributions went to members of the committees that handle maritime legislation. For example, 30 of the 41 present members of the House Merchant Marine and Fisheries Committee received a total of $102,763 in 1976. On August 2, 1977, the committee voted in favor of the oil cargo preference bill by a vote of 31 to 5. Twenty-four members voting for the bill had received a total of $82,263 in maritime contributions in 1976; three of the five dissenters received no donations and the two other members received only $500 each.

According to Common Cause, the leading committee recipient was Chairman John Murphy (D-NY), who introduced the bill on the House floor. He received $11,200 from maritime unions and $5,000 from company executives, plus $9,950 at a fundraiser before the committee vote for a total of $26,150. Second biggest recipient was Leo Zefferetti (D-NY), who received $18,138 from unions and $3,000 from company executives, for a total of $21,138.

Between the committee vote favoring the bill and the floor vote in the House, the news media gave prominent coverage to the Common Cause report on contributions. When the vote came up in the House, several committee members, who had favored the bill in committee and had been identified as recipients of substantial contributions, voted against the bill. The House vote against the bill was 265 to 157.

Following is a list of committee members' votes for and against the bill on the House floor and the amounts they received from maritime unions: (Murphy and Zefferetti both represent Congressional districts that rely heavily on the shipping business.)

VOTED FOR BILL

Akaka (D-HI)	$ 300	Hubbard (D-KY)	$ 1,300
Anderson (D-CA)	1,200	Jones (D-NC)	1,000
Ashley (D-OH)	18,000	Leggett (D-CA)	4,300
AuCoin (D-OR)	7,350	Mikulski (D-MD)	1,900
Bauman (R-MD)	200	Murphy (D-NY	11,200
Biaggi (D-NY)	6,800	Oberstar (D-MN)	2,500
Bonoir (D-MI)	800	Patterson (D-CA)	3,550
Bonker (D-WA)	2,500	Pritchard (R-WA)	0
Bowen (D-MS)	1,000	Rogers (D-FL)	0
D'Amours (D-NH)	800	Rooney (D-PA)	1,000
de la Garza (D-TX)	0	Snyder (R-KY)	500
Dingell (D-MI)	4,725	Trible (R-VA)	0
Eilberg (D-PA)	1,500	Young (R-AL)	1,500
Emery (R-ME)	0	Zeferetti (D-NY)	18,138
Ginn (D-GA)	0	Total:	$92,063

VOTED AGAINST BILL

Breaux (D-LA)*	$2,200
Dornan (R-CA)	0
Evans (R-DE)	0
Forsythe (R-NJ)	0
Hughes (D-NJ)	300
Lent (R-NY)	500
McCloskey (R-CA)	500
Ruppe (R-MI)*	2,700
Studds (D-MA)	1,000
Treen (R-LA)*	0
Not voting on the floor:	
Metcalfe (D-IL)*	3,500
Total	$7,200

* Voted in favor of bill in committee.

In 1978, a House subcommittee headed by Rep. Benjamin Rosenthal (D-NY) reported that officials of the U.S. Maritime Administration routinely served as members of the private National Maritime Council "in utter disregard for conflict-of-interest requirements." The Maritime Administration also contributed services worth $200,000 per year to the group, while the industry was receiving almost $3 billion in subsidies from the government. The Council ties were broken after being reported in the press.

NATIONAL PUBLIC INTEREST GROUPS

CHILDREN

Action for Children's Television (ACT), 46 Austin St., Newton Centre, MA, 02159; 617/527-7870. Seeks to reduce offensive television commercials and programs aimed at young children. Has forced networks to reduce violence and commercial time on Saturday morning and forced ad industry to curb unfair appeals to youngsters.

Children's Foundation, 1028 Connecticut Ave. NW, Suite 1112, Washington, DC, 20036; 202/296-4451. Seeks to make people aware of their right to proper nutrition and monitors federal food assistance programs.

Child Welfare League of America, 1346 Connecticut Ave. NW, Suite 310, Washington, DC, 20036; 202/833-2850. Has helped revise adoption, foster care and day care practices. Two programs are the Adoption Resource Exchange, which finds organizations with homes for handicapped children, and the Foster Parents Project, which helps agencies develop training programs for foster parents.

Council on Children, Media and Merchandising, 1346 Connecticut Ave. NW, Washington, DC, 20036; 202/466-2584. Aims to reform unfair and deceptive television advertising of food and drugs to women and children. Was responsible for forcing cereal companies to fortify 35 widely advertised dry cereals with vitamins and minerals.

COMMUNITY AFFAIRS

Center for Community Change, 1000 Wisconsin Ave. NW, Washington, DC, 20007; 202/338-6310. Provides technical assistance to community organizations on housing, economic development and other grass roots issues.

National Association of Neighborhoods, 1612 20th St. NW, Washington, DC, 20009; 202/332-7766. Aims to raise neighborhood issues of all types to a national level. Also helps develop and coordinate action of neighborhood groups.

National Center for Community Action, 1328 New York Ave. NW, Washington, DC, 20005; 202/667-8970. Clearinghouse for community action groups. Assists in community organizing on issues affecting low-income individuals such as food stamps and fuel.

Shelterforce Collective, 380 Main St., East Orange, NJ, 07918; 201/673-2405. Works on housing issues including tenant rights, redlining and national housing policy. Publishes quarterly journal, *Shelterforce,* and helps organize on local levels.

CONSUMER

American Council on Consumer Interests, 238 Stanley Hall, University of Missouri, Columbia, MO, 65201; 314/882-3817. An organization of professionals and teachers in consumer affairs. Conducts research, holds workshops and publishes monthly *ACCI Newsletter.*

Aviation Consumer Action Project, 1346 Connecticut Ave. NW, Washington, DC, 20036; 202/223-4498. Concerned with airline safety and the rights of airline passengers. Monitors workings of the Civil Aeronautics Board and Federal Aviation Administration.

Center for Auto Safety, 1346 Connecticut Ave. NW, Washington, DC,

20036; 202/659-1126. Concerned with automobile safety issues. Studies problems, issues reports, petitions government for rules changes, pressures manufacturers to adopt stronger safety measures.

Conference of Consumer Organizations (COCO), Box 4277, Tucson, AZ, 85717. A federation of consumer citizens groups which specializes in conducting discussion conferences and educational seminars around the country. Publishes monthly newsletter, *COCO Intercom.*

Consumer Federation of America, 1012 14th St. NW, Washington, DC, 20005; 202/737-3732. A federation of consumer, labor, cooperative and other groups. Holds annual Consumer Assembly, publishes monthly *CFA News* and pamphlets, and lobbies for consumer protection legislation in Congress.

Consumer's Research Inc., Bowerstown Road, Washington, NJ, 07882; 201/689-3300. The original consumer product testing organization. Publishes monthly *Consumer Research Bulletin and Consumer Bulletin Annual.* Takes a jaundiced view of both government regulators and professional consumerists.

Consumers Education & Protective Association, 6048 Ogontz Ave., Philadelphia, PA, 19141; 215/424-1441. An activist organization which conducts demonstrations and mass picketing to obtain justice for inner-city poor. Publishes monthly *Consumers Voice* tabloid.

Consumers Union, 256 Washington St., Mount Vernon, NY, 10550; 914/664-6400. The largest and second oldest independent product-testing organization. Publishes monthly *Consumer Reports* magazine, an annual *Buying Guide* and numerous books. Also produces TV mini-documentaries and educational materials.

Cooperative League of the USA, 1828 L St. NW, Washington, DC, 20036. National membership organization of cooperatives of all types. Conducts research and publishes educational materials of interest to members. Provides "how-to" information on starting coops.

National Consumer Research Center, 1346 Connecticut Ave. NW, Washington, DC, 20036; 202/797-7600. Conducts research and consumer education on regulatory reform issues.

National Consumers League, 1522 K St. NW, Suite 406, Washington, DC, 20005; 202/797-7600. The oldest consumer organization, founded in 1899 to fight sweat shops and child labor by boycotting goods of target companies. Testifies before Congress and federal agencies and publishes monthly newsletter.

National Public Interest Research Group, 1329 E St. NW, Suite 1127, Washington, DC, 20004; 202/347-3811. Provides technical resources to local PIRGs in the areas of personal finance, energy and public utilities. Organizes citizen action groups in specific areas of interest, including Residential Utility Consumer Action Groups (RUCAGs) to monitor local utilities.

DISABLED

American Coalition of Citizens with Disabilities, 1346 Connecticut Ave. NW, Room 817, Washington, DC, 20036; 202/785-4265. Umbrella organization of 45 national, state and local groups concerned with physically, mentally or emotionally handicapped individuals. Represents disabled interests to the federal and state governments.

Disability Rights Center, 1346 Connecticut Ave. NW, Suite 1124, Washington, DC, 20036; 202/223-3304. Monitors federal enforcement of civil rights and consumer protection for the disabled. Issues reports, conducts research on compliance efforts of federal agencies.

Mainstream, Inc., 1200 15 St. NW, Washington, DC, 20005; 800/424-8089. Provides information to facilitate compliance with the Rehabilitation Act of 1973. Maintains a toll-free hotline to answer questions about compliance, and distributes a number of publications.

National Association of the Deaf, 814 Thayer Ave., Silver Spring, MD, 20710; 301/587-1788. Primarily an educational organization, alerts people to the special needs of the deaf and distributes publications relating to deafness.

National Association of the Physically Handicapped, 6473 Grandville Ave., Detroit, MI, 48228. Provides information about transportation, sports, and the removal of architectural barriers.

National Federation of the Blind, 1346 Connecticut Ave. NW, Washington, DC, 20036; 800/424-9700. Lobbies for the rights of blind persons. Maintains a toll-free hotline to assist the blind with social, legal and educational problems.

ELDERLY

National Citizens' Coalition for Nursing Home Reform, 1424 16th St. NW, Suite 204, Washington, DC, 20036; 202/797-8227. Serves as clearinghouse of information and advocate of reform in treatment of patients in nursing homes throughout the U.S.

Gray Panthers, 3700 Chestnut St., Philadelphia, PA, 19104; 215/382-6644. Lobbies and organizes around health care, nursing homes, age discrimination, mandatory retirement, Social Security and other issues involving the aged.

National Center on the Black Aged, 1730 M St. NW, Washington, DC, 20036; 202/637-8400. Research and information clearinghouse on problems of black low-income elderly.

National Council of Senior Citizens, 1511 K St. NW, Washington, DC, 20005; 202/347-8800. Research and information group working on problems of elderly including housing, national health insurance, Medicare and mental health.

National Retired Teachers Association/American Association of Retired Persons, 1750 K St. NW, Washington, DC, 20006. Large membership organization which provides information and services such as low-cost prescriptions.

ECONOMICS

Agribusiness Accountability Project, P.O. Box 5646, San Francisco, CA, 94101; 415/626-1650. Represents small farming interests against large farming conglomerates. Publishes monthly newsletter, *Agbiz Tiller.*

Council on Economic Priorities, 84 Fifth Ave., New York, NY, 10011; 212/691-8550. Studies and issues reports on a wide range of economic issues, from energy and environment to military contracts to social issues raised by corporate stockholders.

Movement for Economic Justice, 1735 T St. NW, Washington, DC, 20009; 202/462-4200. Clearinghouse for information on community action and social change groups. Publishes monthly newsletter, *Just Economics*, covering taxes, utilities, redlining and other issues.

National Taxpapers Union, 625 E. Capital St. SE, Washington, DC, 20003; 202/546-2085. Lobbies to cut deficit financing and wasteful spending by the federal government.

Pension Rights Center, 1346 Connecticut Ave. NW, Washington, DC,

20036; 202/296-3778. Concerned with educating employees about rights under the Employee Retirement Income Security Act of 1974.

Peoples Business Commission, 1346 Connecticut Ave. NW, Room 1010, Washington, DC, 20036; 202/483-8138. Concerned with countering corporate control of the U.S. through educational materials about worker rights, worker-owned businesses.

Public Interest Economic Center, 1714 Massachusetts Ave. NW, Washington, DC, 20036; 202/872-0313. Provides educated analyses of the economic bases for legislation, regulatory action and litigation.

Tax Analysts and Advocates, 2369 N. Taylor, Arlington, VA, 22207; 703/532-1850. A public interest tax law firm and news service. Publishes weekly magazine, *Tax Notes.* Monitors federal tax policy.

Tax Reform Research Group, 133 C St. SE, Washington, DC, 20003; 202/544-1710. Concerned with reform of income and property tax laws. Publishes monthly tabloid, *People and Taxes.*

Taxation With Representation, 2369 N. Taylor, Arlington, VA, 22207; 703/527-6877. Taxpayers' lobby, advocating public interest viewpoint on tax reform.

ENERGY AND ENVIRONMENT

Center for Science in the Public Interest, 1757 S St. NW, Washington, DC, 20009; 202/332-9110. Seeks to protect the public from scientific and health hazards through publication of newsletters, reports and books on issues such as nutrition, food advertising, energy conservation, and toxic chemicals.

Critical Mass, 133 C St. SE, Washington, DC, 20003; 202/546-4790. A Public Citizen-affiliated organization researching the health, safety and economic ramifications of nuclear power. Publishes monthly tabloid, *Critical Mass.*

Defenders of Wildlife, 2000 N. St. NW, Washington, DC, 20036; 202/659-9510. Educates the public on the need to protect all forms of wildlife. Has improved conditions in zoos and has helped expand wildlife preserves.

Energy Action, 1523 L St. NW, Suite 302, Washington, DC, 20005; 202/737-6220. Consumer-oriented group monitoring energy legislation on the federal level.

Environmental Action Foundation, 1346 Connecticut Ave. NW, Suite 724, Washington, DC, 20036; 202/659-9682. Publishes papers on utilities, transportation, solid waste, nuclear power and the B-1 bomber.

Environmental Defense Fund, 1525 18th St. NW, Washington, DC, 20036; 202/833-1484. A public interest law firm seeking to tighten pollution control standards and ban harmful substances from the environment. Was successful in banning the carcinogen DES from cattle feed and banning DDT.

Environmental Policy Center, 324 C St. SE, Washington, DC, 20003; 202/547-6500. Provides economic and political analyses on environmental problems and lobbies for bills and regulations particularly dealing with solar energy and other non-polluting alternatives.

Environmentalists for Full Employment, 1785 Massachusetts Ave. NW, Washington, DC, 20036; 202/347-5590. Coalition of several hundred environmental and labor groups advocating that environmental quality and full employment are compatible goals. Holds regional seminars and conferences.

Friends of the Earth, 620 C St. SE, Washington, DC, 20003; 202/543-4312. Lobbies for environmental legislation. Educates the public about alternative sources of energy. Works through courts to stop strip mining, nuclear power plants and international whale hunting and to create new national parks and wildlife refuges.

National Wildlife Federation, 1412 16th St. NW, Washington, DC, 20036; 202/797-6800. Educates public and government leaders to the problems of wildlife preservation, overpopulation and energy. Monitors legislative activities, is active in court suits and petitions federal regulatory agencies.

Natural Resources Defense Council, 15 W, 44th St., New York, NY, 10036; 212/869-0150. Conducts studies and files legal suits to block harmful substances in foods, beverages, air and water.

Sierra Club, 530 Bush St., San Francisco, CA, 94108; 415/981-8634. Aims principally to keep unspoiled sections of the country in their natural state through law suits and lobbying activities.

The Wilderness Society, 1901 Pennsylvania Ave. NW, Washington, DC, 20006; 202/293-2732. Focuses on land preservation and protection of endangered species. Monitors federal regulatory agencies, participates in law suits, and trains citizens in the politics of environmental protection.

HEALTH AND NUTRITION

Bread for the World, 110 Maryland Ave. NW, Washington, DC, 20002; 202/544-3820. Lobbies on issues relating to food stamps and other federal food programs.

Community Nutrition Institute, 1146 19th St. NW, Washington, DC, 20036; 202/833-1730. Provides information and technical assistance on a wide range of food program and policy issues. Publishes newsletter to nutritionists and school lunch program personnel.

Health Research Group, 2000 P St. NW, Washington, DC, 20036; 202/872-0320. Concerned with improving the quality of medical care, removing harmful chemicals from food and eliminating dangerous drugs from the market.

Food Research and Action Center, 2011 I St. NW, Washington, DC, 20006; 202/452-8250. Provides legal assistance, organizing aid, training and information on how to expand and improve federal food programs such as food stamps, school lunch programs and WIC.

Nutrition Action, 1755 S St. NW, Washington, DC, 20009; 202/332-9110. Provides public with information about food contents and hazards, and about the food industry and government regulation of food.

LAW AND GOVERNMENT

American Civil Liberties Union, 22 E. 40th St., New York, NY, 10016; 212/725-1222. Concerned with protecting and educating individuals on their basic constitutional rights. Provides free legal aid in test cases. Publishes monthly newsletter, *Civil Liberties.*

Center for Law and Social Policy, 1751 N St. NW, Washington, DC, 20036; 202/872-0670. Represents citizens before regulatory bodies and the courts on public interest issues such as women's rights, miners' health and safety and other issues.

Center for the Study of Responsive Law, PO Box 19367, Washington, DC, 20036; 202/833-3400. The original organization established by Ralph Nader. Includes the Housing Research Group and Freedom of Information Clearinghouse. Is the main receiving point for letters to Nader.

Initiative America, 1316 Independence Ave. SE, Washington, DC, 20003; 202/347-5959. Provides organizing and technical assistance to groups seeking rights of initiative, referendum and recall on local issues. Working towards national law on citizen initiatives.

Institute for Public Interest Representation, 600 New Jersey Ave. NW, Washington, DC, 20001; 202/624-8390. Seeks to make regulatory agencies more responsive to the public interest.

National Legal Aid and Defender Association, 2100 M St. NW, Suite 601, Washington, DC, 20037; 202/452-0620. Helps provide the poor with quality legal services. Won a court case which established that people in mental institutions have a constitutional right to rehabilitative treatment.

National Paralegal Institute Inc., 2000 P St. NW, Washington, DC, 20036; 202/872-0655. Trains paralegals for public law. Also provides technical assistance for legal service programs.

National Resource Center for Consumers of Legal Services, 1302 18th St. NW, Washington, DC, 20036; 202/659-8514. Works towards creating better public access to lawyers and assists in establishing prepaid legal plans.

MEDIA AND COMMUNICATIONS

American Women in Radio and Television, 1321 Connecticut Ave. NW, Washington, DC, 20036; 202/296-0009. Acts as a national forum for exchange of ideas concerning women and the broadcast industry. Works for equal status for women in broadcast jobs and encourages women to enter media careers.

Cable Television Information Center, 2100 M St. NW, Washington, DC, 20037; 202/872-8888. Information clearinghouse about all aspects of cable TV. Provides consultation on starting stations including technical data.

Media Access Project, 1609 Connecticut Ave. NW, Washington, DC, 20036; 202/232-4300. Forces government agencies to grant public access to important information and seeks to have broadcasters give coverage for all candidates running for public office.

National Black Media Coalition, 2027 Massachusetts Ave. NW, Washington, DC, 20036; 202/797-7474. Coalition of more than 70 black media reform groups. Seeks to represent minority needs in programming and employment in media jobs. Publishes research and intervenes on minority interests before FCC.

National Citizens Committee for Broadcasting, 1028 Connecticut Ave., Washington, DC, 20036; 202/466-8407. Aims to educate and encourage citizens and organizations to participate more in the media and its regulatory processes.

Office of Communication of the United Church of Christ, 289 Park Ave S, New York, NY, 10010; 212/475-2127. Helps racial minorities and women achieve recognition in broadcast programming and employment. Provides field staff assistance to local community groups.

Public Interest Satellite Association, 55 W. 44th St., New York, NY 10036; 212/730-5172. Educates consumers on use of satellites for telecommunications. Assists consumer and public interest groups in utilizing telecommunications technology and obtaining access to existing systems.

Public Media Center, 2751 Hyde St., San Francisco, CA, 94109; 415/885-0200. Develops advertising and media campaigns for public interest groups and movements. Assists nonprofit groups with creating, producing and distributing ads.

WOMEN

Center for Women Policy Studies, 2000 P St. NW, Suite 508, Washington, DC, 20036; 202/872-1770. Provides analyses of legal and economic problems which relate to women, such as the role of the hospital in treatment of rape victims, the rights of policewomen, educational rights and sex discrimination in employment.

National Abortion Rights Action League, 705 G St. SE, Washington, DC, 20003; 202/347-7774. Lobbies for abortion services and improved health education for women, particularly those from deprived backgrounds. Helps stop legislation barring federal funds for abortions and works to defeat anti-abortion candidates.

National Organization for Women, 706 7th St. SE, Washington, DC, 20003; 202/347-2279. The oldest and largest feminist organization, NOW aims to sensitize the country to the problems of women and gain equality for them through lobbying, legislation, litigation and publications.

National Women's Political Caucus, 1921 Pennsylvania Ave. NW, Washington, DC, 20006; 202/347-4456. Supports women seeking public office and lobbies for the Equal Rights Amendment.

Women's Equity Action League, 377 National Press Building, Washington, DC 20045; 202/638-1961. Seeks to protect working women and those attending school from sex discrimination.

Helping Yourself

In This Chapter
- **Getting Results With Complaints**
- **Common Frauds and Deceptions**
- **Better Business Bureaus**
- **Business and Professional Sources of Help**
- **Public Law Centers**
- **State and Local Consumer Groups**

"Let the seller beware," the reverse of the ancient saying, is the battle cry of today's consumers. Inflation has forced many people to work harder than ever to get their money's worth and to complain more loudly than before when they don't get satisfaction.

Most confrontations take place at the retail level, where businesses are most conscious of maintaining customer loyalty. But surveys show that only about half of all complaints are resolved by retailers, causing consumers to seek help elsewhere.

When problems are not resolved immediately, many people don't go further because they are unaware of other avenues of redress. Those who press on often waste time and money spinning their wheels, calling or writing to the wrong places and appealing to organizations which cannot or will not provide assistance.

Sixty-five per cent of people surveyed in a 1977 Lou Harris poll found it "very difficult" to get results with complaints. Eighty-one per cent of government consumer representatives and 53 per cent of consumer representatives in business agreed that dissatisfied buyers have difficulty getting redress. As a result, not all people with legitimate complaints bother to protest. While 6.2 per cent of those surveyed by Harris said they wanted to complain about a product or service, only 47 per cent actually did so.

INDIVIDUALS LEFT MORE TO OWN DEVICES

At the same time, individuals are expected to look out for themselves more now than only a few years ago. Widespread complaints about government spending and allegedly excessive regulations have caused many states to slash public services, such as California did following passage of Proposition 13. In addition, several federal agencies have begun to cut back on their rules in response to complaints from business that regulations limit competition and discourage new enterprises. These events have shifted more responsibility onto private individuals to resolve their own problems in the marketplace.

This chapter focuses on ways to do just that with information on how and where to complain when things go wrong. In recent years, Americans have gained many new rights (see previous chapter). But these rights are worthless if not exercised by individuals. Among organizations ready to help consumers help themselves are Better Business Bureaus, business and professional associations, public law centers and a network of citizen groups. (Government sources of help, including small claims courts, are discussed in the next chapter.)

One of the best ways consumers can protect themselves is by becoming aware of the types of products and services which cause the most problems and the types of business firms most likely to resolve complaints amicably. This chapter describes common frauds and deceptions as well as marketplace trends.

PROBLEMS WITH HOME REPAIR RISING FAST

In 1979, the Council of Better Business Bureaus, a federation of local BBBs, reported that the biggest change in consumer problems was an increased concern about home remodeling, construction and maintenance. These three subjects accounted for more than 30 per cent of the 5 million inquiries to BBBs in 1978. Complaints about such businesses rose about 30 per cent in only two years, added the Council.

"Caution," said the Council, "is clearly warranted for consumers considering home repairs and improvements as well as new home purchases." Ranking just below home remodelers in number of inquiries were insurance companies, followed in order by mail-order firms, auto dealers, trade and vocational schools, roofing contractors, heating and air conditioning companies, new home builders, moving and storage companies and auto repair shops, not including transmission shops.

MAIL ORDER COMPLAINTS LEAD ALL OTHERS

Among complaints filed with BBBs, mail-order companies again led all others, as they did in past years. (See accompanying table of the most frequent complaints.) However, the volume of complaints about mail orders dropped slightly from the previous year. So did complaints in the second- and third-ranked categories: franchised auto dealers and home furnishing stores. Significant increases in complaints were reported for independent auto repair shops, roofing contractors and home remodelers. Complaints dropped substantially for television service and mail-order subscriptions.

Businesses doing the best to resolve complaints were banks, which settled 92.1 per cent of problems involving them. Next most effective were department stores, chain food stores, insurance companies, credit card companies, hospitals and clinics, airlines, small local firms and utilities.

Most frequent type of complaint was about delivery of merchandise. Unsatisfactory service and unsatisfactory repair were the next most frequent, followed by quality and performance problems, credit billing, warranties, refunds, selling practices, advertising practices and discontinued businesses.

Products most often involved in complaints were, in order, automobiles, clothing and accessories, furniture, appliances, television sets, roofing, floor coverings, watches and clocks, storm windows and doors and home heating devices.

USE OF ARBITRATION GROWING

A major trend in complaint resolution is the increase in the use of arbitration, a legally-binding alternative to court action. A third party mediator, usually a BBB or private organization, is selected by both parties in a dispute to hear the case and make a fair judgment.

The American Arbitration Association (AAA), a private organization which mediates disputes for a fee, reports its programs are on the rise. In addition to individual disputes, the AAA runs arbitration programs for numerous companies, including many in the home remodeling and construction business. It also administers the Home Owners Warranty program (see Housing chapter) for the National Association of Home Builders.

Ninety-four BBBs offer some sort of arbitration program. In 1978, the CBBB also initiated two pilot arbitration programs in conjunction with General Motors (GM) to settle automobile disputes in Western New York and Minnesota. GM entered into the arrangement with the CBBB in order to determine which resolution procedures "are most effective and leave the car owner with the highest possible level of satisfaction." The Council reports that both programs have been met with enthusiasm and that others are being considered.

BETTER BUSINESS BUREAUS

Better Business Bureaus, first established by business leaders in 1912, are chartered to "build and conserve public confidence in advertising and in business generally." Local BBBs are financed and operated by business people and membership is voluntary.

For many years, BBBs gave only lip service to their self-appointed role as the watchdog of the marketplace. In 1970, they succumbed to the role demanded of them by the increasing number of consumer complaints and inquiries. Local BBBs federated into the Council of Better Business Bureaus (CBBB) with a tripled annual budget and a commitment to greater action. In 1978, nearly 8 million people called on the nation's 143 BBBs for help. The total was down slightly from the record 8.2 million registered the year before. But it was still far higher than the number handled by other private groups. BBBs have become the leading processor of consumer complaints outside government.

BBBs A MAJOR SOURCE OF INFORMATION

Two-thirds of the inquiries to BBBs in 1978 were requests for information about specific companies. Files are maintained on every business that is the subject of an inquiry. A person who asks about a business's reputation is usually told that it (1) has a satisfactory record and meets the BBB standards, (2) has been the subject of complaints which have been answered, (3) does not meet the BBB standards, (4) is new in the area and has not yet established a record, (5) has not responded to requests for information, or (6) has no information on file but a report is in progress. Such information is not always helpful and may even be deceptive.

Seldom does a company with a notoriously poor track record gain a satisfactory rating, but it does happen. Some companies resolve all complaints forwarded by the BBB so that their record will reflect satisfactory service. Their customers don't necessarily get the same attention, however.

MANY COMPLAINTS REFERRED ELSEWHERE

Of the 920,000 requests to BBBs for help with complaints in 1978, 233,800 were referred to other sources (attorneys, courts, regulatory agencies). Bureaus require people to fill out a written form and only look into problems which a complainant has failed to resolve on his or her own. Less than 50 per cent of those who contacted BBBs bothered to pursue their case in writing.

While many people have found that BBBs are slow to take action in case of disputes, their services are improving. Arbitration is one service being offered by an increasing number of bureaus. In 1978, 2,125 hearings were held and decided by arbitration, with the average amount in dispute being $946.

BBBs use arbitration only after trying to mediate problems first. Companies in the programs pledge to arbitrate any disputes not resolved informally and include a statement to that effect in their contracts.

Persons who do not have a BBB in their area may write the Council of Better Business Bureaus for the location of the nearest office. Its address is 1150 17th St. NW, Washington, DC, 20036.

TOP 15 COMPLAINTS

Type of Business	1978			1977		
	Rank	Number	Percent of Total	Rank	Number	Percent of Total
Mail-Order Companies	1	61,321	15.19	1	63,150	15.41
Franchised Auto Dealers	2	25,071	6.21	2	25,408	6.20
Home Furnishings Stores	3	13,135	3.25	3	13,331	3.25
Auto Repair Shops (Independent)	4	12,517	3.10	7	10,744	2.62
Misc. Home Maintenance	5	11,967	2.96	4	11,538	2.81
Home Remodeling Contractors	6	11,337	2.81	8	10,110	2.46
Department Stores	7	11,169	2.77	5	11,370	2.77
Magazine Subscriptions	8	9,781	2.42	6	11,222	2.74
Insurance Companies	9	8,366	2.07	10	8,515	2.07
Television Servicing	10	7,481	1.85	9	9,113	2.22
Dry Cleaning/Laundry	11	7,385	1.83	11	8,041	1.96
Misc. Automotive	12	7,256	1.80	13	7,322	1.78
Apparel & Accessory Shops	13	6,899	1.71	12	7,420	1.81
Roofing Contractors	14	6,725	1.66	18	5,725	1.39
Appliance Stores	15	6,617	1.64	15	7,275	1.77

Source: Council of Better Business Bureaus

MERCHANDISING MIRACLES
Schemes That Stretch the Truth for Profit

The person who invents and sells a cream to remove wrinkles, a tonic to grow hair, a strawberry plant as big as a man, or a diet pill that soaks away fat in bath water will probably become a millionaire in a hurry.

Claims for such non-existent products are already making shady entrepreneurs rich; and they will continue to make money as long as it pays them to produce, package and promote their miracles through the mass media. Consumers tend to have faith in dream merchants because they believe that the government would never allow a fraudulent product to be sold and that the media would not carry an advertisement with untrue claims.

But regulators and the media protect people only to a certain degree. Agencies do not generally take action until there is a broad pattern of abuse and strong evidence that a large number of people have been cheated. Many schemes are considered victimless crimes because the amount of money involved is minimal and the major injury is embarrassment.

The Federal Trade Commission and the U.S. Postal Service are the principal guardians of the marketplace. They try to insure that advertising is not false or deceptive, but neither agency has the power to prevent ads from appearing initially. Often, a product is advertised widely and sold for some time before the ad ever comes to the government's attention. And it may take many years before a case is finally concluded.

Although some newspapers and radio and television stations screen ads for accuracy, theirs is by no means a universal practice. Advertising provides the funds that allow the media to exist, and only rarely will a newspaper or television station bite the hand that feeds it.

Smooth-talking con artists and advertisements that hide the truth are not likely to disappear from the marketplace. The best defense against them is to suspect a wolf beneath the sheep's clothing. Most consumer frauds are time-honored traditions; although different wolves appear on the scene regularly, they usually wear the same old costumes.

Following are some of the more common schemes which people are likely to encounter. There are legitimate firms offering such goods and services, but it is not always easy to distinguish them from the less scrupulous ones. Instances of consumer abuse also occur in connection with land sales, vocational schools, funeral services, commodities trading, insurance, auto repair and many other areas. These and others are discussed elsewhere in this book. (See subject headings in the index for page references.)

People who are victims of consumer fraud or who suspect a practice is illegal should contact a local or state consumer protection agency, post office or regional office of the Federal Trade Commission. Although such agencies may not resolve individual complaints, they can take measures to prevent the scheme from injuring other people.

SUPER PLANTS—A GROWING PROBLEM

Shady mail-order and nursery offers crop up regularly. Ads in comic books, Sunday comic pages and magazines make grossly exaggerated growth claims and say plants will survive in any environment. Two plants which were widely promoted by a number of firms in 1979 were zoysia grass and giant strawberries. Claims for both products have been called untrue by plant scientists, but business continues. Although the Postal Service took action to stop ads for American Nursery Sales' "Giant Climbing Strawberries," the company began advertising "Giant Man-High Strawberries" just two weeks later. TIP: Check with an agricultural extension agent to determine if claims are valid.

DIET PLANS—THINNING DOWN THE WALLET

According to ads in national publications, doctors have discovered a myriad of ways to achieve effortless, speedy weight loss. Thera-Slim-100 protein supplement "burns away more fat each 24 hours than if you ran 14 miles a day." Astro-trimmer is "guaranteed to reduce your waistline two to four inches in just three days." And a testimonial for W-L-40, a liquid for the bath, boasts:

"I lost 61 pounds of excess fat by just relaxing in my bathtub." Food and Drug Administration officials have called such claims untrue. Some diet plans are not only ineffective but dangerous. Yet regulators cannot keep up with all the new products which flood the market. The USPS stopped sales of W-L-40 in December, 1978, but only after hearing complaints that people had not received their shipments. As with many diet plans, few who received the miracle product notified authorities, probably because they were embarrassed to admit they had been taken. TIP: Consult a physician to verify claims or recommend other treatment.

HOME REMODELING—PUTTING BUYERS IN A FIX

Roof, furnace and chimney repair, basement waterproofing and new siding are among services offered by door-to-door contractors. Some schemers approach homes with offers to inspect various features free and then recommend extensive repair or remodeling. In addition to paying a large amount for poor service, many people wind up with a lien on their property. One company offered a special discount for certain improvements and required one-third payment on signing, one-third on delivery of materials and one-third on completion. Soon after materials were delivered, a salesman would collect the second payment and the homeowner would receive notice of a lien which had to be paid to the materials supplier. Before the contractor was indicted for mail fraud in March, 1978, he had collected $47,000. Another area which is ripe for deception is sale of solar energy equipment. Because the demand for such products is high and the number of qualified contractors limited, the FTC says people should be especially cautious in making such purchases. TIP: Get a number of estimates before contracting such work and check the firm's reputation with the BBB, neighbors and previous customers.

WORK-AT-HOME SCHEMES—PROFITS OUT THE WINDOWS

Opportunities which appear often in classified ads involve stuffing envelopes and clipping newspapers. Companies claim that their own employees are too busy to do such duties and they are therefore looking for outside help. Ads usually require a $10 to $15 deposit for information. People who send money may receive instructions for starting their own stuffing business by making the offer to others. In one case, the American Homeworkers Association, which claimed to be affiliated with 1,000 large corporations, offered lifetime memberships for $55 to $375 to stuff envelopes for its affiliates. Once the money was paid, no materials were supplied. The company was convicted of mail fraud in January, 1978.

A new scheme cited by the BBB is indoor decorative plant growing. People are asked to buy a backyard greenhouse, equipment, plants, soil and fertilizer and the seller offers to buy back the plants later. Investors pay from $3,000 to $6,000 over a period of time and are supposed to be able to make up to $700 a month. But the agreement is subject to the seller's approval of the plants, and many people end up having all plants rejected. TIP: Avoid offers that require payment in advance. For more information, order *Work-At-Home Schemes* from the Council Of Better Business Bureaus, 1150 17th St. NW, Washington, DC, 20036.

COMPUTER DATING—AUTOMATED ATTRACTION

The dancing school con artists of yesteryear have discovered a new way to tap the lonelyhearts market. Computer dating services charge from $15 to $25 to match people with the "perfect" companion. But many firms do not use computers; they provide the same names to everyone who signs up. One elderly woman reported receiving names of men ranging from 20 to 66 years old, all of whom lived far from her home. More costly are video dating services, in which daters get to screen prospective mates before entering into a "meaningful relationship." People who use them stand to lose still more if the company proves to be disreputable. TIP: Ask for a profile of past clients first; be wary of any firm which accepts all applicants and doesn't require references.

INVENTION PROMOTERS—SOMETIMES THE WRONG IDEA

"Ideas, inventions wanted! Can be turned into cash!" This familiar slogan appears in magazines and newspapers nationwide. People answering such ads are told that for a fee of at least $250 a firm will evaluate the marketability of their invention. Once the firm has collected that, it usually asks for at least $1,000 more to promote the idea to manufacturers. Such firms seldom determine that a similar product is already on the market or that the invention has no sales potential. The Federal Trade Commission has taken action against several invention marketing firms which collected millions of dollars and produced no results. One firm, the Raymond Lee Organization, admitted to the FTC that only three of its 30,000 clients had made a profit. TIP: Choose a firm that requires no advance fee. For more information write the Center for the Advancement of Invention and Innovation, 131 Gilbert Hall, University of Oregon, Eugene, OR, 97403.

MAIL-ORDER DIAMONDS—GLIMMERING DECEPTION

"Boiler rooms" in the U.S. and Canada have begun to use WATS lines to sell diamonds and other gems at inflated prices. Although it is true that real diamonds appreciate in value, many of those being sold are of inferior quality and are difficult to resell. London Merchants Inc., one firm no longer in business, told prospective buyers that diamonds appreciated 34 per cent in the past year and could be resold at a handsome profit. People who purchased diamonds were contacted a few months later and told that their diamonds had already gone up in value. The firm discouraged them from selling, however, and usually managed to convince buyers to purchase more. The second shipment seldom arrived. TIP: Get an independent appraisal before buying. For more information, write for *Buying Diamonds*, published by the Federal Trade Commission, Office of Consumer Protection, Washington, DC, 20580.

VACATION DISCOUNTS—WHERE "FREE" MAY BE COSTLY

"You have been selected by computer for a free vacation . . ." begins a standard promotional letter. People who read on discover that the free vacation is available for a $10 to $25 registration fee. Only after paying the fee, and sometimes even taking the trip, people discover the offers do not include transportation, can be used only during certain weeks of the year and are subject to room availability. The biggest vacation scheme in recent years was run by Columbia Research Inc., which promised trips to Las Vegas and Florida for

$15.95. Millions of letters were sent out nationwide beginning in 1974, and numerous complaints were received by state attorneys general afterward. Despite much legal action, the company was still in business in 1979.

Land developers are frequent users of vacation offers to promote their property. Literature doesn't always disclose that people are required to take a tour of the community and be subjected to a high-pressure sales pitch or they will be presented with a stiff bill for accommodations. TIP: Find out exactly what the trip covers and who it is sponsored by; don't put much faith in a money-back guarantee.

CHAIN LETTERS—LINKS TO NEVER-NEVER LAND

Although chain letters that involve the mailing of money or any other item of value are against the law, they still flourish. Promoters find that people are still willing to take chances for easy financial reward. A chain letter widely circulated in 1978/79 was the "Circle of Gold." Recipients were asked to pay $50 to receive the letter and then send $50 to the first person on a list of 12 names. The buyer then was to remove the top name, add his/her name to the bottom and sell two copies of the letter for $50 each. If he sold both letters, no money was lost.

The USPS filed formal complaints and reached some consent agreements by May, 1979. While Circle of Gold originators made money, people who received the letter after it had been widely circulated had difficulty selling it, especially at the $50 price. And people whose names appeared on the list at any time face the possibility of a postal service complaint. TIP: Make the Postal Service the next recipient of any chain letter you receive.

PUZZLE CONTESTS—ELUSIVE PRIZES

Lotteries and promotional games are monitored by the U.S. Postal Service and most states, but some promoters have developed contests to snare gambling consumers while avoiding regulators. Puzzle contests purport to require some skill and therefore are not considered lotteries. Ads for such contests are placed primarily in comic books and invite readers to complete a series of puzzles to win cash prizes. Once a small fee is paid, contestants receive a simple puzzle ("Name the first President of the United States," for example) which they must return to the promoter when completed. When that puzzle is judged correct, contestants are told that they can continue in the contest by paying a larger fee to receive the second set of puzzles. As many as ten puzzles may comprise a single contest, each puzzle being more expensive than the last. People are encouraged by early winnings and often pay extra money to be eligible for a cash "bonus" or to receive tips on winning the grand prize. But even those chosen as winners often lose. One woman who invested nearly $75 in a Florida contest was cited as a $100 winner, but never received any prize money.

REFUNDS AVAILABLE FOR VICTIMS

Thanks to a relatively new law, the Magnuson-Moss Act, the Federal Trade Commission (FTC) now has the authority to obtain refunds for victims of various selling schemes. Following are cases involving refunds resulting from FTC Actions in the past two years. For more information, contact any FTC office.

REFUNDS AVAILABLE FOR VICTIMS OF VARIOUS SELLING SCHEMES

Thanks to a relatively new law, the Magnuson-Moss Act, the Federal Trade Commission (FTC) now has the authority to obtain refunds for victims of various selling schemes. Below are cases involving refunds resulting from FTC Actions in the past two years. For more information, contact any FTC office.

COMPANY	PRODUCT/SERVICE	SETTLEMENT TERMS	WHO IS ELIGIBLE
BELL AND HOWELL SCHOOLS	electronics and accounting correspondence courses	$1.4 million in refunds. Contact: FTC, 6th and Penn. Ave. NW, Washington, DC, 20580.	Students who failed to get a job in the field, dropped out or were terminated. Only those who have made payments since May, 1974, but enrolled as early as January, 1971.
FEDDERS CORP.	split-system heat pumps manufactured between Nov., 1975, and June 1, 1978	Extended warranties to May, 1980. Reimbursement for prior repairs. Free replacement of defective part. Contact: FTC (see above)	All owners of Fedders CKH and Climatrol brands.
NORTH AMERICAN CORRESPONDENCE SCHOOLS	conservation and ecology correspondence courses	Up to $200 per student per course. Contact: FTC Regional Office, Los Angeles, CA, 213/824-7575	Students who enrolled to get a job in conservation or ecology and failed to do so within two years of terminating the course. Only those enrolled between March 26, 1973 and March 25, 1976 who had paid full tuition by June 30, 1977.
UNIVERSAL TRAINING SERVICE, INC.	vocational training of heavy equipment operators, motel managers, welders, flight attendants, insurance adjusters, etc.	$750,000 in refunds. Contact: FTC (see above)	Students who graduated between January, 1975, and January, 1978, and who meet requirements laid out by the company.

NURSERY BARN, SAVAGE FARMS NURSERY, McMINNVILLE TREE FARM, AMERICAN NURSERY AND SEED CO. AND MORRISON NURSERY	mail-order plants	$200,000 in refunds. Contact: FTC Regional Office, Atlanta, GA.	People who ordered plants that died or were never received and have cancelled checks or money orders proving merchandise was purchased after July 1, 1975.
HERTZ CORP.	rental cars	Refunds of unclaimed credit balances. Contact: FTC (see above)	Persons who had unclaimed credit from October, 1975, due to overcharges or duplicate payments.
FORD MOTOR COMPANY	repossessed cars	$100,000 in refunds Contact: FTC (see above)	Persons whose cars were repossessed by some 200 Ford dealers and resold by them for surplus profit since May, 1974.
RYDER SYSTEM INC.	truck driving and heavy equipment vocational courses	$1.5 milion in refunds. Contact: FTC (see above)	Persons who completed truck driving programs between January 1, 1970 and December 31, 1972, but could not find employment. And persons who completed heavy equipment courses from Jan. 1, 1970, to December 31, 1973 but could not find employment.
AUSLANDER DECORATOR FURNITURE	furniture	$60,000 in refunds. Contact: FTC (see above)	Customers who paid for undelivered merchandise since May 29, 1974.
BANKERS LIFE AND CASUALTY CO. (San Luis Valley Ranches, Rio Grande Ranches, Top of the World, Larwill Costilla Ranches, Hartsel Ranch and Estates of the World)	land sales in Texas and Colorado	$14 million. Contact: FTC (see above)	Purchasers of land from January 1, 1971, to January 1, 1974, eligible for up to 70 per cent of amount paid.

GETTING RESULTS WITH COMPLAINTS
About Products and Services

When you encounter a problem with a product or service, the results you get will depend greatly on how you present your case. Here are a few simple rules suggested by experienced consumer experts:

FIRST STEP: Telephone or visit the person or organization which sold the item in question. Provide sales slips, warranties and other supporting data to back up your case. Displaying anger sometimes helps, but a calm and firm demeanor is usually more effective. If an important issue is at stake, make clear that you are not going to let the matter drop even if you are rebuffed at this primary level. Don't take the first "no" as a final answer. But be willing to settle minor disputes, and consider the toll that much wasted energy and frustration can have on you personally. If you do not get anywhere with store clerks and department heads, go to the store manager or owner.

GO TO THE TOP: If you still don't succeed, and the company operates regionally or nationally, write a letter to the president of the firm. Letters are usually much more effective than telephone calls. Names and addresses of companies and their principal officers can be obtained from numerous sources, including Standard & Poor's annual directories available at most libraries. They can also be obtained in the *Consumer Complaint Guide* (Macmillan, $10.95) and *EM Complaint Directory,* available for $1.25 from Everybody's Money, Box 431B, Madison, WI, 53701. Send copies, not originals, of all key documents.

FOLLOW UP: If you receive no response within three weeks, follow up with a registered letter asking what is being done about the matter. Be sure to ask for a signed receipt.

WHERE TO WRITE: If no apparent law violation is involved, and you have failed to get satisfaction on an important matter, write a detailed letter to a local "action line" (see separate listing) with copies and personally signed cover letters to other organizations listed on the original letter. Consider sending carbon copies to one or more of the following, in addition to the company involved: the local Better Business Bureau; Chamber of Commerce; a state, city or county consumer office; a federal agency with jurisdiction in the subject area; a trade association active in the industry; a citizen organization dealing with consumer affairs; your state legislator; and your representative or senator in the U.S. Congress. (For help in determining where to send it, look up the subject of your complaint in this book's index.)

CONSIDER ARBITRATION: If you can get the company to agree to a hearing, you can hire an independent agency to arbitrate your dispute. There is a fee for this service (as much as $100 minimum) but you may be able to divide it between yourself and the company. Some companies have arbitration clauses already in their contracts. For more information contact the nearest regional office of the American Arbitration Association, or your local Better Business Bureau.

CONTACT ATTORNEY GENERAL: If there may be a law violation, send details to your state attorney general and/or consumer protection agency along with supporting materials.

CONSIDER COURT: If you get no response within three or four weeks, consider taking the case to small claims court. You can obtain information about these civil courts and their requirements, including the maximum amounts eligible, by consulting the index of this book.

LEGAL SERVICE: If considerable money is involved, you may want to hire a lawyer on either a fee or contingency basis. In the latter case, the lawyer does not collect any fee unless he wins for you. If you cannot afford a lawyer, you may qualify for free or reduced-rate assistance either through a government-funded legal service office or from the Legal Aid Society. For details consult an attorney or bar association.

GROUP ACTION: If yours is one of many similar complaints you know about in the area, you might consider starting a group or class action. The latter requires the services of a lawyer. The former requires much hard work by dedicated people with time to spare. A helpful publication is *How to Form a Consumer Complaint Group* (75 cents) from Consumer Federation of America, Suite 901, 1012 14th St., NW, Washington, DC, 20005. The booklet describes how residents of Cleveland resolved 1,000 disputes in four years through organized action. Another approach is represented by the Consumers Education & Protective Association International Inc. (CEPA) headquartered at 6048 Ogontz Ave., Philadelphia, PA, 19141. It has compiled a long record of success in getting results, including refunds or replacements for defective autos, through organized picketing.

DON'T GIVE UP: If you have a just case, don't give up trying to get justice. Don't let early rebuffs and disappointments stand in your way. Action line editors will vouch for the fact that many companies will make exceptions to their own rules in refunds, warranty terms and repair policies in order to silence a persistent customer with a legitimate gripe. One of the reasons why satisfaction is frequently so difficult to obtain is the willingness of many consumers to let their legitimate complaints and their money go down the drain without a struggle.

DON'T PANIC: Don't be frightened into paying a bill you don't think you owe. If you are overcharged, refuse to pay, or stop making payments. Ominous threats from collection agencies rarely result in suits for amounts under $200, sometimes not even for amounts several times that, because of the expense involved. If you are sued, you can still fight in court. And you can see that your credit bureau record reflects your side of the story. If a product becomes defective and you cannot get the seller to fix it, you may be protected from suit by a new federal rule in case you stop making payments to gain leverage.

INFLATION-FIGHTING TACTICS
For Those Who Want to Go Beyond the Obvious

Frazzled consumers who are over-extended with credit, unable to meet monthly bills and frustrated by gasoline lines, wage controls and other beasts of inflation are being told and retold by a growing number of "experts" to "cut back on beef," "shop around for advertised specials" and other painfully obvious things which most people have already considered and tried.

Such advice merely puts salt on the wounds, leaving many people still struggling to find ways to control their own finances in the face of escalating

living costs. In an effort to help find other ways, the staff of Consumer New
Inc. in Washington has drawn up some inflation-fighting tactics that won't b
found in the usual literature or broadcast tips. They also have the potential o
greater savings than the run-of-the-mill variety can produce.

The suggestions may not be useful for everyone, and some require an initia
investment to save in the long run. But each tactic could prove effective t
some extent.

● **Pool savings with friends or relatives.** Small savers who keep thei
money in regular savings accounts lose money at the present rate of inflation
If you can collect people who can pool $10,000 and are able to keep that mucl
money out of circulation for six months, you can earn top rates by purchasin
a money market certificate.

● **Borrow to buy real estate.** It may be worth going into debt for sucl
a sure-fire investment. The market should stay hot due to "baby-boom" childrei
who are now parents and looking for family homes. Rental property is als
a good bet; high rents can carry mortgage payments until you're ready to sell

● **If selling your house don't use a real estate broker.** Many broker
now charge 7 per cent sales commission, which can be a substantial chunl
of your profits. You will probably need a lawyer to handle the closing an
prepare necessary documents, but a lawyer's fee for such procedures is onl
a fraction of what you would pay a real estate firm.

● **Switch to a lower octane gasoline.** If your engine gives you a smootl
ride with your current gasoline, try lower grades until you hear "knocking."
Then switch to the next higher grade; your car won't know the difference bu
your wallet might.

● **Get an energy audit of your home.** For a fee, your utility compan
will determine how your home can be more energy efficient and recommen
improvements that will pay for themselves in a short time.

● **Don't retire at 65.** If you hold off a few years, your Social Securit
payments will be higher and you may collect more from company pensions.

● **Make air travel arrangements through a travel agent.** Most agent
don't charge a fee for such service and may be more willing than airlines t
tell you the cheapest fares. They are also likely to know more about recen
changes and special deals than you do.

● **Handle your own uncontested divorce.** Even most lawyers agree tha
you don't need them to handle the paper work in an uncontested divorce whei
there are no children or property complications. You can get the forms at ;
local business supply store for less than it costs to walk into a lawyer's office
Other legal chores most people can do themselves include wills, name change:
and small claims court cases.

● **Get a second or third opinion before any recommended surgery**
Some insurance plans cover second opinion check-ups but even if you are no
covered, it is probably worth the trouble; you may find out you don't nee
the operation at all.

● **If buying a new car, purchase the manufacturer's extended warranty.** Major auto makers are offering service above and beyond the standar
new vehicle warranty. You have to pay for it, but it is a one time fee tha
is likely to keep you covered for major repairs when the costs of parts an
labor inevitably are higher.

● **If you don't make many calls, get economy phone service.** For abou
half the monthly fee for regular residential service, you can receive unlimite

incoming calls and pay a few cents for each call you make.

● **Don't let doctors and dentists take unnecessary X-rays.** X-rays as part of a routine physical check-up, hospital admission or yearly dental exam are usually unnecessary and always expensive. If they must be taken, be sure they are localized. Don't allow a full-mouth X-ray for a problem with a left incisor. Ralph Nader' Health Research Group recommends full-mouth X-rays no more frequently than every three to five years.

● **Avoid doctors as much as practical** in order to avoid their charges. A recent book by two doctors (Donald Vickery and James Fries) estimates that as much as 70 per cent of all visits to doctors are unnecessary. They also suggest that annual medical checkups are not necessary for people who have no reason to think they have a serious ailment.

● **Avoid costly dental surgery** by taking good care of your teeth and gums. Much advice to the public on these subjects has been erroneous. A new crop of "preventive" dentists now offer advice well worth their fees. Essential to good dental health is regular brushing of the teeth sideways and up and down close to the gums, thorough flossing, gum massage and prophylaxis at least once every six months.

● **Consider more exercise** to avoid physical problems. Strenuous exercise has been found to be better than the passive kind in protecting people from serious physical ailments, such as high blood pressure and heart attacks.

● **Buy generics in both foods and drugs.** The Food and Drug Administration says there is no difference in quality or effectiveness between approved generic drugs and their brand name equivalents. Generic food products are not as high in quality as most brands but just as wholesome, and the savings can be high.

● **If you have cash value insurance,** switch to term and invest the difference. The Federal Trade Commission found that the average return on the savings portion of cash value insurance was about 3 per cent, a very low rate compared to what can be earned from other investments.

● **Avoid credit insurance where possible.** It is often required in installment purchases, but if you have life or health/accident insurance already, the extra policy may be duplicative. Premiums are usually inflated far beyond actual costs and include a kickback to the seller.

● **If you are arranging a funeral, comparison shop.** Cremation is much less expensive than burial. If burial is preferred, ask for specific services instead of a "packaged deal." Contact a memorial society for the best rates. Also consider donations of body organs to research. (See chapter on death and burial.)

● **Don't buy title insurance unless required.** Some lenders require it but government studies indicate that the actual risk of problems is too small for title insurance to be worth the cost in a real estate sale. If the title is checked thoroughly, there should be no need to buy insurance.

BUSINESS SOURCES OF HELP
When You Strike Out at the Sales Counter

A number of industry and trade associations offer to help resolve complaints which cannot be solved directly by sellers or manufacturers. Such associations usually establish standards of practice and have a code of ethics which members pledge to uphold.

The effectiveness of business associations in resolving complaints varies.

They have no legal power to enforce their own codes and can often do no more than threaten members with expulsion from the organization if they fail to take action. While some associations have established consumer affairs departments or Consumer Action Panels (CAPs), most simply forward complaints to appropriate individuals.

The first CAP—and still the largest and most effective—is the Major Appliance Consumer Action Panel (MACAP). It and a few similar trade organizations that have followed suit attempt to settle consumer complaints through a panel of supposedly independent, objective people.

However, the creation of CAPs has slowed down, and some have gone out of business. Most industry representatives say they disagree with the basic principles set up by the Federal Trade Commission for settling disputes. The FTC says that programs to resolve complaints must not be limited to cases first handled directly by the company involved. Industry representatives disagree. They say CAPs should serve only as a final resort after all other remedies have been exhausted.

As a result, virtually no new CAPs have been established since 1976. One group, the Carpet and Rug Institute's CRICAP, ceased operations as a result of budget cutbacks.

Others have grown in size and effectiveness. AUTOCAPs—sponsored by the National Automobile Dealers Association to handle complaints against new car dealers—have doubled in number during 1977. They also have been strengthened by endorsements from Ford and General Motors. GM recommended to its 17,000 dealers that they actively participate and cooperate with the AUTOCAP process.

GETTING THE BEST RESULTS

Many of the associations listed below will not handle complaints about which the customer has not previously made sincere efforts to settle at the retail level. (See previous two pages on "Getting Results with Complaints.") If you have a problem, write, don't telephone, the organizations listed. Briefly state the nature of your problem including attempts you have already made at settling the dispute through direct contact with store managers, regional offices, and, when possible, through the company headquarters.

If you do not find a trade association listed below that can handle your complaint, it does not necessarily mean that no help is available. Many other trade associations informally pass complaints on to company officials. However, the groups listed below are in the forefront of efforts to improve business-customer relations.

AMERICAN COLLECTORS ASSOCIATION

Handles complaints against its member firms, professional bill collectors. ACA will also arbitrate disputes at a member's request. ACA, 4040 W. 70th St., Box 35106, Minneapolis, MN, 55435; 612/926-6547.

AMERICAN HOTEL AND MOTEL ASSOCIATION

A federation of state and regional associations which forwards complaints to hotels and motels but claims to have no authority over members. AHMA, 888 7th Ave., New York, NY, 10019; 212/265-4506.

ASSOCIATION OF HOME APPLIANCE MANUFACTURERS

Operates the Major Appliance Consumer Action Panel (MACAP) in conjunction with the American Retail Association and the Gas Appliance Manufacturers Association. MACAP, the oldest and most effective program of this kind, is made up of citizen advisors not affiliated with the industry. It will investigate complaints about sellers of refrigerators, stoves, freezers, washers, dishwashers, dryers, air conditioners, garbage disposals, microwave ovens, humidifiers, dehumidifiers, compactors and water heaters. MACAP, 20 N. Wacker Dr., Chicago, IL, 60606; 312/236-3223.

AMERICAN MOVERS CONFERENCE

Has a Consumer Assistance office to handle complaints against local, intrastate and interstate movers of household goods. AMC, 1117 N. 19th St., Suite 806, Arlington, VA, 22209; 703/524-5440.

AMERICAN SOCIETY OF TRAVEL AGENTS

Has chapters throughout the U.S., Canada and Mexico and maintains a consumer affairs department to handle complaints. Persons should be sure to include copies of all supporting documents; failure to do so slows the resolution process considerably. ASTA also maintains a file of complaints and can provide information about the reliability of certain firms. ASTA, 711 Fifth Ave., New York, NY, 10022; 212/486-0700.

BLUE CROSS AND BLUE SHIELD ASSOCIATIONS

Maintains a Consumer Affairs office to help resolve complaints not solved by a state or local BC/BS office regarding hospital payments. BCBS, 1700 Pennsylvania Ave. NW, Washington, D.C., 20006; 202/785-7932.

CARPET AND RUG INSTITUTE

Had a consumer panel to handle complaints but it was disbanded. CRI claims it still tries to help people but in many cases will only "attempt to educate the consumer" or suggest that the problem be taken to the retailer involved. CRI, Director of Consumer Affairs, P.O. Box 2048, Dalton, GA, 30720; 404/278-3176.

DIRECT MAIL MARKETING ASSOCIATION

Maintains a Mail Order Action Line (MOAL) which claims a high success rate. But mail-order complaints still top the list of BBB and government inquires, and many such firms do not belong to the DMMA. In addition to MOAL, DMMA offers a Mail Preference Service (MPS) which will add or delete individual names on request from mailing lists used by member firms. DMMA, 6 E 43 St., New York, NY, 10017.

DIRECT SELLING ASSOCIATION

Represents firms which sell products door-to-door and at in-home parties. DSA has a strong code of ethics and good enforcement. DSA, Code of Ethics Administrator, 1730 M St. NW, Suite 610, Washington, DC, 20036; 202/293-5760.

ELECTRONIC INDUSTRIES ASSOCIATION

Investigates complaints about televisions, radios, stereos, tape decks, calculators, and CB radios sold by member and non-member firms. Inquiries are handled by Consumer Affairs department, and follow-up is good. EIA, 2001 Eye St. NW, Washington, DC, 20036; 202/457-4900.

INTERNATIONAL FABRICARE INSTITUTE

Does not accept inquiries directly from consumers. But a BBB, consumer affairs office, or member firm can ask this organization of retail dry cleaning firms to chemically analyze a garment in question to determine the nature of any damage. The fee for this service is $6. IFI, 12251 Tech Rd., Silver Spring, MD, 20904.

MANUFACTURED HOUSING INSTITUTE

Forwards complaints to member firms, manufacturers of mobile homes, but seldom presses for resolution. MHI, 1745 Jefferson Davis Hwy., Suite 511M, Chantilly, VA, 22201; 703/979-6620.

NATIONAL ADVERTISING DIVISION

The Council of Better Business Bureaus operates the NAD to improve the truthfulness of advertising. It forwards complaints and its own request for substantiation of claims to the advertiser involved and determines whether the company violated NAD's code of ethics. NAD may request that the ad be changed or discontinued. In many cases, the advertiser drops the ad or claims that the ad campaign has run its course. NAD then reports back to the complainant who can appeal the case to the National Advertising Review Board (NARB), a panel of private citizens and representatives of the ad business. NAD, 845 Third Ave., New York, NY, 10022.

NATIONAL ASSOCIATION OF FURNITURE MANUFACTURERS

Will forward complaints to member firms but says it does not receive many and that most problems can be resolved at the retail level. NAFM, Consumer Affairs, 8401 Connecticut Ave. NW, Washington, DC, 20015; 202/657-4442.

NATIONAL ASSOCIATION OF PERSONNEL CONSULTANTS

Investigates complaints against member and non-member employment agencies. Members are those involved in job placement, not counseling. NAPC, 1012 14th ST. NW, Washington, DC, 20005; 202/638-1721.

NATIONAL ASSOCIATION OF SECURITIES DEALERS

Has an arbitration department to settle disputes between its broker-members and investors. In cases where a regulatory agency or other organization may be better able to resolve the problem, NASD will refer complaints. NASD does not have the authority to remit funds, reverse securities transactions or require specific performance of any kind, but it may impose fines, suspend or expel a member that does not resolve disputes satisfactorily. NASD, 1735 K St. NW, Washington, DC, 20006.

NATIONAL AUTOMOBILE DEALERS ASSOCIATION

Operates Automobile Consumer Action Panels (AUTOCAPS) throughout the country to resolve complaints against new car dealers. Most complaints concern warranties. While some AUTOCAPS include consumers on arbitration panels, others are made up solely of industry representatives or utilize a single mediator. (For a complete list of state and local AUTOCAPS, see automobile chapter.) NADA, 8400 Westpark Dr., McLean, VA, 22101; 703/821-7000.

NATIONAL HOME STUDY COUNCIL

Grants accreditation to correspondence schools. Will investigate complaints against schools which have been accredited as well as those which have not. NHSC, 1601 18th St. NW, Washington, DC, 20015; 202/234-1500.

NATIONAL ROOFING CONTRACTORS ASSOCIATION

Members are primarily commercial and industrial contractors. NRCA will help consumers with residential complaints in some cases. NRCA, 1515 N. Harlem Ave., Oak Park, IL, 60302; 312/383-9513.

NATIONAL TIRE DEALERS AND RETREADERS ASSOCIATION

Forwards complaints to state Consumer Action Panels or to companies involved. Two successful CAPs operate in Wisconsin and Indiana. NTDRA, 1343 L St. NW, Washington, DC, 20005; 202/638-6650. State CAPs: Independent Tire Dealers and Retreaders Assn., P.O. Box 2104, Indianapolis, IN, 46203; 317/531-8124; Wisconsin Independent Tire Dealers and Retreaders Assn., 1109 N. Mayfair Rd., Wauwatosa, WI, 53226; 414/774-6590.

PHOTO MARKETING ASSOCIATION

Maintains Consumer Affairs department to handle complaints about cameras and film. Members are retailers and photo finishers. PMA, 603 Lansing Ave., Jackson, MI, 49202; 517/783-2807.

PUBLISHERS CLEARING HOUSE

Operates a Magazine Action Line (MAL) which has been very effective. Magazine complaints of any kind are handled, but MAL does not provide refunds. In cases where a person has unwittingly ordered a non-existent publication, MAL will offer its own list of substitutes at no charge. PCH is a mail-order seller of discount magazine subscriptions. MAL, 382 Channel Dr., Port Washington, NY, 11050; 516/883-5432.

SOUTHERN FURNITURE MANUFACTURERS ASSOCIATION

Operates the Furniture Industry Consumer Advisory Panel (FICAP). Cases are usually resolved by replacement or repair; refunds are rare. FICAP does not represent the entire industry, however, and effectiveness varies due to the subjective nature of complaints. FICAP, P.O. Box 951, High Point, NC, 27261; 919/885-5065.

PROBLEMS WITH PROFESSIONALS

WHERE TO SEND COMPLAINTS

Complaints involving licensed professionals should first be directed to the state or local licensing board. Such boards may be helpful if the complaint involves a legal issue, but questions of ethical practice should probably be directed to the professional association. Although such associations are anxious to maintain high ethical standards, they rarely censure fellow members. Only in cases where there is evidence of gross negligence or ineptitude do such associations intervene.

Not all licensed professionals belong to an association. But those who do swear to uphold the standards established by their peers. If an association feels that a grievance is justified, it may revoke membership but will not be able to collect damages for the complainant. In some cases, expulsion from the organization is extremely detrimental to a professional's reputation; in others, such an action is meaningless.

Licensing varies by state and is not limited to occupations that involve the public's health and safety. Louisiana, for example, licenses weathermen, decorators, engravers and jewelers. Hawaii licenses tattoo artists and New Hampshire, lightning rod salesmen. State licensing boards often are dominated by those who are licensed, so punitive action is rarely taken.

Major professional associations include:

AMERICAN MEDICAL ASSOCIATION, 535 N. Dearborn St. Chicago, IL, 60610; 312/751-6000.

AMERICAN DENTAL ASSOCIATION, 211 E. Chicago Ave., Chicago, IL, 60601; 312/440-2500.

AMERICAN CHIROPRACTIC ASSOCIATION, 2200 Grand Ave., Des Moines, IA, 50312.

AMERICAN INSTITUTE OF ARCHITECTS, 1735 New York Ave. NW, Washington, DC, 20006; 202/785-7300.

NATIONAL SOCIETY OF PUBLIC ACCOUNTANTS, 1717 Penn. Ave. NW, Washington, DC, 20006; 202/298-9040.

NATIONAL FUNERAL DIRECTORS ASSOCIATION, 135 W. Wells St., Milwaukee, WI, 53203; 414/276-2500.

AMERICAN BAR ASSOCIATION, 1155 E. 60th St., Chicago, IL, 60637; 312/947-3885.

AMERICAN OPTOMETRIC ASSOCIATION, 7000 Chippewa St., St. Louis, MO, 63119; 314/832-5770.

AMERICAN PHARMACEUTICAL ASSOCIATION, 2215 Constitution Ave. NW, Washington, DC, 20037; 202/628-4410.

AMERICAN PSYCHOLOGICAL ASSOCIATION, 1200 17th St. NW, Washington, 20036; 202/833-7600.

NATIONAL ASSOCIATION OF REALTORS, 430 Michigan Ave., Chicago, IL, 60611; 312/440-8000.

DIRECTORY OF PUBLIC INTEREST LAW CENTERS

Following is a list of more than 100 public interest law centers. All are non-profit, tax-exempt groups devoted to providing legal representation to otherwise unrepresented interests in court or government agency proceedings.

In most cases, "legal representation" means more than just lawsuits. It also encompasses such activities as formal participation in rulemaking proceedings as well as informal monitoring of government activities. Some groups listed rely not only on the expertise of attorneys but also use scientists, engineers, economists, doctors and other professionals to develop the policies on which their legal actions are based. Some centers also lobby, produce investigative research reports and conduct public education compaigns.

The public interest law centers are separated into primary fields of interest. The list was furnished by the Council for Public Interest Law, 1333 Connecticut Ave. NW, Washington, DC, 20036, a national clearinghouse for public interest law firms.

RACIAL/ETHNIC MINORITY LAW CENTERS

ASIAN LAW CAUCUS, 1608 San Pablo, Oakland, CA, 94612. Works for equal rights for Asian-Americans in employment, education and housing.

LAWYERS' COMMITTEE FOR CIVIL RIGHTS UNDER LAW, 733 15th St. NW, Washington, DC, 20005. Represents disadvantaged minorities in such areas as voting rights, employment discrimination, educational opportunities and criminal justice reform.

LAWYERS' COMMITTEE FOR CIVIL RIGHTS UNDER LAW OF THE BOSTON BAR ASSOCIATION, 15 State St., Boston, MA, 02109. Represents disadvantaged minorities on matters involving fair housing, criminal justice reform and generally, problems of racial and poverty discrimination.

MEXICAN AMERICAN LEGAL DEFENSE AND EDUCATION FUND, 145 Ninth St., San Francisco, CA, 94103. Works for equal rights for Mexican Americans in employment, education and voting.

NAACP LEGAL DEFENSE AND EDUCATION FUND, 10 Columbus Circle, New York, NY, 10019. Challenges discriminatory practices against black people in employment, education, housing, voting rights and in the criminal justice system.

NATIONAL COMMITTEE AGAINST DISCRIMINATION IN HOUSING, 1425 H St. NW, Washington, DC, 20005. Works to eliminate housing discrimination against racial minorities.

NATIONAL CONFERENCE OF BLACK LAWYERS, 126 W. 119th St., New York, NY, 10026. Bar association with active public interest law program working for criminal justice reform and to eliminate discrimination in education, employment and in the military.

NATIVE AMERICAN RIGHTS FUND, 1506 Broadway, Boulder, CO, 80302. National Indian law center focusing on protecting Indian treaty rights, lands, water, minerals and other natural resources, civil rights and insuring independence of Indian tribes.

NORTHWEST LABOR AND EMPLOYMENT LAW OFFICE, 105 14th Ave., Seattle, WA, 98122. Works to eliminate discrimination against blacks, Chicanos and Native Americans in farm work, cannery work and other industries.

PUERTO RICAN LEGAL DEFENSE AND EDUCATION FUND, 95 Madison Ave., New York, NY, 10016. Priorities are obtaining equal employment opportunities, bilingual education and voting rights for Puerto Ricans and other Spanish-speaking Americans.

WOMEN'S LAW CENTERS

CONNECTICUT WOMEN'S EDUCATIONAL AND LEGAL FUND, 614 Orange St., New Haven, CT, 06511. Challenges sex discrimination in employment, education, credit lending and insurance.

EQUAL RIGHTS ADVOCATES, 433 Turk St., San Francisco, CA, 94102. Advocates elimination of sex discrimination in employment, health care and criminal justice.

WOMEN'S LAW FUND, 620 Keith Bldg., Cleveland, OH, 44155. Challenges sex discrimination, particularly in the employment area.

WOMEN'S LAW PROJECT, 112 S. 16th St., Philadelphia, PA, 19139. Priorities are obtaining equal rights for women in employment, education, family planning and health care.

WOMEN'S LEGAL DEFENSE FUND, 1010 Vermont Ave. NW, Washington, DC, 20005. Focuses on removal of discriminatory practices in employment, credit lending, housing and domestic relations.

WOMEN'S RIGHTS LITIGATION CLINIC, Rutgers University School of Law, Newark, NJ, 07102. Challenges discrimination in abortion laws, prisons, name changes and domestic relations.

LAW CENTERS FOR THE HANDICAPPED

COMMUNITY CLINICAL LAW PROJECT, Columbia University School of Law, New York, NY, 10027. Advocates rights of the mentally handicapped in housing, welfare benefits and health care matters.

DISABILITIES RIGHTS CENTER, 1346 Connecticut Ave. Suite 1124, Washington, DC, 20036. Works in behalf of the handicapped, particularly in the employment area.

MARYLAND DEVELOPMENTAL DISABILITIES LAW PROJECT, University of Maryland Law School, Baltimore, MD, 21201. Priorities include desinstitutionalization of disabled persons, equal access to buildings, transportation systems, employment and medical services.

MENTAL HEALTH LAW PROJECT, 1220 19th St. NW, Washington, DC, 20036. Has established patients' rights to treatment, challenged use of patients as unpaid workers and established right of mentally handicapped children to a public education.

NATIONAL CENTER FOR LAW AND THE DEAF LEGAL DEFENSE FUND, 7th and Florida Aves. NE, Washington, DC, 20002. Legal representation, information and educational opportunities for the deaf and hearing-impaired.

NATIONAL CENTER FOR LAW AND THE HANDICAPPED, 1235 N. Eddy St., South Bend, IN, 46617. Concerned with equal employment and educational opportunities, health care, access to transportation systems and removal of architectural barriers.

WESTERN LAW CENTER FOR THE HANDICAPPED, 849 S. Broadway, Los Angeles, CA, 90014. Advocates equal rights in education and employment, removal of architectural barriers and quality of care in state hospitals.

OTHER MINORITY LAW CENTERS

AMERICAN CIVIL LIBERTIES UNION FOUNDATION, 22 E. 40th St., New York, NY, 10016. Has projects on rights of women, prisoners, juveniles, farmworkers, sexual privacy and voting.

BEVERLY HILLS BAR FOUNDATION PUBLIC COUNSEL, 300 S. Beverly Dr., Beverly Hills, CA, 90212. Works for the rights of minorities in jury selection procedures, use of the death penalty and school segregation.

CONSTITUTIONAL LITIGATION CLINIC, Rutgers School of Law,

Newark, NJ, 07102. Challenges unequal allocation of public funds for education in the state, government misconduct and employment discrimination.

EMPLOYMENT RIGHTS PROJECT, Columbia University School of Law, New York, NY, 10027. Works for equal employment opportunities for women and racial and ethnic minorities.

LAMBDA LEGAL DEFENSE AND EDUCATION FUND, PO Box 5448, New York, NY, 10017. Works for equal rights for homosexuals.

LEAGUE OF WOMEN VOTERS EDUCATION FUND/LITIGATION DEPARTMENT, 1730 M St. NW, Washington, DC, 20036. Challenges restrictive state and local residency requirements, absentee voting laws and other voting rights issues.

LEGAL ACTION CENTER, 271 Madison Ave., New York, NY, 10016. Advocacy for ex-convicts and former drug users, particularly in the equal employment area.

NATIONAL MILITARY DISCHARGE REVIEW PROJECT, 511 E St. NW, Washington, DC, 20001. Focuses on military law reform and military discharge review procedures, generally as they affect minority servicemen.

PRISONERS' RIGHTS PROJECT, 2 Park Square, Boston, MA, 02116. Addresses prison and criminal justice reform issues on a statewide basis.

PUBLIC ADVOCATES, 433 Turk St., San Francisco, CA, 94115. Represents disadvantaged minorities in consumer protection, employment discrimination, health care, women's rights, children's rights and land use matters.

PUBLIC INTEREST LAW CENTER, 1315 Walnut St., Philadelphia, PA, 19107. Representation for disadvantaged minorities. Concerned with juvenile justice, employment discrimination, rights of the handicapped and health care.

SANTA CLARA COUNTY BAR ASSOCIATION PUBLIC INTEREST LAW FOUNDATION, San Jose, CA, 95110. Representation for disadvantaged minorities. Issues include price advertising for prescription drugs, the right of indigent defendants to counsel in criminal matters and other criminal justice reform issues.

URBAN LEGAL CLINIC, Rutgers School of Law, Newark, NJ, 07102. Works in the employment, education, fair housing, civil liberties and consumer protection areas.

POVERTY LAW CENTERS

ADVOCATES FOR BASIC LEGAL EQUALITY, 740 Spitzer Bldg., Toledo, OH, 43614. Issues include public utilities, fair housing issues, rights of the disabled, welfare reform, health care, consumer rights and employment discrimination.

APPALACHIAN RESEARCH AND DEFENSE FUND, 1116-B Kanawha Blvd., Charleston, WV, 25301. Involved with utility rate reform, environmental protection and welfare benefit matters.

APPALACHIAN RESEARCH AND DEFENSE FUND OF KENTUCKY, PO Box 152, Prestonsburg, KY, 41653. Issues include environmental protection, housing, education, welfare benefits and black lung benefits.

CENTER ON SOCIAL WELFARE POLICY AND LAW, 95 Madison Ave., New York, NY, 10016. Legal Services support center concentrating on welfare policy issues.

CHILDREN'S DEFENSE FUND, 1520 New Hampshire Ave. NW, Washington, DC, 20036. Concerned with national social welfare issues as they affect children: right to an education, a child's right to privacy, health care, juvenile justice and rights of children to comprehensive development services.

CONCERNED CITIZENS FOR JUSTICE, PO Box 1409, Wise, VA, 24293. Community-based law project working on consumer protection, occupational health and safety and welfare benefit issues.

EAST TENNESSEE RESEARCH CORPORATION, PO Box 436, Jacksboro, TN, 37757. Works on environmental protection matters, state tax reform, utility rate reform, black lung benefits and delivery of health care services.

FOOD RESEARCH AND ACTION CENTER, 2011 Eye St. NW, Washington, DC, 20006. Specializes in food benefit matters: food stamps, national school breakfast and lunch programs and special nutritional programs for indigent pregnant women, infants and children.

GREATER UPSTATE LAW PROJECT, 80 W. Main St., Rochester, NY, 14614. Statewide legal services support center with emphasis on welfare matters.

HARVARD CENTER FOR LAW AND EDUCATION, Harvard University, Cambridge, MA, 02138. Legal Services support center working on issues involving special education for emotionally disturbed or retarded children, desegregation of schools, bilingual education and students' rights.

INDIANA CENTER ON LAW AND POVERTY, 129 E. Market St., Indianapolis, IN, 46204. Provides policy-oriented representation on such issues as welfare benefits, utility rate reform, employment and criminal justice reform.

LEGAL ACTION SUPPORT PROJECT, 1990 M St. NW, Washington, DC, 20036. Legal Services support center. Provides social science research services in areas of poverty law litigation and reform and participates in administrative agency proceedings.

LEGAL RESEARCH AND SERVICES FOR THE ELDERLY/ NATIONAL COUNCIL OF SENIOR CITIZENS, 1511 K St. NW, Washington, DC, 20006. Representation before federal, state or local administrative agencies concerned with the welfare of senior citizens.

LEGAL SERVICES FOR THE ELDERLY POOR, 2095 Broadway, New York, NY, 10023. Legal Group concerned with problems of the elderly: Social Security and health benefits, age discrimination, pension rights, housing and nursing homes.

LOUISIANA CENTER FOR THE PUBLIC INTEREST, 1222 Maison Blanche Bldg., New Orleans, LA, 70122. Focuses on consumer protection, employment, welfare benefits and health care issues as they affect the elderly.

MASSACHUSETTS ADVOCACY CENTER, 2 Park Square, Boston, MA, 02116. Works on educational and social welfare issues affecting children: right to an education, special education and child health.

MASSACHUSETTS CENTER FOR PUBLIC INTEREST LAW, 2 Park Square, Boston, MA, 02116. Focuses on education and other child welfare issues on a statewide basis.

MASSACHUSETTS LAW REFORM INSTITUTE/VOLUNTARY DEFENDERS COMMITTEE, 2 Park Square, Boston, MA, 02116. Issues include consumer protection, housing, community development, welfare benefits, education and juvenile justice.

MICHIGAN LEGAL SERVICES, 900 Michigan Bldg., Detroit, MI, 48226. Statewide support center. Issues include consumer protection, employment and education.

MIGRANT LEGAL ACTION PROGRAM, 1910 K St. NW, Washington, DC, 20006. Works in behalf of migrant workers on housing, welfare benefit, health care and occupational safety and health issues. and health issues.

NATIONAL CONSUMER LAW CENTER, 11 Beacon St., Boston, MA, 02108. Consumer protection issues include truth-in-lending, product warranties, collection practices, unfair and deceptive sales practices and public utility deposit and termination practices.

NATIONAL EMPLOYMENT LAW PROJECT, 423 W. 118th St., New York, NY, 10027. Concerned with racial discrimination in employment, unemployment insurance benefits, labor relations, manpower programs and minimum wage provisions.

NATIONAL HEALTH LAW PROGRAM, 10995 LeConte Ave.. Los Angeles, CA, 90024. Concerned with accessibility of quality health care for poor people and with government funded health programs.

NATIONAL HOUSING AND ECONOMIC LAW DEVELOPMENT PROJECT, University of California, Berkeley, CA, 94704. Concerned with landlord/tenant relations, public housing, housing construction and rehabilitation of housing, federal and state tax and securities law, and the law of nonprofit organizations, charitable corporations and charitable trusts.

NATIONAL JUVENILE LAW CENTER, St. Louis University School of Law, St. Louis, MO, 63108. Challenges unlawful practices and conditions in juvenile institutions, educational matters and other juvenile justice issues.

NATIONAL SENIOR CITIZENS LAW CENTER, 1709 W. 8th St., Los Angeles, CA, 90017. Legal services support center addressing issues affecting the elderly: pension rights, health services and the regulation of nursing homes.

OHIO STATE LEGAL SERVICES ASSOCIATION, 8 E. Broad St., Columbus, OH, 43215. Statewide support center providing representation on a wide range of issues.

SOUTHERN POVERTY LAW CENTER, 19 S. McDonough St., Montgomery, AL, 36101. Concentrates on criminal justice reform and elimination of state death penalty statutes for Southern rural poor.

WESTERN CENTER ON LAW AND POVERTY, 1709 W. 8th St., Los Angeles, CA, 90017. Legal services support center for Southern California on consumer protection, employment rights, housing and welfare benefits issues.

YOUTH LAW CENTER AND WESTERN STATES PROJECTS, 693 Mission St., San Francisco, CA, 94105. Legal services support center representing interests of children in juvenile law, mental health law and educational matters.

CONSUMER PROTECTION LAW CENTERS

CALIFORNIA CITIZEN ACTION GROUP, 2315 Westwood Blvd., Los Angeles, CA, 90064. Interested in general consumer protection issues: food and drug pricing and energy policy.

CENTER FOR AUTO SAFETY, 1346 Connecticut Ave. NW, Washington, DC, 20036. Works for safer cars, trucks, mobile homes and highways.

CONNECTICUT CITIZEN RESEARCH GROUP, PO Box 6465, Hart-

ford, CT, 06106. General consumer protection orientation: posting of prescrip
tion drug prices, regulation of sale of hearing aids, utility rate reform.

CONSUMERS UNION, 1714 Massachusetts Ave. NW, Washington, DC
20036. Works on range of consumer protection matters: utility rate reform, product safety, food and drug advertising; also challenging restrictions on competition among professionals.

KENTUCKY PUBLIC INTEREST RESEARCH GROUP, University of
Louisville, Louisville, KY, 40208. Works on issues involving environmental protection, consumer protection and education.

PUBLIC CITIZEN, 1346 Connecticut Ave. NW, Washington, DC, 20036.
Funds a number of organizations, two of which engage in legal advocacy: Litigation Group, which works on consumer protection and corporate and governmental accountability matters; and Health Research Group, which focuses on health
care delivery, occupational health and safety, safety of foods, drugs and
pesticides and general product safety.

ENVIRONMENTAL PROTECTION LAW CENTERS

ENVIRONMENTAL DEFENSE FUND, 1525 18th St. NW, Washington
DC, 20036. Challenges use of toxic chemicals and pesticides, fights for conservation of natural resources, utility rate reform, enforcement of clean air and water
laws.

NATIONAL WILDLIFE FEDERATION/RESOURCES DEFENSE DIVI-
SION, 1412 16th St. NW, Washington, DC, 20036. Works for protection of fish
and wildlife, sewage and waste disposal policy, land use policy and wildlife
management.

NATURAL RESOURCES DEFENSE COUNCIL, 15 W. 44th St., New
York, NY, 10036. Combats air and water pollution, works for water management
policy, nuclear safety and energy policy.

NORTHWEST ENVIRONMENTAL DEFENSE CENTER, 10015 SW Ter-
williger Blvd., Portland, OR, 97219. Environmental concerns include land use,
coastal land zoning policy, energy policy, noise pollution and forestry.

1,000 FRIENDS OF OREGON, 519 SW Third, Portland, OR, 97204.
Works to implement and enforce Oregon's land use laws at the state and local
levels.

SIERRA CLUB LEGAL DEFENSE FUND, 311 California St., San Francisco, CA, 94104. Environmental protection issues include air and water quality,
wilderness protection and highway construction.

OTHER ISSUE-ORIENTED PUBLIC INTEREST LAW CENTERS

ACTION ON SMOKING AND HEALTH, 2000 H St. NW, Washington
DC, 20006. Worked for establishment of smoking and non-smoking sections in
airplanes and for the removal of cigarette commercials from radio and TV.

ARIZONA CENTER FOR LAW IN THE PUBLIC INTEREST, PO Box
2783, Phoenix, AZ, 85002. Concentrates on consumer protection, government
accountability and utility rate reform issues.

BUSINESS AND PROFESSIONAL PEOPLE FOR THE PUBLIC IN-
TEREST, 109 N. Dearborn St., Chicago, IL, 60602. Focuses on nuclear power
safety, environmental protection and fair housing issues.

CENTER FOR LAW AND SOCIAL POLICY, 1751 N St. NW
Washington, DC, 20036. Issues include consumer protection, health problems of

the poor, environmental protection, women's rights, international law and mine safety.

CENTER FOR LAW IN THE PUBLIC INTEREST. 10203 Santa Monica Blvd., Los Angeles, CA, 90067. Provides legal advocacy in the environmental protection, corporate accountability and employment discrimination areas.

CENTER FOR PUBLIC REPRESENTATION, 520 University Ave., Madison, WI, 53703. Advocates equal rights for ex-offenders, fair credit standards for women, land use policy, governmental accountability, health care and corporate responsibility.

CITIZENS COMMUNICATIONS CENTER, 1914 Sunderland Pl. NW, Washington, DC, 20036. Works for increased representation of women and racial minorities in the electronic media in employment opportunities, program scheduling and program content.

COMMON CAUSE/LEGAL AFFAIRS DEPARTMENT, 2030 M St. NW, Washington, DC, 20036. Has litigated for election campaign reforms and challenged the misuse of franking privileges by members of Congress.

EDUCATION LAW CENTER, 605 Broad St., Suite 800, Newark, NJ, 07102. Provides legal advocacy on educational matters: parental access to pupil records, racial and sexual equality in schools, adequacy, availability and quality of educational programs, school facilities and school personnel.

GREAT PLAINS LEGAL FOUNDATION, 127 W. 10th St., Kansas City, MO, 64105. Work covers range subjects, with focus on government regulation of business and industry.

INSTITUTE FOR PUBLIC INTEREST REPRESENTATION, Georgetown University Law Center, Washington, DC, 20001. Works primarily at federal and District of Columbia administrative agency level on environmental protection, consumer protection, housing and Freedom of Information Act matters.

MARYLAND PUBLIC INTEREST RESEARCH GROUP, University of Maryland, College Park, MD, 20742. Areas of interest include energy conservation, consumer protection and environmental protection.

MEDIA ACCESS PROJECT, 1609 Connecticut Ave. NW, Washington, DC, 20009. Works to assure that electronic media keep public fully and fairly informed on environmental, consumer affairs, civil rights, economic and political issues.

MID-AMERICA LEGAL FOUNDATION, 20 N. Wacker Dr., Chicago, IL, 60606. Work covers wide range of issue areas, generally focusing on government regulation of business and industry.

PACIFIC LEGAL FOUNDATION, 455 Capitol Mall, Sacramento, CA, 95814. Legal representation supporting corporate and government positions on issues such as welfare reform, national defense, environmental concerns, land use and property rights and national energy policy.

PUBLIC COMMUNICATIONS, 1910 Parnell Ave., Los Angeles, CA, 90025. Representation for citizens' groups in matters relating to the media.

SOUTHEASTERN LEGAL FOUNDATION, PO Box 95132, Atlanta, GA, 30347. Defends policy interests of private business and government in such areas as energy policy, environmental protection and land use.

TAX ANALYSTS AND ADVOCATES, 2369 N. Taylor St., Arlington, VA, 22207. Concentrates on federal tax reform issues.

UCLA COMMUNICATIONS LAW PROGRAM, UCLA Law School, Los Angeles, CA, 90024. Focuses on communications law and media reform.

CALL FOR ACTION

Call For Action is not-for-profit referral and action service affiliated with and supported by broadcast organizations. Staffed by 2500 volunteers, Call For Action helps about 360,000 people a year.

When a person calls with a problem, a volunteer records the information—which is kept confidential—and refers the caller to a place where he can receive help. Two weeks later, CFA calls the client back to see what results were achieved. If the client is satisfied, the case is closed. If not, Call For Action will step in.

Headquarters of Call For Action is located at 575 Lexington Ave., New York, NY, 10022; 212/355-5965. Radio and television stations participating in the program are:

WAKR	Akron, OH	WELI	New Haven, CT
WROW	Albany, NY	WMCA	New York, NY
WFBG	Altoona, PA	KWTV	Oklahoma City,
WBAL	Baltimore, MD	WOW/KEZO	Omaha, NE
WYDE	Birmingham, AL	WDBO	Orlando, FL
WBZ	Boston, MA	WRAU-TV	Peoria, IL
WIVB—TV	Buffalo, NY	WFIL	Philadelphia, PA
WIND	Chicago, IL	KPHO-TV	Phoenix, AZ
WJKW—TV	Cleveland, OH	KDKA	Pittsburgh, PA
WBNS—TV	Columbus, OH	WJAR	Providence, RI
WDZ	Decatur, IL	WRAL-TV	Raleigh/Durham
KLZ	Denver, CO	CJRN	St. Catherines, C
WJR	Detroit, MI	KMOX	St. Louis, MO
WOWO	Ft. Wayne, IN	KGTV	San Diego, CA
WTLV—TV	Jacksonville, FL	WGSM	Suffolk Country,
KCMO	Kansas City, KS	WHEN	Syracuse, NY
KARK—TV	Little Rock, AR	KTKT	Tucson, AZ
KFWB	Los Angeles, CA	WTLB	Utica, NY
WDIA	Memphis, TN	WTOP	Washington, DC
WCIX—TV	Miami, FL	WWVA	Wheeling, WV
CJAD	Montreal, CAN	WFMJ	Youngstown, OF
WBSM	New Bedford, MA		

NON-GOVERNMENT CITIZEN GROUPS

ALASKA: Alaska Public Interest Research Group Inc., Box 1093, Anchorage, AK, 99510, 907/278-3661; Fairbanks Consumer Group, P.O. Box 483, Fairbanks, AK, 99707.

ARIZONA: Arizona Consumers Council, 6480 Camino DeMichael St., Tucson, AZ, 85718, 602/626-4856; Human Action for Chandler, 100 W. Boston, Suite #2, Chandler, AZ, 85224, 602/963-4321.

ARKANSAS: Arkansas Consumer Research, 1842 Cross St., Little Rock, AR, 72206, 401/374-2394; Ark-Tex Chapter, American Association of Retired Persons, Route 4, Box 325, Texarkana, AR, 75502, 401/772-2136; Association of Community Organizations for Reform Now (ACORN): 217 Davis #1, Conway, AR, 72032, 501/327-3193; 10 E. Rock, Fayetteville, AR, 72701, 501/521-7990; 718 S. 22nd St., Fort Smith, AR, 72901, 501/782-6714; 126 Hawthorne, Hot Springs, AR, 71901, 501/624-2508; 306½ Carson, Jonesboro, AR, 72401, 501/932-0163; 523 W. 15th St., Little Rock, AR, 72202, 501/376-7151; 318 W. 5th St., Pine Bluff, AR, 71601, 501/536-6300; 503 C. E. 4th, Stuttgart, AR, 72160, 501/673-7776.

CALIFORNIA: Accountants for the Public Interest, Ft. Mason Center, Bldg. 310, San Francisco, CA, 94123, 415/771-0410; American Consumers Council, P.O. Box 24206, Los Angeles, CA, 90024, 213/476-2888; California Citizen Action Group, 2315 Westwood Blvd., Los Angeles, CA, 90064, 213/475-0417; California Citizen Action Group, 909 12th St., Sacramento, CA, 951814; California Consumer Club, 523 W. 6th Street, Suite 642, Los Angeles, CA, 90014, 213/624-3961; California Public Interest Research Group of the L.A. Region, 301 Kerckhoff Hall, 308 Westwood Plaza, Los Angeles, CA, 90024, 213/825-4584; California Public Interest Research Group, 3000 E St., San Diego, CA, 92102, 714/236-1508; California Council Against Health Frauds, Inc., Box 1276, Lomalinda, CA, 92354, 714/796-0141 ext. 411; Citizens Action League, 814 Mission St., San Francisco, CA, 94103, 415/543-4101; Coalition for Economic Survival, 5520 W. Pico Blvd., Los Angeles, CA, 90019, 213/938-6241; Consumer Action, 26 7th St., San Francisco, CA, 94103, 415/626-4030; Consumer Federation of California Los Angeles-Orange County Chapter, 621 S. Virgil Ave., Los Angeles, CA, 90005, 213/380-1450; Consumer Protection Project Office of Environmental & Consumer Affairs, 308 Westwood Plaza, Los Angeles, CA, 90024, 213/825-2820; Consumer Panel of America, 1424 Windsor Dr., San Bernardino, CA, 92404, 714/885-5393; Consumers Cooperative of Berkeley, Inc., 4805 Central Ave., Richmond, CA, 94804, 415/526-0440; Consumers United of Palo Alto, Inc., P.O. Box 311, Palo, Alto, CA, 94302, 415/325-1924; Davis Consumer Affairs Bureau, 364 Memorial Union, Room 358, Davis, CA, 95616, 916/752-6484; El Concilio for the Spanish Speaking, 339 W. Side Plaza, Modesto, CA, 95351, 209/521-2033; The Group, 457 Haight St., San Francisco, CA, 94115, 415/861-6840; Northern California Public Interest Research Group, Inc., P.O. Box 702, Santa Clara, CA, 95052, 408/984-2777; Organize, Inc., 21115 Beverley Blvd., Los Angeles, CA, 90057, 213/483-6530; Pasadena Consumer Action Center, 1020 N. Fair Oaks, Pasadena, CA, 91104, 213/794-7194; People's Action Research, 1206 S. Gramercy Pl., Los Angeles, CA, 90019; 213/735-4969; People's Lobby, 3456 W. Olympic Blvd., Los Angeles, CA, 90019, 213/731-8321; Public Media Center, 2751 Hyde St., San Francisco, CA, 94109, 415/885-0200; Interfaith Service Bureau, 3720 Folsom Blvd., Sacramento, CA, 95816, 916/456-3815; Self-Help for the Elderly, 3 Old Chinatown Lane, San Francisco, CA, 94108, 415/982-9171; Stanislaus County Commission on Aging, P.O. Box 42, Modesto, CA, 95353, 209/526-6720; Toward Utility Rate Normalization, 2209 Van Ness Ave., San Francisco, CA, 94109, 415/441-7777; Watts Labor Community Action Committee, 11401 S. Central Ave., Los Angeles, CA, 90059, 213/564-5901.

COLORADO: Associated Students Consumer Protection Office, Student

Center, Fort Collins, CO, 80523, 303/491-5931; Associated Students Renter's Information Office, Student Center, Fort Collins, CO, 80523, 303/491-5931; Colorado League for Consumer Protection, 8230 W. 16th Pl., Lakewood, CO, 80215, 303/233-5891; Colorado Public Interest Research Group, 1111 W. Colfax Ave., P.O. Box 83, Denver, CO, 80204, 303/629-3332; Colorado Public Interest Research Group, UMC - Room 420, Boulder, CO, 80302, 303/492-5086; Colorado Public Interest Research Group, Inc., University Center - Room 207, Greeley, CO, 80639, 303/351-4504; Crusade for Justice, P.O. Box 18347, Denver, CO, 80218, 303/832-1145; East-Side Action Movement, 2855 Tremont Pl. - Room 201, Denver, CO, 80205, 303/534-6228; Environmental Action of Colorado, 2239 East Colfax Ave., Denver, CO, 80206, 303/321-1645; Mt. Plains Congress of Senior Citizens, 431 West Colfax Ave., Suite 2A, Denver, CO, 80204, 303/629-7270.

CONNECTICUT: Connecticut Citizen Action Group, 130 Washington St., P.O. Box G, Hartford, CT, 06106, 203/527-7191; Connecticut Consumers' Group, 53 Wildwood Ave., Milford, CT, 06460, 203/878-0414; Connecticut Public Interest Research Group, 248 Farmington Ave., Hartford, CT, 06105, 203/525-8312; Connecticut Public Interest Research Group, Box U-8, Storrs, CT, 06268, 203/486-4525; Consumer Information Services, One Landmark Square, Suite 100, Stamford, CT, 06901, 203/359-2112.

WASHINGTON, DC: Auto Owners Action Council, 1411 K St., NW, Suite 800, Washington, DC, 20005, 202/638-5550; Aviation Consumer Action Project, P.O. Box 19029, Washington, DC, 20036, 202/223-4498; Consumer Affairs Committee of the Americans for Democratic Action, 3005 Audubon Terrace, NW, Washington, DC, 20008, 202/244-4080; Consumer HELP, 2000 H St., NW, Suite 100, Washington, DC, 20052, 202/785-1001; Consumer Protection Center, National Law Center, Washington, DC, 20052, 202/676-7585; D.C. Community Research Foundation, P.O. Box 19542, Washington, DC, 20036, 202/676-6968; D.C. Public Interest Research Group, Box 19542, Washington, DC, 20036, 202/676-7388; Consumer Federation of America, 1012 14th St., NW, Suite 901, Washington, DC, 20005, 202/737-3732; Consumers Union of the U.S.—Regional Office, 1714 Massachusetts Ave., NW, Washington, DC, 20036, 202/785-1906; National Center on the Black Aged, 1424 K St., NW, Suite 500, Washington, DC, 20005, 202/637-8400; National Consumers League, 1522 K St., NW, Suite 406, Washington, DC, 20005, 202/797-7600, National Council on the Aging, 1828 L St., NW, Suite 504, Washington, DC, 20036, 202/223-6250; National Council on Senior Citizens, 1511 K St., NW, Washington, DC 20005, 202/783-6850; National Consumer Assistance Center, AARP/NRTA, 1909 K St., NW, Washington, DC, 20049, 202/872-4890; Neighborhood Legal Services, 310 6th St., NW, Washington, DC, 20001, 202/628-9161; Metropolitan Washington Housing & Planning Association, 1225 K St., NW, Washington, DC, 20005, 202/737-3700; National Center for Urban Ethnic Affairs, 1521 16th St., NW, Washington, DC, 20036, 202/232-3600; Far East Community Services, 5929 East Capitol St., SE, Washington, DC, 20019, 202/583-6000; Housing Research Group, P.O. Box 19367, Washington, DC, 20036, 202/833-3400; National Urban League, Washington Bureau, 425 13th St., NW, Suite 515, Washington, DC, 20004, 202/393-4332; National Congress of American Indians, 1430 K St., NW, Washington, DC, 20005,

202/347-9520; National Urban Coalition, 1201 Connecticut Ave., NW, Washington, DC, 20036, 202/331-2400; National Association of Spanish-Speaking Elderly, 1801 K St., NW, Suite 1021, Washington, DC, 20006, 202/466-3595; National Association of Retired Federal Employees, 1533 New Hampshire Ave., NW, Washington, DC, 20036, 202/234-0832; Urban Elderly Coalition (Ethnics), 1828 L St., NW, Suite 505, Washington, DC, 20036, 202/857-0166; D.C. Cooperative Extension Service, 1351 Nicholson St., NW, Washington, DC, 20011; National Association of Community Health Centers, 1625 Eye St., NW, Suite 420 Washington, DC, 20006, 202/833-9280; Ad Hoc Low-Income Housing Coalition, 215 8th St., NE, Washington, DC, 20002; Commission for Racial Justice, 1029 Vermont Ave., Suite 208, Washington, DC, 20005, 202/737-2600; Berry Farm, 1101 Eaton Rd., SE, Washington, DC, 20020, 202/889-5341; National Council of Negro Women, 1346 Connecticut Ave., NW, Suite 832, Washington, DC, 20523, 202/223-2363; AFL-CIO, Department of Community Services, 815 16th St., NW, Washington, DC, 20006, 202/637-5000; Joint Center for Political Studies, 1426 H St., NW, Suite 926, Washington, DC, 20008, 202/638-4477; National Tribal Chairmen's Association, 1701 Pennsylvania Ave., NW, Washington, DC, 20006, 202/343-9484; Universidad Boricua—Puerto Rican Research and Resources Center, Inc., 1766 Church St., NW, Washington, DC, 20036, 202/667-7940; NAACP Washington Bureau, 733 15th St., NW, Washington, DC, 20005, 202/638-2269; National Public Interest Research Group, 1329 E St., NW, Suite 1127, Washington, DC, 20004, 202/347-3811.

FLORIDA: American Consumer Assn., Inc., P.O. Box 24141, Fort Lauderdale, FL, 33307, 305/933-3882; Consumer Committee on Utility Rates and the Environment, P.O. Box 10578, St. Petersburg, FL, 33733, 813/393-1106 or 813/393-7917; and Consumers Cure Inc. of Florida, P.O. Box 10578, St. Petersburg, FL, 33733, 813/393-1106 or 813/393-7917; Florida Consumers Federation, Clematis Building, Suite 600, 208 Clematis St., West Palm Beach, FL, 33401, 305/832-6077; Florida Public Interest Research Group, University Union, Room 331, Tallahassee, FL, 32306, 904/644-1811; N.E. Florida Community Action Agency, 135 Riverside Ave., Jacksonville, FL, 32202, 904/358-7474; Leon County CAP, Inc., P.O. Box 1775, Tallahassee, FL, 32301, 904/222-2043; Student Consumers Union, University Union, Room 334, Tallahassee, FL, 32306, 904/644-1811.

GEORGIA: Georgia Citizens' Coalition on Hunger, Inc., 201 Washington St., SW, Atlanta, GA, 30303, 404/659-0878; The Georgia Conservancy, Inc., 3110 Maple Dr., Suite 407, Atlanta, GA, 30305, 404/262-1967.

HAWAII: Citizens Against Noise, 205 Merchant St., Rm. 18, Honolulu, HI, 96813, 808/537-3490; Kokua Council, 2535 S. King St., Honolulu, HI, 96814, 808/732-0455 or 373-3879; Life of the Land, 404 Piikoi St., Rm. 209, Honolulu, HI, 96814, 808/521-1300.

IDAHO: Idaho Consumer Affairs, Inc., 106 N. 6th St., 3 Pioneer Bldg., Old Buise, ID, 83792, 208/343-3554.

ILLINOIS: Business and Professional People for the Public Interest, 109 N. Dearborn St., Suite 1001, Chicago, IL, 60602, 312/641-5570; Chicago

Consumer Coalition, 5516 S. Cornell, Chicago, IL, 60601, 312/955-0197; Citizens for a Better Environment, 59 E. Van Buren St., #2610, Chicago, IL, 60605, 312/939-1984; Community Action Program, 2200 N. Lincoln, Chicago, IL, 60614; Consumer Coalition, P.O. Box 913, Highland Park, IL, 60035, 312/679-8735; Consumer Information for Low Income Consumers, Southern Illinois University, Box 130, Edwardsville, IL, 62025, 618/692-2420; Food and Cooperative Project, 5516 S. Cornell, Chicago, IL, 60601, Illinois Public Interest Research Group, Southern Illinois University, Carbondale, IL, 62901, 618/536-2140; Midwest Academy, 600 W. Fullerton, Chicago, IL, 60614, 312/953-6525; Pollution and Environmental Problems, Box 309 Palatine, IL, 60067, 312/381-6695; Public Action, 59 East Van Buren, Suite 2610, Chicago, IL, 60605, 312/427-6262; Citizen Labor Energy Coalition, 600 E. Fullerton, Chicago, IL, 60614, 312/953-6525; People United to Save Humanity (PUSH), 930 E. 50th St., Chicago, IL, 60615, 312/373-3366.

INDIANA: Citizens Action Coalition, 3620 N. Meridian St., Indianapolis, IN, 46208, 317/923-2494; Indiana Consumer Center, 730 East Washington Blvd., Fort Wayne, IN, 46802, 219/422-7630; Indiana Public Interest Research Group, 406 N. Fass St., Bloomington, IN, 47401, 812/337-7575; Indiana Public Interest Research Group, 1825 Northside, South Bend, IN, 46624; New World Center, 611 W. Wayne St., Fort Wayne, IN, 46802, 219/422-6821.

IOWA: Citizens United for Responsible Energy (CURE), 1342 30th St., Des Moines, IA, 50311, 515/277-0253; Iowa Consumers League, Box 189, Corydon, IA, 50060, 515/872-2329; Iowa Public Interest Research Group, Student Activities Center, Iowa Memorial Union, Iowa City, IA, 52242, 319/353-2121; ACORN, Insurance Exchange Bldg., Suite 201, 2nd and Pershing, Davenport, IA, 52801, 319/322-6176; ACORN, 617 E. Grand, Des Moines, IA, 50300, 515/288-2740; ACORN, 3177 South Grand, St. Louis, Missouri, 63118, 314/865-3833.

KANSAS: Can Help, P.O. Box 4253, Topeka; KS, 66616, 913/235-3434; Consumer Assistance and Information for the Aging, 217 S. Seth Childs Rd., Manhattan, KS, 66502, 913/776-9294 or 800/432-2703; El Centro De Servicios Para Mexicanos, Inc., 204 NE Lime, Topeka, KS, 66616, 913/232-8207; Kansas Home Economics Association Extension Service, 21 E. Des Moines Ave., South Hutchinson, KS, 67505, 316/663-5491; Kansas National Consumer Information Center, 315 N. 20th St., Kansas City, KS, 66102, 913/342-4574; Manhattan Consumer-Business Relations Center, c/o KSU Consumer Relations Board S.G.A., Manhattan, KS, 66506, 913/532-6541; Mid-Kansas Community Action Program (MIDKAP), P.O. Box 1034, Eldorado, KS, 67042, 316/321-6373; Older Citizens Information Center, 1122 Jackson, Topeka, KS, 66616, 913/232-9037; Peoples Energy Project, P.O. Box 423, Lawrence, KS, 66044, 913/843-7592; Shawnee County Community Assistance and Action, Inc., 603 Topeka Ave., Topeka, KS, 66603, 913/235-9561; Lawrence Kansas Consumer Affairs 819 Vermont, Lawrence, KS, 66044, 913/843-4608; Consumer Affairs Association, Box W, Kansas Union, Lawrence, KS, 66044; Consumer United Program 8410 W. Highway #54, Wichita, KS, 67209, 316/722-4251; Kansas National Consumer Information Center, 315 N. 20th St., Kansas City, KS, 66102 913/342-4574; Community Information Service, Topeka Public Library, 1515 10th St., Topeka, KS, 66606, 913/233-4636; Topeka Housing Information Center, 3120 East 6th St., Topeka, KS, 66607, 913/234-0217.

KENTUCKY: Community Incorporated, 222 N. 17th St., Louisville, KY, 40203, 502/583-8385; Concerned Consumers, P.O. Box 325, 747 Liberty St., Newport, KY, 41071, 606/491-4444; Louisville and Jefferson County Community Action Agency, 305 W. Broadway, Fin Castle Bldg., Louisville, KY, 40202, 502/585-1631.

LOUISIANA: Gulf Coast Area NCIC, P.O. Box 5122, Alexandria, LA, 71301, 318/442-1614; Louisiana Center for the Public Interest, Suite 700, Maison Blanche Bldg., New Orleans, LA, 70112, 504/524-1231 or 8182; Louisiana Consumers' League, Inc., 144 Elks Pl., Suite 1202, New Orleans, LA, 70112, 504/568-9281; Louisiana Consumers' League, Capital Area Chapter, P.O. Box 14301, Baton Rouge, LA, 70808, 504/293-3088; New Orleans Council on Aging, 705 Lafayette St., Rm. 103, Gallier Hall, New Orleans, LA, 70130, 504/586-1221; New Orleans Legal Assistance Corp., 226 Carondelet St., Suite 601, New Orleans, LA, 70130, 504/529-1000; ACORN, 628 Baronne St., New Orleans, LA, 70113, 504/523-1691; Opportunities Industrialization Center, 315 N. Broad St., New Orleans, LA, 70119, 504/821-8222; Tulane Consumer Center, 308 Alcee Fortier Hall, New Orleans, LA, 70115, 504/866-0849.

MAINE: Citizens Committee on the Maine Economy (CCME), Box 2066, Augusta, ME, 04330; Consumer Affairs Program Task Force on Human Needs, 12 Park Hill Ave., Auburn, ME, 04210, 207/786-2481; Maine Public Interest Research Group, Colby College, Waterville, ME, 04901; Maine Public Interest Research Group, 68 High St., Portland, ME, 04101, 207/774-3066; Northeast COMBAT, Inc., 33 Idaho Ave., Bangor, ME, 04401, 207/947-3331; Pine Tree Legal Assistance, 146 Middle St., Portland, ME, 04101, 207/774-8211; Safe Power for Maine, P.O. Box 774, Camden, ME, 04843, 207/236-3610.

MARYLAND: Baltimore Urban League Consumer Services Department, 1150 Mondawmin Concourse, Baltimore, MD, 21215, 301/423-8150; Cambridge Park East Tenants Assn., 600 Greenwood Ave., Apt. 201, Cambridge, MD, 21613, 301/228-8581; Dorchester Community Development Corporation, P.O. Box 549, 445 Race St., Cambridge, MD, 21613, 301/228-3600; Garrett County Community Action Committee, Inc., P.O. Box 149, Oakland, MD, 21550, 301/334-9431; Maryland Action, Inc., 3120 Fenton St., Suite 300, Silver Spring, MD, 20910, 301/681-5101; Maryland Association of Housing Counselors, P.O. Box 549, Cambridge, MD, 21613, 301/228-3600; Maryland Citizens Consumer Council, P.O. Box 34526, Bethesda, MD, 20034, 301/299-5400, 301/448-9552; Maryland Public Interest Group, 3110 Main Dining Hall, College Park, MD, 20742, 301/454-5601; Neighborhoods Uniting Project, Inc., 3501 Bunker Hill Rd., Mt. Rainier, MD, 20822, 301/277-7085; North Arundel Consumers Assn., 106 Thomas Rd., Glen Burnie, MD, 21061, 301/761-0106; St. Ambrose Housing Aid Center, Inc., 321 E. 25th St., Baltimore, MD, 21218, 301/235-5770; Southeast Community Organization, 10 S. Wolfe St., Baltimore, MD, 21231, 301/327-1626; United Communities Against Poverty, Inc., 3708 Dodge Park, Suite 300, Landover, MD, 20705, 301/322-5255.

MASSACHUSETTS: Consumer Action Center, 721 State St., Springfield, MA, 01109, 413/736-3210; Massachusetts Community Center, 304 Boylston St., Boston, MA, 02116, 617/266-7505; Massachusetts Consumer Association, c/o Boston College, 140 Commonwealth Ave., Chestnut Hill, MA, 02167,

617-969-011 ext. 3674; Massachusetts Public Interest Research Group, 233 N. Pleasant St., Amherst, MA, 01002, 413/256-6434; Massachusetts Public Interest Research Group, 120 Boylston St., Rm. 320, Boston, MA, 02116, 617/423-1796; National Consumer Law Center, Inc., 11 Beacon St., Boston, MA, 02108, 617/969-1576; Springfield Action Commission, 721 State St., Springfield, MA, 01109, 413/736-3210.

MICHIGAN: The Calhoun Community Action Agency, P.O. Box 1026, Battle Creek, MI, 49016, 616/965-7766; Citizens for Better Care, 163 Madison St., Detroit, MI, 48226, 313/962-5968; Consumer Affairs Bureau Kalamazoo County Chamber of Commerce, 500 W. Crosstown, Kalamazoo, MI, 49008, 616/381-4004; Consumer Research Advisory Council, 51 W. Warren Ave., #310, Detroit, MI, 48201, 313/831-2290/313-865-9557; Greater Lansing Area Citizens for Saginaw, 1514 W. Saginaw St., Lansing, MI, 48915, 517/482-1297; Greater Lansing Association for Retarded Citizens, 855 Grove St., East Lansing, MI, 48823, 517/351-9592; Legal Aid of Central Michigan, 300 N. Washington Ave., P.O. Box 14171, Lansing, MI, 48901, 517/485-5411; Housing Assistance Foundation, 935 N. Washington Ave., Lansing, MI, 48502, 517/487-6051; Legal Aid of Western Michigan, 430 Federal Square Bldg., Grand Rapids, MI, 49503, 616/774-0672; Landlord Tenant Clinic, 144 W. Lafayette - 2nd Fl., Detroit, MI, 48226, 313/963-1375; Mediation Services, 1011 Student Activity Bldg., Ann Arbor, MI, 48104, 313/763-7455; Memorial Society of Greater Detroit, 4605 Cass, Detroit, MI, 48201, 313/TE3-9107; Michigan Citizens Lobby, 19111 10 Mile Rd., Suite 227, Southfield, MI, 48075, 313/559-9260; Michigan Consumer Council, 414 Hollister Bldg., Lansing, MI, 48933, 517/373-0947; Michigan Consumer Education Center, 215-A University Library, Ypsilanti, MI, 48197, 313/487-2292; Michigan Tenant Rights Coalition, 749 Eastern, SE, Grand Rapids, MI, 49503, 616/241-6429; Oakland/Livingston Human Services Agency, 196 Oakland Ave., Pontiac, MI, 48020, 313-858-5134; Public Interest Research Group in Michigan, 590 Hollister Bldg., Lansing, MI, 48933, 517/487-6001; Tenants Resource Center, 855 Grove St., East Lansing, MI, 48823, 517/337-9795; West Michigan Environmental Action Council, 1324 Lake Dr., SE, Grand Rapids, MI, 49506, 616/451-3051; Grand Rapids Urban League Tenants Union, 745 Eastern SE, Grand Rapids, MI, 49503, 616/241-6429; Association of Community Organizations for Reform Now (ACORN), 43 E. Willis, Detroit, MI, 48201, 313/831-3155; Association of Community Organizations for Reform Now (ACORN), 28½ Jefferson, Grand Rapids, MI, 49503, 616/454-1055.

MINNESOTA: Alternative Sources of Energy Magazine, Route 2, Box 90A, Milaca, MN, 56353, 612/983-6892; Minnesota Public Interest Research Group, Coffman Student Union, Duluth, MN, 55802, 612/376-7498; Minnesota Public Interest Research Group, 3036 University Ave., SE, Minneapolis, MN, 55414, 612/376-7554; Northeastern Minnesota Consumer's League, 206 W. 4th St., Duluth, MN, 55806, 218/727-8973 ext. 5.

MISSISSIPPI: Harrison County Neighborhood Service Center/Consumer Awareness and Action Agency, P.O. Box 519, Gulf Port, MI, 39501, 601/864-3421; Mississippi Consumer Association, 375 Culley Dr., Jackson, MS, 39206, 602/362-6643.

MISSOURI: Community Services, Inc., 214 W. Third, Maryville, MO, 64468, 816/582-3114; Human Resources Corporation, 3205 Woodland, Kansas City, MO, 64109, 816/923-7907; Legal Aid Society of the City and County of St. Louis-Legal Services of Eastern Missouri, 607 N. Grand, St. Louis, MO, 63103, 314/533-7900; Missouri Public Interest Research Group, Box 8276, St. Louis, MO, 63156, 314/361-5200; Missouri A.C.O.R.N., 3177 S. Grand, St. Louis, MO, 63104, 314/865-3835; Utility Consumers Council of Missouri, Inc., 7710 Carondelet, Suite 503, Clayton, MO, 63105, 314/361-5725.

MONTANA: Center for Public Interest, P.O. Box 931, Bozeman, MT, 59715, 406/587-0906; Montana State Low Income Organization, 225 Wheeler Vill Ave., Missoula, MT, 59602, 406/543-5245; Student Action Center, University Center, Missoula, MT, 59801, 406/243-2451; Montana Consumer Affairs Council, Inc., 68 Missoula Ave., Butte, MT, 59701, 406/792-3981; Student Action Center, University Center, Missoula, MT, 59801, 406/243-2451.

NEBRASKA: Consumer Alliance of Nebraska, Nebraska Center, 33rd and Holdrege, Lincoln, NE, 68583, 402/472-2844; Nebraska Public Interest Research Group, Nebraska Union, Rm. 117, Lincoln, NE, 68508, 402/472-2448.

NEVADA: Consumers League of Nevada, 3031 Garnet Court, Las Vegas, NV, 89121, 702/457-1953; KOLO-TV, News Department, 4850 Ampere Dr., Reno, NV, 89502, 702/786-2932; Poor People Pulling Together, 1285 W. Miller, Las Vegas, NV, 89106, 702/648-4645.

NEW HAMPSHIRE: Newmarket Regional Health Center, Inc., 14 Elm St., Newmarket, NH, 03857, 603/659-3106; Utility Consumer Advocate of New Hampshire, Room 401, L.O.B., Concord, NH, 03301.

NEW JERSEY: Community Relations Office City, Plainfield, NJ, 07061, 201/753-3229; Consumers League of New Jersey, 20 Church St., Rm. 11, Montclair, NJ, 07042, 201/744-6449; Gray Panthers of South Jersey, 408 Cooper St., Camden, NJ, 08102; National Consumer Advisory Council, 217 13th Ave., Belmar, NJ, 07719, 201/681-7494; New Jersey Public Interest Research Group, Rutgers Law School, 5th and Penn Sts., Camden, NJ, 08102; Clean Water Action Project, Douglas Student Center, New Brunswick, NJ, 08903, 201/932-9277; New Jersey Public Interest Research Group, 32 W. Lafayette St., Trenton, NJ, 08608, 609/393-7474; Ocean Community Economic Action Now, Inc., 40 Washington St., P.O. Box 1029, Toms River, NJ, 08753, 201/244-5333; Office of Economic Opportunity, 525 Penn St., Camden, NJ, 08102, 609/541-7675; Paterson Task Force for Community Action, Inc., 240 Broadway, Paterson, NJ, 07501, 201/271-7400; Public Information Office, 57 Sussex Ave., Newark, NJ, 07103, 201/622-6044.

NEW YORK: A.C.C.O.R.D., 264 East Onondaga St., Syracuse, NY, 13202, 315/422-2331; Bi-County Consumer Coalition of Long Island, 23 Roberts St., Farmingdale, NY, 11735; Brinkerhoff Action Association, Inc., 174-16 110th Ave., St. Albans, NY, 11433, 212/739-8281; Citizens Energy Council of Western New York, P.O. Box 564, Wilson, NY, 14172, 716/751-6227; Consumer Action Now, Inc., 49 East 53rd St., New York, NY, 10022, 212/752-1220; Consumer Action Program, 16 Court St., Brooklyn, NY, 11201,

212/643-1580; Council on Environmental Alternatives, 355 Lexington Ave., New York, NY, 10017, 212/682-8915; Empire State Consumer Association, Inc., 109 Heather Dr., Rochester, NY, 14625, 716/381-2758; Flatbush Tenants' Council, 1604 Newkirk Ave., Brooklyn, NY, 11226, 212/859-4717; GET Consumer Protection, P.O. Box 355, Ansonia Station, New York, NY, 10023; Harlem Consumer Education Council, Inc., 1959 Madison Ave., New York, NY, 10035, 212/926-5300; Irate Consumers of Ulster County, Box 419, Saugerties, NY, 12477, 914/246-4021; National Coalition to Fight Inflation, 160 Fifth Ave., New York, NY, 10011, 212/673-3700; Neighborhood Council Action Service System, 105-19 177th St., Jamaica, NY, 11433, 212/291-8115; New Frontier Consumer Council, 723 Steven Court, East Meadow, NY, 11554; New York City Community Development Agency, 349 Broadway, New York, NY, 10013, 212/433-2143; New York Public Interest Research Group, 295 Main St., Buffalo, NY, 14203; 716/847-1536; New York Public Interest Research Group, College of Staten Island, Building C, Rm. 131, '715 Ocean Terrace, Staten Island, NY, 10301, 212/981-8986/212/390-7538; New York Public Interest Research Group, Box 295, Hunter College, 695 Park Ave., Manhattan, NY, 10021, 212/570-5324; New York Public Interest Research Group, City College - Downer 203, 100 33rd St. & Convent Ave., Manhattan, NY, 10031, 212/234-1628; American Council on Science and Health, 1995 Broadway, New York, NY, 10023, 212/362-7044; Oswego County Consumer Protection League, Route 8, Oswego, NY, 13126, 315/342-3850; New York Consumer Assembly, 465 Grand St., New York, NY, 10002, 212/674-5990; New York Public Interest Research Group, Inc., 1 Columbia Pl., Albany, NY, 12207, 518/436-0876; New York Public Interest Research Group, University Union, SUNY - Binghamton, Binghamton, NY, 13901, 607/798-4971; New York Public Interest Research Group, Inc., 1479 Flatbush Ave., Brooklyn, NY, 11210, 212/338-5906; New York Public Interest Research Group, Queens College, Student Union, Rm. B-34, Flushing, NY, 11367, 212/520-8616; New York Public Interest Research Group, Inc., 5 Beekman St., New York, NY, 10038; 212/349-6460; New York Public Interest Research Group, 1004 E. Adams St., Syracuse, NY, 13210, 315/476-8381; Consumer Commission on the Accreditation of Health Services, 377 Park Ave., S., New York, NY, 10016, 212/689-8959.

NORTH CAROLINA: Carolina Action, Box 1985, Durham, NC, 27702, 919/682-6076; I CARE, INC., Consumer Affairs, P.O. Box 349, 502 S. Center St., Statesville, NC, 28677, 704/872-8141; Institute for Southern Studies, P.O. Box 230, Chapel Hill, NC, 27514, 919/929-2141; The North Carolina Consumers Council, Inc., P.O. Box 1246, Raleigh, NC, 27602, 919/828-8744; North Carolina Public Interest Research Group, P.O. Box 2901, Durham, NC, 27705, 919/286-2275; North Carolina Senior Citizens Federation, P.O. Box 1516, Henderson, NC, 27536, 919/492-6031; Operation Breakthrough, Inc., P.O. Box 1470, Durham, NC, 27702, 919/688-8111.

NORTH DAKOTA: Area Low Income Council, 1219 College Dr., Devils Lake, ND, 58301, 701/662-5388; Quad County Consumer Action, 27½ S. 3rd St., Grand Forks, ND, 58201, 701/772-8989.

OHIO: Cleveland Consumer Action Foundation, Inc., 532 Terminal Tower, Cleveland, OH, 44113, 216/687-0525; Cleveland Consumer Action, Inc., 532

Terminal Tower, Cleveland, OH, 44113, 216/687-0525; Community Action Commission of the Cincinnati Area, 801 Linn St., Cincinnati, OH, 45203, 513/241-1425; Consumer Conference of Greater Cincinnati, 6701 Highland Ave., Cincinnati, OH, 45236, 513/791-6515; Consumer Protection Association, 3134 Euclid Ave., Cleveland, OH, 44115, 216/881-3434; Consumers League of Ohio, 513 Engineers Bldg., Cleveland, OH, 44114, 216/621-1175; Free Stores, Inc., 2270 Vince St., Cincinnati, OH, 45219, 513/241-1064; Humanity House, 475 W. Market St., Akron, OH, 44303, 216/253-7151; Lake County Branch, NAACP, Suite B303, New Market Mall, Painesville, OH, 44077, 216/354-2148; Montgomery County Community Action Agency, 3304 N. Main St., Cottage 10, Dayton, OH, 45405, 513/276-5011; Ohio Consumer Association, P.O. Box 52, North Bend, OH, 45002, 513/941-4289; Ohio Public Interest Research Group, 65 Fourth Ave., Columbus, OH, 43215, 614/461-0136; Ohio Public Interest Research Group, Box 25, Wilder Hall, Oberlin, OH, 44074, 216/775-8137; Dayton Tenants Organization, Box 577, Dayton, OH, 45469, 513/229-2110; Student Consumer Union, 405C Student Services Bldg., Bowling Green, OH, 43403, 419/372-0248.

OKLAHOMA: Delta Community Action Foundation, 1024 Main St., Duncan, OK, 73533, 405/255-3222; Association of Community Organizations for Reform Now, 544 S. Norfolk, Tulsa, OK, 74120, 918/599-9106.

OREGON: Consumers' Food Council, Route 1, Box 842, Beaverton, OR, 97005, 503/628-1227; Multnoma County Legal Aid Service, 310 SW 4th Avenue, Room 1100, Portland, OR, 97204, 503/224-4086; Oregon Consumer League, 519 SW Third, Room 412, Portland, OR, 97204, 503/227-3882; Oregon Student Public Interest Research Group, 918 SW Yamhill, Portland, OR, 97205, 503/222-9641; Portland Neighborhood Services, 9 Chatham Court, Portland, OR, 97217, 503/227-5110; RAIN (magazine), 2270 NW Irving, Portland, OR, 97210, 503/227-5110.

PENNSYLVANIA: Action Alliance of Senior Citizens of Greater Philadelphia, 401 N. Broad, Rm. 800, Philadelphia, PA, 19108, 215/574-9050; Areas of Concern, P.O. Box 47, Bryn Mawr, Pa., 19010, 215/525-1129; Bucks County Consumer Organization, 30 Spice Bush Rd., Levittown, PA, 19056, 215/945-3373; Bucks County Opportunity Council, Nesshaminy Manor Center, Doylestown, PA, 18901, 215/343-2800 ext. 360; Cumberland County Bureau of Consumer Affairs, 35 East High St., Carlisle, PA, 17013, 717/249-1133 ext. 251 or 252; Citizens Choice Coalition, 73 West Ross St., Wilkes Barre, PA, 18702, 717/823-6439; Concerned Citizens of The Delaware Valley, P.O. Box 47, Bryn Mawr, PA, 19010, 215/LA 5-1129; Consumer Action of Berks County Inc., City Hall, 8th and Washington Sts., Reading, PA, 19601, 215/373-5111 ext. 369 or 370; Consumer Education and Protective Assn., 6048 Ogontz Ave., Philadelphia, PA, 19141, 215/424-1441; Consumers United Together (CUT), 1022 Birch St., Scranton, PA, 18505; Council of Spanish Speaking Organs., 709 Franklin St., Philadelphia, PA, 19123, 215/574-3535; Institute for Community Services, Edinboro State College, Edinboro, PA, 16412; Temple-Law Education & Participation of Temple University Law Center, 1719 N. Broad St., Philadelphia, PA, 19122, 215/787-8953; Lehigh Valley Committee Against Health Fraud, Inc., Chairman, Board of Directors, P.O. Box 1602, Allentown, PA, 18105, 215/437-1795; National Students Consumer Protection Council, 328

Bartley Hall, Villanova, PA, 19085, 215/527-2100 ext. 331; North West Con
sumer Council, Box 725, Edinboro, PA, 16412, 814/732-2451; Northwes
Tenants Organization, c/o Summit Presbyterian Church, Greene & Western Sts.
Philadelphia, PA, 19144, 215/849-7111; Pennsylvania Public Interest Researcl
Group, Bldg., 20 Hetzel Union Bldg., University Park, PA, 16802, 814/865
6851; Delaware Valley Coalition for Consumer Education & Cooperation, 55
Carpenter Lane, Philadelphia, PA, 19119, 215/843-6945 (W) 215/849-4326
Pennsylvania Consumers Board, Houston Hall, 3417 Spruce St., Philadelphia
PA, 19174, 215/243-6000; Pennsylvania Citizens Consumers Council, Bo
17019, Pittsburgh, PA, 15235; Pennsylvania League for Consumer Protection
P.O. Box 1266, Harrisburg, PA, 17108, 717/233-5704; Philadelphia Consume
Services Cooperative, 1008 River Park House, Philadelphia, PA, 19131
215/GR3-0482; Taxpayers Information Project, 330 Race St., Philadelphia, PA
19106, 215/922-6890; Tenant Action Group, 5710 Germantown Ave., Phila
delphia, PA, 19144, 215/849-8877; United Consumers of the Alleghenies, Inc.
P.O. Box 997, Johnstown, PA, 15907, 814/535-8608; Association of Communit
Organizations for Reform Now (ACORN), 2015 Fairmount Ave., Philadelphia
PA, 19130, 215/235-8686.

PUERTO RICO: Committee for Consumer Action, W-3 Loma Alta
Garden Hills, Guaynabo, PR, 00657.

RHODE ISLAND: Coalition for Consumer Justice, 410 Broad St., Centra
Falls, RI, 02863, 401/723-3147; Rhode Island Public Interest Research Group
Brown University - Box 2145, Providence, RI, 02912, 401/863-4343; Rhod
Island Handicapped Action Committee, 410 Broad St., Central Falls, RI, 02863
401/723-3147; Workers Association to Guarantee Employment, 410 Broad St.
Central Falls, FI, 02863, 401/722-1148; Rhode Island Workers Association, 37
Broadway, Providence, RI, 02909, 401/751-2008; Urban League of Rhod
Island, 246 Prairie Ave., Providence, RI, 02905, 401/351-5000.

SOUTH CAROLINA: Midlands Human Resources Development Com
mission, 650 Knox Abbott Dr., Cayce, SC, 29033, 803/791-1345; South Caro
lina Public Interest Research Group, Furman University, Greenville, SC, 29613
803/294-2174.

SOUTH DAKOTA: ACORN, 611 S. 2nd Ave., Sioux Falls, SD, 57104
605/332-2328; Consumers League, Rapid City, SD, 57701, 605/343-6836; NE
South Dakota Community Action Program, 610 Second Ave., E., Sisseton, SD
57262, 605/698-7654; South Dakota Consumers League, P.O. Box 106, Ma
dison, SD, 57042, 605/256-4536.

TENNESSEE: Community Services Administration, 444 James Robertso
Parkway, Nashville, TN, 37219, 615/741-2615; Elk and Duck Rivers Commu
nity Association, 606 Lee Ave., Fayetteville, TN, 37334, 615/433-7182; The
Highlander Center, Route 3, Box 370, New Market, TN, 37820, 615/933-3443

TEXAS: Community Action Resource Services, Inc., 1510 Plum St.
Texarkana, TX, 75501, 214/794-3386; Dallas Community Action, 2208 Mai
St., Dallas, TX, 75201, 214/742-2500; Senior Citizens Service, Inc., of Texar

kana, P.O. Box 619, Texarkana, TX, 75501, 214/792-5131; West Texas Legal Services, 406 W. T. Waggoner Bldg., Ft. Worth, TX, 76102, 817/334-1435; Texas Consumer Association, 711 San Antonio, Austin, TX, 78701, 512/477-1882; Texas Citizen Action Group, 2226 Guadalupe, Austin, TX, 78705; Texas Public Interest Research Group, Box 237-UC, University of Houston, Houston, TX, 77004, 713/749-3130; Bowie County Economic Advancement Corporation, Texarkana, TX, 75501; Association of Community Organizations for Reform Now (ACORN), 503 W. Mary, Austin, TX, 78704, 512/442-8321; 4415 San Jacinto, Dallas, TX, 75204, 214/823-4580; 1322 Hemphill, Ft. Worth, TX, 76104, 817/924-1401; 4600 S. Main, Houston, TX, 77002, 713/523-6989.

UTAH: League of Utah Consumers, Division of Food and Consumer Services, 147 N. 200 W., Salt Lake City, UT, 84103, 801/533-4124; Ogden Area Community Action Center, 206 24th St., Ogden, UT, 84401, 801/399-9281; Salt Lake Community Action Agency, 2033 S. State, Salt Lake City, UT, 84115, 801/582-8181; Utah Consumer Advisory Committee, 147 N. Second W., Salt Lake City, UT, 84103, 801/533-4124; Utah Consumers Organization, 203 E. 7th S., Salt Lake City, UT, 84111, 801/531-9039; Utah Home Economics Association, 444 S. 300 W., Salt Lake City, UT, 84101, 801/533-5745; Utah Issues and Information, 2024 Annex - University of Utah, Salt Lake City, UT, 84114, .801/581-7208; Utah Nutrition Council, 218 E. 1800 S., Orem, UT, 84057.

VERMONT: Consumer Association for the Betterment of Living (CABOL), Box 77, Danby, VT, 05739, 802/293-5462; Vermont Alliance, 5 State St., Montpelier, VT, 05602, 802/229-9104; Vermont Public Interest Research Group, Inc., 26 State St., Montpelier, VT, 05602, 802/223-5221.

VIRGINIA: Concerned Citizens for Justice, Inc., P.O. Box 1409, Wise, VA, 24293, 703/328-9239; Consumer Congress of the Commonwealth of Virginia, 3122 W. Clay St., Suite 205, Richmond, VA, 23230, 804/355-6947; North Anna Environmental Coalition, P.O. Box 3951, Charlottsville, VA, 22903, 804/293-6039; Office of Appalachian Ministry, Catholic Diocese of Richmond, Box 1376, Wise, VA, 24293, 703/328-6800; Catholic Diocese of Richmond, Hull Bldg., 554 S. Main, Marion, VA, 24354, 703/783-3981; Pittsylvania County Community Action Agency, P.O. Box 936, Chatham, VA, 24531, 804/432-8250; Total Action Against Poverty Consumer Education Program, 702 Shenandoah Ave., N.W., Roanoke, VA, 24001, 703/345-6781 ext. 319; Virginia Citizens Consumer Council, 823 E. Main St., Richmond, VA, 23219, 804/643-2511 or 649/7664; Virginia Citizens Consumer Council Richmond Chapter, P.O. Box 5462, Richmond, VA, 23220, 804/266-2534; Virginia Citizens Consumer Council Roanoke Chapter, 702 Shenandoah Ave., N.W., Roanoke, VA, 24016, 703/345-6781 ext. 319; Virginia Citizens Consumer Council Northern Virginia Chapter, P.O. Box 777, Springfield, VA, 22150, 703/941-1441; Virginia Home Economics Association, 706 N. Frederick St., Arlington, VA, 22203.

WASHINGTON: Washington Committee on Consumer Interests, 2701 First Ave., Suite 300, Seattle, WA, 98121, 206/682-1174; Washington Public Interest Research Group, FK-10, Seattle, WA, 98195, 206/543-0434.

WEST VIRGINIA: Appalachian Research and Defense Fund, 1116 B Kanawha Blvd., E., Charleston, WV, 25301, 304/344-9687; Council of the Southern Mountains West Virginia Branch, 125 McDowell St., Welch, WV, 24801, 304/436-2185; Multi-County Community Action Against Poverty, P.O. Box 3228, Charleston, WV, 25332, 304/343-4175; North-Central West Virginia Community Action Assn. Inc., 208 Adams St., Fairmont, WV, 26554, 304/363-2170; West Virginia Citizens Action Group, Inc., 1324 Virginia St., E., Charleston, WV, 25301, 304/346-5891; West Virginia Public Interest Research Group, Box 198, Wesleyan College, Buchhannon, WV, 26201; West Virginia Public Interest Research Group, S.O.W. Mountainlair, Morgantown, WV, 26506, 304/293-2108.

Source: U.S. Office of Consumer Affairs

Public Sources of Help

Government agencies at almost all levels are continuing to expand and improve their direct services to individuals, especially in consumer matters. And despite cries mostly from the business community for less government, individuals and organizations of all types, including business itself, continue to turn increasingly to government for assistance.

At the federal level, the Carter Administration increased the momentum of previous administrations toward involving the public more in government decision-making. It ordered all agencies to step up efforts to include individuals and citizen groups especially in official proceedings, hold more hearings outside Washington and increase use of public funds to pay legitimate expenses of witnesses representing diverse viewpoints. The Administration also took other steps to open up government more by disclosing more information about officials and making more files available for inspection.

The Administration went further than previous ones in appointing representatives of public interest organization to key positions in regulatory agencies. Previous administrations followed a policy of filling regulatory posts largely with representatives of the industries that were supposed to be regulated by those commissions. This practice led to growing criticism, especially in Congress. A survey by the General Accounting Office, an arm of Congress, determined that only 10 per cent of some 120 key appointees "demonstrated a significant sensitivity to the interest of consumers."

President Carter not only tried to reverse this trend but also endorsed establishment of a quasi-independent consumer agency to watch over the regulators. But Congress defeated the long-sought proposal of consumer groups in early 1978, and the Carter Administration did not attempt to revive it in 1979.

SERVICES TO PUBLIC FOUND VARIABLE

Despite all the activity to improve public services, however, private citizens still find it difficult to get government help in many cases. Individuals often expect more than they should, and they often contact the wrong agency for assistance, according to government officials. They advise people to try to resolve individual problems in other ways before going to a federal agency.

Few agencies have the power to resolve individual cases. But they are all interested at least to some degree in knowing whether there is a pattern of abuse that should be addressed by new rules, changes in rules or other corrective measures. Thus, while an individual may get little or no immediate personal aid by contacting the government, he or she might help correct a problem affecting many people.

When contacting the government at any level letters are usually far more effective than phone calls. Results are much more likely if the proper agency is contacted in the first place. Much of the work of bureaucrats consists of forwarding misdirected complaints and inquiries to appropriate offices.

In fact, the only government-wide consumer office at the federal level began in 1979 to phase out all complaint resolution efforts and refer all inquiries and complaints to other federal offices.

COMPLAINT HANDLING GETS LOW SCORE

That decision of the U.S. Office of Consumer Affairs (OCA) was made after receiving the final report of a four-year study of government handling of citizen complaints and inquiries. The study was done by contract by Technical AssistanceResearch Programs (TARP), a private firm.

The report said in effect that if you have a consumer problem, write, don't call, especially if you want help from OCA itself. The report said OCA may not even note your telephoned complaint so that follow-up can occur.

Over a third of the agencies checked were found to lag significantly in some or many aspects of effective complaint handling.

VISIT WASHINGTON, COURTESY UNCLE SAM
Government Will Pay Expenses for Views on Certain Issues

An increasing number of federal agencies have programs to pay the costs of public participation in official proceedings. In general, the agencies will do so for views and information deemed essential for a full and fair resolution of controversial issues.

Expenses paid include those for travel, meals, hotel, research and attorney fees involved in the preparation and presentation of testimony.

Agencies with such programs are listed below along with addresses and telephone numbers for interested persons:

Civil Aeronautics Board: Office of General Counsel, 1825 Connecticut Ave. NW, Washington, DC, 20428; 202/673-5442.

Consumer Products Safety Commission: Office of Public Participation, Washington, DC, 20207; 202/254-6241.

Economic Regulatory Administration: Utility Consumer Office, Department of Energy, 1111 20th st. NW, Washington, DC, 20036; 202/254-9755.

Environmental Protection Agency: Office of Toxic Substances, 401 M st. SW, Washington, DC, 20406; 202/755-4880.

Federal Trade Commission: Regional offices or Office of General Counsel, 6th and Pa. ave. NW, Washington, DC, 20580; 202/523-3796.

National Highway Traffic Safety Administration: Administrator, 400 Seventh st. SW, Washington, DC, 20590; 202/426-9522.

National Oceanic and Atmospheric Administration: Office of General Counsel, Dept. of Commerce, Room 5816A, Washington, DC, 20230; 202/377-4080.

Other agencies actively considering such programs include: the Department of Agriculture, Federal Communications Commission, Food and Drug Administration and Department of Interior.

Several other agencies were credited with having made "dramatic improvements" since the first phase of the study in 1975. These agencies included the Food and Drug Administration, Federal Communication Commission, Federal Trade Commission and Deparmtent of Housing and Urban Development. Continuing with good records throughout the study were the Securities and Exchange Commission, U.S. Postal Service and Civil Aeronautics Board.

Agencies with overall unsatisfactory records included the Office of Education, Rehabilitation Services Administration, Veterans Administration, Department of Energy and the Employment and Training Administration. The first two had not even installed basic complaint-handling systems by December, 1978, when the final TARP report was issued.

SUBJECTS MOST COMPLAINED ABOUT

Each year, the OCA tabulates the major types of complaints received in broad categories. And each year, complaints about automobiles and trucks have led the list by a wide margin. Problems with mail order have always been second.

Other changes include more frequent complaints about banking and credit, insurance, housing, appliances and energy, including utilities. On the other hand, problems regarding travel, magazines and time pieces have moved down the list, indicating fewer problems in comparison with the rest.

However, the categories are not precise and have occasionally been revised. So precise comparisons cannot be made. Following are the top 20 complaint categories, according to letters received by OCA in 1978:

TOP TWENTY COMPLAINTS
Received by Federal Consumer Office

Rank	Category	Number of complaints in 1978	Per cent of total, 1978
1	Automobiles and trucks	2,102	35.1
2	Mail Order	582	9.7
3	Banking and Credit	319	5.3
4	Appliances	289	4.8
5	Housing	285	4.8
6	Insurance	192	3.2
7	Publications	182	3.0
8	Food	158	2.6
9	Home Entertainment Equip.	137	2.3
10	Home Furnishings	117	2.0
11	Transportation Service (passenger)	115	1.9
12	Recreation and Travel	114	1.9
13	Energy and Utilities	109	1.8
14	Transportation Equipment (except autos & trucks)	90	1.5
15	Transportation, freight	82	1.4
16	Equipment and Tools	74	1.2
17	Government Services	72	1.2
18	Time Pieces	69	1.2
19	Clothing and Accessories	63	1.1
20	Retail stores	61	1.0

Source: U.S. Office of Consumer Affairs, 1979.

FEDERAL CONSUMER SERVICES

Many of the agencies listed below have regional offices. Consult your phone directory under "United States Government" for local listings, or call a local Federal Information Center listed on preceding pages.

DEPARTMENT OF AGRICULTURE (USDA)

Agriculture Research Service provides technology for farmers to produce efficiently, conserve the environment and meet the food and fiber needs of the American people. 202/447-4561.

Animal and Plant Health Inspection Service conducts regulatory programs to protect the wholesomeness of meat and poultry products for human consumption, including meat and poultry inspection. 202/447-3861.

Economic Research Service carries out research on all aspects of food production, consumption and prices. 202/447-4839.

Extension Service in coorperation with state and county governments, conducts continuing education programs in agricultural production, home economics, family life and related subjects. 202/727-2004.

Farmers Home Administration provides credit for those in rural America who are unable to get credit from other sources at reasonable rates and terms. 202/447-4323.

Food and Nutrition Service administers the USDA's food assistance programs, such as food stamps and child nutrition programs. 202/447-8138.

Forest Service provides for the conservation and use of the nation's forest and land resources, including recreational uses. 202/447-3760.

Office of Governmental and Public Affairs provides information on all programs of the USDA, including publications available free or for a minimal charge. Produces movies, film strips, slides and exhibits for public information. 202/447-6311.

Rural Development Service coordinates social and economic development programs in rural areas of the nation, including a wide range of assistance measures for communities of 10,000 population or less. 202/447-7595.

All other questions, complaints or comments to the Office of Information, USDA, Washington, DC, 20250; 202/447-6311.

DEPARTMENT OF COMMERCE

National Bureau of Standards develops specifications, rating schemes, and label designs to provide information on the energy efficiency of major household appliances. Provides technical assistance in developing safety standards to reduce risk of injury associated with consumer products. Director, National Bureau of Standards, Department of Commerce, Washington, DC, 20234; 301/921-3181.

National Fire Prevention and Control Administration monitors residential fire detectors and related equipment; encourages owners and managers of certain types of buildings to prepare fire safety effectiveness statements; and assists in the development of fire safety standards for consumer products. Department of Commerce, Washington, DC, 20230; 202/634-7658.

National Marine Fisheries Service is involved with inspection and grading, developing standards of quality and packaging for fishery products. Department of Commerce, Washington, DC, 20240; 202/634-7281.

Patent and Trademark Office administers the trademark registration system to protect the consumer from confusion and deception in brand identification. Department of Commerce, Washington, DC, 20231; 703/557-3268.

Inquiries, complaints or comments can be made to the Director of Consumer Affairs, Room 3800, Department of Commerce, Washington, DC, 20230; 202/377-3176.

DEPARTMENT OF ENERGY

Economic Regulatory Administration monitors prices, production of all energy sources and compliance and enforcement of federal regulations. Audits refineries and other energy producers and creates emergency programs, such as gas rationing. 202/254-8690.

Energy Information Administration compiles data on all aspects of energy production and use. Does research and issues reports. 202/633-8184.

Energy Regulation Commission, formerly the Federal Power Commission, regulates wholesale rates and service of natural gas and electric companies. Allocates supplies during shortages and licenses non-federal hydroelectric plants. 202/275-4006.

Office of Conservation and Solar organizes programs for developing solar and other alternative power sources. Involved in all aspects of energy conservation. 202/376-4934.

Office of Consumer Affairs handles all complaints and comments directed at the agency and provides information to consumers on a wide range of energy-related topics. 202/755-8830.

Correspondence to all offices should be addressed to Department of Energy, Washington, DC, 20545.

DEPARTMENT OF HEALTH, EDUCATION AND WELFARE (HEW)

Office of Education provides leadership and assistance to improve the quality and relevance of educational opportunity at every level. Its **Office of Consumer Education** provides support to States, local education agencies, institutions of higher education and nonprofit organizations (including libraries) for consumer education projects. Emphasis is on model programs, curriculum development and personnel training.

Consumer and Homemaking Education Program provides funds to States on a formula grant basis to assist them in developing consumer and homemaking education programs. Funds also are available to higher education institutions. Instruction programs are designed to prepare persons at every age level—kindergarten through adult—for the dual role of homemaker and wage earner. Publications for this program are available from the Supervisor of Vocational Home Economics Education, Department of Education in each state capital. Washington, DC, 20202; 202/653-5983.

Office for Civil Rights is responsible for the administration and enforcement of departmental policies under laws that prohibit discrimination with regard to race, color, national origin, religion, mental and physical handicap and sex.

Inquiries or complaints should be directed to the Regional Offices for Civil Rights in Atlanta, Boston, Chicago, Dallas, Denver, Kansas City, New York, Philadelphia, San Francisco and Seattle, or Office for Civil Rights, Washington, DC, 20201; 202/245-6700.

Office of Consumer Affairs coordinates federal activities in the consumer field and seeks ways to aid and protect the consumer. OCA conducts investigations, conferences and surveys on the problems of consumers; handles consumer complaints and conducts meetings with state officials, consumer groups and individuals to discuss common problems and possible solutions. Office of Consumer Affairs, Washington, DC, 20201; 202/755-8875.

Office of Human Development organizes planning and resources for Americans with special needs: children and youth, the aged, physically and mentally disabled persons, Indians and Alaskan Natives and persons living in rural areas. Units are: **Office for Handicapped Individuals, President's Committee on Mental Retardation, Office of Rural Development, Office of Manpower, Office of Volunteer Development, Office of Veterans Affairs and the Federal Council on the Aging, Washington, DC, 20201.**

Six other units grant funds to assist certain groups:

● **Administration on Aging** administers grants to states for planning, coordination and provision of community services, including nutrition programs; grants to organizations, institutions and individuals for research and demonstration projects; and grants to public and nonprofit organizations for training. It operates a central clearinghouse of information on services and opportunities available to the elderly. Washington, DC, 20224; 202/245-0827.

● **Development Disabilities Office** assists state and local public agencies and private nonprofit organizations serving persons who have a disability resulting from mental retardation, cerebral palsy, epilepsy, autism or severe dyslexia that originates before age 18. 3070 Switzer Building, Washington, DC, 20201; 202/245-0335.

● **Office of Child Development** consists of the **Office of the Director, the Head Start Bureau** and the **Children's Bureau.** In each of 10 HEW regional offices, a Director for OCD supervises a staff carrying out Head Start and Children's Bureau projects in the area. OCD serves as a point of coordination for federal programs, with emphasis on children who have special problems.

For information about Head Start Bureau and Children's Bureau, activities of the **National Center on Child Abuse and Neglect,** or **Education for Parenthood,** write Division of Public Education, P.O. Box 1182, Washington, DC, 20013; 202/755-7547 or 202/755-7724.

● **Office of Native American Programs** assists American Indians, Alaskan Natives and Native Hawaiians to attain social and economic self-sufficiency through a policy of self-determination. Washington, DC, 20201; 202/426-3960.

● **Office of Youth Development** assists states, localities and private nonprofit organizations in providing tempory shelter care and counseling services to youth under the age of 18. Washington, DC, 20201; 202/245-2859, National Runaway Switchboard: 800/621-4000.

● **Rehabilitation Services Administration** provides federal support for state and federal programs of vocational rehabilitation serving physically and mentally handicapped citizens. Disabled persons should apply to their state vocational rehabilitation agency or contact: Project Grants and Management Division, Rehabilitation Services Administration, Washington, DC, 20201; 202/245-0474.

Public Health Service consists of six operating agencies that directly affect consumers:

● **Alcohol, Drug Abuse and Mental Health Administration** leads the na tional effort to prevent and treat alcohol abuse and alcoholism, drug abuse and mental and emotional illness. 5600 Fishers Lane, Rockville, MD, 20852; 301/443-3783.

● **Center for Disease Control** directs programs designed to improve the health of the people of the United States. 1600 Clifton Rd. NE, Atlanta, GA, 30333; 404/283-3286.

● **Food and Drug Administration** enforces laws and regulations to prevent distribution of adulterated or misbranded foods, drugs, medical devices, cosmetics and veterinary products. 5600 Fishers Lane, Rockville, MD, 20852; 301/443-4177.

● **Health Resources Administration** identifies, develops and makes use of the nation's health resources. 5600 Fishers Lane, Rockville, MD, 20852; 301/436-8988.

● **Health Services Administration** works to reach underserved populations; improves quality of health care; and fosters effective and efficient health service delivery. 5600 Fishers Lane, Rockville, MD, 20852; 301/443-2086.

● **National Institutes of Health** works to improve human health by acquiring new scientific knowledge. 9000 Rockville Pike, Bethesda, MD, 20014; 301/496-5787.

Inquiries, complaints or comments should be addressed to any of the previously listed offices, or to: Office of Public Affairs, U.S. Public Health Service, 5600 Fishers Lane, Rockville, MD, 20852; 301/443-2155.

Social Security Administration provides monthly benefits to insured persons and their dependents in the event of retirement, disability or death and provides health insurance to persons 65 and over (to some under age 65 who are disabled). SSA administers a federal program of cash assistance payments to the needy, aged, blind and disabled.

For information and service, call any of the 1,300 Social Security offices listed in local telephone directories. If there is no office in your community, consult the local post office for the schedule of visits of Social Security representatives. For further information and service, contact Division of Public Inquiries, Social Security Administration, 6401 Security Boulevard, Baltimore, MD, 21235; 301/953-3600.

DEPARTMENT OF HOUSING AND URBAN DEVELOPMENT (HUD)

Crime Insurance enables businessmen and residents of houses and apartments to purchase burglary and robbery insurance in states where crime insurance is difficult to obtain or not affordable in the private market. For more information, call toll-free 800/638-8780. In metropolitan Washington, DC, call 301/652-2637.

Fair Housing and Equal Opportunity. HUD investigates complaints of discrimination and attempts to resolve them through conciliation. Any person aggrieved by a discriminatory housing practice may file a complaint with HUD. 202/755-7252.

Flood Insurance is available in eligible communities for one- to four-family residential properties and small business properties for which the insured owner will pay a subsidized rate and the government will pay the difference between that rate and the full premium rate. 202/755-5581.

Housing Assistance. HUD insures mortgages to finance the construction, purchase or improvement of one- to four-family houses for low- and moderate-income families, including those people displaced by HUD-assisted programs and natural disasters. HUD-insured, low-interest loans may be used to buy mobile home units or condominiums or to buy a house or membership in a cooperative housing project designed for low-income families. HUD also insures mortgages to finance the repair, rehabilitation, construction or purchase of housing in older, declining neighborhoods and urban renewal areas. HUD requires subsidized project owners to notify tenants of their intention to request a rental increase from HUD and to provide a 30-day comment period. HUD provides special housing programs to the elderly and handicapped. At all field offices, free counseling services are provided. 202/755-5656.

Interstate Land Sales Registration. HUD requires that developers of subdivisions file a statement of record with HUD and furnish a printed property report to the consumer at least 48 hours before signing an agreement to buy or lease subdivision property. 202/755-5989.

Minimum Property Standards provides a sound technical basis for the planning and design of housing under HUD programs, defining the minimum level of quality acceptable to HUD. Standards for carpets were developed to increase the quality standards for material used in carpeting. HUD also has developed the Mobile Home Construction and Safety Standards to reduce personal injuries and deaths, insurance costs and property damage resulting from mobile home accidents.

Mortgage Credit Assistance for Homeownership provides mortgage insurance to finance homeownership for low- and moderate-income families whose credit history does not qualify them for insurance under normal standards.

Real Estate Settlement Procedures. HUD is authorized to assure that consumers are provided with better and more timely information on the nature and cost of closing and settlement of housing purchases. 202/755-7038.

Structural Defect Repairs. HUD provides for federal reimbursement, in certain circumstances, for the repair of defects affecting safety and habitability of certain HUD-insured houses in older, declining urban neighborhoods.

Individuals with complaints and inquiries relating to Fair Housing and Equal Opportunity may call the toll-free number: 800/424-8590. All other correspondence and calls may be directed to the Assistance Secretary for Consumer Affairs, HUD, Suite 4100, Washington, DC, 20410; 202/755-6887, or any regional office.

DEPARTMENT OF THE INTERIOR

Bureau of Land Management administers public lands in the western states and Alaska. Washington, DC, 20240; 202/343-4151.

Bureau of Outdoor Recreation provides financial grants for recreational development. Washington, DC, 20240; 202/343-5726.

Fish and Wildlife Service conserves migratory bird resources and other types of wildlife refuges. Washington, DC, 20240; 202/343-5634.

Geological Survey prepares and sells topographic, geologic and hydrologic maps. Standard topographic quadrangle maps of the United States are issued. National Center, Reston, VA, 22092; 703/860-7211.

Indian Arts and Crafts Board provides guidance for purchasers of authentic Indian and Eskimo arts and crafts. Washington, DC, 20240; 202/343-2773.

National Park Service maintains a network of 300 natural, historical, and recreational areas for public campsites; lectures and tours by professional guides; boating and swimming facilities; and fire prevention and police protection. Washington, DC, 20240; 202/343-5731.

Inquiries, complaints or comments should be addressed to the previously listed units or Office of Communications, Department of the Interior, Washington, DC, 20240; 202/343-8331.

DEPARTMENT OF JUSTICE

The department is the principal law enforcement arm of the federal government. Through its prosecuting divisions and local United States Attorneys' offices, it enforces federal laws through criminal and civil prosecutions in federal courts. The Federal Bureau of Investigation is the department's principal investigating arm.

The department also enforces federal laws for consumer protection through cases referred to it by other agencies and enforces antitrust laws aimed at preventing restraints of trade and concentrations of economic power that may lead to monopoly and unfair pricing.

Alleged violations may be reported in writing to Office of Policy and Planning, Room 4236, Department of Justice, Washington, DC, 20530; 202/633-2000.

DEPARTMENT OF LABOR

Bureau of International Labor Affairs represents the interests of American workers in trade and tariff matters and administers a trade adjustment assistance program for workers adversely affected by import competition. 202/523-6259.

Bureau of Labor Statistics collects, analyzes and publishes data relating to wages, prices, productivity, employment and the performance of the nation's economy. Publishes a monthly Consumer Price Index. 202/523-1913.

Employment and Training Administration assists the unemployed or those seeking new or improved employment opportunities by providing training, placement services and unemployment compensation through a federal and state system. 202/376-6905.

Employment Standards Administration enforces laws and regulations by setting employment standards, providing workers' compensation to those injured on their jobs and requiring federal contractors to provide equal employment opportunity. Also seeks to upgrade the status of working women, minorities and the handicapped. 202/523-8743.

Labor-Management Services Administration enforces laws affecting certain activities of unions and private pensions and welfare benefit plans as well as veterans' re-employment rights. Also works to improve labor and management relations. 202/523-7408.

Occupational Safety and Health Administration sets and enforces job safety and health standards for workers. Trains employers and employees in proper occupational safety and health practices. Enforcement through regional and field investigations. 202/523-8151.

Inquiries or comments should be directed to regional or local offices of the respective units or to the office of information, Department of Labor, Washington, DC, 20210.

DEPARTMENT OF STATE

The department issues passports to U.S. nationals for use in travel to foreign countries. All first-time passport applications must be made in person before a Department of State passport agent, before a clerk of a federal court; clerk of a state court of record; a judge or clerk of any probate court; or certain postal employees as designated by the Postmaster of selected post offices. Passport agencies are in Boston, Chicago, Honolulu, Los Angeles, Miami, New Orleans, New York, Philadelphia, San Francisco, Seattle and Washington, DC. A person who has been issued a passport in his own name within the past eight years may, under certain circumstances, obtain a new passport by mail. Passport Office, 1425 K St. NW, Washington, DC, 20534; 202/783-8200.

DEPARTMENT OF TRANSPORTATION (DOT)

Coast Guard enforces federal laws on the high seas and navigable waters of the United States. The Coast Guard Auxiliary, a nonmilitary organization, provides, upon request, courtesy examination of boats for compliance with standards and requirements and offers courses in small boating. 202/426-1080.

Federal Aviation Administration establishes safety standards for air operation. Conducts research into all phases of aviation safety. 202/426-1960.

Federal Highway Administration is concerned with improvement and development of the total operation and environment of highway systems. 202/426-0585.

Federal Railroad Administration is responsible for a safe, efficient and progressive railroad system and oversees operation of the Alaskan Highway. 202/426-0881.

National Highway Traffic Safety Administration works to reduce highway deaths, injuries and property losses through enforcement of federal performance standards for cars, motorcycles, small trucks and vehicle equipment and development of highway safety standards. 202/426-0670.

Office of Consumer Affairs seeks to provide information to consumers that will enable them to become more knowledgeable buyers and users of transportation. 202/426-4518.

Urban Mass Transportation Administration assists communities throughout the country in meeting residents' needs for safe and efficient mass transit systems. 202/426-4043.

For information, write to the appropriate unit, Department of Transportation, Washington, DC, 20590 (FAA's Zip code is 20591).

DEPARTMENT OF THE TREASURY

Bureau of Alcohol, Tobacco and Firearms monitors content, labeling and reuse of alcoholic beverage containers and classification and labeling of tobacco products. Enforces and administers regulations for firearms and explosives. Washington, DC, 20226; 202/566-7777.

Internal Revenue Service provides taxpaper assistance. (Check your tax form for the address of offices or check your phone directory for local IRS numbers.) Offers education courses and bilingual assistance. Other problems can be directed to district and regional directors of IRS or to Commissioner, Internal Revenue Service, Washington, DC, 20224; 202/488-3100.

Comptroller of the Currency oversees the 4,600 national banks and controls a staff of 2,000 bank examiners who are responsible for auditing banks to insure financial solvency and to protect bank depositors. Consumers may contact regional administrators or Comptroller of the Currency, Washington, DC, 20219; 202/447-1600.

U.S. Customs clears all persons and merchandise entering the United States. Washington, DC, 20229; 202/566-8195.

U.S. Savings Bonds promotes the sale and retention of U.S. Savings Bonds and provides information on lost or destroyed bonds. Washington, DC, 20226; 202/634-5377. Local banks and regional U.S. Savings Bonds offices can also be of assistance.

NON-CABINET OFFICES

ACTION

Action is the nation's volunteer service agency consisting of six major programs:

Peace Corps is an international volunteer program in which Americans spend time (usually about two years) teaching or supplying needed skills to underdeveloped countries.

VISTA (Volunteers In Service To America) is a domestic volunteer service program, in which individuals live in low-income communities and teach new skills.

Foster Grandparents is a program for older Americans where senior citizens work with younger ones in mental institutions, hospitals and other institutions for the disadvantaged.

RSVP (Retired Service Volunteer Program) uses senior citizens' talents and experience in performing community service, such as consulting small business-persons.

Senior Companion Program is designed for senior citizens to give companionship to other older Americans in hospitals, nursing homes and other institutions.

University Year for Action sends college students into low-income communities for one year to perform needed services in exchange for academic credit.

For more information, write to Action, Washington, DC, 20525, or call toll-free 800/424-8580.

CIVIL AERONAUTICS BOARD (CAB)

Office of the Consumer Advocate handles consumer complaints against airlines, attempts to resolve consumer problems by contact with company involved, publishes monthly statistical reports detailing complaints received by the office and participates in Board proceedings. Civil Aeronautics Board, Washington, DC, 20428; 202/673-5990.

COMMISSION ON CIVIL RIGHTS

The commission's purpose is to encourage constructive steps toward equal opportunity for minority groups and women. It conducts fact-finding hearings, research and investigations relating to the denial of equal protection of the laws because of race, color, religion, sex or national origin. Topics of interest include: voting rights, employment, education, housing, administration of justice and the federal effort to further equal opportunity. It reports findings of facts and makes recommendations, but it has no enforcement authority. Washington, DC, 20425; 202/254-6600 or 202/254-7381.

COMMODITY FUTURES TRADING COMMISSION

Regulates trading of options on agricultural and metal futures. Registers firms selling options and investigates cases of fradulent operations. Has toll-free hot-line for information on buying futures, on the reputation of specific firms, and information on how to file a complaint against a firm. 2033 K St. NW, Washington, DC, 20581; 800/424-9383.

COMMUNITY SERVICES ADMINISTRATION

The federal anti-poverty agency, it sponsors five major programs:

Community Action Agencies are set up in nearly 900 communities. They are locally organized, nonprofit groups that conduct a wide variety of anti-poverty programs such as Head Start and manpower projects.

Office of Economic Development is responsible for funding community development corporations (CDCs) in economically depressed areas. CDCs organize businesses to provide programs such as job training and counselling.

Energy Conservation and Weatherization assists low-income homeowners to weatherize and insulate their homes by providing materials and training or labor.

Community Food and Nutrition supplements federal food stamp programs and funds projects such as community food gardens and food cooperatives. Assists individuals in applying for food stamps and other programs.

Senior Opportunity and Services is designed to create programs for senior citizens at the local levels, such as senior citizen centers and job-training.

For more information about CSA programs, write Office of Public Affairs, 1200 19th St. NW, Washington, DC, 20506; 202/254-5840.

CONSUMER PRODUCT SAFETY COMMISSION (CPSC)

The Consumer Product Safety Commission (CPSC) seeks to protect citizens against unreasonable risks associated with consumer products; to assist in evaluating the comparative safety of consumer products; to develop uniform safety standards for consumer products and minimize conflicting state and local regulations; and to promote research and investigations into product-related deaths, illnesses and injuries.

CPSC invites consumers to participate in the standards-setting procedures. A weekly Public Calendar which lists meetings, hearings and other notices of public interest can be obtained from the Office of the Secretary. Persons can have their names placed on the Consumer Roster in the Office of the Secretary, from which volunteers are selected to participate in CPSC activities. Citizens are encouraged to volunteer as Consumer Deputies to assist in surveys to identify unsafe products in stores. Consumers can submit petitions to the Office of the Secretary to begin proceedings to issue, amend or revoke a consumer product safety rule. To report complaints about the safety of a consumer product or product-related injuries, call toll-free: 800/638-2666 (in Maryland: 800/492-2937).

ENVIRONMENTAL PROTECTION AGENCY (EPA)

EPA's enforcement, standard setting, monitoring and research activities include: developing regulations for air pollution control, national standards for air quality and emission standards for hazardous pollutants; identifying and regulating noise sources and establishing control methods; maintaining a national surveillance and inspection program for measuring radiation levels in the environment; performing technical assistance for development, management and operation of solid waste management activities and for analysis on the recovery of useful energy and resources from solid waste; developing regulations for water pollution control and water quality standards and effluent guidelines; regulating pesticides and their use to assure human safety.

These functions are performed through technical assistance, guidance and support; training; grants; technical and public information materials and programs; legal and regulatory processes; and legal proceedings, such as conferences and public hearings. Requests for information may be addressed to: Office of Public Affairs, Washington, DC, 20460; 202/755-0700.

EQUAL EMPLOYMENT OPPORTUNITY COMMISSION (EEOC)

EEOC is responsible for guaranteeing equal opportunity for employment without regard to race, color, sex, religion or national origin. EEOC has jurisdiction over private employers and unions with 15 or more employees or members, agencies of state and local governments and public and private educational institutions, but not federal agencies.

EEOC investigates charges of discrimination. If facts show probable cause to believe that discrimination exists, EEOC attempts to persuade the employers to voluntarily eliminate that discrimination. If conciliation attempts fail, EEOC then files suit in federal courts. If persons feel they have been discriminated against in an employment situation, they should contact the nearest district office of the EEOC or: The Commissioner, EEOC, Washington, DC, 20506; 202/634-7040.

FEDERAL COMMUNICATIONS COMMISSION (FCC)

Regulates the number and type of radio and TV stations and cable television—also known as community antenna television services (CATV)— and licenses individual users. Sees that holders of licenses to operate radio and TV stations are responsive to needs of citizens in their geographic areas, that their broadcasts do not present only one side of public controversial issues, that their broadcasts observe reasonable standards as to length, number and loudness of commercials and that stations avoid broadcast of misleading advertising.

Regulates companies that provide interstate and foreign communications via wire, radio, cable or satellite to assure adequate facilities and reasonable rates. FCC does not have responsibility for telephone companies operating entirely in one state.

Grants licenses for other radio services, such as marine and aviation safety, police and fire, business radio and the citizens radio service. Insures that these licensees observe regulations concerning their operation.

Complaints concerning broadcasting stations should be directed to the Complaints Division, Broadcast Bureau; 202/632-7048. Cable television complaints to the Cable Complaint Service of the Special Relief and Microwave Division, Cable Television Bureau; 202/632-9703. Common carrier complaints to the Complaints and Services Standards Branch, Common Carrier Bureau; 202/932-7553.

Complaints about particular broadcast programs or practices should be made initially to the stations or firms involved. The Commission's Field Operations Bureau maintains offices open to the public in 28 cities where complaints may be filed and applications for radio licenses, commercial licenses and other information concerning the FCC may be obtained. For information, contact: Office of Public Information, Washington, DC, 20554; 202/632-7260.

FEDERAL DEPOSIT INSURANCE CORPORATION (FDIC)

FDIC's purpose is to protect depositors in the nation's banks, to help maintain confidence in the banking system and to promote sound banking practices. FDIC runs an insurance program to protect deposits of individuals up to $40,000 in member banks.

Office of Bank Customer Affairs serves and protects the interests of bank customers in state-chartered banks supervised and examined by the FDIC. This office receives all bank customer complaints and inquiries sent to FDIC and is responsible for prompt investigation and appropriate disposition of complaints. In addition, the Board of Directors proposes regulations and policy statements applicable to non-member banks in such areas as equal credit opportunity, fair housing lending, bank advertising practices and real estate settlement practices. On the recommendation of the Office of Bank Customer Affairs, the FDIC Board of Directors may institute formal enforcement actions against non-member banks where previous efforts at voluntary compliance with the requirements of "consumer legislation" or bank customer regulations and policy statements have been unsuccessful.

Complaints and inquiries regarding state-chartered, non-member banks should be directed to Office of Bank Customer Affairs, FDIC, Washington, DC, 20429; 202/389-4427.

FEDERAL HOME LOAN BANK BOARD (FHLBB)

The FHLBB is responsible for the operation of the Federal Home Loan Bank System, Federal Home Loan Mortgage Corp. (FHLMC) and Federal Savings and Loan Insurance Corp. (FSLIC). Savers in FSLIC-insured savings and loan associations are protected against loss up to a maximum of $40,000. Insurance of accounts—a major factor in obtaining and keeping accounts—can be terminated or withheld. Cease and desist orders may also be issued to stop unsound practices. Washington, DC, 20552; 202/377-6000.

FEDERAL MARITIME COMMISSION (FMC)

Assures that cargo moves as quickly, efficiently and economically as possible. Guards against and investigates cases of discrimination, excessively high or low rates and various other illegal activities. Assures financial responsibility of passenger vessels to protect passengers embarking at United States ports for failure to perform a voyage or for personal injury or death. Assists in environmental protection by determining the financial responsibility of vessel for the cost of cleaning up discharges of oil or hazardous substances in the waters of the United States. Regulates and licenses ocean freight forwarders, who provide for the transportation of commercial cargoes sold and bought by consumers, and private cargoes, such as household goods shipped by consumers.

FEDERAL RESERVE SYSTEM (FRS)

The Federal Reserve System, comprises the Board of Governors (also known as "the Fed"); the Federal Open Market Committee; 12 Federal Reserve Banks and their 25 branches; and some 5,800 banks, and their branches, which are members of the system. The FRS serves as the nation's central bank, whose main responsibilities are to regulate the flow of money and credit and to perform supervisory services and functions for the public, the U.S. Treasury and the commercial banks. The Board of Governors is responsible for issuing regulations implementing several titles of the Consumer Credit Protection Act to prohibit discrimination in credit transactions on the basis of sex or marital status. Another title is the Truth in Lending Act, relating to consumer credit cost disclosures. The board also has responsibility for writing rules relating to unfair or deceptive acts or practices by banks. The responsibility for enforcement of these regulations is split among federal agencies. The Board's specific responsibility for enforcement is limited to state chartered banks that are members of the FRS. In addition, the Board has responsibility for enforcement of the Fair Credit Reporting Act. Federal Reserve System, Washington, DC, 20551; 202/452-3204.

FEDERAL TRADE COMMISSION (FTC)

Enforces antitrust laws and acts to curb deceptive advertising, packaging and selling. Assures truthful labels on textile products. Requires proper disclosures in credit transactions. In performing these functions, the FTC monitors television, radio and printed advertisements for possible deception and fraud; investigates complaints of false advertising, oral misrepresentation, misbranding, restraint of trade and unfair business practices; holds industry conferences and issues advisory opinions and guidelines designed to achieve voluntary observance of the law through improved business practices; makes economic studies of anti-competitive practices where they are found to exist. Consumer education activities are conducted through regional offices. Consumer protection specialists provide guidance to business, consumers, consumer groups and state and local officials as to the requirements of the laws prohibiting false advertising, misrepresentation and other deceptive acts and practices and unfair restraints of trade.

Anyone accused by the FTC of using an unlawful practice may agree to a consent order and stop the practice without admitting any violation of law. If an agreement to a consent order is not made, the FTC may issue a formal complaint and hearings would be held before an administrative law judge who makes an initial decision. A respondent may appeal an adverse decision to the full Commission. Violation of an FTC order carries a potential $10,000 fine for each violation each day.

While the FTC is not empowered to seek refunds or adjustments in individual consumer matters, the Magnuson-Moss Warranty-Federal Trade Commission Improvement Act of 1975 authorizes the FTC to obtain refund of money lost, sue for damages, legal termination of contracts or reformation. The FTC may adopt Trade Regulations Rules (after appropriate public hearings) that have the force of law. The FTC also has the power to obtain civil penalties and consumer redress in situations other than violations of a specific trade regulation.

Anyone can file a complaint with the FTC. As much supporting evidence as possible should accompany the complaint, which should be directed to: Secretary, Federal Trade Commission, Washington, DC, 20580; 202/523-3625.

GENERAL SERVICES ADMINISTRATION (GSA)

GSA is the government's "housekeeper." It buys food, buildings, cars, etc.

It also stockpiles strategic and critical materials for use in national emergencies; disposes of surplus land and personal property to organizations and consumers; coordinates the federal government's civil emergency preparedness program; runs the federal data processing and telecommunications programs; and distributes federal information for consumers.

Consumer Information Center collects information useful to consumers and makes recommendations for new publications of consumer interest. This information is listed in a quarterly catalog, *Consumer Information*. The catalog lists hundreds of publications, many of which are free. The center also provides information through press releases to newspapers and magazines, through monthly scripts for broadcasters and through occasional public service announcements to radio and television stations. For a free *Consumer Information Catalog,* write Consumer Information Center, Pueblo, CO, 81009.

Federal Information Centers provide information to consumers on all aspects of the federal government. FIC offices are located around the country. Consumers can get information by making a local phone call. The FIC information service helps consumers to locate the right agency—usually federal, but sometimes state and local agencies—for help with their problems. Washington, DC, 20269; 202/755-8660.

GOVERNMENT PRINTING OFFICE (GPO)
Operates 24 bookstores throughout the country and supplies 1,18? Depository Libraries with copies of federal government publications for public use. All inquiries and orders should be addressed to the Superintendent of Documents, U.S. Government Printing Office, Washington, DC, 20402. Information on the price and availability of publications may be obtained from the order desk by telephone: 202/783-3238. Complaints or inquiries on orders for publications or subscriptions should be addressed to the Customer Information Branch Services Section, Government Printing Office, Stop SSO, Washington DC, 20401; 202/275-3050. All inquiries, complaints or suggestions relating to the overall GPO operation should be addressed to Special Assistant to the Public Printer, U.S. Government Printing Office, Stop P, Washington, DC, 20401 202/275-2958.

INTERSTATE COMMERCE COMMISSION (ICC)
The ICC regulates operating certification, rates, finance and control of interstate railroads, trucks, buses, barges, ships, oil pipelines, express delivery companies and freight forwarders. It also seeks to ensure that regulated carriers provide consumers with adequate transportation service at reasonable charges under fair and equitable conditions. Requires carriers to maintain proper insurance for the protection of the public. Of direct concern to consumers are ICC rules for moving household goods, complaint procedures for railroad and bus passengers public disclosure of carriers' rates and fares, discontinuance of rail passenger service, abandonment of tracks and settlement of loss and damage claims Washington, DC, 20423; 202/343-4761. Toll-free hotline: 800/424-9312. Report complaints to ICC headquarters in Washington, DC, or to field offices in principal cities.

LIBRARY OF CONGRESS

Books and other reference material are available for use by the public in the Library's 16 reading rooms. When consumers cannot obtain a certain book in a local library, the local library may borrow the book from the Library of Congress through the inter-library service.

The **Division for the Blind and Physically Handicapped,** in cooperation with 54 regional libraries, administers a national program supplying Braille and "talking" (recorded) books and recorded tape cassettes to those who cannot read conventional print.

Consumers may register their personal creative works (such as books and music) with the Library's **Copyright Office.** The **Science and Technology Division** answers brief technical inquiries entailing a bibliographic response. This division also provides free referral service through its **National Referral Center for Science and Technology** by directing those who have a question concerning a particular subject to organizations or individuals that can provide the answer.

The **General Reference and Bibliography Division** answers written inquiries, insofar as the pressures on staff permit, to consumers who have exhausted local, state and regional reference sources. Consumers requiring services that cannot be provided by the Library will be supplied with the names of private researchers who can do the work on a fee basis. Other activities include a continuing series of exhibitions, literary programs and concerts that the public may attend free of charge. Some of its literary and musical programs are broadcast in other cities.

Guides to the use of the Library and information on its services may be obtained from the Publications Distribution Unit, Central Services Division, Library of Congress, Washington, DC, 20504; 202/426-5000. Division for the Blind and Physically Handicapped, 1291 Taylor St. NW, Washington, DC, 20542; 202/426-5100. Copyright Office, Crystal Mall, 1921 Jefferson Davis Highway, Arlington, VA, 20559; 703/557-8700. General Reading Division, (state reference topic, such as U.S. History), Library of Congress, Washington, DC, 20540; 202/426-5530.

NATIONAL CREDIT UNION ADMINISTRATION (NCUA)

Grants federal charters to qualified groups and supervises and examines established federal credit unions throughout the country. Insures accounts of all federal credit unions and of those state chartered credit unions that want such coverage. For information about forming a credit union and getting a federal charter and for other questions, complaints or comments, contact National Credit Union Administration, Washington, DC, 20056; 202/254-9800.

NUCLEAR REGULATORY COMMISSION

Oversees licensing, construction and safety of nuclear-powered electric generating plants, and all other non-military uses of nuclear energy, such as radio isotopes used in medical diagnosis and other scientific uses. Holds hearings on issues of safety, environmental impact, waste storage and other aspects of nuclear power. Inquiries and complaints should be made to Office of Public Affairs, Washington, DC, 20555; 202/492-7715.

PENSION BENEFIT GUARANTY CORPORATION (PBGC)

PBGC insures basic vested benefits—within statutory limits—of participants

GOVERNMENT CONSUMER PUBLICATIONS

The federal government, through the General Services Administration, has available hundreds of useful publications, many of them free. Subjects include Automobiles, Budget, Children, Clothing, Consumer Education, Food, Health, Housing, Insurance, Landscaping, Recreation and Senior Citizens.

A free quarterly list of publications is available in both English and Spanish. Write to: Consumer Information, Pueblo, CO, 81009.

in defined benefit pension plans (plans containing a formula by which any participant can calculate what he will receive when he retires—such as $10 a month for life times the number of years he worked for a company). PBGC can order the appointment of a trustee for a plan that appears financially unsound. PBGC advises consumers who are interested in establishing Individual Retirement Accounts (IRAs). Washington, DC, 20006; 202/254-4817.

U.S. POSTAL SERVICE (USPS)

Provides mail service; insures valuables sent through the mail; sells U.S. Savings Bonds in small communities where no other facilities are available; sells postal money orders; processes passport applications.

Operates the Postal Inspection Service to enforce postal laws, protecting postal customers from dangerous articles, contraband, fraud and pornography. Through its Consumer Protection Program, the Postal Inspection Service acts to resolve unsatisfactory mail-order transactions even where no fraud has occurred.

Report unresolved mail service complaints to Consumer Advocate, U.S. Postal Service, Washington, DC, 20260; 202/245-4514. Report suspected postal violations, including failure to receive ordered merchandise, to your local postmaster or the Chief Postal Inspector, U.S. Postal Service, Washington, DC, 20260; 202/245-4514.

SECURITIES AND EXCHANGE COMMISSION (SEC)

Protects the public in the investment and trading of securities by requiring disclosure of information by companies having publicly held securities, overseeing the operations of the securities markets and taking enforcement action through court actions or administrative proceedings or both. Reviews complaints about stock and bond sales (not the value of securities or market fluctuations) and provides assistance in the identification of possible corrective action.

Complaints may be submitted to: Office of Investor Services, SEC, Washington, DC, 20549; 202/523-5516. Education publications and other information may be obtained from Office of Public Information, SEC, Washington, DC, 20549; 202/755-4846.

SMALL BUSINESS ADMINISTRATION (SBA)

Insures that small business concerns receive a fair share of government contracts, subcontracts and property. Makes loans to small firms, state and local development companies and victims of floods and other disasters. Licenses, regulates and lends to small business investment companies. Improves management skills of small business owners. Contact nearest SBA office or Office of Public Information, SBA, Washington, DC, 20416; 202/655-4000.

VETERANS ADMINISTRATION (VA)

Provides medical care, home nursing care, out-patient medical and dental care and prosthetic devices to eligible veterans and dependents. Provides funds for educational assistance to qualified veterans, orphans and widows of veterans, children and wives of certain seriously disabled veterans and certain categories of active duty personnel. Provides monthly compensation for service-connected disability and monthly pension for nonservice-connected disability if it is total and permanent.

Provides monthly compensation or pension to qualified dependents of living or deceased veterans. Provides loan guarantees ("GI loans") or, in certain conditions, direct loans, to qualified veterans for purchase of houses, condominiums and mobile homes. Provides burial in national cemetaries, grave and memorial headstones or markers, funds toward costs of burial in non-national cemetaries and flags for eligible veterans and their dependents. Administers five life insurance programs for veterans, makes loans on permanent plan policies, and pays insurance disability benefits to beneficiaries.

SMALL CLAIMS COURTS
Justice for the Little Guy

By 1979, every state had some type of court procedure designed to settle small claims. All but eight states had a separate system of informal small claims courts, while five had such courts only for certain urban areas, according to a study done by John C. Ruhnka and Steven Weller of the National Center for State Courts in Williamsburg, Va.

States without a separate system of informal courts are Arizona, Delaware, Louisiana, Mississippi, South Carolina, Tennessee, Virginia and West Virginia. States where such courts are only in designated urban areas are Arkansas, Georgia, Kentucky, Montana and New Mexico. (See table for further details.)

Small claims courts originated over 50 years ago to provide simplified settlement systems for wage earners and small businesses to collect wages or accounts due them. The essence of the procedure was and is informality, including little or no paper work, waiver of trial procedures and rules of evidence and no requirement for a formal answer from a defendant beyond appearing in court.

Although such courts give the consumer or business an opportunity to achieve justice, the courts have frequently found their calendars crowded by corporations, collection agencies and loan companies. Furthermore, while a litigant or defendant need not be represented by an attorney, those who find themselves opposed by an attorney face uneven odds.

Among recent reform efforts reported by Ruhnka and Weller are the barring of assignees and collection agencies, limitation on the use of attorneys at trials, use of paralegals or law students to help litigants and more workable methods of collection.

The 1979 edition of a book first published in 1978 by Nolo Press (P.O. Box 544, Occidental, CA, 95465. Price $5.95) offers practical guidance for handling small claims cases in each state. The 236-page paperback is entitled: "Everybody's Guide to Small Claims Court." Author is Ralph Warner.

SMALL CLAIMS COURTS

State	Type of Court	Maximum Claim	Minimum Age	Lawyers: Permitted/or Required	Appeals Permitted by Plaintiff	Defendant	Typical Filing and Service Costs
Alabama	Small Claims	$500	21	Permitted	yes	yes	$10-$15
Alaska	Small Claims	1000	18	Corps: Required Others: Permitted	yes	yes	7-15
Arizona	Justice Court	999	21	Corps: Required Others: Permitted	yes	yes	3-6
Arkansas	Municipal Court	100-300	(12)	Permitted	yes	yes	3-10
California	Small Claims	750	(13)	Not permitted	no	yes	2-5
Colorado	Small Claims	500	18	Not permitted	yes	yes	7-10
Connecticut	Common Pleas	750	21	Permitted	no	no	6-15
Delaware	Justice of Peace	1500	19	Permitted	yes	yes	10
District of Columbia	Small Claims	750	21	Permitted[1]	yes	yes	2-10
Florida	Small Claims	1500-2500[14]		Permitted	yes	yes	5-10
Georgia	Small Claims or Justice of Peace	200-300	18	Permitted	(2)	(2)	2-15
Hawaii	Small Claims	300	21	Permitted[3]	no	no	7
Idaho	Small Claims	500	21	Not permitted	yes	yes	5-10
Illinois	Small Claims (State)	1000	18	Corps: Required Others: Permitted	yes	yes	7-11
	Cook County[4]	300					
Indiana	Small Claims	3000	21	Corps: Required Others: Permitted	yes	yes	6-10
Iowa	District Court	1000	19	Permitted	yes	yes	3-5
Kansas	Small Claims	300	18	Not permitted	yes	yes	10
Kentucky	Small Claims[5]	500	18	Permitted	yes	yes	6.50
Louisiana	City Courts	25	21	Permitted	no	no	10-20
	Justice of Peace	300					
Maine	Small Claims	800	21	Permitted	yes	yes	5
Maryland	District Court	500	21	Permitted	yes	yes	5-10
Massachusetts	Small Claims	400	21	Permitted	no	yes	2-3
Michigan	Small Claims	300	21	Not Permitted	no	no	7-12
Minnesota	Conciliation Court	500-1000	21	Not permitted[9]	yes	yes	3

State	Court	Amount	Min. Age	Lawyers			
Missouri	Small Claims	500	21	Permitted	yes	yes	9-11
Montana	District Court	1500	19	Permitted	yes	yes	2.50
Nebraska	Small Claims	500	19	Not permitted	yes	yes	4
Nevada	Small Claims	300	(12)	Permitted	yes	yes	5-7
New Hampshire	Small Claims	500	21	Permitted	yes	yes	3
New Jersey	Small Claims	500	21	Permitted	yes	yes	3-5
New Mexico	Small Claims[6]	2000	18	Permitted	yes	yes	6-14
New York	Small Claims	1000	21	Permitted[7]	yes	yes	3-4
North Carolina	Small Claims	500	18	Permitted	yes	yes	7-12
North Dakota	Small Claims	200-500	18	Permitted	no	no	3
Ohio	Small Claims	300	21	Permitted	yes	yes	2.75
Oklahoma	Small Claims	600	(12)	Permitted	yes	yes	5-10
Oregon	Small Claims	500	21	Not permitted[8]	no	yes	15
Pennsylvania	Small Claims	1000	None	Permitted	yes	yes	6-12
Rhode Island	Small Claims	300	21	Corps: Required / Others: Permitted	no	yes	2
South Carolina	Magistrate Court	200-3000	21	Permitted	yes	yes	varies
South Dakota	Magistrate Court	1000	18	Permitted	no	no	2-4
Tennessee	Justice of Peace	3000	18	Permitted	yes[10]	yes	25 bond
Texas	Small Claims	150-200	18	Permitted	yes[10]	yes[10]	5-8
Utah	Small Claims	200	(12)	Permitted	no	yes	5-7
Vermont	Small Claims	250	18	Permitted	(10)	yes	3-6
Virginia	District Court	5000	None	Permitted	(10)	(10)	3-5
Washington	Small Claims	300	18	Not permitted	no	(11)	3-5
West Virginia	Magistrate Court	1500	18	Permitted	yes	yes	7.50
Wisconsin	Small Claims	500	21	Permitted	yes	yes	5-7
Wyoming	Justice of Peace	200	21	Permitted	yes	yes	2-6

[1] Law students allowed to represent parties; [2] Appeals allowed only for amounts over $50; [3] Lawyers not permitted in security deposit cases; [4] Lawyers not permitted in Cook Co. Pro Se Court. Corporations, partnerships and associations not permitted to use court; [5] In Jefferson Co., Consumer Court, for consumer plaintiffs only; [6] Small Claims Court in Albuquerque only; [7] Corporations, assignees, partnerships, associations and insurers not permitted as plaintiffs; [8] Lawyers may appear only with consent of judge; [9] Lawyer permitted in Minneapolis and St. Paul only; [10] Appeals allowed only for amounts over $20; [11] Appeals allowed only for amounts over $100; [12] Minimum age is 18 for females, 21 for males; [13] Minimum age 18 for married individuals, 21 for single individuals; [14] Lawyer required for claim over $1,500.

Source: Dept. of Policy Research, Yegge, Hall & Evans, Denver, CO, 80202.

STATE LAWS GOVERNING DECEPTIVE AND UNFAIR TRADE PRACTICES

State	(a) Restitution	(b) Civil Penalties	(c) Class Actions	(d) Private Actions	(e) Rules and Regulations
Alabama(f)					
Alaska	X	X	X	X	X
Arizona	X	X		X	
Arkansas	X				
California		X	X	X	
Colorado	X			X	
Connecticut	X	X	X	X	X
Delaware	X				X
D.C.	X	X		X	
Florida	X			X	X
Georgia	X	X		X	X
Hawaii	X	X		X	X
Idaho	X			X	X
Illinois	X	X		X	X
Indiana	X		X	X	
Iowa	X				X
Kansas	X	X	X	X	
Kentucky	X	X		X	
Louisiana	X			X	X
Maine				X	X
Maryland	X	X		X	X
Massachusetts	X		X	X	X
Michigan	X	X	X	X	X
Minnesota	X	X		X	X
Mississippi	X	X		X	
Missouri	X		X	X	
Montana	X	X		X	X
Nebraska	X			X	
Nevada	X	X		X	X
New Hampshire	X	X	X	X	X
New Jersey	X	X	X	X	X
New Mexico	X	X			X
New York	X	X	X		
N. Carolina	X			X	
North Dakota	X				X
Ohio	X		X	X	
Oklahoma	X				
Oregon	X	X	X	X	X
Pennsylvania	X	X		X	X
Rhode Island	X		X	X	
S. Carolina	X	X		X	X
S. Dakota	X	X		X	X
Tennessee	X			X	
Texas	X	X	X	X	
Utah	X		X	X	X
Vermont	X	X		X	X
Virginia				X	
Washington	X	X		X	
West Virginia				X	
Wisconsin	X	X		X	X
Wyoming			X	X	

(a) Restitution may be obtained by the administering of enforcement official on behalf of consumers. (b) Civil penalties may be assessed for violations. (c) Class action suits by consumers are authorized. (d) Private actions by consumers, sometimes including minimum recovery of $100 or $200, sometimes including double, treble or punitive damages, and usually including costs and attorney fees, are authorized. (e) Rules and regulations are authorized to be issued for implementing statutes similar to the Federal Trade Commission Act. (f) Alabama does not have deceptive trade laws, but has consumer complaint clearinghouses to facilitate the taking of action under existing laws and to recommend new legislation.
Source: Federal Trade Commission, 1979

STATE CONSUMER OFFICES
With Addresses and Telephone Numbers

ALABAMA. State Offices: GENERAL: Governor's Office of Consumer Protection, 138 Adams Ave., Montgomery, AL, 36130; 205/832-5936; 800/392-5658. Office of Attorney General, 669 S. Lawrence St., Montgomery, AL, 36104; 205/834-5150. AGING: Commission on Aging, 740 Madison Ave., Montgomery, AL, 36104; 205/832-6640. BANKING AND CREDIT: Superintendent of Banks, 64 North Union St., Room 651 Montgomery, AL, 36130; 205/832-6256. ENERGY: Alabama Energy Management Board, Montgomery, AL, 36130; 205/832-5010. INSURANCE: Commissioner of Insurance, Administration Bldg., Montgomery, AL, 36104; 205/832-6140. TRANSPORTATION/UTILITIES: Alabama Public Service Commission, P.O. Box 991, Montgomery, AL, 36130; 205/832-3421 and 603 Frank Nelson Bldg., Birmingham, AL, 35203; 205/251-2881.

ALASKA. State Offices: GENERAL: Office of Attorney General, 420 L St., Suite 100, Anchorage, AK, 99501; 907/276-3550. Branch Offices: 604 Barnette, P.O. Box 1309, Fairbanks, AK, 99701; 907/456-8588 and Pouch K, State Capitol, Juneau, AK, 99801; 907/586-5931. AGING: Office on Aging, Department of Health and Social Services, Pouch H, Juneau, AK, 99811; 907/586-6153. BANKING AND CREDIT: Director of Banking and Securities, Pouch D, Juneau, AK, 99801, 907/465-2521. ENERGY: State Energy Office, Mackay Bldg., 338 Denali St., Anchorage, AK, 99501; 907/272-0527. INSURANCE: Director of Insurance, Pouch D, Juneau, AK, 99801; 907/465-2515. TRANSPORTATION/UTILITIES: Alaska Transportation Commission, 1000 MacKay Bldg., 338 Denali St., Anchorage, AK, 95501; 907/279-1451. Alaska Public Utilities Commission, 1100 MacKay Bldg., 338 Denali St., Anchorage, AK, 99501; 907/276-6222. Consumer Protection Section, 420 L St., Suite 100, Anchorage, AK, 99501; 907/279-0428.

ARIZONA. State Offices: GENERAL: Economic Protection Division, Department of Law, 200 State Capitol Bldg., Phoenix, AZ, 85007; 602/255-5763. Branch Office: Economic Protection Division, 100 N. Stone Ave., Suite 1004, Tucson, AZ, 85701; 602/882-5501. AGING: Bureau on Aging, 543 E. McDowell, Rm. 217, Phoenix, AZ, 85004; 602/271-4446. BANKING AND CREDIT: Commerce Bldg., Rm. 101, 1601 W. Jefferson St., Phoenix, AZ, 85007. ENERGY: Office of Economic Planning and Development, Capitol Tower, Rm. 507, Phoenix, AZ, 85007; 602/271-3303. INSURANCE: Director of Insurance, 1601 W. Jefferson, Phoenix, AZ, 85007; 602/271-4862. TRANSPORTATION/UTILITIES: Arizona Corporation Commission, 2222 W. Encanto Blvd., Phoenix, AZ, 85009; 602/271-3624. Economic Protection Division, Office of Attorney General, State Capitol, Phoenix, AZ, 85007; 602/255-5763.

ARKANSAS. State Offices: GENERAL: Consumer Protection Division, Justice Bldg., Little Rock, AR, 72201; 501/371-2341 and 800/482-8982. AGING: Office on Aging and Adult Services, 7107 W. 12th, P.O. Box 2179, Little Rock, AR, 72203; 501/371-2441. BANKING AND CREDIT: State Bank Commissioner, University Tower Bldg., Suite 200, Little Rock, AR, 72204; 501/371-1117. ENERGY: Energy Conservation and Policy Office, 960 Plaza West Bldg., Little Rock, AR, 72205; 501/371-1370. INSURANCE: Insurance

Commissioner, 400-18 University Tower Bldg., Little Rock, AR, 72204; 501/371-1325. Consumer Affairs Coordinator, Department of Insurance, 12th and University, Little Rock, AR, 72204; 501/371-1811. TRANS-PORTATION/UTILITIES: Arkansas Public Service Commission, Justice Bldg., Little Rock, AR, 72201; 501/371-1451. Arkansas Transportation Commission, Justice Bldg., Little Rock, AR, 72201; 501/371-1341. Division of Energy Conservation and Rate Advocacy, Suite 122, National Old Line Bldg., Little Rock, AR, 72201; 501/371-1967. Office of Attorney General, Justice Bldg., Little Rock, AR, 72201; 501/371-1967.

CALIFORNIA. State Offices: GENERAL: Department of Consumer Affairs, 1020 N St., Sacramento, CA, 95814; 916/445-0660 and 800/952-5210. Branch Offices: 107 S. Broadway, Rm. 8020, Los Angeles, CA, 90012; 213/620-2003 and 30 Van Ness Ave., Rm. 2100, San Francisco, CA, 92104; 415/557-2046. Public Inquiry Unit, Office of Attorney General, 555 Capitol Mall, Sacramento, CA, 95814; 800/952-5225. AUTOMOBILES: Dept. of Consumer Affairs, 1020 N St., Sacramento, CA, 95814; 800/952-5210. AGING: Department of Aging, Health and Welfare Agency, 918 J St., Sacramento, CA, 95814; 916/322-3887. BANKING AND CREDIT: Superintendent of Banks, 235 Montgomery St., Suite 750, San Francisco, CA, 94104; 415/557-3535. ENERGY: California Energy Commission, 1111 Howe Ave., Sacramento, CA, 95825; 916/920-6811, 800/852-7516. INSURANCE: Insurance Commissioner, 600 S. Commonwealth, Los Angeles, CA, 90005; 213/736-2551. TRANS-PORTATION/UTILITIES: California Public Utilities Commission, 350 McAllister St., San Francisco, CA, 94102; 415/557-1487.

COLORADO. State Offices: GENERAL: Assistant Attorney General, 1525 Sherman St., 3rd Floor, Denver, CO, 80203; 303/839-3611. Consumer and Food Specialist, 1525 Sherman St., Denver, CO, 80203; 303/839-2811. Uniform Consumer Credit Code, 1525 Sherman St., 3rd Floor, Denver, CO, 80203; 303/839-3611. AGING: Division of Services for the Aging, 1575 Sherman St., Denver, CO, 80203; 303/892-2651. BANKING AND CREDIT: State Bank Commissioner, State Office Bldg., Rm. 325, Denver, CO, 80203; 303/839-3131. ENERGY: State Energy Office, State Capitol, Denver, CO, 80203; 303/839-2507. INSURANCE: Commissioner of Insurance, 106 State Office Bldg., Denver, CO, 80203; 303/839-3201. TRANS-PORTATION/UTILITIES: Colorado Public Utilities Commission, 500 State Services Bldg., 1525 Sherman St., Denver, CO, 80203; 303/839-3154.

CONNECTICUT. State Offices: GENERAL: Department of Consumer Protection, State Office Bldg., Hartford, CT, 06115; 203/566-4999 and 800/842-2649. Consumer Protection, Rm. 177 State Office Bldg., Hartford, CT, 06115; 203/566-3035. AGING: Department on Aging, 90 Washington St., Rm. 312, Hartford, CT, 06115; 203/566-7725. BANKING AND CREDIT: Bank Commissioner, State Office Bldg., Rm. 239, Hartford, CT, 06115; 203/566-7580. ENERGY: Energy Division, 80 Washington St., Hartford, CT, 06115; 203/566-2800. INSURANCE: Insurance Commissioner, Rm. 425 State Office Bldg., Hartford, CT, 06115; 203/566-5275. TRANSPORTATION/UTILITIES: Connecticut Public Utilities Control Authority, 165 Capitol Ave., Hartford, CT, 06115; 203/566-7384. Division of Consumer Counsel of Connecticut, Rm. 545

State Office Bldg., 165 Capitol Ave., Hartford, CT, 06115; 203/566-7287. Public Utilities Control Authority, 165 Capitol Ave., State Office Bldg., Hartford, CT, 06115; 203/566-7287.

DELAWARE. State Offices: GENERAL: Consumer Affairs Division, 820 N. French St., 4th Floor, Wilmington, DE, 19801; 302/571-3250. Department of Justice, 820 N. French St., Wilmington, DE, 19801; 302/571-2500. AGING: Division of Aging, 2413 Lancaster Ave., Wilmington, DE, 19805; 302/571-3481. BANKING AND CREDIT: State Bank Commissioner, 15 The Green, Kirk Bldg., Dover, DE, 19901; 302/678-4235. ENERGY: Energy Affairs, P.O. Box 1401 - Townsend Bldg., Dover, DE, 19901; INSURANCE: Insurance Commissioner, 21 The Green, Dover, DE, 19901; 302/678-4251. TRANS-PORTATION/UTILITIES: Delaware Public Service Commission, 1560 S. DuPont Highway, Dover, DE, 19901; 302/678-4247. Office of Public Advocate, 820 N. French St., 4th Floor, Wilmington, DE, 19801; 302/571-3250.

DISTRICT OF COLUMBIA. State Offices: GENERAL: D.C. Office of Consumer Protection, 1407 "L" St., NW, Washington, D.C., 20005; 202/727-1308. Office of the People's Counsel of the District of Columbia, 917 15th St., NW, 10th Floor, Washington, D.C., 20005; 202/727-3071. AGING: Office of Aging, Suite 1106, 1012 14th St., NW, Washington, D.C., 20005; 202/724-5623. ENERGY: Municipal Planning Office, Rm. 409, District Bldg., 13th & E Sts., NW, Washington, D.C., 20004; 202/629-5111. INSURANCE: Superintendent of Insurance, 614 H St., NW, Suite 512, Washington, D.C., 20001; 202/727-1273. TRANSPORTATION/UTILITIES: District of Columbia Public Service Commission, 1625 I St., NW, Washington, D.C., 20006; 202/727-1000.

FLORIDA. State Offices: GENERAL: Division of Consumer Services, 110 Mayo Bldg., Tallahassee, FL, 32304; 904/488-2221 and 800/342-2176. Consumer Protection and Fair Trade Practices Bureau, Department of Legal Affairs, State Capitol, Tallahassee, FL, 32304; 904/488-8916. Branch Offices: County Regional Service Center, 401 NW 2nd Ave., Suite 820, Miami, FL, 33128; 305/377-5441. Assistant Attorney General, 1313 Tampa St., 8th Floor, Park Trammell, Tampa, FL, 33602; 813/...272...2670. **State Offices:** Office of Public Counsel, Holland Bldg., Rm. 4, Tallahassee, FL, 32304; 904/488-9330. Department of Business Regulation, The Johns Bldg., Tallahassee, FL, 32304; 904/488-9820. AGING: Program Office of Aging and Adult Services, 1323 Winewood Blvd., Tallahassee, FL, 32301; 904/488-2650. BANKING AND CREDIT: Comptroller of Florida, State Capitol Bldg., Tallahassee, FL, 32304; 904/488-0370. ENERGY: State Energy Office, 108 Collins Bldg., Tallahassee, FL, 32304; 904/488-6764. INSURANCE: Insurance Commissioner, State Capitol, Tallahassee, FL, 32304; 904/488-7056. Bureau of Consumer Research and Education, State Capitol, Suite 53, Tallahassee, FL, 32304; 904/488-6085. TRANSPORTATION/UTILITIES: Florida Public Service Commission, 700 S. Adams St., Tallahassee, FL, 32304; 904/488-1234. Public Counsel of Florida, Rm. 4, The Holland Bldg., Tallahassee, FL, 32304; 904/488-9330. Public Service Commission, The Fletcher Bldg., Tallahassee, FL, 32304; 904/488-7238 and 800/342-3552.

GEORGIA. State Offices: GENERAL: Governor's Office of Consumer Affairs, 225 Peachtree St., NE, Suite 400, Atlanta, GA, 30303; 404/656-4900 and 800/282-4900. Deceptive Practices, 132 State Judicial Bldg., Atlanta, GA, 30334; 404/656-3391. BANKING AND CREDIT: Commissioner of Banking and Finance, 148 International Blvd. NE, Suite 640, Atlanta, GA, 30303; 404/656-2050. ENERGY: Office of Planning & Budget, 270 Washington St., SW, Atlanta, GA, 30334; 404/656-3874. INSURANCE: Insurance Commissioner, 238 State Capitol, Atlanta, GA, 30334; 404/656-2056. TRANSPORTATION/UTILITIES: Georgia Public Service Commission, 162 State Office Bldg., 244 Washington St., SW, Atlanta, GA, 30334; 404/656-4501. Consumers' Utility Counsel of Georgia, 15 Peachtree, Suite 933, Atlanta, GA, 30303; 404/656-3982.

HAWAII. State Offices: GENERAL: Consumer Protection, 250 S. King St., P.O. Box 3767, Honolulu, HI, 96811; 800/548-2560 and 800/548-2540. AGING: Executive Office on Aging, 1149 Bethel St., Rm. 311, Honolulu, HI, 96813; 808/548-2593. BANKING AND CREDIT: Regulatory Agencies, P.O. Box 541, Honolulu, HI, 96809; 808/548-7505. ENERGY: Department of Planning and Economic Development, P.O. Box 2359, Honolulu, HI, 96804; INSURANCE: Insurance Commissioner, P.O. Box 3614, Honolulu, HI, 96811; 800/548-7505. TRANSPORTATION/UTILITIES: Hawaii Public Utilities Commission, 1164 Bishop St., Suite 911, Honolulu, HI, 96813; 800/548-3990. Public Utilities Division, 1010 Richards St., Honolulu, HI, 96813; 800/548-7550.

IDAHO. State Offices: GENERAL: Consumer Protection Division, State Capitol, Boise, ID, 83720; 208/384-2400 and 800/632-5937. AGING: Idaho Office on Aging, Statehouse, Boise, ID, 83720; 208/384-3833. BANKING AND CREDIT: Director of Finance, Statehouse Mail, Boise, ID, 83720; 208/384-3313. ENERGY: Idaho Office of Energy, State House, Boise, ID, 83720; 208/384-3258. INSURANCE: Director of Insurance, 700 W. State St., Boise, ID, 83720; 208/384-2250. TRANSPORTATION/UTILITIES: Idaho Public Utilities Commission, State House, Boise, ID, 83720; 208/384-3143. Idaho Electrical Consumers Office, State House, Boise, ID, 83720; 208/384-2964.

ILLINOIS. State Offices: GENERAL: Consumer Advocate Office, 160 N. LaSalle St., Rm. 2010, Chicago, IL, 60601; 312/793-2754. Consumer Fraud Section, 228 N. LaSalle St., Rm. 1242, Chicago, IL, 60601; 312/793-3580. Branch Offices: 2151 Madison, Bellwood, IL, 60104; 312/344-7700. 50 Raupp Blvd., Buffalo Grove, IL, 60090; 312/459-2500. 1104 N. Ashlaw Ave., Chicago, IL, 60622; 312/793-5638. 4750 N. Broadway, Rm. 216, Chicago, IL, 60640; 312/769-3742. 7906 S. Cottage Grove, Chicago, IL, 60619; 312/488-2600. 800 Lee St., Des Plaines, IL, 60016; 312/824-4200. 901 Wellington St., Elk Grove Village, IL, 60007; 312/439-3900. Evanston Library, 1703 Orrington, Evanston, IL, 60204; 312/475-6700. P.O. Box 752, 71 N. Ottawa St., Joliet, IL, 60434; 815/727-3019. 1603 North Ave., McHenry, IL, 60050; 815/385-1703. 6300 N. Lincoln Ave., Morton Grove, IL, 60050; 312/967-4100. 1000 Schaumberg Rd., 217 S.Civic Dr., Schaumberg, IL, 60172; 312/884-7710. 5127 Oakton St., Skokie, IL, 60077; 312/674-2522. Consumer Protection Division, 500 S. Second St., Springfield, IL, 62706; 217/782-9011. 103 S. Washington, Suite 12, Carbondale, IL, 62901; 618/457-7831. 818 Martin Luther King Dr., E. St. Louis, IL, 62201; 618/874-2238. 500 Main St., Peoria, IL, 61602; 309/671-3191. 208 18th St., Rock Island, IL, 61201; 309/786-3303. 401 W.

State St., Suite 701, Rockford, IL, 61101; 815/965-8635. Consumer Protection Section, 527 E. Capitol Ave., Springfield, IL, 62706; 217/782-2024. AGING: Department on Aging, 2401 W. Jefferson, Springfield, IL, 62706; 217/782-5773. BANKING AND CREDIT: Banks & Trust Companies, Reisch Bldg., Rm. 400, 117-119 S. Fifth St., Springfield, IL, 62701; 217/782-7966. ENERGY: Institute of Natural Resources, 309 W. Washington St., Chicago, IL, 60606; 312/793-3870. INSURANCE: Consumer Market Branch, 215 E. Monroe, Springfield, IL, 62767; 217/782-4395. TRANS-PORTATION/UTILITIES: Illinois Commerce Commission, Leland Bldg., 527 E. Capitol Ave., Springfield, IL, 62706; 217/782-7295. 160 N. LaSalle St., Chicago, IL, 60601; 312/793-2844. Illinois Office of Consumer Services, Springfield, IL, 62706; 217/785-3196.

INDIANA. State Offices: GENERAL: Consumer Protection Division, 215 State House, Indianapolis, IN, 46204; 317/633-6496/6276 and 800/382-5516. AGING: Commission on Aging and Aged, 215 N. Senate Ave., Indianapolis, IN, 46202; 317/633-5948. BANKING AND CREDIT: Division of Consumer Credit, 1024 Indiana State Office Bldg., Indianapolis, IN, 46204; 317/633-6297 and Department of Financial Institutions, Indiana State Office Bldg., Rm. 1024, Indianapolis, IN, 46204; 317/633-4365. ENERGY: Indiana Energy Group, 115 N. Pennsylvania St., 7th Fl., Indianapolis, IN, 46204; 317/633-6753. INSURANCE: Commissioner of Insurance, 509 State Office Bldg., Indianapolis, IN, 46204; 317/633-4892 and Consumer Services Dvision, State Office Bldg., Rm. 509, Indianapolis, IN, 46204; 317/633-6338. TRANSPORTATION/UTILITIES: Indiana Public Service Commission, 901 State Office Bldg., Indianapolis, IN, 46204; 317/633-5359 and Office of Public Counselor, 807 State Office Bldg., Indianapolis, IN, 46204; 317/633-4659.

IOWA. State Offices: GENERAL: Consumer Protection Division, 1209 E. Court, Des Moines, IA, 50319; 515/281-5926 and Citizens' Aid Ombudsman, 515 E. 12th, Des Moines, IA, 50319; 515/281-3592. AGING: Commission on Aging, 415 W. 10th St., Jewett Bldg., Des Moines, IA, 50319; 515/281-5187. BANKING AND CREDIT: Superintendent of Banking, 418 Sixth Ave., Rm. 530, Des Moines, IA, 50309; 515/281-4014. ENERGY: Iowa Energy Policy Council, 707 E. Locust St., Des Moines, IA, 50319; 512/281-4420. INSURANCE: Commissioner of Insurance, State Office Bldg., Des Moines, IA, 50319; 515/281-5705 and Citizen Complaints and Inquiries, Lucas State Office Bldg., Des Moines, IA, 50319; 515/281-4241. TRANSPORTATION/UTILITIES: 300 Fourth St., Des Moines, IA, 50319; 515/281-3631. Iowa State Commerce Commission, State Capitol, Des Moines, IA, 50319; 515/281-5309. Public Utilities Division, Valley Bank Bldg., Des Moines, IA, 50319; 515/281-5979. Consumer Protection Division, 1209 East Court, Executive Hills, West, Des Moines IA, 50319; 515/281-5926.

KANSAS. State Offices: GENERAL: Consumer Protection Division, Kansas Judicial Center, 310 W. 10th 2nd Floor, Topeka, KS, 66612; 913/296-3751. AGING: Department of Aging, Biddle Bldg., 2700 W. 6th St., Topeka, KS, 66606; 913/296-4986. BANKING AND CREDIT: State Bank Commissioner, 818 Kansas Ave., Suite 600, Topeka, KS, 66612; 913/296-2266. ENERGY: State of Kansas Energy Office, 503 Kansas Ave., Rm. 241, Topeka, KS, 66603; 913/296-2496. INSURANCE: Commissioner of Insurance, State

Office Bldg., Topeka, KS, 66612; 913/296-3071 and 800/432-2484. TRANS-PORTATION/UTILITIES: Kansas State Corporation Commission, State Office Bldg., Topeka, KS, 66612; 913/296-3324.

KENTUCKY. State Offices: GENERAL: Consumer Protection Division, Frankfort, KY, 40601; 502/564-6607 and 800/372-2960. AGING: Center for Aging and Community Development, 403 Wapping St., Frankfort, KY, 40601; 502/564-6930. BANKING AND CREDIT: Commissioner of Banking and Securities, 911 Leawood Dr., Frankfort, KY, 40601; 502/564-3390. ENERGY: Kentucky Department of Energy, Capitol Plaza Tower, 9th Fl., Frankfort, KY, 40601; 502/564-7070. INSURANCE: Insurance Commissioner, 151 Elkhorn Ct., Frankfort, KY, 40601; 502/564-3630. TRANSPORTATION/UTILITIES: Kentucky Department of Transportation, Senate Office Bldg., Frankfort, KY, 40601; 502/564-4890. Kentucky Railroad Commission, Tenth Floor, State Office Bldg., Frankfort, KY, 40601; 502/564-4640. Consumer Protection Division, 209 St., Clair St., Frankfort, KY, 40601; 502/564-2196. Kentucky Public Service Commission, P.O. Box 615, 730 Schenkel Ln., Frankfort, KY, 40602; 502/564-3940.

LOUISIANA. State Offices: GENERAL: Governor's Office of Consumer Protection, P.O. Box 44091, Suite 1218, Capitol Station, Baton Rouge, LA, 70804; 504/925-4401 and 800/272-9868 and Consumer Protection Section, 1885 Wooddale Blvd., Suite 1208, Baton Rouge, LA, 70806; 504/925-4181. Branch Offices: Consumer Protection Section, 234 Loyola Ave., 7th Fl., New Orleans, LA, 70112; 504/568-5575 and Bureau of Marketing, P.O. Box 44302, Capitol Station, Baton Rouge, LA, 70804; 504/292-3600. AGING: Bureau of Aging Services, P.O. Box 44282, Capitol Sta., Baton Rouge, LA, 70804; 504/389-2171. BANKING AND CREDIT: Commissioner of Financial Institutions, P.O. Box 44095, Capitol Station, Baton Rouge, LA, 70804; ENERGY: Department of Conservation, P.O. Box 44275, Baton Rouge, LA, 70804; 504/389-5161 and Department of Natural Resources, P.O. Box 44156, Baton Rouge, LA, 70804; 504/389-2771. INSURANCE: Commissioner of Insurance, P.O. Box 44214, Baton Rouge, LA, 70804; 504/342-5328. TRANSPORTA-TION/UTILITIES: Louisiana Public Service Commission, One American Place, Suite 1630, Baton Rouge, LA, 70804; 504/389-5867.

MAINE. State Offices: GENERAL: Consumer and Anti-Trust Division, State Office Bldg., Rm. 505, Augusta, ME, 04333; 207/289-3716 and Bureau of Consumer Protection, State Office Bldg., Augusta, ME, 04333; 207/289-3731 AGING: Bureau of Maine's Elderly, Community Services Unit, State House Augusta, ME, 04333; 207/289-2561. BANKING AND CREDIT: Bank Superintendent, State Office Bldg., Augusta, ME, 04333; 207/289-3231. ENERGY Office of Energy Resources, 55 Capitol St., Augusta, ME, 04339; 207/868-2196 INSURANCE: Superintendent of Insurance, Capitol Shopping Center, Augusta ME, 04330; 207/289-3141 and Consumer Service Division, Bureau of Insurance State Office' Bldg., Augusta, ME, 04333; 207/289-3141. TRANS PORTATION/UTILITIES: Maine Public Utilities Commission, State House Augusta, ME, and Department of Attorney General, Augusta, ME, 04333 207/289-3051.

MARYLAND. State Offices: GENERAL: Consumer Protection Division, 131 E. Redwood St., Baltimore, MD, 21202; 301/383-5344. Branch Offices Consumer Protection Division, 5112 Berwyn Rd., 3rd Fl., College Park, MD

20740; 301/474-3500 and Consumer Protection Division, 138 E. Antietam St., Hagerstown, MD, 21740; 301/791-4780. AGING: Office on Aging, 301 W. Preston St., Baltimore, MD, 21201; 301/383-5064. BANKING AND CREDIT: Bank Commissioner, 1 N. Charles St., Rm. 2005, Baltimore, MD, 21201; 301/383-2480 and Office of Consumer Credit, One S. Calvert St., Rm. 601, Baltimore, MD, 21202; 301/383-3656. ENERGY: Energy Policy Office, 301 W. Preston St., Suite 1302, Baltimore, MD, 21201; 301/383-6810. INSURANCE: Insurance Commissioner, One S. Calvert Bldg., Baltimore, MD, 21202; 301/383-5690. TRANSPORTATION/UTILITIES: Maryland Public Service Commission, 904 State Office Bldg., 301 W. Preston St., Baltimore, MD, 21202; 301/383-2374 and People's Counsel of Maryland, 301 W. Preston St., Rm. 900, Baltimore, MD, 21202; 301/383-2375.

MASSACHUSETTS. State Offices: GENERAL: Executive Office of Consumer Affairs, John W. McCormack Bldg., One Ashburton Pl., Boston, MA, 02108; 617/727-7755. Self-Help Consumer Information Office, John W. McCormack Bldg., One Ashburton Pl., Boston, MA, 02108; 617727-7780. Consumer Protection Division, One Ashburton Pl., 19th Fl., Boston, MA, 02108; 617/727-8400. Branch Office: Consumer Protection, 235 Chestnut St., Springfield, MA, 01103; 413/785-1951 and MA Consumers' Council, 100 Cambridge St., Rm. 2109, Boston, MA, 02202; 617/727-2605/2606. AGING: Department of Elder Affairs, 110 Tremont St., Boston, MA, 02108; 617/727-7750. BANKING AND CREDIT: Commissioner of Banks, 100 Cambridge St., Boston, MA, 02202; 617/727-3120. ENERGY: Massachusetts Energy Policy Office, 73 Tremont St., Rm. 700, Boston, MA, 02108; 617/727-4732. INSURANCE: Commissioner of Insurance, 100 Cambridge St., Boston, MA, 02202; 617/727-3333. TRANSPORTATION/UTILITIES: Massachusetts Department of Public Utilities, 100 Cambridge St., Boston, MA, 02202; 617/727-3500 and Energy Regulatory Impact Program, Public Protection Bureau, McCormack Bldg., One Ashburton Pl., Boston, MA, 02108; 617/727-1085.

MICHIGAN. State Offices: GENERAL: Consumer Protection Division, 670 Law Bldg., Lansing, MI, 48913; 517/373-1140 and Michigan Consumers Council, 414 Hollister Bldg., 106 N. Allegan St., Lansing, MI, 48933; 517/373-0947 and 800/292-5680. AGING: Office of Services to the Aging, 300 E. Michigan, P.O. Box 30026, Lansing, MI, 48909; 517/373-8230. BANKING AND CREDIT: Financial Institutions Bureau, P.O. Box 30224, Lansing, MI, 48909; 517/373-3460. ENERGY: Michigan Energy Administration, Law Bldg.—4th Fl., Lansing, MI, 48913; 517/374-9090. INSURANCE: Commissioner of Insurance, P.O. Box 30220, Lansing, MI, 48909; 517/374-9724 and Office of Consumer Protection, 1048 Pier Pont, Lansing, MI, 48912; 517/373-0240 and 800/292-5943. TRANSPORTATION/UTILITIES: Michigan Office of Electric Utility Consumer Affairs, 632 Law Bldg., Lansing, MI, 48913; 517/373-1123. Public Service Commission, P.O. Box 30221, Lansing, MI, 48909; 517/373-8729 and 800/292-9555. Michigan Public Service Commission, Mercantile Bldg., 6545 Mercantile Way, P.O. Box 30221, Lansing, MI, 48909; 517/373-3244.

MINNESOTA. State Offices: GENERAL: Consumer Protection Division, 02 State Capitol, St. Paul, MN, 55155; 612/296-3353 and Office of Consumer Services, 7th & Roberts Sts., St. Paul, MN, 55101; 612/296-4512 and 612/296-331. Branch Office: Duluth Regional Office, 604 Alworth Bldg., Duluth, MN,

55802; 218/723-4891. AGING: Minnesota Board of Aging, Suite 204, Metro Square Bldg., 7th and Robert Sts., St. Paul, MN, 55101; 612/296-2544. BANKING AND CREDIT: Commissioner of Banks, Metro Square Bldg., 5th Fl., 7th & Robert Sts., St. Paul, MN, 55101; 612/296-2715. ENERGY: Minnesota Energy Agency, 740 American Center Bldg., 160 E. Kellogg Blvd., St. Paul, MN, 55101; 612/296-6424. INSURANCE: Commissioner of Insurance, Metro Square Bldg., St. Paul, MN, 55101; 612/296-6907. TRANSPORTATION/UTILITIES: Minnesota Department of Transportation, 411 Transportation Bldg., St. Paul, MN, 55155; 612/296-3131. Office of Consumer Services, Residential Consumer Utility Unit, 1st Fl., Metro Square Bldg., 7th & Robert Sts., St. Paul, MN, 55101; 612/296-4512. Minnesota Public Service Commission, 7th Fl., American Center Bldg., Kellogg & Robert Sts., St. Paul, MN, 55101; 612/296-7107.

MISSISSIPPI. State Offices: GENERAL: Consumer Protection Division, Justice Bldg., P.O. Box 220, Jackson, MS, 39205; 601/354-7130 and Consumer Protection Division, High & President Sts., P.O. Box 1609, Jackson, MS, 39205; 601/354-6258. AGING: Council on Aging, P.O. Box 5136, Fondren Station, 510 George St., Jackson, MS, 39216; 601/354-6590. BANKING AND CREDIT: Department of Bank Supervision, P.O. Box 731, Jackson, MS, 39205; 601/354-6106. ENERGY: Mississippi Fuel and Energy, Woolfolk State Office Bldg., Rm. 1307, Jackson, MS, 39302; 601/354-7406. INSURANCE: Commissioner of Insurance, P.O. Box 79, Jackson, MS, 39205; 601/354-7711. TRANSPORTATION/UTILITIES: Mississippi Public Service Commission, Walter Sillers State Office Bldg., 19th Fl., P.O. Box 1174, Jackson, MS, 39205; 601/354-7474.

MISSOURI. State Offices: GENERAL: Consumer Protection Division, Supreme Court Bldg., P.O. Box 899, Jefferson City, MO, 65102; 314/751-3321. Branch Offices: Consumer Protection Division, 75 Olive St., Suite 1323, St. Louis, MO, 63101; 314/241-2211. Consumer Protection Division, 615 E. 13th St., Kansas City, MO, 64106; 816/274-6686. MO Consumer Information Center, P.O. Box 1157, Jefferson City, MO, 65102; 314/751-4996. 615 E. 13th St., Kansas City, MO, 64106; 816/274-6381. 330 Mansion House Center, St., Louis MO, 63102; 314/241-8318. AGING: Office of Aging, Broadway State Office Bldg., P.O. Box 570, Jefferson City, MO, 65101; 314/751-2075. BANKING AND CREDIT: Commissioner of Finance, P.O. Box 716, Jefferson City, MO 65101; 314/751-3397. ENERGY: Missouri Energy Program, P.O. Box 1309 Jefferson City, MO, 65101; 314/751-4000. INSURANCE: Division of Insurance 515 E. High St., Box 690, Jefferson City, MO, 65101; 314/751-4126 and Director of Insurance, P.O. Box 690, Jefferson City, MO, 65101; 314/751-2451 TRANSPORTATION/UTILITIES: Missouri Public Service Commission, Jefferson Bldg., P.O. Box 360, Jefferson City, MO, 65101; 314/751-3234 and Office of the Public Counsel, P.O. Box 1216, Jefferson City, MO, 65102; 314/751-4857.

MONTANA. State Offices: GENERAL: Consumer Affairs Division, 805 N. Main St., Helena, MT, 59601; 406/449-3163 and Missoula County Attorney County Courthouse, Missoula, MT, 59801; 406/543-3111. AGING: Aging Services Bureau, Dept. of Social and Rehabilitation Services, P.O. Box 1723 Helena, MT, 59601; 406/449-3124. BANKING AND CREDIT: Department of

Business Regulation, 805 N. Main St., Helena, MT, 59601; 406/449-3163. ENERGY: Montana Energy Office, Capitol Station, Helena, MT, 59601; 406/449-3750. INSURANCE: Commissioner of Insurance, Capitol Bldg., Helena, MT, 59601; 406/449-2040. TRANSPORTATION/UTILITIES: MT Consumer Counsel, 34 W. Sixth Ave., Helena, MT, 59601; 406/449-2771 and Montana Public Service Commission, 1227 11th Ave., Helena, MT, 59601; 406/449-3017.

NEBRASKA. State Offices: GENERAL: Consumer Protection Division, State House, Lincoln, NE, 68509; 402/471-2682. Consumer Protection Dvision, Department of Justice, 605 S. 14th, Lincoln, NE, 68509; 402/471-2682. Consumer Consultant, 301 Centennial Mall South, 4th Fl., P.O. Box 94941, Lincoln, NE, 68509; 402/471-2341. AGING: Commission on Aging, State House Station 94784, P.O. Box 95044, Lincoln, NE, 68509; 402/471-2307. BANKING AND CREDIT: Banking and Finance, P.O. Box 95006, Lincoln, NE, 68509; 402/471-2171. ENERGY: Nebraska Energy Office, P.O. Box 95085, Lincoln, NE, 68509; 402/471-2867. INSURANCE: Director of Insurance, 301 Centennial Mall South, P.O. Box 94699, Lincoln, NE, 68509; 402/471-2201. TRANSPORTATION/UTILITIES: Nebraska Public Service Commission, 301 Centennial Mall South, P.O. Box 94927, Lincoln, NE, 68509; 402/471-3101.

NEVADA. State Offices: GENERAL: Consumer Affairs Division, 2501 E. Sahara Ave., 3rd Fl., Las Vegas, NV, 89158; 702/386-5293 and Consumer Affairs Dvision, 2501 E. Sahara Ave., Las Vegas, NV, 89158; 702/386-5293. Branch Office: Consumer Affairs Dvision, Nye Bldg., Rm. 325, Capitol Complex, Carson City, NV, 89710; 702/885-4340 and 800/992-0900. AGING: Division for Aging Services, 505 E. King St., Kinkead Bldg., Rm. 600, Carson City, NV, 89710; 702/885-4210. BANKING AND CREDIT: Superintendent of Banks, 406 E. Second St., Capitol Complex, Carson City, NV, 89710; 702/885-4260. ENERGY: Nevada Department of Energy, 1050 E. Will, Suite 405, Carson City, NV, 89710; 702/805-5157. INSURANCE: Insurance Commissioner, Nye Bldg., Carson City, NV, 89710; 207/885-4270. TRANSPORTATION/UTILITIES: Nevada Public Service Commission, 505 E. King St., Carson City, NV, 89710; 702/885-4180. Division of Consumer Relations, 505 E. King St., Carson City, NV, 89710; 702/885-5556. Consumer Division, P.O. Box 1130, Reno, NV, 89520; 702/785-5652. Las Vegas City Attorney's Office, 400 Stewart Ave., Las Vegas, NV, 89101; 702/386-6201.

NEW HAMPSHIRE. State Offices: GENERAL: Consumer Protection Division, Statehouse Annex, Concord, NH, 03301; 603/271-3641. AGING: Council on Aging, P.O. Box 786, 14 Depot St., Concord, NH, 03301; 603/271-2751. BANKING AND CREDIT: Bank Commissioner, 97 N. Main St., Concord, NH, 03301; 603/271-3561. ENERGY: Governor's Council on Energy, 26 Pleasant St., Concord, NH, 03301; 603/842-2121. INSURANCE: Insurance Commissioner, 169 Manchester, Concord, NH, 03301; 603/271-2261. TRANSPORTATION/UTILITIES: Public Utilities Commission, 8 Old Sun Cook Rd., Concord, NH, 03301; 603/271-2452 and Utility Consumer Advocate of New Hampshire, Rm. 401, L.O.B., Concord, NH, 03301; 603/271-2762.

NEW JERSEY. State Offices: GENERAL: Division of Consumer Affairs, 1100 Raymond Blvd., Rm. 504, Newark, NJ, 07102; 201/648-4010. Public

Advocate, P.O. Box 141, Trenton, NJ, 08625; 609/292-7087 and 800/792-8600. Department of Law and Public Safety, 1100 Raymond Blvd., Rm. 316, Newark, NJ, 07102; 201/648-3945. Division of Consumer Complaints, Legal and Economic Research, P.O. Box CN040, Trenton, NJ, 08625; 609/292-5374. AGING: Division on Aging, P.O. Box 2768, 363 W. State St., Trenton, NJ, 08625; 609/292-4833. BANKING AND CREDIT: Commissioner of Banking, 36 W. State St., Trenton, NJ, 08625; 609/292-3420. ENERGY: Department of Energy, 101 Commerce St., Newark, NJ, 07102-201/648-2744. INSURANCE: Commissioner of Insurance, 201 E. State St., Trenton, NJ, 08625; 609/292-5363 and Division of Consumer Services, P.O. Box 1510, 201 E. State St., Trenton, NJ, 08625; 609/292-5374.

NEW MEXICO. State Offices: GENERAL: Consumer and Economic Crime Division, P.O. Box 1508, Santa Fe, NM, 87501; 505/827-5521. AGING: Commission on Aging, 408 Galisteo - Villagra Bldg., Santa Fe, NM, 87503; 505/827-5258. BANKING AND CREDIT: Financial Institutions Division, Lew Wallace Bldg., Santa Fe, NM, 87503; 505/827-2217 and Department of Energy and Minerals, P.O. Box 2770, Santa Fe, NM, 87501; 505/827-2471. INSURANCE: Superintendent of Insurance, P.O. Box Drawer 1269, Santa Fe, NM, 87501; 505/827-2451. TRANSPORTATION/UTILITIES: New Mexico Public Service Commission, State Capitol Bldg., Santa Fe, NM, 87501; 505/827-2827. New Mexico State Commission, P.O. Drawer 1269, Santa Fe, NM, 87501; 505/827-2277. Attorney General, P.O. Drawer 1508, Santa Fe, NM, 87501; 505/827-5521.

NEW YORK. State Offices: GENERAL: Consumer Protection Board, 99 Washington Ave., Albany, NY, 12210; 518/474-8583. Branch Offices: Consumer Protection Board, Two World Trade Center, Rm. 8225, 82nd Fl., New York, NY, 10047; 212/488-5666 and Consumer Frauds and Protection Bureau, Two World Trade Center, New York, NY, 10047; 212/488-7450. State Office: Consumer Frauds and Protection Bureau, State Capitol, Albany, NY, 12224; 518/474-8686. Branch Offices: Assistant Attorney General in Charge, 10 Lower Metcalf Plaza, Auburn, NY, 13021; 315/253-9765. Office of Attorney General, 44 Hawley Ave., State Office Bldg., Binghamton, NY, 13901; 607/773-7823. Office of Attorney General, 65 Court St., Buffalo, NY, 14202; 716/842-4385. Assistant Attorney General in Charge, Suffolk State Office Bldg., Veterans Memorial Highway, Hauppauge, NY, 11787; 516/979-5190. Office of Attorney General, 48 Cornelia St., Plattsburgh, NY, 12901; 518/561-1980. Office of Attorney General, 65 Broad St., Rochester, NY, 14614; 716/454-4540. Assistant Attorney General in Charge, 333 E. Washington St., Syracuse, NY, 13202; 315/473-8432. Assistant Attorney General, 40 Garden St., Poughkeepsie, NY, 12601; 914/452-7744. Assistant Attorney General in Charge, 207 Genesee St., Box 528, Utica, NY, 13501; 315/797-6120. Assistant Attorney General in Charge, 317 Washington St., Watertown, NY, 13601; 315/782-0100. Branch Offices: 1468 Flatbush Ave., Brooklyn, NY, 11210; 212/434-1900. 2838 Third Ave., Bronx, NY, 11455; 212/993-7770. 98-18 61st St., Jamaica, NY, 11432; 212/526-6600. Department of Consumer Affairs, 120-55 Queens Blvd., Rm. 203, Kew Gardens, NY, 11424; 212/261-2922,2923. 227 E. 116th St., New York, NY, 10029; 212/566-6047. Consumer Complaint Center, Staten Island Bureau Hall, Rm. 119-A, Staten Island, NY, 10301; 212/390-5154. AGING: Office for the Aging, Agency Bldg. #2, Empire State Plaza, Albany, NY, 12223;

518/474-5731. BANKING AND CREDIT: Superintendent of Banks, 2 World Trade Center, 32nd Fl., New York, NY, 10047; 212/488-2310. Branch Office: 2 World Trade Center, Rm. 5036, New York City, NY, 10047; 212/488-6405. ENERGY: New York State Energy Office, Agency Bldg. No. 2, 10th Fl., Empire State Plaza, Albany, NY, 12223; 518/474-8181. INSURANCE: Superintendent of Insurance, Two World Trade Center, New York, NY, 10047; 212/488-4124 and Consumer Complaint Bureau, Two World Trade Center, New York, NY, 10047; 212/488-4005. Branch Office: Consumer Complaint Bureau, State Insurance Department, Albany, NY, 12210; 518/474-4556. TRANSPORTATION/UTILITIES: New York Public Service Commission, Empire State Plaza, Albany, NY, 12223; 518/474-7080. Two World Trade Center, New York, NY, 10047; 212/488-4390. New York State Department of Transportation, 220 Washington Ave., Bldg. #5, State Campus, Albany, NY, 12232; 518/457-1016. New York State Consumer Protection Board, 99 Washington Ave., Albany, NY, 12210; 518/474-5015.

NORTH CAROLINA. State Offices: GENERAL: Consumer Protection Division, Justice Bldg., P.O. Box 629, Raleigh, NC, 27602; 919/733-7741 and Office of Consumer Service, P.O. Box 27647, Raleigh, NC, 27611; 919/733-7125. AGING: North Carolina Division for Aging, 213 Hillsborough St., Raleigh, NC, 27603; 919/733-3983. BANKING AND CREDIT: Commissioner of Banks, P.O. Box 951, Raleigh, NC, 27602; 919/733-3016. ENERGY: Energy Management Division, 215 E. Lane St., Raleigh, NC, 27601; 919/733-2230. INSURANCE: Commissioner of Insurance, P.O. Box 26387, Raleigh, NC, 27611; 919/733-7343 and Consumer Affairs, P.O. Box 26387, Raleigh, NC, 27611; 919/733-2032. TRANSPORTATION/UTILITIES: North Carolina Utilities Commission, 430 N. Salisbury St., Dobbs Bldg., Raleigh, NC, 27602; 919/733-4249. North Carolina Utilities Commission, P.O. Box 991, Raleigh, NC, 27611; 919/733-2435. Consumer Services, P.O. Box 991, Raleigh, NC, 27602; 919/733-4271. Utilities Division, P.O. Box 629, Raleigh, NC, 27602; 919/733-7214.

NORTH DAKOTA. State Offices: GENERAL: Consumer Fraud Division, State Capitol, 1102 S. Washington, Bismarck, ND, 58501; 701/224-3404 and 800/472-2600 and Consumer Affairs Office, P.O. Box 937, Bismarck, ND, 58505; 701/224-2485 and 800/472-2927. AGING: Aging Services, State Capitol Bldg., Bismarck, ND, 58505; 701/224-2577. BANKING AND CREDIT: Commissioner of Banking and Financial Institutions, State Capitol, Rm. 1301, Bismarck, ND, 58505; 701/224-2253. ENERGY: Energy Conservation Coordinator, Capitol Place Office, 1533 N. 12th St., Bismarck, ND, 58501; 701/224-2200. INSURANCE: Commissioner of Insurance, Capitol Bldg., Fifth Fl., Bismarck, ND, 58505; 701/224-2444 and Claims Division, State Capitol Bldg., 5th Fl., Bismarck, ND, 58505; 701/224-2440. TRANSPORTATION/UTILITIES: North Dakota Public Service Commission, State Capitol Bldg., Bismarck, ND, 58505; 701/224-2400 and Office of Attorney General, State Capitol, Bismarck, ND, 58505; 701/224-2210.

OHIO. State Offices: GENERAL: Consumer Frauds and Crimes Section, 30 E. Broad St., Columbus, OH, 43215; 614/466-8831. AGING: Commission on Aging, 50 W. Broad St., Columbus, OH, 43216; 614/466-5500. BANKING AND CREDIT: Superintendent of Banks, Borden Bldg., 14th Fl., 180 E. Broad

St., Columbus, OH, 43215; 614/466-2932. ENERGY: Ohio Energy and Re source Development Agency, State Office Tower - 25th Fl., 30 E. Broad St. Columbus, OH, 43215; 616/466-8102. INSURANCE: Director of Insurance 2100 Stella Ct., Columbus, OH, 43215; 614/466-3584. TRANS PORTATION/UTILITIES: Ohio Public Utilities Commission, 180 E. Broad St. Columbus, OH, 43215; 614/466-3016 and Consumers' Counsel of Ohio, 13 E. State St., Columbus, OH, 43215; 614/466-8574.

OKLAHOMA. State Offices: GENERAL: Department of Consumer Af fairs, Jim Thorpe Bldg., Rm. 460, Oklahoma City, OK, 73105; 405/521-365. and Consumer Protection, State Capitol Bldg., Rm. 112, Oklahoma City, OK 73105; 405/521-3921. AGING: Special Unit on Aging, P.O. Box 25352 Oklahoma City, OK, 73125; 405/521-2281. BANKING AND CREDIT: Ban Commissioner, Malco Bldg., 4100 N. Lincoln Blvd., Oklahoma City, OK 73105; ENERGY: Oklahoma Department of Energy, 4400 N. Lincoln Blvd. Suite 251, Oklahoma City, OK, 73105; 405/521-3941. INSURANCE: Insuranc Commissioner, 408 Will Rogers Memorial Bldg., Oklahoma City, OK, 73105 405/521-2828. TRANSPORTATION/UTILITIES: Oklahoma Corporation Com mission, Jim Thorpe Office Bldg., Oklahoma City, OK, 73105; 405/521-226 and Assistant Attorney General, State Capitol, 112, Oklahoma City, OK, 73105 405/521-3921.

OREGON: State Offices: GENERAL: Consumer Protection Division, 52 S.W. Yamhill St., Portland, OR, 97204; 503/229-5522 and Consumer Service Division, Department of Commerce, Labor and Industries Bldg., Salem, OR 97310; 503/378-4320. AGING: Program on Aging, 772 Commercial St., S.E. Salem, OR, 97310; 503/378-4728. BANKING AND CREDIT: Superintenden of Banks, Department of Commerce, Busick Bldg., Salem, OR, 97310 503/378-4140. ENERGY: Department of Energy, 528 Cottage St. N.E., Salem OR, 97310; 503/378-4131. INSURANCE: Insurance Commissioner, 158 12t St., N.E., Salem, OR, 97310; 503/378-4271. TRANSPORTATION UTILITIES . . . Oregon Public Utility Commissioner, 300 Labor & Industrie Bldg., Salem, OR, 97310; 503/378-6611.

PENNSYLVANIA. State Offices: GENERAL: Bureau of consumer Pro tection, 301 Market st., 9th Fl., Harrisburg, PA, 17101; 717/787-9707. Branc Offices: Bureau of Consumer Protection, 133 N. Fifth St., Allentown, PA, 18102 215/821-0901. Bureau of Consumer Protection, 919 State St., Rm. 203, Erie PA, 16501; 814/871-4371. Bureau of Consumer Protection, 1500 N. 2nd St. Harrisburg, PA, 17101; 717/787-7109. Deputy Attorney General, 1405 Locus St., Suite 825, Philadelphia, PA, 19102; 215/238-6475. Bureau of Consume Protection, 300 Liberty Ave., State Office Bldg., Rm. 1405, Pittsburgh, PA 15222; 412/565-5135. Bureau of Consumer Protection, 1835 Centre Ave. Pittsburgh, PA, 15219; 412/566-1500. Bureau of Consumer Protection, 10 Lackawanna Ave., State Office Bldg., Rm. 105-A, Scranto, PA, 18503 717/961-4913. Regional Manager, Erie Regional Office, Commerce Bldg., Stat & 12th Sts., Erie, PA, 16501; 814/871-4466. Regional Manager, Philadelphi Regional Office, 1400 Spring Garden St., Philadelphia, PA, 19130; 215/238 7240. Regional Manager, Pittsburgh Regional Office, 300 Liberty Ave., Stat Office Bldg., Pittsburgh, PA, 15222; 412/565-5020. Consumer Coordinator, PA Department of Agriculture, 615 Howard Ave., Altoona, PA, 16601; 814/943

1133. Public Utility Commission, Bureau of Consumer Services, North Office Bldg., Harrisburg, PA, 19120; 717/783-1740. Office of Consumer Advocate, 100 Chestnut St., Harrisburg, PA, 17101; 717/783-5048. AGING: Office for the Aging, Health and Welfare Bldg., Rm. 540, P.O. Box 2675, 7th & Forster Sts., Harrisburg, PA, 17120; 717/787-5350. BANKING AND CREDIT: Secretary of Banking, P.O. Box 2155, Harrisburg, PA, 17120; 717/787-6992 and Consumer Affairs Coordinator, P.O. Box 2155, Harrisburg, PA, 17120; 717/787-1854. ENERGY: Governor's Energy Council, State & Third Sts., Harrisburg, PA, 17120; 717/787-9749. INSURANCE: Commissioner of Insurance, 108 Finance Bldg., Harrisburg, PA, 17120; 717/787-5173 and Policy Holders Service and Protection, Finance Bldg., Rm. 408, Harrisburg, PA, 17120; 717/787-1131. TRANSPORTATION/UTILITIES: Pennsylvania Public Utility Commission, P.O. Box 3265, Harrisburg, PA, 17120; 717/783-1740 and Consumer Advocate of Pennsylvania, Suite 102, 100 Chestnut St., Harrisburg, PA, 17101; 717/783-5048.

RHODE ISLAND. State Offices: GENERAL: RI Consumers Council, 365 Broadway, Providence, RI, 02909; 401/277-2764 and Public Protection Consumer Unit, 56 Pine St., Providence, RI, 02903; 401/277-3163. AGING: Division on Aging, 150 Washington Ct., Providence, RI, 02903; 401/277-2858. BANKING AND CREDIT: Chief Banking Administrator, 100 N. Main St., Providence, RI, 02903; 401/277-2405. ENERGY: Energy Capability and Management, State Energy Office, Providence, RI, 02903; 401/277-3374. INSURANCE: Insurance Commissioner, 100 N. Main St., Providence, RI, 02903; 401/277-2223 and Division of Public Utilities and Motor Carriers, 100 Orange St., Providence, RI, 02903; 401/277-2443. TRANSPORTATION/UTILITIES: Rhode Island Public Utilities Commission, 100 Orange St., Providence, RI, 02903; 401/277-3500. Consumer Council of Rhode Island, 365 Broadway, Providence, RI, 02909; 401/277-2764. Attorney General's Office, 56 Pine St., Providence, RI, 02903; 401/277-3163.

SOUTH CAROLINA. State Offices: GENERAL: Office of Citizens Service, State House, P.O. Box 11450, Columbia, SC, 29211; 803/758-3261. Department of Consumer Affairs, 2221 Devine St., Columbia, SC, 29211; 803/758-2040 and 800/922-1594. Assistant Attorney General for Consumer Protection, 2303 Devine St., Columbia, SC, 29205; 803/758-3040. Office of Executive Policy and Program, Brown Bldg., Rm. 434, 1205 Pendleton St., Columbia, SC, 29201; 803/758-2249. AGING: Commission on Aging, 915 Main St., Columbia, SC, 29201; 803/758.2576. BANKING AND CREDIT: Commissioner of Banking, 1026 Sumter St., Rm. 217, Columbia, SC, 29201; 803/758-2186. ENERGY: Energy Management Office, Edgar Brown Bldg., 1205 Pendleton St., Rm. 342, Columbia, SC, 29201; 803/758-2050. INSURANCE: Insurance Commissioner, 2711 Middleburg Dr., Columbia, SC, 29204; 803/758-2185 and Market Conduct Division, 2711 Middleburg Dr., P.O. Box 4067, Columbia, SC, 29204; 803/758-2876. TRANSPORTATION/UTILITIES: South Carolina Public Service Commission, P.O. Box 11649, Columbia, SC, 29211; 803/758-3621 and Consumer Advocate, 2221 Devine St., Columbia, SC, 29250; 803/758-5864.

SOUTH DAKOTA. State Offices: GENERAL: Department of Commerce and Consumer Affairs, State Capitol, Pierre, SC, 57501; 605/773-3177. Branch

Office: Department of Commerce and Consumer Affairs, 408 W. 34th St., Sioux Falls, SD, 57105; 605/339-6691. AGING: Office on Aging, State Office Bldg., Illinois St., Pierre, SD, 57501; 605/224-3656. BANKING AND CREDIT: Banking and Finance, State Capitol Bldg., Pierre, SD, 57501; 605/773-3421. ENERGY: Office of Energy Policy, State Capitol, Pierre, SD, 57501; 605/224-3603. INSURANCE: Director of Insurance, Insurance Bldg., Pierre, SD, 57501; 605/773-3563. TRANSPORTATION/UTILITIES: South Dakota Public Utilities Commission, Capitol Bldg., Pierre, SD, 57501; 605/224-3203 and Public Utilities Commission, First Fl., State Capitol, Pierre, SD, 57501; 605/773-3201.

TENNESSEE. State Offices: GENERAL: Division of Consumer Affairs, Ellington Agriculture Center, P.O. Box 40627, Melrose Station, Nashville, TN, 37204; 615/741-1461 and 800/342-8385 and Consumer Protection, 450 James Robertson Parkway, Nashville, TN, 37219; 615/741-1671. AGING: Commission on Aging, Rm. 102, S&P Bldg., 306 Gay St., Nashville, TN, 37201; 615/741-2056. BANKING AND CREDIT: Commissioner of Banking, Capitol Hill Bldg., Suite 460, 311 7th Ave., North, Nashville, TN, 37219; 615/256-3788. ENERGY: Tennessee Energy Authority, 250 Capitol Hill Bldg., Nashville, TN, 37219; 615/741-1772. INSURANCE: Commissioner of Insurance, 114 State Office Bldg., Nashville, TN, 37219; 615/741-2241. TRANSPORTATION/UTILITIES: Tennesse Public Service Commission, C1 - 102 Cordell Hull Bldg., Nashville, TN, 37219; 615/741-3668.

TEXAS. State Offices: GENERAL: Consumer Protection Division, P.O. Box 12548, Capitol Station, Austin, TX, 78711; 512/475-3288. Branch Offices: Assistant Attorney General, 4313 N. 10th, Suite F, McAllen, TX, 78501; 512/682-4547. Assistant Attorney General, 701 Commerce, Suite 200, Dallas, TX, 75202; 214/742-8944. Assistant Attorney General, 4824 Alberta Ave., Suite 160, El Paso, TX, 79905; 915/533-3484. Assistant Attorney General, County Office Bldg., Suite 312, 806 Broadway, Lubbock, TX, 79401; 806/747-5238. Assistant Attorney General, 200 Main Plaza, Suite 400, San Antonio, TX, 78205; 512/225-4191. Assistant Attorney General, Houston Bar Center Bldg., Suite 610, 723 Main St., Houston, TX, 77002; 713/228-0701. Consumer Center, 201 E. Belknap St., Fort Worth, TX, 76102; 817/334-1788. AGING: Governor's Committee on Aging, 411 W. 13th St., Fls. 4&5, Austin, TX, 78703; 512/475-2717. BANKING AND CREDIT: Banking Commissioner, 2601 N. Lamar, Austin, TX, 78705; Office of Consumer Credit, 1011 San Jacinto Blvd., P.O. Box 2107, Austin, TX, 78768; 512/475-2111. ENERGY: Administrative Assistant for Energy Resources, 7703 N. Lamar Blvd., Austin, TX, 78752; 512/475-5491 and Texas Energy Advisory Council, 7703 N. Lamar Blvd., Austin, TX, 78752; 512/475-7017. INSURANCE: Commissioner of Insurance, 1110 San Jacinto Blvd., Austin, TX, 78786; 512/475-2273. TRANSPORTATION/UTILITIES: Texas Aeronautics Commission, 410 E. 5th St., 1st & Seasonal Fls., P.O. Box 12607, Capitol Station, Austin, TX, 78711; 512/475-4762. Texas Public Utility Commission, 7800 Shoal Creek Blvd., Suite 400 N, Austin, TX, 78757; 512/458-6111. Texas Railroad Commission, P.O. Drawer 12967, Capitol Station, Austin, TX, 78711; 512/475-2439. Assistant Attorney General, P.O. Box 12548, Capitol Station, Austin, TX, 78711; 512/475.3288.

UTAH. State Offices: GENERAL: Division of Consumer Affairs, Department of Business Regulation, 330 E. Fourth South, Salt Lake City, UT, 84111; 801/533-6441 and Consumer Protection Unit, 236 State Capitol, Salt Lake City, UT, 84114; 801/533-5261. AGING: Division of Aging, 150 W. North Temple, Salt Lake City, UT, 84102; 801/533-6422. BANKING AND CREDIT: Commissioner of Financial Institutions, 10 W. Broadway, Suite 331, Salt Lake City, UT, 84101; ENERGY: Energy Office, 231 E. 4th South, Suite 101, Salt Lake City, UT, 84111; INSURANCE: Commissioner of Insurance, 326 S. 500 East, Salt Lake City, UT, 84102; 801/533-5611. TRANSPORTATION/UTILITIES: Utah Public Service Commission, 330 E. 4th South St., Salt Lake City, UT, 84111; 801/533-5522 and Utah Committee of Consumer Services, 330 E. 4th South, Salt Lake City, UT, 84111; 801/533-5511.

VERMONT. State Offices: GENERAL: Consumer Protection Division, 109 State St., Montpelier, VT, 05602; 802/828-3171 and 800/642-5149 and Weights and Measures Division, Montpelier, VT, 05602; 802/828-2436. AGING: Office on Aging, 81 River St., Montpelier, VT, 05602; 802/828-3471. BANKING AND CREDIT: Commissioner of Banking and Insurance, State Office Bldg., Montpelier, VT, 05602; 802/828-3301. ENERGY: Vermont Energy Office, Pavilion Office Bldg., 109 State St., Montpelier, VT, 05602; 802/828-2393. INSURANCE: Commissioner of Insurance, State Office Bldg., Montpelier, VT, 05602; 802/828-3301. TRANSPORTATION/UTILITIES: Vermont Public Service Board, 120 State St., State Office Bldg., Montpelier, VT, 05602; 802/828-2811 and Consumer Affairs Division, VT Public Service Board, 120 State St., Montpelier, VT, 05602; 802/828-2332.

VIRGINIA. State Offices: GENERAL: Division of Consumer Counsel, 11 S. 12th St., Suite 308, Richmond, VA, 23219; 804/786-4075 and Office of Consumer Affairs, 825 E. Broad St., Richmond, VA, 23219; 804/786-2042 and 800/552-9963. Branch Office: Coordinator, 3016 Williams Dr., Fairfax, VA, 22031; 703/573-1286. AGING: Office on Aging, 830 E. Main St., Suite 950, Richmond, VA, 23219; 804/786-7894. BANKING AND CREDIT: Commissioner of Financial Institutions, Blanton Bldg., Rm. 800, Richmond, VA, 23219; 804/786-3657. ENERGY: Office of Emergency & Energy Services, 7700 Midlothian Turnpike, Richmond, VA, 23235; 804/272-1441. INSURANCE: Commissioner of Insurance, 700 Blanton Bldg., Richmond, VA, 23209; 804/786-3741. TRANSPORTATION/UTILITIES: Virginia State Corporation Commission, Blanton Bldg., P.O. Box 1197, Richmond, VA, 23209; 804/786-3601 and Division of Consumer Counsel, 11 S. 12th St., Suite 308, Richmond, VA, 23219; 804/786-4075.

WASHINGTON. State Offices: GENERAL: Consumer Protection and Antitrust Division, 1366 Dexter Horton Bldg., Seattle, WA, 98104; 206/464-7744 and 800/552-0700. Branch Offices: Consumer Protection Division, Temple of Justice, Olympia, WA, 98504; 206/753-6210. Spokane Office of Attorney General, 1305 Old Nat'l Bank Bldg., Spokane, WA, 99201; 509/456-3123. Office of Attorney General, 620 Perkins Bldg., Tacoma, WA, 98402; 206/593-2904. Consumer Specialist, 215 Union Ave., Olympia, WA, 98504; 206/753-0929. AGING: Office on Aging, P.O. Box 1788 - M.S.45-2, Olympia, WA, 98504; 206/753-2502. BANKING AND CREDIT: Supervisor of Banking, General Administration Bldg., Rm. 219, Olympia, WA, 98504; 206/753-6520. ENERGY: Washington Energy Office, 400 E. Union St., 1st Fl., Olympia, WA,

98504; 206/753-2417. INSURANCE: Insurance Commissioner, Insurance Bldg., Olympia, WA, 98504; 206/753-7301. TRANSPORTATION/UTILITIES: Washington Utilities & Transportation Commission, Highways-Licenses Bldg., Olympia, WA, 98504; 206/753-6423.

WEST VIRGINIA. State Offices: GENERAL: Consumer Protection Division, 3412 Staunton Ave., SE, Charleston, WV, 304/348-8986 and Consumer Protection Division, 1900 Washington St., East, Charleston, WV, 25305; 304/348-7890. AGING: Commission on Aging, State Capitol, Charleston, WV, 25305; 304/348-3317. BANKING AND CREDIT: Commissioner of Banking, State Office Bldg. 6, Rm. B-406, 1900 Washington St., East, Charleston, WV, 25305; ENERGY: Fuel and Energy Division, 1262½ Greenbrier St., Charleston, WV, 25305; 304/348-8860. INSURANCE: Insurance Commissioner, 1800 Washington St., E, Charleston, WV, 25305; 304/348-3386. TRANSPORTATION/UTILITIES: West Virginia Public Service Commission, Rm. E-217, Capitol Bldg., Charleston, WV, 25305; 304/348-2182 and Attorney General of West Virginia, Rm. 26E, State Capitol Bldg., Charleston, WV, 25305; 304/348-2021 and 304/348-8986.

WISCONSIN. State Offices: GENERAL: Office of Consumer Protection, State Capitol, Madison, WI, 53702; 608/266-1852. Branch Office: Office of Consumer Protection, Milwaukee State Office Bldg., 819 N. 6th St., Rm. 520, Milwaukee, WI, 53203; 414/224-1867. State Office: Division of Consumer Protection, P.O. Box 8911, Madison, WI, 53708; 608/266-9837. Branch Offices: Northwest District Office, 1727 Loring St., Altoona, WI, 54720; 715/836-2861. Northeast District Office, 1181 A Western Ave., Green Bay, WI, 54303; 414/497-4210. Southeast District Office, 10320 W. Silver Spring Dr., Milwaukee, WI, 53225; 414/464-8581. AGING: Division on Aging, 1 W. Wilson St., Rm. 686, Madison, WI, 53703; BANKING AND CREDIT: Commissioner of Banking, 30 W. Mifflin St., Rm. 401, Madison WI, 53703; 608/266-1621. ENERGY: Office of State Planning and Energy, 1 W. Wilson St., Rm. B 130, Madison, WI, 53702; 608/266-3382. INSURANCE: Commissioner of Insurance, 123 W. Washington Ave., Madison, WI, 53702; 608/266-3585. TRANSPORTATION/UTILITIES: Wisconsin Public Service Commission, 432 Hill Farms State Office Bldg., Madison, WI, 53702; 608/266-1241 and Wisconsin Transportation Commission, Hill Farms State Office Bldg., 4802 Sheboygan Ave., P.O. Box 7957, Madison, WI, 53707.

WYOMING. State Offices: GENERAL: Assistant Attorney General, 123 Capitol Bldg., Cheyenne, WY, 82002; 307/777-7841. AGING: Aging Services, New State Office Bldg., West, Rm. 288, Cheyenne, WY, 82002; 307/777-7561. BANKING AND CREDIT: State Examiner, 819 W. Pershing Blvd., Cheyenne, WY, 82002; ENERGY: State Planning Coordinator, 2320 Capitol Ave., Cheyenne, WY, 82002; 307/777-7574. INSURANCE: Insurance Commissioner, 2424 Pioneer, Cheyenne, WY, 82001; 307/777-7401. TRANSPORTATION/UTILITIES: Wyoming Public Service Commission, Supreme Court Bldg., Cheyenne, WY, 82001; 307/777-7427.

Source: U.S. Office of Consumer Affairs.

Housing and Land

Fast rising prices are leaving more and more Americans with fading dreams of owning their own homes. The price of a new home now is in excess of $63,000, while the price of a previously occupied one exceeds $56,000. Biggest increases have been in urban areas and western states. The average price of a house in Los Angeles, Washington, DC, and numerous other cities exceeds $100,000.

Making matters worse for prospective homeowners has been the tightening of mortgage money. Interest rates rose in most parts of the country to above 11 per cent in 1979, causing the government's FHA and VA mortage guarantee programs to raise their rates to 10 per cent, the highest level on record.

The high prices and interest rates were beginning to depress sales in 1979. Sales of single-family houses in February, 1979, were 11 per cent below what they were in January and 14 per cent lower than a year earlier, according to the Department of Commerce.

GOVERNMENT LAUNCHES NEW PROGRAMS

Meanwhile, the federal government launched numerous efforts to stimulate housing construction and sales. The Department of Housing and Urban Development (HUD) began implementing recommendations of a Task Force on Housing costs. Among the actions taken by the government were:

- *Increased purchases of home mortgages,* especially new ones with graduated payments, by the Government National Mortgage Association (Ginnie Mae). The purpose is to increase the supply of funds available for home mortgages.

- *New money for housing counseling,* expanding HUD's efforts to help low- and moderate-income families to avoid loss of their homes because of financial problems.

- *A new program by the Farmers Home Administration* to make housing more available to low-income and minority people and reduce delinquency among borrowers. Assistance is provided through grants to community-based organizations and other non-profit groups.

- *A study of ways to use vacant or underused land* in cities already serviced by public transportation and utilities.

HELP OFFERED FOR COMMUNITY DEVELOPMENT

At the same time, the federal government continued its program of community revitalization through the Community Development Block Grant program, a joint effort of HUD, the Federal Home Loan Bank board and other agencies. The program folds in several older programs of community assistance, among them Model Cities, and gives the communities themselves the determining voice in how the federal funds will be spent.

In June, 1978, President Carter announced the availability of a loan fund of $10 billion over five years for such purposes through the Community Investment Fund. Eight months later, the Federal Home Loan Bank Board declared the program was already "proving quite successful" in improving housing in inner cities and rural areas.

EXISTING GOVERNMENT AID PROGRAMS

● *Rehabilitation loans.* These loans provide direct financing for renovating privately owned residential and commercial buildings in urban renewal areas. They are not limited to low-income people.

● *Urban homesteading.* Under this program, run-down single-family properties owned by the federal government are deeded to localities and sold at nominal cost, sometimes as low as $1, to people willing to rehabilitate and occupy them.

● *Low rent public housing.* Funds are provided for the construction, purchase and rehabilitation of rental projects owned and managed by state and local government agencies for lower income tenants, who pay lower-than-market rents. Rental and utility charges must not total more than 15 to 25 per cent of adjusted family incomes, depending on the program.

● *Homeownership assistance.* This program provides mortgage assistance to lower-income households for buying new or restored homes. Families with incomes up to 95 per cent of the area median may buy homes at reduced rates of interest—as low as 4 per cent—with HUD making up the difference between the family's payment and the amount due on the mortgage each month.

● *Housing for the elderly and handicapped.* Federal loans are available to non-profit organizations which develop rental housing for the elderly and handicapped. Loan rates are close to conventional rates, but a subsidy can reduce rents to as little as 25 per cent of personal income.

INDUSTRY PRACTICES STIR ACTION BY FTC

The unprecedented demand for new housing has drawn firms into the home construction business in a big way, many for the first time. Some now operate nationally, bringing them under the jurisdiction of federal agencies. Some large projects have resulted in slipshod work and a rash of buyer complaints. Government investigators have discovered that the greater the distance between the new house and the company offices, the more likely there will be unresolved problems.

Complaints about housing defects began pouring into government and private agencies in increasing numbers in 1978 and 1979. The Council of Better Business Bureaus reported an increase of 40 per cent in one year. The nature of the complaints also changed, from relatively minor matters to ones involving inadequate foundations that cause houses to settle at an angle, inadequate drainage leading to basement floodings; absence of waterproofing of basement walls and generally slipshod work on other parts of the house.

In 1978, the Federal Trade Commission (FTC) cracked down on the fifth largest builder of new homes, Kaufman and Broad Inc. and its subsidiaries. A consent order required the firm to repair more than 20,000 houses without charge for problems dating back to January 1, 1972. Sales of the company are nearly $300 million per year.

The FTC disputed numerous claims of the company, including ones promising a five-year warranty that "covers everything" and 24-hour customer service. In contrast, said the FTC, "in many cases, even after proper notice was given . . . (the company) neglected, refused or ignored making repairs under the warranty." The company was also accused of not always building according to good manufacturing practices despite its claims of having a unique quality control program.

USE OF WARRANTIES INCREASES

The increase in complaints about housing was occurring despite increased use of warranties, a relatively new selling device promoted by the housing industry to improve consumer relations. By 1979, however, only 20 per cent of new single-family homes building in the country carried warranties modeled by the Home Owners Warranty (HOW) program of the National Association of Home Builders. The owner of a HOW-warranted home is protected for one year against the cost of defects in both materials and workmanship. (See table.) Some basic parts of the house are covered for nine more years.

Defects have also become a major problem for owners of mobile homes. As a result of complaints to the government, the FTC proposed standards for warranties offered voluntarily or imposed by state laws. There are federal standards for the construction of mobile homes, but conformance is left largely up to manufacturers who certify they meet the standards. The Department of Housing and Urban Development (HUD), which sets the standards, has few inspectors and has been reluctant to prosecute, according to testimony presented at hearings on the matter held by the FTC. (See section on mobile homes.)

COST OF SELLING A HOME ALSO RISING

Closing costs can amount to 10 to 14 per cent of the actual price of a house, according to a survey by HUD. An increasing proportion is now going to real estate agents, whose rates have climbed in some places to 7 and 8 per cent from the 6 per cent charged for many years. These increases have come despite the fact that inflationary increases were included in the traditional 6 per cent figure and despite increased government efforts to prosecute brokers suspected of setting fees in local areas. The Justice Department has prosecuted brokers in Washington, DC, and other areas but has not succeeded in changing practices in any noticeable way. In 1979, the FTC was investigating allegations of fixed fees, deceptive sales forms, denial of access to multiple listing services and boycotts of some lower-fee dealers by others.

House selling has also gone national, with a growing number of countrywide home-selling operations competing with local firms for the lucrative fees. Most of the national firms specialize on higher-priced properties and operate through local brokers. One of them, Previews, has an 11 per cent selling fee, including 2 per cent cash in advance on the asking price and 5 per cent for the local firm. Franchises have also hit the real estate market. Century 21 and Red Carpet pioneered the system on the West Coast and are the largest in the field. Others are Gallery of Homes, Electronic Realty Associates, Better Homes and Gardens, Realty U.S.A. and Neighborhood Realty Group.

The increasing cost of selling a home has spurred many owners to tacke the job themselves. A number of books and phamphlets are available with advice on the subject.

SHOULD TITLE INSURANCE BE REQUIRED?

Among the more controversial items on the list of settlement costs is title insurance. It is usually required by the lender. The buyer of the property usually pays the fee even though the prime beneficiary is the lending institution. In theory, there should be no reason for such insurance if the title is searched properly. In practice, title insurance rarely results in a claim, thus making it an unusually high-profit business.

The Justice Department has found that consumers pay much more than they should for this type of insurance because there is reverse price competition. In order to get a lender's business, title insurance companies compete by paying rebates, referral fees and kickbacks. The stiffer the competition, the higher the fees paid ultimately by the consumer. Congress ordered HUD to study this situation and report back by December, 1979, but delays indicate that the deadline will not be met.

HOMEBUYERS' RIGHTS

Under the Real Estate Settlement Procedures Act (RESPA), a lender must provide a borrower a copy of a booklet: *Settlement Costs: A HUD Guide,* published by HUD. If the lender does not present it in person on the day of application for a loan (mortgage), he must mail it within three days after the application is filed. The free booklet explains real estate settlement procedures and offers advice to the buyer.

It describes a buyer's rights under RESPA. For example, when a buyer files a loan application, the lender must provide a "good faith" estimate of the settlement costs. The lender has three days to mail it if he prefers.

In addition, the lender must allow the borrower to inspect a "Uniform Settlement Statement" one day before settlement. This Statement must itemize the services and fees that will be charged. In any case, the Statement must be given to the borrower at the time of the settlement. If the borrower does not attend the settlement, the Statement must be mailed at that time.

The lender is also required to provide a "Truth-in-Lending" statement disclosing the annual percentage rate of the mortgage. The rate must include not only the interest but also any discount "points," financing charges and certain other fees. The lending statement must be provided when the load is made, not when applied for. But most lenders supply this information at the time of application.

RESPA also protects borrowers against certain unfair practices such as kickbacks for referring business to a particular person or company. It also prohibits fees where no service is provided. Sellers are prohibited from requiring that the borrower use a certain title company. Violating this rule makes the seller liable to pay the buyer three times all charges made for title insurance. In addition lenders are also required to comply with the Fair Credit Reporting Act and Equal Credit Opportunity Act described in the chapter on "Banking and Borrowing."

FAIR HOUSING REQUIREMENTS

Federal laws passed in 1964 and 1968 prohibit discrimination on the basis o race, color, national origin or sex in the sale and rental of housing. But the laws did not give the Department of Housing and Urban Development (HUD) the power to enforce them when a violation is discovered.

A study of the situation in 1978 by the General Accounting Office concluded that not only does HUD have insufficient legal authority for enforcing the fair housing laws but it has not used the little authority it has effectively. HUD's authority is limited to conciliating and mediating complaints. When such efforts do not bring results, the matter is usually dropped, according to the GAO report. Landlords have learned that they can simply ignore HUD letters and phone calls rather than attempt to conciliate.

Of 332 complaints checked by GAO over a 28-month period, 247 were not resolved because of lack of clear evidence of discrimination. Of these, 119 were dropped before an investigation was even begun. In only 57 cases was HUD able to determine that discrimination occurred. Of these, 36 cases were resolved, including 21 cases where housing or monetary compensation was provided. HUD responded by blaming inadequacies of its staff.

In addition to recommending that HUD improve its procedures, the GAO suggested that one way to build up stronger cases is to use testers — such as whites in racial cases — to provide evidence of violations.

SHOULD YOU BUY OR RENT?

Although monthly payments for rent are generally lower than the costs of buying and maintaining a home, other factors are important in determining whether it is more economical to buy or rent housing. Homeowners are able to deduct part of their ownership costs from their federal income tax; renters cannot. On the other hand, the buyer of a house incurs settlement costs averaging between two and six per cent of the sales price, while the renter will probably have to pay only a modest "security deposit."

The amount a homeowner saves on income taxes depends on his or her income. The following example, based on an analysis by the U.S. Department of Labor's Bureau of Labor Statistics, shows how much an owner would save on taxes, and, therefore, homeownership costs, assuming an income of $15,000:

	Renter	Owner
Income Before Taxes	$15,000	$15,000
Less Deductions:		
Real Estate Taxes	—	504
Mortgage Interest	—	2,164
Other Deductions	—	2,000
Standard Deduction	2,000	—
Less Personal Exemptions	3,000	3,000
Taxable Income	$10,000	$8,132
Monthly Tax Liability	$152	$116

In the above example, taxes are the average for FHA-backed loans, and the

mortgage is based on a $27,000 loan at eight per cent interest. The mortgage
interest is based on first-year payments in which interest constitutes most of the
payments. It is likely that the lower interest payments in subsequent years will
be offset by higher taxes and increased income (and, therefore, tax benefit).

Homeownership also provides a return on investment as the home
appreciates in value. This increase needs to be considered when determining
whether it is better to rent or buy. Between 1965 and 1977, the average sale
price of a home more than doubled nationally. This means that homes are
increasing in value by about 15-20 per cent a year.

To determine whether the tax savings plus appreciation in a home results in
cheaper housing than in renting, it is necessary to compare the amount of
interest that the downpayment and settlement costs would earn in a savings
account with the appreciated value of a home. Based on the 10-year increase in
average price from $20,000 to $39,600, it would cost about eight per cent—or
$3,120— of that value to sell the home. In addition, about $16,000 of a 25-year, 8
per cent mortgage will remain. The following table shows the net appreciation:

Sale Price	$39,000
Less:	
Selling Costs	3,120
Mortgage Balance	15,840
Net Proceeds	$20,040

Assuming a 10 per cent downpayment and principal payments of $2,209,
the net appreciation or gain would equal:

Net Proceeds	$20,040
Less Downpayment	2,000
Principal	2,209
Net Appreciation	$15,831

Had the downpayment and settlement costs of purchasing the home
(assumed to be 2½ per cent) been invested at five per cent a year, it would be
worth $4,073 at the end of 10 years. The principal payment of $2,209 is a forced
savings of $18.40 a month. The renter would gain $4,073 by investing the
downpayment. The net gain of ownership thus would be:

Net Appreciation	$15,831
Less:	
Value of Downpayment (5% Interest)	4,073
Value of Forced Savings (5%)	2,834
Net Ownership Gain	$8,924

**A renter would have to save about $75 a month
on the difference between rent and the monthly costs
of homeownership to come out ahead of the homebuyer
in this example.**

Costs are only one factor to consider. The location and condition of the area
and building may be more important than they first appear to be.

WARRANTY PROGRAMS
For New and Old Homes

Warranties for residential housing are a relatively new phenomenon, with an increasing number of programs available for both new and old buildings. Following are details:

NEW HOUSES: The National Association of Home Builders, the largest trade association in the home construction industry, runs a program called HOW, for Home Owners Warranty. The program is available in 45 states through Home Owners Warranty Councils licensed by HOW, which is headquartered at the National Housing Center, 15th and M Sts. NW, Washington, DC, 20005.

A HOW warranty provides protection for 10 years against major structural defects. During the first two years, this is the builder's obligation. The next eight years are covered by a national insurance plan which also covers the first two years if the builder defaults. In the first year, the builder warrants that materials and workmanship meet HOW's standards. In the second year, the builder continues to be responsible for wiring, piping and duct work. The builder pays the one-time insurance premium and warranty administration of $2 per thousand dollars of the selling price.

Some builders not in the HOW program also offer new-house warranties, so it is advisable to ask about them when considering buying a new house.

USED HOUSES: A growing number of companies offer warranties on used (existing) houses, but only five have been approved by the National Association of Realtors. They are: Certified Home Inspection Program, Columbia, MD; First American Home Protection Insurance Co., Kansas City, MO; Homestead Inspection Program, Camden, NJ; St. Paul Home Protection Program, St. Paul, MN; and Soundhome Assurance Program, Newark, NJ.

Under the NAR program, homes for sale are inspected for existing or potential problems involving seven major aspects of structural soundness: central heating, interior plumbing; wiring; exterior and interior walls, floors and ceilings; foundation and basement roof; and central air conditioning. Optional coverage may be provided for items such as water softeners and major appliances.

The cost of inspection varies from company to company, but overall cost of the inspection plus protection is about one-half of one per cent of the sale price, or about $200 for a $40,000 home.

NAR programs are presently available in 19 states, with intentions of becoming nationwide eventually. For more information, contact your local board of realtors of your state association of realtors.

In 1978, the NAR announced plans to add a second warranty program for existing homes. The program would not require inspection in advance and would cover a limited number of items. A basic policy would include these components: central heating system, interior plumbing (including hot water heater), electrical system and central air conditioning. Optional coverage could be added for such things as structural soundness, roof, appliances and septic tanks.

The plan was expected to be available nationwide within two years. For more information, contact NAR, 430 N. Michigan Ave., Chicago, IL, 60511, or a local board of realtors.

DETAILS OF THREE MAJOR HOME WARRANTY PROGRAMS
(See text for more information on programs.)

Major Provisions	Home Owners Warranty (NAHB)	Home Protection Programs (NAR)	Federal Housing Administration
Plan coverage	Covers only operating failures: 1st year—faulty workmanship or materials. 2nd year—heating, plumbing, electrical & air conditioning systems; structural soundness. 3rd-10th years—major structural defects. Plan covers new homes.	Covers only operating failures: Heating, plumbing, electrical & air conditioning systems; structural soundness of exterior & interior walls, including floors & ceilings. Plan covers resale homes.	Covers faulty workmanship or materials Plan covers new homes.
Length of coverage	10-year policy	Certified's coverage is for one year. Soundhome's coverage is for 2 years.	One year
Warranty exclusions	Loss due to fire, flood, other acts of God, normal shrinkage, buyer neglect.	Coverage limited to inspected & approved items. Exterior structures (garage).	Loss due to fire, flood, other acts of God, normal shrinkage, buyer neglect.
Policy transferable	Yes, within 10 year period.	Yes, within the period of contract.	Yes, within the one-year period.
Deductible	None	$100 per element per occurrence.	None
Cost	$2 per thousand with a minimum of $50.	Premium set exclusively by participating companies, usually about $200.	No cost
Covers condominiums	Yes, with some provisions.	Not required. One program does; 2 do not.	Yes
Includes termite inspection	No	No	No
Insulation requirements	House must meet either FHA or local warranty council standards.	Not included in inspection.	House must meet FHA requirements.
Program includes uniform complaint resolution mechanism	Yes, conciliation and arbitration are available at no charge.	No	No
Inspection arrangements	Where adequate building codes & acceptable inspections by FHA, Veterans Administration, or the local municipality exist, local councils' inspections are not necessary. Otherwise, the local warranty council is re-	NAR does not select inspectors; only approved companies engage professional engineers to perform the necessary inspections.	FHA's field staff conducts inspections.

RIGHTS OF TENANTS
Repairing Years of Imbalance

Lawmakers are finally beginning to rectify the imbalance in rights between landlords and tenants. Since the first "tenants" — serfs or small farmers renting land to till — laws have almost always given rights only to landlords and obligations only to tenants.

Most landlord-tenant law is still a hodgepodge of statutes and court decisions. Less than a third of the states have comprehensive laws deemed fair to both parties. Only Virginia has organized its laws into a section of its state code.

Most tenant law reform has come with introduction of the Uniform Residential Landlord and Tenant Act, a piece of model legislation created in 1972 by the National Conference of Commissioners on Uniform State Laws. The Act gives obligations and rights to both parties, and a mechanism with which to resolve disputes. Among its provisions:

● Security deposits must be returned within 14 days after the tenant moves. Deductions must be itemized in writing.

● If a landlord fails to live up to terms of a written agreement, the tenant may recover actual damages.

● If the cost of needed repairs is no more than $100, or one-half the rent, whichever is greater, the tenant may make repairs himself and deduct the expense from his rent.

● A landlord cannot raise the rent, decrease services or evict a tenant for complaining to a government agency, filing suit, joining or organizing a tenants' group.

A booklet containing the model act is available for $2 from the Conference, 645 N. Michigan Ave., Chicago, IL, 60611.

The following states have adopted landlord-tenant laws that are "substantially similar" to the Uniform Residential Landlord and Tenant Act, as of February 1, 1978:

Alaska	Michigan
Arizona	Montana
Connecticut	Nebraska
Florida	New Mexico
Hawaii	Oregon
Iowa	Tennessee
Kansas	Virginia
Kentucky	Washington

OTHER REFORMS AGAIN ACCEPTANCE

Although only 16 states have adopted the model law dealing with landlords and tenants, parts of it have been accepted more widely. Over 30 states and the District of Columbia have adopted the "warranty of habitability" clause, which changes the basic landlord-tenant relationship from a feudal one to a contractual one. It requires that if the landlord does not maintain an apartment properly, the tenant does not have to pay the rent.

Another clause, allowing tenants to deduct the amount of minor, necessary repairs from rent payments, has been adopted by more than two dozen states.

Many states also have some form of law on security deposits. Provisions include a maximum of one month's rent, payment of interest, itemization of deductions and a limit on how long a landlord can wait before returning the deposit.

Acceptance of more basic changes in the landlord-tenant relationship has been rare and usually has depended on where there is a strong tenant organization in the area. Thus, the state with the strongest protection for tenants is New Jersey, where the oldest and largest tenant organization exists. The New Jersey Tenant Association has managed to win legislation protecting tenants from unfair evictions and requiring landlords to post bonds which can be used by local communities to fix hazardous conditions if the landlord refuses to do so. It is the only state with the latter law.

SEPARATE COURTS NOW IN SIX CITIES

Another growing concept is separate courts for resolving disputes between tenants and landlords. By 1978, six major cities had established some form of housing courts, although they differ somewhat from each other. They are New York, Boston, Pittsburgh, Detroit, Baltimore and Minneapolis.

Other types of changes include organizing tenants into unions for collective bargaining, establishing cooperatives to take over property about to change hands or be made into a condominium and legislative control of rents. Rent control continues to exist in some large cities, including Boston, New York and Washington, DC. In 1979, Santa Monica, California, voted for rent control after tenants accused landlords of refusing to pass through tax cuts received as a result of Proposition 13. Citizen groups in other California communities were threatening to do the same.

Several organizations have published guides for tenants. One is the New Jersey Tenant Organization, P.O. Box 1142, Fort Lee, NJ, 07024. Its booklet, "Tenant Laws," is available free to N.J. residents, 50 cents to others. Another is the New York State College of Human Ecology. Its "Renter's Guide," written in both English and Spanish, is also available for state residents and costs 50 cents to others, from Mailing Room, Building 7, Research Park, Cornell University, Ithaca, NY, 14853.

ALUMINUM ELECTRICAL WIRING HAZARDS
Some Shocking Details Revealed

About 2 million private homes in the U.S. have aluminum electrical wiring, most of which was installed between 1965 and 1973. In 1977, the Consumer Product Safety Commission asked a U.S. District Court to declare such wiring an "imminent hazard" because of fire hazards and to require manufacturers to warn homeowners of the danger.

In addition to the suit, the Commission issued a pamphlet describing the fire hazards of the wiring, but as the result of a counter-suit by an aluminum wiring manufacturer, the court prohibited the Commission from distributing the pamphlet. The manufacturer claimed that the CPSC pamphlet was misleading and that aluminum wiring, properly installed, presented no fire hazard. In a successful attempt to circumvent the court order, one congressman inserted the CPSC pamphlet into the *Congressional Record.*

The complete booklet is available only by writing to the Freedom of Information Officer, CPSC, Washington, DC, 20207. You must cite the Freedom of Information Act and request "a copy of the draft booklet describing how to detect faulty aluminum wiring in homes, found in Exhibit 1 in CPSC vs. Anaconda."

Excerpts from the pamphlet follow:

THE PROBLEMS WITH ALUMINUM WIRE

Dangerous overheating may occur where aluminum wire connects to outlets or switches. When this happens, fire is a possibility. House wiring to appliances such as dishwashers, room air conditioners and refrigerators may also share the same problem.

If your home or apartment has a 15 and 20 amp. aluminum wire system there may be a fire hazard. Signs of trouble are:

- Cover plates on switches and outlets which are warm or hot to the touch;
- Smoke coming from outlets or switches;
- Sparks or arcing at switches and outlets;
- Strange odors, especially the smell of burning plastic, in the area of outlets or switches;
- Lights which flicker periodically (in some cases, faulty appliances or other unrelated causes may result in light flickering);
- Outlets, lights, or entire circuits which fail to work.

IDENTIFYING PROBLEM WIRING

Homes built between 1965 and 1973 or any additions to homes made during that time may have aluminum wire.

In 1972, manufacturers altered both aluminum wire and switches and outlets to make aluminum electrical systems safer. If your house was built after 1972, this does not mean that the system in your home has the newer equipment, since the sale of the old types of wire, outlets, and switches continued after 1972.

If you think your home may have aluminum wire, follow these precautions:

- Do not remove cover plates on switches or outlets;
- Do not try to check the wiring in electrical panels or boxes;
- Do not try to check the wiring on your appliances.

If there are areas in the basement, attic or garage where the wiring is open to view, check to see if the letters "AL" or the word "aluminum" is printed or stamped every few feet on the outside jacket of the wire insulation.

If neither of these is used, the wire is probably not aluminum.

Since some houses are partly wired with aluminum and partly with copper wire, be alert for signs of trouble described even if you do not find either marking.

If no wiring is visible, call the electrical contractor who wired your home and ask him if the wiring is aluminum. The builder of your home may be able to supply the name of the contractor.

You can also find out if you have aluminum wiring by having a qualified electrican come to your home to make a visual inspection. If you live in an apartment, ask the resident manager or maintenance man if the unit has aluminum wire.

SMOKE DETECTORS
Fire Hazards vs. Detector Hazards

A lively controversy has arisen over the relative safety of a home-safety device to warn occupants of fire. The issue is whether smoke detectors using an ionization process and a radio-active metal, americium, give off too much radiation. Smoke detectors are electrical devices to set off an alarm before a fire progresses too far for the safe exit of occupants. There are two basic types: ionization and photoelectric.

The controversy began when Ralph Nader's Health Research Group (HRG) released a letter to the Nuclear Regulatory Commission (NRC) requesting a ban and recall of all ionization-type detectors. According to the NRC, there are more than 4 million such devices in use, mostly in private homes. HRG Director Sidney Wolfe contended that americium, a known carcinogen, is too hazardous for long-term use in such devices. He said that although the amount of radiation is very small, it adds to the combined amount received over a lifetime and is avoidable with the use of a photoelectric detector.

Adding fuel to the controversy was an article in the October , 1976, issue of *Consumer Reports* urging buyers not to worry about radiation. The magazine rated an ionization device, Guardion FB-1 as the best of 15 tested because of "its rapid response to both flaming and smoldering fires." The article said photoelectric devices are not as effective as ionization ones with flaming fires but are just as good for smoldering fires.

The National Bureau of Standards (NBS) contends that both types are "equally effective" as smoke detectors in the home. NBS and NRC issued statements assuring the public that the small amount of radiation emitted by ionization devices is not a health hazard.

For a free pamphlet showing where to place smoke detectors in a house, ask for *Smoke Detectors* from Consumer Information Center, Pueblo, CO, 81009.

FEDERAL GUIDELINES FOR CONDOMINIUMS
To avoid more than your share of trouble

One of the biggest sources of trouble in the housing field in recent years is the sale of condominiums. Fed by the increasing demand for housing and the rush of apartment landlords to convert to a more profitable operation, condominium units have grown at a rapid pace.

Under ideal conditions, a condominium can offer many advantages of home ownership at a more reasonable price than a separate house would command. However, few condominium arrangements come close to the ideal. Most common problems include lack of full disclosure of financial obligations for maintenance, recreational facilities such as swimming pools, and other benefits.

Once a purchase is made, the owner becomes locked into the terms of the fine print. If he becomes disappointed and decides to sell, he may find that the unfavorable contract may reduce the resale value far below the original price.

BUYING TIPS FROM GOVERNMENT TASK FORCE

As a result of rising complaints from buyers, a whole network of laws and regulations have come into being around the country. Congress began to move a few years ago. It ordered the Department of Housing and Urban Development to study the situation and make recommendations. The study cited numerous abuses and a lack of uniform regulations. The Condominium Task Force was formed to develop uniform rules to strengthen buyers' rights. Its recommendations were published in February, 1977. A person contemplating buying a condominium could benefit from reading the main points of the report, including recommendations:

● That the owners' association have the right to terminate, without penalty and upon not more than 90 days' notice, any recreation lease or management contract or any other agreement made between the association and the developer or his affiliates;

● That control of the owners' association be given to the purchasers within 120 days after the owners control 75 per cent of the total votes or within a reasonable period of time not exceeding three years;

● That the developer assure that future sections of the same condominium will be compatible in style, quality, size and cost;

● That there may be no "right of first refusal" since a unit owner shall have the right to sell his unit without restriction;

● That books and records of the association and a copy of the audit report, if prepared, be open to inspection of all unit owners;

MOBILE HOMES
Slow Progress on Defects, Safety Hazards

Mobile homes have grown so much in popularity that they now account for more than half of all new housing sold in the United States to people with $15,000 annual income or less, according to the Bureau of the Census. In 1970, the average income of owners was only $7,000. The large numbers of people and their limited buying power have added urgency to quality and safety factors. Yet such factors have been scarce in many units.

In the rush to catch up to the demand for inexpensive housing, many manufacturers have produced mobile homes with major defects and then failed to respond adequately to requests for corrections. Efforts to police the industry by manufacturers themselves and by various government agencies have also been deficient. As a result, mobile homes have caused much public dissatisfaction as shown by the relatively high proportion of complaints.

A survey of nearly 2,000 mobile home owners in Ohio by Housing Advocates Inc., a non-profit group, found that "almost every (home) had at least one serious defect and most had several."

FEDERAL STANDARDS ESTABLISHED

In response to the problems, Congress passed the National Mobile Home Construction and Safety Standards Act of 1974. The law required the Department of Housing and Urban Development (HUD) to set up minimum standards of construction and safety and make an annual report to Congress about conditions in the industry. Federal standards became effective June 15, 1976. Homes manufactured since that date have been required to meet the standards in order to be sold. They have also been required to display an official seal near the electric panel denoting compliance.

The standards require certain minimums in structural strength and design, including alternative means of escape in case of a fire that blocks the door, a relatively frequent occurrence in older homes. The standards also prohibit use of extremely flammable materials. The fatality rate from fires in mobile homes has averaged nearly four times that of a normal residential home, largely because of the difficulty of escaping.

Under HUD rules, each buyer of a mobile home must be given an owner's manual much like the one given to new car buyers. The booklet describes the warranty and tells what is covered and what is not covered. It also advises owners of their rights to be notified of any newly found safety hazards. In serious cases, owners have the right to get the defect corrected by the manufacturer without charge or have the entire home replaced or have the price refunded.

INSPECTION SYSTEM ALSO DEFECTIVE

The federal program also calls for states to help inspect manufacturing plants and monitor dealers to see that the standards are met. (For a list of states with programs approved by HUD, see "States with Pro-Consumer Laws," in the first chapter of this book.) As of 1978, 34 states had agencies with such approval.

Homes not meeting the standards are subject to recall. But recalls have been few, largely because of an inspection system with more defects than the homes themselves. In testimony before the Federal Trade Commission in November, 1977, the head of federal inspection efforts observed that "a very small number" of manufacturers comply with the standard. John S. Mason. chief of the Enforcement Branch of HUD's Office of Mobile Home Standards, said many state inspectors ignore violations by not reporting them as required. He said California had the best state program.

When asked what HUD does to help complainants, he said his agency usually telephones owners for further details, then calls the manufacturer if there is an apparent failure to conform to the federal standards. "Sometimes," he said "that results in a joint inspection, which is between the HUD inspectors and manufacturer, of the actual condition in the home." He said it may bring agreement as to what the manufacturer will and will not do. That is followed, he added, with "a letter from us to the owner describing that agreement and suggesting that if that does not solve the entire problem, additional action can be taken through the warranty or state enforcement." He said the "great majority of complaints" are...settled by the manufacturer without referral to either HUD or the state agency. State agencies, he said, settle "another large quantity" of complaints. Despite these efforts, he said, the number of complaints to HUD has been increasing.

GOVERNMENT PROPOSES NEW WARRANTY SYSTEM

In May, 1975, the Federal Trade Commission proposed a trade regulation rule to better protect buyers of mobile homes. One section of the rule would require manufacturers who offer warranties to establish a performance system assuring that all obligations are fully performed within certain time periods at the home site. Manufacturers would be given three days to correct any defects that could affect safety or make the home uninhabitable. Dealers would have two days to pass along consumer complaints to manufacturers. Defects of lesser importance would have to be passed on within five days by dealers, acted on within seven business days by manufacturers and be completed within 30 days.

The rule would also require manufacturers to inspect the home prior to or at the time of delivery to the buyer and to arrange for or perform reinspection at the home site within 90 days. Forms certifying these actions would have to be submitted to buyers for signature. In case of a dispute between manufacturer and dealer, the manufacturer must make the repairs needed or replace the home or refund the purchase price within a reasonable time. This provision is designed to eliminate situations where the consumer is left to suffer with his defect while the manufacturer and the dealer spend weeks or months arguing over which is to bear the repair burden.

The hearings in 1977 were held by the FTC following publication of a final notice of rulemaking in May of that year. Final action on the rule, however, must await filing of a staff report, various rebuttals, and commission consideration, all of which could take several more years.

LAND FOR SALE
Lots of Trouble for Buyers

The demand for living space and the desire for second homes have begun to leave their mark, unmistakably and often brutally, on the American landscape. Commercial developers, with persuasive advertising appeals, have pockmarked the countryside with unfinished communities and vacation sites, leaving millions of people owning land they want to sell but cannot do so at any price. Happy owners of such lots are a rarity. Despite increased efforts to protect such buyers and the landscape itself by state and federal government agencies, sales of this type continue to grow at a steady pace.

Tensions also have been increasing between conservationists and business firms over the use of unspoiled land for lumbering, mining and other commercial purposes. The controversy, which has simmered for many years, became inflamed in September, 1978 when President Carter proposed to add substantially to the number of protected acres in the U.S. He asked Congress to add 42 million acres of virgin land in Alaska to the National Park System, add 45 million acres also in Alaska to National Widlife Refuges and add another 5 million acres to the National Wild and Scenic River System and National Forests.

In April, 1979, he reversed course. Under pressure from commercial interests wanting to exploit government land, Carter proposed allowing 36 million acres of the 62 million acres of roadless and undeveloped National Forest lands to be used for such purposes as oil and gas exploration, mining, logging and recreation. He recommended transferring 15.4 million acres to the National Wilderness Preservation System and further study of the remaining 10.6 million acres.

GOVERNMENT ACTIONS PUT PRESSURE ON PRICES

Almost as controversial was legislation in Congress to double the size of the Redwood National Park in California. That controversy aroused lumber interests and led to several acts of wanton destruction of redwoods in the area. As both state and federal governments continue to buy land and set aside usable acres, they reduce the amount of land available for private uses, fanning further the inflationary trends in land sales. (For more on land use, see the Environment chapter.)

Local restrictions in the form of zoning laws, building codes and sewer moratoriums have the same effect. Although they are designed to slow down commercial and residential development, their efforts often boomerang in the form of higher prices. The battle to slow down what are considered undesirable developments is a losing one in most areas of the country.

LAND DEVELOPERS BOUNCE BACK

The year 1978 proved to be a turning point for developers of vacation and retirement communities. After passage of the Interstate land Sales Full Disclosure Law in 1968, many of these businesses became incensed at increasing government requirements governing land sales. Working with friendly members of Congress, they nearly succeeded in getting legislation virtually wiping out these federal regulations. They vowed to try harder in 1979.

Meanwhile, the Office of Interstate Land Sales Registration (OILSR) got the message and began relaxing its rules. Revised regulations published in April, 1979, by the Department of Housing and Urban Development, the parent agency of OILSR, gave developers new options on what they must disclose and increased the number of developments exempted from the rules altogether. Newly exempted were local offerings of less than 200 lots and certain others of relatively small size. Some paperwork was also eliminated.

INFORMATION FOR BUYERS IN PROPERTY REPORT

Federal law still requires most sellers of 50 or more lots in a subdivision to register with OILSR and offer prospective customers a Property Report containing certain information. The information covers the right to cancel the contract, title data, physical condition of the land, plans for roads and utlities and other characteristics of the development. Buyers have:

● The right to cancel a sale and get a refund if the Property Report has not been registered with OILSR (HUD);

● The right to cancel a sale and get a refund if the report is not presented to the buyer at least 48 hours before the contract is signed; and

● The right to sue the developer if a Property Report contains untrue statements or if fraud or misrepresentation is present.

Property Reports can be obtained well in advance of purchase from all developers subject to federal law. They also can be obtained for $2.50 from OILSR by providing the name of the developer and the location to HUD/ OILSR, 451 Seventh St. SW, Room 4108, Washington, DC, 20410. Also available is a free folder: *Get the Facts Before Buying Land.*

FEDERAL EFFORTS TO SINGLE OUT WORST OFFENDERS

Ironically, HUD has prosecuted few cases, mostly against small firms. In two years, OILSR suspended only 225 developers for varying periods of time for violations of disclosure and registration requirements. Only a few were fined or jailed.

The Federal Trade Commission (FTC) has been more effective against large companies but has acted against even fewer firms. In the past few years, the FTC has investigated 35 companies, issued four formal complaints, held two trials and issued five consent orders, including some requiring large refunds. Among recent cases handled by the FTC have been:

● A consent agreement with Cavanagh Communities Corporation of

Miami in January, 1979, following complaints by the FTC that the firm had falsely represented the value of lots in Florida and Arizona. Florida subdivisions included Rotonda, Palm Beach Heights, Paradise Hills and Perdido Bay Country Club Estates. The Arizona subdivision was Twin Lakes Country Club Estates. Cavanagh was required to offer a 10-day cooling-off period for purchasers to cancel contracts and get full refunds for any reason and to disclose to prospective purchasers that the purpose of holding dinner parties, awarding fee gifts and other promotions is to sell land. The firm was required to send "truth letters" to certain buyers, stop representing that purchasers must complete their contract payments and stop taking legal action to recover unpaid balances.

● A change in an order originally issued in 1974 against GAC Corp. requiring the firm to improve uninhabitable Florida land it had sold for homesites. Instead, the FTC decided in February, 1979, to allow the company to give refunds or alternate sites to some owners in Golden Gate Estates. The previous order was eased because GAC was going through reorganization under bankruptcy laws.

● A consent order requiring Bankers Life and Casualty Co. of Chicago to refund payments or cancel debts totalling $14 million to buyers of land in Texas and Colorado. Purchasers of land from January 1, 1971, to January 1, 1974, were eligible. Subdivisions involved included San Luis Valley Ranches, Rio Grande Ranches, Top of the World, Larwill Costilla Ranches, Hartsel Ranch and Estates of the World. Buyers who stopped paying were also entitled to refunds. More than 7,600 buyers were eligible for up to 70 per cent of what they paid.

In addition, buyers of these and other lots could save millions of dollars in federal income tax for contracts cancelled for non-payment after January 1, 1975, without refunds. For further information, ask for an FTC leaflet entitled Facts for Consumers dated 4/8/78 or contact the Internal Revenue Service.

SUGGESTED READINGS ON HOUSING AND LAND

Mobile Homes: The Low-Cost Housing Hoax, by the Center for Auto Safety; Grossman Publishers, $10.95.

Questions About Condominiums: What to Ask Before You Buy, a free booklet from HUD.

Wise Home Buying, a 1974 pamphlet free from HUD.

Mobile Home Manual, by "Plain Jane" Conrad, P.O. Box 21222, Denver, CO, 80221. Price $1.

Buying Lots from Developers, (HUD-357-1(4), Department of Housing and Urban Development, 50¢, Government Printing Office.

Get the Facts Before Buying Land, free from HUD.

Promised Lands Vol. 1, Subdivision in Deserts and Mountains, Vol. 2, Subdivisions in Florida's Wetlands and *Vol. 3, Subdivision and the Law,* $20 each from INFORM, 25 Broad St., New York, NY, 10004.

My House Has a Flat: Mobile Homes, part of "Consumer Survival Kit" published by the Maryland Center for Public Broadcasting, Owings Mills, MD, 21117; $1.

The Great Land Hustle, a 1972 report on irresponsible land selling, by Morton Paulson; Regnery Publishers, 114 West Illinois St., Chicago, IL, 20210; $7.95.

Clothing and Furnishings

Since the start of the 1970s, attitudes toward clothing have changed greatly. Buyers have built up an unprecedented resistance to "fad" fashions engineered by the industry and ready-to-wear designers. Interest has shifted markedly away from the frivolous and temporary and toward basic utility and permanence.

At the same time, technology has expanded buyer choices from the once-dominant basics of cotton, linen, wool and silk to include 17 man-made alternatives. The new fibers, plus the proliferation of synthetic and natural combinations, have created vast confusion in the public mind. Biggest problems have been in evaluating quality, durability, cleanability and flammability in order to get the most for one's money.

Meanwhile, manufacturers have begun to settle on certain combinations of natural and synthetic fibers that present the least problems. For example, 100 per cent polyester fabric, which popularized the "easy care" qualities of man-made fibers, was found impractical. Difficulties with stains, static electricity and lack of absorbency overshadowed the easy-care properties. Likewise, all-cotton clothing, despite its absorbent and static-free qualities, became unacceptable for many uses because of its inability to hold a crease and tendency to wrinkle.

The result has been development of a popular fabric that combines the best properties of both, with 35 per cent polyester and 65 per cent cotton. This is the combination most often used now in making sheets, pillow cases, shirts and many other garments with easy-care properties. Wool also has had a comeback, particularly in combination with synthetic fibers.

With so many new combinations on the market, it is more important than ever to check labels before buying. Federal law requires all clothing and textile furnishings to be labeled with the percentage of fiber content. Learning the characteristics of the new fabrics can help considerably in choosing textiles for ease of care, durability and confort as well as cost.

CHARACTERISTICS OF COMMON FIBERS

NATURAL FIBERS

COTTON

Cotton is a natural plant fiber and the world's most versatile. It may be treated, blended, sanforized (pre-shrunk) or mercerized (to strengthen fiber and add luster).

BEST CHARACTERISTICS: Absorbent, color fast, resistant to heat, moths, perspiration, soft but strong.

WORST CHARACTERISTICS: Poor crease retention, mildews easily, aged by sunlight and wrinkles easily.

FLAMMABILITY: Burns readily, not self-extinguishing. Cotton must be treated to become flame resistant but loses durability and softness.

LINEN

Linen, a product of the flax plant, has a rough, uneven texture. Hand labor has made linen an expensive fabric recently. Linen does not produce lint, although over time the fibers will crack if the fabric is constantly creased in the same place.

BEST CHARACTERISTICS: Absorbent, color fast, durable, resistant to heat, moths and perspiration.

WORST CHARACTERISTICS: Will not hold a crease, winkles easily and is not resistant to mildew.

FLAMMABILITY: Ignites readily and is not self-extinguishing. Linen can be treated but loses some durability.

SILK

Silk is the only natural continuous (filament) fiber. It is obtained from unwrapping the silk worm cocoon. Fabrics labeled as "pure silk" or "all silk" cannot contain more than 10 per cent by weight of dyes or finishing materials.

BEST CHARACTERISTICS: Absorbent, color fast, wrinkle resistant and strong when dry.

WORST CHARACTERISTICS: Poor crease retention, weakened by heat and perspiration, not durable. Poor strength when wet. Yellowed by age, strong soap and sunlight.

FLAMMABILITY: Does not ignite readily, but any materials or dyes added to silk may change this property.

WOOL

Wool fibers are animal hairs from sheep, lamb, Angora or Cashmere goats, alpaca, or llama. "Virgin" wool is new wool. "Reprocessed" wool has fibers that have been reclaimed from unused products such as remnants. "Reused" wool has fibers reclaimed from worn or used textiles.

A "worsted" fabric contains longer, smoother fibers that crease more readily than unworsted wools.

BEST CHARACTERISTICS: Absorbent, color fast, warm, resistant to wrinkles.

WORST CHARACTERISTICS: Pills (forms fuzzy balls) easily, may be allergenic, poor resistance to moths, bleaches, perspiration and is damaged by strong soaps.

FLAMMABILITY: In most weaves will not burn readily and is self-extinguishing.

MAN-MADE FIBERS

ACETATE

Acetate is made from cellulose, a plant fiber, but has been changed chemically to form either long continuous filaments or short spun yarns. Taffeta, satin, crepe, brocade all contain acetate.

BEST CHARACTERISTICS: Silk-like appearance, soft or crisp, resistant to mildew and moths.

WORST CHARACTERISTICS: Not absorbent, does not keep a crease, but wrinkles easily, not strong or durable, does not wash well.

FLAMMABILITY: Acetate ignites easily and is not self-extinguishing. Melts at high temperatures. Can be made flame retardant, but loses some of the desirable characteristics.

TRIACETATE

Similar to acetate but is more resistant to heat damage, so fabrics can have pleats or creases heat-set.

BEST CHARACTERISTICS: Soft, resistant to heat and wrinkles.

WORST CHARACTERISTICS: Not absorbent, not durable.

FLAMMABILITY: Ignites readily and melts at high temperatures. Can be made flame retardant, but loses some desirable properties.

ACRYLIC

Acrylic has many wool-like properties, but it can be used for a variety of fabric from fake furs to smooth fabrics.

BEST CHARACTERISTICS: Color fast, moth and mildew resistant, holds a crease but resists wrinkles, warm and not damaged by the sun.

WORST CHARACTERISTICS: Pills, not strong or absorbent and holds static.

FLAMMABILITY: Burns readily.

ANIDEX

Anidex is a new, man-made elastic, that is most often used in combination with all other fabrics to permit stretching without sag.

BEST CHARACTERISTICS: Good stretch and recovery, resistant to bleaches drycleaning solvents, heat and perspiration.

WORST CHARACTERISTICS: Cannot withstand extreme heat.

FLAMMABILITY: Does not ignite readily, but will burn once ignited.

GLASS

Glass fibers are often used in home furnishings such as drapes and for industrial purposes. The glass fibers are barely visible but can easily puncture and enter the skin, so glass is not suitable for clothing.

BEST CHARACTERISTICS: Color fast, strong, resistant to heat, mildew, moths sunlight and wrinkling.

WORST CHARACTERISTICS: Non-absorbent, wears poorly.

FLAMMABILITY: Non-flamable.

METALLIC

A metallic fiber is either totally metal or metal coating a plastic or another fiber Metallic fibers are brittle and expensive, but add luster to apparel and furnishings.

BEST CHARACTERISTICS: Lustrous appearance, resists weathering, chlorine bleaching and salt water.

WORST CHARACTERISTICS: Non-absorbent, brittle.

FLAMMABILITY: Heat-sensitive. Plastic components will soften and shrink.

MODACRYLIC

This "modified" acrylic fiber can be heat set into a variety of patterns or tex tures, and requires little ironing. Pile fabrics resembling natural furs are also modacrylics

BEST CHARACTERISTICS: Color fast, warm, soft, resistant to moths, mildew wrinkling and chemicals.

WORST CHARACTERISTICS: Pills, not very strong and easily loses shape.

FLAMMABILITY: Flame resistant and self extinguishing. Stiffens and discolor at high temperatures.

NYLON

First introduced in 1939, Nylon is one of the strongest man-made fibers. It i very light weight and versatile.

BEST CHARACTERISTICS: Color fast, retains shape, elastic, resists mildew moths, perspiration, strong, durable.

WORST CHARACTERISTICS: Pills, not absorbent, wrinkles and is damaged by sunlight.

FLAMMABILITY: Nylon burns, melts and drips at high temperatures.

OLEFIN

Olefin fibers are derived from petroleum gases and are not often used for clothing except for thermal insulation.

BEST CHARACTERISTICS: Resistant to abrasion, chemicals, mildew, perspira tion, will not pill, stain, and is not affected by sunlight or weather.

WORST CHARACTERISTICS: Not absorbent and difficult to dye.

FLAMMABILITY: Olefin burns, melts and drips once ignited.

POLYESTER

Polyester is the key to easy-care fabrics and clothing. It is used extensively alone and in combination with many other man-made and natural fibers. The blend of 65 per cent cotton and 35 per cent polyester combines the best characteristics of both fibers: wrinkle resistant but lightweight and absorbent.

BEST CHARACTERISTICS: Color fast, retains shape, crease resistant, resists mildew, moths, perspiration, and wrinkling, and is strong.

WORST CHARACTERISTICS: Pills, not absorbent, oily stains are difficult to remove.

FLAMMABILITY: Polyester does not ignite readily but when lit, it melts and drips.

RAYON

Rayon is the first and perhaps the least expensive man-made fiber. It is made by chemically altering cellulose fibers. Rayon combines well with most other fibers and new processing techniques permit rayon to be more sheer with greater strength.

BEST CHARACTERISTICS: Absorbent, color fast.

WORST CHARACTERISTICS: Not resistant to mildew, wrinkles, does not hold shape and is not very strong.

FLAMMABILITY: Rayon ignites readily but can be made flame resistant.

RUBBER

Natural rubber comes from certain plants. Synthetic rubber is a petroleum by-product. Rubber is usually wrapped in other fibers to give fabrics elasticity.

BEST CHARACTERISTICS: Good strength and holding power.

WORST CHARACTERISTICS: Not resistant to perspiration, or body oils, and may be decomposed by age or light.

FLAMMABILITY: Does not ignite readily, but when lit, burns with a heavy smoke.

SARAN

Saran is used for home furnishings, carpeting and blankets in a many-filament form. It has very limited use in clothing.

BEST CHARACTERISTICS: Resistant to chemicals, fading, mildew, staining, sunlight and weathering.

WORST CHARACTERISTICS: Non-absorbent, poor resistance to heat and is not washable at warm or high temperatures.

FLAMMABILITY: Saran does not support combustion.

SPANDEX

Spandex has great elasticity and almost always is combined with other fibers. In home sewing, spandex will not break as other elastic fibers do when punctured by the sewing needle.

BEST CHARACTERISTICS: Resistant to body oils, cosmetics, and sunlight. Very elastic.

WORST CHARACTERISTICS: Yellows with age and is sensitive to higher temperatures.

FLAMMABILITY: Melts at high temperatures.

VINYON

Vinyon is rarely used alone, but can be blended and felted with other fibers for use in carpeting and non-woven textiles.

BEST CHARACTERISTICS: Resistant to alcohols, bacteria, fungi, mildew, moths and chemicals. Elastic.

WORST CHARACTERISTICS: Poor resistance to heat, not strong.

FLAMMABILITY: Vinyon does not support combustion.

MANUFACTURERS OF SYNTHETIC FABRICS

Trademark	Generic Name	Company
Acrilan	acrylic, modacrylic	Monsanto Textiles Company
Anso	nylon	Allied Chemical Corp., Fibers Div.
Antron	nylon	E.I. du Pont de Nemours & Co., Inc.
Ariloft	acetate	Eastman Kodak Company Tennessee Eastman Co. Division
Arnel	triacetate	Celanese Fibers Marketing Co. Celanese Corp.
Avlin	polyester	Avtex Fibers Inc.
Avril	rayon (high wet modulus)	Avtex Fibers Inc.
Beau-Grip	rayon	Beaunit Corporation
Beaunit Nylon	nylon	Beaunit Corporation
Bi-Loft	acrylic	Monsanto Textiles Company
Blue "C"	nylon, polyester	Monsanto Textiles Company
Cadon	nylon	Monsanto Textiles Company
Cantrece	nylon	E.I. du Pont de Nemours & Co., Inc.
Caprolan	nylon, polyester	Allied Chemical Corp., Fibers Div.
Celanese	nylon, acetate	Celanese Fibers Marketing Co., Celanese Corp.
Chromspun	acetate	Eastman Kodak Company Tennessee Eastman Co. Division
Coloray	rayon	Courtaulds North America Inc.
Cordura	nylon	E.I. du Pont de Nemours & Co., Inc.
Courtaulds Nylon	nylon	Courtaulds North America Inc.
Crepeset	nylon	American Enka Company
Creslan	acrylic	American Cyanamid Company
Cumuloft	nylon	Monsanto Textiles Company
Dacron	polyester	E.I. du Pont de Nemours & Co., Inc.
Elura	modacrylic	Monsanto Textiles Company
Encron	polyester	American Enka Company
Enkaloft	nylon	American Enka Company
Enkalure	nylon	American Enka Company
Enkasheer	nylon	American Enka Company
Enkrome	rayon	American Enka Company
Estron	acetate	Eastman Kodak Company Tennessee Eastman Co. Division
Fibro	rayon	Courtaulds North America Inc.
Fina	acrylic	Monsanto Textiles Company
Fortrel	polyester	Fiber Industries Inc., Marketed by Celanese Fibers Marketing Co., a Division of Celanese Corp.
Herculon	olefin	Hercules Inc., Fibers Division
Hollofil	polyester	E.I. du Pont de Nemours & Co., Inc.
Kevlar	aramid	E.I. du Pont de Nemours & Co., Inc.
Kodel	polyester	Eastman Kodak Company Tennessee Eastman Co. Division
Lanese	acetate, polyester	Celanese Fibers Marketing Co. Celanese Corp.
Loftura	acetate	Eastman Kodak Company Tennessee Eastman Co. Division

Trademark	Generic Name	Company
Lurex	metallic	Dow Badische Company
Lycra	spandex	E.I. du Pont de Nemours & Co., Inc.
Marvess	olefin	Phillips Fibers Corp., Subsidiary of Phillips Petroleum Co.
Monvelle	biconstituent nylon/spandex	Monsanto Textiles Company
Multisheer	nylon	American Enka Company
Nomex	aramid	E.I. du Pont de Nemours & Co., Inc.
Orlon	acrylic	E.I. du Pont de Nemours & Co., Inc.
Polyloom	olefin	Chevron Chemical Co., Fibers Div.
Qiana	nylon	E.I. du Pont de Nemours & Co., Inc.
Quintess	polyester	Phillips Fibers Corp., Subsidiary of Phillips Petroleum Co.
SEF	modacrylic	Monsanto Textiles Company
Shantura	polyester	Rohm and Haas Co., Fibers Div.
Shareen	nylon	Courtaulds North America Inc.
Spectran	polyester	Monsanto Textiles Company
Strialine	polyester	American Enka Company
Teflon	fluorocarbon	E.I. du Pont de Nemours & Co., Inc.
Textura	polyester	Rohm and Haas Co., Fibers Div.
Trevira	polyester	Hoechst Fibers Industries
Twisloc	polyester	Monsanto Textiles Company
Ulstron	nylon	Monsanto Textiles Company
Ultron	nylon	Monsanto Textiles Company
Vecana	nylon	Chevron Chemical Company
Vectra	olefin	Vectra Corp., Subsidiary of Chevron Chemical Company
Verel	modacrylic	Eastman Kodak Company Tennessee Eastman Co. Division
Vycron	polyester	Beaunit Corporation
Xena	rayon (high wet modulus)	Beaunit Corporation
X-Static	nylon, metallic	Rohm and Haas Co., Fibers Div.
Zantrel	rayon (high wet modulus)	American Enka Company
Zeflon	nylon	Dow Badische Company
Zefran	acrylic, nylon, polyester	Dow Badische Company

REMOVING CARPET STAINS

If a stain occurs on a carpet, blot up as much of it as possible. Most stains can be removed by sponging with a solution of one teaspoon of mild detergent to one teaspoon of white vinegar in a quart of warm water.

Oily stains can be removed with a very small amount of drycleaning fluid such as trichloroethylene. Most manufacturers suggest professional carpet cleaning, but will provide home-care information upon request.

LAWS TO PROTECT CLOTHES BUYERS

When buying clothing, whether fabric, fur or woolen, read the label. It should tell who manufactured the garment, what it is made of and how to care for it. To protect buyers against deceptive labeling, Congress has passed the following laws and given the Federal Trade Commission the authority to enforce them:

WOOL PRODUCTS LABELING ACT: Effective since 1940, this law requires the label to specify the type of wool and all other fibers making up five per cent or more of the fabric content. The FTC has standardized these definitions:

"Reprocessed wool" refers to fibers previously woven or felted into a wool product that was never used by consumers. "Reused wool" means fibers reclaimed from a used wool product and reworked into another garment. "Virgin wool" or "wool" is any animal fleece that has never been used to make another product.

FUR PRODUCTS LABELING ACT: This law, passed in 1951, requires furriers to label the type of animal fur, the country of origin, whether the fur is imported, if the fur has been dyed or colored and if the garment is made of scraps of fur.

TEXTILE FIBER PRODUCTS IDENTIFICATION ACT: In 1960 the FTC defined 17 generic groups of man-made textiles (listed elsewhere in this chapter) and required manufacturers of natural and man-made textile products to label the fiber content in percentage terms by the generic name. If less than five per cent of a fiber is used, it does not need to be labeled.

In 1978 and 1979, the Commission noted a number of problems with the labeling of down-filled garments. It found that many jackets, vests, etc., which were labeled "down" were actually composed of more than 20 per cent water-fowl feather.

A 1971 guideline under the Act requires that all such garments be labeled with percentages of down and water fowl feather if the filling is less than 80 per cent down. Percentages of synthetic fibers must also be stated on the label. The FTC took action in a number of cases to eliminate the practice and attributed the increase in problems to the increase in popularity of down-filled clothes.

PERMANENT CARE LABELING: Since 1972, the Federal Trade Commission has used its rule-making authority to require manufacturers to include instructions for "normal" care on labels of all textile garments. For example: Machine wash warm, tumble dry. In January, 1976, the FTC proposed to expand this rule to require more complete labeling and expand care labeling to other textiles.

The revised rule would require clearer, more descriptive instructions and include all methods of care. Some manufacturers have been "low labeling" items: citing only the most conservative method of care maintenance, such as "Dry Clean Only" when a garment could be hand washed or "Do Not Bleach" when bleaching would not harm the garment.

Permanent care labels would be required for the first time on suede and leather apparel, upholstered furniture, draperies, sheets and spreads, table cloths, towels and slipcovers. The rule would also require labels to be supplied to fabric, carpet and rug retailers to pass along to consumers.

The revision has not been finalized.

FLAMMABILITY

Although a law designed to reduce the hazards of flammable fabrics was passed in 1953, an estimated 250,000 injuries and a quarter of a billion in damages are related to or caused by flammable fabrics every year.

Regulations require that children's sleepwear, mattresses and mattress pads and carpets and rugs be flame retardant, but there is no such requirement for upholstered furniture, which is associated with many household and office fires. The Consumer Product Safety Commission (CPSC) has been trying for five years to curb dangers from flammable upholstery.

In 1977, it decided that mandatory standards were necessary. But it delayed action until its staff had determined whether costs would be reasonable and whether other alternatives might be better. It finally held hearings on a proposed standard in 1978. The standard would require the most flammable upholstery fabrics, including heavyweight cottons, rayons and linens, pass certain flammability tests before being used in upholstery.

Industry representatives said they could control the problem with voluntary standards now in effect and added that the real fire hazards were smoking and drinking, not furniture. They said the answer lay in promoting smoke detectors and cigarette controls. No commission action has been taken.

TRIS PULLED OFF THE MARKET, SHIPPED ABROAD

In April, 1977, the CPSC banned the use of "Tris," a flame retardant which had been found to be carcinogenic. But the chemical is still a major problem—outside the U.S.

Many manufacturers who were forced to take back Tris-treated children's sleepwear and dispose of items on the shelves tried to recoup their losses by exporting the hazardous products.

In May, 1978, the Commission prohibited the export of Tris products that had been sold or offered for sale in domestic commerce. It said Tris-treated children's sleepwear was so dangerous "that the risks it poses transcend national boundaries." But much of the banned sleepwear had already been "dumped," and the export ban was not enforced. The situation sparked Congressional hearings on the export of other hazardous products such as drugs, pesticides, medical devices, foods and additives and various consumer products.

There are many flame retardants which have been designated safe, however, and they are being used not only for children's sleepwear but for such items as nurses and waitresses uniforms, nightgowns, pajamas and shirts. Public reluctance to buy such items seems to be diminishing.

REGULATIONS CONCERNING FLAMMABLE FABRICS

The standards listed below require fabrics used in the specified textile product to be "flame retardant." This means using a natural fiber that does not readily burn or a chemical treatment to make the material resist flames. Such treatment is designed to make the fire go out when the flame source is removed and make the flame spread more slowly if its source is kept on the textile.

The GENERAL WEARING APPAREL STANDARD was adopted in 1954 to prohibit extremely flammable apparel, such as rayon sweaters, from the marketplace.

Since 1971, LARGE AND SMALL CARPETS AND RUGS have had to be flame retardant. The standard simulates a match dropping on a carpet. Small carpets and rugs that do not restrict and self-extinguish a flame within the limits, must be labeled with a warning. All carpets and rugs treated to be flame retardant must be labeled with a "T." The standard does not include linoleum or floor tile.

MATTRESSES AND MATTRESS PADS but not pillows, box springs or upholstered furniture, were first required to meet flame retardant standards in 1973. The standard simulates a burning cigarette dropped onto the surface. Mattresses and pads that fail to meet the standard must be labeled with a warning. Mattresses meeting the standard need no label, but pads must be labeled with a "T" if treated.

CHILDREN'S SLEEPWEAR (sizes 0 to 6X) and any related sleep garment except underwear and diapers have been required to be fire retardant since 1973. This standard was developed to prevent a child's garment from catching fire if it comes in contact with a flame or match. A flame retardant treatment must last for at least 50 washings. Care labels indicating any special laundering instructions are required.

In 1975 the CHILDREN'S SLEEPWEAR standard was expanded to include sizes 7 to 14.

IN CASE OF CLEANING DAMAGE

The International Fabricare Institute, successor to the American Institute of Laundering and National Institute of Drycleaning, is a trade association that will analyze a garment or furnishing to determine why it was ruined.

IFI is headquartered in Joliet, IL, with a Research Center and Drycleaning Analysis Laboratory at 12251 Tech Rd., Silver Spring, MD, 20904. IFI will accept textiles for analysis if referred by a professional drycleaner or launderer who is an IFI member, a retail store, Better Business Bureau or government consumer affairs office. The Lab will not test textiles sent by individuals or non-member laundries or drycleaners.

For a $6 fee, the lab will analyze the textile and determine what ruined it. The results can help the consumer, retailer, manufacturer and cleaner conclude who is at fault.

The responsible party will usually honor a request for replacement or reimbursement after the IFI makes a report. A person should contact the retailer where the garment was purchased or the cleaner and ask that it be sent to the IFI. Retailers are given credit when a damaged garment is returned to the manufacturer. Some retailers such as Montgomery Ward, Sears and Penneys maintain their own testing labs to test damaged garments or furnishings.

If the retailer balks, contact the manufacturer. The address is usually on the hang tags or can be located through a Better Business Bureau. After the manufacturer has been given ample time to respond, contact any BBB or consumer protection agency and ask it to forward the textile to IFI.

REMOVING STAINS FROM FABRICS

Simple home treatment can remove many stains from washable fabric without a trace.

Treatments for 50 common stains are described below. Before using any of the home treatments, test the detergent or chemicals on a hem or seam of the garment to make sure the fabric will not be damaged by the stain removal process. In cases where rubbing alcohol is suggested, test to make sure the dye will not run.

Chemicals such as oxalic acid, acetic acid, perchloroethylene and other grease solvents (trichloroethane, trichloroethylene, petroleum naphthas, petroleum distillates and petroleum hydrocarbons) are available at drug stores. Sodium thiosulfate is available at photo supply stores. Most of the other preparations can be purchased at a grocery store. Read directions carefully, because some of these chemicals are poisonous.

Care labels on clothing will indicate if chlorine bleach (usually for white clothes) or peroxygen bleach (for colors) may be used. Peroxygen bleaches include those containing sodium perborate and potassium monopersulfate.

Silks and woolens are very delicate fibers, and professional dry cleaning is usually the best method of stain removal. Bleaches are not recommended for these two natural fibers, and when ammonia is suggested, dilute to half strength. Acetate is a delicate man-made fiber. When alcohol is suggested, dilute to at least half-strength.

Some stain removal methods are safe for dry cleanables, but for best results, consult a reliable dry cleaner. And when taking garments to be dry cleaned, point out all stains to the dry cleaner.

Listed 'first is the most common method of removing non-greasy stains. It should work also for ones not listed here. Other types of stains are listed alphabetically.

ITEM-BY-ITEM STAIN REMOVAL

NON-GREASY STAINS: CANDY, CASEIN GLUE, CATSUP, CHOCOLATE, COCOA, COFFEE, CREAM, DYES, EGG, FOOD COLORING, GRAVY, ICE CREAM, MAYONNAISE, MEAT JUICE, PERFUME, SALAD DRESSING, SCORCH, SOFT DRINKS, TEA, TOMATO STAINS, VEGETABLES, WRITING INK—Soak 30 minutes or more in cool water. Rub stain with a detergent paste and rinse. If stain remains, wash in chlorine or peroxygen bleach according to directions on package. Or, if safe for fabric, use acetone, alcohol or amyl acetate (for acetate fabrics) or turpentine directly on the stain.

ACID: Rinse immediately and apply house-hold ammonia. Rinse.

ADHESIVE TAPE: Scrape away gummy adhesive and sponge with perchlorethyl ene or trichloroethane or trichloroethylene (except on acetates) or other grease solvent.

ALCOHOLIC BEVERAGES: Where stain has not caused dye to run, sponge with rubbing alcohol, diluted to half strength for acetates. Wash with chlorine or peroxygen bleach. Or use a grease solvent such as perchloroethylene.

ALKALIES: (ammonia, lye)—Sponge with white vinegar.

ANTIPERSPIRANTS OR DEODORANTS: Rub in detergent paste. Use half strength ammonia to restore color.

ARGYROL: If stain is fresh, wash in detergent. Or, put tincture of iodine on stain, let stand for a few minutes and either soak in cool water, moisten and hold stain over steam or sponge on alcohol.

BLOOD: If no set, wash with soap or detergent. Or put a few drops of ammonia on stain and wash.

BLUING: Use acetone (amyl acetate on acetate fabrics) or alcohol.

BUTTER OR MARGARINE: Wash, sponge on perchloroethylene or other grease solvent.

CANDLE WAX AND PARAFFIN: Place stain between layers of absorbent paper

RECOMMENDED TYPES OF FABRIC CARE

Method		Cotton	Linen	Silk	Wool	Acetate	Tri-acetate	Acrylic	Anidex	Glass	Metallic	Moda-crylic	Nylon	Olefin	Polyester	Rayon	Rubber	Saran	Spandex	Vinyon
Hand Wash	Warm	●	●	●	●	●	●	●		●	●	●	●		●	●			●	●
	Cold	●		●	●										●			●		
Machine Wash	Hot	●	●																	
	Warm	●	●				●	●	●	●		●	●	●	●		●	●	●	●
Tumble Dry	Hot/Normal	●	●												●					
	Warm/Delicate	●					●		●			●	●	●	●	●			●	
Drip Dry	Flat Surface				●	●					●				●					
	Line Dry	●	●	●		●					●	●	●	●	●	●	●	●	●	●
Dry Clean				●	●			●		●	●			●	●	●			●	
Do Not Use a Strong Detergent				●	●	●					●					●	●	●	●	
Do Not Bleach			●	●	●	●					●					●	●		●	
Iron	Low Heat Set								●			●								
	Medium Set	●						●	●				●		●	●				
	High Set	●	●				●													
No Ironing Required										●				●	●		●	●	●	●

Source: National Bureau of Standards

and press with warm iron, or if safe for fabric, pour boiling water through spot. Or use perchloroethylene or other grease solvent on stain.

CARBON PAPER OR TYPEWRITER RIBBON: Use a few drops of ammonia on the stain and wash in detergent. For stains from duplicating paper use alcohol, diluted to one-third strength for acetate.

CHEWING GUM: Harden gum with ice and scrape off as much as possible. Sponge on perchloroethylene or other grease solvent.

CHLORINE: For yellow stains on resin-finished fabrics, soak at least 30 minutes in solution of one teaspoon sodium thiosulfate per quart of warm water.

COSMETICS: For eye shadow, lipstick, mascara, blusher, powder, eye liner, rub with undiluted liquid detergent or detergent paste or sponge with perchloroethylene or reliable grease solvent.

CRAYON: Rub with undiluted liquid detergent or detergent paste or sponge with perchloroethylene or reliable grease solvent.

FINGER NAIL POLISH: Sponge stain with acetone or amyl acetate (for acetate fabrics).

FISH SLIME, MUCUS OR VOMIT: Sponge stain with solution of salt water (one-fourth cup salt per quart of water) and treat as non-greasy stain.

FRUIT JUICES: Sponge with cool water immediately and treat as non-greasy stain.

FURNITURE POLISH: Rub stain with detergent paste, let stand overnight. If stain remains, treat with perchloroethylene or a petroleum distillate.

GLUE, MUCILAGE OR ADHESIVE: For airplane glue, sponge with acetone or amyl acetate (for acetate fabrics). For hardened plastic glue, immerse in boiling vinegar up to 15 minutes. For rubber cement, scrape stain, sponge on perchloroethylene or other grease solvent.

GREASE, LARD OR OIL: Rub detergent paste on stain, let stand for several hours and wash. Sponge on perchloroethylene. If a yellow stain remains, wash in chlorine or peroxygen bleach solution. Of if safe for fabric, wash in sodium perborate.

INK, BALLPOINT: Sponge repeatedly with acetone or amyl acetate (for acetates). If stain remains wash in bleach solution.

INK, INDIA: Treat stain as soon as possible. Rinse away loose pigment, wash in warm, soapy water, then soak overnight in warm suds and one to four tablespoons of ammonia per quart of water.

IODINE: First, treat as non-greasy stain. If stain remains after treatment, soak in solution of one tablespoon of sodium thiosulfate per pint of warm water. Or moisten stain and hold in steam from a boiling kettle. Or soak with alcohol for several hours (diluted to half strength for acetates).

LACQUER: Sponge with acetone or amyl acetate (for acetates).

MAYONNAISE OR SALAD DRESSINGS: Soak in cool water at least 30 minutes. If stain persists sponge with perchloroethylene or another reliable grease solvent.

METAL stains caused by tarnish: Do not bleach. Dampen stain and rub with lemon juice, white vinegar or 10 per cent acetic acid or oxalic acid solution. Rinse well.

MILDEW: Wash in chlorine or peroxygen bleach, let dry in the sun.

MUSTARD: Soak in hot detergent solution for several hours. Wash in chlorine or peroxygen bleach solution.

PAINT OR VARNISH: Treat promptly by washing with detergent. Sponge with turpentine. For aluminum paint stains, use trichloroethylene (not on acetates). While stain is still wet from solvent, work in detergent paste and let stand overnight.

PERSPIRATION: Rub in detergent paste. If discolored, sponge with ammonia or white vinegar. Bleach yellow stains with chlorine or peroxygen bleach or if safe for fabric, sodium perborate.

PLASTIC marks from hangers: Sponge with amyl acetate or trichloroethylene. Do not use trichloroethylene on acetates.

RUST: Moisten stain with solution of one tablespoon oxalic acid in one cup of water. If stain remains, heat solution and repeat. Rinse thoroughly. Or spread stain over a pan of boiling water and squeeze lemon juice on the stain. Or sprinkle salt on stain, squeeze lemon juice on it and dry in the sun.

SHELLAC: If color safe, sponge stain with alcohol, diluted to half strength for acetate, or use turpentine.

SHOE POLISH: Rub detergent paste into stain. If stain persists, sponge with perchloroethylene or turpentine. If stain still remains wash in solution of chlorine or peroxygen bleach.

SOOT OR SMOKE: Rub with detergent paste or use perchloroethylene or another grease solvent.

TOBACCO: Sponge with alcohol, diluted to half strength for acetates. If stain remains wash in a solution of chlorine or peroxygen bleach.

TRANSFER PATTERNS: Rub in detergent and let stand overnight. If stain remains, sponge with perchloroethylene or grease solvent.

URINE: If fabric has yellowed, sponge with ammonia, white vinegar or 10 per cent acetic acid solution. If stain remains, bleach with chlorine or peroxygen bleach.

WALNUT, BLACK: For fresh stains, boil in hot soapy water. If stain is set, mix equal parts of either chlorine bleach or sodium perborate bleach with water and apply to stain.

WAX (floor or car): Rub with detergent paste and let stand overnight. Or apply perchloroethylene or other grease solvent.

YELLOW or brown stains: Wash in weak chlorine or peroxygen bleach solution. If stain remains use a stronger solution, or dissolve one tablespoon oxalic acid crystals in warm water (hot water for stubborn stains) and apply to stain. Or treat as chlorine stain.

Source: USDA (Home and Garden Bulletin No. 62)

HOW TO BUY CARPETING

Buying a carpet may be hazardous to your pocketbook. The carpeting industry is one of the few industries that has resisted most attempts to grade or standardize quality and durability of its products. And for most carpets, there is no manufacturer's guarantee.

But since 1975, the Federal Housing Administration has had a formal testing and certification program for carpets used in FHA-mortgaged homes. Although homes with FHA loans constitute only a small portion of the market, the standards affect 85 per cent of the carpets marketed.

FHA has authorized three independent companies to administer carpet testing. Carpets with FHA certification must meet standards for wear of fibers and backing, resistance to fading, flammability and static.

But only carpets carrying the stamp of one of the three independent test administrators meet the FHA standards. Manufacturers have no authority to stamp carpeting with FHA approval. The three companies are:

Electrical Testing Laboratory Inc., (ETL), 2 East End Ave., New York, NY, 10021; Associated Dallas Labs (ADL), P.O. Box 15705, Dallas, TX, 75215, and Metallurgical Engineers of Atlanta Inc. (MEAI), 3480 Oak Cliff Rd., Atlanta GA, 30340.

These companies have directories for sale which list certified manufacturers and styles of carpeting. Approved carpeting is retested yearly, and during the year the independent company must make at least two spot checks of carpet samples in the field.

The stamp of approval from one of these three testing companies is perhaps a buyer's best measure of over-all carpet quality. Another consideration is the reputation of the retailer, which can be as important as the brand of carpet itself. The retailer may offer his own guarantee. A local consumer protection agency or Better Business Bureau will know if the retailer honors the warranty.

COMPARING FURNITURE MAKERS

For several years, a large trade association has polled retailers to determine how manufacturers compare in these respects. The first such poll by the National Home Furnishing Association (in 1974) showed Henredon Furniture Industries with the highest rating among furniture makers, followed by Sumter Cabinet Co., Tell City Chair Co., Hooker Furniture Corp., White Furniture Co., Heywood-Wakefield Co., American Drew Inc., Century Furniture Co., Dixie Furniture Co. and Temple-Stuart Co. in the top ten.

From the bottom, in order, were Barwick Furniture Ltd., Lea Industries Inc., Singer Furniture, Bassett Furniture and Pennsylvania House.

In 1976, the Association took another poll but has refused to release the results to non-members of the organization. Interested consumers might inquire at a store to see if it belongs to the Association and has a copy of the latest survey for inspection.

Cosmetics

In This Chapter
- **New Regulations**
- **Carcinogenic Ingredients**
- **Hazards of Common Products**

Much recent controversy over the safety of hair dyes has increased public awareness to two basic facts about cosmetics:
- There is growing evidence that many types of cosmetics pose serious health hazards to users;
- Yet manufacturers are not required to test products for safety either before or after putting them on sale.

Debate over the health consequences of cosmetics reached a new peak in 1978 when the government's General Accounting Office (GAO) reported that nearly 200 cosmetic ingredients may cause cancer, birth defects and other serious ailments. The GAO severely criticized the Food and Drug Administration (FDA) for failing to do a better job of regulating these products. At the same time, the GAO acknowledged that federal law was too weak to be effective. In essence, the FDA cannot take action against any product until after it causes injury to a significant group of people. The agency also has no power to force a manufacturer to furnish records of injuries.

The GAO found approximately 125 cosmetic ingredients on a list of suspected carcinogens at the National Institute of Occupational Safety and Health. Another two dozen substances in cosmetics are suspected of causing birth defects. And 20 more are suspected of damaging nerves. Evidence of cancer-causing abilities was obtained from animal studies. There is no conclusive evidence that these substances also can cause cancer in humans. However statistical studies indicate that beauticians who frequently handle hair dyes have higher cancer rates than the normal population.

CONTACT DERMATITIS IS MOST COMMON INJURY

Most cosmetic injuries consist of contact dermatitis, a redness and inflammation of the skin caused by exposure to chemicals. Irritants and allergens are the two main groups of chemical causes. An estimated 31 million Americans have some form of allergy, according to the National Institute of Allergy and Infectious Diseases.

In addition to the above problems are:
- **Flammable ingredients.** Among the most likely to ignite are perfumes and colognes, because of high levels of alcohol; nail polish removers, which contain such flammable substances as acetone and ethyl acetate; hairsprays and nail polishes.
- **Bacterial contamination.** The FDA has received reports of loss of vision resulting from the use of contaminated cosmetics, such as shampoos, lotions, creams and eye makeup. A 1969 survey by the FDA disclosed microbial contamination in 20 per cent of products sampled.
- **Lack of warnings.** Non-cosmetic products must carry warnings on label

when ingredients include amonia, ammonium hydroxide, toluene, xylene and turpentine by order of the Consumer Product Safety Commission. But when they appear in cosmetics, no such warning is required by the FDA.

● **Ingredients banned elsewhere but not in U.S.** Among cosmetic ingredients banned in several other countries but not in the U.S. are antimony, potassium tartrate, barium sulfide, brucine, iodine, phenol, stramonium, tetrachloroethylene and Vitamin D.

● **Drugs that escape regulation in cosmetics.** Drugs can be used in cosmetics without being subject to regulations as long as the product is not "intended" or understood to have a drug effect. Among the 90 or so drugs in cosmetics are those which induce vomiting, relieve pain, fight infections, remove pigmentation from the skin or destroy living tissue.

COSMETIC SAFETY TESTING BLOCKED

In recent years, Congress has shown an increased interest in cosmetic problems. Legislation to provide the FDA with the power to regulate cosmetics more effectively has been introduced into Congress every year for more than a decade, but it has always been sidetracked, largely because of industry objections.

The great majority of cosmetic products pose no health hazard in normal use. The proportion of products associated with various adverse reactions is relatively small, according to surveys taken by the government. Most large firms test new products before selling them. But the large volume of sales — approximately $10 billion annually — and the large number of people of both sexes who use cosmetics means that even a small chance of injury could involve millions of people. It is estimated, for example, that more than 33 million women use hair dyes.

Leaving out the possibility of getting cancer, which may take years to develop, the chances of getting an immediate adverse reaction is about 2 per cent, according to a survey by the American Academy of Dermatology and the FDA. Of the reactions reported, 76 per cent were considered mild, 11 per cent moderate and 13 per cent severe. Products with the highest rate of reactions, in order, were depilatories (chemical hair removers), deodorants and antiperspirants, moisturizers and lotions, bubble bath and oil preparations, hair sprays and lacquers, mascara, eye cream, hair dyes, facial creams and cleaners and nail polish. Other products that have caused a significant number of bad reactions are hair straighteners, skin lighteners and permanent wave items.

PACKAGE LABELS BECOME MORE INFORMATIVE

For many years, cosmetic manufacturers have resisted government and con-

---

AEROSOLS CANNED

December 15, 1978, was the last date on which manufacturers could distribute aerosol products containing chlorofluorocarbons as propellants. The government has found that "continued unrestricted use" of such products "poses an unacceptable risk for present as well as future generations." Scientists have determined that these gases can destroy part of the ozone layer protecting the earth from harmful solar radiation. By April 15, 1979, stores were prohibited from selling non-essential aerosol products, such as cosmetics, containing chlorofluorocarbons.

sumer efforts to require the listing of ingredients on labels. But in 1977, a federal court upheld a FDA regulation requiring ingredients to be listed on the label in descending order of their presence in the product. Notable exceptions are fragrances, flavors and bonafide trade secrets.

The FDA also has been successful in getting some warnings on cosmetic labels to alert users to injury hazards. Cosmetics in aerosol form are required to have the following notice:

> **"WARNING — AVOID SPRAYING IN EYES, CONTENTS UNDER PRESSURE. DO NOT PUNCTURE OR INCINERATE. DO NOT STORE AT TEMPERATURES ABOVE 120 DEGREES FAHRENHEIT. KEEP OUT OF REACH OF CHILDREN."**

Manufacturers are further required to warn users about any ingredients about which safety has not been "adequately substantiated." Labels of products containing such ingredients must say the following prominently and conspicuously:

> **"WARNING — THE SAFETY OF THIS PRODUCT HAS NOT BEEN DETERMINED."**

Efforts of the FDA to restrict claims for so-called hypoallergenic cosmetics, however, ended in March, 1978, after a federal court ruled against its legality. The FDA had proposed to restrict use of the term, "hypoallergenic", to cases where scientific studies show fewer adverse reactions than for competing products. Contrary to popular conception, "hypoallergenic" does not mean complete absence of allergic reactions.

COSMETIC CONTENTS AND HAZARDS
How to Minimize the Risks

BABY PRODUCTS
- **Baby Shampoo** is a synthetic detergent of either the amphoteric or amphotericanionic type. These detergents are comparatively stingless and non-irritating. They do not normally contain added ingredients such as perfumes, which may irritate the eyes. However, adverse reactions reported to the FDA include eye and scalp irritation.
- **Baby Oil** usually contains mineral oil, palmitate, lanolin, vegetable oils, and lanolin derivatives. According to pediatricians, mineral oil or vegetable oil will protect and soothe the skin as effectively. A thin film of baby oil or mineral oil is good for insulating and protecting skin in very cold weather. It is also good for makeup removal—precleaning the skin for washing. Adverse reactions reported to the FDA include irritation to the urogenital tract.
- **Bubble Bath** in liquid form contains TEA-dodecylbebzene sulfonate (which may be irritating to the skin), fatty acid alkanolamides, perfume, about 70% water and methylparaben (antimicrobial and preservative which is nontoxic in small amounts but may cause allergic skin reactions). The powdered form contains sodium lauryl sulfate (nontoxic detergent, wetting agent and emulsifier which may dry skin), sodium chloride (table salt—used as an astringent and an-

tiseptic) and perfume. Ingestion may cause gastrointestinal disturbances and skin irritations.

Reports to the FDA cite skin irritation, urinary and bladder infections, brain damage, stomach distress, irritation and bleeding of genital area, inflammation of the genitals, and eye injury. Bubble bath rated third highest on FDA's list of consumer complaints and among the top ten cosmetics causing adverse reactions in FDA-AAD (American Academy of Dermatology) survey with 14 adverse reactions per 10,000 products used.

In 1976, the FDA ordered that labels of bubble bath products carry a warning:

> **CAUTION: USE ONLY AS DIRECTED. EXCESSIVE USE OR PROLONGED EXPOSURE MAY CAUSE IRRITATION TO SKIN AND URINARY TRACT. DISCONTINUE USE IF RASH, REDNESS OR ITCHING OCCUR. CONSULT YOUR PHYSICIAN IF IRRITATION PERSISTS. KEEP OUT OF REACH OF CHILDREN.**

CLEANSING CREAMS AND LOTIONS

● **Cold cream** contains water soluble materials which evaporate to give "cold" effect while loosening grime particules and easing dirt removal. Cold creams contain mineral oil, beeswax and borax (water softener, preservative and texturizer). Borax may be toxic and application to rough skin should be avoided. Complaints to the FDA include facial skin dermatitis and eye irritations.

● **Washing creams** contain mineral, petrolatum and paraffin oils which melt on contact with the skin, leaving an oily film to loosen grime. Rinsing skin with water removes oily residues.

Dermatologists and the American Medical Association say soap and water serve the same purpose at less expense and less risk of allergy. According to Dr. Bedford Shelmire, Jr.'s *The Art of Being Beautiful,* soaps, rinsable cleansers and alcohol are the most effective, while nonrinsable oils, greases, creams and lotions are the least effective.

DEODORANTS

Deodorants are classified as cosmetics because they have no effect on bodily functions. Deodorants employ perfumes as "coverups," while antiperspirants use organic compounds as germicidals to inhibit the growth of odor-causing microorganisms on the skin. Aluminum, alcohol and zinc salts in these products can cause skin irritations and other disorders. (See antiperspirants in drug section of "Health Care" chapter.)

Adverse reactions include stinging, burning, itching, cysts, enlarged sweat glands, underarm pimples and lung and throat irritations. Deodorants and antiperspirants had the second highest number of complaints sent directly to the FDA from consumers and headed the list of products rated in the FDA-AAD survey for verified adverse reactions.

DEPILATORIES

● **Depilatories** contain strong chemicals that remove hair by eating through the hair's shaft. Sulfides, particularly hydrogen sulfides, are the most effective hair remover, but have an obnoxious odor that is hard to cover up. Most sulfides have been replaced by thioglycollic acid salts which are slower acting, but less irritating and less unpleasant than sulfides. Ingestion may cause severe gastrointestinal irritation. Adverse reactions include skin irritations, burns, rashes, scars on legs and headaches. Depilatories ranked third on the industry product experience reports and second on the FDA-AAD consumer survey list for causing adverse reactions.

● **Cream depilatories** dissolve hair and can cause numerous adverse reactions as well. Calcium thioglycolate in the depilatories can cause skin problems on the hand or scalp and have produced thyroid problems in animals. Calcium hydroxide can cause skin and eye burns, and accidental ingestion can cause throat and esophagus burns, and possible death from shock and asphyxia due to swelling of the glottis. Other ingredients include cetyl alcohol and sodium laurel sulfate, a detergent which may dry skin.

EYE MAKEUP

Eye makeup is one of the most potentially hazardous cosmetics since it comes into contact with the eye. The most severe problem with eye makeup is bacterial contamination. Pseudomonas, a type of bacteria that can cause eye infections, and other hazardous microorganisms can grow in eye makeup upon the deterioration of the cosmetic's preservatives and the eye's natural protecting mechanisms. If the eye is scratched, the bacteria can enter the eyeball, causing infection, inflammation and possible blindness.

● **Eyeliner** is used to outline and accentuate eyes. Ingredients include: alkanolamine (no known toxicity); a fatty alcohol (low toxicity); polyvinylpyrrolidone (PVP's ingestion may produce gas and fecal impaction, damage to lungs and kidneys. It may last in the system several months to a year. Modest intravenous doses in rats produced tumors); cellulose ether; methylparaben (antimicrobial and preservative—nontoxic in small amounts but can cause allergic skin reactions); antioxidants (prevents rancidity of oils or fats or deterioration of other materials by inhibiting oxidation); perfumes; titanium dioxide (white pigment with no known toxicity with external use).

Do not apply eyeliner to the upper and lower borders of the eyelids (as opposed to the eyelid behind the lashes) because permanent pigmentation of the mucous membrane lining the inside of the eyelids, as well as redness, itching, tearing, and blurring of vision may occur.

● **Mascara** colors and thickens lashes. Ingredients include: salt of stearic acid (natural fatty acid—possible sensitizer for allergic people); pigments and/or lanolin (absorbs and holds water to skin, a common skin sensitizer causing allergic reactions); paraffin (pure paraffin is harmless to the skin, although impure paraffin may give rise to irritations, eczemas and precancerous or cancerous conditions); and carnauba wax (texturizer which rarely causes allergic reactions).

● **Shadow** is used to color the eyelid. The waterless type contains colors, titanium dioxide, a lightening agent with no known toxicity when used externally. However, high concentrations of the dust may cause lung damage; lanolin; beeswax (non-toxic emulsifier); ceresin (substitute for beeswax and paraffin which may produce an allergic reaction); calcium carbonate (white coloring with no known toxicity); mineral oil (no known toxicity); sorbitan oleate (an emulsifying agent with no known toxicity) and talc (white to grayish-white mineral insoluble in water and used as a coloring agent. It gives a slippery sensation to powders and creams. Prolonged inhalation causes lung problems.) Shadow's iridescence is achieved by adding very pure aluminum.

FEMININE DEODORANT SPRAYS

These were introduced in the U.S. in 1966 to prevent the development of odor in the external genital area. Advertisements convinced hundreds of thousands of women they needed the sprays to insure personal hygiene. But the FDA has found no hygienic or therapeutic advantage and has banned the term "hygienic" in advertising and labeling.

Two types of odor can be present in the genital area: bacterial odor from the skin and odor from internal areas. The latter is not affected by a product made exclusively for external use. **For cleanliness, soap and water are the most effective and safest.**

Ingredients include: perfume, alcohol, propellant or aerosol talcum. Since nearly all of the products contain propellants, holding the spray too close to the body could cause burning, itching, rash, infection, inflammation of the urinary tract, allergic reactions, dermatitis of the thighs, swelling and inflammation of the vulva.

The FDA says, "These sprays offer no medical usefulness, no hygienic benefits and, in many instances, do not adequately destroy, neutralize or mask unpleasant body odors so as to be accurately labeled as a deodorant." The FDA requires this warning on the label:

> **CAUTION: FOR EXTERNAL USE ONLY. SPRAY AT LEAST 8 INCHES FROM THE SKIN. DO NOT APPLY TO BROKEN, IRRITATED OR ITCHING SKIN. PERSISTENT, UNUSUAL ODOR OR DISCHARGE MAY INDICATE CONDITIONS FOR WHICH PHYSICIANS SHOULD BE CONSULTED. DISCONTINUE USE IMMEDIATELY IF RASH, IRRITATION, OR DISCOMFORT DEVELOPS.**

FRESHENERS

Fresheners are designed to make skin feel cool and refreshed. Ingredients: witch hazel (freshener and astringent whose ingestion in large amounts may produce nausea, vomiting, impaired perception, coma and death); camphorated alcohol, alcohol (dries skin when used in excess; toxic in large doses); and citric acid (astringent with no known toxicity). Fresheners may also contain arnica (never to be used on broken skin because it is an active irritant; ingestion produces intestinal upset, nervous disturbances, irregular heartbeat and collapse); bay rum (can cause allergic reactions); boric acid (possible toxicity with severe poisonings from ingestion and topical application to abraded skin); brucine sulfate (as poisonous as strychnine when ingested); chamomile (ingestion of large amounts causes vomiting; used to soothe skin irritations—no known toxicity); glycerin (in concentrated solutions it is irritating to the mucous membranes); lactic acid (caustic in concentrated solutions when taken internally or applied to the skin) magnesia (no known toxicity); menthol (nontoxic in low doses; but in concentrations of 1 per cent or more it can irritate layers of mucous membrane); lavender oil (allergic skin reactions and possible adverse reactions in sunlight); phosphoric acid (no known toxicity except in concentrated solutions); talc (white to grayish-white mineral insoluble in water and used as a coloring agent; prolonged inhalation causes lung problems); benzoin (possible allergic reactions); and aluminum salts (possible skin irritations).

Many fresheners contain chemical irritants that can harm the skin, irritating small blood vessels, and attacking the outer portion of the skin causing it to swell.

A safer, cheaper and more effective freshener can easily be made at home by mixing one part rubbing alcohol to four parts water.

HAIR PREPARATIONS

Bleaches strip color from the hair and are usually the first step in other dyeing procedures. Hydrogen peroxide is the most widely used bleach. Ingredients include hydrogen peroxide solution; quarternary ammonium compound; adipic acid; and sodium stannate. Adverse reactions include nausea, hives, burned scalp, severe allergic reactions and face swelling.

To minimize hair damage, bleaching should be limited to once a month and curling or teasing should be avoided. Conditioners formulated for use with bleach are recommended.

Hair dyes change the hair color until the hair grows out, is washed, or is cut off. They are also absorbed by the skin and bloodstream, thus becoming hazards to body health. The degree of absorption depends on the type of dye used and the chemicals in it.

There are essentially three types of hair dyes: temporary, semi-permanent and permanent. According to the Cosmetic, Toiletry and Fragrance Association, the leading trade group of manufacturers, about 33 million women and untold millions of men use hair dyes. Most of the dyes used by women are permanent coal tar or petroleum derivatives; most dyes used by men are temporary, such as metallic ones.

Temporary dyes are rinses to add brightness or highlight natural color and disguise grayness. They are usually applied directly to the hair and combed through it. Since they do not penetrate the hair, they can be shampooed out.

Semi-permanent dyes penetrate the hair but wear off after several shampoos. They are used to blend streaked hair and to improve tones. They are usually applied in a liquid base, which is left on the hair for 20 to 40 minutes before being rinsed out. No chemical reaction occurs, so they do not affect the structure of the hair itself.

Permanent dyes work through chemical processes. Ingredients are colorless chemical agents which produce color after they are oxidized inside the hair fiber by hydrogen peroxide. The colors are not readily removed by shampooing but must be reapplied periodically for new hair growth. Permanent hair dyes account for $3 out of every $4 spent on hair dyes in the United States.

The Food, Drug and Cosmetic Act of 1938 says a cosmetic is adulterated if it contains any poisonous or deleterious substance that may cause injury under normal use. But coal-tar hair dyes were exempted as long as they carried instructions for giving a skin patch test and a warning saying:

> **CAUTION: THIS PRODUCT CONTAINS INGREDIENTS WHICH MAY CAUSE SKIN IRRITATION ON CERTAIN INDIVIDUALS AND A PRELIMINARY TEST ACCORDING TO ACCOMPANYING DIRECTIONS SHOULD FIRST BE MADE. THIS PRODUCT MUST NOT BE USED FOR DYEING THE EYELASHES OR EYEBROWS; TO DO SO MAY CAUSE BLINDNESS.**

This warning, however, does not mention numerous hazards that scientists have associated with coal-tar hair dyes in recent years. Clinical data assembled by the Environmental Defense Fund (EDF) indicates that skin absorption is much greater than originally believed and that potential health hazards include cancer, birth defects and inherited cell changes. The EDF cited animal tests showing such effects from coal-tar substances found mostly in permanent hair dyes.

In addition, statistical studies have indicated that beauticians and others who work closely with such dyes have higher rates of cancer. One test found that 87 per cent of breast cancer victims had used hair dyes, while only 26 per cent of healthy women had used them.

As a result, the EDF called on Congress in 1978 to eliminate the legal exemption for coal-tar dyes. It said the "array of evidence clearly establishes the risk to consumers posed by" these products. It pointed out that not only are hair dye manufacturers (like other cosmetic producers) not required to test products for safety before marketing but they are also not required to submit a list of ingredients or test data to the Food and Drug Administration, which is supposed to regulate cosmetics.

In January, 1978, six suspected carcinogens were identified in hair dyes by officials of the National Cancer Institute in testimony before a House commerce subcommittee. They were: 2,4 diaminoanisole (2,4 DAA); 2,5-toluene diamine (2,5 TDA); 2-amino-2-nitrophenol; 2-nitro-1.4 phenylenediamine, all found in permanent hair dyes; and the benzidine derivatives, Direct Black 38 and Direct Blue 6, found mostly in semi-permanent colorings.

The first one — 2,4 DAA — has been used as a main ingredient in various Clairol, Revlon and L'Oreal products, among others, according to EDF. FDA proposed a warning label for products with this ingredient saying:

> **"WARNING: CONTAINS AN INGREDIENT THAT CAN PENETRATE YOUR SKIN AND HAS BEEN DETERMINED TO CAUSE CANCER IN LABORATORY ANIMALS."**

The agency also proposed that posters containing the same warning be placed on display in beauty parlors. Patrons of such establishments may want to ask whether dyes contain any of the substances mentioned earlier. If the salon does not have such information, it might be obtained by writing to the manufacturer listed on the product package.

To assist dye users who want to avoid known dangers, the EDF has published a nine-page folder summarizing the health problems of 2,4 DAA — also known as 4-methoxy-m-phenylenediamine (4MMPD), — and listing products and brands containing it. The folder can be obtained from EDF, 1525 18th St. NW, Washington, DC, 20036. Hair dyes not containing 4-MMPD or lead acetate, according to EDF, include Clairol's Great Day, Great Day Concentrate, Happiness, Clairesse and Loving Care.

In the face of all this adverse information, the cosmetic industry association (CFTA) insists that, in its own words, "any fair evaluation of all the available evidence shows that cosmetics do not present risk or harm to consumers." Cosmetics, including hair dyes, are "among the safest products...consumers can buy," added the association in a news release in January, 1978. Any more controls would amount to "over-regulation," said the CFTA, and Congress and the American people would reject them.

However, by 1979, many hair dyes had been reformulated voluntarily by manufacturers to eliminate the suspected carcinogenic substances and thus avoid having to print the warning on labels. Among major producers, only Clairol changed labels to indicate that formulas were new. Clairol sells about two out of every three packages of hair dyes.

Home users of hair dyes can tell whether a product carries the suspected carcinogens (noted above) by examining the label. Some of the new formulas look clearer than the old ones and were causing some problems in attaining the same hair color as obtained from the older formulas.

Hair straighteners are probably the roughest treatment that can be applied to hair. The two principal processes are:

● **Pomades,** which coat hair and glue it straight. They are the least effective and least damaging.

● **Chemical straighteners,** which are more effective but can cause burns, irritations, and hair damage. They contain either thioglycolic acid compounds or alkalies (sodium hydroxide, ploythylene glycol), cetyl alcohol, stearyl alcohol, a triethanolamine, propylene glycol, perfume and water. The glycols and alcohols may be corrosive.

The straightening process involves applying a waving lotion to break the curly pattern of the molecules. The pull of gravity makes the hair stand straight. Then a neutralizer locks the hair into its new form and new bonds are made. The process should be done by a professional.

Alkali straighteners contain strong burning ingredients, and first to third degree burns can occur. They can also cause allergic reactions, swelling and eye damage.

HAND LOTIONS

These are emollients, which must apply easily, soften skin, leave a pleasant scent and not leave a sticky feeling. Most contain lanolin, stearic acid and water. They also might have cetyl alcohol, mineral oil, glycerin, potassium hydroxide, perfume, methylparaben, triethanolamine and glycerly monostearate. Newer formulas also contain healing ingredients such as allantoin and water-repellent silicones to protect hands from irritants like water, wind or detergents.

Adverse reactions reported by consumers include rashes and blisters Moisturizers and lotions ranked third on the FDA-AAD list with 18.2 adverse reactions per 10,000 products used.

LIPSTICK

Lipstick is a mixture of oil and wax with red staining, certified dyes dispersed in the oil, red pigments similarly dispersed, flavoring and perfume. Bromo acid, D&C Red #21 and related dyes are most often used. Other dyes used are D&C Red #27 and insoluble dyes, known as "lakes," D&C #34 calcium lake and D&C Orange #17 lake. Pinks are made by mixing titanium dioxide with various reds Oils and fats used include olive, mineral, sesame, castor, butyl stearate, polyethylene glycol, cocoa butter, lanolin, petrolatum, lecithin, hydrogenated vegetable oils, carnauba, candelilla, beeswax, ozokerite and paraffin.

Adverse reactions to lipstick include burns, cheilitis (cracks, lacerations, dry and peeling lips—an allergic reaction to bromo acid dyes), numbness, rash and swollen gums. Almost all of the symptoms have been found to be caused by in delible dyes. Those who are allergic may solve the problem by changing brands or by using hypoallergenic lipsticks that do not contain lanolin, perfume and dibromoflourescein.

Some of the dyes found in lipstick have caused cancer in animals. It has also been suggested that lipsticks are unsafe because of the chance of pesticides in the vegetable oils and waxes. Lipstick may also cause gastrointestinal disorders in some women.

MANICURE PRODUCTS

Nail hardeners are supposed to keeep nails from breaking and chipping. Ironically, formaldehyde, the primary ingredient, has been found to produce cracking of nails in addition to discoloration and sometimes loss of nails. FDA reports that nail peeling, burning, inflammation, deformation and damage to the nerves at the base of the nails are possible adverse reactions. Base coats of nail polish are also hazardous, causing discoloration, bleeding, separation of nail from nail bed, pain, and sealing of the skin of the fingertips. A formaldehyde-based resin and the synthetic rubber in the products are primarily responsible.

Nail polish (enamels) are mixtures of glass, dust and oil ground into paste to which plasticizers and resins are added for smoothness. Nail polish contains cellulose nitrate, butyl acetate, ethyl acetate, toluene, dibutyl phthalate, alkyl esters, dyes, glycol derivatives, gums, hydrocarbons (aromatic and aliphatic), ketones (acetones, methyl, ethyl), lakes and phosphoric acid. Common dyes include D&C Red #19 and 31.

FDA reports cite irritation to the nail area, discolored nails (in some cases nails were permanently stained), nausea, pain, bleeding under the nails, loosening or loss of nails, softened or inflamed nail bed, dryness, and cuticle irritation. Skin rashes to eyelids, lesions around the eyes, neck and back of ears are common to those allergic to nail polish.

SHAMPOO

Shampoo is made of synthetic detergents which remove dirt, oil and other material from the scalp, and allow the material to be rinsed away. Synthetic detergents tend to foam better and rinse out more completely than natural detergents. They also function well in hard water, not forming bonds with the calcium in the water as natural soaps do. Liquid shampoos contain triethanolamine dodecylbenzene sulfonate (detergent), ethanolamide of lauric acid, perfume and water. Cream lotion shampoos contain pacifying agents like stearyl and ceryl alcohol. Sequestering agents are often used to make the water soft to remove the foam and to make hair shinier. Finishing agents (mineral oil and lanolin) may be added to make hair lustrous.

Shampoos made specifically for "normal," "dry," or "oily" hair are made by controlling the strength or amount of the synthetic detergent—whose "defatting" action removes oil from the hair—and of the conditioning additives that alleviate or offset this action.

Conditioning additives include eggs, protein derivatives, glycerin or propylene glycol and ethyl alcohol. Conditioners claim to provide lustre, softness, smoothness, manageability, body and texture. Separate conditioner products (not shampoo-conditioners combined) are needed to conceal damage to the hair from dyes, bleaches, waving or straightening chemical treatments, or from intense heat used to curl or straighten hair.

Perfume and preservatives in shampoos, mainly from the methyl and propyl group, may cause allergic reactions. FDA reports irritation to the eyes and scalp. Shampoo was first on the FDA's list of direct consumer complaints of adverse reactions to cosmetics and seventh on the NEISS data list with 32 reported cases.

SOAP
Under federal regulations, soap is considered a cosmetic if it makes no germ-killer claim. Soap with such a claim is considered a drug.

Soap is usually a mixture of sodium salts of various fatty acids. Sodium hydroxide makes a strong soap, fatty acids a mild soap. So-called "neutral" soaps actually are alkaline with pH around 10 (skin pH is 6 to 6.5) when dissolved in water.

Superfatted soaps, which are among the most popular brands, are promoted as skin moisturizers because they contain added cream or lotion. These ingredients, along with such additives as deodorant, perfume, lanolin and cocoa butter, reduce the cleansing effectiveness of soaps. Gift soaps with heavy fragrances should be avoided, as should germicidals ("deodorants" soaps), especially for use on the face.

Dr. Bedford Shelmire, author of *The Art of Being Beautiful*, recommends Ivory, Lux and Camay as brands of soap having none of the previously mentioned drawbacks. He recommends Ivory soap over the others because it is unperfumed, inexpensive and without coloring agents.

Adverse reactions to soap include scaly, itchy eruptions on the face, hands and other parts of the body. Soap topped the NEISS data list with 65 adverse reactions, 51 per cent of which were diagnosed as dermatitis.

SUNSCREENS
Sunscreens are composed of chemicals which selectively block out the ultraviolet rays of sunlight that damage and cause changes in complexion such as wrinkles, dryness and freckles. According to Shelmire, different age groups require different preparations for protection against the sun:

● **Children:** Use screens with oily or greasy bases—they stay on better when swimming and help prevent dryness. Shelmire recommends *Bain de Soleil Suntan Creme*. Also, use a lip pomade containing amyl demethyl PABA (para-amino-benzoic acid) for best protection.

● **Teenagers:** Use PABA sunscreens like *PRE-SUN* and *Ultrabloc*. These contain alcohol which has a drying effect on oily adolescent skin. The screen should be applied liberally to all exposed areas, protecting against a burn *and* a tan.

● **Young adults:** Use benzophenone screens. They are effective in protecting the skin against deep damage that causes wrinkles. According to Shelmire, liberal application of the sunscreen to the face, neck and hands will help prevent "liver spots." *Solbar* and *Uval* are recommended brands.

● **Middle age:** Use sunscreens with moisturizing bases. Shelmire recommends *Swedish Tanning Secret Lotion*.

● **Older people:** Use sunscreen products without oily or greasy bases. The doctor recommends *Eclipse Sunscreen Lotion*.

In August, 1978, an advisory committee to the Food and Drug Administration recommended that all sunscreen products carry a notice citing the dangers of overexposure to the sun and adding: "the liberal and regular use of this product may reduce the chance of premature aging of the skin and skin cancer."

The group also recommended that such products be rated numerically from 2 to 8 according to their ability to protect the skin. A product with a "3" rating would allow a person to stay in the sun three times longer than with no protection. Some manufacturers have started to use the recommended system.

According to Shelmire, effective sunscreen chemicals are PABA, PABA-derivatives and the benzophenones. Homosalate, cinoxate, menthyl anthranilate, digalloyl trioleate and triethanolamine salicylate are also acceptable but have a lower average screening ability. When using a product containing a less potent screen, either a very thick first coat or several coats should be applied. If using a sunscreen product which dries on the skin (meaning it is composed of a water or alcohol base), apply a second coat.

Sunscreens that are compatible with makeup, according to Dr. Shelmire, are *Pre-Sun, Swedish Tanning Secret Lotion* and *Eclipse*.

In addition, these precautions are recommended:

● Sunbathe in moderation. Light skinned persons should begin with 15 minutes exposure, 20 minutes for medium-skinned persons. Increase exposure daily, allowing for a gradual building of skin thickness.

● Certain drugs can affect a person's susceptibility to sunburn. For example, tranquilizers, diuretics (used to rid the body of excess fluids), oral hypoglycemic agents (for diabetes) and estrogens increase susceptibility.

● See a doctor if your burn is severe. Sunburn can make you sick from blisters, chills, fever and even delirium. For moderate burns, apply gauze dipped in a solution of one tablespoon of baking soda, one tablespoon corn starch and two quarts of cool water to the burn.

TANNING PREPARATIONS

These are perfumed alcohol-water solutions with dyhydroxyacetone and a small amount of acetone. The former ingredient is supposed to give a browning effect without exposure to the sun by staining the dead cells of the outer skin.

A few complaints have been received about the development of a spotty appearance when the tan starts to wear off. Mottled areas may result from uneven applications and fade after a few days. One danger is that since the tan is artificial, the skin has not thickened as it would with a natural tan, and therefore offers little protection from the sun.

Baby oil, cocoa butter, coconut oil, and similar products are incorrectly thought to protect skin from burning and increase tanning. These products neither protect against the sun nor affect the rate of tanning. No product makes skin tan faster than it would without a tanning preparation.

Suntan oil contains salicylates, sesame oil and mineral oil, perfume, color and an antioxidant. Preparations may also contain alcohol, p-aminobenzoic acid and derivatives, benzy salicylate, cinnamic acid derivatives and coumarin.

Suntan creams contain para-aminobenzoic acid, mineral oil, sorbitan stearate, poloxamers and water.

Suntan ointments consist of petrolatum, stearyl alcohol, mineral and sesame oil and calcium stearate.

Tanning lotions contain methyl anthranilate, propylene glycol, ricinoleate, glycerin, alcohol and water.

FOR MORE INFORMATION
  AMA Book of Skin and Hair Care, Linda Allen Schoen, ed.; J.B. Lippincot
Company, New York, 1976.
  Art of Being Beautiful, Bedford Shelmire, Jr.; St. Martin's Press, Nev
York, 1976.
  Consumer's Dictionary of Cosmetic Ingredients, Ruth Winter; Crow
Publishers, New York, 1976.
  Cosmetics: Trick or Treat?, Toni Stabile; Arco, New York, 1969.
  Handbook of Nonprescription Drugs; American Pharmaceutical Associa
tion, Washington, DC.
  The Medically Based No-Nonsense Beauty Book, Debora Chase; Alfred A
Knopf, New York, 1975.
  The Skin You're In, Consumer Survival Kit, Maryland Center for Publi
Broadcasting, Owings Mills, MD, 21117.

WHERE TO COMPLAIN
  Reports about bad experiences with cosmetics should be reported to th
Food and Drug Administration, either by calling or writing a regional office, o
the FDA, Division of Cosmetic Technology, Washington, DC, 20204. Com
plaints may also be made directly to the product's manufacturer.

Food and Nutrition

Food shopping has become a series of shocks for most Americans. What was once considered a pleasant experience, enlivened by the advent of supermarkets and packaged dinners, has turned into a potfull of frustrations because of phenomenal price increases. Few of the traditional cost-saving devices work any more, even for the smartest shoppers. In the first half of 1979, prices rose at almost double the 10 percent increase registered for all of 1978. Some items rose four times as fast as they did in 1978. Prices of meat, poultry, fish and eggs jumped 4.1 per cent in April alone, pushing prices of those products 40 per cent above what they were three months earlier (on an annual percentage basis). Price increases moderated during the summer.

Yet there were no signs of the massive resistance that arose in 1973 when beef prices skyrocketed. Perhaps the main reason was the absence of any reasonably priced alternatives. When pork prices declined in April, 1979, after six months of steady increase, government officials cried out: "Buy pork, not beef." Yet earlier shifts of food buyers from beef to cheese and eggs for protein sources helped raise those prices to the point where benefits were virtually wiped out.

The government itself was caught politically between farmers and processors, who were enjoying the price increases, and consumers, who were not. President Carter decided to lift the curbs on meat imports only slightly, thus relieving some of the pressure on prices but not enough to stop them from rising. The government also stopped buying large quantities of some crops but only after prices had reached many times what they were in 1967. Tariff agreements with other countries opened new markets for export, putting further pressure on supplies and prices of meat, tobacco, fruits, vegetables and nuts in this country.

BIGGEST BITE FOR MIDDLEMEN

The biggest proportion of price increases goes to so-called middlemen, who account for all the expenses of moving food from the farm to the store. These costs include processing, packaging, advertising, transportation, storage and advertising. Nearly all of these operations have grown both in size and cost. Foods are more thoroughly processed and wrapped in layers of plastic or paper; and they are transported over longer distances as production areas become more concentrated and distribution becomes more national.

By July, 1979, the farmer's share of the retail food dollar was only 38.4 per cent, based on a market basket of food items analyzed by the U.S. Department of Agriculture. The farmer's share of meat prices was 53.7 per cent and was 66.2 per cent of egg prices, but it was only 16.0 per cent of cereal and bakery prices and 19.3 per cent of processed fruits and vegetables.

By July, 1979, retail food prices were 229.0 per cent of 1967 levels, prices received by farmers were 246.0 per cent, and the difference (spread) between the two was at 223.4 per cent of what it was in 1967.

FEWER FIRMS CONTROL FOOD BUSINESS

Even more significant than the farm-price spread in understanding the rapid rise in prices is the increasing dominance of the food industry by large firms. The number of farms continues to grow smaller each year. In 30 years, more than 30 million farms have gone out of business, leaving only 2.3 million in 1979.

Many have been swallowed up by large corporations seeking control of the food chain, from the farm to store. More and more companies are now vertically integrated in this way, giving them the power to control both the prices paid for crops and the prices paid by the consumer or retailer.

Vertically integrated companies now control 92 per cent of the poultry business, 95 per cent of sweet corn production, 90 per cent of snap beans, 50 per cent of cantaloupes, 95 per cent of tomatoes and 90 per cent of popcorn. Only 50 of the estimated 32,000 food manufacturing firms in the U.S. account for 75 per cent of the industry's profits, according to Jim Hightower in his book, *Eat Your Heart Out: How Food Profiteers Victimize the Consumer* (Crown Publishers Inc., New York, $8.95.).

Growing control by large firms also has tended to concentrate production and processing of certain foods in a few areas of the country. Examples are lettuce and other vegetables in California, cherries in Michigan and citrus fruit in Florida and California. As production becomes more confined geographically, national distribution requires greater distances. Demand for storage facilities and preserving processes also grows.

These processes push costs above what they would be if food production were spread more evenly throughout the country. The smallest farms are not economically efficient; indeed, a study was begun in 1979 by the Department of Agriculture to determine what size farm is the most efficient. But efficiency does not improve above a certain size, according to agriculture experts. Nor does it necessarily improve when a company integrates diverse operations under one roof or buys a competitor.

CONCENTRATION BRINGS INFLATED PRICES

The increasing power of fewer firms in the food business is helping to inflate prices, according to testimony taken by the Senate Subcommittee on Antitrust and Monopoly in April, 1979. Russell C. Parker, an economist with the Federal Trade Commission, estimated that one per cent of the 20,000 food manufacturing firms control over 80 per cent of total food manufacturing assets. He pointed out that by increasing the size of processing operations, they make it more difficult for smaller firms to enter the business.

Concentration also is increasing at the retail level, reducing price competition there. According to Willard F. Mueller of the University of Wisconsin, a former staff member of the FTC, the proportion of metropolitan markets with four chains controlling 60 per cent or more of food sales grew five fold between 1954 and 1972.

Not only do a few firms have more control than ever to set prices, they also have more control over the number and quality of food products. Edward Kennedy, chairman of the Senate Judiciary Committee, expressed concern about this fact, saying "the time has come for Congress to act to protect consumers and small farmers and to preserve the integrity and diversity of our free economic system."

MORE UNIFORM PRODUCTS ON THE MARKET

Control by large companies also brings increased use of chemicals to help in processing, storage and transportation. Chemicals are used to preserve foods longer, make them tough enough to withstand rough handling over long distances and add color and body to help make them look better than they really are.

Billions of dollars of government money have gone into development and testing of new varieties of food that are more efficient to market and more profitable. New varieties and more chemical treatment, however, have not always improved food products from the consumer point of view. Taste and nutrition have often suffered in the process as products have become more uniform.

Yet, foods with the least nutrition tend to be promoted the most. That is because large companies concentrate on items that bring the largest profit. A survey of television ads in 1976 by two Northwestern University students (Lynne Masover and Jeremiah Stamler) showed that 70 per cent of weekday advertising and 85 per cent of weekend advertising were devoted to foods high in fat, cholesterol, salt and sugar, items most criticized for health reasons.

SURVEYS SHOW NUTRITIONAL LEVELS GETTING WORSE

The combination of poor nutrition education and powerful advertising messages for non-nutritional products has deprived many people of rudimentary knowledge needed to maintain healthful diets. A survey by the USDA indicated that 60 per cent of families interviewed in 1955 were getting 100 per cent of the U.S. Recommended Daily Allowances (RDAs) but only 50 per cent were in 1965. Surveys by the Food and Drug Administration showed a similar downtrend. In 1973, 71 per cent of those interviewed rated their own nutrition knowledge as moderate to high; two years later, the proportion declined to 64 per cent. During the same time, the proportion of shoppers who preferred nutritional labeling to recipes on packages declined from 79 to 58 per cent.

But in some respects, food shoppers have become more discriminating. Forty-six per cent of the people questioned in the FDA surveys reported changes in shopping habits over the previous year such as using more ad coupons, watching for special sales, buying cheaper meat cuts, using less meat in general and buying fewer snacks and sweets. But answers indicated that many of these changes were influenced more by price than by nutritional concerns. Those checking for specials, for example, far outnumbered those checking ingredients before buying a product.

GOVERNMENT FAILS TO OFFSET EFFECTS OF ADVERTISING

One force capable of counteracting the impact of massive food advertising and promotion is the federal government. But it has done little in this regard despite 30 government agencies and 19 Congressional committees concerned with nutrition education. According to Rep. Fred Richmond (D-NY), they lack coordination, direction and funding.

RECOMMENDED DIETARY ALLOWANCES

(Years) From Up to	Weight (kg)	Weight (lbs)	Height (in)	Energy (cal)	Protein (g)	Fat-Soluble Vitamins Vitamin A Activity (IU)	Vitamin D (IU)	Vitamin E Activity (IU)	Water-Soluble Vitamins Ascorbic Acid (mg)	Folacin (mg)	Niacin (mg)	Riboflavin (mg)	Thiamin (mg)	Vitamin B$_6$ (mg)	Vitamin B$_{12}$ (mg)	Minerals Calcium (mg)	Phosphorus (mg)	Iodine (mg)	Iron (mg)	Magnesium (mg)	Zinc
INFANTS																					
0.0-0.5	6	14	24	kg x 117	kg x 2.2	1400	400	4	35	50	5	0.4	0.3	0.3	0.3	360	240	35	10	60	3
0.5-1.0	9	20	28	kg x 108	kg x 2.0	2000	400	5	35	50	8	0.6	0.5	0.4	0.3	540	400	45	15	70	5
CHILDREN																					
1-3	28		34	1300	23	2000	400	7	40	100	9	0.8	0.7	0.6	1.0	800	800	60	15	150	10
4-6	44		44	1800	30	2500	400	9	40	200	12	1.1	0.9	0.9	1.5	800	800	80	10	200	10
7-10	66		54	2400	36	3300	400	10	40	300	16	1.2	1.2	1.2	2.0	800	800	110	10	250	10
MALES																					
11-14	97		63	2800	44	5000	400	12	45	400	18	1.5	1.4	1.6	3.0	1200	1200	130	18	350	15
15-18	134		69	3000	54	5000	400	15	45	400	20	1.8	1.5	2.0	3.0	1200	1200	150	18	400	15
19-22	147		69	3000	54	5000	400	15	45	400	20	1.8	1.5	2.0	3.0	800	800	140	10	350	15
23-50	154		69	2700	56	5000	—	15	45	400	18	1.6	1.4	2.0	3.0	800	800	130	10	350	15
51+	154		69	2400	56	5000	—	15	45	400	16	1.5	1.2	2.0	3.0	800	800	110	10	350	15
FEMALES																					
11-14	97		62	2400	44	4000	400	12	45	400	16	1.3	1.2	1.6	3.0	1200	1200	115	18	300	15
15-18	119		65	2100	48	4000	400	12	45	400	14	1.4	1.1	2.0	3.0	1200	1200	115	18	300	15
19-22	128		65	2100	46	4000	400	12	45	400	14	1.4	1.1	2.0	3.0	800	800	100	18	300	15
23-50	128		65	2000	46	4000	—	12	45	400	13	1.2	1.0	2.0	3.0	800	800	100	18	300	15
51+	128		65	1800	46	4000	—	12	45	400	12	1.1	1.0	2.0	3.0	800	800	80	10	300	15
PREGNANT																					
				+300	+30	5000	400	15	60	800	+2	+0.3	+0.3	2.5	4.0	1200	1200	125	18+	450	20
LACTATING																					
				+500	+20	6000	400	15	80	600	+4	+0.5	+0.3	2.5	4.0	1200	1200	150	18	450	25

IU stands for International Unit.
1 kilogram (kg) = 2.2 pounds (lbs)
1 kilocalorie (kcal) = 1,000 calories
1 gram (g) = 1,000 milligrams (mg)

In March, 1978, the General Accounting Office released a massive study agreeing with Richmond and recommending a central point in the government for review of nutrition materials. The GAO estimated that the government spends $73 to $117 million a year on human nutrition research, equivalent to only about 3 per cent of the $3 billion spent on all agriculture and health research.

Failure of the government to do more has put an extra burden on parents and teachers. But they have not been able to make any significant headway in correcting wrong impressions obtained largely from the advertising media. Most victimized have been children too young to distinguish the truth and evaluate ad claims. In March, 1978, the Federal Trade Commission found evidence of unfair and deceptive practices in television advertising aimed at young children. The agency proposed to ban all TV ads aimed at children under the age of 8, ban TV ads to children under 12 for products most likely to cause tooth decay and require TV ads for sugary products aimed at children under 12 to balance ads with dental and nutritional information.

For many years, parents and teachers have accepted nutritional themes that have recently come into serious question. One of these themes is that eating at least one item from each of "four basic food groups" daily will provide an adequate supply of vitamins, minerals and other essential elements. The four groups are meat and fish; fruits and vegetables; dairy products; and bread and cereal. But a person following these guidelines can fail to get proper nutrition because of the wide variety of choices within each group. The groups do not take into consideration the need for many people to reduce their consumption of fat, meat, sugar and other items.

RESTAURANT MENUS FOUND HALF-BAKED

By now, anyone who has eaten at a restaurant knows not to believe everything on the menu. "Home made" is rarely true anymore. And the "cream" for coffee is often a chemical potion, while the "cream" with cereal and fruits is more likely to be half and half or milk. "Fresh" orange juice is often frozen, and butter is really margarine in many places.

Small deceptions like these are so commonplace that few people bother to complain about them, and few in authority ever try to boil them down to credible proportions.

One notable exception is Bailus Walker, director of the District of Columbia Environmental Health Administration. What he found in 141 eating establishments may not be much different than in restaurants elsewhere:

● Most often suspect were references to seafood. Every one of the shrimp advertised as fresh turned out to have been frozen. The same was true of many other seafood products on the menus.

● Bakery items were also overdone, especially when represented as freshly made when they actually were from commercial bakeries. One-fourth of the places falsely claimed that the cheesecakes they served were their own.

● More than 70 per cent of the fruit salads and cocktails advertised as fresh had at least some commercially-packed segments, plus preservatives.

● Beef labeled as prime rib turned out to be choice grade in 90 per cent of the cases. None of the restaurants could prove their menu references to breed of animal, such as Black Angus Beef, New Jersey Pork Chops, Maryland Milk-Fed Chicken and Maine Lobster.

NEW EMPHASIS ON NUTRITION BY GOVERNMENT

As a result of Congressional criticism and pressure, the government launched new efforts to improve public nutrition in 1979. In May, Assistant USDA Secretary Rupert Cutler announced "a rebirth of human nutrition research in USDA," largely due to evidence of a relationship between diet and many leading causes of death.

While other parts of the buget were being cut, funds for nutrition research were increased by $7.8 million. The USDA allocated $26 million to the states for nutrition education and training for 1979.

The Department also expanded its Nutrition Information Center at Beltsville, MD, and made it more consumer oriented. The Center was opened to educators, dietitians, nutritionists, cooperative extension personnel and other interested people. It is located in Room 304 of the National Agricultural Library.

By 1979, there were signs that government feeding programs were beginning to raise nutritional levels. A study by the Field Foundation Medical Team reporting finding far fewer cases of severe malnutrition among Americans than 10 years earlier. It gave most of the credit to the Head Start programs of the Department of Health, Education and Welfare and the school breakfast and lunch programs and Women-Infant-Children (WIC) programs of USDA. (See chapter on Financial Assistance for details about the feeding programs.)

WAS EARLY MAN A VEGETARIAN?

Recent findings and studies of early humans indicate that they had teeth designed for eating fruits, not the meat of large animals. Scientists have found ways to trace the wear of teeth on early jawbones to dietary habits.

The implications are that today's diet heavy in animal proteins and fat is not what the human body was designed for and therefore cannot be as healthy as a lighter diet. Studies have shown that people who don't eat meat have lower rates of heart disease, high blood pressure, obesity and cancer.

WHAT IS 'HEALTH' FOOD?
Government Tries to Clear Up Confusion

Is it necessary to eat "natural" or "organic" food products in order to get proper nutrition and stay healthy? Millions of people apparently think so. At least, they believe advertisements enticing them to buy so-called health food usually at higher prices than similiar items cost at a non-health food store. Sales are now near $3 billion a year.

The most common claim is that a food is "natural" or that all its ingredients are "natural." Can a fruit drink that contains only 30 per cent fruit juice plus artificial color be called natural? And can ice cream with refined sugar be called natural? These are among the approximately 200 food items making such claims.

In addition, there are widespread notions that organic fertilizers produce more nutritious produce, that natural vitamins are better than synthetic ones and other equally questionable assertions.

So much confusion developed that the Federal Trade Commission announced a regulation that would ban the use of words such as "organic," "natural" and "health food" because they are too vague and therefore may deceive buyers. At public hearings, the agency's proposals were supported by many experts in the scientific community but opposed strongly by representatives of the health food industry.

Ruth Leverton, a former nutritionist at the USDA, testified that the terms "natural" and "organic" were meaningless. She said foods grown with organic fertilizers such as manure are not superior to foods grown with commercial fertilizers. She added that since pesticide residues are present to some degree in almost all foods, it is wrong to claim that any food is free of pesticides.

Other witnesses suggested that public ignorance is what makes the health food industry so profitable. A survey by the Food and Drug Administration also indicates that many people want "superhealth" rather than "average" good health or merely the absence of serious ailments. For many people, good health "implies something beyond the norm and therefore unnaturally good," according to the survey data submitted at the FTC hearings.

The FTC rules have not yet been made final.

NUTRITION AND HEALTH

The typical American diet got a big helping of criticism in January 1977, when the Senate Committee on Nutrition and Human Needs issued a report entitled *Dietary Goals for the United States*. The report concluded that the country was suffering under a "wave of malnutrition" affecting all income classes. The Subcommittee, headed by Sen. George S. McGovern (D-SD), found substantial over-consumption of fats, sugar, cholesterol and salt in the typical diet and a substantial lack of complex carbohydrates such as those in cereals, grains, fruits and vegetables.

The report concluded that a great deal more and better nutrition education was necessary to "enable food growers, processors, wholesalers, retailers and consumers to make more healthful food choices." The report urged that nutrition education be improved particularly in schools and that ways be found to convey it on television. It recommended that food labels be required to disclose percentages and types of fats, percentage of sugar, milligrams of cholesterol and salt, caloric content per serving, nutritive values and food additives.

The report proposed a number of dietary goals to improve nutritional levels. The goals included increasing the average consumption of complex carbohydrates to about 55 to 60 per cent of daily energy (caloric) consumption, reducing overall fat consumption from about 40 to 30 per cent of calorie intake, reducing cholesterol intake to about 300 milligrams a day, reducing refined sugar by about 40 per cent to account for only 15 per cent of calories, and reducing salt consumption by about 50 to 85 per cent to approximately 3 grams a day.

OPPOSITION RISES FROM AFFECTED INDUSTRIES

Considerable opposition soon arose, however, mostly from industries directly affected by the recommendations. Leaders of the meat, dairy and egg industries demanded new public hearings, which they received, as well as alterations in the report itself, which they also received. They were joined by the American Medical Association, which objected to the dietary goals on the grounds that any such wholesale recommendations would threaten to disrupt doctor-patient relationships.

As a result of the complaints, especially from farmers in McGovern's largely agricultural home state, a "second edition" of the report was published in December, 1977, over the objections of one staff member who resigned because of the changes. The new edition changed the recommendation to "decrease consumption of meat and increase consumption of poultry and fish" to read "decrease consumption of animal fat and choose meats, poultry and fish which will reduce saturated fat intake." The recommendation to "decrease consumption of butterfat, eggs and other high cholesterol sources" was supplemented by a sentence reading: "Some consideration should be given to easing the cholesterol goal for pre-menopausal women, young children and the elderly in order to obtain the nutritional benefits of eggs in the diet." Other recommendations were also softened in regard to meat, egg and dairy products.

POOR DIETS LINKED TO POOR HEALTH

Before issuing the first report, the Subcommittee had held a series of hearings on nutrition and health. Testimony indicated that Americans are eating more food with high calorie levels and becoming less active and thus are not burning up the extra calories.

Sources of calories have also changed over the years. In the beginning of the century, almost 40 per cent of caloric intake came from fruits, vegetables and grains. Today, these products account for only 20 per cent of calories consumed. Since sugars and fats provide relatively few vitamins and minerals, the result may be severe—though sometimes subtle—malnutrition and undernourishment. In many respects, Americans are killing themselves by eating improper diets.

Subcommittee testimony noted the strong links between overconsumption of fat, cholesterol, sugar, salt and alcohol and killer diseases such as heart attacks, strokes, cancer, diabetes, hardening of arteries and cirrhosis of the liver. These are six of the ten leading causes of death in America. Diet, of course, is not the only factor in contracting these diseases, but it is one factor which can be modified.

BENEFITS OF BETTER DIETS

The Senate Nutrition Subcommittee says its recommended diet could have the following benefits, based on USDA statistics:
- 50 per cent fewer infant deaths per year,
- 80 per cent reduction in cases of obesity,
- 25 per cent fewer cases of heart disease,
- 20 per cent fewer respiratory diseases per year,
- 50 per cent of diabetes cases improved or avoided,
- 50 per cent fewer cases of arthritis,
- 90 per cent fewer cases of asthma due to milk and gluten,
- 20 per cent fewer people with allergies,
- 33 per cent fewer deaths per year due to alcoholism,
- 20 per cent fewer people with impaired vision and
- 75 per cent fewer cases of osteoporosis.

Dr. Gio Gori, of the National Cancer Institute, told a subcommittee hearing of a strong correlation between diet and cancer. He cited epidemiological studies indicating that approximately 40 per cent of American male cancer cases and 60 per cent of female cases are related to diet. The types of cancer related to nutrition include: stomach, breast, prostrate, liver, large and small intestines, and colon. Gori concluded that, next to smoking, nutrition is the single most important factor in cancer. His view was confirmed by another hearing witness, Dr. D. M. Hegsted of the Harvard School of Public Health. He said evidence was overwhelming that "the major causes of death and disability in the United States are related to the diet we eat."

PESTICIDES AND DRUGS IN YOUR DIET

The federal government has set limits (tolerance levels) for chemical residues in food. But excessive amounts continue to be found regularly in meat and poultry, according to quarterly reports of the U.S. Department of Agriculture (USDA).

Data for 1978, for example, show that 9.7 per cent of some 6,687 hogs sampled had illegal residues of sulfa drugs, which are used to prevent disease and foster growth. The USDA has been trying for years without success to get farmers to restrict their use of sulfonamides in hog products. The violation rate has remained at about 10 per cent a year.

The Department has no power to penalize farmers other than to require pretesting before marketing if violations persist. Meat from which samples are taken for regular monitoring purposes is allowed to be sold regardless of test results.

Antibiotics are another serious problem because of the possibility that even at low levels they may lessen the effect of antibiotics in people who eat meat. Like sulfa drugs, antibiotics are used to stimulate growth and prevent disease. Reports for 1978 showed 46 of 1,796 cattle samples with excessive antibiotic residues and 94 of 1,409 calf samples.

Excessive amounts of DES (diethylstilbestrol), a growth hormone that can cause cancer in humans, were found in 9 of 1,329 cattle samples. And 10 of 967 cattle samples showed excessive amounts of halocarbons, mostly pesticides.

Most significant for meat eaters is the fact that these residues tend to concentrate in the kidney and liver, which are consumed in large quantities by many people.

FOR A MORE NUTRITIONAL DIET

For nearly 25 years, nutritionists have followed the government's basic formula for providing proper nutrition in the daily diet. The formula, known as the "Basic Four," calls for each person to include at least some foods from each of four groups: beans, grains and nuts; fruits and vegetables; milk products; and meat, fish and egg products.

But the formula has met increasing criticism because of its lack of clear instruction and its failure to account for new evidence of health risks in certain foods, particularly animal fat, cholesterol, salt and sugar. So the U.S. Department of Agriculture is reviewing the situation.

In the meantime, the Center for Science in the Public Interest, a private research group, has adjusted the "Basic Four" to fit present needs of individuals more precisely, as follows:

GUIDE TO A BALANCED DIET

EAT:	ANYTIME	IN MODERATION	NOW AND THEN
GROUP 1 BEANS, GRAINS & NUTS	Barley Beans Bread & rolls (whole grain) Bulghur Lentils Oatmeal Past Rice Whole grain cereal (except granola)	Granola cereals Nuts Peanut butter Soybeans White bread and Cereals	
FOUR OR MORE SERVINGS/DAY			
GROUP II FRUITS & VEGETABLES	All fruits and vegetables except those listed on right Unsweetened fruit juices Unsalted vegetable juices Potatoes, white or sweet	Avocado Fruits canned in syrup Salted vegetable juices Sweetened fruit juice Vegetables canned with salt	French fries Olives Pickles
FOUR OR MORE SERVINGS/DAY			
GROUP III MILK PRODUCTS CHILDREN: 3 TO 4 SERVINGS OR EQUIVALENT ADULT: 2 SERVINGS (Favor ANYTIME column for additional servings.)	Buttermilk Farmer or pot cheese Lowfat cottage cheese Milk with 1% milkfat Skim milk ricotta Skim milk	Frozen lowfat yogurt Ice milk Lowfat milk with 2% milkfat Lowfat (2%) yogurt, plain or sweetened Regular cottage cheese Part-skim mozarella and ricotta	Hard cheeses: blue, brick, camembert, cheddar, Ice cream Processed cheeses Whole milk Whole milk yogurt
GROUP IV POULTRY, FISH, EGG & MEAT PRODUCTS	POULTRY Chicken or turkey (no skin)	FISH Herring Mackerel Salmon Sardines	POULTRY & FISH Deep fried and breaded fish or poultry

ANYTIME		NOW AND THEN
		RED MEATS
(Favor ANYTIME column for additional servings. If a vegetarian diet is desired, nutrients in these foods can be obtained by increasing servings from Groups I & III.)	Flank steak Ham* Leg of lamb* Loin of lamb* Plate beef* Round steak* Rump roast* Sirloin steak* Veal*	Bacon Corned Beef Ground beef Hot dogs Liver Liverwurst Pork: loin Pork: Boston butt
Cod Flounder Haddock Rockfish Shellfish, except shrimp Sole Tuna, water-packed		
Egg whites		Egg yolk or whole egg
MISCELLANEOUS		
FATS	**FATS**	**FATS**
(none)	Mayonnaise Salad oils Soft (tub) margarines	Butter Cream Cream cheese Lard Sour cream
SNACK FOODS	**SNACK FOODS**	**SNACK FOODS**
(none)	Angel food cake Animal crackers Fig bars Gingerbread Ginger snaps Graham crackers	Chocolate Coconut Commercial pies, pastries and doughnuts Potato chips Soda pop

NOTE: Snack foods should not be used freely, but the middle column suggests some of the better choices.

*Trim all outside fat. "Anytime" foods contains less than 30 per cent of calories from fat and are usually low in salt and sugar. Most of the "now and then" foods contain at least 50 percent of calories from fat—*and* a large amount of saturated fat. Foods to eat "in moderation" have medium amounts of total fat and low to moderate amounts of saturated fat *or* large amounts of total fat that is mostly unsaturated. Foods meeting the standards fall in the middle category, as are refined cereal products. For example, pickles have little fat, but are so high in sodium that they fall in the "now and then" category. To cut down on salt intake, chose varieties of foods listed here that do not have added salt, such as no-salt cottage cheese, rather than the regular varieties. This guide is not appropriate for individuals needing very low-salt diets.

Source: Center for Science in the Public Interest, 1979. A poster-size version of the above is available for $2.00 from the Center, 1755 S St. NW, Washington, DC, 20009.

CARBOHYDRATES

IMPORTANCE: Provide energy for the central nervous system; regulat the body's digestion of foods and metabolism of protein and fat.

MAIN SOURCES: Grains, cereals, baked products, starchy vegetables potatoes, sugar, syrup, honey and other sweets.

CONSUMPTION TRENDS: Consumption of complex carbohydrates, which do not include sugar, has steadily decreased over the past 30 years. Accordin, to a USDA study, consumption of dark green and deep yellow vegetables ha decreased 6.3 pounds a year per person since the late 1940s, and consumptio: of all other vegetables has decreased by 12 pounds. Use of cereal and flou products has fallen 31 pounds, and non-citrus fruits 30 pounds. Only citru fruits have increased in usage.

Carbohydrates used to be the main provider of energy, but they have bee: largely replaced by fat and protein. One possible reason for this shift i increased income which allows people to move away from diets high i: vegetables, beans and whole grains and towards processed, convenience foods Another reason may be the relatively small amount of advertising of fruits vegetables, and whole grains in comparison with that of snack foods and highl: processed foods high in sugar and salt.

PRINCIPAL HEALTH HAZARDS: Testimony before the Senate Nutritio: Subcommittee revealed some serious health hazards associated with diet lacking complex carbohydrates, such as starchy vegetables. Drs. William an Sonja Connor, in *Present Knowledge In Nutrition,* and Dr. Jeremiah Stamle: chairman of the Department of Community Health and Preventive Medicine a Northwestern University, reported a direct relationship between diets high i complex carbohydrates and reduced heart disease. Other studies indicate th societies with low incidence of coronary heart disease and relatively low levels c cholesterol consume many more carbohydrates than Americans do. Comple: carbohydrates, such as vegetables and grain, represent 65 to 85 per cent of tot: energy intake in these societies, compared to only 20 per cent in the U.S.

A diet high in complex carbohydrates may also reduce atherosclerosi (hardening of the arteries) because these products tend to lower cholesterol an saturated fat levels. Such a diet can also improve glucose tolerance levels.

Fiber, a complex carbohydrate, is not absorbed by the body but increase bulk in the intestinal tract. Dr. Beverley Winikoff, assistant director for healt sciences of the Rockefeller Foundation, told the Senate Nutrition Subcommitte that low fiber consumption may be related to high rates of inflammator diseases of the colon, appendicitis, hemmorhoids, arteriosclerosis and diabete:

These differences in calories lead to another hazard — obesity. D: Theodore Cooper, of the U.S. Department of Health, Education and Welfar: told the Senate Nutrition Subcommittee that approximately 20 per cent of a American adults are so overweight as to injure health and reduce longevit:

SUGGESTED DIETARY CHANGES: While fruits and vegetables are goo sources of complex carbohydrates, nutrient levels decrease with processing Foods eaten straight from the garden provide maximum nutrients, but it : questionable whether all fresh fruits and vegetables in supermarkets are mor nutritious than their processed counterparts. Frozen and fresh vegetables ar nearly equal in nutritional value. Increasing consumption of fresh produce would also increase dietary fiber and decrease consumption of food additives.

Highly processed foods should not be considered nutritional equivalents of food in its fresh form. For example, one baked potato provides 4 grams of protein, 32.8 grams of carbohydrate, and .2 grams of fat, while 10 potato chips contain only 1.1 grams of protein, 10 grams of carbohydrates, and 8 grams of fat. As the following table shows, the cost of various forms of potatoes does not coincide with the nutrient.

Increased consumption of grain products as a source of complex carbohydrates is also recommended. Bread is the most widely eaten grain product, but consumption is decreasing mainly because of the belief that it is fattening. An experiment by Dr. Olaf Mickelson, of Michigan State University, concluded that this assumption is incorrect. When slightly overweight men each ate 12 slices of bread a day in addition to their meals, average weight loss was 12.7 pounds per person. Bread tends to decrease one's appetite.

Fiber is also present in whole gain and bran type cereals, peas and other legumes, nuts, fruits and vegetables. It is not present in foods of animal origin. So-called natural or health cereals do not contain significantly more major nutrients than other dry cereals and generally provide 20 to 30 more calories. They also tend to have higher fat content (three to four grams per serving). However, they do provide many trace nutrients and fiber which refined, enriched cereals lack, and they do not contain the artifical additives used in refined cereals.

COMPARATIVE COST OF VARIOUS FORMS OF POTATOES

Product	Package Size	Price*	Price Per Pound
Fresh potatoes	10 lb	$ .98	$ .10
Del Monte, canned whole	16 oz	.28	.28
Bel-Air southern style	32 oz	.59	.30
Bel-Air Tater Treats	16 oz	.45	.45
Orelda Tater Tots	16 oz	.49	.49
Bel-Air frozen fries	9 oz	.28	.50
Orelda dinner fries	24 oz	.77	.51
Orelda frozen shoestring	12 oz	.45	.60
Idahoan instant mashed	8 oz	.37	.74
Pillsbury artificial mashed	16 oz	.85	.85
Butterfield shoestring	16 oz	1.19	1.19
Betty Crocker potato buds	5 oz	.41	1.31
Granny Goose chips	8 oz	.75	1.50
French's potato pancakes	6 oz	.57	1.52
McDonald's small fries	3 oz	.32	1.69
Betty Crocker augratin	5.5 oz	.59	1.71
Procter & Gamble's pringles	4.5 oz	.49	1.72
Nabisco potato snacks	5 oz	.62	1.98
Nabisco tater puffs	5 oz	.64	2.05
Granny Goose chip packets	6 oz	.95	2.52

*Prices in San Francisco, July, 1976.   Source: *AgBiz Tiller*, August, 1976.

SUGAR

IMPORTANCE: Sugar is 99.9 per cent carbohydrate and is the only food that provides calories but no nutrition. It is converted to simple sugar glucose by digestive juices. Glucose is used as energy in the body's breathing, heartbeat, cell growth, brain, nervous system and muscles. A small amount of glucose is converted to glycogen and stored in the liver and muscles. Excess amounts are converted to fat.

SOURCES: Sugars are of two types: monosachharides (simple sugars) found in fruits and vegetables and easily digested; and disaccharides (complex, double sugars) found in table sugar, molasses, maple sugar and syrup.

CONSUMPTION TRENDS: As previously mentioned, sugar has displaced starch as the chief source of carbohydrates in today's diet. Yearly sugar consumption amounts to more than 100 pounds per person. The main reason for increased sugar consumption is the addition of sugar to processed food.

In the early years of this century about 70 per cent of each person's annual sugar intake was through direct consumer use. By 1976, use in commercially prepared foods represented 63 per cent of total sugar deliveries. Refined sugar for non-commercial use represented only 36 per cent of total consumption. Beverage use accounted for nearly 23 per cent of the processed total.

But sugar is not only added to such foods as candy, baked goods, sweetened cereals, desserts and beverages. It is added to almost all processed foods, including catsup, mayonnaise, salad dressing, soup, crackers and even salt packages. Sugar is used increasingly by processors to create more desirable products.

Manufacturers have successfully resisted consumer attempts to have the amount of sugar in products revealed. In 1974, the Center for Science in the Public Interest petitioned the FDA to require disclosure of sugar percentages in cereal products and when the amount exceeded 10 per cent to have the product labeled with a warning. The FDA denied the petition.

In June, 1979, the U.S. Department of Agriculture Human Nutrition Center estimated the sugar content of 62 ready-to-eat breakfast cereals. The 62 cereals, which represent about 90 per cent of the cereal sales to U.S. consumers, were analyzed for the presence of the five main food sugars: sucrose or table sugar, the sugar most commonly used in cereals; fructose, glucose, lactose, and maltose. The study found two cereals with over 50 per cent sugar and failed to find any added sugar in three. (See table).

PRINCIPAL HEALTH HAZARDS: The story of sugar's harmful effects on humans has not been told in much detail to the American people mainly because food advertisers, who provide substantial financial support for the major news media, would not stand for it. At the same time, the other side of the story, the glories of sweet tasting food, is told over and over again in persuasive advertising messages and publicity releases.

The sugar industry frequently claims that sugar is a good food. In November, 1975, the National Advertising Division of the Council of Better Business Bureaus challenged the claim of Amstar Corporation, the largest sugar company, that said: "When it comes to good taste, Domino Sugar isn't just good flavor; it's good food." NAD dropped its challenge, however, when

PERCENTAGE OF SUGAR IN CEREALS

Product	% Sugar	Product	% Sugar
Sugar Smacks (K)	56.0	Raisin Bran (K)	29.0
Apple Jacks (K)	54.6	C.W. Post, Raisin, (GF)	29.0
Froot Loops (K)	48.0	C.W. Post (GF)	28.7
Raisin Bran (GF)	48.0	Frosted Mini Wheats (K)	26.0
Sugar Corn Pops (K)	46.0	Country Crisp (GF)	22.0
Super Sugar Crisp (GF)	46.0	Life, Cinnamon (QO)	21.0
Crazy Cow, chocolate (GM)	45.6	100% Bran (N)	21.0
Corny Snaps (K)	45.5	All Bran (K)	19.0
Frosted Rice Krinkles (GF)	44.0	Fortified Oat Flakes (GF)	18.5
Frankenberry (GM)	43.7	Life (QO)	16.0
Cookie Crisp, vanilla (R-P)	43.5	Team (N)	14.1
Cap'n Crunch, crunch berries (QO)	43.3	40% Bran (GF)	13.0
Cocoa Krispies (K)	43.0	Grape Nuts Flakes (GF)	13.3
Cocoa Pebbles (GF)	42.6	Buckwheat (GM)	12.2
Fruity Pebbles (GF)	42.5	Product 19 (K)	9.9
Lucky Charms (GM)	42.2	Concentrate (K)	9.3
Cookie crisp, chocolate (R-P)	41.0	Total (GM)	8.3
Sugar Frosted Flakes of Corn (K)	41.0	Wheaties (GM)	8.2
Quisp (QO)	40.7	Rice Krispies (K)	7.8
Crazy Cow, strawberry (GM)	40.1	Grape Nuts (GF)	7.0
Cookie Crisp, Oatmeal (R-P)	40.1	Special K (K)	5.4
Cap'n Crunch (QO)	40.0	Corn Flakes (K)	5.3
Count Chocula (GM)	39.5	Post Toasties (GF)	5.0
Alpha Bits (GF)	38.0	Kix (GM)	4.8
Honey Comb (GF)	37.2	Rice Chex (R-P)	4.4
Frosted Rice (K)	37.0	Corn Chex (R-P)	4.0
Trix (GM)	35.9	Wheat Chex (R-P)	3.5
Cocoa Puffs (GM)	33.3	Cheerios (GM)	3.0
Cap'n Crunch, peanut butter (QO)	32.2	Shredded Wheat (N)	0.6
Golden Grahams (GM)	30.0	Puffed Wheat (QO)	0.5
Cracklin' Bran (K)	29.0	Puffed Rice (QO)	0.1

(K) Kellogg, (GF) General Foods, (GM) General Mills, (R-P) Ralston-Purina, (QO) Quaker Oats, (N) Nabisco.

Source: U.S. Department of Agriculture, 1979.

Amstar said it had no intention of repeating the claim. The Sugar Association, Inc., earlier agreed to drop a similar claim when challenged by the NAD. In 1972 the Federal Trade Commission forced the Association to run "corrective" advertising admitting that there is no evidence that eating sugar before meals will help a person lose weight.

The large increase in sugar consumption during this century has been linked to numerous health problems. Not only does sugar lack essential nutrients, it may even increase the body's need for some that are needed to digest carbohydrates. These include vitamins, such as thiamin, and the mineral chromium.

In his book, *Sweet and Dangerous,* Dr. John Yudkin, a physician and professor at Queen Elizabeth College in England, offers a comprehensive indictment

PERCENTAGE OF SUGAR IN MISCELLANEOUS FOODS

Food	Per Cent Sugar (Sucrose) Added	Food	Per Cent Sugar (Sucrose) Added
Del Monte canned peaches (water pack)	0	General Foods Jello	13
		Dannon blueberry yogurt	14
Del Monte canned pineapple (juice pack)	0	Wyler's beef bouillon cubes	15
		Hunt-Wesson snack pack pudding	16
Del Monte canned pineapple (heavy syrup)	9	Duncan Hines angel food cake	17
		Del Monte pudding cup - vanilla	17
Bird's Eye Orange Plus	7	100% bran cereal	18
Del Monte canned peaches (light syrup)	7	Libby's canned peaches	18
		Sealtest chocolate ice cream	21
Borden's Cool 'n Creamy	8	Hamburger Helper	23
Skippy peanut butter	9	Borden's Cool Whip	24
Hunt-Wesson Snack Pack fruit cup	9	Kellog's Pop Tarts	26
Coca-Cola	9	Heinz catsup	29
Bird's Eye Awake	11	Russian dressing	30
Del Monte whole kernel corn	11	Ralston-Purina sandwich cookie	35
Kool-Aid	11	Hostess Sno-Ball	42
Hi-C orange drink	11	Duncan Hines brownies	50
Ritz Crackers	12	Shake & Bake chicken	51
Duncan Hines blueberry muffins	12	Hershey bar	51
Tang	13	Cremora	60
Granola with raisins	15	Coffee-mate	65
Applesauce, sweetened	13	Borden's Cracker Jack	68
Del Monte fruit cup	13		

Source: Center for Science in the Public Interest.

of sugar as a health hazard. Yudkin believes that substance is so harmful that it should be banned. He cites numerous surveys and tests, including many of his own, to show that sugars may be the principal cause of heart disease and other serious ailments. He reports tests showing increased levels of cholesterol and triglyceride (fat) in the blood when animals are fed extra quantities of sugar.

Other studies have shown that people with excess fat are more likely than others to get diabetes after maturity, and that excessive intake of sugar is one of the main causes of obesity. Yudkin refers to studies by Dr. A. M. Cohen, associate professor at Hebrew University, Jerusalem, disclosing a close statistical relationship between high rates of diabetes and high levels of sugar intake an animals and people.

Diabetes now affects about 10 million Americans and is the third leading cause of death in the United States. Diabetes cases increased 50 per cent from 1965 to 1973.

Studies done by Richard A. Ahrens of the University of Maryland indicate that sudden increases in sugar in students tend to raise blood pressure levels significantly, a sign that the body is having difficulty handling the sweet substance.

More well known is sugar's role in tooth decay, the most widespread disease. The American Dental Association has estimated that 95 per cent of the population has tooth decay.

Children generally eat much more sugar than adults do. It is estimated that youngsters consume three or four pounds per week, compared to the average for the whole population of nearly two pounds per week. Some commercially prepared baby foods contain as much as 30 and 40 per cent sugar. Some parents make matters worse by using candy and sugary desserts as rewards for good behavior. As a result, many people develop an early craving for sugar. Some nutritionists suspect that high-sugar diets at early ages may set in motion adverse physical patterns. Tests conducted by the U.S. Department of Agriculture appear to confirm this suspicion.

SUGGESTED DIETARY CHANGES: According to the Senate Nutrition Subcommittee sugar consumption should be reduced to 15 per cent of caloric intake. One area in need of major reduction is soft drink consumption which has doubled since 1960. The average American drank 295 twelve-ounce cans of soft drinks in 1975, equal to 21.5 pounds of sugar. Cutting out soft drinks would achieve at least half the recommended reduction in sugar consumption.

Another area which could be controlled is consumption of baked goods, the largest source of sugar in today's diet. A shift from commercially prepared to homemade baked goods would cut sugar intake substantially.

Replacing snack "junk" foods with fresh foods would also reduce sugar and provide needed nutrients.

FATS AND CHOLESTEROL

IMPORTANCE: Fats are the body's most concentrated source of energy. They are essential for carrying fat-soluble vitamins through the body, for helping absorb vitamin D which brings calcium to bones and teeth and for slowing down the digestion process. Fat deposits protect the body organs, keep them in place, insulate the body from temperature changes and help the body retain heat.

Fatty acids are either saturated or unsaturated; most fats are combinations of both. Cholesterol, a common component of fats, is needed to form bile (which is necessary for fat digestion), adrenal hormones and vitamin D.

SOURCES: Fats are found in butter, margarine, lard, whole milk, eggs, salad and cooking oils, bacon and fatty meats, nuts, seeds, avocados and chocolate. Animal sources and coconut oil are usually high in saturated fats. (See table.) Unsaturated fats are more common in vegetable sources. Cholesterol is obtained from animal foods and the sun's rays. It is also produced by the body and is present in most body cells.

CONSUMPTION TRENDS: The amount of fat available per person per day rose from about 125 grams in the beginning of this century to 157 grams in 1976. Fat increased from 30 per cent to nearly 45 per cent of caloric intake. Today's consumption is equivalent to more than 24 pounds of fat a year.

According to an Agriculture Research Service report, the major sources of fat have also changed. In the early years, salad and cooking oils were the major sources, followed by margarine, shortening and meat respectively. The report found that in the past seven years, meat has contributed the largest increase in fat consumption, followed by salad and cooking oils and shortening.

Fat content of meat ranges from as low as 11 per cent for canned ham to 49 per cent for bacon. Cholesterol content for three ounces of beef is 75 milligrams

FAT CONTENT OF SELECTED FOODS

Food	Total fat	Total saturated	Total monoun-saturated	sa
Animal fats:				
Chicken	100.0	32.5	45.4	
Lard	100.0	39.6	44.3	
Beef tallow	100.0	48.2	42.3	
Avocado	15.0	2.0	9.0	
Beef products:				
T-bone steak (cooked, broiled—56 percent lean, 44 percent fat)	43.2	18.0	21.1	
Chuck, 5th rib (cooked or braised—69 percent lean, 31 percent fat)	36.7	15.3	17.5	
Brisket (cooked, braised, or pot roasted—69 percent lean; 31 percent fat)	34.8	14.6	16.7	
Wedge and round-bone sirloin steak (cooked or broiled—66 percent lean; 34 percent fat)	32.0	13.3	15.6	
Rump (cooked or roasted—75 percent lean; 25 percent fat)	27.3	11.4	13.1	
Round steak (cooked or broiled—82 percent lean; 18 percent fat)	14.9	6.3	6.9	
Cereals and grains:				
Wheat germ	10.9	1.9	1.6	
Oats (puffed, without added ingredients)	5.5	1.0	1.9	
Oats (puffed, with added nutrients, sugar covered)	3.4	.6	1.2	
Barley (whole grain)	2.8	.5	.3	
Domestic buckwheat (dark flour)	2.5	.5	.8	
Cornmeal, white or yellow (whole-ground, unbolted)	3.9	.5	.9	
Shredded wheat breakfast cereal	2.5	.4	.4	
Wheat (whole grain, Hard Red Spring)	2.7	.4	.3	
Wheat flakes breakfast cereal	2.4	.4	.3	
Rye (whole grain)	2.2	.3	.2	
Wheat meal breakfast cereal	1.4	.3	.1	
Wheat flour, all purpose	1.4	.2	.1	
Rice (cooked brown)	.8	.2	.2	
Bulgur from Hard Red Winter wheat	1.5	.2	.2	
Oatmeal or rolled oats, cooked	1.0	.2	.4	
Rye flour	1.4	.2	.1	
Cornstarch	.6	.1	.1	
Rice (cooked white)	.2	.1	.1	
Farina (enriched, regular, cooked)	.2	---	---	
Corn grits, cooked	.1	---	---	
Dairy products:				
Nondairy coffee whitener (powder)	35.6	32.6	1.0	---
Cream cheese	33.8	21.2	9.4	
Cheddar cheese	32.8	20.2	9.8	
Light whipping cream	32.4	20.2	9.6	
Muenster cheese	29.8	19.0	8.7	
American pasteurized cheese	28.9	18.0	8.5	
Swiss cheese	27.6	17.6	7.7	
Mozzarella cheese	19.4	11.8	5.9	
Ricotta cheese (from whole milk)	14.6	9.3	4.1	
Vanilla ice cream	12.3	7.7	3.6	
Half and half cream	11.7	7.3	3.4	
Chocolate chip ice cream	11.0	6.3	2.6	
Canned condensed milk (sweetened)	8.7	5.5	2.4	
Ice cream sandwich	8.2	4.7	2.6	
Cottage cheese (creamed)	4.0	2.6	1.1	
Yogurt (from whole milk)	3.4	2.2	.9	
Cottage cheese (uncreamed)	.4	.2	.1	---
Eggs:				
Fried in margarine	15.9	4.2	7.2	
Scrambled in margarine	12.6	3.7	5.5	
Fresh or frozen	11.3	3.4	4.5	
Fish:				
Eel, American	18.3	4.0	9.0	
Herring, Atlantic	16.4	2.9	9.2	
Mackerel, Atlantic	9.8	2.4	3.6	
Tuna, albacore (canned, light)	6.8	2.3	1.7	
Tuna, albacore (white meat)	8.0	2.1	2.1	
Salmon, sockeye	8.9	1.8	1.5	
Salmon, Atlantic	5.8	1.8	2.7	
Carp	6.2	1.3	2.7	
Rainbow trout (United States)	4.5	1.0	1.5	
Striped bass	2.1	.5	.6	
Ocean perch	2.5	.4	1.0	
Red snapper	1.2	.2	.2	
Tuna, skipjack (canned, light)	.8	.2	.2	
Halibut, Atlantic	1.1	.2	.2	

Food	Total fat	Fatty acids Total saturated	Total monoun- saturated	Total polyun- saturated
Chicken (broiler/fryer, cooked or roasted dark meat)	9.7	2.7	3.2	2.4
Turkey (cooked or roasted dark meat)	5.3	1.6	1.4	1.5
Chicken (broiler/fryer, cooked or roasted light meat)	3.5	1.0	.9	.9
Turkey (cooked or roasted light meat)	2.6	.7	.6	.7
b and veal:				
Shoulder of lamb (cooked or roasted, 74 percent lean; 26 percent fat)	26.9	12.6	11.0	1.6
Leg of lamb (cooked or roasted, 83 percent lean; 17 percent fat)	21.2	9.6	8.5	1.2
Veal foreshank (cooked or stewed, 86 percent lean; 14 percent fat)	10.4	4.4	4.2	.7
:				
Coconut	35.5	31.2	2.2	.7
Brazil nut	68.2	17.4	22.5	25.4
Peanut butter	52.0	10.0	24.0	15.0
Peanut	49.7	9.4	22.9	15.0
Cashew	45.6	9.2	26.4	7.4
Walnut, English	63.4	6.9	9.9	41.8
Pecan	71.4	6.1	43.1	17.9
Walnut, black	59.6	5.1	10.8	40.8
Almond	53.9	4.3	36.8	10.1
products:				
Bacon	49.0	18.1	22.8	5.4
Sausage, cooked	32.5	11.7	15.1	3.9
Deviled ham, canned	32.3	11.3	15.2	3.5
Liverwurst, braunschweiger, liver sausage	32.5	11.0	15.5	4.1
Bologna	27.5	10.6	13.3	2.1
Pork loin (cooked or roasted, 82 percent lean; 18 percent fat)	28.1	9.8	13.1	3.1
Ham (cooked or roasted, 84 percent lean; 16 percent fat)	22.1	7.8	10.4	2.4
Fresh ham (cooked or roasted, 82 percent lean; 18 percent fat)	20.2	7.1	9.5	2.2
Canadian bacon (cooked and drained)	17.5	5.9	7.9	1.8
Chopped ham luncheon meat	17.4	5.7	8.3	2.2
Canned ham	11.3	4.0	5.3	1.2
d and cooking oils:				
Coconut	100.0	86.0	6.0	2.0
Palm	100.0	47.9	38.4	9.3
Cottonseed	100.0	26.1	18.9	50.7
Peanut	100.0	17.0	47.0	31.0
Sesame	100.0	15.2	40.0	40.5
Soybean, hydrogenated	100.0	15.0	23.1	57.6
Olive	100.0	14.2	72.5	9.0
Corn	100.0	12.7	24.7	58.2
Sunflower	100.0	10.2	20.9	63.8
Safflower	100.0	9.4	12.5	73.8
lfish:				
Eastern oyster	2.1	.5	.2	.6
Pacific oyster	2.3	.5	.4	.9
Ark shell claim	1.5	.4	.3	.3
Blue crab	1.6	.3	.3	.6
Alaska king crab	1.6	.2	.3	.6
Shrimp	1.2	.2	.2	.5
Scallop	.9	.1	----------	.4
ps:				
Cream of mushroom (diluted with equal parts of water)	3.9	1.1	.7	.8
Cream of celery (diluted with equal parts of water)	2.3	.6	.5	1.0
Beef with vegetables (diluted with equal parts of water)	.8	.3	.3	----------
Chicken noodle (diluted with equal parts of water)	1.0	.3	.4	.2
Minestrone (diluted with equal parts of water)	1.1	.2	.3	.5
Vegetable (diluted with equal parts of water)	.9	.2	.3	.4
Clam chowder, Manhattan style (diluted with equal parts of water)	.9	.2	.2	.5
le spreads:				
Butter	80.1	49.8	23.1	3.0
Margarine (hydrogenated soybean oil, stick)	80.1	14.9	46.5	14.4
Margarine (corn oil, tub)	80.3	14.2	30.4	31.9
Margarine (corn oil, stick)	80.0	14.0	38.7	23.3
Margarine (safflower oil, tub)	81.7	13.4	16.1	48.4
etable fats (household shortening)	100.0	25.0	44.0	26.0

Source: Consumer and Food Economics Institute, U.S. Department of Agriculture, Agricultural Research Service, Hyattsville, Maryland. "Comprehensive Evaluation of Fatty Acids in Foods," *Journal of The American Dietetic Association*, May 1975; July 1975; August 1975; October 1975; March 1976; April 1976; July 1976; September 1976; November 1976; January 1977; unpublished data on shellfish and margarine.

and increases to 370 mgs. for beef liver. Despite high percentages of fat and cholesterol, meat consumption has continued to rise.

Fish and poultry, which have lower levels or fat and cholesterol and are generally less expensive, have remained at lower consumption levels (12 pounds per person for fish, and 44 pounds for poultry). However, poultry consumption jumped 16 pounds per person from 1960 to 1976.

PRINCIPAL HEALTH HAZARDS: Fat provides nine calories per gram, compared to four calories per gram for both protein and carbohydrates and seven calories per gram for alcohol. The high proportion of calories in fat creates serious weight problems for those whose fat intake is 45 per cent of total calories, the present average.

According to Dr. Theodore Cooper, obesity raises the chance of heart disease, hypertension, athereosclerosis, hernia, gallbladder disease, latent diabetes and liver disease. He told the Senate Nutrition Subcommittee that death of obese men from cirrhosis is 249 per cent of that expected in non-obese men. Obesity also adds to the hazards of surgery and causes postural derangement. Fat people do not live as long as others.

Dr. Gio Gori and Dr. Ernst Wynder both have testified of a direct association between fat intake and cancer of the colon and breast. Epidemiological studies show a much lower rate of colon and breast cancer in Japan, where fat intake is only 10 per cent of total calories, compared to 45 per cent in the U.S. As the Japanese diet is becoming more westernized, incidence of colon and breast cancer is increasing.

The majority of doctors testifying before the Federal Trade Commission hearings in 1976 on nutrition labeling of foods agreed that saturated fat is directly related to cholesterol levels, which have been associated with heart disease. Dr. Cooper reported that people with advanced atherosclerosis or established coronary heart disease have elevated blood fat and cholesterol levels. He said substitution of unsaturated fat for saturated fat markedly lowers cholesterol levels.

These conclusions have been disputed by the American National Cattlemen's Association and the National Livestock Feeders Association. They contend that there is no valid basis for claiming a direct relation between beef consumption and heart disease.

SUGGESTED DIETARY CHANGES: According to the Senate Nutrition Subcommittee most fat and cholesterol enter the diet through eating protein, mainly red meat. The subcommittee, therefore, recommended that more protein be acquired through alternative sources, such as fish, poultry, vegetables and whole grains. Eggs are also a good protein source but cholesterol content is so high that consumption should be limited. One egg yolk contains 250 mg. of cholesterol, or 50 mg. less than the recommended daily limit. Since only foods of animal origin contain cholesterol, increased consumption of vegetables would have a positive effect on cholesterol levels.

Other recommended changes in diet include selection of foods within the fish, poultry and vegetable groups relatively low in fat and cholesterol, reduction of foods high in fat and substitution of polyunsaturated fat for saturated fat.

CHOLESTEROL CONTENT OF SELECTED FOODS

Food	Amount	Cholesterol
		Milligrams
Milk, skim, fluid or reconstituted dry	1 cup	5
Cottage cheese, uncreamed	½ cup	7
Lard	1 tablespoon	12
Cream, light table	1 fluid ounce	20
Cottage cheese, creamed	½ cup	24
Cream, half and half	¼ cup	26
Ice cream, regular, approximately 10% fat	½ cup	27
Cheese, cheddar	1 ounce	28
Milk, whole	1 cup	34
Butter	1 tablespoon	35
Oysters, salmon	3 ounces, cooked	40
Clams, halibut, tuna	3 ounces, cooked	55
Chicken, turkey, light meat	3 ounces, cooked	67
Beef, pork, lobster, chicken, turkey, dark meat	3 ounces, cooked	75
Lamb, veal, crab	3 ounces, cooked	85
Shrimp	3 ounces, cooked	130
Heart, beef	3 ounces, cooked	230
Egg	1 yolk or 1 egg	250
Liver, beef, calf, hog, lamb	3 ounces, cooked	370
Kidney	3 ounces, cooked	680
Brains	3 ounces, raw	more than 1700

Source: "Cholesterol Content of Foods," R. M. Feeley, P. E. Criner, and B. K. Watt. J. Am. Diet. Assoc. 61:134, 1972.

SALT

IMPORTANCE: Salt is 40 per cent sodium chloride, which is a mineral necessary in conjunction with potassium for maintaining a normal balance of water and fluids between cells. Sodium and potassium are important for nerve health.

SOURCE: Salt is present naturally and synthetically in most foods, especially processed foods. It is also present in baking powder, baking soda, water, milk products and seafood.

CONSUMPTION TRENDS: Salt consumption today is estimated to be between 6 to 18 grams a day per person. However, according to Drs. George

Meneely and Harold Battarbee, the average amount needed is only one-half a gram. The National Academy of Science has prescribed three grams per day, equal to about three-fifths of a teaspoon.

Like sugar use, individual salt use has declined while increasing amounts are being added by manufacturers to processed foods.

PRINCIPAL HEALTH HAZARDS: Salt has been shown to cause hypertension (high blood pressure) in children and adults. Meneely and Battarbee contend that the imbalance of sodium and potassium may be a factor in hypertension, which effects an estimated 20 per cent of Americans. High blood pressure also often occurs with heart disease and stroke. Reduction of salt, say Meneely and Battarbee, could reduce suffering and increase the "duration and quality of life for many millions of people." Salt levels have also been linked with kidney disease. Dr. Theodore Cooper reported that regulation of salt intake in persons with kidney disease can prolong the normal life of kidneys for years.

Some doctors have also found a connection between sodium intake and heart disease. According to the Subcommittee report, researchers have found that increases in sodium from 4 to 24 grams a day altered the ability to clear intravenously administered fat from the bloodstream.

Other serious health hazards associated with high salt intake include alterations in gastric acid secretion, stomach cancer and cerebrovascular disease. An experiment conducted by Dr. George Brainard concluded that reduction of salt had a positive effect on migraine headaches.

SUGGESTED DIETARY CHANGES: The goal of three grams of salt a day could be met without the addition of any salt to food or the consumption of foods with salt visible. Salt needs may vary with personal lifestyle. Large amounts of salt are excreted with perspiration so that larger quantities may be necessary in the summer and during heavy exercise. Milk, meats, fish, cheese and eggs are high in sodium, while vegetables, bread and cereals have average amounts. Fruits and fats are low in sodium.

Highly salted snacks should be avoided, and the amount of salt, soy sauce, monosodium glutamate and seasonings which have high salt contents should be halved in cooking and table use.

The nutrition subcommittee prepared the following list of foods according to their sodium content.

SODIUM CONTENT OF SELECTED FOODS

LOW IN SODIUM
    Fruits: all fruits and fruit juices.
    Fats: Avocado, Butter, margaine, Cooking oils or fats (except bacon fats), Cream sweet or sour, Mayonnaise, and Unsalted nuts.

MODERATELY HIGH IN SODIUM
    Vegetables: all kinds except those listed under "Foods to avoid."
    Breads and Cereals: Barley, Bread, (white and whole wheat), Biscuits, Muffins Matzo, Grits, Cornbread, Cornmeal, Cornstarch, Wheat meal, Rolled wheat, Oatmeal Rice, Tapioca, Farina, Dry cereal, Crackers, Griddle cakes and waffles, Macaroni Noodles, and Spaghetti.

HIGH IN SODIUM

Milks: Whole, Skim, Buttermilk, Powdered, and Evaporated.

Meats: Beef, Pork, Lamb, Veal, Rabbit, Brain, Kidney, Liver, Tongue, Chicken, Duck, Quail, and Turkey.

Fish: All kinds, except those listed under "Food to avoid."

Cheese: (lightly salted) Swiss, American, Cottage.

Eggs: in moderation.

Other foods: Alcoholic beverages, fountain beverages, Baking chocolate, Cocoa, Candy, Coffee or coffee substitute, Gelatin, Pudding mixes, Syrups, Honey, Molasses, Leavening agents such as Baking powder, Baking soda, Potassium bicarbonate, and Yeast.

VERY HIGH IN SODIUM

Meats: Salted or smoked, Bacon, Bologna, Corned beef, Ham, Luncheon meats, Sausage, and Salt pork.

Fish: Salted or smoked, Anchovies, Sardines, Caviar, Dried cod, and Herring.

Peanut butter, unless low-sodium dietetic.

Flavorings: Commercial boullion, Catsup, Celery, onion or garlic salts, Chili sauce, Meat extracts, sauces or tenderizers, unless low-sodium dietetic, Prepared mustard, Relishes, Salt substitutes, Cooking wine.

Cheeses: Processed cheese, Cheese spreads, Roquefort, Camembert, and other strong cheeses.

Vegetables: Salted or packed in brine, Pickles, sauerkraut, etc.

Miscellaneous: Breads with salt topping, Potato chips, Popcorn, Other salted snacks, Bacon and bacon fat, Pretzels, Salted nuts, and Olives.

COST OF 20 GRAMS OF PROTEIN FROM MEATS AND ALTERNATIVES

Food	Unit	Price per unit[1]	Part of unit giving 20 grams of protein[2]	Cost of 20 grams of protein
Dry beans	lb	$0.43	3.8 oz	$0.10
Peanut butter	12 oz	.72	2.8 oz	.17
Beef liver	lb	.72	3.8 oz	.17
Bread, white enriched[3]	lb	.35	8.2 oz	.18
Chicken, whole, ready-to-cook	lb	.55	5.9 oz	.20
Hamburger	lb	.86	3.8 oz	.21
Milk, whole fluid[4]	½ gal	.83	2.3 cups	.24
Turkey, ready-to-cook	lb	.70	5.6 oz	.25
Eggs, large	doz	.97	3 eggs	.25
Chicken breasts	lb	1.07	4.0 oz	.27
Pork, picnic	lb	.84	5.1 oz	.27
Bean soup, canned	11.25 oz	.31	11.0 oz	.30
Chuck roast of beef, bone in	lb	.93	5.6 oz	.32
American process cheese	8 oz	.88	3.0 oz	.33
Round beefsteak	lb	1.75	3.5 oz	.38
Ham, whole	lb	1.35	4.6 oz	.39
Frankfurters	lb	1.13	5.8 oz	.41
Pork loin roast	lb	1.27	5.3 oz	.42

Food	Unit	Price per unit[1]	Part of unit giving 20 grams of protein[2]	Cost of 20 grams of protein
Liverwurst	8 oz	.74	4.8 oz	.44
Rump roast of beef, boned	lb	1.75	4.2 oz	.45
Salami	8 oz	.92	4.0 oz	.46
Sardines, canned	4 oz	.54	3.8 oz	.51
Ham, canned	lb	2.13	3.8 oz	.51
Sirloin beefsteak	lb	1.90	4.5 oz	.53
Bologna	8 oz	.77	5.8 oz	.56
Ocean perch, fillet, frozen	lb	1.61	5.8 oz	.58
Rib roast of beef	lb	1.80	5.3 oz	.59
Pork chops, center cut	lb	1.72	5.6 oz	.60
Haddock, fillet, frozen	lb	1.72	5.6 oz	.61
Veal cutlets	lb	3.09	3.4 oz	.66
Pork sausage	lb	1.32	8.3 oz	.68
Bacon, sliced	lb	1.45	8.3	.76
Porterhouse beefsteak	lb	2.36	5.4 oz	.80
Lamb chops, loin	lb	2.89	5.0 oz	.89

[1] Average retail prices in U.S. cities in January, 1977, Bureau of Labor Statistics, U.S Department of Labor. [2] One-third of the daily amount recommended for a 20-year-ol man. [3] Bread and other grain product, such as pasta and rice, are frequently used with small amount of meat, poultry, fish or cheese as main dishes in economy meals. In thi way the high quality protein in meat and cheese enhances the lower quality of protein i cereal products. [4] Although milk is not used to replace meat in meals, it is an economica source of good quality protein.

Source: U.S. Department of Agriculture.

PROTEINS

IMPORTANCE: Most abundant substance in the body, next to water. Essential for healthy growth and development of body tissues, muscles, blood blood clots, milk (during lactation), skin, hair, nails, bones, brain, heart an other internal organs; neutralization of the acid in blood and tissues; regulation of the body's water balance; formation of hormones (which regulate body growth, sexual development, and an individual's rate of metabolism); formation of enzymes (which quicken or retard bodily reactions such as digestion an metabolism), and for the formation of antibodies for fighting body infections

BODY USE: Protein molecules are broken up into similar units, amino acids, during digestion. There are about 22 known amino acids. Of these, 1 cannot be produced in the body. Excess protein is changed into fat and stored i body tissues. Fluid imbalance in the body can be the result of too much protein because body water is directly proportional to the amount of protein that mus be metabolized.

VITAMINS

Vitamins are essential organic compounds necessary for human life and growth. Because the body does not produce them in sufficient quantities, they must be acquired in the diet. Vitamins play a vital role in the metabolism of other nutrients, but they have caloric value.

Vitamins can be divided into two groups: fat-soluble ones (vitamins A, D, E, and K) and water-soluble ones (thiamin, riboflavin, niacin, folic acid, vitamin B_{12}, B_6, pantothenic acid and vitamin C).

FAT-SOLUBLE VITAMINS

Fat-soluble vitamins are dissolvable in fats or oils but not in water. Because these vitamins can be stored in the body, daily dosages are not necessary. Hypervitaminosis (vitamin toxicity) can result from too much of any one vitamin, particularly vitamins A, D and K. Toxicity symptoms are headache, nausea, weakness and fatigue.

Following is a summary of information on each vitamin, including its role, major sources, signs of deficiency, toxicity, plus ways to preserve vitamins in food preparation:

VITAMIN A — Importance: Essential for healthy hair, complexion and eyesight; development of eye tissue and visual purple, which enables eyes to see at night; resistance to infection; repair and functioning of body tissues; protection of skin linings of eyes, nose, mouth, throat, lungs, from infection. **Major Sources:** Liver, spinach, carrots, broccoli, beets, kale, dandelion greens, peppers, tomatoes.

VITAMIN D — Importance: Regulates amount of calcium and phosphorus, minerals necessary for healthy development of bones and teeth, absorbed and utilized by the blood. **Major Sources:** Sun's ultra violet rays which activate a form of cholestrol present skin that absorbs vitamin into bloodstream, fish-liver oils, milk, and egg yolks.

VITAMIN E — Importance: Prevents fats and fat-soluble vitamins from breaking down and combining with substances that may be harmful to the body; unites with oxygen and helps the body's red blood cells resist oxidizing agents that rupture cells; combats heart disease, circulatory problems and emphysema; helps heal burns, bruises, wounds, scars, and treat cancer. **Major Sources:** Salad oils, shortening, margarine, whole grains, eggs, fruits, vegetables and organ meats (e.g., liver, kidneys).

VITAMIN K — Importance: Essential for producing prothrombin, a chemical necessary for blood clotting. Often given to pregnant women during last month of pregnancy and to babies in their first week of life so that hemorrhaging will not occur. **Major Sources:** Green leafy vegetables and fats. **Deficiency Symptoms:** Hemorrhaging.

WATER-SOLUBLE VITAMINS

All of the water-soluble vitamins except Vitamin C are part of the B complex which contains at least 11 vitamins. Eight of the most essential are B_1, B_2, B_6, B_{12}, biotin, folic acid, niacin and pantothenic acid. Water-soluble vitamins cannot be stored in the body because excess amounts are excreted. They are therefore not toxic in large amounts.

VITAMIN C (ASCORBIC ACID) — Importance: Essential for body resistance to some infections and allergies; for speeding recovery from wounds, scars and fractures; for preventing an iron deficiency in the body; and for forming and maintaining collagen, a protein necessary for the growth of skin, ligaments, and bones. **Major Sources:** Broccoli, green peppers, citrus fruits and juices, tomatoes.

VITAMIN B COMPLEX — **Importance:** Converts carbohydrates into glucose, their simplest form, which the body burns for energy; important for health of nervous system, skin, hair, eyes, mouth and liver. **Major Sources:** Because B vitamins are so inter-related in function, they must be taken together, rather than in individual doses. Best sources are natural foods such as whole grains, green leafy vegetables, brewer's yeast and organ meats.

VITAMIN B$_1$ (THIAMIN) — **Importance:** Stored mainly in the heart, liver, kidneys, skeletal muscles and brain. Essential for a healthy appetite; the metabolism of carbohydrates; and nerve functioning. **Major Sources:** Enriched, restored and whole-grain cereal products, organ meats, pork, eggs, milk, legumes and nuts.

VITAMIN B$_2$ (RIBOFLAVIN) — **Importance:** Essential for maintaining smooth, uncracked skin, clear vision and for helping cells use oxygen. **Major Sources:** Milk, cheeses, leafy green vegetables, meats and whole-grain cereal products. Riboflavin is often used to enrich baked goods.

VITAMIN B$_6$ (PYRIDOXINE) — **Importance:** Essential for utilization of carbohydrates, fats and proteins; for the release of glycogen from the liver and muscles to produce energy; for production of red blood cells and substances that fight diseases in the blood stream; and for regulation of brain and nervous tissues. **Major Sources:** Liver, pork, muscle meats, whole grains, cereals, nuts and vegetables.

VITAMIN B$_{12}$ (COBALAMIN) — **Importance:** Essential for normal functioning of all body cells, principally those of the bone marrow, intestine and nervous tissue; for creation of red blood cells; and for metabolism of fats, carbohydrates and proteins. "Intrinsic factor," a substance secreted by the stomach, and calcium usually combine with B$_{12}$ so that it may be easy for the blood to absorb this vitamin. **Major Sources:** Liver, eggs, milk, salt-water fish and muscle meats.

BIOTIN — **Importance:** Produces fatty acids and burns them up along with carbohydrates for body heat and energy. **Major Sources:** Organ meats, muscle meats, milk, egg yoke, most vegetables, whole grains and brewer's yeast.

FOLIC ACID (FOLACIN) — **Importance:** Essential in the formulation of red blood cells and nucleic acid, which is necessary for body growth and reproduction. **Major Sources:** Green leafy vegetables, liver and yeast.

NIACIN — **Importance:** Generates body energy by breaking down sugar, proteins and fats; contributes to physcial and mental well-being and a healthy digestive system, tongue and skin. There are two forms of niacin: (1) what appears in foods, and (2) what the body produces itself (tryptophan). The combination is known as "niacin equivalent." **Major Sources:** Lamb, lean meat, poultry, shellfish, fish, peanuts, flour and whole grain and enriched cereal products.

PANTOTHENIC ACID — **Importance:** Essential for body growth; healthy skin and nerves; formation of cholesterol and fatty acids; breakdown of carbohydrates, fats and proteins to create body energy. **Major Sources:** Liver, kidney, heart, eggs, lean muscle meats, legumes, cereals, milk, vegetables and fruit.

MINERALS

Minerals may be separated into two categories: (1) Macrominerals—present in body tissues in relatively high amounts; and (2) Trace Elements—essential for the body, but which appear in minute amounts.

MACROMINERALS

CALCIUM: Combines with phosphorus to form and maintain strong bones and teeth; helps blood to clot; essential for muscular contraction, heartbeat regulation, metabolism and body utilization of iron. Major sources are milk, cheese, citrus fruits, dry legumes, green leafy vegetables and oysters, sardines, salmon.

MAGNESIUM: Necessary for healthy functioning of nerve impulses, heart contractions, and other muscles; for speeding up the body's utilization of carbohydrates, fats, protein, calcium, phosphorus and vitamin D. Major sources include nuts, whole grains, dark green vegetables and seafoods.

PHOSPHORUS: Needed to maintain a calcium-phosphorus balance in the bones; essential for the body's production of energy; for utilization of carbohydrates, fats and proteins in cell growth and repair; for cell division, reproduction and transfer of hereditary traits; healthy bones and teeth; muscle contraction (particularly of the heart); and absorption of B vitamins. Major sources are meat (especially organ meats), fish, dry legumes, milk products and eggs.

POTASSIUM: Essential in the body's conversion of glucose to glycogen for liver storage and helps stimulate nerve response and maintain a balance of water between fluids and cells. (See section on salt for more information on the role of potassium in conjunction with sodium.) Major sources of potassium are meats, whole grains, fruits and vegetables.

SULFUR: Essential for proper functioning of B vitamins in the body; for tissue formation and respiration. Major sources include meat, fish, legumes and nuts.

TRACE MINERALS

COBALT: Essential for funtioning and maintenance of red blood cells and other body cells in the bone marrow, nervous system and gastro-intestinal tract and for activating enzymes which regulate body reactions. Cobalt is found in meat, leafy vegetables, cereals and fruits.

COPPER: Essential for skin and hair coloring and for the body's absorption of iron and formation of red blood cells and hemoglobin, which carries oxygen from the lungs to body tissues for energy. Major sources are meats, shellfish, nuts, raisins and dried legumes.

IRON: Works with protein and copper to form hemoglobin and is also important for the formation of myoglobin, which is necessary for supplying oxygen to the muscle cells for muscle contractions. Major sources of iron are dark green, leafy vegetables, organ meats, dried fruits, egg yolks, whole grains and enriched cereals and breads. Vitamin C changes iron to a form that is easier for the body to absorb so foods containing these nutrients should be eaten together.

MANGANESE: Essential for normal bone development and structure for the body's utilization of thiamine and fat production; and for formation of blood, milk and urea. Major sources are tea, blueberries, nuts, seeds, meat, whole grains, leafy green vegetables and beans.

NUTRITION AND FOOD LABELS:
The Emerging Truths

Any manufacturer who makes a nutritional claim is required by the Food and Drug Administration to disclose some details. They include percentages of five vitamins (vitamins A and C, thiamin, riboflavin and niacin) and two minerals (calcium and iron) in one serving. The amount of calories, protein, carbohydrates and fat content must also be given.

In order to provide a method of comparing the nutrients in a particular food to total daily nutritional requirements, a system was devised by the National Academy of Sciences called the RDA (Recommended Dietary Allowance). (See table.) RDAs have been set for every significant nutrient needed daily by infants, children and adults of various age groups.

To simplify for labeling purposes, nutritionists have condensed the RDA to the U.S. RDA (United States Recommended Daily Allowance). The U.S. RDA takes the maximum amount of each nutrient needed for four broader categories: infants, children, all children over age four and adults, and pregnant and lactating women.

For example, the amount of vitamin A for males ages 11 and up was adopted as the standard, even though children and women do not need that much. The U.S. RDA uses a larger quantity that the dietary allowance specifies when there is evidence that the population is lacking in that nutrient. An example is riboflavin.

On food meant for only infant or children, nutritional labels use the U.S. RDAs for that age group. All other nutritional labeling is based on the U.S. RDA for adults and children over 4 years old. Following is that list of U.S. RDAs:

Protein	65 grams	Vitamin B6	2 mg.
Vitamin A	5,000 units	Folacin	0.4 mg.
Vitamin C	60 mg.	Vitamin B12	6 mcg.
Thiamin	1.5 mg.	Phosphorus	1 g.
Riboflavin	1.7 mg.	Iodine	150 mcg.
Niacin	20 mg.	Magnesium	400 mg.
Calcium	1 gram	Zinc	15 mg.
Iron	18 mg.	Copper	2 mg.
Vitamin D	400 units	Biotin	0.3 mg.
Vitamin E	30 units	Pantothenic Acid	10 mg.

Why did the FDA choose to use the highest RDAs for labels rather than the averages? Since only 13 items are required on the label, the higher figure is intended to provide a safety margin for other vitamins and minerals that are not mentioned. The maximums are intended to assure that everyone will receive the necessary amounts of nutrients if the guideline is followed.

To complicate matters further, nutritional labels are not exact percentages of U.S. RDAs. If a food contains more than 50 per cent of a nutrient, the percentage is listed to the nearest 10 per cent. If the nutrient satisfies between 10 and 50 per cent of the U.S. RDA, it is listed to the closest five per cent. For amounts between two and ten per cent, the U.S. RDA is listed to the closest two per cent.

FOOD INSPECTION

The federal government and many states have food inspection programs. The following are federal programs:

MEAT AND POULTRY

The Meat Inspection Act of 1906 requires inspection of meat packaging plants for sanitation and carcass inspection for contamination. A similar act mandating inspection of poultry plants was passed in 1957. Federal inspection was only for plants selling across state lines.

Not until the Wholesome Meat Act in 1967 and the Wholesome Poultry Act of 1968 were uniform inspection procedures adopted for meats shipped within as well as between states. State inspection services were required to have an inspection program comparable to that of the federal government.

In the first few years after the 1967 amendment, the USDA took over inspection duties from some states because of inferior quality of the state inspections. Most states have turned over their inspection duties for economic reasons.

Together, the Wholesome Meat and Poultry Acts and the Meat and Poultry Inspection Acts require continuous inspection of processing plants for cleanliness. Meat may be inspected anywhere along the processing line for wholesomeness and contamination. Processed foods containing meat or poultry are also under USDA supervision.

Following are meat (left) and poultry (right) inspection seals which appear on products which have passed USDA inspection standards.

FISHERY PRODUCTS

Some fresh, frozen, canned, breaded or otherwise processed fish products are inspected and graded by the National Marine Fishery Service in the Department of Commerce. But the program is voluntary, authorized by the Agriculture Marketing Act of 1946.

Inspectors check the processing plant for cleanliness and the product for wholesomeness and adherence to the product's standard recipe. The federal inspector may also grade products. A processor may elect whether to have a federal inspector on the premises and whether to have the inspector inspect only a particular product lot. But such lots cannot be labeled as USDC inspected.

Fish products that carry a federal stamp must be packed under the continuous supervision of a federal inspector or packed in a plant that meets a quality assurance standard. In the quality assurance program, a federal inspector's supervision is not continuous.

Fishery products certified under the voluntary program are stamped in one of the following ways: "U.S. Department of Commerce, Packed Under Federal Inspection," (below left) indicates the product was inspected, statistically sampled and found to be safe, wholesome and of good quality.

The Grade A Shield (above left) is given only to top quality products. They must be uniform in size, have no defects and be fresh in flavor and odor.

FOOD GRADING

The chore of grading foods is done almost entirely by the Department of Agriculture (USDA). The USDA began issuing standards of quality in 1917 when it first graded potatoes. Since then the scope has broadened to include meat and meat products, poultry, eggs, butter, cheddar cheese, instant nonfat dry milk, fresh and processed fruits and vegetables, dried beans, peas and rice.

The meat group (beef, veal, calf, lamb and mutton), is graded for eating quality; poultry is measured in terms of the edible portion of meat and the "finish" or appearance. Eggs are graded for appearance and suitability for various types of cooking. Butter and cheddar cheese are ranked for flavor, texture and body. Nonfat dry milk is measured for color uniformity, bacteria count, milkfat and solubility. Fruits and vegetables, both fresh and processed, are graded for color, shape, size and maturity, as are dried beans.

SUMMARY OF FEDERAL FOOD GRADES

Food	Best	Second Best	Third Best	Fourth Best
Beef	Prime	Choice	Good	Standard
Lamb	Prime	Choice	Good	Utility
Pork	Acceptable	Unacceptable	---	---
Poultry	A	B	---	---
Fish*	A	B	C	---
Eggs and butter	AA	A	B	---
Fresh fruits and vegetables**	U.S. Fancy	U.S. No. 1	U.S. No. 2	U.S. No. 3
Canned fruits and vegetables**	A	B	C	Substandard

Source: U.S. Department of Agriculture, Agriculture Marketing Service

  *U.S. Department of Commerce grades.

**Grade designations vary from these for some products.

The U.S. grade shield (above left) may be used on canned, frozen and dried fruits and vegetables. It may also be used on related products such as frozen concentrated juices and jams. If a product makes a claim to be of a certain grade and does not have the inspection seal it must still measure up to that quality.

The shield (above right) is used on fresh fruits and vegetables. The range of grades is U.S. Fancy, U.S. No. 1 and U.S. No. 2. Although most are sold at wholesale on the basis of these grades, not many are so marked in grocery stores.

STANDARDS FOR MEAT AND POULTRY PRODUCTS

MEAT PRODUCTS

All percentages of meat are on the basis of fresh uncooked weight unless otherwise indicated.

Baby Food
High Meat Dinner—At least 26% meat.
Meat and Broth—At least 61% meat.
Vegetable and Meat—At least 8% meat.
Bacon (cooked)—Weight of cooked bacon can't exceed 40% of cured, smoked bacon.
Bacon and Tomato Spread—At least 20% cooked bacon.
Barbecued Meats—Weight of meat when barbecued can't exceed 70% of the fresh uncooked meat. Must have barbecued (crusted) appearance and be prepared over burning or smouldering hardwood or its sawdust. If cooked by other dry heat means, product name must mention the type of cookery.
Barbecue Sauce with Meat—At least 35% meat (cooked basis).
Beans and Meat in Sauce—At least 12% meat.
Beans in Sauce with Meat—At least 20% cooked or cooked and smoked meat.
Beans with Bacon in Sauce—At least 12% bacon.

Beans with Frankfurters in Sauce—At least 20% franks.
Beans with Meatballs in Sauce—At least 20% meatballs.
Beef and Dumplings with Gravy or Beef and Gravy with Dumplings—At least 25% beef.
Beef and Pasta in Tomato Sauce—At least 25% beef.
Beef Burger Sandwich—At least 35% hamburger (cooked basis).
Beef Burgundy—At least 50% beef; enough wine to characterize the sauce.
Beef Sauce with Beef and Mushrooms—At least 25% beef and 7% mushrooms.
Beef Sausage (raw)—No more than 30% fat. No byproducts, no extenders.
Beef Stroganoff—At least 45% fresh uncooked beef or 30% cooked beef, and at least 10% sour cream or a "gourmet" combination of at least 7½% sour cream and 5% wine.
Beef with Barbecue Sauce—At least 50% beef (cooked basis).
Beef with Gravy—At least 50% beef

(cooked basis)./Gravy with Beef—At least 35% beef (cooked basis).

Breaded Steaks, Chops, etc.—Breading can't exceed 30% of finished product weight.

Breakfast (frozen product containing meat)—At least 15% meat (cooked basis).

Breakfast Sausage—No more than 50% fat.

Brown and Serve Sausage—No more than 35% fat and no more than 10% added water.

Brunswick Stew—At least 25% of at least two kinds of meat and/or poultry.

Must contain corn as one of the vegetables.

Cabbage Rolls with Meat—At least 12% meat.

Cannelloni with Meat and Sauce—At least 10% meat.

Cappelletti with Meat in Sauce—At least 12% meat.

Chili Con Carne—At least 40% meat.

Chili Con Carne with Beans—At least 25% meat.

Chili Hot Dog with Meat—At least 40% meat in chili.

Chili Macaroni—at least 16% meat.

Chili Pie—At least 20% meat; filling must be at least 50% of the product.

Chili Sauce with Meat or Chili Hot Dog Sauce with Meat—At least 6% meat.

Chop Suey (American Style) with Macaroni and Meat—at least 25% meat.

Chopped Ham—Must be prepared from fresh, cured, or smoked ham, plus certain kinds of curing agents and seasonings. May contain dehydrated onions, dehydrated garlic, corn syrup, and not more than 3% water to dissolve the curing agents.

Chow Mein Vegetables with Meat and Noodles—At least 8% meat and the chow mein must equal 2/3 of the product.

Creamed Dried Beef or Chipped Beef—At least 18% dried or chipped beef.

Corned Beef and Cabbage—At least 25% corned beef (cooked basis).

Corned Beef Hash—At least 35% beef (cooked basis). Must contain pota-toes, curing agents, and seasonings. May contain onions, garlic, beef broth, beef fat or others. No more than 15% fat; no more than 72% moisture.

Country Ham—A dry-cured product frequently coated with spices.

Crepes—At least 20% meat (cooked basis) if the filling has other major characterizing ingredient, such as cheese.

Croquettes—At least 35% meat.

Curried Sauce with Meat and Rice (Casserole)—At least 35% meat (cooked basis) in the sauce and meat part; no more than 50% cooked rice.

Deviled Ham—No more than 35% fat.

Dinners (Frozen Product Containing Meat)—At least 25% meat or meat food product (cooked basis) figured on total meal minus appetizer, bread and dessert. Minimum weight of a consumer package—10 ozs.

Dumplings and Meat in Sauce—At least 18% meat.

Egg Foo Yong with Meat—At least 12% meat.

Egg Rolls with Meat—At least 10% meat.

Enchilada with Meat—At least 15% meat.

Entrees: Meat or Meat Food Product and One Vegetable—At least 50% meat or meat food product (cooked basis).

Meat or Meat Food Product, Gravy or Sauce, and One Vegetable—At least 30% meat or meat food product (cooked basis).

Frankfurter, Bologna, and Similar Cooked Sausage—May contain only skeletal meat. No more than 30% fat, 10% added water and 2% corn syrup. No more than 15% poultry meat (exclusive of water in formula).

Frankfurter, Bologna and Similar Cooked Sausage with Byproducts or Variety Meats—Same limitations as above on fat, added water and corn syrup. Must contain at least 15% skeletal meat. Each byproduct or variety meat must be specifically named in the list of ingredients. These include hearts, tongue, spleen, tripe, stomachs, etc.

Frankfurter, Bologna and Similar Cooked Sausage with Byproducts or

Variety Meats and Which Also Contain Nonmeat Binders—Product made with the above formulas and also containing up to 3½% nonmeat binders (or 2% isolated soy protein). These products must be distinctively labeled, such as "frankfurters with byproducts, nonfat dry milk added."

Fritters—At least 35% meat. A breaded product.

Goulash—At least 25% meat.

Gravies—At least 25% meat stock or broth, or at least 6% meat.

Ham—Canned—Limited to 8% total weight gain after processing.

Ham—Cooked or Cooked and Smoked (not canned)—Must not weigh more after processing than the fresh ham weighs before curing and smoking; if contains up to 10% added weight, must be labeled "Ham, Water Added"; if more than 10%, must be labeled "Imitation Ham."

Ham and Cheese Spread—At least 25% ham (cooked basis).

Hamburger, Hamburg, Burger, Ground Beef or Chopped Beef—No more than 30% fat; no extenders.

Ham Croquettes—At least 35% ham (cooked basis).

Ham Salad—At least 35% ham (cooked basis).

Ham Spread—At least 50% ham.

Hash—At least 35% meat (cooked basis).

Lasagna with Meat and Sauce—At least 12% meat.

Liver Products Such as Liver Loaf, Liver Paste, Liver Pate, Liver Cheese, Liver Spread and Liver Sausage—At least 30% liver.

Macaroni and Beef in Tomato Sauce—At least 12% beef.

Macaroni and Meat—At least 25% meat.

Macaroni Salad with Ham or Beef—At least 12% meat (cooked basis).

Manicotti (containing meat filling)—At least 10% meat.

Meat and Dumplings in Sauce—At least 25% meat.

Meat and Seafood Egg Roll—At least 5% meat.

Meat and Vegetables—At least 50% meat.

Meatballs—No more than 12% extenders (cereal, etc.—including textured vegetable protein). At least 65% meat.

Meat Casseroles—At least 25% fresh uncooked meat or 18% cooked meat.

Meat Loaf (Baked or Oven-Ready)—At least 65% meat and no more than 12% extenders including textured vegetable protein.

Meat Pies—At least 25% meat.

Meat Ravioli—At least 10% meat in ravioli.

Meat Salads—At least 35% meat (cooked basis).

Meat Soups
Ready-to-Eat—At least 5% meat.
Condensed—At least 10% meat.

Meat Spreads—At least 50% meat.

Meat Tacos—At least 15% meat.

Mince Meat—At least 12% meat.

Omelet with Ham—At least 18% ham (cooked basis).

Pate De Foie—At least 30% liver.

Pepper Steaks (Chinese)—At least 30% beef (cooked basis).

Pizza with Meat—At least 15% meat.

Pizza with Sausage—At least 12% sausage (cooked basis) or 10% dry sausage, such as pepperoni.

Pork Sausage—Not more than 50% fat; may contain no byproducts or extenders.

Pork with Barbecue Sauce—At least 50% pork (cooked basis).

Pork and Dressing—At least 50% pork (cooked basis).

Salisbury Steak—At least 65% meat and no more than 12% extenders including textured vegetable protein.

Sandwiches (containing meat)—At least 35% meat in total sandwich; filling must be at least 50% of the sandwich.

Sauce with Chipped Beef—At least 18% chipped beef.

Sauce with Meat, or Meat Sauce—At least 6% meat.

Sauerbraten—At least 50% meat (cooked basis).

Scalloped Potatoes and Ham—At least 20% ham (cooked basis).

Scallopine—At least 35% meat (cooked basis).

Scrapple—At least 40% meat and/or meat byproducts.

Shepherd's Pie—At least 25% meat; no more than 50% mashed potatoes.

Sloppy Joe (sauce with meat)—At least 35% meat (cooked basis).

Spanish Rice with Beef or Ham—At least 20% meat.

Stuffed Peppers with Meat in Sauce—At least 12% meat.

Sukiyaki—At least 30% meat.

Sweet and Sour Pork or Beef—At least 25% meat and at least 16% fruit.

Sweet and Sour Spareribs—At least 50% bone-in spareribs (cooked basis).

Swiss Steak with Gravy—At least 50% meat (cooked basis)./Gravy and Swiss Steak—At least 35% meat (cooked basis).

Tamales—At least 25% meat.

Taquitos—At least 15% meat.

Tongue Spread—At least 50% tongue.

Tortellini with Meat—At least 10% meat.

Veal Fricassee—At least 40% meat.

Veal Parmagiana—At least 40% breaded meat product in sauce.

Veal Steaks—Can be chopped, shaped, cubed, frozen. Beef can be added with product name shown as "Veal Steaks, Beef Added, Chopped, Shaped and Cubed" if no more than 20% beef, or must be labeled "Veal and Beef Steak, Chopped, Shaped and Cubed." No more than 30% fat.

Vegetable and Meat Casserole—At least 25% meat.

Vegetable Stew and Meat Balls—At least 12% meat in total product.

Won Ton Soup—At least 5% meat.

POULTRY PRODUCTS

All percentages of poultry—chicken, turkey, or other kinds of poultry—are on cooked deboned basis unless otherwise indicated. When standard indicates poultry meat, skin, and fat, the skin and fat are in proportions normal to poultry.

Baby Food

   High Poultry Dinner—At least 18¾% poultry meat, skin, fat, and giblets.

   Poultry with Broth—At least 43% poultry meat, skin, fat, and giblets.

Cabbage Stuffed with Poultry—At least 8% poultry meat.

Canned Boned Poultry

   Boned (kind), Solid Pack—At least 95% poultry meat, skin and fat.

   Boned (kind)—At least 90% poultry meat, skin and fat.

   Boned (kind), with Broth—At least 80% poultry meat, skin and fat.

   Boned (kind), with Specified Percentage of Broth—At least 50% poultry meat, skin, and fat.

Creamed Poultry—At least 20% poultry meat. Product must contain some cream.

Eggplant Parmagiana with Poultry—At least 8% poultry meat.

Egg Roll with Poultry—At least 2% poultry meat.

Entree:

   Poultry or Poultry Food Product and One Vegetable—At least 37½% poultry meat or poultry food product.

Poultry or Poultry Food Product with Gravy or Sauce and One Vegetable—At least 22% poultry meat.

Poultry a la King—At least 20% poultry meat.

Poultry Barbecue—At least 40% poultry meat.

Poultry Burgers—100% poultry meat, with skin and fat.

Poultry Burgundy—At least 50% poultry; enough wine to characterize the product.

Poultry Cacciatore—At least 20% poultry meat, or 40% with bone.

Poultry Casserole—At least 18% poultry meat.

Poultry Chili—At least 28% poultry meat.

Poultry Chili with Beans—At least 17% poultry meat.

Poultry Chop Suey—At least 4% poultry meat./Chop Suey with Poultry—At least 2% poultry meat.

Poultry Chow Mein, without Noodles—At least 4% poultry meat.

Poultry Croquettes—At least 25% poultry meat.

Poultry Dinners (a frozen product)—At least 18% poultry meat, figured on total meal minus appetizer, bread and dessert.

Poultry Fricassee—At least 20% poultry meat.

Poultry Hash—At least 30% poultry meat.

Poultry Lasagna—At least 8% poultry meat (raw basis).

Poultry Livers with Rice and Gravy—At least 30% livers in poultry and gravy portion or 17½% in total product.

Poultry Pies—At least 14% poultry meat.

Poultry Roll—No more than 3% binding agents, such as gelatin, in the cooked product; no more than 2% natural cooked-out juices./Poultry Roll with Natural Juices—Contains more than 2% natural cooked-out juices./Poultry Roll with Broth—Contains more than 2% poultry broth in addition to natural cooked-out juices./Poultry Roll with Gelatin—gelatin exceeds 3% of cooked product.

Poultry Soup
  Ready-to-Eat—At least 2% poultry meat.
  Condensed—At least 4% poultry meat.

Poultry Stew—At least 12% poultry meat.

Poultry Stroganoff—At least 30% poultry meat and at least 10% sour cream or a "gourmet" combination of at least 7½% sour cream and 5% wine.

Poultry with Gravy—At least 35% poultry meat./Gravy with Poultry—At least 15% poultry meat.

Poultry with Noodles or Dumplings—At least 15% poultry meat, or 30% with bone./Noodles or Dumplings with Poultry—At least 6% poultry meat.

Poultry with Noodles Au Gratin—At least 18% poultry meat.

Poultry with Vegetables—At least 15% poultry meat.

Stuffed Cabbage with Poultry—At least 8% poultry meat.

Sauce with Poultry or Poultry Sauce—At least 6% poultry meat.

Source: U.S. Department of Agriculture

STANDARDS FOR NON-MEAT PRODUCTS

Catsup—Concentrated tomato liquid, salt, vinegar, spices and flavorings, sweetened with sugar or sugar syrup.

Cheddar Cheese—Not more than 39% moisture, at least 50% milkfat. Harmless artificial coloring. Optional ingredients: mold-inhibiting ingredient not to exceed 0.3%.

Cheese Food, Pasteurized, Process—At least 51% of one or more cheeses plus milk products, fat content of at least 23% and moisture content not more than 44%. Optional ingredients: not more tnan 3% emulsifier, acidifying agent, water, salt, colorings, flavorings, mold inhibitors.

Cheese Spread, Pasteurized Process—At least 51% ot one or more cheeses plus milk products, fat content at least 20% and moisture content between 44 and 60%, up to 3% emulsifying ingredients. Optional ingredients: up to 8% carob bean gum, guar gum, carrageen or similar substances, acidifying agent, sweetener, water, salt, coloring and flavoring.

Cottage Cheese—At least 4% milkfat and not more than 80% moisture.

Cream Cheese—At least 33% milkfat and not more than 55% moisture.

Dressing, French—At least 35% vegetable oil plus either vinegar or lemon/lime juice, seasonings and emulsifying agents. Optional ingredients: color additives and no more than 75 parts per million (ppm) EDTA, salt, nutritive sweeteners, MSG and spices.

Dressing, Salad—30% vegetable oil, vinegar or lemon juice, egg yolks and flour paste. Optional ingredients: seasonings and emulsifiers, nutritive sweeteners.

Frozen Cherry Pie—Drained fruit content at least 25% of weight of pie. Optional ingredients: food and color additives, ingredients which perform useful functions in preparing of filling, pastry and topping. Artificial sweetener not considered a suitable ingredient.

Fruit Cocktail—30-50% peaches, 25-45% pears, 6-16% pineapples, 6-20% grapes, 2-6% cherries.

Ice Cream—At least 10% milkfat and 20% milk solids. Optional ingredients: spices, flavorings, chocolate, sugar, corn or maple syrup, honey, eggs and additives.

Ice Cream, French, Frozen Custard—At least 10% milkfat and 20% milk solids, but at least 1.4% egg yolks solids. Optional ingredients: spices, flavorings, sweeteners, additives.

Ice Milk—2-7% milk fat, 11% milk solids, food solids equal at least 1.3 pounds per gallon. Optional ingredients: caseinates may be added when milk solids weigh at least 11%, flavorings, colorings.

Lemonade, Frozen Concentrate—Fresh lemon juice, concentrated or natural strength and sugar or sugar syrup. Optional ingredients: artificial sweetener, colorings.

Light Cream—18-30% milkfat. Optional ingredients: stabilizers, emulsifiers, nutritive sweeteners, flavorings and colorings.

Mayonnaise—65% edible vegetable oil and vinegar, lemon/lime juice, egg yolks. Optional ingredients: spices, colorings, flavorings, EDTA, MSG, salt, nutritive sweeteners.

Milk, Evaporated—At least 7.5% milkfat and 25.5% milk solids, 25 units of Vitamin D per oz. Optional ingredients: Vitamin A, emulsifiers, stabilizers.

Milk, Lowfat—0.5% to 2.0% milkfat, at least 2000 units of Vitamin A. Optional ingredients: Vitamin D, concentrated skim milk, nonfat dry milk or other milk, coloring and flavoring, emulsifiers and stabilizers.

Milk, Nonfat Dry—Not more than 5% moisture and 1.5% milkfat unless indicated. Optional ingredients: coloring and flavoring.

Milk, Skim—Less than 0.5% milkfat, at least 2000 Units Vitamin A per quart, not less than 8.25% milk solids. Optional ingredients: Vitamin D, concentrated skim milk, nonfat dry milk or other milk, stabilizers, nutritive sweetener, emulsifiers, and flavorings and colorings.

Milk, Sweetened, Condensed—At least 8.5% milkfat, and 28% milk solids nutritive sweetener. Optional ingredients: coloring, flavorings.

Mixed Nuts—2 to 80% of each nut ingredient used. No color additives.

Oleomargrine—80% rendered animal vegetable fat, and milk products or soybeans in water. Optional ingredients: colorings, flavorings Vitamins A and D, preservatives, salt nutritive sweeteners.

Orange Juice, Frozen Concentrate—At least 11.8% orange juice and sugar or sugar syrup. Optional ingredients: preservatives.

Peanut Butter—Blanched or unblanched peanuts and not more than 10% stabilizing seasoning ingredients, total fat content not to exceed 55%.

Sherbet—At least 2% milk solids, weigh not less than 6 pounds per gallon. Optional ingredients: 1-2% milkfat fruit and juices—at least 2% citrus fruit, 6% berries, 10% for other fruits and sweeteners, eggs, additives.

Shrimp, Frozen Raw Breaded—At least 50% shrimp (whole or pieces), and breading. Optional ingredients: preservatives.

Shrimp, Frozen, Raw Lightly Breaded—At least 65% shrimp (whole or pieces), breading. Optional ingredients: preservatives.

Sour Cream—At least 14.4% milkfat 0.5% lactic acid. Optional ingredients: not more than 0.1% sodium citrate, rennet, nutritive sweeteners salt, flavoring and coloring.

Syrup, Maple—At least 66% maple sap

Syrup, Table—At least 65% soluble sweetener solids. Optional ingredients: additional sweeteners, honey butter, edible fats and oils, color additives, salt, preservatives, emulsifiers.

Water Ices—Weight at least 6 pounds per gallon. Optional ingredients: fruit juices—2% for citrus flavor, 6% for berry, 10% for other fruits, sweeteners and additives.

Source: Food and Drug Administration

CONVENIENCE FOODS: THE REAL COSTS

Each year Americans eat more and more convenience foods—those foods that are fully or partially prepared before sale. Most believe the convenience item costs more than preparing the same food from scratch.

However, in a comparison of convenience and home-prepared foods completed by the USDA, the surprising results showed that over one-third of the convenience foods were cheaper.

The comparison rates the cost of the convenience versus home-prepared foods using similar ingredients. For vegetables, 16 of the canned or frozen convenience forms were less expensive than fresh vegetables. Frozen concentrate orange juice was cheaper than any fresh or fabricated counterpart.

The beef, poultry and chicken skillet main dishes often promoted as "economical" food stretchers are more expensive than comparable home-prepared dinners using similar recipes. The convenient chicken dishes were up to 60 per cent more expensive than the home-prepared versions.

The following charts show the cost of servings rounded to the nearest ounce and the nearest cent. The costs do not include the cost of fuel used to prepare the food or any compensation for the preparer's time to cook the food.

COST OF 'CONVENIENCE' VS. HOME-MADE FOODS

Product	Cents Per Serving			
	Fresh or Home-Made	Frozen	Canned	Other
FRUITS AND BERRIES				
Cherries, red sour, pitted—4 oz.	22		22	
Coconut—3 oz.	2		3	
Cranberry sauce, strained—2 oz.	7		6	
Cranberry sauce, whole—2 oz.	6		6	
Grapefruit sections—3 oz.	12		14	
Lemon juice—1 oz.	8			3 (B)
Orange juice—4 oz.	12	4		7 (B)
Orange drink—4 oz.		3		4 (C)
Peaches—4 oz.	15	27	17	
Pineapple—3 oz.	12		13	
Raspberries—3 oz.	23	34	24	
Strawberries, sweetened, whole—4 oz.	20	22	45	
Strawberries, sweetened, sliced—4 oz.	20	27		
FISH AND SHELLFISH				
Crabcakes—3 oz.	60	52		
Crab-deviled—3 oz.	29	40		
Haddock dinner—12 oz.	56	100		
Pollock fish sticks—3 oz.	34	22		
Shrimp, cooked—2 oz.	61	50	50	
Shrimp, breaded—3 oz.	40	45		
Shrimp, newburg—4 oz.	69	113		
Shrimp, breaded—7 oz.	38	60		
Tuna noodle casserole—8 oz.	26	67		23 (S)

	Cents Per Serving			
Product	Fresh or Home-Made	Frozen	Canned	Other
MEAT AND POULTRY				
Beef				
Chili-macaroni, skillet main dish—9 oz.	28			30 (S)
Dinner—11 oz.	51	79		
Lasagne—10 oz.	52	84		
Lasagne, skillet main dish—9 oz.	35			26 (S)
Patties—3 oz.	21	28		
Pie—8 oz.	20	40		
Sloppy joe sauce—3 oz.	11		17	
Stew—9 oz.	21		34	
Stroganoff, skillet main dish—8 oz.	46			47 (S)
Meat loaf dinner—9 oz.	41	70		
Chicken				
A-la-king—6 oz.	22	37		
Braised, whole—2 oz.	25		26	
Chow mein—7 oz.	39	54	33	
Batter dipped, deep fat fried—2 oz.	12	39		
Meat—2 oz.	10		31	
Pie—8 oz.	29	36		
Salad spread—3 oz.	19		33	
Fried dinner—10 oz.	40	63		
Turkey				
Dinner—13 oz.	30	71		
Tetrazzini—8 oz.	42	79		
Pork				
Sweet and sour—6 oz.	32	52		29 (P)
Link sausage—2 oz.	39	29	31	
VEGETABLES				
Asparagus spears—2 oz.	23	20	20	
Beets—3 oz.	13		9	
Broccoli spears—3 oz.	13	16		
Broccoli spears in butter sauce—4 oz.		22		
Broccoli spears in Hollandaise sauce—4 oz.	18	25		
Broccoli spears, au gratin—5 oz.	26	36		
Brussel sprouts—3 oz.	14	12		
Butter beans—4 oz.	4		12	
Carrots, sliced—3 oz.	7		10	
Corn, cut—3 oz.	12	11	12	
Corn-on-the-cob—6 oz.	13	13		
Green beans—2 oz.	8	9	10	
Green bean casserole—4 oz.	21	25		
Green peas—3 oz.	27	11	11	
Lima beans—3 oz.	29	11	14	
Pork and beans—7 oz.	13		14	
Potatoes, au gratin—5 oz.	8	25		12 (D)
Potatoes, boiled, whole—4 oz.	3		13	
Potatoes, french fried—2 oz.	10	9		
Potatoes, hash browned—4 oz.	5			12 (D)

(B) Bottled; (C) Crystals; (D) Dehydrated; (P) Packaged combination; (S) Skillet main dish mix.

Source: U.S. Department of Agriculture

BIG MACS COMPARED TO HOME-COOKED

Though McDonald's guarantees that you can get change back from your dollar with the purchase of a hamburger, french fries, and soft drink, you could get more change back if you prepared the same food at home. According to a USDA analysis, cost of prepared foods are less by 20 per cent for a hamburger and by 72 per cent for an apple pie. Calories and protein were found about equal although the calories provided from fats vary; a chocolate shake at McDonald's provides half as many calories from fat as does one prepared at home. The additional fat from home-prepared shakes comes from the use of pure milk and ice cream, whereas a McDonald's shake is prepared from a processed mix. The following table compares the cost and nutritive values of various items on the McDonald's menu with their home-prepared counterparts.

Food and Source	Calories	Calories from fat	Protein[1]	Cost[2] (cents)
Hamburger:				
McDonalds'	260	94	20	30
Homemade	338	125	28	24
Cheeseburger:				
McDonald's	312	128	25	38
Homemade	390	160	34	29
Big Mac				
McDonald's	546	284	40	75
Homemade	546	229	40	37
¼-lb Hamburger				
McDonald's	416	171	41	65
Homemade	468	201	43	34
Fillet of Fish				
McDonald's	416	204	24	55
Homemade	338	125	23	29
French Fries				
McDonald's	208	87	4	30
Homemade	182	69	3	13
Apple Pie				
McDonald's	260	133	3	25
Homemade	208	77	3	07
Chocolate Shake				
McDonald's	312	62	17	40
Homemade	286	123	15	15
Soft Drink				
McDonald's	104	0	([3])	20
Homemade	104	0	([3])	08

[1] Protein as percentage of U.S. Recommended Daily Allowance; [2] Prices in Washington, DC area, July, 1976; [3] Insignificant amount of nutrient present.

FOOD ADDITIVES

The increasing amounts of chemicals getting into food are causing health problems for consumers. Almost all foods contain either natural or man-made additives. Some are put there directly; others get there indirectly.

Those that are added directly include a wide variety of substances designed to improve saleability and reduce marketing problems. They range from chemicals used to beautify the product and retard spoilage during transportation and storage to ones used to provide consistency and improve nutritional value. (See "Functions of Food Additives" elsewhere in this chapter.)

DIRECT ADDITIVES

Most of the substances added directly for such purposes are safe in the amounts used, but their large variety and number pose increasing health risks. For one thing, some chemicals react differently when in the presence of other chemicals, causing what is known as a "synergistic" effect. Thus, a chemical that appears to be safe by itself may become a significant health hazard when used in combination with others that are in the same product or are already in the body.

An example is sodium nitrite, a red coloring agent that also inhibits the growth of botulism germ in hot dogs, bacon and other luncheon meats. Tests have shown that when sodium nitrite joins with naturally produced amines (proteins), the result can be nitrosamines, which are known to produce cancer in animals. Nitrosamines have been found in significant amounts in bacon, particularly crisp bacon.

Another problem with additives is the possibility that small amounts taken over a long period of time may be carcinogenic (cancer-causing) by themselves. Relatively little is known about such effects, since cancer takes as long as 40 years to develop and controlled tests are impractical for such a time. Tests linking a substance to excessive cancer rates in animals do not necessarily mean that the substance will cause cancer in humans. But nearly all substances known to cause cancer in people also have been found to cause cancer in animals. So scientists reason that the reverse is also true.

An example of this problem is saccharin. Numerous animal tests have provided evidence that this artificial sweetener, the only one still approved for use in the United States, is carcinogenic. The "cancer" dose in one study was equivalent to only 1.6 bottles of diet soda per day. There is no evidence that any person who used saccharin over the years has gotten cancer as a direct result. Such a result may have occurred, but it would be virtually impossible to prove because of so many other substances consumed by individuals. On the other hand, evidence does show that a small amount of carcinogen taken regularly is more harmful than a one-time exposure to a large dose.

HOW ADDITIVES ARE CLASSIFIED

In an effort to gain some control over potentially dangerous substances added to food, Congress granted authority to several government agencies to regulate the use of additives that cross state lines. Meat products generally come under the jurisdiction of the U.S. Department of Agriculture, while other food products are regulated by the U.S. Food and Drug Administration.

Before 1958, manufacturers had no legal obligation to test additives for safety before putting them into foods. Amendments passed that year by Congress require pre-market testing of new additives. The burden of proving their safety was placed for the first time on the manufacturers.

Additives in common use before 1958 were exempted from this requirement and placed on one of two lists: *GRAS* (Generally Recognized As Safe) and those given *Prior Sanction.* Items on these lists were assumed safe because they had withstood the test of time without causing apparent health problems. Sodium nitrite was on the "Prior Sanction" list, and saccharin was on the GRAS list. (See partial GRAS list on following pages.)

Additives tested after 1958 have been either not approved for use or placed on the *Approved* list. If an additive already on the market is found hazardous, it is placed on the *Banned* list. (See "Banned" list on following pages.) When serious doubts are raised about the safety of an item on the *GRAS, Prior Sanction* or *Approved* lists, it is placed on an *Interim* list. Such items can continue to be used until conclusive tests are completed and a decision is made to ban it.

QUESTIONS ABOUT 'GRAS' ITEMS

Numerous direct additives have had their safety questioned, including the following:

BROMINATED VEGETABLE OIL — an emulsifier and clouding agent used in soft drinks. Its GRAS status has been questioned by Michael Jacobson, director of the Center for Science in the Public Interest, because residues have been found in human fat.

BUTYLATED HYDROXYANISOLE (BHA) and **BUTYLATED HYDROXYTOLUENE (BHT)** — both are antioxidants used mostly in cereals, chewing gum, potato chips and oils. Jacobson says BHA has not been tested thoroughly enough and that BHT is a suspected carcinogen and causes allergic reactions. In May, 1977, the FDA proposed removal of BHT from the GRAS list while new safety tests are conducted.

MONOSODIUM GLUTAMATE (listed under glutamate on GRAS list), a common flavor enhancer, often found in soup, seafood, poultry and Chinese dishes. Large amounts of MSG fed to infant mice and monkeys destroyed nerve cells. Public pressure forced baby food manufacturers to stop using MSG. Adverse reactions include tightness of the chest, burning sensation in the back of the neck and forearms and headaches.

QUININE, a flavoring in quinine and tonic water. Although it can cure malaria, it is suspected of causing birth defects when consumed by pregnant women.

DELANEY CLAUSE

When a direct additive is found carcinogenic in animals, federal law requires that it be banned from human food. The authority for this is the so-called Delaney Clause of the 1958 amendments. It is named for the sponsoring congressman, James Delaney of New York. It says: "No additive shall be deemed... safe if it is found to induce cancer when ingested by man or animals." The clause does not cover substances that are considered "unavoidable."

Most additives banned since 1958 have drawn action under the Delaney Clause or the general safety provisions of the Food, Drug and Cosmetic Act. The most celebrated have been cyclamates and saccharin. Cyclamates were banned in 1970 when tests showed that the artificial sweeteners caused bladder tumors in rodents. The FDA proposed a ban on saccharin in 1977 when Canadian tes showed a high rate of cancer in rats. A public furor arose, fed by a massive adve tising campaign by large soft-drink manufacturers. In response, Congress vote an initial 18-month delay, since extended, in FDA procedures and required warning. The FDA ordered the following warning on all labels of foods an drinks containing saccharin, effective with products shipped in interstate con merce after February 21, 1978:

USE OF THIS PRODUCT MAY BE HAZARDOUS TO YOUR HEALTH. THIS PRODUCT CONTAINS SACCHARIN WHICH HAS BEEN DETERMINED TO CAUSE CANCER IN LABORATORY ANIMALS.

When the 18-month delay ended in May, 1979, and congress had not acted on th matter, the FDA announced that it would not take further action until Congre made a decision.

SODIUM NITRITE FOUND CARCINOGENIC

Another problem affected by the Delaney Clause is the use of sodium nitri as a direct additive in meat. The chemical is used to help keep meat free fro botulism germs and to add a red color for greater buyer acceptance. But a grov ing body of research since 1963 indicates that nitrite can combine with amines i the stomach or elsewhere to form nitrosamines, a known carcinogen. Some tes showed the presence of nitrosamines in bacon packages.

As a result, government and industry officials began struggling to find way to reduce the level of nitrite or eliminate it for a suitable substitute. I March, 1978, the U.S. Department of Agriculture (USDA) decided to reduce th maximum level of sodium nitrite in bacon from 200 parts per million (ppm) to 4 ppm plus .26 per cent of potassium sorbate.

But in May, a massive study funded by the government at the Massachuset Institute of Technology (MIT) confirmed suspicions that nitrite itself was carci ogenic, causing cancer to the lymphatic system of test rats. The FDA calculate that on the basis of the MIT data, a person who eats 1.6 ounces of cured me each day (equal to one hot dog or bologna sandwich) stands a 1- in-3700 chan of getting cancer.

But in March, 1979, before the reduced limit became final, the Justice D partment ruled that the Delaney Clause does not allow a reduced limit, only a outright ban when and if the MIT findings were confirmed. Upon receivir that ruling, both the USDA and FDA submitted legislation to Congress to r solve the matter. Under considerable pressure from the meat industry and i friends in Congress, the agencies proposed further review of a possible substitu preservative while delaying a final rule at least three years.

Congress was receptive to the idea, but some consumer groups were e raged. The Community Nutrition Institute, a public interest group in Washin ton, published a booklet, *Nitrite: Why the Debate?*, contending that there a several suitable substitutes for sodium nitrite in bacon and that use of the would not cause any real economic damage to the industry.

Both the saccharin and nitrite issues added further sentiment in Congress eliminate or greatly limit the Delaney Clause.

FOOD COLORS

Food colors fall under the Color Additive Amendments added to the Food, Drug and Cosmetic Act in 1960. Before then, only informal approval was needed before any color could be used. Colors made from potentially harmful chemicals now must be certified by the FDA before they can be used.

Colors informally approved before 1960 and believed safe were given *Provisional* listing. Those for which adequate data were submitted on their safety were given *Permanent* listing. Those considered unsafe were banned.

This process takes a long time, which is often made longer by the necessity of conducting more tests and by legal maneuverings of commercial interests. Red No. 2 is an example. It was on the Provisional list for 15 years before it was finally declared unsafe and banned in 1976. During that time, it was one of the most common food colors. And since food items with the color were not recalled from sale, many continued to be sold legally until used up.

Numerous other artificial colors continue to be used in human food although questions have been raised about their safety. Among them are:

Citrus Red No. 2, used to color some Florida oranges;

Red No. 3, used in candy, puddings, frosting and cookies;

Red No. 40, used in soda, pastry, sausage, pet foods and ice cream; banned in Canada;

Blue No. 1, used in beverages, candy and baked goods; banned in Britain;

Blue No. 2, used in food, beverages, candy and pet food;

Green No. 3, used in candy and beverages;

Orange B, used in hot dogs and sausage casings;

Yellow No. 5, the most extensively used coloring, found especially in gelatin, pet foods, candy; and

Yellow No. 6, used in beverages, sausage and candy.

INDIRECT ADDITIVES

As technology improves and pollution increases, another type of additive not directly added to foods has become a substantial health problem. This is the indirect additive, such as a chemical that is used in packaging material and "leeches" into the contained food. Polyvinyl chloride, a suspected carcinogen, is an example. Another example is acrylonitrile, a chemical that was used in plastic beverage bottles, margarine tubs, food wraps and other plastic containers.

Another is DES (diethylstilbestrol), a hormone used to stimulate growth in cattle. DES has been linked to human cancer. Its use as a drug in women (to prevent pregnancy and morning sickness) has been severely curtailed. But it continues to turn up in small amounts in meat and meat products, particularly liver. In 1976, the FDA proposed to ban its use, but it still is being used by cattle and poultry growers while they fight the FDA in court. (The Delaney Clause does not apply because DES is not a direct additive.)

The FDA has chosen to regulate indirect additives by setting up tolerance levels. A tolerance level, expressed in parts per million or billion, is the amount the FDA feels would be a safe limit in food. Tolerance levels are more formal and easier to enforce than earlier informal action levels.

But what is a safe amount? Many experts argue that no amount of a hazardous substance, particularly a carcinogen, can be safe because nobody knows what the effect of small amounts built up over the years would have on any particular person. What may be safe for one person may not be safe for another.

Following is a list of indirect additives (other than those discussed earlier) about which questions of safety have been raised in recent years: (For a color-coded 18x24-inch wall poster separating food additives into ones that are safe, ones to be cautious about and ones to avoid, ask for "Chemical Cuisine" from the Center for Science in the Public Interest, P.O. Box 3099, Washington, DC, 20010. Price is $1.75.)

ACRYLONITRILE — a substance that gets into beverages from plastic bottles. In 1976, the National Resource Defense Council asked the FDA to ban plastic bottles containing this chemical because tests indicated that it damaged adrenal glands of animals. In 1977, the FDA banned the use of plastic bottles containing this substance.

AFLATOXIN — A natural, highly poisonous toxin in mold found on corn and peanut products. It has been linked to liver cancer in animals. In 1975, the Health Research Group petitioned the FDA to ban aflatoxin. Instead, the FDA has proposed setting a tolerance level of 15 parts per billion in peanuts. And in 1977, it set a tolerance of 0.5 ppb for milk.

ANTIBIOTICS — used in animal feed to speed growth and prevent disease, mostly in chickens, turkeys and swine. In August, 1977, the FDA proposed to ban the routine use of penicillin in animal feeds. The agency agreed with critics that long-term ingestion of small amounts in food can cause the body to develop resistance to antibiotics. The FDA said other antibiotics less likely to produce bacterial resistance can be substituted for penicillin.

FUNGICIDES — chemicals used to prevent mold, blight, rust and other diseases in more than 60 types of vegetables, fruits and nuts, including potatoes, tomatoes, spinach, celery, cucumbers, apples and cantaloupes. In 1977, the Environmental Protection Agency began a public review of the hazards of fungicide ingredients called ethylenebisdith-iocarbamates (ETU), including AmobamR, maneb, nabam, metiram and zineb. The agency said tests on rodents indicate that ETU may cause cancer and birth defects.

LEAD — a metal that sometimes leeches from the can in evaporated milk. In 1975, the Health Research Group proposed that lead in evaporated milk be eliminated. The FDA proposed a tolerance level of 0.3 parts per million (ppm) and has been considering a ban.

MERCURY — a metal long known for its harmful effect on the central nervous system. It is found especially in fish and shellfish, which get it from industrial pollutants. The FDA has proposed a tolerance level of 0.5 ppm.

PESTICIDES — Numerous pesticides have been found in small amounts in food. Among the most common are DDT and Mirex. The latter was found in Lake Ontario alewife, a type of herring, along with 19 chlorinated organic chemicals, all of which accumulate in body fat and are known to be carcinogenic.

POLYCHLORINATED BYPHENYLS (PCBs) — common industrial chemicals often found in fish, dairy products and eggs. In 1975, the Environmental Resources Defense Fund asked the FDA to ban PCBs, which had received Prior Sanction by the agency with a different tolerance for each type of food. In 1977, the FDA proposed to lower tolerance levels to 3 ppm for poultry, .3 ppm for eggs and 2 ppm for fish and shellfish.

POLYVINYL CHLORIDE (PVC) — a common ingredient of food wrapping and packaging materials. PVC is a known carcinogen. In 1975, the FDA proposed to ban its use in food containers. But the ban is not yet final.

FUNCTIONS OF FOOD ADDITIVES

ACIDS, ALKALIES, BUFFERS AND NEUTRALIZERS: The degree of acidity or alkalinity is a very important property of many processed foods. In the baking industry, for example, acids are used to produce carbon dioxide to make batter porous and give the finished product volume.

The tart taste of soft drinks other than colas is characterized by the addition of natural or synthetic acids. Buffering agents are used to control the acidity in soft drinks.

Adjustment of acidity and alkalinity is necessary in the production and use of some dairy products. Acids are used also as flavoring agents in confections; alkalies may be employed in the processing of chocolate.

BLEACHING AND MATURING AGENTS, BREAD IMPROVERS: Wheat flour in its natural freshly-milled state has a pale yellowish tint. However, during storage, flour slowly becomes white and undergoes an aging process that improves its baking qualities. About 50 years ago it was discovered that certain oxidizing agents added to the flour would accelerate this process.

Some additives bleach; others have both bleaching and maturing or improving properties. Bleaching agents may also be used in other foods, such as cheeses, to improve the appearance of the finished product.

EMULSIFYING, STABILIZING AND THICKENING AGENTS: Emulsifying agents are used in baked goods, cake mixes, ice cream, frozen desserts and confectionary products. In bakery products, emulsifiers give the product a fine, even texture. The whipping properties and physical nature of frozen desserts are improved by emulsifiers. In candies, emulsifiers give the product an even texture and improve storage life. Emulsifiers also retard "bloom," the whitish deposits on chocolate candies.

The texture of ice cream and other frozen desserts is dependent on the size of the ice crystals in the product. This can be controlled by the addition of stabilizing agents. Stabilizers are used in chocolate milk to prevent the settling of cocoa particles.

Sugar-sweetened beverages normally possess a certain amount of "body." Since beverages that are sweetened with non-nutritive sweeteners do not have this property, "bodying agents" or thickeners are used.

FLAVORING MATERIALS: A wide variety of spices, natural extracts and essential oils are used in processed foods. Flavor chemists have also produced many synthetic flavors. Both are used extensively in soft drinks, baked goods, ice cream and candy. Many flavorings used in synthetic preparations are also found naturally. Most often, however, flavorings are used to replace natural ingredients, such as fruit.

Some chemicals, most commonly monosodium glutamate, are added to enhance food flavors.

PRESERVATIVES, ANTIOXIDANTS: Preservatives added to foods prevent or inhibit bacterial or microbial growth. The type of preservative used depends on the type of spoilage involved.

Baked goods are exposed to bacteria in the air and on baking equipment. If preservatives are not added, mold will grow.

Preservatives are commonly used in margarine, certain fruit juices, pickles and confections to inhibit bacterial or mold growth.

Sugar, salt and vinegar are also effective in preventing spoilage.

Fat molecules in fatty foods combine with oxygen or oxidize, producing off-flavors or off-odors. The substances used to prevent this type of spoilage are antioxidants. Certain acids enhance the properties of the antioxidants and are frequently used in combination with them. Antioxidants also prevent discoloration of frozen fruits.

MISCELLANEOUS ADDITIVES:

Clarifying agents remove small particles and minute traces of copper and iron in the production of vinegar and certain beverages.

Sequestering agents combine with metallic ions found naturally in some foods and added to other foods during processing. The sequestering agents form chemically inactive compounds with the metals and permit the metals to pass through digestion untasted.

Humectants prevent confections from drying out. Without a humectant, shredded coconut would not remain soft and pliable.

Glazes and waxes coat confections to give luster to an otherwise dull surface.
Anticaking agents are used in table and garlic salt.

Firming agents are added to processed fruit and vegetable products in order to improve their texture. Canned tomatoes, potatoes and apple slices tend to become soft and fall apart.

PARTIAL LISTING OF GRAS FOOD ADDITIVES
(GRAS: Generally Recognized As Safe)

Name	Function	Often Used In
acacia (gum arabic)	thickener	chocolate drinks, confections, ice cream, dressings, cheese
acetic acid	acid	flavoring, syrups
calcium diacetate	emulsifier	baked goods
sodium acetate	antioxidant	licorice candy
sodium diacetate	mold inhibitor	baked goods, breads
acetate	sequestrant, buffer	general
acetone peroxide	maturing & bleaching	flour
adipic acid	buffer neutralizing	confections
agar-agar	thickener, stabilizer	beverages, baked goods, ice cream
alginic acid & salts	stabilizers, water	beverages, ice cream, desserts, meat, condiments, dressings
ammonium	retainer	
potassium		
calcium		
sodium		
aluminum compounds	acid	milling, baking, cereals, baking powder
ammonium sulfate		
potassium sulfate		
sodium sulfate		
sulfate		
ammonium salts		
bicarbonate	alkali	leavening agent, thin baked goods
carbonate	alkali	leavening agent, thin baked goods
chloride	yeast food, dough conditioner	bread, rolls, buns
hydroxide	alkali	cacao, leavening agent
phosphate, dibasic	buffer	leavening agent, bakery goods
phosphate, mono-basic	buffer	leavening agent, bakery goods
sulfate	buffer	leavening agent, bakery goods
ascorbic acid	antioxidant	fruit juices, carbonated beverages, candy, milk products, cured meats, flavorings, beer, canned mushrooms
ascorbyl palmitate		
calcium ascorbate		
sodium ascorbate		

Name	Function	Often Used In
beeswax	glaze	candy glaze & polish
benzoic acid (sodium benzoate)	antimicrobial preservative	baked goods, beverages, icings, candy
butylated hydroxyanisole (BHA)	antioxidant	beverages, ice cream, candy, dry cereals, dry mixes, gelatins
butylated hydroxytholuene (BHT)	antioxidant	chewing gum base, potato flakes, dry breakfast cereal
caffeine	stimulant	beverages
calcium citrate	firming agent, buffer	jelling ingredient
calcium salts	firming agent, nutrient	potatoes, canned tomatoes
caprylic (octanoic) acid	flavoring	beverages, baked goods, candy
caranuba wax	glaze	candy
carbonate, calcium	alkali	baking powder, confections
carboxymethyl-cellulose	stabilizer	beverages, confections, baked goods, chocolate, cheese spreads
carob bean gum (locust bean)	thickener, stabilizer	chocolate milk, syrups, cheeses, confections, ice cream
carrageenan	stabilizer, emulsifier	chocolate products, syrups, cheeses, milks, salad dressings
caseinate, sodium	texturizer	ice cream, sherbets
cellulose	stabilizer, thickener, emulsifier	non-dairy topping, beverages, baked goods, beer, dietetic products
chloride calcium	firming agent, alkali	jelling ingredient, cheeses, confections
cholic acid desoxycholic acid glycocholic acid ox bile extract taurocholic acid	emulsifier	dried egg whites
dextrin	stabilizer	beer foam
dilauryl thiodi-propionate	antioxidant	general food use
diacetyl tartaric acid	emulsifier	bakery products, animal fat
erythorbate, sodium	color fixative, anti-oxidant	processed meats, ham, beverages, baked goods
erythorbic acid	antioxidant	pickling brine, beverages, baked goods
ethyl formate	yeast & mold inhibitor	raisins, nuts, chewing gum
ghatti gum	flavoring	butter, butterscotch, fruit
gluconate calcium sodium	sequestrant	salad & cooking oil
glucono-delta-lactone	acid	leavening agent, jelly
glutamic acid & salts monoammonium monopotassium monosodium	flavoring	intensifiers, salt substitutes, meats, spices
glycerin (glycerol)	humectant, solvent, coating	marshmallows, solvents for colorings, flavorings, beverages, confections
glyceryl triacetate (triacetin)	flavoring	butter, butterscotch, fruit, spice
guar gum	thickener, stabilizer	frozen fruit, icings, binder for meats, confections, cheeses
gum guaiac	antioxidant	beverages, rendered animal, vegetable fat
hydrolyzed vete-table protein (HVP)	flavor enhancer	soup, beef stew, gravy
isopropyl citrate	sequestrant, antioxidant	margarine, salad oil
karaya gum	flavoring	citrus, spice
lactic acid	acid, flavoring	brewing, brines, cheeses, breads, butter, lime, chocolate
lecithin	antioxidant, emulsifier	breakfast cereals, candy, chocolate, breads, margarine
magnesium salts carbonate	alkali, drying agent, color fixitive, bleaching, anti-caking agent	cacao products, bleaching, neutralizer, salt, flour, cheeses
chloride	color fixative, firming agent	canned peas
hydroxide	drying agent, color fixative	curd formation in cheese
oxide	alkali	neutralizer, dairy products
sulfate	water corrective	brewing industry
mannitol	dusting, anti-sticking agent, texturizer	chewing gum, candy

Name	Function	Often Used In
methyl cellulose	thickener, stabilizer	beverages, dietetic products, toppings, beer-foam
mono- and di-glycerides	emulsifier, defoaming agent	beverages, lard, toppings, ice cream, margarine, chocolate, bakery products
nitrous oxide	propellant	dairy & vegetable-fat toppings
papain	tenderizer	meat
pectinate, sodium	stabilizer, thickener	cyclamate beverages, syrups, confections, jelly
phosphate	buffer	prepared mixes, leavening ingredient, chocolate products, beverages, confections, baked goods
calcium mono-sodium		
di-calcium		
tri-		
phosphoric acid	sequestrant	animal & vegetable fat
	acid	self-rising flour & prepared mixes
potassium citrate	buffer	confections, jellies, preserves
potassium salts		
carbonate	alkali	baking powder, neutralizer, confections
chloride	yeast food	brewing industry, jelly
	salt substitute	dietetic foods
hydroxide	alkali	peeling agent, extraction of color
iodate, iodide	dietary supplement	table salt
phosphate	yeast food	beer, champagne, sparkling wines
sulfate	water corrective	brewing industry
propanoic acid	flavoring	butter, fruit
propyl gallate	flavoring	lemon, lime, fruit, spice
	antioxidant	lard, prepared cereal, candy
propylene glycol	solvent, wetting agent, humectant	confections, chocolate, ice cream, flavor & color solvent
silicates	anti-caking agent	table salt, vanilla powder, baking powder, dried egg yolk, meat dry-curing
aluminum calcium		
calcium		
magnesium		
sodium alumino		
sodium calcium alumino		
silica gel		
tric alcium		
sodium citrate	buffer	frozen dairy products, frozen fruit drinks, confections
sodium salts		
aluminum phosphate	buffer	self-rising flour, prepared mixes
	emulsifier	cheeses
bicarbonate	alkali	leavening
carbonate	alkali	neutralizer for butter, milk products
hexametaphosphate	emulsifier, sequestrant texturizers	breakfast cereals, angel food cake beverages, cheese, jelly, pudding
phosphate (mono-, di-, tri-)	emulsifier, texturizer, sequestrant	evaporated milk
pyrophosphate	emulsifier, texturizer	cold water puddings, processed cheese
thiosulfate	antioxidant	protect sliced potatoes from browning
sorbid acid & salts	fungistats	beverages, baked goods, chocolate, syrups, fruit cocktail, cheesecake, cake, jelly
calcium potassium sodium		
sorbitol	sequestrant, bodying agent	confectionary, oils
	stabilizer, sweetener	nonstandardized frozen desserts
	humectant, texturizing agent	dietetic fruits & drinks, shredded coconut, frozen desserts
stearate		
potassium	defoaming agent	powdered mixes
sodium	emulsifier	prepared mixes
magnesium, calcium	anti-caking agent	onion & garlic salts
sulfate	alkali, yeast food	breads
stannous chloride	antioxidant	canned asparagus
succinic acid	acid	brewing industry
sulfur dioxide	antioxidant	wine, corn syrup, jelly
	anti-browning agent	dried fruit, beverages, soups
potassium bisulfate	antioxidant	ale, beer, wine, maraschino cherries
potassium metabi-sulfate	anti-browning agent	general
tartaric acids & salts	acid, buffer	baking powder, dried egg whites, confec…
potassium (cream of tartar)	acid, buffer	baking powder, dried egg whites, confec…
sodium potassium	buffer	confections, jelly, cheese
thiethyl citrate	antioxidant	dried egg whites
thiodipropionic acid	antioxidant	general food use
tragacanth gum	thickener, stabilizer	jelly, icing, salad dressing

FILTH ALLOWED IN FOOD

Although government regulations generally prohibit impurities in food, they have been bent slightly to accommodate certain types of filth that food processors find impossible to avoid and which are not considered hazardous to health.

Since 1911, the government has required limits on filth, such as hair, excreta, insect parts, rot, mold and plain dirt. The data were kept secret until 1972, when the Food and Drug Administration (FDA) released the data in response to reporters' demands.

The FDA has the authority to seize and destroy food containing more than the allowed limits of filth. FDA officials point out that most food items contain far less than the limits and are usually cooked, thus destroying any harmful bacteria, before consumption.

Following are examples of filth limits for food sold in interstate commerce. Levels are averages from random samples inspected.

CHIPS & SPECIALTY ITEMS

POTATO CHIPS: Up to 6% of the chips by weight with rot.

CHOCOLATE, CHOCOLATE PRODUCTS

CHOCOLATE, CHOCOLATE LIQUOR: Up to 60 microscopic insect fragments per 100-gram sample or up to 100 fragments in one sample. Or an average of 1.5 rodent hairs in each sample or up to 4 rodent hairs in any one sample.

COCOA POWDER (press cake): An average of 75 microscopic insect fragments per 50-gram sample or up to 125 fragments in one sample. An average of 2 rodent hairs in the samples or up to 5 hairs in any one lot. Or 2% by weight consisting of nibs.[1]

COCOA BEANS: 4% of the beans with mold or insect infestation or damage.

COFFEE BEANS: 10% insect infested, damaged or molded.

EGG PRODUCTS

DRIED WHOLE EGGS, DRIED EGG YOLKS: Bacteria count of 100 million per gram.

FISH, SHELLFISH & SEAFOOD

BLUE FIN, FRESH WATER HERRING: In fish weighing 1 lb. or less: 60 cysts[2] per 100 fish. For fish over 1 lb.: 60 cysts per 100 lbs.

ROSE FISH (red fish, ocean perch): 3% of the fillets containing one copepod.[3]

FRESH, FROZEN FISH: 5% of fish or fillets with "definite odor of decomposition" over 25% of fish area. Or 20% of the fish fillets with "slight odor of decomposition" over 25% of their fish areas.

FLOUR & CORNMEAL

CORN MEAL: 25 insect fragments or one rodent hair per 25 grams. Or one whole insect or one rodent excreta fragment per 50 grams.

FRUIT

APRICOTS (canned): 2% insect infested or damaged.

BLACKBERRIES, RASPBERRIES (frozen or canned): Average of 60% showing mold or 4 larvae or 10 insects in a 500-gram sample.

CHERRIES: Brined or Maraschino: Average of 5% containing larvae. Fresh, Canned or Frozen: 7% rot or 4% insect infested.

CITRUS FRUIT JUICES (canned): Mold count averaging 10% or either 5 fly eggs or 1 fly larvae in 250 milliliters.

CURRANTS: Average of 5% containing larvae.

DATES: Whole or Pitted: 5% mold, dead insects, insect excreta, sour, dirty or worthless dates. Pitted: 2 pits or fragments per 100 dates.

DATE MATERIAL (chopped, sliced or macerated): 10 insects in any one sample; average of 5 insects per 100 grams, or 2 pits or fragments per 900 grams.

FIGS: 10% insect infested, moldy or dirty.

OLIVES: Pitted: Average of 1.3% pit fragments. Salad: Average of 1.3% of olives with pits or fragments or 9% insect infested.

OLIVES (imported): Black: Average of 10% with insect damage. Green: 7% of olives insect damaged.

PEACHES (canned): Either 5% wormy or moldy fruit.

PINEAPPLE (canned or crushed): Mold count of 30%.

PLUMS (canned): 5% of plums with rot spots larger than 12 millimeters in diameter.

PRUNES: Dried, Dehydrated or Low Moisture: Average of 5% insect infested, moldy or dirty. Pitted: 2% containing whole pits or fragments.

RAISINS: 5% of raisins showing mold; average 40 milligrams of sand, grit in 100 grams or 10 insects per 8 ounces of golden bleached raisins.

STRAWBERRIES (frozen, whole, sliced): Mold count of 55% in half of the samples.

GRAINS

POPCORN: In six 10-ounce samples either one rodent pellet or one rodent hair per sample; 2 rodent hairs or 20 gnawed grains per lb. with hairs in 50% of samples or 5% by weight of field corn in popcorn.

WHEAT: One rodent pellet per pint, or 1% by weight of insect damaged kernels.

JAMS, JELLIES, FRUIT BUTTERS & FIG PASTE

APPLE BUTTER: Mold count averaging 12%, or in 100 gm. samples either 4 rodent hairs or 5 whole insects (not counting mites aphids, thrips,[4] or scales).

CHERRY JAM: Mold count averaging 30%.

BLACK CURRANT JAM: Mold count averaging 75%.

FIG PASTE: 13 insect heads in two 100-gram samples.

NUTS

TREE NUTS: Any sample infested, rancid, moldy, gummy, shriveled or with empty shells above the following limits: Unshelled: Almonds—5%, brazils—10%, green chestnuts—15%, baked chestnuts—10%, filberts—10%, pecans—10%, pistachios—10%, walnuts—10%, lichee nuts—15%. Shelled: Almonds, brazils, cashews, dried chestnuts, filberts, pecans, pistachios, walnuts—5%.

PEANUTS: Unshelled: 10% insect infested, moldy, decomposed, blanks or shriveled nuts. Shelled: 5% insect infested, moldy, decomposed or shriveled nuts or 20 insects (or equivalent) in a 100 lb. bag.

PEANUT BUTTER: 30 insect fragments per 100 grams or one rodent hair or 25 milligrams of dirt, sand.

SPICES

ALLSPICE: Average of 5% moldy berries by weight.

BAY LEAVES (laurel): Average of 5% moldy or insect-infested pieces by weight or 1 milligram of excreta per lb. (after processing).

CASPSICUM POWDER (cayenne, chilli pepper): 50 insect fragments or 6 rodent hairs per 25 grams or mold count of 20%.

CINNAMON (whole): Average of 5% moldy or insect infested by weight or 1 milligram of excreta per lb.

CLOVES: Average of 5% stems by weight.

CONDIMENTAL SEEDS (other than fennel and sesame): 3 milligrams of excreta per lb.

CUMIN SEED: Average of 9.5% ash or 1.5% acid insoluble ash.

CURRY POWDER: In 25 gram samples, average of 100 insect fragments or 4 rodent hairs.

FENNEL SEED: 20% of samples containing excreta or insects.

GINGER (whole): Average of 3% moldy or insect infested by weight or 3 milligrams of excreta per lb.

HOPS: Average of 2500 aphids per 10 grams.

LEAFY SPICES (other than bay leaves): Average of 5% insect infested or moldy pieces by weight or 1 milligram of excreta per lb. (after processing).

MACE: Average of 3% insect infested or moldy pieces by weight or 1.5% foreign matter.

NUTMEG: 10% insect infested or pieces with mold.

PEPPER: Average of 1% insect infested or mold by weight or 1 milligram of excreta per lb.

SESAME SEEDS: 5% insect infested or decomposed by weight; up to 5 milligrams of excreta per lb. or 0.5% foreign matter by weight.

VEGETABLES

ASPARAGUS (canned or frozen): 10% of spears infested with 6 asparagus beetle eggs; either 40 thrips[4] or 5 insects in 100-gram samples.

BEETS (canned): 5% by weight of dry rot.

BROCCOLI (frozen): Averaging 60 aphids, thrips[4] or mites per 100 grams.

BRUSSEL SPROUTS (frozen): Averaging 30 aphids or thrips[4] per 100 grams.

CORN (sweet, canned): 2 larvae or skins of corn ear worm or corn borer per 24 lbs.

GREENS (canned): Average of 10% of leaves with mildew ½-in. in diameter.

MUSHROOMS (canned): In 100-gram samples, either 20 larvae or 75 mites. Or 10% decomposition.

PEAS, BLACK-EYED (cowpeas, field peas): Canned or Dried: 10% insect damaged.

PEAS, BEANS (dried): Average of 5% insect infested or damaged.

SPINACH (canned or frozen): In 100-gram samples, either 50 aphids, thrips[4] or mites or 8 leaf miners; 2 spinach worms or 10% decomposition.

TOMATOES, TOMATO PRODUCTS

TOMATOES (canned): In 500-gram samples, either 10 fly eggs, 5 fly eggs and a larva or 2 larvae. With or without tomato juice: Microscopic mold count of drained juice averaging 12%. Packed in tomato puree: Mold count averaging 25% of drained weight.

TOMATO CATSUP: Mold count averaging 30%.

TOMATO JUICE: In 100-gram samples, either 10 fly eggs, 5 fly eggs and a larva or 2 larvae. Or mold count averaging 20%.

TOMATO PASTE (Pizza and other sauces): In 100-gram samples, either 30 fly eggs, 15 eggs and a larva, or 2 larvae. Or mold count averaging 40% (30% for pizza sauce).

TOMATO PUREE: If 100-gram samples containing either 20 fly eggs, 10 eggs and a larva or 2 larvae. Or mold count averaging 40%.

TOMATO SAUCE (undiluted): Mold count averaging 40%.

TOMATO SOUP, OTHER TOMATO PRODUCTS: Mold count averaging 40%.

[1] Fragments of crushed cocoa beans.
[2] Sac containing liquid secretion, parasitic larva, etc.
[3] Parasitic worm that forms a cyst.
[4] Small insect.

Source: Food and Drug Administration

FOOD STORAGE LIMITS
To Maintain Frozen Foods at 0° in Home Freezer

Food	Months
FRESH MEATS	
Beef and lamb roasts and steaks	8 to 12
Veal and pork roasts	4 to 8
Chops, cutlets	3 to 6
Variety meats	3 to 4
Ground beef, veal or lamb and stew meats	3 to 4
Ground pork	1 to 3
Sausage	1 to 2
CURED, SMOKED AND READY-TO-SERVE MEATS	
Ham—whole, half or sliced	1 to 2
Bacon, corned beef, frankfurters and wieners	Less than 1
Ready-to-eat luncheon meats	Freezing not recommended
COOKED MEAT	
Cooked meat and meat dishes	2 to 3
FRESH POULTRY	
Chicken and turkey	12
Duck and goose	6
Giblets	3
COOKED POULTRY	
Cooked poultry dishes and cooked poultry slices or pieces covered with gravy or broth	6
Fried chicken	4
Sandwiches of poultry meat and cooked slices or pieces not covered with gravy or broth	1
FRESH FISH	6 to 9
COMMERCIALLY FROZEN FISH	
Shrimp and fillets of lean type fish	3 to 4
Clams, shucked, and cooked fish	3
Fillets of fatty type fish and crab meat	2 to 3
Oysters, shucked	1
FRUITS AND VEGETABLES, most	8 to 12
Home-frozen citrus fruits and juices	4 to 6
MILK PRODUCTS	
Cheddar type cheese—one pound or less, not more than one inch thick	6 or less
Butter and margarine	2
Frozen milk desserts, commercial	1
PREPARED FOODS	
Cookies	6
Cakes, prebaked	4 to 9
Combination main dishes and fruit pies	3 to 6
Breads, prebaked and cake batters	3
Yeast bread dough and pie shells	1 to 2

Source: U.S. Department of Agriculture

Health Care

In This Chapter
- **Unnecessary Surgery**
- **Surgical Fees Compared**
- **How to Choose a Doctor**
- **Patients' Rights**
- **Your Chances of Cancer**
- **Nursing Homes**
- **Dental Care**

Health care continues to go up in price faster than the average of all living costs despite the combined efforts of the federal government and the medical community. President Carter's efforts to put a mandatory limit on hospital cost increases have been successfully defeated in Congress by organized doctors and hospitals who preferred voluntary cost-cutting efforts.

The continued cost increases have spurred new efforts to enact a national health insurance program, an issue which has been bouncing around Washington for decades. In 1979, both President Carter and Senator Kennedy, a prospective rival for the Presidency, submitted comprehensive plans, largely dependent on the existing insurance and health care industries.

For many years, the government has been encouraging the training of more doctors through government grants, a program that organized medicine has generally resisted. As more doctors have become available, including a big influx from foreign countries, however, costs have gone up instead of down. One reason is that doctors and hospitals have virtually no competition and have been able to avoid any serious challenge to their fee schedules. Doctors have been able to control the principal insurance system, Blue Cross and Blue Shield, and effectively have kept the Blues from resisting cost increases. To make matters worse, the government has provided financial incentives for expansion of existing hospitals and construction of new hospitals to the point that excess beds have become a major problem. The cost of maintaining empty beds, an estimated 25 per cent of all hospital beds, is borne by the general public.

Hospitals have also insisted on acquiring all the latest medical and surgical devices even though many are left idle for large parts of the time. Most controversial has been the so-called CAT scanner, an X-ray device that costs more than $500,000. Hospitals have rushed to purchase these machines without having enough patients to keep them busy.

QUALITY OF CARE DRAWS INCREASING DEBATE

To an increasing degree, Americans are questioning the quality of medical care they get from doctors and hospitals. This suspicion is reflected in the rapid rise in malpractice suits, which in turn have forced doctors and hospitals to raise their fees to pay for skyrocketing premiums.

Stark evidence that hospitals have dropped in quality of care was a report of the Joint Commission on Accreditation of Hospitals in December, 1977. Instead of issuing the usual two-year approvals, it issued one-year accreditations to some of the most distinguished institutions in the nation, including Massachusetts General, the Medical College of Virginia Hospitals, the University of Chicago Hospital, Walter Reed Army Medical Center and the Naval Medical Center in Bethesda, Maryland. The Commission said 60 per cent of 2,730 hospitals surveyed were substandard in safety and medical operations.

Private medical labs also came in for severe criticism as a result of an investigation by the Food and Drug Administration (FDA). In September, 1977, the agency said it had found evidence indicating that many tests on drugs had been faked and distorted by such labs. As a result, it said, some products approved as "safe" may not be. Evidence of possible fraud at three of these firms was turned over to the Justice Department. In August, 1977, the Environmental Protection Agency said it had found evidence of "deficiencies" at one lab that had tested 3,400 pesticides. It said it had serious questions about four other firms that had done 4,000 animal tests for pesticide manufacturers.

BASIC CONFLICTS IN MEDICAL CARE

Many problems involving health care stem from basic conflicts of interest within the medical profession. Doctors who charge fees for their services, as opposed to working for a fixed salary as is done in prepaid group programs, stand to gain financially if they decide that an operation or further visits are indicated. Although most doctors can be counted on to make decisions not influenced by monetary factors, many others tend to resolve marginal cases on a financial, rather than professional basis.

Organized medicine, as epitomized by the American Medical Association, also has fundamental conflicts. For example, the AMA has become dependent on drug advertising to finance its weekly *Journal*. This has lead to charges that some articles critical of drugs have been suppressed for no clear professional reason. On the national political scene, the AMA and the drug industry have worked together secretly for common goals, according to an AMA insider who revealed internal AMA memos in 1975.

A more serious conflict is the pressure on individual doctors not to speak critically or testify against medical colleagues even in cases where the colleagues may be clearly in the wrong. The AMA refuses to admit that there is anything significantly wrong with doctors. It called the House report on unnecessary surgery "unscientific" and "invalid." As a result, the medical profession has failed to weed out incompetent and unscrupulous doctors, and it has failed to police standards strictly. It is estimated that as many as 15,000 doctors are unsuited to practice medicine. Government licensing boards rarely go beyond the routine paper shuffling of sending out forms and recording statistics. Almost all effort of the federal government to set standards for federal programs have been opposed by organized medicine on the grounds that a doctor should be free to proceed without pressure from government.

WAYS TO AVOID MEDICAL MISERIES

In the absence of significant steps by the profession or the government to protect people from excessive charges, incompetence and unethical practices, what can an individual do to protect himself? Here are a few tips from experts on the subject:

● Many trips to the doctor can be avoided by maintaining good health with proper exercise and nutrition. Some medical experts estimate that as much as 7 per cent of doctor visits are unnecessary. That is the figure used by Drs. Donald M. Vickery and James F. Fries in their book, *Take Care of Yourself: A Consumer's Guide to Medical Care* (Addison-Wesley Publishing Co., 1976, $5.95).

Not only is exercise good, but vigorous exercise is better, according to a study of 17,000 Harvard alumni reported in November, 1977. Researchers found that strenuous exercise, which causes perspiration, has a protection effect even for a person with high blood pressure and excess weight.

● Don't go running to a doctor with every little ache or pain. Constant advertising for pills and tonics has given Americans a tendency to be hypochondriacs, with fears that each change in the body is a sign of serious illness that must be treated with surgery or powerful chemicals. Yet the body has a remarkable ability to cure itself if given enough time and the right conditions. Preventive measures can be more effective than cures.

● Once you decide to see a doctor, try to choose a competent and honest one with reasonable fees. Your first choice should be a general practitioner or internist. Ask friends, neighbors, even other doctors and dentists for names. If you are told you need an operation, ask the general practitioner or internist to recommend several names of surgeons. Then check to see which may have the best record and reputation. Also make certain that the one you choose is board certified and a member of the American College of Surgeons, two signs of competence.

● If the surgeon you choose recommends an operation, go to another for a second opinion. In several states, Blue Cross now pays for a second opinion. Even a third opinion may be worth the trouble and cost it saves you from a needless operation.

● Avoid X-rays wherever possible. There are obvious cases where X-rays are necessary to determine the extent of internal damage or diseases. But there are many other times when such measures are unnecessary. When you are X-rayed, be sure that you are provided with a lead apron to protect parts of the body not being surveyed. Radiation accumulates in the body and can cause cancer many years later.

● Ask to be told about all alternatives open to you, especially if surgery is advised. Don't accept the decision of a doctor without understanding what it means to you in every respect. Ask for as much information as you need for your own satisfaction. And don't sign any statement relinquishing your right to file a suit if something goes radically wrong.

CONFIDENTIAL PERSONAL RECORDS AVAILABLE

Personal data on approximately 11 million Americans are kept on a computer file run by the Medical Information Bureau for the use of more than 700 life insurance companies. The information includes medical information obtained from insurance applications, hospital records and data on personal finances, hazardous sports activities, driving records and other matters.

There is no law requiring disclosure, but in response to rising demands for public access, the once-secret Bureau will furnish non-medical information on file to anyone upon written request. Medical data will be furnished only to a person's private physician. As of February 1, 1977, the Bureau expunged all data relating to personal habits. For information, write to the Bureau, P.O. Box 105, Essex Station, MA, 02112, or telephone 617/426-3660.

UNNECESSARY SURGERY
Big Cuts for Doctors

One of the biggest problems is unnecessary surgery — operations that could be avoided but which are done simply because they are profitable for the surgeon. Unnecessary surgery also includes cases where the need for minor cutting is turned into a major performance because it brings a larger fee. Such cases are far more common than many people suspect. For many years, estimates put the number of such operations in the U.S. at about 2 million per year. But a study in 1973 by Dr. Eugene G. McCarthy, professor of public health at Cornell University, indicated that 17.6 per cent of all surgical operations were unnecessary. If that figure is applied to the 18.4 million operations done in this country each year, the number of unnecessary ones per year is closer to 3.2 million. At a cost of $1,500 per operation, the national cost is $4.8 billion.

More important is the number of deaths and permanent disabilities caused by useless cutting. Based on a mortality rate of one-half of one per cent for elective surgery, some 16,000 people may die each year because of incompetence or greed of surgeons. But the toll may be even higher. Dr. John Bunker, a Stanford University professor, reported in 1970 that the U.S. had twice as many surgeons and twice as many operations per person as the United Kingdom. Three other studies have indicated that in insurance groups where one surgeon's decision to operate is subjected to review by another, the number of operations performed is only half that of other population groups. On that basis, more than 9 million operations per year in this country may be needless.

MOST COMMON OPERATIONS IN QUESTION

The most common unnecessary operations are hysterectomies, appendectomies, cholecystectomies (removal of gall bladder), tonsillectomies, prostatectomies and inguinal herniorrhaphy (hernia). In testimony before a subcommittee of the House Interstate and Foreign Commerce Committee in 1975, Dr. Sidney Wolfe cited studies showing that while the number of operations involving appendices, varicose veins, hemorrhoids and tonsils dropped from 1965 to 1973, the number of other questionable operations increased substantially. Numbers increased 74 per cent for disc operations, 25 per cent for hysterectomies, 20 per cent for prostate problems and 22 per cent for all operations.

Wolfe, director of Public Citizen's Health Research Group, compared the frequency of questionable operations for the whole country and for federal employees under a prepaid Health Maintenance Organization, which specializes in preventive care and requires surgical decisions to be reviewed before being implemented. He found frequencies considerably lower for the HMO group, as the following table shows:

CHANCES OF HAVING A GIVEN OPERATION BY AGE 70

Operation	U.S. Average[1]	Group (HMO)[2]
Hysterectomy (female)	45.3%	16.8%
Primary appendectomy	11.5%	7.0%
Tonsillectomy	30.1%	10.5%
Pronstatectomy (male)	17.5%	7.7%
Hernia (male)	32.6%	21.0%

A study of nine geographic areas by the Federal Trade Commission issued in July, 1977, found that HMOs tend to lower hospital costs in the area, not just for members of HMOs. The agency also found that the presence of a HMO also tends to increase the package of medical benefits of Blue Cross plans in the vicinity. By December, 1977, there were 184 HMOs around the country with 6.5 million members. Although originally opposed by doctors groups, HMOs were gaining increasing support from such quarters.

SURGERY RATE 2,000% HIGHER IN SOME STATES

Many doctors have gotten rich on Medicaid. In an effort to determine whether the rate of surgery has been higher for Medicaid patients than for others, the House Commerce Committee conducted a survey of state commissioners of the Medicaid program in 1975. Results from 26 states showed that the rate of operations on Medicaid patients for a 12-month period was more than double that for the general population, 18,716 compared to 7,940 per 100,000 persons.

Results also showed huge variations in the surgery rate from state to state. For example, the rate of surgery cases per 100,000 people in North Carolina was reported as 44,887, while the rate for Missouri was only 2,819. The rate for tonsillectomies varied from a low of 78 per 100,000 population in Mississippi to 1,709 in Nevada, more than 2,000 per cent higher.

Citing "intolerably high levels" of unneeded surgery, the federal government announced "major" action in November, 1977, to reduce the toll of injury and death. It said it would begin paying for second medical opinions for Medicare patients before surgery is performed. HEW Undersecretary Hale Champion told a House subcommittee that his department was removing legal barriers to allow second opinions to people who want them. If two doctors do not agree, he said, the government would pay for a third opinion if desired.

WIDE DISPARITY AMONG SURGEONS' FEES

Some surgeons charge four times what others charge for the same operations, and the difference has no relation to quality of work, according to a 1979 study by the Health Research Group, a Ralph Nader organization.

It was the first public comparison of surgical fees anywhere, and it even mentioned surgeons' names. The data were collected from the Blue Shield plan for Washington, D.C. Like other Medicare carriers, it is required to calculate and make public each year "customary" charges—median charges—for each physician serving Medicare patients. The figures are for 1976 and may be low compared to what they are now, but the rankings "are unlikely to have changed significantly since" then, said HRG.

Examples of surgeons' fees for common procedures include:
- One surgeon charged $2,110 for hysterectomies; another charged $550;
- One surgeon charged $500 for 26 abortions, while the Women's Medical Center did 24 for an average of $125;
- Charges for gall bladder removals ranged from $950 to $340; and
- Charges for tonsillectomies varied from $325 to $113.

Considerable savings could be obtained by shopping around, but this is not often done because the patient rarely is the one paying the bills. In the D.C. area itself, HRG estimated that $40 million could be saved if the lowest fees were charged by all surgeons. Nationally, the savings could be $3 to $6 billion.

The ranges of costs in D.C. were called similar to those elsewhere in the U.S. For gall bladder removal, for example, the national range in 1976 was from $1,030 to $450; for appendectomies, the range was $560-$305 for the U.S. and $450-$250 for D.C.; for hemorrhoidectomies, $509-$229 for U.S., $560-$225 for D.C.; hernia repair, $699-$276 for U.S., $715-$275 for D.C.; prostatectomies, $1,287-$533 for U.S., $1,070-$550 for D.C.; and lens extraction (cataracts), $1,211-$506 for U.S., $900-$450 for D.C.

The study attacked the common arguments for higher fees. "Physicians," said HRG, "often claim that the doctors who charge higher fees have higher costs, treat more difficult cases or render higher quality care." But, said HRG, "there is no evidence to support any of these assertions. The cost argument does not apply to a single metropolitan area . . . Because the surgical procedures shown (in the Guide) are all relatively common, routine and narrowly defined, their difficulty should vary little if at all from patient to patient and surgeon to surgeon. Finally," said HRG, "if there is any evidence that those surgeons charging high fees are better surgeons—have lower rates of complications and mortality—then it has not been disclosed to the public."

HRG called on the federal government to encourage similar studies in other parts of the country. In a letter to HEW Secretary Joseph Califano, HRG Director Sidney Wolfe urged him to direct all Medicare carriers to produce a "consumer's directory" of fees and physicians for common procedures .

Copies of the HRG study, "Cutting Prices: A Guide to Washington Area Surgeons' Fees," can be obtained for $3.50 from Health Research Group, Dept. 241, 2000 P St. NW, Suite 708, Washington, DC, 20036.

HOW TO CHOOSE A DOCTOR

Finding a doctor who will tend your health needs as well as maintain your trust is a task which cannot be accomplished through a referral service. Following are experts' suggestions for selecting a physician suited for your individual needs. Begin by looking for a doctor who:

● Is a general practitioner or internist; he or she can refer you to specialists if necessary;

● Is part of a group practice; prices may be cheaper due to shared facilities and equipment and the physician can call on partners for advice;

● Has teaching responsibilities at a hospital; he or she will have the respect of their colleagues and be aware of new developments;

● Is board certified in his/her specialty; this indicates several years of training after medical school and successfully passing a national exam;

● Shares "on-call" duties with at least one other doctor; otherwise, you might not be able to get emergency attention on nights and weekends; and

● Can admit patients at both a community and university (if available) hospital, according to patient needs.

You should also compare such things as charges for routine check ups and follow-up visits, and the usual wait for an appointment for a full physical or other non-emergency problem. And ask if the doctor gives advice over the phone to regular patients.

Other questions cannot be answered by the doctor. Check with other patients to determine:

● If the doctor takes time to explain symptoms and treatment;

- If it is easy to talk to the doctor about medical concerns; and
- If the doctor understands symptoms when they are described to him by patients.

LEGAL RIGHTS OF PATIENTS

Following are excerpts from a "Model Patient's Bill of Rights" issued by the American Civil Liberties Union and published in a paperback, *The Rights of Hospital Patients,* by George J. Annas (Avon Books, $1.50).

Patients have often been treated as though they have no rights. But they have many, including the right to know what research is done, what alternatives are available, the identity of all professions providing service and the right to have visitors and communication with people outside the health facility.

Patients also have established legal rights, according to the ACLU, including the right:

- To informed participation in all decisions involving his health care;
- To privacy respecting the source of payment for treatment and care;
- To prompt attention, especially in emergency situations;
- To a clear, concise explanation of all proposed procedures in understandable terms, including the risk of death or serious side effects and not be subjected to any procedure without his voluntary, competent and understanding consent;
- To a clear, complete and accurate evaluation of his condition and prognosis before being asked to agree to any test or procedure;
- To all information contained in his medical record while in the health-care facility and to examine the record upon request;
- To refuse any particular drug, test, procedure or treatment;
- To leave the health care facility at will regardless of physical condition or financial status although he may be requested to sign a release stating he is leaving against the medical judgment of his doctor.

GETTING YOUR MEDICAL RECORD

"Seeing your medical records will make you a more informed patient, help you establish a more open physician-patient relationship, provide you with continuity of care when you change doctors and help you protect your privacy by allowing you to see and correct the information that will be passed on to others," according to Public Citizen's Health Research Group. Patients in federal facilities and in 14 states* have the legal right to obtain this information. Almost all states which do not grant this right also do not deny it.

The Health Research Group has published a book, *Getting Yours: A Consumer's Guide to Obtaining Your Medical Record,* explaining how to take advantage of this right. It includes a state-by-state description of medical record access laws and a step-by-step guide to getting and using patient records. To get a copy send $2.00 and a large, self-addressed envelope to Health Research Group, Department MR, 2000 P Street, NW, Suite 708, Washington, DC, 20036.

*Colorado, Connecticut, Florida, Hawaii, Illinois, Indiana, Massachusetts, Minnesota, Nevada, New York, Oklahoma, Oregon, Virginia and Wisconsin.

REDUCING YOUR CHANCES OF CANCER

In a highly industrialized society, it is impossible to avoid some exposure to cancer-causing substances, because they permeate much of the air, water, food and other products we consume. But since the incidence of cancer usually depends on the intensity of exposure and the time involved, it is possible to reduce the hazard to some extent. The following are ways in which people can reduce their chances of becoming exposed to carcinogens:

● Avoid living so near a plastics or chemical plant that you breathe its polluted air or drink water processed from its wastes.

● Avoid occupations where you come in constant contact with materials either known to be carcinogenic or suspected as such. If you are not sure, check with the National Cancer Institute.

● Avoid habitual use of processed foods containing known cancer agents. Examples are: Maraschino cherries, which contain Red Dye No. 4, a known carcinogen, and crisp bacon, which may contain nitrosamines from sodium nitrite, a red coloring agent.

● Avoid eating carcinogenic pesticides and insecticides by thoroughly washing, rather than merely rinsing, fresh fruits and vegetables before eating especially in crevices and stem areas.

● Women should avoid taking DES as a "morning after" pill to avoid conception or to cure "morning sickness" in pregnancy.

● Avoid smoking cigarettes, particularly in large quantities. If you cannot stop smoking, switch to a brand low in tar. Do not smoke down to the smallest butt size since the tobacco as well as the filter help screen out harmful tars. If you must smoke, reduce your pollution with maximum ventilation.

● Avoid excessive or unnecessary radiation from natural sources such as the sun. Skin cancer rates for white skinned people are much higher in the southern states, where sun rays are stronger, than in the North.

● Don't allow doctors or dentists to X-ray your body unless there is a clear need to know and a strong suspicion of a serious ailment. Full-mouth X-rays by dentists are not necessary on a regular basis for persons whose physical condition is obviously good.

● If X-ray is indicated, be sure that the equipment has a conical device to narrow the beam of radiation and insist on a lead apron to protect vital body organs from radiation leakage.

● Avoid sitting too close to a color television set and try to keep children at least six feet away from the screen. If you have an old set, ask your local public health department to measure the amount of radiation. To check on whether your set has been recalled because of radiation problems, contact the U.S. Consumer Product Safety Commission. (See list of government offices for toll free number.)

● During pregnancy, women should avoid X-rays unless there is a strong suspicion of abnormal conditions that cannot be diagnosed in any other way.

● Eat plenty of fresh fruits and vegetables, also foods high in fibre to reduce chances of cancer of the colon. Studies show that people who eat no meat have lower cancer rates than others.

FREE CANCER INFORMATION

The National Cancer Institute has established free hotline information centers throughout the country in order to get the facts to the public concerning the risks of cancer. Callers are provided with such services as translations of information provided by physicians, source material on current research or simple emotional support and reinforcement.

Following are numbers arranged alphabetically by state: California—for area codes 213, 714 and 805, call 1-800/252-9066; rest of state call 213/226-2374. Colorado—1-800/332-1850. Connecticut—1-800/922-0824. Delaware—1-800/523-3586. District of Columbia area—202/232-2833. Florida—1-800/432-5953; in Dade County, call 305/547-6920. For Spanish callers in Dade County, call 305/547-6960, others call 1-800/432-5955. Hawaii—In Oahu, call 536-0111; elsewhere ask operator for Enterprise 6702. Kentucky—800/432-9321. Illinois—800/972-0586; in Chicago, call 312/346-9813. Maine—1-800/225-7034. Maryland—800/492-1444. Massachusetts—1-800/952-7420. Minnesota—1-800/582-5262. Montana—1-800/525-0231. New Jersey—800/523-3586. New Mexico—1-800/525-0231. New York—1-800/462-7255; in New York City, call 212/794-7982. North Carolina—1-800/672-0943; in Durham County, call 919/684-2230. Ohio—800/282-6522. Pennsylvania—1-800/822-3963. Texas—1-800/392-2040; In Houston, call 713/792-3245. Vermont—1-800/225-7034. Washington—1-800/552-7212. Wisconsin—800/362-8038. Wyoming—1-800/525-0231. Alaska, Puerto Rico and Virgin Islands—800/638-6070.

NURSING HOMES
Where The Elderly Are Taken

Nursing homes for the elderly are an outgrowth — some would say an open sore — of modern American society. At best, such institutions can substitute for some services, care and companionship of a family home. At worst, they can be uncaring facilities that gobble up Social Security checks and spit out little but contempt and abuse in return. News accounts in recent years have reported lurid examples of greed, inadequate facilities and inferior service, often for relatively high fees.

Before passage of the Social Security Act in 1935, there were few nursing homes in this country. Up to that time, elderly people were almost always cared for by close relatives. It was traditional for the elderly to live with family until they died. This pattern is still largely true, but a whole new industry has emerged, fueled by federal funds.

By 1979, there were approximately 25,000 nursing homes in the U.S. with more than 1.2 million patients, mostly in their seventies and eighties. Of the facilities, about 5,000 are non-profit, and the rest are run for profit. Nearly half are skilled nursing facilities for people who require close personal attention. The remainder provide a wide range of services but little more than room and board in most cases. According to the AFL-CIO, approximately one out of every five establishments is owned by one of some 100 corporations. Nearly half of their total revenue comes from Medicaid (about 45 per cent) and Medicare (about 3 per cent).

A survey by the Department of Health, Education and Welfare found that more than two-thirds of the patients had less than $3,000 annual income, and another 22 per cent had no income at all. It also indicated that up to 400,000 residents had no real need for nursing care but were there for other reasons. Once they cross the threshold, the elderly often have little chance of leaving even if they want to. Most die in nursing homes, according to the HEW survey, and many suffer abuses far beyond the mere shortage of loving care.

POOR FACILITIES, MANY ABUSES

Hearings held by the Senate Special Committee on Aging in 1976 revealed many substandard facilities and a wide variety of abuses. The subcommittee estimated that at least half of all nursing homes do not meet minimum standards because of at least one or more "life-threatening conditions." Among the more serious deficiencies listed were lack of adequate fire protection, unsanitary conditions and lack of safety devices for showers, baths, stairs and beds. Many other places were reported without enough nurses on duty to handle the workload or without any nurse or medical expert on duty for long hours of the day and night.

Why are these conditions allowed to continue? One reason is the split nature of supervision. Although federal funds are the largest source of revenue, and although HEW has set some minimum standards, nursing homes are licensed by the states and theoretically are supervised by state officials. In most states, enforcement is a joke. Even if rules were enforced, there are none to prohibit conflicts of interest that arise when nursing home operators also own drug stores, food services and therapy equipment.

A study by the AFL-CIO concluded that "most of the problems in nursing homes can be traced to the profit motive." Researchers found abuses in profit-making institutions worse than elsewhere. This finding was challenged by the American Health Care Association, the largest federation of proprietary and non-profit nursing homes in the U.S. The Association said other research has shown that the profit status of a nursing home has no correlation with the quality of care given to patients.

HOW TO SELECT A GOOD NURSING HOME

Choosing a good nursing home is not an easy task, but it is not impossible. An increasing amount of information is available to help anyone faced with that decision. The first step is to inquire about local establishments from relatives or friends of patients in them. The next step is to call or visit a few institutions with the best reputations. To help compile pertinent information, take along a checklist of questions such as the ones listed in *Nursing Home Care,* a free federal pamphlet listed below.

It is now possible to consult annual inspection reports of such facilities at the 1,300 Social Security offices around the country. The reports are filled out by state inspectors working under contrct with the federal government. They check facilities with emphasis on professional services, staffing size, fire safety, food preparation facilities and cleanliness. The reports are called "Summaries of Deficiencies" and can be forwarded from regional offices to local offices upon request. The full reports are available for inspection at regional offices.

ALTERNATIVES TO NURSING HOMES

There are many alternatives to nursing homes services, including a wide variety of programs designed for elderly people. Among them are:

● **Meals-on-Wheels** providing a hot meal every day for people unable to prepare their own food and unable to leave their homes.

● **Day Care Centers** providing facilities during the day for people who want companionship, simple meals, transportation, recreation and exercise.

● **Elderly Citizen Groups** providing the means to participate in political action and, through membership, obtain low-cost travel, prescription drugs, insurance and the like. National organizations offering such services include the National Council of Senior Citizens, 1511 K St. NW, Washington, DC, 20005, and the National Retired Teachers Association/American Association of Retired Persons (NRTA/AARP), 1909 K St. NW, Washington, DC, 20036.

A new organization specializing in nursing home problems is the National Citizens' Coalition for Nursing Home Reform. It seeks to exchange information about nursing homes and improve the welfare of patients. It is located in Room 204, 1424 16th St. NW, Washington, DC, 20036.

In addition, there are numerous clinics, counseling services and other facilities available for the elderly in many communities.

TAKING THE PAIN OUT OF FINDING A DENTIST
How to Extract the Truth

How do you find a good dentist? Until a few years ago, there was little information available to consumers to let them evaluate rates and services among dentists. Recently, some help has arrived. In 1975, the Health Research Group (HRG) published *Taking the Pain Out of Finding a Good Dentist,* a guide to dentists for consumers. The booklet compares rates and services of 68 dentists in the Washington, DC, area. It also includes questions to ask of a prospective dentist and how to judge the answers.

Since publication of the HRG booklet, other groups — particularly Public Interest Research Groups — have published similar guides.

Another publication is *How to Become a Wise Dental Consumer,* a free pamphlet from the American Dental Association (ADA), Bureau of Public Information, 211 E. Chicago Ave., Chicago, IL, 60611. The pamphlet offers advice on finding a good dentist, reducing dental bills and buying dental health aids. But many dental authorities — including the Health Research Group — disagree with some of the ADA's advice. For example, the ADA suggests that you find a dentist that uses x-rays regularly in his diagnosis. But the HRG recommends limiting routine full-mouth x-rays to once every 3-5 years, and suggests you "ask the dentist to explain the necessity for any x-rays." Others believe x-rays should be taken only when there are signs of trouble needing further analysis.

Below are excerpts from the HRG booklet. The entire booklet is available for $2 from HRG, 2000 P St. NW, Washington, DC, 20036.

SELECTING A DENTIST
The specific details on the quality of a dentist's services are almost impossible to judge on your own. However, you should be aware of his overall office procedures and attitudes. During an initial appointment, you should acquire a reasonable idea of the dentist's philosophy.

At the initial appointment, the dentist should first obtain a medical history, either by interview or through a questionnaire. This information is essential to prevent any harm to you during treatment. For example, allergies to drugs and other medication or past diseases will help a dentist prescribe safe and effective medicines.

A dentist should also inquire about your dental history, with special references to problems such as swelling, bleeding of the gums, tooth aches and problems encountered in previous dental treatment. A record of past dental treatment and x-rays should be obtained from your previous dentist.

The initial examination should include the following:

● **Soft Tissue:** such areas of the mouth as the tongue, lips, cheeks, salivary glands, muscles and throat should be examined for abnormalities. Two to five per cent of all cancer occurs in these areas.

● **Hard Tissue:** The dentist should evaluate the condition of each tooth as well as the relationship of the upper and lower teeth to each other.

● **Periodontal:** The dentist should make note of bleeding gums, tooth looseness, unusual coloring, or bad breath. He should also examine the space between gums and teeth as an indication of the gums health.

● **X-Rays:** X-rays should be taken only for diagnostic purposes to detect

HOW TO RATE YOUR DENTIST

The following questions from the Health Research Group can help you rate your dentist's services. They should be answered only after at least one appointment. A good dentist will get "yes" answers to nearly all of the following questions:

Were your records released to you or another dentist when sought?

Did the dentist take a medical and dental history during the initial appointment?

Did the dentist conduct a soft tissue and gum examination for oral cancer?

Is a full set of x-rays taken no more than every 3-5 years or for the initial appointment when you could not supply x-rays?

Did the dentist cover you with a lead apron when taking x-rays (without being asked to do so)?

Did the dentist answer any questions you asked regarding x-rays taken?

Did the dentist perform endodontic therapy rather than extract your tooth that was infected?

Did the dentist give you a complete diagnosis of your oral condition with a *written* treatment plan outlining costs?

Were you given instructions on home care with emphasis on ways to eliminate your type of dental disease?

Does the dentist have a plaque control program?

Did the dentist recommend a soft toothbrush, floss, and disclosing tablets or solution?

Does the dentist have you on an automatic recall program tailored to your individual needs?

Were you sent or given an itemized statement of all services provided with the cost of each service?

Is your dentist's home phone listed so you could call during an emergency?

Does the dentist have oxygen in the office?

Did the dentist wait until you were totally numb before beginning your treatment?

Does your dentist take continuing education courses?

Is your dentist in favor of relicensing or review of the treatment?

cavities, bone loss, abcesses, cysts and tumors that may be suspected. It may be impossible to make an adequate diagnosis of some situations without x-rays. However, since radiation is potentially hazardous, your dentist should take the following precautions:

Use a lead apron for patient protection; use ultraspeed dental film to reduce exposure time; and require previous x-rays from your former dentist (these are your property when paid for and must be released upon your request).

PREVENTIVE AND CORRECTIVE MEASURES

Your dentist should suggest a treatment plan that consists of four parts: the results of your examination; preventative measures you should take; corrective measures that you need; and an outline of costs.

Your dentist should not perform any major restorative work (crowns and bridges) before your mouth is clean and healthy. You may want to obtain a written treatment plan detailing the four parts mentioned above.

You should select a dentist who has a plaque control program. The program may vary among dentists but should consist of the following at a minimum:

● An explanation of what plaque is. Plaque is a sticky film of bacteria on teeth that leads to tooth decay and periodontal disease.

● Techniques for removing plaque. This should include showing how to use dental floss (preferably unwaxed); instructing you in the proper use of a toothbrush; and checks on your progress during subsequent visits. Flossing is extremely important because most cavities occur between teeth.

● Nutrition advice. Your dentist may recommend a drastic reduction in your sugar consumption or other changes in your diet.

● Cleaning and scaling. The dentist or hygienist may clean your teeth, removing hard, bacteria-laden, calcified material and tartar from the surfaces of the teeth. This should be done twice a year.

COSTS AND FEES

When the dentist presents your treatment plan it should contain an itemization of the costs and fees. However, more than half the dentists surveyed by the Health Research Group did not routinely do this. A good dentist will provide such information upon request.

If the total cost of the ideal treatment plan is too great, you should ask whether a payment plan can be arranged and if there are optional but acceptable treatment plans.

A dentist should provide a list of fees for regular services (x-rays, cleaning, simple fillings, etc.), to the public. Fees range widely among dentists, sometimes by a factor of five.

Drugs and Devices

In This Chapter
- **Prescription Drugs**
- **Major Controversial Drugs**
- **Unproven Drugs on the Market**
- **Vaccines**
- **Non-prescription Drugs**
- **Birth Control Methods**

Many Americans have become addicted to drugs, either narcotics or medical, or both. News reports have focused mostly on the former, but the latter may do more total damage and include more people.

Americans like to think that a pill will solve all of their problems. More than 19 billion aspirin pills alone are consumed each year in this country. That is more than 80 for each man, woman and child. Yet aspirin is not the only pain killer taken in large quantities. Many others are prescribed by doctors, including some of the most dangerous drugs on the market.

Betty Ford dramatized the type of drug dependency that affects many people when she was hospitalized in 1978 for the effects of excessive drugs and alcohol, a common combination. Like many others, her case began with prescriptions for legitimate medical complaints, then led to a dependency that involved excessive use, later an effort to ease the pain by drinking. The National Institute on Drug Abuse (NIDA) has estimated that there are 1 to 2 million women who are drug abusers. Men are affected in fewer numbers.

TRANQUILIZERS WIDELY USED

Tranquilizers are the biggest problem. Often prescribed for minor tension, muscle spasms and other relatively minor complaints, they can become dangerous when used with other drugs or with alcohol. NIDA says 42 per cent of American women have taken tranquilizers, and 27 per cent of men. Millions of men and women also have sedatives prescribed, not to mention the millions who have taken non-prescription sedatives, such as sleeping pills. Many of these purchases are unnecessary; others are continued long after they are needed.

Until recent years, medical schools paid little attention to adverse effects of drugs. Much of the questioning of drug safety and effectiveness has come from public interest groups such as the Health Research Group, headed by Dr. Sidney Wolfe in Washington, DC. Doctors, often lulled into accepting what they are told by drug manufacturers, have continued to prescribe drugs long after they have been found ineffective or unsafe for the purposes intended. Other doctors have failed to keep up to the latest research.

Donald Kennedy, recent head of the Food and Drug Administration, told the University of California Medical School: "The most serious problem physicians have in making the case that their judgment about drugs should be trusted is in the manner in which they use drugs. It is a discouraging experience to try to explain to Congress how it is that physicians prescribe as they do."

MANY UNAWARE OF PRICE DIFFERENCES

Prescription drugs are expensive enough without having to take them unnecessarily. Yet many people are still unaware that they can save substantial sums because of differences in prices from brand to brand and store to store. Many others fail to urge doctors to prescribe lower-priced generic products, where they are available, rather than high-priced branded drugs.

In an effort to keep sales of branded drugs up, the big drug makers have conducted an intensive campaign to denigrate generic drugs. They have used the mass media in every possible way, mostly through the Pharmaceutical Manufacturers Association in Washington, DC. The large manufacturers also have fought efforts by the government to buy the cheaper generics for federal programs.

In response to this concerted effort, government officials have investigated and found no significant differences in quality between branded and generic drugs. Both have frequently been on recall lists for defective products. And both must meet the same FDA standards for strength, purity and effectiveness. All manufacturers also are subject to inspection by the FDA. In testimony before a Senate subcommittee, FDA Commissioner Kennedy said his agency studies have found "no evidence of widespread differences between the products of large and small firms or between brand name and generic name products."

MEDICAL DEVICES SUFFER FROM DEFECTS

Ninety per cent of the 232 recalls of medical devices between October, 1976, and November, 1977, "were caused by poor manufacturing practices and could have been prevented," according to FDA Commissioner Kennedy. Since then, the FDA has established new quality standards for these devices with authority granted by new legislation.

The new requirements, which describe the general procedures necessary to make safe and effective products, apply to all medical devices, ranging from bandages and tongue depressors to pacemakers, pregnancy test kits and heart-lung machines.

PRESCRIPTION DRUGS
The Dangers and Costs

Although medicine does not constitute a large proportion of all health care costs, the expense can be devastating for some people, particularly those with chronic ailments. Yet buyers have little control over cost. Doctors decide whether to prescribe, which drug to choose, which brand and whether a generic (unbranded) equivalent can be used. In many states, laws prevent druggists from substituting cheaper drugs when they are available. The ultimate user is not often in a position to shop around among stores for the best buy except for repeat orders. As a result, the buyer may have to pay much more than necessary.

These laws and customs have made the drug industry extremely profitable. Since 1961, it has always ranked at the top or next to the top of the annual list of industry profitability rates reported by the Federal Trade Commission. A few large companies that specialize in high-price, brand-name items consistently dominate the market, while firms that produce lower-priced drugs of the same chemical composition have to battle for the left-overs. The company with the highest price often corners the market because of its greater financial ability to woo doctors.

SOME WHOLESALE RATES 1,000% ABOVE OTHERS

The large profit margin in medical drugs has been dramatized in bids to supply government agencies. According to testimony before a Senate subcommittee, prices charged to drug stores for reserpine were sometimes 1,000 per cent above those charged to the Defense Supply Agency. Yet the government spends millions more than necessary each year on prescriptions for various assistance programs. When the Department of Health, Education and Welfare proposed in 1975 to start paying only for the lowest price drug available, the large pharmaceutical firms decided to fight the move in court.

Testimony before the subcommittee also indicated that many drugs are prescribed for no justifiable reason. One study found 22 per cent of antibiotics prescribed in hospitals to be unnecessary. In addition, some drugs found ineffective by government advisers are still being prescribed 14 years after passage of a law banning such drugs. The subcommittee heard allegations of widespread doctor ignorance about drugs, unethical gifts and favors accepted by doctors from drug companies, inadequate testing for drug safety and falsified reports to government regulators about drug reactions that have proved fatal or disabling to many people. Adverse reactions from drugs account for as much as 10 per cent of hospital cases, according to some studies.

ARE GENERIC DRUGS LOWER IN QUALITY?

The debate over drug quality heated up in 1977 as large prescription drug manufacturers intensified their campaign to denigrate lower priced generic drugs. Through massive advertising and other publicity, makers of brand-name drugs sought to convince the general public that generic drugs (which are chemically equivalent to branded products) are not reliable and therefore dangerous to use. Drug makers were peeved at a 1975 federal decision to buy only the lowest cost drugs for government programs (see list of wholesale prices of competing drug elsewhere in this chapter).

In response, Senator Gaylord Nelson, who had conducted a 10-year investigation of medical drugs, held a series of hearings in November, 1977. The only witness to back the anti-generic theory was a representative of the large brand-name manufacturers, Joseph Stetler, head of the Pharmaceutical Manufacturers Association. Officials of state and federal government agencies agreed that there was no evidence of any significant difference in quality between generic and brand-name prescription drugs.

Another major complaint of large drug makers in recent years is that important new medical discoveries have been kept from public use by cumbersome government red tape. But in March, 1978, the Health Research Group reported an internal FDA survey showing just the opposite. The FDA review of 171 drugs approved for marketing from October, 1975, through December, 1977, indicated only 11 (6.4 per cent) offered "important therapeutic gains" and 77 per cent offered "little or no therapeutic gain."

WAYS TO REDUCE THE COST OF MEDICINE

There is virtually no way for the average person to completely avoid needless and harmful medicines that are prescribed. But there are ways to reduce the financial pain:

● **Get your doctor to prescribe generically where possible.** The only drug available under their generic (chemical) name are those whose patents have ex pired. When a drug is first marketed, its manufacturer patents a brand name and sets as high a price as the market will bear. Once the patent expires, other manufacturers are free to produce the drug under the generic name. At this point, prices usually drop substantially.

Several books offer details about drug products, listing names of brand and generic products, summarizing benefits and adverse reactions and listing prices. The most recent and most comprehensive is *The Essential Guide to Prescription Drugs,* by Dr. James W. Long. It was published in 1977 by Harper & Row, 10 East 53rd St., New York, NY, 10022, and sells for $8.95.

● **Get your doctor to prescribe a reasonable quantity.** Many prescriptions are written for more of a drug than the patient will need. Although it is not always possible to determine the optimum quantity, it is possible to renew a prescription. However, if you may be on a drug for a long time, it is cheaper to buy it in large quantities. The price per capsule drops as the quantity increases.

● **Shop around for the lowest price.** Numerous surveys show a wide variety of prices for the same drug among competing pharmacies. Some stores will give prices over the phone. Others may post or advertise their prices where state laws permit. Another possibility is to buy drugs from a discount mail-order house. Prices average about 20 to 25 per cent below chain store prices. See the accompanying table comparing drug prices of mail-order firms.

SHOPPING FOR DRUGS BY MAIL
With Prices That are Easy to Swallow

Following is a comparison of mail-order prescription drug prices for the 40 biggest sellers. Both brand-name and generic equivalents are listed for packages of 100 pills. Generics are in capital letters.

All three companies also sell non-prescription items, vitamins and devices in addition to prescriptions, including many others not listed here. Some also offer more specialized services. For example, if requested, prescriptions filled by NRTA/AARP pharmacies will not use the hard-to-open "safety caps" on prescriptions.

The three mail-order drug firms compared are:

● **NRTA/AARP:** The National Retired Teachers Association/American Association of Retired Person, 1224 24th St. NW, Washington, DC, 20037. The pharmacy is for members of NRTA/AARP. Membership fee for qualifying members (retired teachers for NRTA, anyone over age 55 for AARP) is $3. Eight regional service centers offer mail-order and walk-in service in: Long Beach, CA; St. Petersburg, FL; East Hartford, CT; Kansas City, MO; Washington, DC; Indianapolis, IN; Portland, OR; and Warminster, PA. NRTA/AARP pays postage on all orders. No minimum order, but a charge of 35 cents is added for quantities less than 100 pills.

● **Getz Prescription Co.,** 916 Walnut St., Kansas City, MO, 64199; Sells directly to the public. Service charge of 25 cents for orders under $2.50. No postal charges.

● **Pharmaceutical Services,** 127 W. Markey Rd., Belton, MO, 64012. Sells directly to the public. Gives 10 per cent discount to members of the National Education Association and to people who pay one-time $40 charge for 10 years of discounts. No charges for postage and handling.

TOP 40 MAIL-ORDER DRUGS

	NRTA-AARP	GETZ	PHARM. SERVICES
Aldacetazide Tab	$12.50	$17.25	$16.20
SPIRONOLACTONE-		12.50	11.00
HYDROCHLOROTHIAZIDE (HCT)	N.A.	N.A.	N.A.
Aldactone 25 mg. Tab	13.30	16.15	14.90
SPIRONOLACTONE 25 mg.	N.A.	11.75	10.00
Aldomet 250 mg. Tab	8.50	10.60	18.40
METHYLDOPA 250 mg.	N.A.	N.A.	N.A.
Aldomet 500 mg. Tab	16.95	N.A.	N.A.
METHYLDOPA 500 mg.	N.A.	N.A.	N.A.
Aldoril-15 mg. Tab	11.00	12.80	12.90
METHYLDOPA-HCT	N.A.	N.A.	N.A.
Aldoril-25 mg. Tab	10.95	14.60	14.40
METHYLDOPA-HCT	N.A.	N.A.	N.A.
Antivert 12.5 mg. Tab	6.00	8.35	7.10
MECLIZINE 12.5 mg.	2.45	4.70	2.98
Apresoline 25 mg. Tab	6.30	8.15	7.80
HYDRALAZINE 25 mg.	2.70	4.30	2.50
Arlidin 6 mg. Tab	8.95	12.50	11.00
NYLIDRIN 6 mg.	3.35	6.50	2.70
Atromid-S Cap	7.60	10.15	9.30
CLOFIBRATE	N.A.	N.A.	N.A.
Benemid 0.5 Gm. Tab	8.35	9.80	9.40
PROBENECID 0.5 Gm.	5.95	7.25	7.50
Coumadin 5 mg. Tab	6.35	8.00	7.40
WARFARIN SODIUM 5 mg.	N.A.	N.A.	N.A.
Cyclospasmol 200 mg. Cap	8.45	11.85	10.10
CYCLANDELATE 200 mg.	4.85	7.45	4.10
Darvon Comp. 65 mg. Cap	8.50	10.95	8.40
PROPOXYPHENE COMP. 65 mg Cap	3.75	5.95	5.70
Diabinese 250 mg. Tab	13.00	19.45	17.50
CHLORPROPAMIDE 250 mg.	N.A.	12.95	9.50
Dilantin 100 mg. Cap.	3.60	6.00	4.90
PHENYTOIN 100 mg.	1.75	2.95	N.A.
Diuril 500 mg. Tab	5.95	7.40	7.10
CHLOROTHIAZIDE 500 mg.	4.70	5.75	6.40
Donnatal Tabs	2.40	3.15	3.60
Dyazide Cap	8.75	12.80	11.20
TRIAMTERPENE-HCT	N.A.	N.A.	N.A.
Equanil 400 mg. Tab	8.30	8.50	8.80
MEPROBAMATE 400 mg.	1.85	4.50	2.40
Hydrodiuril 50 mg. Tab	5.95	7.60	7.30
HYDROCHLOROTHIAZIDE (HCT) 50 mg.	2.45	4.25	2.50
Hygroton 50 mg. Tab	10.45	13.50	12.00
CHLORTHALIDONE	N.A.	N.A.	N.A.

	NRTA-AARP	GETZ	PHARM. SERVICES
nderal 10 mg. Tab	4.70	6.45	6.00
PROPRANOLOL 10 mg.	N.A.	N.A.	N.A.
nderal 40 mg. Tab	8.75	10.45	9.20
PROPRANOLOL 40 mg.	N.A.	N.A.	N.A.
ndocin 25 mg. Cap.	11.35	13.65	13.60
INDOMETHACIN 25 mg.	N.A.	N.A.	N.A.
sordil 10 mg. Oral Tab	5.65	8.15	7.20
ISOSORBIDE 10 mg. Oral	2.95	5.10	2.60
anoxin 0.25 mg. Tab	1.40	1.65	2.10
DIGOXIN 0.25 mg.	1.35	N.A.	N.A.
asix 40 mg. Tab	9.00	12.60	11.80
FUROSEMIDE 40 mg.	N.A.	9.50	N.A.
ibrium 10 mg. Cap	8.60	10.75	10.60
CHLORDIAZEPOXIDE 10 mg.	3.95	6.30	3.50
Motrin 400 mg. Tab	13.35	16.20	15.60
IBUPROFEN 400 mg.	N.A.	N.A.	N.A.
Orinase 500 mg. Tab	9.75	11.95	12.60
TOLBUTAMIDE 500 mg.	7.75	8.50	9.80
Pavabid 150 mg. Cap	9.85	13.65	10.90
PAPAVERINE 150 mg. L.A. Caps	3.95	7.25	4.60
Peritrate SA 80 mg. Tab	11.95	N.A.	14.50
PETN SA 80 mg.	N.A.	N.A.	4.90
Persantin 25 mg. Tab	11.50	14.60	12.00
DIPYRIDAMOLE 25 mg.	N.A.	11.00	9.00
Deltasone 5 mg. Tab	3.75	N.A.	N.A.
PREDNISONE 5 mg.	1.95	N.A.	N.A.
Quinora 200 mg. Tab	13.00	N.A.	N.A.
QUINIDINE SULFATE 200 mg.	7.95	N.A.	N.A.
alutensin Tab	14.85	17.40	15.60
HYDROFLUMETHIAZIDE-RESPERINE	N.A.	N.A.	N.A.
er-Ap-Es Tab	11.00	15.60	13.60
H.R.H. Tab	3.25	N.A.	4.00
low-K 600 mg. Tab	6.75	8.15	7.50
POTASSIUM CHLORIDE S.R.	N.A.	N.A.	N.A.
THYROID 1 gr. Tab (Armour)	1.25	1.50	2.20
alium 2 mg. Tab	7.28	9.50	8.80
DIAZEPAM 2 mg.	N.A.	N.A.	N.A.
alium 5 mg. Tab	9.60	13.45	12.60
DIAZEPAM 5 mg.	N.A.	N.A.	N.A.
asodilan 10 mg. Tab	11.75	15.20	12.50
ISOXSUPRINE 10 mg.	N.A.	6.95	7.60
asodilan 20 mg. Tab	16.95	24.10	18.10
ISOXSUPRINE 20 mg.	N.A.	11.50	12.90

N.A. — Not Available. Capital letters indicate generic equivalents.
All quantities are for 100 pills. Prices in effect as of May, 1979.

MAJOR CONTROVERSIAL DRUGS

In recent years, serious questions have been raised about the effectiveness and safety of a growing number of widely used medicines. Much of the questioning has come from one public interest group, the Health Research Group, established by Ralph Nader.

Other important sources of serious analysis of prescription drugs have been some Congressional committees, the New England Journal of Medicine and the Medical Letter on Drugs and Therapeutics. Despite much greater sources of funds for research and analysis, government agencies have not provided much initiative in reviewing the value of medical drugs in use. In fact, many government reviews and studies have come in response to groups such as those mentioned and to laws requiring certain drug reviews. In effect, groups like these serve as front-line troops in the battle to get government regulators to do their job. These groups also tend to counteract efforts of the drug industry to slow down or neutralize what regulatory activities are undertaken.

Among the prescription drugs that have been most seriously questioned in recent years are the following:

CHLORAMPHENICOL

This drug is a potent antibiotic, better known by its brand name, Chloromycetin. Millions of prescriptions were written for it in the 1950s and early 1960s before it was found to cause a fatal form of anemia. While use has declined 248,000 prescriptions were written for chloramphenicol in 1978. According to William Schaffner, Wayne Ray and Charles Federspiel of Vanderbilt University virtually all prescriptions were unjustified. The drug does serve a legitimate purpose in the treatment of a few serious illnesses, but has been used mostly for minor ailments.

CIMETIDINE

Cimetidine is widely used in the treatment of peptic ulcers. But laboratory tests conducted by David H. Van Thiel at the University of Pittsburgh indicated that the drug can cut the sperm count of most men in half. It can also cause sterility in about 10 per cent of its users, although Van Thiel found no evidence of permanent damage.

CLOFIBRATE (Amotrid-S)

A chloesterol-reducing drug, taken to decrease the possibility of heart attacks, clofibrate has been banned in West Germany because of evidence that it has serious and sometimes fatal side effects. One study found that reducing chloresterol levels with clofibrate did reduce the risk of nonfatal heart attacks but did not reduce the risk of fatal heart attacks. The study also raised the possibility that clofibrate increases the risk of death from liver, gall bladder and intestinal disease. A 1977 report by the National Institutes of Health found that clofibrate users had a 54 per cent greater risk of gall-bladder disease than non users. In 1977, Ralph Nader's Health Research Group estimated clofibrate sales to be $30 million.

DARVON

A mild pain killer, Darvon is one of the nation's most frequently prescribed drugs. According to Eli Lilly and Company, the major manufacturer, over 20 billion doses have been prescribed during the past 21 years. In 1978, 31.2 million of the 1.4 billion prescriptions in U.S. retail pharmacies were for Darvon or products containing propoxyphene, its generic equivalent.

Dr. Sidney Wolfe, director of the Health Research Group, called Darvon the nation's "deadliest prescription drug," during hearings held by the Senate Select Committee on Small Business in early 1979. Wolfe and others testifying at the hearings on the drug said Darvon was less effective than aspirin but caused more deaths than heroin and morphine combined. A study by the Mayo Clinic in Rochester, NY, found that Darvon was only slightly more effective than sugar pills. Aspirin was found to be most effective in reducing pain.

Darvon was implicated in 590 deaths in 1977, according to figures compiled by the Justice Department's Drug Abuse Warning Network. This was a 25 per cent increase over the number of Darvon-related deaths in 1976. According to Wolfe, a "substantial portion" of Darvon-related deaths are due to accidental overdoses rather than suicide. Because the drug is relatively weak, patients often take it in excess. In large amounts, or in combination with alcohol or other drugs, Darvon can be disabling or lethal. Eli Lilly has denied charges that the drug is dangerous, stating that it "knows of no death that has occurred" when the drug was properly used.

Most doctors are unaware of Darvon's dangers, according to Dr. Page Hudson, Chief Medical Examiner in North Carolina. Darvon is more expensive than its generic equivalents, and aspirin sells for a fraction of its cost. Former Secretary of Health, Education and Welfare Joseph Califano stated that he was aware of Darvon's dangers, but he refused to ban the drug, pending further studies.

In August, 1979, the major manufacturers agreed voluntarily to include warnings in all packages about the risk of continued use and use with alcoholic beverages.

ESTROGENS

Estrogen is a female hormone secreted by the ovaries. In various forms it has been prescribed to millions of women throughout their adult lives to treat acne, to prevent pregnancy, to prevent miscarriages and to ease the discomforts of menopause. Estrogen is also a potent carcinogen whose immediate and delayed effects have caused harm to both users and their offspring.

Middle aged women have been given estrogen to reduce symptoms of menopause. According to Dr. Sidney Wolfe of the Health Research Group, an estimated 10 million women have used these drugs. Studies have found that women who use estrogen during menopause run five to 10 times greater risk of uterine cancer than nonusers. The higher the dose and the longer the drug is used, the greater the risk. Users also run a greater risk of gall bladder disease and breast cancer.

A study done at Johns Hopkins University concluded: "(Estrogens) can be valuable in treating for a short time some of the most severe symptoms of menopause. But there is no evidence they are effective for many of the purposes for which they have been used." Estrogens have been proven to be effective in treating hot flashes. They have not been found to reduce simple nervousness and depression, to help keep skin soft, or to make women feel younger, all of which have been claimed. Menopausal estrogens are sold under a variety of names, including Premarin, Hormonin, Estratab, Evex, Menest, Femogen and Ogen.

DES (DIETHYLSTIBESTROL) is a synthetic estrogen used to prevent pregnancy or miscarriage. Its carcinogenicity has raised "serious concern" among government officials. According to former Food and Drug Administration Commissioner Donald Kennedy, DES is "grossly overused as a morning after contraceptive." While use of the drug to prevent miscarriages has dropped, an estimated 2 million women have taken the drug. Prescriptions for DES continued to be written for over 25 years after a study found no substantial evidence that it prevented miscarriages.

DES has been linked to cancer of the breast, uterine, cervix, lining of the uterus, and ovaries. It has been linked to cancer in the daughters of women who took it while pregnant, and has been traced to reproductive problems, including low sperm counts, among users' sons. The FDA now requires patient labeling for all estrogens.

ORAL HYPOGLYCEMIC DRUGS

These drugs are prescribed for diabetics to restore blood sugar to normal ranges. According to ex-Food and Drug Administration Commissioner Donald Kennedy, "even the most avid supporter of their use agrees (they) are grossly misused." A 1978 study by Ralph Nader's Health Research Group concluded that the nearly 2 million diabetics who still take these drugs should stop doing so for their own health. Dr. Sidney Wolfe, director of the Group, called the pills "dangerous and ineffective." A report by the Senate Select Committee on Small Business confirmed that these drugs have been overprescribed and that other treatments have been "neglected."

Tolbutamide, one of the oral hypoglycemics, has been linked to an increased risk of death from heart attacks and strokes in a study sponsored by the National Institutes of Health. The FDA has proposed a labeling rule recommending that oral diabetes drugs be used only where dietary restrictions or insulin have failed. In addition to tolbutamide, oral drugs for diabetes include chlorpropamide, acetohexamide and tolazamide.

PROGESTRINS

These hormones are used by women with menstrual disorders or abnormal bleeding of the uterus. When taken during early pregnancy, the drug may increase the risk of heart defects or deformed limbs among offspring. As with estrogens, labeling for patients using progestrins is now required.

SLEEPING PILLS

The most widely prescribed sleeping medication is flurazepan, or Dalmane, which is taken by an estimated 8.5 million people a year. A study by the National Academy of Science found Americans' heavy consumption of them to be on the whole medically unjustified and possibly dangerous. The study group, part of the Academy's Institute of Medicine, said the pills' effectiveness is limited to short periods of time. After breaking down, they linger in the body and can make driving or operating machinery difficult. "It is difficult to justify much of current prescribing of sleeping medication," the report said.

UNPROVEN DRUGS STILL BEING SOLD
Despite 1962 Law Banning Ineffective Drugs

Millions of drugs are being prescribed and used by the American public each year despite the fact that they are ineffective or lacking evidence of effectiveness. The states and federal government spend hundreds of millions of dollars each year for such medicines. The Health Research Group estimated that Americans spent more than $130 million in 1977 on nearly 20 million prescriptions for only 10 of these drugs.

The result is not only a huge waste of money and lower quality medical care but additional health hazards for people who unnecessarily subject their bodies to these powerful chemicals. Because of possible side effects and unknown health effects, drugs that don't work as intended are potentially unsafe as well as ineffective.

In 1962, Congress passed a law prohibiting the sale of medicines that are not effective for their intended uses. Earlier laws prohibit drugs not proven safe. The U.S. Food and Drug Administration (FDA) has been conducting a massive review of drugs on the market, with the help of the National Academy of Sciences, to determine which ones to order off the market. The FDA has banned many drugs that lack evidence of effectiveness.

But hundreds remain in use. Some are exempt from banning because safe and effective substitutes are not available while effectiveness is being determined. These exempted drugs are listed alphabetically below, with brand names of those still on the market as of June, 1979. Also listed in separate alphabetical lists are prescription drugs declared unsafe, ineffective, or less than fully effective, all still on the market as of June, 1979, pending final decisions on manufacturers' challenges of FDA designations.

UNPROVEN DRUGS EXEMPT FROM BANNING

Achromycin w/HC, Actified (also -C Expectorant), Adroyd (2.5, 5., 10 mg.), Ambenyl Expectorant, Amodrine, Amphocortrin, Anadrol, Asminyl, Bacitracin-Poly-Ned-HC, Beclysyl with Dextrose, Benadryl with Ephedrine, Beonquin ointment, Bentyl and Bentyl/Phenobarbital, Benylin Expectorant, Berocca-C (also 500), Betolake Forte, Blephamide Liquifilm, Breonex-L and -M.

Caldecort, Cantil w/Phenobarbital, Clor-Trimeton, Cloromycetin-HC, Clistin Expectorant and R-A, Co-Pyronil and co-Pyronil Pediatric, Coditrate, Cor-oticin, Cor-Tar-Quin (0.5 and 1%), Cordran-N, Coricidin/Codeine, Cortisporin (also -G), Cortomycin, Cremothalidine.

Dactil and Dactil/Pehnobarbital, Daricon PB, Deca-Durabolin, Decaspray, Di-Hydrin, Dianabol (2.5 and 5 mg.) Dimetane (also Expectorant and Expectorant DC), Dimetapp (also Extentab), Disomer, Disophrol, Duotrate 45, Durabolin (25 and 50 mg./cc).

Enarax (5 and 10), Erythocin, Florinef-S, Folbesyn, Forhistal, HC .5% (also 1, 1.5, 2.5%) with Neomycin 5 mg., Hispril, Hista-Clopane, Histadyl and Ephed (1 and 2), Histionex 50, Hycodon, Hydrocortisone/Heomyc, Hydroderm.

Ilotycin, Isopto PHN .5 and 1.5%, Isordil (also Sublingual and Tembids), Kenalog-S, Kryl Tab, MVI, Manibee (also C 500), Mannitol Hexanitrate, Maxitate, Metamine, Methyl Androstenediol, Meti-Derm and Neomycin, Metimyd (also with Meomycin), Metranil, Milpath (200 and 400), Mycolog (also 100,000 units), Myconef.

Neo-Aristocort, Neo-Aristoderm, Neo-Cort-Dome (.5 and 1%), Neo-Cortef (.5, 1, 1.5 and 2.5%), Neo-Cortell, Neo-Decadron, Neo-Delta-Cortef, Neo-Deltef, Neo-Deomeform-HC, Neo-Hydeltrasol, Neo-Hytone, Neo-Magnacort, Neo-Medrol (.25 and 1%), Neo-Nystra-Cort, Neo-Oxylone, Neo-Polycin HC, Neo-Resulin-F, Neo-Synlar, Neo-Tarcortin, Neodecadron, Neomycin Sul/HC (1 and 2.5%), Neomycin-HC (.5 and 1.%), Neosone, Neosporin (also G), Nilevar, Nitranitol, Nitretamin.

Predmycin P, Pro-Banthine with Phenobarbital, Proternol (30 mg.), Pyribenzamine Eph/Coex (also Eph^{c}Exp), Robinul-PH (also PH Fote), Soluzyme, Stendiol (25 and 50 mg/cc), Sufathalidine, Terra Cortil, Tetrasule-80, Theophorine Exp/Cod/Pap, Trasentine-Phenobarbital, Tuss-Ornade, Tussionex, Ulogesic, Ulominic, Vi Syneral (als0 10 ML/vials), Vioform-HC Mild and with Hydrocortisone, Winsteroid, and Winstrol.

DRUGS WITH UNPROVEN SAFETY

Di-ademil-K, Naturetin w/K (2.5, 5 mg.), Rautrax (also Rautrax Improved, -N, -N Modified) and Travamin/Dextrose.

DRUGS DECLARED INEFFECTIVE BY FDA

Achrostatin V, Adrenosem Salicylate, Aerosporin, Alevaire, Ananase, Arlidin, Aureomycin Triple Sulfate, Avazyme, Azo Gantanol, Azotrex, Betadine, Biozyme Ointment, Butiserpazide (25 and 50), Butizide (25 and 50), Carbrital (also Carbrital Half Strength), Cartrax (10 and 20), Chymolase, Chymoral, Combid, Comycin, Cyclospasmol.

Deaner (25 and 100 mg.), Declostatin, Deprol, Dibenzyline, Diutensen, Duo-Medihaler, Equagesic, Equanitrate, (10 and 20), Eskatrol Spansules, Ilidar, Isordil with Phenobarbital, Lidosporin, Marax, Migral, Milprem (200 and 400 mg.), Miltrate, Mysteclin F (also -125 and V).

Octin, Onycho-Phytex, Orenzyme, Orthoxine, Otobione, Otobiotic, Oxaine, Oxsoralen, Papase, Pathilon, Pathilon/Phenobarbital, Paveril Phosphate, Peritrate w/Phenobarbital, PMB (200, 400), Polycline with Triple Sulfate), Potaba (0.5 and 2 gm.), Priscoline, Pro-Banthine with Dartal, Propion Gel.

Roniacol, Solusponge (Cone and Strip), Terrastatin, Tetrastatin, Tetrex Triple Sulfate, Tral Gradument, Trocinate, Vasodilan, Wilzyme, Wyanoids HC, Zactane, Zactirin.

DRUGS POSSIBLY OR PROBABLY EFFECTIVE

AVC Improved, Mepergan, Mepergan Fortis, Parafon, Parafon Forte, Supertah H-C and Tarcortin.

DRUGS DECLARED LESS THAN FULLY EFFECTIVE

Benadryl, Coumadin (2 to 75 mg.), Cytoxan (50, 100, 200 and 500 mg.), Darbid, Gantrisin, Mellaril and Mellaril Concentrate, Merpectogel, Pathilon, Premarin, Ritalin, Solu-Medrol, Stelazine, Sultrin, Tacaryl (3.6, 4 and 8 mg.), Temaril (2, 2.5 and 5 mg.), Thio-Tepa, Thorazine (10 to 200 mg. and Thorazine Concentrate), Torecan, Trilafon and Trilafon Concentrate, Vosol and Vosol HC, Westhiazole Applicator.

Source: Food and Drug Administration.

VACCINES
Public Reactions Bug Mass Programs

Negative public reactions to the swine flu program of 1976, the biggest failure in the U.S. history of mass innoculations, continue to frustrate efforts of health officials to fight virus diseases through vaccines. Not only did the effort to get all adults vaccinated fall far short of its goal but the vaccine itself proved more dangerous than the disease it was designed to prevent.

Since then, officials of the health community have been fighting to regain public confidence in vaccines, particularly those for children. Conferences were held in 1978 and 1979 to help overcome these problems. And the Department of Health, Education and Welfare launched a program to increase participation in child vaccination programs, which suffered from the reactions to the flu fiasco.

Another result has been a paring down of flu programs. The aim now is to concentrate on the oldest and youngest people, the ones most vulnerable to flu strains, which vary from year to year. But even these more limited approaches drew criticism at one conference from Dr. Albert B. Sabin, developer of the oral polio vaccine. He said flu represented less of a hazard than generally assumed by public health officials and that flu vaccines cannot be sufficiently effective even under ideal situations. He contended that the incidence of bed-disabling influenza rises only from 58 to 62 per cent of the entire population from non-epidemic to epidemic years. Thus, he concluded, "even a 100 per cent effective vaccine .... could be expected to have a very limited impact."

Public worries about childhood vaccines are very real, not just apathy, said Sarah Newman, vice Chairman of the National Consumers League at the same conference, the Symposium on Public Concerns of Immunization, sponsored by Georgetown University in Washington in November, 1978. She said the public has become worried about serious side effects, including: convulsions in 1 of every 5,000 DPT shots (for diphtheria, pertussis or whooping cough and tetanus); the abnormal screaming syndrome resulting from 1 of 12,000 pertussis shots; temporary arthritis in 1 out of 10 rubella (German measles) shots, nerve damage in 1 of 10,000 rubella shots and brain damage in 1 of 1 million rubella shots. She declared that Americans were not saying to stop all vaccinations, only that "we haven't been leveled with. We have not been given all the information we should have had to make an informed rational decision."

Partly in response to such concerns, public health officials now provide much more information in most areas. They have also gone on the offensive to defend the record of childhood vaccines. Dr. Jean Lockhart, director of health services and government affairs of the American Academy of Pediatrics, says standard childhood vaccines "have a track record of remarkable efficacy, and side effects are either mild (sore arm) or infrequent." In referring to the 1 in a million chance of a child getting encephalitis from measles shots, she pointed out that thousands of children would get encephalitis from measles if not for the shots.

She also points out that many other countries have better infant mortality rates than the United States because they have better immunization rates. She urges parents to request information sheets if they are not given them before their children are immunized. The sheets list possible side effects and other data.

Following are vaccine recommendations of the American Academy of Pediatrics:

RECOMMENDED VACCINATION SCHEDULE

DIPHTHERIA

Procedure: 3 vaccinations at 2-month intervals.(in a combination with pertussis and tetanus vaccine).
When Given: Starting at age 8 weeks.
Boosters: At age 1½ and at entry into school; at age 14-16, a combination of tetanus and diphtheria.
Length of Protection: For life.

PERTUSSIS (Whooping Cough)

Procedure: 3 vaccinations at 2-month intervals, in combination (DTP).
When Given: Starting at age 8 weeks.
Boosters: At age 1½ and at entry into school.
Length of Protection: Into adulthood.

TETANUS (Lockjaw)

Procedure: 3 vaccinations at 2-month intervals as DTP.
When Given: Starting at age 8 weeks.
Boosters: At age 1½ and at entry into school; then at age 14-16 as tetanus and every 10 years for life; after an injury only if wound is dirty and last shot was 5 or more years ago.
Length of Protection: 10 years per vaccination.

POLIO

Procedure: Oral vaccine 2 times at 2 months and 4 months.
When Given: Starting at age 8 weeks.
Boosters: At age 1½ and at entry into school.
Length of Protection: Possibly for life.

MEASLES

Procedure: One vaccination (can be a combination shot with mumps and rubella vaccine).
When Given: 15 months.
Boosters: None.
Length of Protection: Probably for life.

MUMPS

Procedure: One vaccination.
When Given: Between ages 15 months and 12 years, but before puberty.
Boosters: None.
Length of Protection: Probably for life.

RUBELLA (German Measles)

Procedure: One vaccination.
When Given: Between ages 15 months and 12 years, but never to women who may be pregnant or plan to be within 2 months.
Boosters: None; most adults are immune, but a woman of childbearing age should be tested for immunity.
Length of Protection: Probably for life.

NON-PRESCRIPTION DRUGS
Less Cost But No Less Risk

The high cost of doctors and prescription drugs poses a tough question for people with what seem to be minor ailments: Should they risk the expense of professional medical help or risk misinterpreting their problems by choosing less costly non-prescription drugs, often referred to also as over-the-counter (OTC) products?

There is a common misconception that all dangerous drugs require a doctor's prescription. Only the most dangerous ones do; many non-prescription drugs are also dangerous. For people seeking relief at drug stores, it may be possible to get adequate information and professional advice from pharmacists. They often know more about drugs, both prescription and non-prescription, than doctors.

Most over-the-counter drugs, however, have little therapeutic value yet can cause serious side effects if taken too frequently or in too large a dose. Since the entry of federal regulators onto the scene a generation ago, most dangerous fakes have been taken off the market. But television has replaced the early hawkers of patent medicine, raising sales to the $8 billion level with ads that are often deceptive and misleading.

Federal regulators have been fighting a losing battle against the flood of ads. Questions of safety and effectiveness have also worried Congressional investigators. Through public hearings and reports, they have focused attention on numerous problems which have yet to be resolved by government regulators.

In 1962, Congress passed the Kefauver-Harris Act, which required the government to approve the effectiveness of drugs as well as their safety. Since then, the Food and Drug Administration (FDA) has been reviewing the status of OTC drugs on the market. Numerous advisory committees have been formed to check on the safety and effectiveness of various groups of products. But although many drugs have been found to have their safety and effectiveness unproven, hundreds are still being sold.

Following are details not mentioned in ads about major controversial OTC drugs and devices:

ANALGESICS

Aspirin (acetylsalicylic acid) is the closest thing to a "magic pill" there is today. It is inexpensive and effective in lowering temperature, easing pain and reducing inflammation, but doctors do not know precisely how it works. Aspirin also causes stomach bleeding to varying degrees, though the ads rarely warn users for whom this could be a serious problem. Thus, aspirin may be risky for a person with a tendency to have excess acidity, stomach distress or ulcers. Since aspirin can cause slight loss of blood in healthy individuals, taking plenty of liquid, preferably milk, with aspirin can reduce this effect.

For many years, makers of Bayer aspirin have tried to indicate that Bayer is significantly better than other aspirin products, the makers of Bufferin have tried to show that it is better than aspirin because of its buffering agents (to reduce acidity); and makers of Anacin, Execedrin and other analgesics have claimed to be superior to each other. But many tests cited by manufacturers to support these claims have been contradicted by evidence that there is no significant difference among aspirins in their ability to relieve pain or cause stomach distress. This means that such products can be purchased by price rather than brand name. An aspirin substitute, acetaminophen, has been growing in popularity because it has less tendency to cause bleeding and yet is as effective in relieving pain.

In July, 1977, an FDA advisory panel recommended new warnings on labels of aspirin and acetaminophen. The panel proposed a ban on all claims for the relief of arthritis or rheumatism for aspirin products on the ground that consumers should not treat themselves for such ailments. It also proposed warning pregnant women that these drugs can cause prolonged labor and cause bleeding if taken during the last three months of pregnancy. In addition, the panel recommended that labels warn users to stop taking the medicines if ringing in the ear occurs, or while having stomach distress or ulcer problems, or while taking taking drugs for thinning the blood, diabetes, gout or arthritis, except on a doctor's advice.

Acetaminophen labels, said the panel, should warn users not to exceed the recommended dosage because large doses can cause serious liver damage. It said that, contrary to the impression of some ads, acetominophen is no safer than aspirin.

The panel further recommended that the standard dosage for both aspirin and acetaminophen be 325 milligrams (5 grains) per tablet.

ANTACIDS

Antacids are promoted for relief of stomach distress caused by over-eating, nervousness and other conditions. They became the subject of the first advisory panel set up by the FDA in 1972. The antacid panel was ordered to review the numerous products on the market to determine whether they were effective and safe.

In 1973, the panel reported that all products should be relabeled and some (those containing anticholinergics) should be banned unless they were reformulated. The panel found no fault with claims for relief from "heartburn," "sour stomach," and "acid indigestion." But it proposed elimination of claims for relief of "nervous emotional disturbances," "nervous tension headaches," "cold symptoms," "overconsumption of alcoholic beverages" and "food intolerance."

The panel also was critical of antacids with other major ingredients. For example, it said that although the simethicone in Digel definitely broke up large gas bubbles into smaller ones, there was no proof that this helped. The panel was also critical of Alka-Seltzer because of its combination of sodium bicarbonate, an effective antacid, with aspirin, a known irritant to the stomach. The panel decided to approve the product for two years while awaiting supporting evidence of claims that it is good for "upset stomach." Meanwhile, Miles Laboratories has introduced a new product without aspirin.

ANTI-ACNE PREPARATIONS

People who are looking for something to cure acne won't find it among non-prescription products. Ads for these items do not claim much more than an anti-bacterial or cleansing action to "fight" acne or the spread of acne. Plain soap and water would provide some tough competition for these products. In fact, water is listed as an "active" ingredient in some products, and "scrubbing" is listed as the way some products work.

These facts were contained in voluminous materials filed with the Federal Trade Commission in 1976 in response to FTC requests for documentation of advertising claims. Most of the companies trying to prove anti-bacterial action merely cited tests comparing their anti-bacterial action products with regular soap or other products without anti-bacterial agents. All these tests showed that anti-bacterial products were more effective than soap in reducing germs on the skin and reducing the spread of germs which spawn acne. But keeping the skin clean does not cure acne, and none of the companies make such a claim, though some ads come close to suggesting it.

ANTISEPTICS

Five antibiotic first-aid ointments have been approved by the FDA as safe and effective in killing bacteria in minor cuts. But the FDA panel of advisors which studied the matter said it found no proof that the products speed up the healing process.

The five products are: Bacitracin, Polymixin B sulfate (when combined with another antibiotic) and three varieties of tetracycline (chlortetracycline hydrochloride, oxytetracycline hydrochloride and tetracycline hydrochloride). These antibiotics are in some 50 non-prescription products including the following:

Neosporin Ointment, Bacitracin Ointment, Neomycin Ointment, Neo-Polycin, Aschromycin Ointment, Aureomycin Ointment, Bacimycin Ointment, Bacitracin Antibiotic Ointment, Terramycin Ointment, Spectrocin Ointment, Baciguent Ointment, Myciguent Cream and Ointment and Mycitracin Ointment.

The panel recommended that labels warn not to use these products more than one week or for longstanding skin conditions.

ANTIPERSPIRANTS

Antiperspirants are considered drugs because they are intended to stop the body's perspiration process. Deodorants are not considered drugs, and therefore are not subject to safety and effectiveness requirements, because they are merely scents that do not aim to reduce perspiration itself. Many products are both deodorants and antiperspirants.

In 1973, the FDA set up a scientific panel to review claims made by antiperspirant products. The following year, the panel concluded that the main problem with such products was an ingredient called zirconium. Products containing it included Sure, Secret and Arrid. The panel said manufacturers had been unable to provide sufficient evidence that these products were safe. Zirconium, when inhaled, has been found to produce fibrous growths that can cause lung disease. The panel urged that the products be banned. Later, the FDA proposed to ban such products but took no final action on the mater. Manufacturers quietly eliminated zirconium because of the publicity.

COLD AND COUGH REMEDIES

Of the 50,000 products sold over the counter without prescription for treatment of the common cold, not one can cure, prevent or even shorten the course of a cold.

That is the conclusion of a panel of scientists called together by the FDA to evaluate the cold, cough, allergy, brochodilator and antiasthmatic drug products. In a report to the FDA in 1976, the panel said that although some products can be effective in relieving symptoms such as a runny nose, cough and sinus congestion, no product will cure any of these conditions. The panel saw "no valid evidence" that antihistamines or vitamins are effective in treating cold symptoms.

The panel also was critical of labeling. It said labeling "tends to be overly complicated, vague, unsupported by scientific evidence and in some cases misleading." It called for prohibitions against claims that one product is superior to, stronger than, or contains more active ingredients than another, or is specially formulated. It would ban such phrases as "cold medicine," "cold formula" or "for the relief of colds."

As to cough medicines, the panel felt that sore throats are often signs of serious ailments, and that to treat them with non-prescription products may be worse than nothing if it delays treatment of a serious problem or masks symptoms of a serious situation. Claims should be limited to relief of "minor throat irritations," said experts.

Time-release products also drew the panel's fire. It found a wide variation in the rate at which ingredients dissolved, due to differences in individual patient reactions and product quality. The panel said such products cannot be relied on. It recommended that no time-release claims be allowed except when thoroughly documented.

The scientists grouped 52 ingredients into three categories: generally recognized as safe and effective, not generally recognized as safe and effective and ones for which there was insufficient evidence to determine safety and effectiveness.

Among the more common ingredients in cough remedies classified as safe and effective are codeine and dextromethorphan; ingredients not recognized as safe and effective include chloroform, hydrocodone bitartrate and oil of turpentine. In the third group are camphor, cod liver oil, elm bark, eucalyptus oil, horehound, menthol and thymol. The FDA banned group two products but gave manufacturers three to five years to make new tests on group three items.

Among nasal decongestant ingredients found safe and effective are ephedrine and phenylpropanolamine maleate. Mustard oil and oil of turpentine were placed into group two. In group three, the panel put camphor, eucalyptus oil, menthol and thymol.

The panel found no safe and effective ingredients in expectorants or anticholinergics (to dry up runny eyes and noses).

One thing not considered by the panel was ordinary hot drinks as treatment for the common cold. Several medical experts who testified at 1972 Senate hearings on cold and cough "remedies" suggested that chicken soup is more effective than any non-prescription cold or cough medicine.

DIET AIDS

Many products claim to be able to reduce weight, but none can do so without the assistance of stringent reduction in food intake. The files of the FTC and U.S. Postal Service contain numerous cases of products found to have been advertised falsely because they did not include mention of the need to cut down on eating while taking the advertised item. As a result of these cases, most ads and labels now contain some reference to the need to go on a diet.

"The only way to lose weight is to eat fewer calories than your body burns." That was the conclusion of Dr. James Ramey, clinical professor of medicine at George Washington Medical School, from a 1976 study he made of non-prescription dieting aids for Americans for Democratic Action. The only thing you will lose with such products, he said, is money. Ones that act as appetite inhibitors, he said, present unacceptable medical risks in the long run; ones that are diuretics are too weak to produce more than a slight loss of fluid and may have harmful side effects. Combinations of candy and vitamins, such as Ayds, are not unsafe but are not effective either without a diet, according to Ramey.

During 1977, there were increasing news reports of deaths and illnesses in people who had taken liquid protein to lose weight. The reports prompted the FDA to issue a warning against "unsupervised and uninformed use" of these substances. Some are advertised as new ways to reduce "without drugs;" one of the best known is called the "Last Chance" diet.

The FDA received 16 reports of deaths and additional reports of severe illnesses associated with predigested liquid protein. All involved people who subsisted on the diet without other nourishment for weeks or months. The FDA said the diet "may be extremely hazardous for some people." The agency said it had asked manufacturers to add a warning label on such products saying:

"DO NOT USE FOR WEIGHT REDUCTION OR MAINTENANCE WITHOUT MEDICAL SUPERVISION. DO NOT USE WITHOUT MEDICAL ADVICE IF YOU ARE TAKING PRESCRIPTION MEDICATIONS. NOT FOR USE BY INFANTS, CHILDREN OR PREGNANT OR NURSING WOMEN."

EYEGLASSES

Nearly half of all Americans wear eyeglasses regularly; almost everyone needs them as they get older. Most eyeglasses are sold by prescription but are purchased over the counter from retailers who usually buy the completed glasses from wholesalers.

Glasses can be expensive. It is not uncommon to encounter prices ranging from $50 to $90 for a pair of glasses. Yet the wholesale price is often only one-tenth of the retail price, according to a study issued by the Federal Trade Commission in 1976. Retail prices have been found to vary considerably. Surveys in New York and New Jersey found prices ranging from $16 to $55 for essentially the same pair of glasses.

Recently, the Federal Trade Commission (FTC) adopted new rules which should make it easier to effectively shop for glasses and contact lenses. In June, 1978, the FTC removed nearly all public and private restraints on the advertising of price and the availability of eye exams and prescription lenses. The Commission also ruled that consumers who have their eyes examined must receive a copy of their prescription. In January, 1979, the FTC ordered that consumers be given a copy of their prescription even when it matches the glasses they now wear, but do not need to be given a prescription when it is recommended that corrective lenses need not be worn.

While glasses are expensive, those suffering from presbyopia, the gradual decrease in focusing power which affects most people over 40, have an inexpensive alternative. Ready-to-wear glasses, sold in many department, drug and novelty stores, cost about $10 per pair. These glasses do not correct visual defects requiring a prescription but do help those with presbyopia. The major brand, Vision Aid Magnifiers, comes in 10 focus powers, which can be translated into diopters, the standard prescription unit.

HEARING AIDS

Hearing aids have been a continuing subject of controversy. Dealers have frequently been accused of failing to fit customers properly and failing to adjust devices to customers' satisfaction. There also have been many complaints about price, which numerous surveys have found to vary widely among dealers for the same brands and styles in the same marketing area. The average retail price is about $350 for a hearing aid that costs $50 at wholesale.

The FTC has reported numerous cases of allegedly false claims. Typical have been claims that certain aids are "guaranteed" to improve a person's hearing despite the fact that many people have structural defects that cannot be corrected with such a device. In 1975, the FTC proposed a rule that would require hearing aids to be sold on a 30-day trial basis to allow the customer to return the device and get his money back during that time. Shortly after the rule was announced, three of the largest manufacturers — Zenith, Dahlberg and Audiotone — announced that they were voluntarily instituting the 30-day trial period on sales of their products.

In August, 1977, rules of the FDA restricting the selling of hearing aids went into effect. They require a prescription from a doctor before a hearing aid may be sold although people over 17 may waive this requirement as long as the seller does not encourage such a waiver. The rules also require manufacturers to provide a detailed brochure for each device telling consumers what the device will and will not do. The brochure must make clear that hearing aids can only amplify sound, not restore hearing or prevent further loss. The FDA estimates that 15 million Americans suffer from hearing impairment, but that more than 10 million have never had any medical evaluation. About 3 million use hearing aids.

Each year, the Veterans Administration publishes results of its own evaluations of hearing aids it has purchased on bids for the use of military veterans. The VA rates the devices on the basis of effectiveness, price and other factors. Absence of a certain brand from the list, however, does not necessarily mean it flunked the tests. The VA tests only those submitted by companies on bids. Non-veterans who would like the name and address of a nearby hearing clinic may obtain it from the American Speed & Hearing Assn., 9030 Old Georgetown Rd., Bethesda, MD, 20014; Tel. 301/530-3407.

Following is the latest VA list of approved hearing aids:

GOVERNMENT PURCHASED HEARING AIDS
Approved for Issue to Veterans

Manufacturer	Model	Type	Category[1]	Index[2]
ACOUSTICON SYSTEMS CORP. SHELTER ROCK LANE DANBURY, CT 06810	A-69OUP	Over Ear	Hi-Pass	
AUDIOTONE 2422 W. YOLLY PHOENIX, AZ 85009	A-31 HF	Over Ear	Hi-Pass	
	A-32 HF	Over Ear	Hi-Pass	
	A-24 DHF	Over Ear	Hi-Pass	
	A-31	Over Ear	Compression	134.5
	A28 H	Over Ear	Bone Conduction	
BELTONE ELECTRONICS CORP. 4201 WEST VICTORIA ST. CHICAGO, IL. 60646	Minuet Dir AGC	Over Ear	Compression	123.7
DAHLBERG ELECTRONICS INC. P.O. BOX 549 MINNEAPOLIS, MN 55404	VA 2551	Eye Glass	Cros	
	HG 1250	Eye Glass	Bicros	110.9
	SZ 2535	Over Ear	Hi-Pass	
	TQ 2536	Over Ear	Compression	134.1
DANAVOX INC. 1905 3RD AVE., SOUTH MINNEAPOLIS, MN	735 SH	Over Ear	Hi-Pass	
	743 UH2	Over Ear	Hi-Pass	
	735 DC	Over Ear	Compression	64.4
	745 DAGC	Over Ear	Compression	53.1
FIDELITY ELECTRONICS LTD. 5245 west diversey ave. CHICAGO, IL 60639	F-490C	Eye Glass	Cros	
	F-38	Over Ear	Hi-Pass	
	F-184	Over Ear	Hi-Pass	
	F-36	Over Ear	Compression	65.5
	227		Bone Conduction	
HC ELECTRONICS PHONIC EAR 240 CAMINO ALTO MILL VALLEY, CA 94941	801C	Over Ear	Compression	104.3
	801DC	Over Ear	Compression	92.8
	810 AGC	Over Ear	Compression	61.1
LEHR INSTRUMENT CORP. P.O. BOX 445 1666 NEW TORK AVE. HUNTINGTON STATION, NY 11746	44 HAGC	Over Ear	Hi-Pass	
	6 DRC	Over Ear	Hi-Pass	
NORTH AMERICAN PHILIPS CO. 100 EAST 42ND ST. NEW YORK, NY 10017	HP 8409	Over Ear	Hi-Pass	
	HP 8269 HFR VTC	Over Ear	Hi-Pass	
	HP 8274C LIM TI	Over Ear	Compression	134.9
	HP 84 LIM TI TC	Over Ear	Compression	101.7

GOVERNMENT PURCHASED HEARING AIDS
Approved for Issue to Veterans

Manufacturer	Model	Type	Category[1]	Index[2]
OTICON CORPORATION	S14V	Eye Glass	Cros	
999 STONE ST.	E11HC	Over Ear	Hi-Pass	
P.O. BOX 1511	E11H	Over Ear	Hi-Pass	
UNION, NJ 07083	E15C	Over Ear	Compression	100.6
QUALITONE, DIV. OF	SWA	Over Ear	Hi-Pass	
SEEBURG CORP.	TSWM	Over Ear	Hi-Pass	
4931 WEST 35TH ST.	TCM	Over Ear	Compression	108.3
MINNEAPOLIS, MN 54416	CA	Over Ear	Compression	94.8
RADIOEAR CORPORATION	1010	Eye Glass	Cros	
375 VALLEY BROOK ROAD	1067	Over Ear	Hi-Pass	
CANONSBURG, PA 15317				
SIEMENS MEDICAL OF	173 PC	Over Ear	Hi-Pass	
AMERICA INC.	66 H	Over Ear	Hi-Pass	
186 WOOD AVE.	176 H-AGC	Over Ear	Compression	100.4
SOUTH ISELIN, NJ 08830	27 PP-AGV-1	Over Ear	Compression	54.1
SONOTONE CORPORATION	50-3 Bx	Eye Glass	Bicross	126.5
SAWMILL RIVER ROAD	36-23	Over Ear	Compression	101.7
ELMSFORD, NY 10523	36-13	Over Ear	Compression	99.8
STARKEY LABS INC.	BC 1		Bone Conduction	
6700 WASHINGTON AVE.	SP-X		Bone Conduction	
EDEN PRAIRIE, MN 55343	B-12		Bone Conduction	
TELEX COMMUNICATIONS	402 Wireless	Eye Glass	Cros	
9600 ALDRICH AVE.	338 Wireless	Over Ear	Cros	
S. MINNEAPOLIS, MN 55420	338 Wireless	Over Ear	Bicros	57.5
	331 HI	Over Ear	Hi-Pass	
UNITRON INDUSTRIES INC.	695U	Over Ear	Hi-Pass	
1017 HURON AVE.	615H	Over Ear	Hi-Pass	
PORT HURON, MI 48060	905	Over Ear	Compression	97.6
	695	Over Ear	Compression	91.8
VICON INSTRUMENT CO.	E322LC-AO	Over Ear	Hi-Pass	
828 WOOTEN ROAD	E533 Standard	Over Ear	Hi-Pass	
P.O. BOX 1676	OE159	Over Ear	Compression	97.4
COLORADO SPRINGS, CO				
80901				
VIENNATONE OF AMERICA,	AOC/SS	Over Ear	Hi-Pass	
INC.	AOC/PC	Over Ear	Compression	73.0
5245 W. DIVERSEY AVE.	AN		Bone Conduction	
CHICAGO, IL 60639				
WIDEX HEARING AID CO.	F8+H	Over Ear	Hi-Pass	
INC.	A9+H	Over Ear	Hi-Pass	
36-14 ELEVENTH ST.	A9+T	Over Ear	Compression	160.1
LONG ISLAND CITY, NJ 11106	A8+T	Over Ear	Compression	153.3

GOVERNMENT PURCHASED HEARING AIDS
Approved for Issue to Veterans

Manufacturer	Model	Type	Category[1]	Index[2]
ZENITRON INC.	Cros	Eye Glass	Cros	
6501 W. GRAND AVE.	Command 100H	Over Ear	Hi-Pass	
CHICAGO, IL 60635	Command 100	Over Ear	Compression	103.9

(1) *Cros*—for people with no usable hearing in one ear and only mild high-frequency loss in the other; *Bicros*—for people with no usable hearing in one ear but significant loss in the other; *Hi-Pass*—amplification of frequencies above middle pitch range; *Compression*—for people with hearing loss throughout the range but who need loud noises suppressed; *Directional*—with special microphone to pick up sounds better from front than side; *Bone conduction*—for people with chronic ear disease who cannot wear ear molds.

(2) The index of characteristics is the average score of each model for seven tests indicating total performance in relation to other models. Numbers above 100 represent better than average performance. Index scores were not obtained for Cros and Hi-Pass categories because of a lack of relevant data.

Source: Veterans Administration, Information Bulletin 13-2, 1979.

LAXATIVES

Laxatives are a big waste, according to the scientific panel formed by the FDA to study their safety and effectiveness. In a report issued in 1975, the panel said it found only 45 of 81 laxative ingredients to be both safe and effective. It found 20 both unsafe and ineffective and 16 lacking in sufficient proof for any determination.

The panel said 98 per cent of people do not need such products, yet total sales are an estimated $300 million per year. According to the panel: "Prolonged laxative use can in some instances seriously impair normal bowel function. Use of laxatives for acute abdominal pain, vomiting and other digestive tract symptoms can lead to serious life-threatening situations." According to the panel, the best treatment for simple constipation is proper diet, adequate fluid intake and prompt response to the urge to evacuate the bowels. The panel urged people to consult a physician if they notice a sudden change in bowel habits.

Examples of ingredients cited by the panel as safe and effective were phenolphthalein (in Ex-lax and Correctol), magnesium hydroxide and saline (in Milk of Magnesia and Haley's MO), psylliummethylcellulose (in Serutan) and yellow phenolphthalein (in Feen-a-mint). Examples of ingredients considered unsafe and ineffective were calomel, jalap and podophyllum.

MOUTHWASHES

Testimony before the Select Senate Committee on Small Business was overwhelmingly critical of mouthwashes. Medical witnesses generally agreed that plain water was the best mouthwash. They contended that products that claim no antiseptic action are nothing but pleasant tasting rinses with no medical effect, while products that claim to be antiseptic are either not strong enough to be effective or are too strong. A mouthwash that is too powerful in killing bacteria, according to witnesses, may upset the balance of bacterial flora and make the mouth more vulnerable to growth of harmful bacteria. Recently, manufacturers have been removing boric acid from these products at the request of the FDA because of potential toxicity to users.

Listerine, the biggest selling mouthwash, lost a six-year battle in March, 1978, when the Supreme Court upheld an order of the Federal Trade Commission (FTC) requiring corrective advertising for claims found to be misleading. As a result, Warner Lambert Co., the manufacturer, must stop advertising the product or spend $10 million in ads saying that, despite earlier claims, Listerine "will not help prevent colds or sore throats or lessen their severity." It was the first time the Supreme Court had ruled on the issue of corrective advertising, which the FTC says is necessary when there have been years of misleading claims made to the public. Listerine had been on the market for 99 years by 1978, when its sales accounted for nearly half of the $200 million spent each year on mouthwash products. The FTC did not dispute the Listerine claim that it could kill bateria but found no evidence that it could kill viruses that cause colds.

SEDATIVES

In 1975, the Select Senate Committee on Small Business heard medical witnesses criticize the safety and effectiveness of sleeping pills and sedatives. One witness, Dr. Anthony Kales, professor of psychiatry at Pennsylvania State University, reported a study which he said showed that commonly used sleeping pills not only had no effect but tended to make pill takers awaken more often than others during the night. Taking too much of these drugs, said several witnesses, could cause hallucinations, headaches and precipitate glaucoma, an eye disease. Ninety-five per cent of the advertising for sleeping pills and sedatives on television was said to be false.

The following month, a panel of experts working for the FDA reported that many ingredients in sleeping pills were unsafe or of questionable value. The FDA was urged to ban numerous claims, including ones saying these products will help "nervous irritability," "simple nervousness due to common everyday overwork and fatigue," "calming down and relaxing," "gently soothe away the tension" and "nervous tension headache." The only claim approved by the experts was that such products may help "occasional simple nervous tension." But they said this claim should be tested.

In June, 1979, the FDA announced a voluntary recall of over-the-counter sleeping aids containing methapyrilene, an antihistamine, after tests showed that the ingredient caused liver cancer in animals. Sleeping aids which contained the drug include Sominex, Compoz, Excedrin P.M., Sleep-Eze and Nytol. Manufacturers immediately reformulated these products, replacing methapyrilene with pyrilamine, a weaker antihistamine.

VITAMINS AND MINERALS SOLD AS NON-PRESCRIPTION DRUGS

Use of vitamins and minerals as supplements to the daily diet has caused continuing controversy for both safety and economic reasons. When sold separately, rather than in foods and beverages, they become drugs that may be sold by prescription or freely over the counter.

Vitamins and minerals are essential to human survival. (See a description of them in the chapter on Food and Nutrition.) But their effects on human health are not entirely clear despite numerous studies over the years. There is considerable disagreement among scientists on what amounts of which may be necessary and what amounts might be harmful in some cases. Most medical authorities feel that a normal person can get all the vitamins and minerals needed for proper health in a normal diet.

But others claim that extra amounts of certain ones may be necessary for some people to maintain good health. Because of the mystery about some vitamins and minerals, some claims for them go far beyond reality. The result is that many people wind up spending lots of money on items of questionable value and potential harm to their health.

In an effort to protect such people, federal officials have tried for years to restrict sales of some products. First efforts were to propose what the industry called a "crepe label," saying in effect that vitamin and mineral supplements are not necessary for a normal person who eats a normal diet. But vitamin and mineral businesses and devotees created such a storm of protest that the government's Food and Drug Administration (FDA) shelved its proposals. It threw the issues into the lap of an advisory board of scientists and other experts.

That group issued a report in March, 1979, with recommendations that the FDA restrict sales of some products because of health reasons. It said vitamins and minerals, when sold over the counter as non-prescription drugs, should be labeled only for the prevention or treatment of deficiencies. Labels, the advisors said, should make clear that the products should be used only "when the need for such therapy has been determined by a physician." The panel did not address the use of these products as dietary supplements.

But it said deficiencies in vitamins and minerals occur mainly among special groups of people such as pregnant and nursing women, heavy drinkers and patients taking other drugs that might interfere with the body's absorption processes. The group named nine vitamins and three minerals that could be sold singly as non-prescription drugs to treat deficiencies. The vitamins are Vitamin C, B12, folic acid, niacin, B6, riboflavin, thiamine, A and D. The three minerals are calcium, iron and zinc.

The group also recommended stricter rules for labeling and advertising. For example, it said such terms as "stress," "super potency," or "geriatric" should not be allowed as part of a brand name. And it advised against calling any product "natural" because there is no evidence that "natural" forms of vitamins and minerals are any better than synthetic ones. The so-called "sex" vitamin (E), it said, should not be sold by itself as a non-prescription drug because it has no proven therapeutic value, and deficiency of this vitamin is virtually unknown. Some vitamins, it added, can be dangerous in large amounts. For example, said the panel, large amounts of Vitamin A taken over a long period can cause irreversible liver and bone damage, and excess amounts of Vitamin C can interfere with a common test for sugar in the urine of diabetics.

Following is a summary of the panel's recommendations:

VITAMINS ON RESTRICTED LIST

The following vitamin may be sold only on a prescription:
Vitamin K could be hazardous to individuals taking anticoagulant drugs. It should only be taken when a physician has determined the need for such therapy.

The following four vitamins shall not be sold as single-ingredient over-the counter drug products because deficiency is virtually non-existent.

Biotin is available in the diet from numerous sources and is synthesized by intestinal microorganisms which assures against a biotin deficiency.

Choline is fully manufactured in the body using a number of dietary sources as precursors.

Vitamin E, although safe, has no proven therapeutic value as a single ingredient drug. However, at a daily dose of 30 I.U. (International Units) it may be added to combination drugs designed to prevent multiple vitamin deficiencies. There is no evidence that it increases fertility or is useful against cardiovascular disease, peripheral vascular disease, or leg cramps.

Pantothenic acid may be included in doses of 5 to 20 milligrams in combination drugs used to prevent multiple vitamin deficiencies.

The following nine vitamins may be sold as non-prescription drugs and should be taken only when a physician has determined the need for such therapy.

Vitamin C (Ascorbic Acid) doses of 50 to 100 milligrams daily are sufficient to prevent deficiency. Doses of more than 1,000 milligrams a day may cause kidney and bladder problems. They also can produce false results in some diagnostic tests, such as the test for sugar in the urine of diabetics. Manufacturers should not claim that Vitamin C is useful for treating such conditions as the common cold, atherosclerosis, allergy, mental illness, corneal ulcers, thrombosis, anemia or pressure sores.

Niacin should be used in the form of niacinamide or niacinamide ascorbate, because they are less toxic than the other form, nicotinic acid. Daily doses of niacinamide should range between 10 and 20 milligrams for prevention of deficiency and 25 to 50 milligrams for treatment of deficiency.

Vitamin B$_6$ (Pyridoxine) doses of 1.5 to 2.5 milligrams daily are recommended for preventing deficiency and 7.5 to 25 milligrams for treatment. Patients taking L-dopa for Parkinsonism should not take this drug without a doctor's supervision. There is no evidence that Vitamin B$_6$ is useful for preventing kidney stones or controlling vomiting in pregnant women.

Vitamin B$_2$ (Riboflavin) Recommended daily doses are 1 to 2 milligrams for prevention of deficiency and 5 to 25 milligrams for treatment.

Vitamin B$_1$ (Thiamine) doses of 1 to 2 milligrams are sufficient to prevent deficiency and 5 to 25 milligrams are sufficient for treatment. There is no proof that thiamine helps stimulate mental response or is useful in treating such conditions as skin disease, multiple sclerosis, infections, cancer or impotence.

Vitamin A should be taken only when a physician has determined the need for such therapy. Daily preventive doses should range from 1,250 to 2,500 I.U. (International Units) and treatment doses from 5,000 to 10,000 I.U. Drugs for treatment of deficiency should warn that excessive doses may be harmful. Levels above 2 million I.U. can cause acute toxicity, characterized by severe headache, dizziness, nausea, and red and swollen skin. Long term use can cause enlarged liver and spleen, painful swelling under the skin, permanent liver damage and stunted bone growth. There is no proof that Vitamin A is of any value against plantar warts, acne and other skin diseases, dry and wrinkled skin, stress ulcers, respiratory infections, or eye disorders.

Vitamin B$_{12}$ dose to prevent deficiency is 3 to 10 micrograms daily for most people.

Folic Acid doses to prevent deficiency are 0.1 to 0.4 milligrams for most people. For pregnant and lactating women and persons who consume alcohol to excess, the daily dose is 1 milligram.

Vitamin D daily dose of 400 I.U. (International Units) is sufficient to prevent deficiency in healthy infants and growing children up to 18 years of age. For most other adults over 18 years of age, the recommended daily dose is 200 I.U. Some studies indicate that doses greater than 1,000 to 1,200 I.U. daily may contribute to kidney stones and heart attacks. There is no reliable evidence that vitamin D lowers blood cholesterol levels or prevents or cures osteoporosis in the elderly.

MINERALS ON RESTRICTED LIST

The panel said the following should not be sold as over-the-the-counter drugs because deficiency is rare: copper, fluoride, iodine, magnesium, manganese, phosphorus, potassium. High doses of copper, iodine and manganese also pose some risk of toxicity. Treatment of deficiency requires prescription status and a doctor's supervision.

The panel said the following three minerals can be sold as nonprescription drugs:

Calcium doses for five different age groups and for pregnant and lactating women were recommended only when the need has been determined by a physician. Taking more than 2,500 milligrams daily may produce excessive calcium in the blood and rapid deterioration in kidney function.

Iron deficiency is more likely to occur among menstruating, lactating, and pregnant women and children under age five. The panel recommended specific daily doses for these groups, as well as for other adults and children over five when the need has been determined by a physician. Since there is some evidence of iron deficiency among both men and women over 60 and among adolescent males, the panel said a nonprescription drug containing a daily dose of 10 to 20 milligrams of elemental iron should be made available on a provisional basis for five years.

Zinc sulfate is the only safe and effective form of elemental zinc for use in a nonprescription drug to prevent deficiency when the need for such therapy has been determined by a physician. The daily dose is 10 to 25 milligrams.

The best source of information for the layman about non-prescription drugs is the *Handbook of Nonprescription Drugs*. It is published every two years and contains details about more than 30 types of products, from antacids to foot care items. Publisher is the American Pharmaceutical Association, 2215 Constitution Ave. NW, Washington, DC, 20037.

BIRTH CONTROL METHODS COMPARED BY UNCLE SAM
For Effectiveness and Health Hazards

In January, 1978, the Food and Drug Administration (FDA) published a detailed statement that must be included, with a summary, in packages of birth control pills purchased by patients. The statement lists the relative health hazards and effectiveness of various methods.

Its main emphasis is on the hazards of oral contraceptives. It points out that the pill is 99 per cent effective in preventing pregnancies but may cause some serious ailments, including blood clots in the legs, lungs, brain, heart and other organs, as well as liver tumors, birth defects (if the pill is taken while a woman is pregnant), high blood pressure and gallbladder disease.

Women who smoke face an added risk of heart and circulatory problems that increase with age and the number of cigarettes smoked per day. In short, says the FDA, "women who use oral contraceptives should not smoke." Other women who should not use them, says the agency, are those who have had clotting disorders, cancer of the breast or sex organs, unexplained vaginal bleeding, stroke, heart attack, angina pectoris or those who suspect they are pregnant already.

Other, less serious side effects include nausea, vomiting, bleeding between menstrual periods, weight gain and breast tenderness.

COMPARING THE EFFECTIVENESS OF CONTRACEPTIVES

The FDA's detailed labeling statement includes the following estimates of relative effectiveness of birth control methods in terms of pregnancies per women:

- **Intrauterine device (IUD), less than 1 to 6;**
- **Diaphragm with spermicidal products such as creams and jellies, 2 to 20;**
- **Condom (rubber), 3 to 36;**
- **Aerosol foams, 2 to 29;**
- **Jellies and creams, 4 to 36;**
- **Rhythm method by calendar, 14 to 47;**
- **Rhythm method by temperature, 1 to 20;**
- **Rhythm method with intercourse only in post-ovulatory phase, less than 1 to 7;**
- **Rhythm method, mucus system, 1 to 25;**
- **No contraceptive, 60 to 80.**

The FDA explains that the estimates vary widely because of the wide difference in how people use each method. "Very faithful users of the various methods," says the agency, "obtain very good results, except for users of the calendar method of periodic abstinence (rhythm). Sterilization was not included as an option, but it is estimated 10 per cent of young couples have employed this method.

COMPARING THE DANGERS OF CONTRACEPTIVES

Also included in the FDA's detailed package statement for birth control pills is a comparison of health risks for various age groups of women.

It indicates that until age 40, the biggest risk of fatality is from using no method and suffering the consequences of pregnancy and birth. The FDA says the rate of fatality for ages 15 to 24 is less than 2 per 100,000 women for abortion, the pill, IUD, traditional methods alone (diaphragm or condom) and traditional methods plus abortion, while the fatality rate for no method is about 5 per 100,000. At age 30 to 34, the no-contraceptive fatality rate is nearly 14 per 100,000, while the rate for pill users who smoke is above 10, traditional methods about 3, non-smoking pill users about 2 and traditional methods about 3. At age 40, the fatality rate for pill users who smoke zooms above 58, while the rate for no method hits 22, non-smoking pill users are 7, traditional method users are 4 and others are still below 2 per 100,000.

Largely because of the hazards and news stories about them, the number of women taking the pill has dropped from about 12 to 8 million in recent years.

WARNINGS ISSUED ABOUT IUDs

Following are excerpts from a similar package statement required by the FDA to be given to all buyers of intrauterine devices (IUDs) since November, 1977:

"The following adverse reactions and side effects have been reported after an IUD is inserted:

"Anemia; backache; blood poisoning (septicemia); bowel obstruction; cervical infection; complete or partial expulsion; cysts on ovaries and tubes; delayed menstruation; difficult removal; embedment; fainting at the time of insertion or removal; fragmentation; intermenstrual spotting; internal abdominal adhesions; pain and cramps; painful intercourse; pelvic infection; perforation of the uterus (womb) or cervix; pregnancy; pregnancy outside the uterus (tubal or ovarian); prolonged or heavy menstrual flow; septic abortion (infected miscarriage) followed in some cases by blood poisoning (septicemia) which can lead to death; spontaneous abortion (miscarriage); vaginal discharge and infection...

"Some women become pregnant while using an IUD. If you miss your menstrual period, or if you have a scanty flow during your period, or if you suspect that you might be pregnant, see your doctor right away. Serious complication of sepsis (severe infection), septic abortion (infected miscarriage) and death have occurred when a pregnancy continues with an IUD in place..."

SIDE EFFECTS THAT MAY OCCUR WITH IUDs

Some bleeding occurs following insertion in most women. Because of this, your doctor may choose to insert your IUD during or at the end of your menstrual period. This also reduces the possibility that you are pregnant at the time of IUD insertion.

● Bleeding between menstrual periods, usually in the form of spotting, may occur during the first 2 or 3 months after insertion. The first few menstrual periods after the insertion may be heavier and longer. If these conditions continue for longer than 2 or 3 months, consult your doctor.

● Pain, usually in the form of uterine cramps or low backache, may occur at the time of insertion and last for a few days. Simple pain medication usually relieves the cramping.

● Fainting may occur at the time of insertion or removal of an IUD. This passes quickly and is not usually serious.

● The IUD may be expelled during the first two or three menstrual cycles following insertion. Expulsion increases the risk of an unplanned pregnancy.

COMMON PRESCRIPTION SYMBOLS

Abbreviation	Latin	Meaning
ad lib.	ad libitum	freely, as needed
a.c.	ante cibos	before meals
b.i.d.	bis in die	twice a day
caps.	capsula	capsule
gtt.	gutta	drop
h.s.	hora somni	at bedtime
P.O.	per os	orally
q.4 h.	quaque 4 hora	every 4 hours
q.i.d.	quater in die	4 times a day
t.i.d.	ter in die	3 times a day
Ut dict., UD	ut dictum	as directed

Education

In This Chapter
- **The Crisis in Educational Quality**
- **Factors in Choosing a College**
- **Sources of Student Financial Aid**
- **Vocational Schools**
- **Useful Publications**

Education has run into increasing criticism in the United States after centuries of unquestioning acceptance of both public and private school systems.

Formal educational attainment levels have reached record heights. Between 1960 and 1974, the proportion of adults with a high school diploma rose from 40 to 60 per cent. During the same period, the proportion of adults with four years of college rose from 11 to more than 20 per cent.

On the other hand, American literacy levels are lagging behind those of many other countries, including the Soviet Union, and achievement test scores are trailing those in Germany, Japan and Britain. A survey in 1975 by the U.S. Office of Education found evidence that many Americans are functionally illiterate, meaning that they have poor ability to do basic things such as counting money, converting weights and measures and doing simple arithmetic. The survey indicated that almost 30 per cent of Americans performed such basic tasks with difficulty and that another 33 per cent were not proficient in comparison shopping, figuring sales or taxes or determining a tip for services. In addition, average scores on standard Scholastic Aptitude Tests have been falling steadily since 1964.

EDUCATION ESSENTIAL TO MANY JOBS
Formal schooling has traditionally been considered essential to getting many jobs. Statistics prove that on the average, the more education one has, the higher the earnings will be. Incomes of college graduates are about 1½ times those of high school graduates. People who drop out of high school before finishing have unemployment rates nearly double those of high school graduates.

But in recent years, employers have generally raised their educational requirements to compensate for the decline in the value of high school and university standards and the increased need for educated people to handle the more technical jobs required by society. A disturbing percentage of blacks and other minorities fail to finish school and are turned down by employers, leaving a large segment of the population open to anti-social pursuits such as crime. Noting these problems in 1978, Senator George McGovern (D-SD) commented: "We have closed the door of education behind poor students and the door of opportunity in front of them."

Education also has had mixed results in preparing Americans for citizenship. There is a general assumption that education is necessary for a healthy democracy. Indeed, voter and citizen participation increases with the level of learning. But the percentage of eligible voters actually casting ballots in this country has declined in recent national elections despite the rise in educational levels. A substantial proportion of Americans cannot identify passages from the

Declaration of Independence and Constitution and do not seem to understand or care about basic rights once considered worthy of mortal combat.

EFFORTS TO REVERSE THE TRENDS

A variety of reasons for the decline in educational values have been offered. They include the drawing power of television over school homework; the move away from disciplined teaching; the trend toward too many courses of questionable value; fewer required courses; elimination of formal grades in many schools; the increased absence of parents from home; a more uncaring society and racial injustice in the schools.

While argument continues over the reasons, efforts to reverse the trends have been launched by numerous elements of society. Colleges have instituted remedial reading and writing courses to make up for failures of high schools to teach these fundamentals. Many states are moving toward setting up standard tests which high school students must pass in order to receive a diploma. And a growing number of schools have returned to the "basics."

In Washington, the government is preparing to carve a separate department of education out of the Department of Health, Education and Welfare to give education a better focus and more funding, especially programs that have had their budgets cut. And there has been a drive in Congress to establish a commission to study the low level of functional literacy and seek solutions.

INCREASING GOVERNMENT ASSISTANCE OF STUDENTS

New rules and laws in Washington have greatly increased money available for students wishing to go beyond high school. In November, 1978, President Carter signed legislation adding more than a million students from middle-income families to those eligible to receive federal aid for college and vocational schools. The law also extended the government program for elementary and secondary education to 2 million more children. The purpose of the changes was to make financial aid easier to obtain for nearly all who want to continue their education beyond high school. In essence, almost anyone can now get some government financial aid. It is no longer necessary to be in the lowest income brackets.

DISBURSEMENT OF FUNDS NOT UNIFORM

However, a review of the four main federal aid programs in May, 1979, by the General Accounting Office (GAO) found many examples of inconsistent treatment of students. Some students got more than their computed needs, while others did not receive enough, according to the GAO. Differences were due to variations in the handling of federal funds by the institutions involved. The GAO found that funds were distributed to states and to schools not on the basis of student needs. Awards to students were also found to be inconsistent.

The Congressional Budget Office, after checking into federal expenditures of $10 billion in 1978, reported that "the disadvantaged and poor are only slightly more likely to be in college today than they were 10 years ago and they are still less than half as likely to attend college as are children from higher-income families." There is no doubt, said the Budget Office, that federal student assistance programs make it possible for many students to attend college and to select institutions that meet their unique needs. But the Office concluded that the increase in aid to middle-income families was not justified by available data.

Meanwhile, tuition fees and other charges continue to go up at a rapid rate.

According to the College Scholarship Service of the College Board, overall ex
penses rose about 8.5 per cent from 1978-79 to 1979-80 for four-year public in
stitutions and about 10.6 per cent for private four-year colleges.

QUALITY OF EDUCATION BEING QUESTIONED MORE

As costs continue to rise and the number of college-aid people tapers off
schools are facing increasing questioning and criticism. The wave of critica
books and reports, which swept over primary and secondary schooling, ha
begun to engulf colleges and universities.

Among those concerned about the trends is the American Assembly of Col
umbia University. It invited some 66 experts on education to Arden House in
Harriman, NY, in March, 1979, to discuss "The Integrity of Higher Educa
tion."

The group found much that it considered wrong. Its Final Report, publishe
later in 1979, found "a certain malaise" creating "an urgent need to deal witl
problems that are both internal and external to the academic community." I
noted that "public confidence in American higher education has been eroded in
recent years." And it concluded that financial resources and enrollments will de
cline unless something drastic is done.

"The public," said the report, "correctly or incorrectly believes that there i
waste in its universities and colleges; they (sic) hear of tenure and conclude that i
has become a job-security device for both the incompetent as well as the compe
tent; they read inflated claims regarding faculty and curriculum only to find tha
one study program is like another;. . . . they see statistics showing that gradu
ates cannot get jobs they were led to expect while, at the same time, institution
recruit vigorously for students; they ask whether the admission of ill-prepare
students or of foreign students is not simply a device to fill classrooms in order t
justify state appropriations or to produce tuition revenue;. . . . they fear that af
firmative action is only a promissory note with no appreciable advance fo
minorities and women within the academy itself."

The report also cited examples of unethical behavior by both faculty mem
bers and students and listed 32 recommendations for improvement. It urged th
academic community to take the initiative in order to prevent further govern
ment involvement.

ETHICAL CRISIS SEEN BY CARNEGIE GROUP

In April, 1979, an even harder hitting report emerged from the Carnegi
Council on Policy Studies in Higher Education. It saw the nation's colleges an
universities as suffering an ethical crisis involving cheating, vandalism and thef
by students, grade inflation by faculty and dishonest advertising by institution
themselves. It found "a general loss of self-confidence and . . . mutual trust (be
tween institutions and students) and a general decline in integrity of conduct o
campus."

It urged state governments to "assume primary responsibility for educatio
within their boundaries" by setting minimum standards, and it recommende
that the federal government screen accrediting organizations more closely.

Prospective students were also urged to look more carefully into institution
before enrolling. (See separate section in this chapter on factors in choosing a
college.) And it suggested that accrediting associations themselves be more rigor
ous in reviewing institutional candidates for approval.

ACCREDITATION FOUND LACKING

Similar criticism of accreditation came also in 1979 from the General Accounting Office, an arm of Congress. After looking into 16 accredited schools that met federal eligibility requirements and state authorizations, the GAO concluded that none of these attainments assured that student or taxpayer interests were protected. It found students admitted with no evaluation of their abilities to undertake the courses applied for, grading policies that did not indicate performance, induced enrollments through false and misleading advertising; failure to provide promised job placement help, refund policies that resulted in little or no money back despite brief attendance; inadequately prepared teachers and failure to advise prospective students and parents of attrition and graduate placement rates.

The report called on the states and the federal Office of Education to tighten up review policies. And it urged Congress to clarify what the Office can or should require of accrediting associations.

FACTORS IN CHOOSING A COLLEGE
Beyond What the Usual Directories Suggest

Choosing a college or graduate school can be a difficult task. Applicants are swamped with choices and sometimes irrelevant information. While test schores, school size, location, and admission criteria may narrow down the field, they do not give the applicant a full picture of an institution. Statistically, many schools look alike.

Students currently attending an institution are good sources of information on their school. Alumni and admissions officers are others sources, from somewhat different points of view. Finally, there are catalogs and guidebooks, including those put out by independent companies as well as one distributed by the schools themselves. These can help narrow down the field.

But there are many factors not often discussed or considered which are potentially important. Following are some in the form of questions for a prospective student to consider in making a choice:

ADMINISTRATION—How accessible is the school administration to the student body? Do students have a voice in administrative decision-making? Is there a forum for students in which to air their gripes? How does the administration define *in loco parentis*? What types of restrictions does it place on student activities?

ADMISSIONS—On what bases are admissions decisions made? What factors does the admissions office consider to be most important? Is there an attempt to admit a diverse student body in age, interests, race, culture, religion and geographic background?

COUNSELING AND GUIDANCE—What kind of counseling facilities are available to students? How accessible are the facilities and people who provide academic and psychological counseling? Is peer counseling available? What type of programs are available to ease the transition newcomers must make? Is counseling available on future educational alternatives?

CURRICULUM—What types of academic requirements does the institution have? Are all students required to take certain "core" courses or to take courses in a variety of areas? What types of offerings are available to students who must meet these requirements? What requirements are there for specific majors? Do students have the opportunity to take a variety of courses? Is it difficult to arrange tutorials, part-time study, visiting semesters, auditing, external degree programs, field work, and other independent courses of study?

ENVIRONMENT—What types of educational, social, cultural and athletic opportunities are available to the students? Do large numbers of students leave campus on weekends? What type of relationship does the institution have with the surrounding community? Is it accessible to other educational or cultural institutions?

FACULTY—Are faculty members available outside the class? Do they hold frequent office hours? Are they willing to meet informally with students or only to talk about specific problems? Do students have access to well-known scholars? What size are most classes? How are faculty members and courses evaluated? Is the emphasis on publishing and academic research and/or teaching? Do students have any input in the evaluation process?

FINANCES—What is the institutions current and expected financial position? How is it dealing with inflationary pressures? If there are cutbacks, who feels the brunt of these? How accountable is the institution? What types of financial aid are available? Does the institution help students take advantage of different programs?

FOOD SERVICE—What choices does the food service offer in hours, menus, alternative meal plans and dietary options? Is there a clear emphasis on good nutrition?

HOUSING—What types of housing options are available both on- and off-campus? What type of rooming situation could a first-year student expect to have? How does this change in later years? Are dormitories coeducational or single-sex? Are there alternative options? How are roommates selected? Are the housing facilities and other buildings well maintained?

JOBS—What types of counseling and placement facilities are there to help students find employment both in school and after graduation? Are there programs to arrange internships and volunteer employment?

COLLEGE DEGREES BY MAIL

College degrees are now available to millions of Americans previously unable to attend college due to an increasing number of home-study programs accredited to grant degrees.

A number of major colleges and correspondence schools have received accreditation for degree programs offered entirely through the mails. According to the National Home Study Council (NHSC), the trend is towards making more such programs available in the near future.

Among the first institutions to offer such programs are Indiana University, Ohio University, University of Minnesota, Brigham Young University, University of Oklahoma and Columbia Union College. Accredited correspondence schools offering college degrees include La Salle Extension University in Chicago, Center for Degree Studies in Scranton, PA., and Grantham College of Engineering in Los Angeles.

In addition, some 200 institutions offer programs in which less than one-fourth of the course work involves in-class or on-campus activity.

STUDENTS AND EMPLOYEES PLEASED

Most students completing such programs are pleased with their experience, according to an unpublished survey by the Bureau of Social Science Research in Washington, D.C. The survey, which questioned 3,000 graduates of accredited home study degree programs, found that the average age of students was about 35. Some students surveyed were in their 70s and 80s.

Employers of such students were also pleased with the programs, according to preliminary impressions of another study by the Bureau. Most employers were found to readily accept such degrees as being as valid as those received by students attending classes on campus.

The accredited programs include both two-year and four-year degrees, although most students are opting for the shorter programs which offer "associate" degrees usually available from community colleges, according to NHSC. The most common programs currently available are those in business and engineering.

Potential students should carefully check claims made by the schools, warns the Council. Hundreds of schools offering degrees by mail are not accredited. Not all schools accredited by NHSC may be recognized by an employer or by another college.

More information on degree-granting home study schools is available in a free packet from NHSC, 1601 18th St. NW, Washington, DC, 20009.

SCHOLARSHIPS, GRANTS AND LOANS

Many different scholarship, grant and loan programs are available for individuals wishing to continue their education after high school. These awards are based on financial need, merit, a combination of both, or other unrelated factors. Some programs are sponsored by the Federal Government, others by states, localities, businesses, organizations, individuals, associations and other private sources.

Academic scholarships are awarded primarily on the basis of scholastic achievement although some are based on financial need. The money does not need to be repaid. Awards can range from $50 or $100 to $3,000 a year, although amounts exceeding $1,500 or $2,000 are unusual since scholarship officials prefer to give funds to as many deserving and qualified students as possible.

Grants and loans are normally made on the basis of financial need. While grants do not have to be repaid, loans must be. Federal programs include the Basic Educational Opportunity Grant Program and the Supplemental Educational Opportunity Grant Program. They are described under "Sources of Financial Aid."

Loans are perhaps the biggest source of financial assistance to students throughout the country. While scholarships are competitive and uncertain, and grants offer limited amounts of money, loans are made on the basis of need. For those qualified, loans are fairly easy to obtain year after year. Educational loans may be obtained from federal and state resources, private organizations and colleges and universities. If obtained under government programs, interest and repayment must begin nine months after graduation, or departure, from college and may extend up to 10 years. If an individual enters graduate school, military service, or certain other government occupations, payment and interest are usually deferred. The two main sources of government loans are the National Direct Student Loan Program and the Guaranteed Student Loan Program.

on the basis of financial need. Many colleges use a standard form of financial analysis which involves comparing a family's current income and assets with statistical data on "normal" family living expenses at various income levels.

GOVERNMENT GRANT PROGRAMS

BASIC EDUCATIONAL OPPORTUNITY GRANT PROGRAM: to be eligible, a student must be an applicant or student at an approved postsecondary educational institution and be on a full-time or half-time basis. Student eligibility is determined by the U.S. Office of Education. These 100 per cent federally funded grants are limited to $1,800 per school year. Applications may be obtained from postsecondary educational institutions, high schools, public libraries, or by writing P.O. Box 84, Washington, D.C. 20044. The deadline for 1979-1980 is March 15, 1980.

SUPPLEMENTAL EDUCATIONAL OPPORTUNITY GRANT PROGRAM: to qualify, a student must have an exceptional financial need and be at least a half-time undergraduate or vocational student. Eligibility is determined by the student's school. Graduate students are not eligible. Grants may not exceed $1,500 per school year.

STATE STUDENT INCENTIVE GRANTS: states and the federal government each contribute 50 per cent of the funds for this grant. Grants may not exceed $1,500 per school year.

COLLEGE WORK-STUDY PROGRAM: enables students to work part-time on and off campus provided they are enrolled in a college at least half-time. The federal government pays 80 per cent of the cost of employment of eligible students; the school funds the remaining 20 per cent. Contact the director of financial aid or student employment office at the school you attend.

FOR FURTHER DETAILS on federal programs, call 800/638-6700; in Maryland, call 800/492-6602.

EDUCATIONAL ASSISTANCE FOR VETERANS

VIETNAM GI BILL: provides the opportunity for financial assistance to male and female veterans of the Army, Navy, Marine Corps, Air Force and Coast Guard who are interested in continuing their education. Individuals are eligible if they served (and were honorably discharged) (1) Continuously on active duty for at least 181 days ending after January 31, 1955; (2) If active duty (less than 181 days) was ended by a service-connected disability; or (3) If individual has had at least 181 days of active duty.

CONTRIBUTORY ASSISTANCE PLAN: requires that men and women who enter the military after January 1, 1977, no longer be entitled to receive full benefits from their GI Bill. Individuals have to contribute a minimum of $50 or a maximum of $75 per month toward their expenses. The VA will contribute double what an individual contributes. In one year, an individual may contribute a maximum of $900 ($75 per month times 12 months) while the VA contributes a maximum of $1,800. The VA will loan a maximum of $2,500 per academic year under its loan program to those requiring additional funds.

To be eligible for this Educational Reimbursement Plan, a person has to have been in the service more than 181 days. An individual may take up to 10 years to participate in this educational assistance program.

DEPENDENTS EDUCATION ASSISTANCE PROGRAM: provides educational opportunities for children, wives and widows of dead or permanently

NATIONAL DIRECT STUDENT LOAN PROGRAM

Students are eligible if they are enrolled at least half-time in a participating post-secondary institution and need a loan to meet educational expenses. They may borrow up to: a) $2,500 if enrolled in a vocational program or if they have completed less than two years of a program leading to a bachelor's degree; b)$5,000 if an undergraduate student who has already completed two years of study toward a bachelor's degree. This amount includes any amount previously borrowed from this program during the first two years of study; c) $10,000 for graduate study. This amount includes any previous amount borrowed during undergraduate study.

Repayment begins nine months after graduation or departure from school. Recipients are allowed up to 10 years to pay back the loan. During the repayment period, 3 per cent interest is charged on the unpaid balance of the loan. Individuals who decide to enter the Armed Forces, Peace Corps or VISTA are allowed to defer payment for up to three years while they serve. Those who enter certain fields of teaching or specified military duty are not required to pay back their loans. Application for this loan should be made through school financial aid officers.

GUARANTEED STUDENT LOAN PROGRAM

Students are eligible if they are enrolled at least half-time in an eligible college or university, a school of nursing, or a vocational, technical trade, business, or home study school. A high school diploma is not necessary in order to borrow. This loan enables individuals to borrow directly from a bank, credit union, savings and loan association, or other participating lender willing to make an educational loan. The loan is guaranteed by a state or private nonprofit agency or insured by the Federal Government.

The maximum that may be borrowed in one year is $2,500. In some states, it is less. Annual interest rates cannot be more than 7 per cent. The total amount a student may borrow for undergraduate or vocational study is $7,500. There is a limit of $10,000 for those in graduate study or who have previously borrowed for undergraduate work.

Many students may be eligible for Federal Interest Benefits when paying back their loans. The Federal Government pays the interest for you during school and for nine to 12 months afterward.

REPAYMENT CAN TAKE 10 YEARS

When applying for a loan, students must submit a notarized statement stating that the money they are borrowing will be used only for educational purposes. The loan repayments must begin nine to 12 months after departure or graduation from school and take no longer than 10 years. Students are entitled to three-year deferments if they chose to continue going to school full-time or to serve in the Armed Forces, Peace Corps, or VISTA (which includes such programs as the University Year for ACTION, ACTION Cooperative Volunteer Programs, Volunteers in Justice and Program for Local Service.)

Information and application forms are available from schools, lenders, state guarantee agencies and regional offices of the U.S. Office of Education which are listed below.

Students may also obtain financial aid directly from their schools in the form of scholarships, loans or grants. Most of the money awarded is determined and totally disabled veterans. Family members are eligible if servicemen have been missing in action or prisoners of war for more than 90 days. Eligible students may get assistance upon completion of high school or on their 18th birthday (whichever comes first). Assistance ends on a student's 26 birthday. Widows and wives may qualify for assistance if their veteran husband is dead or permanently and totally disabled from service-related causes, from being a prisoner of war, or from being missing in action for more than 90 days.

FOR MORE INFORMATION on veteran programs, contact a regional office of the Veterans Administration or call 202/872-1151.

VOCATIONAL AND HOME-STUDY SCHOOLS

Many people who do not have the interest in or academic background for college have found valuable marketable skills through courses at vocational or home-study schools. Approximately 3 million Americans attend or correspond with the estimated 8,000 such schools each year, often with higher hopes than can possibly be fulfilled.

Many are lured by false promises and deceptive sales pitches. When the disappointed student drops out, he or she often finds it impossible to get any advance payments back. Even with completion of the prescribed courses, many students find job opportunities either non-existent or greatly overrated. The Federal Trade Commission estimates that only about 10 to 15 per cent of students complete such programs.

Complaints and reports of abuse have flooded government agencies that provide funds, chiefly the Veterans Administration and the U.S. Office of Education. The latter reports that 99 per cent of the complaints received pertain to vocational and home-study schools.

PROPOSED FTC RULES TO PROTECT STUDENTS

More than four years ago, the FTC responded to the large number of complaints with proposed rules governing vocational and home-study schools. The agency's purpose was to reduce the amount of fraud and deception in this $3 billion business.

The rules would prohibit deceptive representations about facilities, equipment, instructors, job placement ratios, and the value of diplomas, degrees or certificates. They would also prohibit unfair collection and credit practices and failure to disclose facts about graduation and dropout rates.

Students would have 14 days to change their mind and get a refund after having signed up. Schools would have to notify students of this right when they are accepted. If students cancel within 14 days, they would be able to get all their money back even if the course had started. Any equipment received by the student would have to be returned. No rental fee could be charged even if the equipment was used.

Students would be able to cancel at any time during the course for any reason. However, after the first 14 days, they could owe money. Schools could keep a registration fee of not more than $75. They could also charge tuition based on the number of classes or lessons completed. Veterans already have a 10 day cancellation period.

GRADUATION AND PLACEMENT RATES REQUIRED

In order to reduce the chance of deception, the FTC rules would require schools to tell newly enrolled students in writing how many former students dropped out of the course before finishing and how the figure compared to the number enrolled.

If the school makes any claim about the demand for—or the potential earnings of—graduates, a written notice must disclose how many recent graduates were placed in jobs and how much they are earning. Schools would have to stand behind all advertising claims about graduates' jobs and earnings and let students see such records.

The rules are due to go into effect January 1, 1980, but several industry groups have filed legal challenges designed to block them.

Until the rules go into effect, government protection will be minimal. In some cases, the FTC has been able to force schools to provide refunds, but the number of students and money involved has been relatively small compared to the alleged abuses.

PRECAUTIONS ISSUED BY THE FTC

As soon as an individual shows an interest in a school, he or she becomes a target for telephone calls, mail and visits from school sales people. Some states have licensing requirements, but they are relatively easy to meet. Other schools operate across state lines to avoid meeting state requirements. According to the FTC, prospective students should beware of a person who:

● Says he is a school counselor or advisor. (He may only be a salesman whose income is solely dependent on the sales he makes.)

RIGHT TO SEE STUDENT RECORDS

Under a federal law passed in 1974, students and parents of students have certain rights to see school records, get errors corrected and to have the information kept confidential. The Family Educational Rights and Privacy Act grants these rights to parents or students who are 18 or older in school beyond high school.

Among the rights provided are the following:

● A school must allow parents or eligible students to inspect and review all of the student's education records maintained by the school. However, this does not include personal notes of teachers, or, at the college level, medical or law enforcement records. Schools are not required to provide copies of material unless, for reasons such as illness or great distance, it is impossible to inspect the records personally. The school may charge a fee for copies.

● Parents and eligible students may request that a school correct records believed to be inaccurate or misleading. If the school refuses to change the records, the parent or eligible student then has the right to a formal hearing. After the hearing, if the school still refuses the correction, the parent or eligible student has the right to put a note in the record explaining his or her concerns.

● Generally, the school must have written permission from the parent or eligible student before releasing any information from a student's record. But this does not apply to directory-type information such as a name, address or phone number.

If you have any questions the school cannot answer, or if you have problems in securing your rights under this Act, you may call 202/245-7488 or write to Room 526E, South Portal Building, Department of Health, Education, and Welfare, Washington, DC, 20201.

● Offers you a large discount if you pay now, or won't let you think it over and tries to force you to sign before he leaves.

● Makes you feel guilty for not signing up for a course by saying that you will be "depriving" yourself or your children of educational opportunities.

● Assures you that the school is "registered", "licensed", "approved", or "accredited." These words say nothing about how uniform the accredidation standards are among the numerous accrediting associations or how good the school will be in preparing you for a new job or career. A school doesn't have to be accredited to operate.

● Promises a fabulous career or glamorous job and says there are thousands of job openings for someone like you "if you sign up for this course". Find out what percentage of individuals who have taken courses at the school actually found employment and what are their present positions and salaries. Many schools enroll students that aren't adequately prepared to benefit from a course or to obtain employment in jobs for which the course is designed to prepare them.

● "Guarantees" a job or "your money back." Honest schools do not make such guarantees involving employment, and in many states it is illegal to do so.

WHERE TO COMPLAIN

Complaints about private vocational or home study schools should be made to the Office of Education or the Veterans Administration, whichever is funding the student's program of education. If payments to schools are made by private individuals, complaints should go to the State Consumer Protection Division Attorney General's Office or to the Federal Trade Commission, Bureau of Consumer Protection, Washington, DC, 20580. (See list of state, county and city government consumer protection offices elsewhere in this book.)

USEFUL PUBLICATIONS FOR STUDENTS

A large variety of publications await the prospective student in nearly every bookstore. The best course of action is to personally review the latest editions of annual guides and directories to find the type of information most helpful for your purposes.

Other useful publications may be available only by mail, including some listed below. Certain institutions have been selected, the next step is to request free catalogs and other information directly. High school counselors and placement officers may be able to recommend publications as well as institutions to be considered.

The following are selected publications, both free and paid, with names and addresses of publishers. Dates are omitted because of frequent changes. (Free publications are indicated; prices of others are for the most recent editions.)

American Junior Colleges, by Edmund J. Gleazer Jr., American Council on Education, 1 Dupont Circle, Washington, DC, 20009. ($8.50). Descriptions of more than 800 accredited institutions.

Barron's Guide to Two-Year Colleges, Barron's Educational Series Inc., 113 Crossways Park Drive, Woodbury, NY, 11797. ($4.95). Descriptions of more than 1,000 institutions.

Barron's Profiles of American Colleges, Barron's Educational Series Inc.,

113 Crossways Park Drive, Woodbury, NY, 11797 ($6.95). Information about more than 1,400 four-year institutions.

Careers for the Homebound, President's Committee on Employment of the Handicapped, Washington, DC, 20210. Free.

Careers in Music, Music Educators National Conference, 1902 Association Drive, Reston, VA, 22091. ($1.00)

Career Decisions, American Personnel and Guidance Association, 1607 New Hampshire Ave, NW, Washington, DC, 20009. ($1.00) Advice to parents and students planning careers.

College Handbook, The College Board, 888 Seventh St. New York, NY, 10019. ($9.95). Detailed descriptions of 2,000 colleges and brief descriptions of some 800 others.

College Placement and Credit by Examination, The College Board, 888 Seventh Ave., New York, NY, 10019. ($3.50). A list of Advanced Placement and College-Level Examination Program (CLEP) programs at colleges.

Comparative Guide to American Colleges, by James Cass and Max Birnbaum, Harper & Row, 10 East 53d St., New York, NY, 10022. ($6.95). Descriptions of four-year colleges.

Continuing Education Programs and Services for Women, Superintendent of Documents, Washington, DC, 20402. ($1.55). List of institutions offering courses to middle-aged women. 18th St. NW, Washington, DC, 20009. Free.

Counselor's Guide to Home Study Training, A, National Home Study Council, 1601 18th St. NW, Washington, DC, 20009. Free.

Directory of Accredited Private Home Study Schools, National Home Study Council, 1601 18th St. NW, Washington, DC, 20009. Free.

Directory of Cooperative Education, Cooperative Education Association, Drexel University, Philadelphia, PA, 19104 ($6.00)

Directory of Special Programs for Minority Members, Garrett Park Press, Garrett Park, MD, 20766. ($8.95)

Directory of State-Approved Programs of Practical/Vocational Nursing, National Association for Practical Nurse Education and Service, 122 East 42nd St., New York, NY, 10017. Free.

Federal Benefits for Veterans and Dependents, Supt. of Documents, Washington, DC, 20402. (60°).

Guide to American Graduate Schools, by Herbert B. Livesey and Gene A. Robbins, Viking Press, New York, NY. ($8.95). Descriptions of schools.

Guide to Graduate and Professional Study, Chronicle Guidance Publications Inc., Moravia, NY, 13118. ($5.00)

How to Prepare for College Entrance Examinations, Barron's Educational Series Inc., 113 Crossways Park Drive, Woodbury, NY, 11797. ($4.50) Review of skills necessary for SATs along with sample tests.

I Can Be Anything, by Joyce S. Mitchell, The College Board, 888 Seventh St., New York, NY, 10019. ($7.95) Description of careers and colleges for young women.

Index of Majors, The College Board, 888 Seventh St., New York, NY, 10019. ($7.95). List of major programs of study at 2,400 two-and four-year colleges.

Insider's Guide to the Colleges, The, Yale Daily News, New Haven, CT. ($2.50) Informal appraisal of institutions with emphasis on student conditions and relations.

National Association of Trade and Technical Schools, 2021 L St. NW, Washington, DC, 20036. Free. A list of over 400 schools.

Need a Lift?, American Legion, Emblem Sales, P.O. Box 1055, Indianapolis, IN, 46206. ($1.00). Annual detailed directory of sources of financial aid for post-secondary schools.

Pathways to a Career in Dentistry, Technical Education Research Center, 44 Brattle St., Cambridge, MA, 02138. ($4.50).

Practical Nursing Career, National League for Nursing, 10 Columbus Circle, New York, NY, 10019. (50ᶜ).

Student Aid Bulletin—Scholarships Offered by States, Chronicle Guidance Publications Inc., Moravia, NY, 13118. ($6.95).

Tips on Home Study Schools, Council of Better Business Bureaus, 1150 17th St. NW, Washington, DC, 20036. Free.

COMPACT SET OF STUDENT PUBLICATIONS

One organization claims to have a "low-cost cure for every financial aid ailment afflicting the typical student." It is Octameron Associates of Alexandria, VA.

Its packet of compact booklets include *Don't Miss Out: The Ambitious Student's Guide to Scholarships and Loans*, an explanation of the financial aid process. ($2.00); *The As & Bs of Academic Scholarships,* a list of over 40,000 scholarships offered by 600 colleges to bright students. ($2.00); *The Federal Government & Cooperative Education,* a growing program with 12,000 students at 600 institutions ($1.25); *Calculate Your BEOG Eligibility Index,* (75¢); *State Financial Aid Agencies* (30¢); and *State-by-State Contact Addresses for the Guaranteed Student Loan Program* (30¢).

The 1979/1980 edition of each booklet is available for the above prices plus 25 cents for postage and handling from Dept H80, Octameron Associates Inc., P.O. Box 3437, Alexandria, VA, 22303.

Jobs and Careers

For millions of workers, 1979 was a catchup year, a time to push wage rates up to where living costs were going. That was the theme for 4 million workers whose contracts were due to expire. It was also the theme for many other workers without formal contracts.

Purchasing power, which tumbled 3.4 per cent in 1978, headed even lower in 1979. Prices leaped ahead at an annual rate of 13.1 per cent in the first seven months, nearly double the 7 per cent ceiling on wage increases set by the Carter Administration to combat inflation.

As a result, contract increases began to break through the recommended ceilings from one union to another. The Administration assured that prospect by agreeing to a national contract with the teamsters union well above the guideline. It also assured some tense negotiations in other industries and the likelihood of strikes more serious than the one by teamsters.

NEMPLOYMENT RATE STAYS STEADY

While the number of people out of work dropped to 5.6 in June, 1979, the total number of people at work was 2.1 million higher than a year earlier, but increased joblessness in the automobile industry threatened to have reverberations throughout the economy as a recession appeared to begin. Unemployment among teenagers continued rising, especially among black teenagers.

At a time when American workers needed all the friends they could get, support for organized labor was reaching a low ebb in Congress. Legislators were becoming more friendly with business interests and less friendly to labor, according to AFL-CIO leaders.

One of the big issues in 1979 was the Davis-Bacon Act of 1931. This Depression-era law sets minimum wages for construction projects involving federal funds at the prevailing local rate. It applied to about 22 per cent of the $172 billion spent on such work in 1977. A powerful campaign was launched by business interests to repeal the law on the grounds that it is inflationary and does not allow local contractors to compete on government contracts.

Unions in the construction business began a concerted counteroffensive in April, 1979, on Capitol Hill. As a result, prospects of defeating a repeal effort began to look better than for other labor-backed measures.

LABOR PUSHES FOR MORE IMPORT CURBS

Organized labor has also stepped up its campaign to protect jobs of American workers whenever they are threatened by importation of products priced substantially below American-made products. AFL-CIO leaders have become particularly concerned about importation of color television sets, shoes and textile items. Labor leaders succeeded in getting the Carter Administration to negotiate voluntary reductions with nations supplying these and other products to the U.S. market.

Labor unions also have been fighting the loss of jobs to other countries as American corporations set up plants abroad or move to another state. Efforts to pass state laws to require plants to give advance notice—as much as two years—before moving away have met strong business opposition. The most that any state requires is 60 days (Maine and Wisconsin). Efforts to get a federal law have failed.

Organized labor also has not had much success in stemming the outflow of manufacturing operations to other countries where wage rates and taxes are generally much lower.

WOMEN IN LABOR FORCE AT RECORD LEVEL

Some of the reasons for the decline in political influence of organized labor is the changing composition of the American labor force. Women are joining the ranks of workers at a record pace, usually in jobs that have little or no union activity.

From 1970 to 1977, the number of wives at work rose by 24 per cent, according to Labor Department figures. The number of single women with paying jobs has also gone up rapidly. By 1990, women will account for 45 per cent of the total workforce, according to a Commerce Department study released in 1979. They now total 41 per cent.

Meanwhile, Service jobs continue to grow, while production jobs drop in proportion to the total, as the economy continues to shift in that direction.

GETTING HELP IN FINDING THE RIGHT JOB

The U.S. Employment Service and affiliated state agencies operate over 2,400 local offices to serve those seeking employment and those providing it. General services include outreach, interviewing, testing, counseling, and referral to placement, training, and other services in readying individuals for employment. Specialized services for various groups such as the following are also provided:

VETERANS receive priority treatment (with preference for disabled veterans) in all services leading to employment and training.

YOUTH receive such services as counseling, testing, referral to training and other agencies, job development, and placement.

WORKERS OVER 45 receive specialized job counseling, job development, referral to training or health and social services, and job placement.

THE HANDICAPPED benefit from special placement techniques that seek to match the physical and mental demands of a job to the capabilities of a worker.

RURAL RESIDENTS AND WORKERS receive year-round assistance in the full range of employment services. They also receive special services in recruitment and placement in farm and woods occupations. Growers receive assistance in meeting critical seasonal labor needs.

DISADVANTAGED INDIVIDUALS receive such services as testing, counseling, referral to training and other supportive services.

EMPLOYERS receive help in obtaining workers for their work force needs.

Private employment services may often be more effective than government ones, but they charge fees which are paid either by the employer or employee. An advertisement saying "fee paid" means that the fee is paid by the employer. If such wording is not present, it may mean that the applicant will have to pay it. Such fees are often as much as 10 per cent of the first year's salary.

WHICH TYPES OF JOBS OFFER THE BEST PROSPECTS

The most recent government review of job prospects shows a brighter picture than ever for people without college degrees and a dimmer picture than ever for those with degrees. The U.S. Labor Department's biennial study, released in March, 1978, found that the vast majority of the 46 million jobs expected to open up between now and 1985 will require less than four years of college training. But a high school education has become what Secretary of Labor Ray Marshall called "the minimum standard for entry into almost all jobs."

Among the many job categories due to grow faster than average are insulation workers, police officers, water treatment plant operators, mechanics, repairmen and health paraprofessionals, such as nursing aides, hospital orderlies and nursing home assistants.

Jobs expected to become harder to get include teachers, particularly, elementary and high school levels; bookkeepers, because of increased computerization; historians; librarians; mathematicians; physicists; and newspaper reporters.

Clerical workers are both the largest and the fasting growing occupational group. Increasing especially fast will be jobs for cashiers, receptionists and secretaries. Also growing rapidly as a group will be service workers such as chefs, guards and cosmetologists. Rising income levels will cause greater use of restaurants, beauty parlors and recreational services.

OTHER SOURCES OF CAREER INFORMATION

The most up-to-date survey of employment opportunities is the Labor Department's 840-page *Occupational Outlook Handbook, 1978-79 Edition.* Every major job and industry is discussed with details including pay scales, qualifications, chances of advancement and estimated numbers of jobs opening up.

The book can be obtained from the Government Printing Office for $8 and can be found in libraries. Reprints of various sections can be obtained for 50 cents from regional offices of the Bureau of Labor Statistics. A free list of sections is also available at BLS offices or from its main office at the Department of Labor, Washington, DC, 20212.

For college graduates, the Labor Department offers *Occupational Outlook for College Graduates, 1978-79 Edition* (Bulletin 1956). It is a 275-page book about more than 100 jobs for which a college education is necessary or useful. The price is $4.50.

Also available from BLS and the Department are five free leaflets focusing on jobs that require specified levels of education. They include: *Jobs for Which*

High School Education is Preferred But Not Essential; Jobs for Which Education is Generally Required; Jobs for Which Apprenticeships are Available; Jobs for Which Junior College, Technical Institute or Other Specialized Training is Usually Required; and *Jobs for Which College Education is Usually Required.*

In addition, BLS and the Labor Department have 11 free leaflets on these types of careers: clerical jobs, ecology, English, foreign languages, health, liberal arts, math, mechanics, outdoors, science and social science.

CAREER INFORMATION FOR SPECIAL GROUPS

People who don't fit easily into the normal job market are the subject of numerous publications and services. Special counseling, training and placement services are available in many communities, particularly through public employment agencies and community service organizations. Among publications of help are:

YOUTH: *Employment and Training for Youth,* fact sheet from Office of Information, Room 10225, Department of Labor, Washington, DC, 20213. *A Message to Young Workers About the Fair Labor Standards Act,* free from Office of Information, Room 4331, Department of Labor, Washington, DC, 20210.

MENTALLY HANDICAPPED: *These, Too, Must Be Equal: America's Needs in Habilitation and Employment of the Mentally Retarded,* from President's Committee on Mental Retardation, 7th and D Sts. SW, Washington, DC, 20201. *Guide to Job Placement of Mentally Retarded Workers* and *Jobs and Mentally Retarded People,* from the President't Committee. Also *Affirmative Action to Employ Handicapped People,* from Office of Information, Room 4331, Department of Labor, Washington, DC, 20210.

PHYSICALLY HANDICAPPED: *Careers for the Homebound* and *People at Work: 50 Profiles of Men and Women with MS,* both from President's Committee on Employment of the Handicapped, Room 600, Vanguard Bldg., 1111 20th St. NW, Washington, DC, 20036.

OLDER WORKERS: *The Law Against Age Discrimination in Employment,* from Office of Information, Room 4331, Department of Labor, Washington, DC, 20210. *Services for Older Workers* and *Memo to Mature Job Seekers,* from Office of Information, Room 10225, Department of Labor, Washington, DC, 20213. *Employment and Volunteer Opportunities for Older People,* from National Clearinghouse on Aging, Room 4146, Department of Health, Education and Welfare, 330 Independence Ave. SW, Washington, DC, 20201.

WOMEN: *Steps to Opening the Skilled Trades to Women* and *Why Not Be an Apprentice and Become a Skilled Craft Worker,* also other publications from the Women's Bureau, Department of Labor, Washington, DC, 20210.

VETERANS: *Out of the Service and Looking for a Job? Here's Help* and *Veterans for Hire,* from Office of Information, Room 10225, Department of Labor, Washington, DC, 20213. Others available from the Veterans Administration, Department of Veterans Benefits, 810 Vermont Ave. NW, Washington, DC, 20420.

MATCHING PEOPLE TO JOBS

A 15-page booklet: "Matching Personal & Job Characteristics" is available free from the U.S. Dept. of Labor, Bureau of Labor Statistics, Washington, DC, 20210. Designed to help those who are seeking a job or changing careers, it can help match personal interests, capacities, abilities and educational qualifications with characteristics of a specific occupation or group of occupations. The pamphlet lists 281 jobs.

TARGETS OF LABOR BOYCOTTS

Following is a partial list of companies, products and brands subject to boycotts officially sanctioned by the AFL-CIO Executive Council as of April, 1979, because of alleged non-union conditions or activities:

American Buildings Inc.: Metal structures including storage buildings, warehouses, etc.

Bartlett-Collins Company: Glass products including drinking glasses, mugs, etc.

Coors Brewery: Beer.

Charles Manufacturing Company: Coffee tables, end tables and similar items sold under **Fox** brand.

Croft Metals Inc.: Aluminum and vinyl doors and windows, including storm doors and windows, bathtub enclosures, patio doors, ladders, camper products and building specialty products.

Dal-Tex Optical Co.: Eyeglass lenses, frames, contact lenses, sunglasses, safety glasses.

Hussmann Refrigerator Co./Pet Inc.: Commercial refrigeration equipment including **Hussman Refrigeration** display cases; food products sold under **Pet, Old El Paso Mexico, Musselman Fruit** and **Downeyflake** brands; **Stuckey's Roadside Stores; 9-0-5 Liquor Stores** in St Louis; and **Vendome Liquor Stores** in Southern California.

J.P. Stevens & Co.: Sheets and pillowcases sold under **Beauti-Blend, Beauticale, Fine Arts, Peanuts, Tastemaker, Utica & Mohawk** brands; carpets under **Contender, Gulistan, Merryweather** and **Tastemaker** brands; Table linen under the **Simtex** brand; hosiery under the **Finesse, Hip-Lets** and **Spirit** brands; Towels under the **Fine Arts, Tastemaker** and **Utica** brands and blankets under the **Frostmann** and **Utica** brands.

Kingsport Press: Books including **World Book, Childcraft** and others published by **Field Enterprises Educational Corporation;** and **Britannica Jr., Great Books of the Western World,** and others published by Encyclopaedia Britannica Inc.

Mason-Tyler Manufacturing Company: Household furniture.

R.J. Reynolds Tobacco Company: Cigarettes under **Winston, Salem, Camel, Doral, Vantage, More, Now,** and **Real** brands; **Winchester Little Cigars;** and **Prince Albert Smoking Tobacco.**

Rylock Company Ltd.: Sliding glass doors, windows.

Winn-Dixie Stores: Retail food stores doing business as **Buddies** in Texas, **Foodway** in New Mexico and **Kwik-Chek** elsewhere.

JOB OUTLOOKS FOR SELECTED OCCUPATIONS
INDUSTRIAL PRODUCTION AND RELATED OCCUPATIONS

Foundry and machining occupations.

MACHINISTS: Employment expected to increase about as fast as average for all occupations due to expansion of metalworking activities and rising demand for machined goods.

MACHINE TOOL OPERATORS: Employment expected to increase about as fast as average as metalworking industries expand. Although changes in machine tools may affect some jobs, opportunities should be plentiful.

MOLDERS, COREMAKERS, PATTERNMAKERS: Employment expected to change little due to laborsaving innovations. However, replacement needs will create hundreds of openings annually.

TOOL-AND-DIEMAKERS: Employment expected to grow about as fast as average for all occupations as result of expansion in metalworking industries.

WELDERS: Employment expected to increase faster than average for all occupations due to favorable outlook for metalworking industries and greater use of welding. Very good opportunities.

Printing occupations.

BOOKBINDERS AND RELATED WORKERS: Employment expected to grow more slowly than average for all occupations because of increasing mechanization of bindery operations.

COMPOSING ROOM WORKERS: Employment expected to decline due to use of high-speed phototypesetting and typesetting computers that require few operators.

LITHOGRAPHIC WORKERS: Employment expected to grow faster than average for occupations as offset presses are increasingly used in place of letter presses.

PHOTOENGRAVERS: Employment expected to decline as result of offset printing, which requires no photoengraving, and other technological advances. Limited opportunities.

PRINTING PRESS OPERATORS: Employment expected to increase more slowly than average because faster and more efficient presses will limit growth.

Other industrial production and related occupations.

ASSEMBLERS: Employment expected to increase faster than average for all occupations due to growing demand for consumer products and industrial machinery and equipment. However, employment is concentrated in durable goods industries which are highly sensitive to changes in business conditions and national defense needs.

BLUE COLLAR WORKER SUPERVISORS: Employment expected to grow about as fast as average. Most of increase in employment due to expansion of nonmanufacturing industries.

BOILER TENDERS: Employment expected to decline as more new boilers are equipped with automatic controls. However, hundreds of openings will arise annually due to replacement needs.

FORGE SHOP WORKERS: Employment expected to grow more slowly than average because of improved forging techniques and equipment, despite expansion in automobile and energy-related industries.

FURNITURE UPHOLSTERERS: Employment expected to grow at a slower rate than average because furniture is being constructed with less upholstery and because of trend toward buying new furniture instead of reupholstering the old.

INSPECTORS (MANUFACTURING): Employment expected to increase faster than average for all occupations because of industrial expansion and growing complexity of manufactured products.

MOTION PICTURE PROJECTIONISTS: Employment expected to grow more slowly than average because of laborsaving innovations in equipment and the limited growth in the number of theatres.

OPHTHALMIC LABORATORY TECHNICIANS: Employment expected to increase much faster than average for all occupations due to rising demand for eyeglasses.

PHOTOGRAPHIC LABORATORY WORKERS: Employment expected to increase faster than average for all occupations due to increasing use of photography in business, government, research and development activities, and growth of amateur photography.

POWER TRUCK OPERATORS: Employment expected to increase about as fast as average as more firms use power trucks in place of hand labor.

PRODUCTION PAINTERS: Employment expected to grow about as fast as average for all occupations, but not keep pace with manufacturing output because of increased use of automatic sprayers and other laborsaving innovations.

STATIONARY ENGINEERS: Employment expected to change little because of increased use of more powerful and centralized equipment.

OFFICE OCCUPATIONS
Clerical occupations.

BOOKKEEPERS: Employment expected to increase at slower rate than average because of increasing automation in recordkeeping.

CASHIERS: Because of very high turnover and average employment growth in response to increased retail sales, thousands of job openings for cashiers expected annually. However, future growth could slow with widespread adoption of automated checkout systems.

COLLECTION WORKERS: Employment expected to grow faster than average as continued expanded use of credit results in increasing numbers of delinquent accounts.

FILE CLERKS: Increased demand for recordkeeping should result in some job openings. However, employment is not expected to grow as fast as in past years due to increasing use of computers.

OFFICE MACHINE OPERATORS: Employment expected to grow more slowly than average as result of more centralized and computerized recordkeeping and processing systems.

POSTAL CLERKS: Employment expected to change little due to modernization of post offices and installation of new equipment which will increase efficiency of clerks.

RECEPTIONISTS: Employment expected to grow faster than average due to expansion of firms providing business, personal, and professional services.

SECRETARIES AND STENOGRAPHERS: The increasing use of dictating machines will limit opportunities for office stenographers. Very good prospects for skilled shorthand reporters and secretaries.

SHIPPING CLERKS: Employment expected to grow about as fast as average as business expansion results in increased distribution of goods.

STATISTICAL CLERKS: Employment expected to grow about as fast as average as numerical data increasingly are used to analyze and control activities in business and government.

STOCK CLERKS: Employment expected to grow about as fast as average as business firms continue to expand.

TYPISTS: Employment expected to grow faster than average as business expansion results in increased paperwork. Very good opportunities, particularly for those familiar with new kinds of word processing equipment.

Computer and related occupations.

COMPUTER OPERATORS: Employment of keypunch operators expected to decline because of advances in data-entry techniques and equipment. Employment of console and auxiliary equipment operators should grow about as fast as average due to expanding use of computers.

PROGRAMMERS: Employment expected to grow faster than average as computer use expands, particularly in accounting and business management firms.

SYSTEMS ANALYSTS: Employment expected to grow faster than average in response to advances in hardware and computer programs resulting in expanded computer applications.

Banking occupations.

BANK CLERKS: Excellent employment opportunities due to large replacement needs and faster than average growth as banking services expand. Best prospects for those trained in computer techniques.

BANK OFFICERS: Employment expected to grow faster than average as increasing use of computers and expansion of banking services require more officers to provide sound management.

BANK TELLERS: Good employment opportunities due to large replacement needs and faster than average employment growth as banking services expand.

Insurance occupations.

ACTUARIES: Employment expected to rise faster than average due to increased volume of insurance sales.

CLAIM REPRESENTATIVES: Employment expected to grow about as fast as average in response to expanding insurance sales and claims.

INSURANCE AGENTS, BROKERS, AND UNDERWRITERS: Employment expected to increase about as fast as average as insurance sales continue to expand. Selling expected to remain competitive, but ambitious people who enjoy sales work will find favorable opportunities as agents and brokers.

Administrative and related occupations.

ACCOUNTANTS: Very good opportunities because of growing complexity of business accounting requirements.

ADVERTISING WORKERS: Employment expected to increase faster than average. Best opportunities in retail advertising.

BUYERS: Slower than average employment growth expected as chain stores increasingly depend on centralized buying.

COLLEGE STUDENT PERSONNEL WORKERS: Tightening budgets in both public and private colleges and universities will limit employment growth.

CREDIT MANAGERS: Employment expected to increase faster than average due to expanded use of credit by both businesses and consumers.

HOTEL MANAGERS AND ASSISTANTS: Employment expected to grow more slowly than average, although additional hotels and motels are being built.

LAWYERS: Employment expected to grow faster than average as a result of increased business activity and population. However, continued increase in number of law school graduates is expected to create keen competition for salaried positions. Prospects best in small towns and expanding suburban areas.

MARKETING RESEARCH: Employment expected to grow much faster than average as marketing activities are stimulated by demand for new products and services.

PERSONNEL: Employment expected to increase faster than average as employers implement new employee relations programs in areas of occupational safety and health, equal employment opportunity, and pensions.

PUBLIC RELATIONS: Employment expected to increase faster than average as organizations expand their public relations efforts. Competition for jobs, however, is likely to be great.

PURCHASING AGENTS: Employment expected to increase faster than average. Strongest demand for those with graduate degrees in purchasing management.

URBAN PLANNERS: Employment expected to grow faster than average in response to need for quality housing, transportation systems, health care, and other social services.

SERVICE OCCUPATIONS

Cleaning and related occupations.

BUILDING CUSTODIANS: Employment expected to grow about as fast as average as construction of office buildings, schools, and hospitals increases demand for maintenance services.

HOTEL HOUSEKEEPERS: Employment expected to grow more slowly than average, but competition is likely to be keen.

PEST CONTROLLERS: Employment expected to grow faster than average because pests reproduce rapidly and tend to develop resistance to pesticides.

Food service occupations

BARTENDERS: Employment expected to increase about as fast as average as many new restaurants, hotels, and bars open.

COOKS AND CHEFS: Employment expected to increase faster than average. Most starting jobs in small restaurants serving simple food.

DINING ROOM ATTENDANTS AND DISHWASHERS: Favorable opportunities due to average employment growth and high replacement needs, particularly for part-time workers.

FOOD COUNTER WORKERS: Favorable opportunities due to average employment growth and high replacement needs, particularly for part-time workers.

WAITERS AND WAITRESSES: Favorable opportunities due to average employment growth and very high replacement needs, particularly for part-time workers.

Personal service occupations.

BARBERS: Employment expected to change little with most openings resulting from replacement needs. Better opportunities for hairstylists.

COSMETOLOGISTS: Employment expected to grow about as fast as average. Good opportunities for both newcomers and experienced cosmetologists.

FUNERAL DIRECTORS: Employment expected to change little.

HOUSEHOLD WORKERS: Despite expected decline in employment, demand is likely to exceed supply.

Protective and related service occupations.

CONSTRUCTION INSPECTORS (GOVERNMENT): Employment expected to increase faster than average. Best opportunities for those with college education and knowledge of specialized type of construction.

FIREFIGHTERS: Employment expected to increase about as fast as average in response to growing need for fire protection and replacement of volunteer fire companies.

GUARDS: Employment expected to grow faster than average due to increased concern over crime and vandalism. Opportunities are best in guard and security agencies and in night-shift jobs.

HEALTH INSPECTORS: Employment expected to increase faster than average in response to public concern for improved quality and safety of consumer products. Employment of health inspectors expected to grow more rapidly than that of regulatory inspectors.

OCCUPATIONAL SAFETY WORKERS: Employment expected to increase faster than average as growing concern for occupational safety and health and consumer safety continues to generate programs and jobs.

POLICE OFFICERS: Employment expected to rise faster than average as law enforcement becomes a higher priority. Good prospects for those with college training in law enforcement.

Other service occupations.

MAIL CARRIERS: Employment expected to change little due to cutbacks in mail delivery, but several thousand openings annually will result from replacement needs.

TELEPHONE OPERATORS: Employment expected to decline due to increased direct dialing and technological improvements.

EDUCATION AND RELATED OCCUPATIONS

Teaching occupations.
COLLEGE TEACHERS: Applicants expected to face keen competition. Number of new master's and Ph.D. degree recipients expected to more than meet the demand for college and university teachers. Best prospects in public colleges and universities.
KINDERGARTEN AND ELEMENTARY TEACHERS: Number of persons qualified to teach in elementary schools will exceed number of openings.
SECONDARY SCHOOL TEACHERS: Supply of teachers expected to exceed demand. Teacher supply is least adequate in mathematics, natural and physical sciences, and some vocational-technical subjects.

Library occupations.
LIBRARIANS: Applicants are likely to face competition for choice positions.
LIBRARY ASSISTANTS: Employment expected to grow faster than average. Best opportunities in large public and college and university libraries.

SALES OCCUPATIONS

AUTOMOBILE PARTS: Employment expected to increase faster than average as more parts will be needed to repair growing number of motor vehicles.
AUTOMOBILE SALESWORKERS: Employment expected to grow as demand for automobiles increases. However, employment may fluctuate from year to year because car sales are highly sensitive to economic conditions.
GASOLINE STATION ATTENDANTS: Employment expected to grow over next few years, although trends toward cars with improved gas mileage and self-service gas stations might limit growth.
MANUFACTURERS' SALESWORKERS: Employment expected to increase about as fast as average because of growing demand for technical products and resulting need for trained sales workers.
MODELS: Employment expected to grow faster than average, but glamour of modeling attracts many more persons than needed.
REAL ESTATE: Employment expected to increase faster than average in response to growing demand for housing and other properties.
RETAIL SALESWORKERS: Employment expected to grow about as fast as average as volume of sales rises and stores continue to remain open longer.
ROUTE DRIVERS. Employment expected to change little.
SECURITIES SALESWORKERS: Employment expected to grow about as fast as average as investment in securities continues to increase.
WHOLESALE SALESWORKERS: Employment expected to grow about as fast as average as wholesalers sell wider variety of products and improve services to their customers.

CONSTRUCTION OCCUPATIONS

ASBESTOS AND INSULATION: Employment expected to grow much faster than average in response to increased construction activity and need for energy-saving insulation.
BRICKLAYERS: Employment expected to grow about as fast as average in response to increased construction activity and expanding use of brick for decorative work.
CARPENTERS: Plentiful opportunities over long run resulting from high replacement needs and increased construction activity.
CEMENT MASONS: Favorable opportunities due to faster than average employment

growth in response to increased construction activity and greater use of concrete.

CONSTRUCTION WORKERS: Employment expected to grow about as fast as average due to increasing construction work.

DRYWALL INSTALLERS: Employment expected to grow faster than average due to increasing use of drywall in place of plaster.

ELECTRICIANS (CONSTRUCTION): Employment expected to increase faster than average as more electrical fixtures and wiring will be needed in homes, offices, and other buildings.

ELEVATOR CONSTRUCTORS: Employment expected to increase faster than average due to growth in number of high rise apartment and commercial buildings.

FLOOR COVERING INSTALLERS: Employment expected to increase about as fast as average due to more widespread use of resilient floor coverings and carpeting.

OPERATING ENGINEERS: Employment expected to grow much faster than average due to increased activity in construction, highway maintenance, and movement of materials in factories and mines.

PAINTERS: Employment of painters expected to grow about as fast as average due to growing need to paint new structures and repaint old ones.

PLASTERERS: Employment expected to change little as drywall materials are increasingly used in place of plaster.

PLUMBERS: Employment expected to grow faster than average due to increased construction activity and growth in areas which use extensive pipework.

ROOFERS: Employment expected to increase faster than average due to increases in construction activity, roof repairs, and waterproofing.

SHEET-METAL WORKERS: Employment expected to increase about as fast as average due to need for air-conditioning and heating ducts and other sheet-metal products in homes, stores, offices, and other buildings.

OCCUPATIONS IN TRANSPORTATION ACTIVITIES

Air transportation occupations

AIR TRAFFIC CONTROLLERS: Employment expected to grow faster than average as number of aircraft increases, but applicants may face keen competition.

AIRPLANE MECHANICS: Employment expected to increase faster than average. Good opportunities in general aviation and federal government.

AIRPLANE PILOTS: Employment expected to grow faster than average but applicants likely to face keen competition.

FLIGHT ATTENDANTS: Employment expected to grow faster than average as number of airline passengers increases.

TICKET AGENTS: Employment expected to grow faster than average due to anticipated increase in airline passengers.

Railroad occupations.

CONDUCTORS: Employment expected to grow more slowly than average as a result of technological innovations which increase efficiency of freight movement.

STATION AGENTS: Employment expected to decline as more customer orders and billing are handled by centrally located stations and as smaller stations are serviced by mobile agents.

TRACK WORKERS: Employment expected to change little due to increased productivity of track workers and installation of improved train control systems requiring less track.

Driving occupations.

INTERCITY BUSDRIVERS: Employment expected to grow about as fast as average due to moderate increase in bus travel.

LOCAL TRANSIT BUSDRIVERS: Employment expected to grow about as fast as average due to improved local bus service in many cities.

LOCAL TRUCKDRIVERS: Employment expected to increase faster than average as a result of growth in the amount of freight to be distributed.

LONG DISTANCE TRUCKDRIVERS: Employment expected to grow more slowly than average as result of increased efficiency of freight movement.

PARKING ATTENDANTS: Employment expected to grow more slowly than average as trend to self-parking systems continues.

TAXICAB DRIVERS: Employment expected to change little, but applicants should find good opportunities due to high replacement needs.

SCIENTIFIC AND TECHNICAL OCCUPATIONS

Conservation occupations.

FORESTERS: Employment expected to grow about as fast as average. However, number of forestry graduates each year expected to exceed number of annual openings.

RANGE MANAGERS: Good employment opportunities expected. Demand stimulated by need to increase output of rangelands while protecting ecological balance.

Engineering occupations.

AEROSPACE ENGINEERS: Employment, largely dependent upon Federal expenditures on defense and space programs, expected to grow more slowly than average. Expenditures expected to increase by mid-1980s.

AGRICULTURAL ENGINEERS: Employment expected to grow faster than average in response to increasing demand for agricultural products, modernization of farm operations and increasing emphasis on conservation of resources.

BIOMEDICAL ENGINEERS: Employment expected to grow faster than average, but actual number of openings not likely to be very large.

CHEMICAL ENGINEERS: Employment expected to grow about as fast as average. Additional engineers will be needed to design, build, and maintain plants and equipment due to growing complexity and automation of chemical processes.

CIVIL ENGINEERS: Employment expected to increase about as fast as average as a result of growing needs for housing, industrial buildings, electric power generating plants, transportation systems, environmental pollution programs.

ELECTRICAL ENGINEERS: Employment expected to increase about as fast as average. Growing demand for computers, communications and electric power generating equipment, military and consumer electronic goods, and increased research and development.

INDUSTRIAL ENGINEERS: Employment expected to grow faster than average due to industry growth, increasing complexity of industrial operations, expansion of automated processes, and greater emphasis on scientific management and safety.

MECHANICAL ENGINEERS: Employment expected to increase about as fast as average resulting from growing demand for industrial machinery and machine tools and increasing complexity of industrial machinery and processes.

METALLURGICAL ENGINEERS: Employment expected to grow faster than average due to need to develop new metals and alloys, adapt current ones to new needs, solve problems associated with efficient use of nuclear energy, and develop new ways of recycling solid waste materials.

MINING ENGINEERS: Employment will grow, spurred by efforts to attain energy self-sufficiency and resulting increase in demand for coal, development of more advanced mining systems, and further enforcement of mine health and safety regulations.

PETROLEUM ENGINEERS: Employment expected to increase faster than average. Efforts to attain energy self-sufficiency will result in growing demand for petroleum and natural gas and will require increasingly sophisticated recovery methods.

Environmental science occupations.

GEOLOGISTS: Employment expected to increase faster than average because of demand for petroleum and minerals.

GEOPHYSICISTS: Employment expected to grow faster than average as petroleum and mining companies need additional geophysicists for increased exploration activities.

METEOROLOGISTS: Favorable opportunities in industry, weather consulting firms, radio and television, government, and colleges and universities.

OCEANOGRAPHERS: Those with Ph.D. degrees should have favorable opportunities.

Life science occupations.

BIOCHEMISTS: Employment expected to grow about as fast as average due to increased funds for research and development. Opportunities are best for advanced degree holders.

LIFE SCIENTISTS: Good opportunities for those with advanced degrees due to increased activities in medical research and environmental protection.

Mathematics occupations.

MATHEMATICIANS: Keen competition expected, particularly for those seeking teaching positions in colleges and universities. Best opportunities are for those seeking employment in government and private industry.

STATISTICIANS: Employment expected to grow faster than average due to increasing use of statistical techniques in business and government.

Physical science occupations.

ASTRONOMERS: Employment expected to grow more slowly than average because funds available for basic research in astronomy not expected to increase enough to create many new positions.

CHEMISTS: Good opportunities for graduates at all degree levels. Increased demand for plastics, manmade fibers, drugs, and fertilizers in addition to activities in health care, pollution control and energy will contribute to need for chemists.

FOOD SCIENTISTS: Favorable opportunities, particularly for those with advanced degrees, in research and product development. Increased demand for food scientists in quality control and production.

PHYSICISTS: Good employment opportunities overall, but keen competition for teaching positions in colleges and universities.

Other scientific and technical occupations.

BROADCAST TECHNICIANS: Employment expected to increase about average as new radio and television stations go on air, and cable television stations broadcast more of their own programs.

DRAFTERS: Employment expected to increase faster than average as more drafters will be needed to support growing number of scientists and engineers. Also, increasingly complex design problems require additional drafters.

SCIENCE TECHNICIANS: Employment expected to grow faster than average as result of industrial expansion and increasingly important role of technicians in research and development.

SURVEYORS: Employment expected to increase faster than average in response to rapid development of urban areas.

MECHANIC AND REPAIRER OCCUPATIONS

Telephone craft occupations.

CENTRAL OFFICE EQUIPMENT INSTALLERS: Employment expected to increase about average because of need to install equipment in new telephone central offices.

LINE INSTALLERS: Employment expected to change little due to laborsaving technological developments.

WORKERS' COMPENSATION LAWS
By State, 1979

State	Maximum Weekly Benefits If Injuries Are			Waiting Period (Number of Days)		Maximum Burial Allowance
	Tem-porary	Perma-nent	Fatal (Spouse and children)	No benefit payment for first	Unless time off exceeds	
Alabama	$128	$128	$128	3	21	$1,000
Alaska	654	654	654	3	28	1,000
Arizona	192	192	192	7	14	1,000
Arkansas	87	87	87	7	14	750
California	154	154	154	3	21	1,000
Colorado	175	175	175	7	21	500
Connecticut	204	204	204	3	7	1,500
Delaware	154	154	154	3	7	700
Dist. of Colum.	396	396	396	3	14	1,000
Florida	130	130	130	7	14	500
Georgia	110	110	110	7	28	750
Hawaii	200	200	200	2	5	1,500
Idaho	173	173	173	5	14	1,500
Illinois	329	329	329	3	14	1,750
Indiana	120	120	120	7	21	1,500
Iowa	265	265	265	3	14	1,000
Kansas	129	129	129	7	21	2,000
Kentucky	121	121	121	7	14	1,500
Louisiana	141	141	141	7	42	1,500
Maine	231	231	231	3	14	1,000
Maryland	220	220	220	3	14	1,000
Massachusetts	211	211	211	3	14	1,200
Michigan	185	185	185	7	14	1,500
Minnesota	209	209	209	3	10	1,000
Mississippi	91	91	91	5	14	1,000
Missouri	115	115	115	3	28	2,000
Montana	188	188	188	7	7	1,100
Nebraska	155	155	155	7	42	1,000
Nevada	211	211	211	5	5	1,200
New Hampshire	180	180	180	3	7	1,000
New Jersey*	156	156	156	7	7	750
New Mexico	186	186	186	7	28	1,500
New York	215	215	215	7	14	1,250
North Carolina	178	178	178	7	28	500
North Dakota	180	180	75	5	5	1,000
Ohio	241	241	241	7	21	1,200
Oklahoma	132	90	90	5	5	1,000
Oregon	224	224	224	3	14	1,000
Pennsylvania	227	227	227	7	14	1,500
Rhode Island	176	176	176	7	14	1,800
South Carolina*	185	185	185	7	14	400
South Dakota	155	155	155	7	7	2,000
Tennessee	100	100	100	7	14	500
Texas*	105	105	105	7	28	1,250
Utah	197	167	167	3	14	1,000
Vermont	181	181	181	3	14	500
Virginia	187	187	187	7	21	1,000
Washington	163	163	163	3	13	1,000
West Virginia	224	224	224	3	7	1,500
Wisconsin	218	218	218	3	7	1,000
Wyoming	211	140	140	3	8	1,100

*Compensation laws are not compulsory in these states
Source: Alliance of American Insurers.

TELEPHONE AND PBX INSTALLERS AND REPAIRERS: Demand for telephones and private branch exchange (PBX) and central exchange (CENTREX) systems will result in employment growth about as fast as average.

Other mechanic and repairer occupations.

AIR-CONDITIONING, REFRIGERATION, AND HEATING MECHANICS: Employment expected to increase much faster than average. Most openings for air-conditioning and refrigeration mechanics.

APPLIANCE REPAIRERS: Employment expected to grow about as fast as average.

AUTOMOBILE BODY REPAIRERS: Employment expected to increase about average as result of rising number of vehicles damaged in traffic accidents.

AUTOMOBILE MECHANICS: Employment expected to grow about average as more automobiles will be equipped with pollution control devices, air-conditioning, and other features that increase maintenance requirements.

BUSINESS MACHINE REPAIRERS: Employment expected to grow faster than average. Opportunities particularly favorable for those with training in electronics.

COMPUTER TECHNICIANS: Employment expected to grow much faster than average due to increased use of computers.

DIESEL MECHANICS: Employment expected to grow faster than average due to expansion of industries which are major users of diesel engines and continued replacement of gasoline engines by diesel engines.

FARM EQUIPMENT MECHANICS: Employment expected to grow about as fast as average as increase in size and complexity of farm equipment will lead to more maintenance requirements.

INDUSTRIAL MACHINERY REPAIRERS: Employment expected to increase much faster than average because of the growing amount of complex factory machinery requiring maintenance and repair.

INSTRUMENT REPAIRERS: Employment expected to increase about as fast as average because of anticipated increased use of instruments for energy conservation and exploration, air and water pollution monitoring, and medical diagnosis.

JEWELERS: Employment expected to grow more slowly than average as jewelry factories, with their improved production methods, are able to meet the increased demand for jewelry.

LOCKSMITHS: Employment expected to grow faster than average as result of more security conscious public.

MAINTENANCE ELECTRICIANS: Employment expected to grow about as fast as average due to increased use of electrical and electronic equipment by industry.

PIANO AND ORGAN TUNERS AND REPAIRERS: Employment expected to change little.

SHOE REPAIRERS: Opportunities best for experienced repairers who can open their own shops.

TELEVISION AND RADIO TECHNICIANS: Employment expected to increase faster than average in response to growing number of radios, television sets, phonographs, tape recorders, and other home entertainment products.

TRUCK AND BUS MECHANICS: Employment of truck mechanics expected to grow about as fast as average but employment of bus mechanics to grow more slowly than average.

VENDING MACHINE MECHANICS: Slower than average employment increase.

HEALTH OCCUPATIONS

Dental occupations.

DENTAL ASSISTANTS: Employment expected to grow much faster than average. Excellent opportunities, especially for graduates of approved programs.

DENTAL HYGIENISTS: Employment expected to grow much faster than average in response to increasing use of hygienists by dentists.

DENTAL LABORATORY TECHNICIANS: Employment expected to grow faster than average in response to increasing demand for dentures.

DENTISTS: Employment expected to grow about as fast as average due to population growth and increased awareness of importance of dental care.

Medical Practitioners.

CHIROPRACTORS: Employment may be difficult due to increasing number of graduates. Best opportunities in small towns and areas with few practitioners.

OPTOMETRISTS: Employment expected to grow about as fast as average.

PHYSICIANS: Very good employment outlook. Particular demand in primary care areas such as general practice, pediatrics, and internal medicine, especially in rural areas.

VETERINARIANS: Favorable employment opportunities as result of growth in pet population.

Medical technologist, technician, and assistant occupations.

ELECTROCARDIOGRAPHIC TECHNICIANS: Employment expected to increase faster than average because of growing reliance on electrocardiograms in diagnosis and physical examinations.

MEDICAL ASSISTANTS: Employment expected to increase faster than average in response to growth of number of physicians. Excellent opportunities, particularly for graduates of accredited junior college programs.

MEDICAL LABORATORY WORKERS: Employment expected to increase faster than average. However, applicants may face competition for choice positions.

MEDICAL RECORD TECHNICIAN: Very good outlook for clerks. Favorable prospects for technicians with at least associate degree.

OPERATING ROOM TECHNICIANS: Employment expected to grow faster than average as technicians increasingly assume more tasks in operating room.

OPTOMETRIC ASSISTANTS: Employment expected to grow much faster than average.

X-RAY TECHNOLOGISTS: Despite faster than average employment growth, even graduates of AMA-approved programs may face competition for choice positions.

Nursing occupations.

LICENSED PRACTICAL NURSES: Very good opportunities as public and private health insurance plans expand and as LPN's assume duties previously performed by registered nurses.

NEW MINIMUM WAGE RATES

A federal law signed in November, 1977, set a uniform minimum wage scale for almost all workers. Previously, separate minimums existed for farm workers and for other types of workers.

The law set the minimum hourly wage at $2.90 on January 1, 1979; $3.10 on January 1, 1980; and $3.35 on January 1, 1981.

Federal law requires overtime work to be paid at 1½ times the regular rate for all hours worked over 40 hours in one work week.

Learners, apprentices and handicapped workers may, under certain circumstances, be paid less than the minimum wage. The same is true for full-time students in retail or service jobs, agriculture or institutions of higher education. Special certificates issued by the Department of Labor, Wage and Hour Administrator, must be obtained by employers wishing to use these provisions.

State wage laws can supercede federal laws if the state has a higher standard. For further information, contact the Wage and Hour Division of the U.S. Department of Labor, Employment Standards Administration, or your state employment division.

UNEMPLOYMENT INSURANCE BENEFITS
By State, January, 1979

State	Weekly Benefits Average Payment	Legal Minimum	Legal Maximum	Duration of Benefits (weeks) Legal Range	1978 Average
Alabama	$ 68,04	$15	$ 90	11-26	10.3
Alaska	84.45	18-28	90-120	14-28	19.6
Arizona	72.92	15	85	12-26	12.7
Arkansas	68.81	15	100	10-26	10.3
California	74.83	30	104	12-26	12.5
Colorado	90.50	25	130	7-26	11.2
Connecticut	84.58	15-20	128-92	26-26	10.8
Delaware	90.56	20	150	17-26	13.8
D.C.	106.09	13-14	172	17-34	19.5
Florida	82.42	10	82	10-26	12.7
Georgia	70.07	27	90	9-26	8.6
Hawaii	89.51	5	134	26-26	16.0
Idaho	80.84	17	116	10-26	10.0
Illinois	96.86	15	121-145	26-26	17.7
Indiana	74.49	35	74-124	4-26	9.9
Iowa	100.91	20	133	10-39	13.5
Kansas	83.05	29	116	10-26	12.3
Kentucky	75.86	12	111	15-26	11.4
Louisiana	91.01	10	141	12-28	14.7
Maine	68.98	12-17	90-135	11-26	10.5
Maryland	74.89	10-13	106	26-26	12.2
Massachusetts	81.31	12-18	122-183	9-30	14.9
Michigan	91.61	16-18	97-136	11-26	10.8
Minnesota	95.17	18	133	13-26	13.7
Mississippi	59.57	10	80	12-26	11.3
Missouri	71.56	15	85	8-26	10.7
Montana	81.16	12	113	12-26	12.3
Nebraska	77.04	12	90	17-26	10.5
Nevada	81.81	16	107	11-26	12.1
New Hampshire	69.63	21	102	26-26	6.9
New Jersey	86.19	20	117	15-26	17.8
New Mexico	68.20	20	98	18-30	15.3
New York	79.84	25	125	26-26	19.5
North Carolina	67.40	15	119	13-26	9.3
North Dakota	86.92	15	121	18-26	13.8
Ohio	98.69	10-16	120-189	20-26	13.5
Oklahoma	74.67	16	116	10-26	11.4
Oregon	80.37	33	119	9-26	13.0
Pennsylvania	91.86	13-18	152-160	30-30	14.2
Rhode Island	74.25	26-31	110-130	12-26	9.2
South Carolina	72.20	10	111	10-26	11.2
South Dakota	74.33	19	102	10-26	10.7
Tennessee	63.77	14	95	12-26	11.7
Texas	66.99	16	91	9-26	12.6
Utah	87.12	10	128	10-22	11.8
Vermont	73.35	18	109	26-26	13.7
Virginia	81.92	38	115	12-26	11.7
Washington	83.52	17	128	8-30	13.8
West Virginia	73.67	18	149	26-26	10.6
Wisconsin	92.94	27	145	1-34	11.6
Wyoming	86.50	24	121	11-26	10.3

Source: U.S. Department of Labor, 1979.

NURSING AIDS: Employment expected to increase faster than average, with many new openings in nursing homes, convalescent homes and other long term care facilities.

REGISTERED NURSES: Favorable opportunities, especially for nurses with graduate education seeking positions as teachers and administrators. Strong demand in some southern states and inner-city locations.

Therapy and rehabilitation occupations.

OCCUPATIONAL THERAPISTS: Employment expected to grow much faster than average due to public interest in rehabilitation of disabled persons and success of established occupational therapy programs.

PHYSICAL THERAPISTS: Employment expected to grow faster than average due to expansion of rehabilitation programs and facilities, particularly in suburban and rural areas.

SPEECH PATHOLOGISTS AND AUDIOLOGISTS: Employment expected to increase faster than average.

Other health occupations.

DIETICIANS: Employment expected to grow increasing demand for expertise in fields of nutrition and food management.

DISPENSING OPTICIANS: Employment expected to increase faster than average in response to growing demand for prescription lenses.

HEALTH SERVICE ADMINISTRATORS: Employment expected to grow much faster than average as quality and quantity of patient services increase and hospital management becomes more complex.

PHARMACISTS: Very good outlook as number of job openings expected to exceed number of pharmacy school graduates.

SOCIAL SCIENCE OCCUPATIONS

ECONOMISTS: Economists with master's and Ph.D. degrees may face keen competition for positions in colleges and universities but may find good opportunities in private industry and government.

GEOGRAPHERS: Favorable employment opportunities for Ph.D.'s in the nonacademic job market.

POLITICAL SCIENTISTS: Ph.D.'s and master's degree holders may face very keen competition for teaching positions, but those with specialized training may find jobs in government and industry.

PSYCHOLOGISTS: Employment expected to grow faster than average. Ph.D's likely to face increasing competition, particularly for teaching positions. Best opportunities are for those trained in clinical counseling and industrial psychology.

SOCIOLOGISTS: Sociologists well trained in research methods, advance statistics, and use of computers are expected to have widest choice of jobs.

SOCIAL SERVICE OCCUPATIONS

Counseling occupations.

COLLEGE CAREER COUNSELORS: Favorable prospects for well-qualified workers.

EMPLOYMENT COUNSELORS: Those with master's degrees or experience in related fields are expected to have competition in both public and private employment agencies.

REHABILITATION COUNSELORS: Employment growth dependent upon government funding to rehabilitation agencies. Favorable prospects for those with graduate work in rehabilitation counseling or related fields.

SCHOOL COUNSELORS: Employment expected to increase more slowly than average due to expected decline in school enrollments coupled with financial constraints.

STATE MINIMUM WATE RATES
(Non-agricultural employment, February, 1979)

State	Min. Wage. Per Hour	Future Increases
Alabama	none	
Alaska	$3.40	$3.60 (1/1/80)
Arizona	none	
Arkansas	2.30	2.55 (1/1/80); 2.70 (1/1/81)
California	2.90	
Colorado	1.90	
Connecticut	2.91	3.12 (1/1/80);3.37 (1/1/81)
Delaware	2.00	
D.C.	(1)	
Florida	none	
Georgia	1.25	
Hawaii	2.65	2.90 (7/1/79); 3.10 (7/1/80)
Idaho	2.30	
Illinois	2.30	
Indiana	2.00	2.15 (7/1/79)
Iowa	none	
Kansas	1.60	
Kentucky	2.00	
Louisiana	none	
Maine	2.90	3.10 (1/1/80); 3.35 (1/1/81)
Maryland	2.90	3.10 (1/1/80); 3.35 (1/1/81)
Massachusetts	2.90	3.10 (1'/1/80); 3.35 (1/1/81)
Michigan	2.90	
Minnesota	2.30	
Mississippi	none	
Missouri	none	
Montana	2.00	
Nebraska	1.60	
Nevada	2.75	
New Hampshire	2.90	3.10 (1/1/80); 3.35 (1/1/81)
New Jersey	2.50	2.90 (3/1/79); 3.10 (1/1/80)
New Mexico	2.30	2.65 (7/1/79); 2.90 (1/1/80); 2.35 (1/1/81)
New York	2.90	3.10 (1/1/80); 3.35 (1/1/81)
North Carolina	2.50	
North Dakota	2.10-2.30	2.55-2.90 (7/1/79); 2.60-3.10 (1/1/80); 2.80-3.10 (7/1/80)
Ohio	2.30	
Oklahoma	2.00	
Oregon	2.30	
Pennsylvania	2.90	3.10 (1/1/80); 3.35 (1/1/81)
Rhode Island	2.30	
South Carolina	none	
South Dakota	2.30	
Tennessee	none	
Texas	1.40	
Utah	2.45(2)	2.60 (1/1/80); 2.75 (1/1/81)
Vermont	2.90	3.10 (1/1/80); 3.35 (1/1/81)
Virginia	2.35	
Washington	2.30	
West Virginia	2.20	
Wisconsin	2.80	3.00 (1/1/80); 3.25 (1/1/81)
Wyoming	1.60	

(1) Minimum rates differ by occupation: Beauticians: $2.50; manufacturing, printing trades: $3.50; laundry and dry cleaning: $3.00; hotel, restaurant employees: $2.80; clerical: $2.90; building service $2.70. (2) Applies to Salt Lake, Weber, Utah and Davis Counties and cities outside these counties with population of 5,000 or more; all other areas: $2.20; 2.35 (1/1/80); 2.50 (1/1/81).
Source. U.S. Department of Labor, Employment Standards Administration.

Other social service occupations.

HOME ECONOMISTS: Although employment is expected to grow more slowly than average, many jobs will become available due to replacement needs.

SOCIAL SERVICE AIDES: Employment expected to grow faster than average as social welfare programs expand. Good opportunities for part-time work.

ART, DESIGN, AND COMMUNICATIONS-RELATED OCCUPATIONS

Performing artists.

ACTORS AND ACTRESSES: Overcrowding in field expected to persist.

DANCERS: Those seeking professional careers likely to face keen competition despite expected average rate of employment growth.

MUSICIANS: Better prospects for those qualified as teachers as well as musicians than for those qualified as performers only.

Design occupations.

ARCHITECTS: Employment expected to increase about as fast as average result of growth of nonresidential construction. Most openings will be in architectural firms.

COMMERCIAL ARTISTS: Talented and well-trained commercial artists may face competition for employment and advancement in most kinds of work. However, artists are needed in areas of visual advertising, such as television graphics and packaging displays, and industrial design.

DISPLAY WORKERS: Employment expected to grow more slowly than average.

INDUSTRIAL DESIGNERS: Employment expected to grow slower than average as the trend away from frequent redesign of household products, automobiles and industrial equipment continues.

INTERIOR DESIGNERS: Best opportunities for talented college graduates who majored in interior design and graduates of professional schools of interior design. Increasing use of design services in businesses and homes is expected to cause employment to grow about as fast as average.

Source: *Occupational Outlook Handbook, 1978-79 edition.*

FEDERAL CHILD LABOR LAW IN NONFARM JOBS

The Fair Labor Standards Act of 1938 requires the following minimum ages for employment:

● **18 years old** for any job at any time for unlimited hours in any occupation declared hazardous by the Secretary of Labor.

● **16 years old** for any job except those declared hazardous by the Secretary of Labor.

● **14 and 15 years old** for various nonmanufacturing, nonmining, nonhazardous jobs under the following conditions: No more than three hours a school day, 18 hours a school week, eight hours a nonschool day or 40 hours a nonschool week. May not work before 7 a.m. or after 7 p.m., except from June 1 to Labor Day, when evening hours are extended until 9 p.m.

● **Any age** for youths who deliver newspapers; act or perform in television, movies, radio, and theatrical productions; work for parents in their solely owned nonfarm business (except in manufacturing, mining and hazardous jobs) gather evergreens and make evergreen wreaths.

Minors younger than 18 may not work in nonfarm jobs declared hazardous by the Secretary of Labor.

Most young workers must be paid at least the minimum wage and overtime pay. Some youths, such as full-time students, student learners and apprentices, may be paid less than the minimum under special Department-issued certificates.

OCCUPATIONAL HAZARDS
Employers Fighting to Stop Safety Programs

On April 27, 1978, a scaffold in Willow Island, West Virginia, fell 167 feet, plunging 51 workers to their death. It was the largest loss of life to occur in the United States from a work-related accident.

Many hazards faced by American workers are not as loud and clear, but they are just as tragic. The threat of cancer alone now faces untold millions of workers though relatively few are aware of the dangers involved. Some workers did not know they were handling carcinogenic substances until after vital parts of their bodies had been eaten away by cancer cells spawned by chemicals they had never suspected were lethal. Some cancers take 20 to 40 years to develop.

Many dangerous products are hidden under brand names. According to the National Institute for Occupational Safety and Health (NIOSH), from 7 to 15 million workers are being exposed to toxic substances known only by their brand names. By 1977, only about half of some 86,000 trade-name substances were identifiable, and about 20,000 were subject to regulation as work hazards. In 1978, NIOSH had made some progress by issuing seven *Current Intelligence Bulletins,* identifying previously unknown or unrecognized information on occupational hazards.

21 MILLION WORKERS EXPOSED

Altogether, an estimated 21 million American workers are believed to be exposed to serious hazards at work. That is roughly about one-fourth of the entire labor force in this country. Injuries range from cuts and sprains to fractures and amputations. Occupational illnesses—such as cancer, kidney and liver disease and urinary dysfunction—are caused by inhalation, absorption, ingestion or direct contact with toxic substances. And as a result of these injuries and illnesses, approximately 100,000 workers die each year.

President Carter appointed Eula Bingham, an industrial safety expert from the University of Cincinnati, as administrator of the Occupational Safety and Health Administration (OSHA) in 1977, to spur the organization into more action. Previously, OSHA had done little to implement the Occupational Safety and Health Act 1970 that set up the agency. Under her leadership, OSHA has increased efforts to control cancer-causing substances in the workplace and has issued and enforced more health standards. Actions included requiring employers to regularly measure the degree of hazard and conduct free medical exams for workers. Other OSHA actions included:

● Effective in March 1978, OSHA set the limit for exposure to benzene at five parts per millions (ppm) for any 15-minute period. The standard also prohibited eye or repeated skin contact with the leukemia-causing chemical. Although some 600,000 workers at 150,000 worksites are affected by the standard, a court ruling in 1979 knocked down the benzene standard because OSHA had failed to prove significant numbers of deaths from benzene exposure and because of the high economic impact on the companies involved. OSHA has appealed the ruling to the Supreme Court, arguing that it should not have to count the number of deaths or go beyond saying workers will die if exposed to more than five ppm of benzene.

● Effective in April 1978, OSHA limited exposure to dibromochloropropane (DBCP) to 50 parts per billion (ppb) for any 15-minute period. DBCP is a pesticide that has been associated with sterility among chemical plant workers. Tests showed that 28 of 79 workers at Occidental Chemical Co. in Lathrop, California, had low sperm counts and four had no sperm after an average of nine years' employment. Under the ruling, employers are required to conduct regular monitoring and provide protective equipment.

● In April, 1978, OSHA alerted 13 plastics manufacturing companies to the hazards of a chemical catalyst known as NIAX Catalyst ESN. Employers were told to notify workers of two reports of urinary dysfunction due to exposure to the chemical. One report found that urinary and other physiological and neurological dysfunctions had occurred among 69 of 101 workers at the William T. Burnett Company in Jessup, Md. Another report cited widespread employee complaints of bladder dysfunction at the Lear Siegler plant in Boston. Since there was no safe limit standard at the time, OSHA requested that all employees be removed from exposure to ESN.

● Effective in August, 1978, OSHA reduced permissible worker exposure to inorganic arsenic from 500 to 10 micrograms per cubic meter for any 15-minute period. The ruling affects employees in the non-ferrous metal smelting, glass and arsenical chemical industries. OSHA's economic impact study estimates that about 660,000 workers are involved in the commercial cycle of arsenic, but that only 12,000 are directly exposed at high levels. The standard was initiated after mortality studies showed excess respiratory and lymphoma cancer deaths among exposed workers.

● The fight against dangerous chemical exposure for workers in the asbestos industry was highlighted in 1979 by a $3 million suit filed by the estate for Ira H. Dishner, who died in 1978 of cancer caused by asbestos manufactured by the Johns-Mansville Corp. Dishner's attorney claims the company did not warn workers adequately about the hazards of asbestos. This case could effect about 40 others claiming more than $300 million.

Asbestos has long been known for its ability to cause lung cancer. Workers in construction and shipbuilding industries and auto mechanics who work on brake linings are regularly exposed to the substance. Yet, the asbestos industry has continuously tried to escape from its responsibility to improve work conditions. The industry has supported a bill that would establish a joint industry-federal fund to pay for the costs of asbestos lawsuits. Critics of the bill include Rep. George Miller (D-Calif.) who claims that federal tax money should not be used for this purpose and that it is up to the industry to provide the funds. Furthermore, he and Rep. Edward P. Beard (D-R.I.) contend that the asbestos manufacturers should turn to substitutes for their product wherever possible.

● Effective September, 1978, OSHA issued rules to reduce the hazard of "Brown Lung" among about 600,000 workers exposed to cotton dust. It is estimated by medical experts that more than 35,000 employed and retired textile workers are disabled by the disease. While the cotton industry has claimed OSHA's standards are too harsh, the textile workers union believes they are too weak. In February 1979, the union appealed the standard, claiming that the limit for yarn manufacturers of 200 micrograms of cotton dust per cubic meter of air is too low in view of scientific studies indicated that 13 percent of these workers suffer from Brown Lung disease at this level of dust. The union wants a 100-microgram level, and has also complained that the standard allows four-year delays in the implementation of engineering controls to reduce dust levels.

● Coal mining injuries and deaths are expected to increase substantially as utilities and industrial plants switch from oil and gas to coal for power. The government's Office of Technology Assessment predicted in 1979 that as many as 370 miners will die and 42,000 will be injured annually by the year 2000 if product triples as expected. Little improvement in injury or death rates has been apparent since passage of the Federal Coal Mine Health and Safety Act of 1969 following a disaster fatal to 78 miners at a Consolidated Coal Company mine the year before. New standards were set for dust levels as a result of the law, but the number of injuries per million hours worked has not changed since the 1950s. The main health problem is pneumoconiosis ("black lung"), but other lung problems are also associated with coal mining.

● The final standard for acrylonitrile, a substance long associated with lung and colon cancer, became effective in November, 1978. NIOSH estimates that 125,000 people are exposed to this chemical at work, mostly at plants of American Cyanamid Co. at Fortier, Louisiana and Linden, New Jersey; DuPont plants at Beaumont, Texas and Memphis, Tennessee; and Monsanto Co. plants in Chocolate Bayou, Texas and at Vistron Corp., a susidiary of Standard Oil Co. of Ohio, at its Lima, Ohio, plant. The standard limits average worker exposure to airborne acrylonitrile to two ppm and to 10 ppm for any 15-minute period.

● Effective in February 1979, OSHA lowered permissible exposure levels of inorganic lead from 200 to 50 micrograms of lead per cubic meter of air over an eight-hour day. Industries involved included lead smelting, manufacturing of lead storage batteries, ship-building, auto manufacturing and printing. They were given from one to three years to reach the final 50-microgram level. Studies have revealed that inhalation or ingestion of lead results in damage to the nervous, urinary and reproductive systems. There is evidence of miscarriage and stillbirth in pregnant women who were exposed to lead or whose husbands were exposed. Children born of exposed parents are also more likely to have birth defects and other abnormalities.

● In April, 1979, OSHA proposed safety regulations to protect 332,000 workers servicing potentially explosive truck, bus and trailer tires with multipiece wheel rims. Of 165 serious accidents reported to the Rubber Manufacturers Association from 1972 to 1975, 22 resulted in deaths and 103 in disabling injuries. OSHA's proposal includes the use of a cage or other restraining device to block the force from an explosive tire-rim separation, other tire servicing equipment, safe operating practices and employee training programs.

● The largest penalty in OSHA's history was ordered in April, 1979. The agency imposed a fine of $340,000 against the Berwick Forge and Fabricating Co. in Berwick, PA, for 273 alleged violations, ranging in seriousness.

OSHA FACING HAZARDS IN CONGRESS

While OSHA is trying to speed up progress, numerous businesses, politicians and organizations are attempting to dismantle the agency. From the beginning, it has been under persistent attack from business interests that either object to efforts to improve occupational safety or object to the large costs and paperwork involved in carrying out its regulations. Groups such as the "Committee to Stop Government Harassment of Business" want to wipe out job safety and health laws.

Each year, several in Congress introduce legislation to repeal OSHA laws. In addition, OSHA has to cope with numerous amendments to its regulations. In

May, 1979, Senator Frank Church (D-Idaho) introduced an amendment that would exempt businesses with ten or fewer workers from OSHA's jurisdiction. The International Association of Machinists and Aerospace Workers estimates that the amendment would exempt about 70 per cent of the business establishments presently covered under OSHA and drop more than 10 million American workers from OSHA's protection.

The General Accounting Office also has been critical. In May, 1979, it said OSHA was not making good use of its accident data collection system. "The industries in which 30 per cent of the fatalities occurred received less than 18 per cent of OSHA's self-initiated inspections," the report said, "and small workplaces received larger share of inspections than their proportion of serious accidents." The GAO also said OSHA inspections were not identifying many serious hazards.

LAW PROTECTS THOSE WHO COMPLAIN

The Occupational Safety and Health Act of 1970 applies to every employer of one or more persons except for workers covered by the Atomic Energy Act and Coal Mine Safety Act and most farmworkers. Employees have the right to file formal complaints directly with OSHA, an agency in the Labor Department, requesting inspection of their workplace. OSHA must comply with requests not to transmit names of complainants to employers. It is illegal for an employer to punish a worker who requests an inspection. Any worker who believes he or she has been discriminated against, discharged or demoted because of a request for inspection can file a complaint with OSHA within 30 days. If OSHA determines that the complaint is valid, the agency can take action against the employer.

Employees also have the right to be informed of OSHA actions. If OSHA decides not to conduct an inspection, the workers have a right to an informal review. They can request an informal conference to discuss the issues raised by an inspection and can become a formal party to proceedings between OSHA and employers. Although all employees have the right to receive information on safety and health hazards at work, they were previously exempt from access to the employer's log of job-related injuries and illnesses. In July, 1979, OSHA revised this ruling, allowing any worker access to the log. On the same day, OSHA proposed a rule that would require employers with medical records of toxic exposure to preserve and provide access to the records to all workers and OSHA and NIOSH officials. Access to these records would continue for five years after the duration of employment.

A federal law signed by President Carter in December, 1977, authorized NIOSH to notify workers who have been exposed to certain hazards on the job. The agency is permitted to obtain from the Internal Revenue Service names and addresses of workers affected. The bill was introduced by Senator Gaylord Nelson (D-Wisc.).

CANCER TOLL COMPARED BY JOB

The National Cancer Institute estimated in 1978 that about 20 per cent of all cancer deaths are from exposure of workers to chemicals on the job. The institute also calculated the number of workers exposed to carcinogens and the number of excess (above normal) cancer cases for each substance as well as the per cent of excess cases per occupation. Several industry groups, however, said the figures were unscientific.

Following are the Institute's figures:

WORKERS EXPOSED AND EXCESS CANCER CASES PER SUBSTANCE

Substances	Number of workers potentially exposed	Excess cancers yearly
Asbestos	8-11 million	67,000
Arsenic	about 1,500,000	2,100—7,300
Benzene	about 2,000,000	240—1,400
Coal tar pitch volatiles	about 60,000	160—800
Chromium	about 1,500,000	2,400—46,000
Iron oxide	about 1,600,000	1,300—5,000
Nickel	about 1,370,000	3,800—5,000
Petroleum distillates	about 3,000,000	2,400—12,000
Vinyl chloride	about 2,260,000	1,940

PER CENT OF EXCESS CANCER CASES PER OCCUPATION

Occupational group	Cancer site	Per cent excess
Coal miners	Stomach	40
Chemists	Pancreas, lymphomas	64
Foundry workers	Lung	50;150
Textile workers	Mouth and pharynx	77
Printing pressmen	Mouth and pharynx	125
Metal miners	Lung	200
Coke by-product workers	Large intestine, pancreas	181;312
Cadmium production workers	Lung, prostate	135;248
Lead workers	Lung	30
Rubber industry—processing	Stomach, leukemia	80,140
—tire building	Bladder, brain	88;90
—tire curing	Lung	61
Leather and shoe workers	Nasal cavity and sinuses, bladder	5000;150

Source: National Cancer Institute 1978.

FOR FURTHER INFORMATION

Job Safety and Health, free Consumer Information Leaflet No. USDL-3. Available from OSHA, Washington, DC, 20210.

Help for the Walking Wounded, by Thomas Mancuso, International Association of Machinists, 1300 Connecticut Ave., NW, Washington, DC, 20036.

Protection for Workers in Imminent Danger, booklet published by OSHA. U.S. Government Printing Office, Washington, DC, 20402, 40 cents.

OSHA: Your Workplace Rights in Action, (OSHA 3032) Free from OSHA, Washington, DC, 20210.

Banking and Borrowing

In This Chapter
- **Checking Accounts**
- **New Rates for Savers**
- **Aid for Credit Problems**
- **Rights of Credit Users**
- **Guide to Bankruptcy**

Soaring living costs have caused many Americans to borrow money or buy on credit beyond their means to pay. No longer is credit used only for necessary purchases. The power of advertising and peer pressure has pushed many people deeply into debt for non-essential things, such as vacations and extra cars and homes, as well as for essential things.

Credit has become so predominant that cash is no longer accepted for some transactions. Many people have discovered that a credit card is preferred to either cash or personal check even though the merchant must pay a fee for credit card services. Even applications for jobs ask for credit references. The ironic result is that the cash customer who once was considered the best credit risk is no longer considered a good one.

The increasing availability of credit has allowed many people to acquire products and services they would not otherwise have and to do so sooner. But it also has brought an increasing string of problems, some of which can hit very hard personally. Among the major developments in the field of personal finance are:

- **Electronic banking.** Automated teller windows are nearly everywhere. Virtually the only roadblock in the way of more rapid expansion has been restrictions on setting up remote banking terminals. The latest step toward a "cashless society" is the introduction of "debit cards," which look like credit cards but are used to deduct purchases and loans directly from savings or checking accounts instead of through monthly bills.

- **Higher yields for smaller savers.** The move to increase interest on savings certificates for small investors, similar to that earned by large savers, got rolling in 1979. The impetus came from the Gray Panthers, a senior citizens lobby, after a direct appeal to the Federal Reserve Board (Fed) found a sympathetic audience.

- **Interest-bearing checking accounts.** By 1979, many banks and savings and loan associations were offering some form of interest-bearing checking accounts. But the future of the plans was unexpectedly thrown into doubt when the Supreme Court ruled that the Fed had not followed proper procedures in approving transfers from savings to checking accounts. The Court ruled that if Congress did not approve the plans, they would all become illegal on January 1 1980.

● **Discounts for consumers who pay cash.** Although cash discounts are legal and seem logical, since merchants must pay a fee for credit card services, businesses have not rushed to offer them. The few which have include airlines and other scattered retail enterprises.

● **A new bankruptcy law.** Effective October 1, 1979, people who go bankrupt are able to keep more for themselves than they were allowed under the old law.

● **New types of mortgages.** In late 1978 and early 1979, government financial agencies approved several new types of home mortgages. One is the graduated mortgage, which allows payments to be stepped up (graduated) each year, beginning with lower than normal payments in the early years in order to help young people swing the large-size loans now required for purchasing houses.

Another new type is the Variable Rate Mortgage (VRM), which allows interest rates to be raised or lowered depending on market rates. Still another is the Reverse Annuity Mortgage (RAM). It allows a person with equity in a house to borrow from it in monthly payments over an extended period. It is designed for older people with considerable equity. Rules prevent the financial institution from selling the house to repay the loan. Refinancing is required when all the equity is gone. However, by late 1979, only a few institutions were offering RAMs since the program was so new.

CHECKING ACCOUNTS
It Pays to Shop Around

Among the changes consumers have won from the banking industry is increased disclosure of terms. Credit terms and savings accounts were the first targets of this movement; checking accounts became the next in 1979.

There are two basic issues: "free" checking accounts, some of which end up costing consumers plenty through hidden costs; and interest-bearing checking accounts, which vary widely in the way interest is calculated and the service charges are levied.

Banks make money from checking accounts, even "free" ones. They know that there will be a predictable amount of deposits and withdrawals on any given day. By figuring the total of all daily account balances, deposits and withdrawals, a banker can determine almost exactly how much "excess" money is available beyond that needed for daily transactions. The "excess" is loaned out at a profit from the interest charged.

But despite the profits they make from checking accounts, most banks still charge customers for the "privilege" of using checks. Such charges can be substantial. A 1979 Federal Reserve Board survey found that nearly three out of five banks offering free checking accounts imposed costly conditions on customers.

Some banks even went as far as to charge a customer $6 a month if the account balance fell below $500. One out of 10 banks that attached conditions to free checking did not mention these "strings" in advertising. The Fed also found that nearly half of the banks in the survey that changed the terms of checking accounts in the past two years did not notify their customers.

INTEREST-PAYING CHECKING

Consumers and savings banks have tried for years to amend the 1933 law that prohibits banks from paying interest on checking accounts. But they are beginning to discover that interest-paying checking may not be worth the fuss. The experiment with NOW (Negotiable Order of Withdrawal) accounts in New England states has found that while these accounts—technically interest-bearing savings accounts on which checks can be written —do earn money for customers, the service fees are high.

For example, assume that an account earns interest at the rate of 5 per cent, compounded daily, and that there is a monthly service charge of $3 plus 15 cents per check. Assume also that the average monthly balance is $500 and that there is an average of 20 checks written each month. In such a case, the monthly interest earnings would be about $2.09, while the service fees would cost $6—a net cost of almost $4 a month, $48 a year, for interest-bearing checking.

ALTERNATIVES ALSO AVAILABLE

Alternatives to interest-bearing checking may be better for consumers. The "automatic savings transfer" account, for example, combines checking and savings by maintaining a checking account, with the provision that checks written for more than the account's balance will be paid out of the savings account. Thus, one can maintain a $0 balance in checking, and checks written would still be paid. In 1979, however, the Supreme Court struck down laws allowing such accounts (effective January 1, 1980), saying that they had not been approved legally by the Fed. Congress is expected to allow such accounts to continue to be available.

Credit union share draft accounts are another interest-bearing account on which one can now write checks. "Share drafts" look like personal checks, but are technically withdrawals against a member's shares in the credit union. Also, unlike checks, share drafts usually are not returned to the customer after they have been processed and paid.

A third alternative is the telephone transfer account, now offered by most savings and loan associations. This allows you to make a phone call authorizing transfer of funds (minimum transfer is usually $100) from a savings account to a checking account—even a checking account at a different financial institution. This allows a person to keep a minimum balance in checking to cover day-to-day needs, keeping the rest in an interest-bearing savings account until needed.

A new twist is the telephone bill-paying account offered by a growing number of savings and loan associations. In such accounts, a telephone call to the savings and loan authorizes certain bills to be paid from your account, usually for a fee of ten cents per check, less than the cost of postage alone. But only certain types of regular payments—charge accounts, rent, loans, and utilities, for example—can be paid this way, and only to merchants who participate with the S&L.

OTHER TYPES OF CHECKING PLANS

The Minimum Balance Plan can be one of the most expensive types of checking accounts. Basically, the plan requires that you maintain a minimum balance in your account in exchange for checking that is "free" or at nominal cost. If your balance falls below the minimum, the cost of the account goes up proportionally.

But as in most free offers, there is a catch. If you maintain a minimum balance of $250 in order to receive free checking you lose money. That $250 could earn $12.50 a year interest in a 5 per cent savings account. So "free" checking costs you $12.50 annually. You should not be required to keep more money in your checking account than you need to cover the checks you write. The bigger your excess balance, the more interest you lose.

The Per Check Plan charges a service fee—usually 10 or 15 cents—for every check you write. There may also be a small monthly service fee. This type of account is good if you write only a few checks each month. In fact, you may handle occasional transactions via a savings account where you can earn interest.

Package Accounts offer checking along with an array of other banking services for a flat monthly fee. A typical account may cost $2 or $3 a month and may include "free" checking, travelers checks, money orders, "courtesy cards" and sometimes credit cards and safe deposit boxes. If you can use these services, this type of plan may be the least expensive. But if you need only a checking account, do not open this type of account.

The Free Checking Account—with no strings attached—is by far the cheapest type of account. Banks make money with your money. Why should you have to pay them? Banks in many cities offer such accounts. But make sure there are no strings such as a monthly charge, per-check charge, or minimum balance requirement.

A "No-Bounce" Account is a form of instant credit. In the typical account, the bank will deposit money in your account if your balance goes below zero. In that case, you should understand, however, that you are being *loaned* money. Usually, the bank will deposit a minimum of $100 even if your account becomes overdrawn by only one cent. Finance charges on the money loaned are figured *daily*. The longer you take to pay back the money, the larger the finance charge.

Here are some other things you should look for when choosing a checking account:

● Interbanking. Can you cash checks at any branch of your bank or only at the branch at which you have your account?

● Postage-paid bank-by-mail.

● The cost of checks. Many banks offer free checks with only your name printed.

● Overdraft and stop-payment charges. Charges for these services vary widely.

TOLL-FREE NUMBERS FOR CREDIT CARD COMPANIES

Many of the major credit card companies have toll-free "800" telephone numbers with which you can contact a company for numerous purposes. Services offered by each company differ, but generally you can notify them of a stolen or lost credit card, make inquiries about your bill or your account, apply for a credit card, and register a change of address.

Bank credit card companies, such as Bankamericard and Master Charge, do not have toll-free numbers, since most business is handled by the issuing banks. However, if you need to contact the bank about any of the above problems, and you are out of the local calling area, try calling collect.

You can obtain toll-free numbers by calling 800/555-1212.

SAVINGS ACCOUNTS
Changes Made In Your Interest

Computation of interest on savings accounts is one of the oldest controversies in banking. Weak federal regulations regarding interest rates have enabled banks to compute interest in more than 40 different ways. Since few banks readily disclose their method of computing interest, shopping around for the best rate is not easy.

There were some signs of improvement in 1979, as several states and the federal government proposed laws to provide "truth in savings." In Kansas, for example, a bill was introduced that would provide "uniform and full disclosure of information with respect to the computation and payment of earnings on individual savings deposits for dissemination to any individual upon request . . ." A "Financial Services Disclosure Act" sponsored in Congress by Rep. Frank Annunzio (D-Ill.) would do substantially the same thing on the federal level.

Differences between banks—and accounts within the same bank—can be substantial. Seemingly insignificant features of an account, such as grace days and minimum balance restrictions, can deplete the interest an account earns. Such variables include:

ANNUAL PERCENTAGE RATE. Not all types of institutions offer the same interest rates. Banks, for example, generally pay less interest on savings accounts than savings and loan associations (see box, "Maximum Interest Rates"). And some institutions pay less than the maximum interest rate allowed by law.

Most banks advertise two annual percentage rates: the "nominal" rate and the "effective" rate. Here is a typical interest rate advertised for a regular passbook account:

"5.25%, yields 5.47%"

The nominal rate in this example is 5.25 per cent. Due to the method used to calculate the interest (in this case, day-of-deposit to day-of-withdrawal), the effective rate (actual yield) is 5.47 per cent.

METHOD OF CALCULATION. There are five basic methods of calculating interest on a savings account:

● **The Low Balance method** yields the least amount of interest. Interest is simply paid on the lowest balance in your account during the interest period.

● **The First-In-First-Out method applied to the beginning balance** is only a little more generous than the Low Balance method. With this method, withdrawals are deducted from the beginning balance of the interest period. Interest is then computed on the reamining amount. If, for example, your balance at the beginning of the period was $1,000, and you withdrew $500 halfway through the period, your interest would be computed as if you had a $500 balance through the entire interest period. In reality, however, you have $1,000 in your account for half of the period. Your money, therefore, would not be earning all that it could.

● **The First-In-First-Out applied to the first deposit of the interest period** has a better yield. The method is similar to the previous method except that withdrawals are deducted from the first deposits of the interest period before the interest is computed. As a result, the balance in the account between the beginning of the interest period and the first deposit earns full interest.

STUDY SHOWS 40 METHODS OF INTEREST CALCULATION

A 1970 master's thesis by Kansas State University student Jackie M. Pinson illustrated how various interest calculations can affect interest yield on savings accounts. Pinson created a hypothetical savings account at 6 per cent interest for one year.

The account was opened with a $1,000 deposit, and over the course of the year had additional deposits totaling $3,000, and withdrawals totaling $2,000. The interest earned by the account was calculated by Pinson in 40 different ways used by savings institutions, varying in yield from $29.95 to $79.13.

Some of the methods and interest yields are:

● **Interest yield: $79.13.** Day-of-deposit to day-of-withdrawal method, compounded quarterly, credited quarterly, 10 deposit grace days at the beginning of each month.

● **Interest yield: $65.20.** Last in-first out method, compounded quarterly, credited quarterly, no deposit grace days, 3 withdrawal grace days.

● **Interest yield: $59.51.** Low balance method, compounded semi-annually, credited semi-annually, 10 deposit grace days at the beginning of each interest period.

● **Interest yield: $44.42.** Low balance method, compounded quarterly, credited quarterly, no grace days, penalty for withdrawals.

● **Interest yield: $29.95.** Low balance method, compounded semi-annually, credited semi-annually, no grace days, penalty for withdrawals.

Pinson's professor, Richard L. D. Morse, has written a 26-page booklet, [1] *Check Your Interest,* that shows how to determine whether you are receiving the maximum amount of interest advertised by a bank. The booklet is available for $2 from Morse Publications, 2429 Lookout Dr., Manhattan, KS, 66502.

withdrawals are deducted from the first deposits of the interest period before the interest is computed. As a result, the balance in the account between the beginning of the interest period and the first deposit earns full interest.

● With the **Last-In-First-Out method,** withdrawals are subtracted from the latest deposit. Deposits made early in the interest period earn more interest than in the previous methods, since they remain in the account longer.

● The best yield comes from the **Day-of-Deposit-to-Day-of Withdrawal method.** With this method, interest is calculated on the actual number of days the money remains in the account.

GRACE PERIODS. Some banks allow a specified number of "grace" days at the beginning and end of an interest period that can affect the amount of interest you receive.

Deposit Grace Days are days at the beginning of an interest period in which you can make deposits and receive credit for those deposits as if they had been deposited by the first day of the interest period. For example, deposits made by the 10th of the month will be credited as if they were deposited by the first of the month. The more grace days, the better.

Withdrawal Grace Days are days allowed at the end of an interest period in which you can withdraw money without losing any interest. Again, the more grace days, the better.

FREQUENCY OF CALCULATION. It's not just how much interest is being given that is important, but how often it is being credited to your account. Here is how much interest is earned at various interest rates credited at six different frequencies:

Interest Rate	Method of Calculation					
	semiannually	quarterly	monthly	weekly	daily	continuously
5¼%	5.3189	5.3543	5.3782	5.3875	5.3898	5.3903
5½	5.5756	5.6145	5.6408	5.6510	5.6535	5.6541
5¾	5.8327	5.8752	5.9040	5.9152	5.9180	5.9185
6	6.0900	6.1364	6.1678	6.1800	6.1831	6.1837
6¼	6.3476	6.3980	6.4322	6.4455	6.4488	6.4494
6½	6.6056	6.6602	6.6972	6.7116	6.7153	6.7159
6¾	6.8639	6.9228	6.9628	6.9783	6.9823	6.9830
7	7.1225	7.1859	7.2290	7.2458	7.2501	7.2508
7¼	7.3814	7.4495	7.4958	7.5138	7.5185	7.5193
7½	7.6406	7.7136	7.7633	7.7826	7.7876	7.7884
7¾	7.9002	7.9782	8.0313	8.0520	8.0573	8.0582

OTHER CONSIDERATIONS: There are other variables, each of which can make a difference in what your savings account earns. They include:
● Free services, such as safe deposit boxes or free travelers checks and money orders;
● Minimum balance restrictions which could tie up funds. Some banks impose a penalty for going below the minimum;
● Charges for withdrawals, levied after a maximum number of withdrawals have been made in an interest period;
● "Inactive" charges, made against accounts which have shown no deposits or withdrawals for a lengthy period of time;
● Conveniences, such as extended and Saturday banking hours, EFTS's (electronic fund transfer systems), which allow you to deposit or withdraw funds anytime from computer terminals located at the bank or in shopping centers;
● Postage-paid banking by mail.
A warning: make sure that any "free" services are not being provided in lieu of a higher interest rate.

BETTER YIELDS FOR SMALLER SAVERS
One consumer breakthrough during 1979 was the increased availability of high-interest savings accounts for savers with relatively small amounts to invest. Previously, investments such as certificates of deposit with interest yields as high as 10 per cent were available only for minimum deposits of $10,000. In April 1979, the government bowed to pressures initiated by the Gray Panthers, a national senior citizens lobby, to make high-yield investments available for those with as little as $500 to invest. The accounts proposed included:
● **An increase in interest rates** for all passbook savings accounts of ¼ per cent.
● **Five-year certificates of deposit** paying one per cent less than U.S. Treasury securities at savings and loan associations and 1¼ per cent less at banks.
● **An increasing-rate certificate** which would receive 6¼ per cent from savings and loan associations and 6 per cent from banks in the first 18 months. The rates would rise ½ per cent during each 18-month period until at the end of five

years, the rates would be 8¼ per cent for savings and loan associations and 8 per cent for banks.

● **Bonus savings accounts** paying an extra ½ per cent on balances held more than a year.

● **Smaller certiticates** than $500 for up to four years, with no minimum deposit required. The minimum for other certificates would be $500.

OTHER INVESTMENT STRATEGIES

An increasing number of alternatives to passbook savings accounts are available. Many mutual funds, for example, are lowering their minimum investment requirements or abolishing minimum requirements altogether. Mutual funds average investment returns of 8 to 9 per cent. Treasury Bills with maturities of four or more years are available to savers with a minimum $1,000 investment; in mid-1979, such bills paid more than 9 percent interest. For more information, call the nearest Federal Reserve Bank.

Among the better kept secrets are high-interest accounts maintained by subsidiaries of large banks such as Citicorp and the Bank of America. B of A, for example, can legally pay only 5 per cent interest on passbook accounts. But FinanceAmerica Thrift, a subsidiary of B of A, pays 6 per cent interest on savings accounts. A Rhode Island-based loan and investment company, Commercial Credit Plan Inc., recently advertised that its "super savings account" paid 8.5 per cent interest on accounts with $2,000 or more, and 6.5 per cent on accounts of at least $500.

The U.S. League of Savings Associations, a trade organization, has endorsed the idea that the minimum denomination on certificates of deposit of one to eight years be lowered from the current $1,000 to $100. The League also approved new open-ended certificates in $50 and $100 denominations with interest rates that would rise gradually over time.

MAXIMUM INTEREST RATES

Interest rates are controlled by the federal government, which sets maximum rates financial institutions can pay on savings accounts. Current trends indicate that those federal ceilings may be removed in the next few years. Meanwhile, here are the maximum nominal interest rates allowed by the federal government.

TYPE OF ACCOUNT	SAVINGS & LOANS	BANKS
Regular savings	5.50 per cent	5.25 per cent
90 day	5.75 per cent	5.50 per cent
1 to 2.5 years	6.50 per cent	6.00 per cent
2.5 to 4 years	6.75 per cent	6.50 per cent
4 to 6 years* (certificates)	7.50 per cent	7.25 per cent
6 to 8 years* (certificates)	7.75 per cent	7.50 per cent
8 years or more* (certificates)	8.00 per cent	7.75 per cent

*Percentages listed for certificates of four years or more are minimum rates. The rates are tied to four-year treasury bond yields; such certificates earned the stated minimum or the treasury rate, whichever is higher at the time of purchase.

LOANS AND CREDIT CARDS
The American Way of Debt

Americans are borrowing more than ever. And they are finding it easier than ever. With the advent of debit and credit cards, an entire new credit industry has emerged.

Traditional loans issued by a bank or finance company are fast giving way to more impersonal transactions. To an increasing degree, people are borrowing from credit card companies, banks, credit unions and finance companies by simply signing their names to a purchase or loan. Without even consulting a credit manager or filling out a form, they are borrowing from "no-bounce" checking accounts, 24-hour electronic tellers and airport vending machines.

But as the inflationary spiral continues, more and more people are reaching maximum tolerance levels. Interest alone is taking up more of the weekly pay check. Not including home mortgages, amounts borrowed now exceed amounts paid by an average of $300 a year for every person over the age of 19. In 1978, the outstanding debt on the nation's 600 million credit cards rose by almost a third over the previous year's total. One result was an increase in bankruptcies, which have doubled since 1970.

FEWER RESTRICTIONS ON CREDIT CARDS

One reason for the sudden surge in credit card use is a stepped-up campaign by credit institutions to encourage their use. Slick advertising campaigns emphasize the pleasures of the "buy now, pay later" lifestyle.

In addition, changes in federal laws have made credit available to more people, including:

● Until a few years ago, banks offering Visa cards could not offer Master Charge cards, and vice versa, due to exclusive contracts with agent banks. In 1976, the Supreme Court ruled those agreements to be restraints of trade. Since then, banks have literally flooded the market with their own credit cards. Citibank of New York sent out solicitation letters to an estimated 60 million Americans in 35 states. These people received second credit cards without investing a 15-cent stamp.

● Recent amendments to the Equal Credit Opportunity Act bar sex discrimination in granting credit and allow married women to establish their own credit histories, with alimony and part-time income considered equally with other income.

● In 1978, the Federal Reserve Board quietly issued a rule to promote the use of credit backed by home mortgages. It allowed banks to issue special checks or cards to be used for purchases of almost anything up to a total of $20,000 without requiring the bank to notify the purchaser after each transaction that the deal could be rescinded within three business days, as required by the Truth-in-Lending law. Credit institutions would still have to notify users of that right at least once a year and each time the maximum allowable credit is increased. But the Fed agreed that disclosure of the three-day right would be impractical in view of the time it takes merely to send out a bill.

The rule ran into opposition, however, in 1979. Some critics, worried about over-extension of credit and possible exploitation of lower-income people, petitioned the Fed to either repeal the rule or modify it. In September, 1979, the Fed repealed the rule, leaving in place the requirement to offer a three-day cooling off period.

BIG DIFFERENCES IN COST OF CREDIT

Not all credit card terms are alike. In 1977, the Washington Center for the Study of Services, a non-profit research group, surveyed rates charged by local lending institutions. One finding was that while the basic interest rate of 18 per cent was uniform for credit card purchases of up to $500, the method of calculating finance charges differed widely.

The least costly method to consumers—and perhaps the least used—is the **adjusted balance method,** in which the finance charge is calculated on the unpaid balance at the time of billing.

The **previous balance method** figures charges based on the amount owed on the billing date of the previous month. This method is more expensive since it does not take into account any payments made or any credits for returned merchandise during the billing period.

Some creditors begin charging interest on unpaid balances as of the day customers are billed. Other creditors begin charging as of the day the purchases are made.

The most common method of calculation is the **average daily balance method.** Interest is figured on the average daily balance during a billing period. This method can be less costly than others if payments are made early in the billing cycle.

COSTS RANGE FROM $6.90 TO $54.97

Charges for services like cash advances varied the most. In the Center's study, the charges ranged from $6.90 on a sample account at one bank to $54.97 on the same sample at another bank. The differences depend on how finance charges are calculated and any grace periods allowed. For example, some banks do not levy any finance charges within 25 days of the billing date; others begin charging interest the day you receive the money.

Similarly, interest rates vary widely on installment loans, especially "small loans" as defined under individual states' laws. Local laws can make big differences in the interest rate charged. For example, in the Washington, DC, area, which comprises the District of Columbia, Maryland, and Virginia, rates vary by as much as 200 per cent. Maryland law sets a maximum annual percentage rate of 18 per cent on loans over $500; Virginia allows lenders to charge up to 30 per cent for the first $500, and up to 18 per cent for amounts over that; DC allows a maximum rate of only 11.5 per cent.

SHOPPING FOR CREDIT

Here are some other factors to consider when shopping for credit:

Downpayment: The larger the downpayment, the less you will have to borrow. You can save money by paying for part of a purchase in cash, and financing only a portion.

Size of payment: Determine the kind of payments best suited to your needs. In most cases, equal monthly payments enable borrowers to set aside a fixed portion of each paycheck to pay off the loan. Watch out for "balloon payments" where small monthly payments may hide a much larger final payment. Even if you make all but the final balloon payment, you may default on the loan.

Repayment in advance: If you are able to pay off the loan in advance of the due date, you should receive a partial refund of finance charges.

Missed payments: Make sure you know what the consequences are if you miss a monthly payment. Some loans provide for grace days, others charge stiff penalties for missed payments. Many require that the entire loan be immediately repaid in full if any payment is missed.

Default: Make sure the terms of a loan spell out collection charges or court costs and whether any item you put up as security for the loan can be repurchased at a later date if you default.

Insurance: Many loans include a charge for insurance that will pay off the debt in the event that you are unable to make payments due to disability or death. Often, lenders imply that purchasing the insurance—which is usually more expensive per $1,000 than comparable life insurance policies—is a requirement for obtaining a loan. Banks and finance companies push the insurance policies because they make large profits from commissions on the insurance premiums. However, if you own enough life insurance to repay the loan and still meet the financial needs of your dependents, you probably will not need additional insurance.

UNDERSTANDING YOUR CREDIT RECORD

Credit managers walk a tightrope between losing sales and issuing credit accounts to risky customers. To set a relatively uniform standard as to who gets credit, they rely heavily on credit bureau reports. If you don't have one—or have a record that contains erroneous information—you may be out of luck, regardless of what you do and how much you make.

If you don't have a credit record but want to obtain credit or open a credit card account, there are always ways to bend the rules. A letter from an employer may help, because the main ingredient of a successful applicant is a stable income. Another way is to get someone more financially stable than yourself—a relative or close friend—to apply for the card and include you as an authorized user, although some companies allow only dependents and close relatives to do this.

WHAT CREDIT REVIEWERS LOOK FOR

There are several things that credit application reviewers look for that can help your case, even if you don't have a record at a credit bureau. Having a telephone in your name helps; it theoretically demonstrates the ability to pay monthly bills, although neither the phone company nor any other utility reports bad accounts to credit bureaus. Having a checking and savings account is a sign that you can manage your money; bouncing a few checks or maintaining a small savings balance won't necessarily hurt.

Living and working in the same places for a year or more are two more pluses. The type of job you have may also be important: some creditors have compiled lists of "low-risk" and "high-risk" occupations. Government employees, for example, are considered good risks because they are almost impossible to lay off or fire. Bartenders and ministers are poor risks, the former because they change jobs frequently, the latter because their incomes are often tied to donations to the church.

As a last resort, you could try taking out a small loan for a year to demonstrate your credit worthiness. Ironically, the best time to borrow the money is when you are financially solvent. If you wait until you need the loan, you are probably already in some financial hot water and may not be approved if your debt load is too high.

MAXIMUM INTEREST RATES ON SELECTED LOANS
By State

	SMALL LOANS				CREDIT CARDS
	Annual Percentage Rates				Monthly Service Charge
State	**$500** (6 Mos.)	**$1,000** (12 Mos.)	**$1,000** (24 Mos.)	**$1,000** (36 Mos.)	**Revolving Accounts** (Merchandise)
AL	x	x	x	x	1½%
AK	36.50	32.92	32.75	x	1½%-$1000-1%
AZ	33.49	28.47	28.28	x	1½%-$1500-1%
AR	x	x	x	x	
CA	23.08	17.76	17.68	x	1½%-$1000-1%
CO	32.87	28.05	27.86	27.60	1½%
CT	24.59	22.84	22.91	x	1¼%-$250-1%
DE	23.46	22.07	22.41	23.78	1½%-$1000-1%
DC	x	x	x	x	1½%-$500-1%
FL	30.00	28.25	28.18	28.07	1½%
GA	53.04	33.00	25.36	23.06	1½%
HI	x	x	x	x	—
ID	36.00	32.22	32.03	31.77	1½%
IL	28.75	25.67	25.56	25.39	1.80%
IN	35.56	30.83	30.61	30.33	1½%
IA	31.99	26.43	26.23	25.96	1½%-$500-1¼%
KS	34.24	29.24	29.01	28.74	1¾%-$300-1½%-$1000-1.20%
KY	36.00	32.47	32.31	32.07	—
LA	36.00	35.45	35.43	35.36	1½%
ME	29.57	26.60	26.49	26.33	1½%
MD	31.12	25.67	25.50	25.25	1½%-$500-1%
MA	27.96	20.62	19.27	18.81	1½%-$500-1%
MI	31.00	25.82	25.69	25.45	1.70%
MN	29.88	24.53	24.37	24.12	1%
MS	36.00	35.40	35.35	35.29	1½%-$800-1¼%-$1200-1%
MO	26.62	21.89	21.82	21.63	1½%-$500-¾%
MT	30.89	26.96	26.90	x	1½%
NB	28.75	25.10	24.99	24.81	1½%-$500-1%
NV	32.87	28.05	27.86	x	1.80%
NH	24.00	22.85	22.81	22.75	—
NJ	24.00	23.42	23.40	23.37	1½%-$700-1% (for Banks 1¼%-$700-1%
NM	29.06	22.10	21.94	21.68	1½%-$500-1%
NY	24.71	21.82	21.75	21.62	1½%-$500-1%
NC	32.25	26.50	26.29	26.01	1½%
ND	28.21	25.29	25.20	x	1½%
OH	26.93	26.18	26.15	25.57	
OK	28.13	25.24	25.14	24.99	1½%
OR	32.87	28.05	27.86	27.60	—
PA	24.59	21.72	22.67	24.38	1¼%
RI	29.98	24.00	24.00	x	1½%
SC	32.87	28.05	27.86	27.60	1½%-$1000-1%
SD	28.75	26.82	26.74	x	1%
TN	32.19	25.24	23.13	23.15	1½%
TX	23.59	19.72	19.87	19.56	1½%-$500-1%
UT	36.00	32.22	32.03	31.77	1½%
VT	23.62	24.91	24.92	24.40	1½%-$500-1%
VA	30.00	26.53	26.42	x	1½%
WA	30.00	26.53	26.42	26.23	1%
WV	31.06	26.78	26.61	26.38	1½%-$750-1%
WI	16.86	18.52	20.40	22.00	1½%-$500-1%
WY	32.87	28.05	27.86	27.60	1½%

CREDIT UNIONS
Improved Services for Members

A bill signed by President Carter in 1977 gave credit unions broader lending savings and investment authority. The law made credit unions more competitive with other banking institutions in rates and services offered.

Credit unions are non-profit savings and lending institutions that provide services only to members, often at better rates than available elsewhere. Members must have a common bond through employment, community or organization. More than 40 million Americans belong to nearly 23,000 credit unions in the U.S.

Credit union members save their money in the form of "shares," which are typically $5 each. From funds accumulated by these shares, loans may be made to credit union members. The board of directors of a credit union has authority to fix the limits for loans and to revise them as the credit union grows. Applications for loans are passed upon by a credit committee elected by the members or by loan officers appointed by the credit committee. Profits from the loans and other sources may be distributed to members in the form of dividends, in addition to regular interest rates paid on savings.

The 1977 law allows credit unions to offer 30-year conventional mortgage loans; 15-year conventional home-improvement loans; self-replenishing lines of credit similar to bank cards such as Visa and Master Charge; and savings plans with variable interest rates and maturities comparable to certificates of deposit offered by savings institutions. In addition, many credit unions feature savings accounts on which members can write "share drafts," which look like and can be used exactly like regular checks—in effect, an interest-bearing checking account.

For more information on credit unions, including how to join or start one, contact the Credit Union National Association, 1730 Rhode Island Ave. NW, Washington, DC, 20036; 202/659-2360.

CREDIT INSURANCE
Added Cost for Duplicate Coverage

The growth of credit has spawned a subsidiary industry of providing credit insurance, to the tune of $3 billion in sales annually. An increasing number of banks, car dealers and merchants require purchasers to buy insurance to automatically cover payment in case of death, illness, accident and even unemployment in some cases. The result is that many buyers pay extra for protection that duplicates existing insurance policies. It is not unusual for a purchaser of a $5,500 car to pay $900 for insurance covering death and disablement only for the life of the loan.

Such rates are many times the cost of similar insurance if bought separately, according to Robert Hunter, Acting Federal Insurance Administrator. Purchasers are often given the impression that the insurance is required for completion of a sale or loan. Few people realize how high the rates are for the rate of claims, which is far below the average for other types of insurance.

The rates include considerable profit for the business firm offering the insurance. In Maryland, for example, residents paid more than $17 million in 1978 for credit insurance, while loan defaults totaled only $3.5 million, leaving a profit of $13.5 million or nearly 80 per cent. Retailers pocket most of the premiums and then add to that profit by including the insurance costs in amounts financed, often at rates of 24 per cent or more.

Insurance industry spokesmen dispute these profit figures and insist that rates charged are reasonable. James Kielty of the Consumer Credit Insurance Association told one reporter that there is no overpayment by consumers and that buyers are not pressured into buying the insurance. He was backed by a study of the Federal Reserve Board.

But a study by Emmett J. Vaughan for the Independent Insurance Agents of America Inc., concluded just the opposite. It said rates tend to be especially high for the service offered and that most consumers who buy it feel pressured into doing so for fear of losing the loan or sale. Other studies going back to 1967, the year when a Senate committee investigated the subject, concluded the same. And the Federal Trade Commission found in 1974 that tying a sale to credit insurance was widespread.

Credit insurance may be required by a merchant or lender. If so, the charges must be disclosed and included in the Annual Percentage Rate (APR), as required by the Truth-in-Lending Act. Many business firms give the impression that credit insurance is required when it is not. All a customer needs to do is to refuse to buy it. A competing firm may be found that does not require credit insurance.

Some types of credit insurance may be advantageous to the consumer. One of the most unusual types is offered by Montgomery Ward, the retail chain, to its customers. For a fee of ½ per cent of monthly bills, it pays future bills if the buyer dies, becomes sick or injured or becomes unemployed. Few companies offer such broad coverage.

AVOIDING FINANCIAL DISASTERS
Where to Go For Help

Being poor, in debt or broke is not a crime in America. Long gone are the days of debtors' prisons that isolated the indigent from the rest of society. Yet there is still a stigma attached to needing financial help. The same society which induces Americans through advertising to "buy now, pay later" frowns upon individuals who go financially overextended in their monthly payments. Corporate executives, who would not think twice about taking advantage of federal bankruptcy laws if they thought it would be to their advantage, point to the disastrous effects of bankruptcy on individuals and the rising cost of welfare payments.

Credit problems are intimately tied to divorce and other family problems. A wife angry at her husband might take his credit cards for a fast and furious buying session. By the time the bills arrive two to six weeks later, the dispute may be long resolved and the arrival of the bills may bring on a rash of new problems.

A financially disorganized life also can lead to a variety of pathologies, according to Dr. M. Harvey Brenner, a psychologist and professor at Johns Hopkins University. Brenner has studied the relationships between the economy and mental health. He has found that economic conditions like unemployment, changes in income and inflation have a measurable impact on mental hospital admissions, cardiovascular illnesses, suicides, and other personal problems.

PLASTIC SURGERY

The hardest thing to do about financial difficulties is to get out of them. Cutting down on credit card use—like dieting or conserving energy—requires a strong will, a radical change in habits and months of discomfort.

Outside help is advised, but a bad choice of counselors can bring even more trouble. One general rule: Stay away from anyone who is out to profit from your financial difficulties. Consumer finance companies, bankruptcy lawyers, and other "financial counselors" often have interests other than yours at heart.

One big source of problems is the company offering a "consolidation" loan designed to reduce your stack of bills into one monthly payment. Consolidation often tends only to delay the problem. First, if you are still carrying credit cards around, no "easy monthly payment" is going to get you off the hook. Second, loans from finance companies carry high interest rates—typically 18 to 36 per cent, sometimes as high as 54 per cent—because such lenders take big risks by catering to people who are in financial trouble. According to the Federal Trade Commission, the unspoken policy of the finance companies is that it is not profitable to make a loan unless they can keep someone as a debtor for at least seven years.

FREE HELP IF YOU'RE IN DEBT

One resource is a network of credit counseling services affiliated with the National Foundation for Consumer Credit Inc. (1819 H St., NW, Washington, DC, 20006, 202/223-2040).

In 1978, the foundation reported that approximately 150,000 people visited its 212 credit counseling centers, about half of whom went only to get advice or information. Of the remainder, about 15,000 were referred elsewhere, and 60,000 were helped to set up a debt management program to pay off about $260 million in debts, excluding mortgages. The average debt per family (excluding mortgages) was $16,000.

Consumer Credit Counseling Services are supported financially by local merchants, banks, savings and loan associations and other business firms with a vested interest in helping consumers pay off their debts rather than wiping them out through bankruptcy. Services are usually free.

Many people find that they can overcome their problems with only a little advice or information. Others may be put into a debt management program. In such cases, the counselor arranges with creditors to stretch payments over longer periods of time than originally scheduled. The debtor then pays each month into a personal trust fund at the counseling office. With this money the office pays off creditors on a pro-rated basis until all outstanding debts are eliminated.

RIGHTS OF CREDIT USERS
Keeping Your Record Clean

Not very long ago, consumers had few legal rights when it came to obtaining and using credit. The abuses and deceptions were numerous, and public outcry resulted in passage of some of the most important consumer legislation of our time. The laws, most of which took effect between 1975 and 1977, gave consumers a redress procedure for billing problems, strengthened the rights of those seeking credit, and sought to eliminate abuses by credit reporting agencies and bill collection firms.

SOLVING BILLING PROBLEMS

In the past, consumers had no legal recourse against stores and credit card companies which allowed only a short time to pay bills before finance charges were applied, or which kept applying penalty fees and interest on purchases for defective or returned merchandise. A frequent result was a bad credit record for innocent consumers.

Such problems have been reduced somewhat. In 1975, the Fair Credit Billing Act placed restrictions on such billing practices and gave new rights to credit customers. The act requires creditors to mail bills at least 14 days before the due date. However, during peak mail periods such as Christmas, it is still possible that a consumer may have only one week between the time a bill is received and the time it must be mailed in order to avoid finance charges.

The act set forth specific procedures for consumers and creditors for settling billing disputes:

● Any customer who believes that a statement of his account contains a billing error and who notifies the credit card company in writing within 60 days after receiving the statement, must receive an acknowledgement from the creditor within 30 days.

● After receiving the complaint, the creditor must either correct the error or send a written explanation to the customer stating why the account is correct. This must be done within two billing cycles.

● During the time the account is in dispute, the customer is not required to pay the disputed amount or any finance charges on it, and the creditor must not close the account for refusal to pay.

● During this time, the creditor must not report the account to a credit bureau without stating that the amount is in dispute.

● If the company fails to follow these procedures, it automatically forfeits the disputed amount, up to $50, regardless of whether the bill was in error.

EQUAL CREDIT OPPORTUNITY

Other acts have strengthened the rights of those seeking credit. The Equal Credit Opportunity Act, which took effect in October, 1975, was intended to prohibit credit discrimination on the basis of sex or marital status. As a result of the act:

● Creditors may not make statements discouraging applicants on the basis of sex or marital status.

● Creditors may not ask the marital status of an applicant, except in a community property state or as required to comply with laws governing finance charge and loan ceilings.

● Creditors must provide reasons for terminating or denying credit to applicants.

● Creditors may not discriminate against a credit-seeker on the basis of race, color, religion, national origin, age or because all or part of the credit-seeker's income comes from public assistance.

● You can require that creditors report the credit history on any account you share with your spouse to credit bureaus in both names. Any accounts opened after June 1, 1977, which both spouses may use or for which both are liable, must be reported by creditors in both names.

CHECKING YOUR CREDIT RECORD

If you have ever owed anyone money, bounced a check, owned life insurance or been arrested, chances are you are one of more than 100 million Americans who has file in a credit reporting agency. The contents of that file indicate how you pay your bills, your credit history and whether you have ever been sued or filed for bankruptcy. But it may also include your neighbor's and friends' views on your character, general reputation and lifestyle, especially if compiled by an investigative reporting agency instead of a credit bureau.

Until 1971, consumers had no way to protect themselves against the circulation of inaccurate or obsolete information, and to make sure that credit reporting agencies used their files in a manner that was fair and equitable. The Fair Credit Reporting Act of 1971 gave new powers to consumers to protect themselves from the use of inaccurate information and provided ways to correct inaccuracies.

Under the Fair Credit Reporting Act, you have the right:

● To be told the name and address of the credit reporting agency responsible for preparing a credit file that was used to deny you credit, insurance or employment or to increase the cost of credit or insurance;

● To be told by a credit reporting agency the nature, substance and sources of the information collected about you;

● To take anyone of your choice with you when you visit a credit reporting agency to check on your file;

● To be told who has received a credit report on you within the past six months, or within the past two years if the report was furnished for employment purposes;

● To have incomplete or incorrect information removed from your file;

● To have the agency notify those who have received the inaccurate information that such information has been deleted from your file;

● To have all adverse information on your file removed after seven years, except bankruptcy information, which can remain for 14 years; and

● To sue a credit reporting agency for damages if it willfully or negligently violates the law.

The law requires only that the credit bureau or investigative reporting agency disclose the "nature and substance" of the file, although some agencies will actually show you the file, and a few will give you a copy of the file, usually for a fee.

In order to obtain the information in your file, you must either go directly to the agency and provide suitable identification, or contact the agency by phone. When contacted by phone, the agency will send you disclosure forms, then will call you to give you the information about your file. You must pay any toll charges resulting from long-distance phone calls.

ENDING DEBT COLLECTION ABUSES

In 1977, the Fair Collections Practices Act was signed into law, making it a federal offense for professional debt collectors to use numerous unfair tactics that had become commonplace in that business.

The law prohibits debt collectors from:
- Threatening debtors with violence, using obscene language, or calling them late at night;
- Contacting a debtor's employer if the collector knows that the employer disapproves of such calls;
- Making repeated telephone calls that annoy recipients;
- Misrepresenting that the collector is affiliated with any state or federal agency;
- Misrepresenting that failure to pay will result in arrest or imprisonment;
- Furnishing information that is false;
- Claiming that documents are from the government or are legal process papers when they are not; and
- Using false or deceptive means to obtain information about a debtor.

Dept collectors who violate the law are liable for actual damages plus civil damages of up to $1,000 or, in a class action suit, $500,000 or 1 per cent of net worth.

WHO HAS ACCESS TO CREDIT FILES?

Not all problems associated with credit files were eradicated with enactment of fair credit reporting and fair collection practices acts. One big problem is in determining who can have access to personal credit files. Those wishing to examine the files of another person need only make vague disclosures about what their purpose is in examining the file. As a result, numerous abuses have occurred.

In 1976, for example, a debt-collection subsidiary of Diners Club was accused by the Federal Trade Commission of obtaining credit information on consumers under false pretenses in order to harass debtors into paying their bills. The subsidiary, National Account Systems, Inc., was charged with misrepresenting itself as a subscriber to credit-information agencies (such as retail stores) in order to obtain information about the debtors.

Reformers also want to place stricter regulations on the way credit files are put together. Hearings before the Senate revealed that some credit reporting agencies have set up quotas on the number of credit reports that employees must make each day and what percentage of the files have to contain adverse information.

With the rapid increase in electronic fund transfers systems, concern is growing over easy access to individual files containing a vast amount of data about a person's life. Such innovations as telephone bill paying and 24-hour banking terminals in shopping centers are creating detailed, computerized files about customers' financial transactions. Congress and federal and state agencies are considering ways to limit access to such data with the hope of heading off abuses.

A CITIZEN'S GUIDE TO BANKRUPTCY
Going for Broke

Declaring bankruptcy is a radical move, but in many cases it can be a lifesaver. The stigma attached to bankruptcy is slowly fading, but major misunderstandings about the process remain.

A frequent concern is that bankruptcy will leave a major blemish on your credit rating. True, but it was the credit rating that caused the problems in the first place. Some people are better off without a credit rating.

A new bankruptcy law, effective October 1, 1979, liberalizes some parts of the bankruptcy process. Among its provisions:

● Increased amounts of money and property are protected from bankruptcy seizure: up to $7,500 in equity in a home and burial plot; your interest, up to $1,200, in a motor vehicle; your interest, up to $200, in any single piece of household goods and furnishings, clothes, appliances, etc.; up to $500 worth of jewelry; any other property worth up to $400, plus the unused part of the $7,500 homestead exemption; up to $750 worth of tools and books needed for a trade; any professionally prescribed health aids.

● In some cases, a creditor's right to repossess certain kinds of exempted property—such as furnishings or tools of a trade—can be invalidated when a debtor has pledged such property as security for a cash loan.

● The law limits a creditor's claim against certain property to the value of the property, regardless of how much is still owed. Suppose, for example, you bought a $500 dishwasher and still owe $350. In bankruptcy, the court would determine the current value of the dishwasher, say $300. You could redeem the washer by paying the court that amount. The other $50 would be discharged.

WHAT WILL IT COST?

A lawyer's fee for a fairly simple bankruptcy may range from $200 to $300. The law requires that lawyers' fees be reasonable and be subject to regulation by the bankruptcy court. In addition, the filing fee in Federal District Court is $60. Those unable to pay the $60 fee in advance may get permission from the Court to pay it monthly.

Many experts feel that a lawyer's fee is well worth it. A good lawyer will fill out the forms, fully advise you and help make sure you will not make any slip-ups that will create serious problems. He will provide you with psychological as well as legal security.

If you have a fairly simple bankruptcy involving only a few debts and no complications, you may be able to do it yourself. If you do so, you should get a book that explains how to proceed. The needed forms can be obtained from a legal stationery store or from publishers of books about credit and bankruptcy. There are different forms for business and personal bankruptcies.

There is a compromise between having a lawyer represent you and doing it yourself. That is to fill out the forms and have them checked by a lawyer before filing. In a simple case you may be able to get a lawyer to look the forms over for $50. Lawyers typically demand fees for bankruptcy cases in advance.

Low-income debtors who cannot afford to pay an attorney may be eligible for free legal advice from organizations like Community Legal Services and the Legal Aid Society.

THE MECHANICS OF BANKRUPTCY

The procedure for bankruptcy consists of filing necessary forms with a Federal District Court, a hearing by the court and a court order that results in wiping out your debts except for the categories previously mentioned.

The forms to commence bankruptcy ask for detailed information about the would-be bankrupt. All debts and assets must be listed and submitted under oath, subject to the penalties of perjury.

This filing, which is referred to as a voluntary petition in bankruptcy, is filed in Federal District Court in the district in which the debtor has his residence or principal place of business for the six months immediately preceding the date of filing. The $60 fee is paid upon filing.

You and your creditors will then be notified by the Court, and a hearing will usually be held a few weeks after filing. At that hearing, the bankruptcy judge makes sure your papers are in order, and the person filing is subject to examination under oath by the judge and creditors. (A creditor, for example, may claim you are concealing assets or submitted erroneous information on your forms.) In the typical case, however, creditors do not show up, and the hearing lasts for only about 15 minutes.

If you have assets which are not exempt, the court will take them over and use them to pay your creditors.

Within about 60 days after the hearing, the court issues what is called a discharge in bankruptcy. This wipes out or discharges all debts (except taxes and other special exceptions). The bankruptcy court can also issue orders to prevent your creditors from trying to collect debts or otherwise harrassing you.

A LEGAL ALTERNATIVE TO BANKRUPTCY

There is one other legal procedure for those in debt over their heads: a Chapter 13 Procedure, also called a Wage Earner Plan.

Under Chapter 13 of the Federal Bankruptcy Law, the bankruptcy court takes a portion of each paycheck and distributes it to your creditors. Unlike a regular bankruptcy, there is no wiping out of debts. Instead they are paid pursuant to the plan. Nor does the debtor surrender his assets as in bankruptcy. The debtor maintains control of his assets.

For purposes of Chapter 13, a wage earner is defined as one who earns more than 50 percent of his income from wages or commissions.

A Wage Earner Plan contemplates liquidating all of your debts in three years. The court, which administers the plan, has authority to protect you from lawsuits and harassment by creditors and stop service charges, interest and other charges on debts.

The Wage Earner Plan must be approved by the court, by all secured creditors (those with mortgages and other security interests) and by a majority of unsecured creditors (those whose debts are not secured by mortgages or other security devices).

Procedures for filing and legal expenses are about the same as a regular bankruptcy (but the filing fee is only $15). At any point, a Wage Earner Plan can be converted into a regular bankruptcy. Some debtors prefer a Wage Earner Plan because they object to bankruptcy on moral or other grounds.

A Wage Earner Plan may prolong the agony of getting rid of debts. It may be better to get it over with by bankruptcy. Any debtor who wishes to pay his debts can do so even after bankruptcy.

Bankruptcy has one other advantage over a Wage Earner Plan. By going through bankruptcy and getting a fresh start, you may actually improve your credit rating. Under a Wage Earner Plan the debts still hang over you.

Wage Earner Plans account for about 15 per cent of bankruptcies.

Insurance and Investments

In This Chapter

- Life Insurance
- Health Insurance
- Automobile Insurance
- Homeowner & Tenant Insurance
- Flood & Crime Insurance
- Personal Retirement Plans
- Investments

Insurance remains a deep mystery for most people. They tend to buy it without comparing prices, largely because:

- They don't realize that prices for the same coverage vary greatly among competing companies; and
- Few people understand insurance well enough to make any comparisons, or even ask intelligent questions.

As a result, Americans pay much more than they need to for almost every kind of insurance. For example, 80 per cent of those with life insurance policies have a form of cash value insurance that costs from two to five times the cost of the simplest type of life insurance. Auto insurance is also substantially overpriced, costing Americans several billion dollars more than simple no-fault insurance would cost for the same coverage. Health and accident insurance, except through the non-profit Blue Cross/Blue Shield organizations, has been loaded with gimmicks costly to consumers. One of the most expensive in terms of value is credit insurance, which insures the life of the borrower and is often forced on him by lenders even though he already has life insurance. The worst buy of all is title insurance, which is often added to real estate settlement costs to cover a risk that is virtually non-existent.

When risks and costs increase, insurance companies often tend to overreact by raising premiums many times actual increased costs. When medical malpractice and product liability suits began to result in large jury awards, insurance firms took advantage of the publicity not only to raise premiums but to seek legislative relief from legitimate court suits. As a result, several states have restricted the filing of liability suits. However, two extensive government studies have concluded that the problem of large settlements has been greatly exaggerated, and that the awards were well deserved by the victims and their survivors.

INSURANCE INDUSTRY EXEMPT FROM FEDERAL REGULATION

One of the basic problems is the lack of effective regulation. Since 1945, insurance companies have been exempt from federal antitrust regulation. That was the year when the McCarran-Ferguson Act turned over the regulatory job to the states. The industry obtained the exemption from Congress after the Supreme Court decided that the industry should be subject to federal supervision.

There is wide agreement outside the industry that all but a few states have failed to do an adequate job in supervising the selling of insurance. Industry representatives have customarily dominated conventions and meetings of state regulators, even paying for many of the expenses. To make matters worse, state insurance commissions have been hamstrung by inadequate funds and small staffs that are dwarfed by the lobbying and legal resources of private companies. Efforts to correct these inequities have been defeated by legislatures heavily populated by lawyers and insurance agents.

But by 1979, growing public disenchantment with the industry and state regulation was beginning to raise the possibility of eventual federal intervention. A task force working for the Justice Department concluded that federal exemption for the insurance industry should be ended. In March, 1978, a subcommittee of the House Committee on Small Business released a study recommending that a Federal Insurance Commission be created "to regulate the insurance industry in those instances where state regulation is deficient." In the same month, Rep. John Moss (D-Calif.) and Senator Howard Metzenbaum (D-Ohio), chairmen of other Congressional committees with interests in insurance matters, asked the General Accounting Office to conduct a comprehensive study of state regulation. They cited an "enormous" public interest in insurance problems raised in committee hearings and suggested that regulatory efforts have been woefully deficient in protecting buyers of insurance.

INDUSTRY LACKS SELF-REGULATION

Compared to other industries, the insurance industry has done relatively little to rid itself of unethical practices and unscrupulous operators that add unnecessary billions to the cost of the insurance. For nearly a decade, for example, life insurance companies have known of a study by their own experts acknowledging that a common selling method grossly misleads customers. Yet many agents and companies continue to use it without criticism of their colleagues or prosecution by regulatory agencies. However, much of the deception is done innocently by people who don't know what they are doing.

For two years, a small portion of the industry tried to conduct a complaint-resolving program called ICAP (Insurance Consumer Action Panel). But the program was discontinued in 1978 for lack of support from the industry.

The only hope for policyholders with problems unresolved in direct contacts with agents or companies is a state insurance commission. In a few states, such agencies seek to resolve individual disputes and take vigorous action against the worst offenders when indicated by a pattern of complaints. But most insurance commissions have too little money or staff to even monitor public problems, and many that do have the resources lack the will to act. Legal action against an insurance company is rare.

LIFE INSURANCE

Of all products sold, life insurance is perhaps the least understood. Consequently, it is much more expensive than it needs to be for many people.

The late Senator Philip A. Hart, while chairman of the Senate Antitrust and Monopoly Subcommittee, summed up the situation: "The life insurance market abounds with waste, inefficiency and overcharges, and consumers are not getting clear, accurate, reliable and adequate information about the cost and value of the policies they buy...Policyholders are wasting millions of dollars yearly because they are terminating (lapsing) their cash value policies too early...coming up short in getting death — or income — protection."

GROWING ROLE FOR FEDERAL GOVERNMENT

The 1973 hearings kindled a growing interest in the selling practices of the life insurance business. Among events focusing on this subject were:

● A task force study by the Justice Department concluding that the exemption from federal antitrust laws for the insurance industry should be ended. The task force found that although policy costs vary widely from company to company, buyers do not have such information readily available at the time of purchase. In addition, buyers are often too confused by insurance to make valid comparisons among competing products even when cost figures are disclosed. The task force concluded that true competition does not occur because the larger firms dominate the market so much through larger advertising budgets and sales forces.

● A Federal Trade Commission study concluding in July, 1979, that too little information about life insurance is disclosed to buyers and that "most consumers have great difficulty understanding how to compare the cost of one life insurance policy to another." The agency found that the average return on the savings portion of policies in 1977 was only 1.3 per cent and that only 15 per cent of each dollar spent on life insurance comes back in the form of death benefits.

Hart and his staff conducted history's only comprehensive investigation of the life insurance industry. At public hearings in 1973, a parade of expert witnesses called life insurance everything from "a national scandal" to "a consumer fraud." The Subcommittee found little public awareness of the wide differences in policy costs among competing companies. It also heard from a number of industry critics contending that although term insurance is a better buy for most people, more than four out of five buyers of life insurance choose other types of policies without realizing they may be paying two to five times more for equivalent coverage.

THE TWO BASIC KINDS OF LIFE INSURANCE

There are essentially two kinds of life insurance: term and cash value.

Term insurance is pure protection. Like fire insurance, it pays a certain amount in case of loss (death of the policyholder). Since the risk of death increases with age, the annual premium rises steadily. For one-year term insurance, the rate goes up yearly; for five-year term, the rate rises every five years. Some policies are written with level premiums and declining coverage; this kind is called declining term insurance. Another variety is deposit term which requires an initial deposit above the premium.

Term insurance is sometimes called "temporary" insurance because it usually terminates at age 65 or 70, when it can usually be converted to a cash value policy or dropped. Actually, the insurance needs of most people decline over the years as children grow up, go to school or college and establish their own homes.

Cash value insurance assumes that the policyholder will own the policy for his entire life. The increasing premiums associated with term insurance are averaged out, creating a level premium over the life of the policy. As a result, cash value premiums are higher than term premiums in early years and lower in later years.

Cash value insurance is also for people who want to start a low-return savings plan as well as buy death protection. Annual premiums are set high enough to pay for both the death protection and to accumulate a "cash value" as well as provide profit for the company and agent. If the policyholder drops the policy, he gets back the cash value portion. Or, he can borrow from the cash value at relatively low interest. Other names for cash value insurance are "permanent," "whole," "ordinary" or "endowment" insurance. Many insurance "packages" include both term and cash value.

Life insurance policy may also bring "dividends," which are excess premiums returned by the company. Companies that pay "dividends" are called "participating" or "par;" companies that don't pay "dividends" are called "non-participating" or "non-par." Par companies tend to have higher premiums but lower net costs to policyholders in the long run than non-par companies.

The reason for the quotation marks around the word, "dividends," is that they are not true dividends, such as those earned on common stock. They are merely returned premiums that are not needed by an insurance company for expenses and profits. For this reason, they are not considered taxable by the Internal Revenue Service.

COMMON MISCONCEPTIONS ABOUT LIFE INSURANCE

Cash value insurance is more lucrative for agents and companies because it involves much higher premiums at the start. This means higher commissions for selling policies and larger amounts for insurance companies to invest for the benefit of stockholders. For these reasons, sellers of cash value insurance are likely to call term insurance bad names, such as "temporary insurance." And they are likely to make cash value insurance look better than it really is.

For example, cash values are often misrepresented as extra benefits from the company for use in emergencies in later years, such as college expenses or major health bills. It is not always made clear that in order to obtain the cash value, the policyholder must forfeit the entire policy and its protection. A slightly smaller amount can be borrowed at interest, but if death should occur before the loan is paid back, the beneficiary will get only the difference between the amount borrowed and the face value (total amount) of the policy.

Since the cash value is made of excess premiums plus the interest earned by them, it belongs to the policyholder and represents no risk for the company. As a policy's cash value grows, the proportion of the face value protected by the company declines. Consequently, the cost per $1,000 of insurance protection goes up steadily for this kind of policy, just as it does for term life insurance.

In fact, the cost per thousand dollars of protection tends to be substantially higher for cash value policies than for term policies because of the much higher premiums paid in the early years of the policy. Even at the point where term insurance premiums become larger than level cash value premiums — usually in a person's mid-fifties — the cost per thousand dollars of protection usually continues to be higher for cash value insurance.

However, many companies and agents claim falsely that term insurance becomes more expensive at that point because the premium becomes larger. They choose to ignore the accumulated payments plus interest, which are likely to be several times greater for a cash value policy than for term.

Cash value insurance is often referred to by its salesmen as a good investment. They offer tables showing impressive cash value buildups and "dividends" without pointing out that the actual return is rarely over three or four per cent a year, less than the same amount of money could earn in an ordinary savings account. Another point made by sellers of cash value insurance has more validity. It is the fact that relatively few people have enough discipline to stash away a regular amount in savings every month. For people like that, a three per cent return is better than no return at all. This "forced savings" feature is the biggest advantage of cash value life insurance.

MISLEADING TYPES OF COST COMPARISONS

One of the most common ways of selling life insurance is called the "traditional net cost method." It simply means adding up premiums paid over the years and subtracting any projected cash values or "dividends" that might be received by the policyholder, then dividing the amount by the number of years involved to get the "net cost" per year. In cases where premiums are especially high, the amount paid back may exceed the total premiums paid. Some agents maintain that in such cases, the insurance has been "free."

But insurance is not free. Premiums are only part of the picture. One of the biggest cost factors is interest, the amount that could be earned elsewhere with the same amount of money paid out. In the previous paragraph, it was investment earnings that allowed the company to pay back more in "dividends" and cash value than was paid in premiums. The constant compounding of interest over the years can make a substantial difference.

Nearly a decade ago, a group of concerned executives of the life insurance industry made a study and issued a report severely criticizing the use of the traditional net cost method of comparing costs of policies over the years. The group, headed by E.J. Moorhead, a respected life insurance executive concluded that any comparison of true life insurance costs must include an interest factor. They endorsed what has become known as the "interest-adjusted" system. It means that over a 10-year period, for example, the true cost is the total of premiums, less dividends, plus interest. Interest is applied to the net payments to indicate what could have been earned on the same money elsewhere. To explain interest cost further, assume that you kept $1,000 in a mattress for a year when you could have deposited it in a savings account paying five per cent. The cost of hiding it in a mattress, therefore, was $50 in lost interest.

Since the Moorhead study was released, nearly every state insurance commission has required that cost comparisons use the interest-adjusted system. Some states have even published booklets comparing interest-adjusted policy costs of various companies licensed to sell insurance in those states. (See data from New York State booklet in this section.) Herbert Denenberg started this practice in 1972 with his "shoppers guides" for buyers of life insurance in Pennsylvania where he was insurance commissioner.

But the interest-adjusted system can also be misleading. It is accurate only in comparing term policies to each other and in comparing certain cash value policies. The system does not provide a true comparison of costs between a cash value and a term life insurance policy or between a cash value policy that is cashed in and one that provides a death payment. That is because the system does not reflect the declining proportion of protection provided by the company as the cash value rises. Instead, it erroneously assumes that the amount of protection always remains equal to the face value. It also ignores the protection received before a policy is cashed in.

WHICH COMPANIES OFFER THE BEST VALUES?

Over the last 10 years, in which the interest-adjusted system has become widely used, the companies with the lowest net costs for cash value policyholders have included (in alphabetical order) Bankers Life of Iowa (not to be confused with Bankers Life & Casualty of Chicago), Connecticut Mutual, Massachusetts Mutual, National Life of Vermont, Northwestern Mutual and Provident Mutual.

A comprehensive study by the Senate Antitrust and Monopoly Subcommittee in 1973 ranked companies for costs per $1,000 for many ages and amount of cash value policies. Starting with the lowest cost companies, they were Connecticut Mutual, Provident Mutual, Northwestern Mutual, Allstate (Sears Roebuck), Bankers Life of Iowa, Southwestern Life, Central Life Assurance, Massachusetts Mutual, Home Beneficial and Phoenix Mutual.

The Subcommittee did not compare term policies. But Herbert Denenberg did while insurance commissioner of Pennsylvania in 1972. He found Canadian companies generally lower than American ones for sample policies.

A study by the New York State Insurance Department in 1977 showed large differences in interest-adjusted costs among companies doing business in that state. For example, a $25,000 cash value policy for a 35-year-old man had costs ranging from $9.63 to $24.06 per $1,000 of death payments. (See table.) The average for all companies surveyed was $16.46. The Department published its findings in a 94-page booklet, *Consumers Shopping Guide for Life Insurance.*

BOOKLET CONTAINS ERRORS, DEFECTS

However, authors of the booklet fell into some of the same traps that have made similar studies misleading. The major defect of the New York and other studies is that they do not adjust cost index figures to reflect the declining element of risk protection in cash value policies as the cash value builds up. They assume erroneously that the full face value is insured for the life of the policy although only the difference between it and the cash value is so protected by the company.

Writers of the New York booklet also fell into other errors that have afflicted such studies in the past. For example, they accepted the large insurance companies' misleading description of term insurance as "temporary" and cash value insurance as "permanent." They also accepted the false notion that term insurance is, in their words, "considerably more expensive than cash value insurance in advanced years," presumably because premiums are higher. They ignore the higher accumulated costs for cash value insurance over a normal lifetime. Furthermore, they listed the absence of cash value as a "disadvantage" of term life insurance. They did not consider it a disadvantage to have to surrender an insurance policy in order to obtain the cash value in it. They also listed the increasing premiums of term insurance as a "disadvantage" even though the cost of equivalent cash value insurance also increases each year and at a faster rate. But the booklet's comparisons of term and cash value costs for death payments are valid.

The accompanying two tables are taken from the New York booklet. One shows the interest-adjusted index per $1,000 of $25,000 in term insurance for both a 25- and a 35-year-old man and for 10- and 20-year periods. The other table shows the interest-adjusted index per $1,000 of $25,000 in cash value

(COMPARISON OF $25,000 TERM LIFE INSURANCE POLICIES
Per interest-adjusted cost per $1,000 over 10 and 20 years [5,6]

Company	20-Year-Old Male			35-Year-Old Male		
	Average Premium	10-Year Index	20-Year Index	Average Premium	10-Year Index	20-Year Index
Bankers Life Co.[2,9]	$5.43	$4.10	$3.90	$9.71	$5.49	$6.73
Berkshire Life[1,4,9]	4.49	3.13	3.18	9.38	4.52	5.95
Columbian Mutual[1,10]	5.01	4.39	4.34	8.80	5.07	6.51
Connecticut Mutual[1,4,9]	4.04	3.60	3.64	8.14	4.73	6.40
Continental Amer.[1,9]	4.41	3.61	3.81	8.25	5.05	6.87
Empire State Mutual[1,9]	4.33	3.51	3.66	8.66	5.10	6.75
Equitable Life Assur.[1,4,9]	3.75	3.10	3.30	7.90	4.84	6.46
Farm Family Life[1,9]	3.88	2.81	2.96	7.92	4.29	5.88
Farmers & Traders Life[1,9]	6.43	3.57	3.70	11.72	5.35	7.22
Fidelity Mutual Life[1,4,9]	3.87	3.16	3.34	7.94	4.75	6.61
Guardian Life of Amer.[1,4,9]	4.73	3.67	3.85	9.20	5.43	7.19
Home Life[1,4,9]	4.78	2.93	2.97	9.22	4.43	5.87
John Hancock Mutual[1,9]	5.26	3.38	3.57	9.65	5.37	6.67
Loyal Protective Life[1,9]	4.54	3.64	3.73	9.04	4.94	6.59
Lutheran Mutual Life[2,9]	4.48	3.31	3.38	8.59	4.49	6.11
Manhattan Life[1,4,9,10]	4.09	3.27	3.43	8.06	4.73	6.10
Massachusetts Mutual[1,4,9]	4.48	3.33	3.43	8.76	4.96	6.35
Metropolitan Life[2,3,4,9]	4.85	3.66	3.51	10.32	5.67	7.16
Mutual Life of NY[1,4,9]	4.58	3.18	3.36	8.92	5.02	6.73
Mutual Trust Life[1,9]	5.01	3.61	3.80	9.49	5.01	6.91
National Life[1,4,9]	4.40	3.59	3.58	8.31	4.70	5.92
New England Mutual[1,4,9]	3.77	3.25	3.30	7.93	4.70	6.35
New York Life[1,4,9]	4.35	3.10	3.32	9.21	4.50	5.90
Penn Mutual Life[1,4,9]	4.63	3.62	3.60	9.09	5.28	6.78
Phoenix Mutual Life[1,4,9]	4.47	3.70	3.89	8.72	5.10	6.73
Provident Mutual of Phil.[1,9]	4.51	3.24	3.41	8.89	4.88	6.54
Prudential of Amer.[2,3,9]	4.61	3.14	3.05	10.01	4.75	6.16
Savings Banks Life Ins.[1,8,11]	3.19	2.28	2.10	6.90	3.59	4.53
Security Mutual of NY[1,9]	4.67	3.86	3.58	8.81	4.84	6.36
State Mutual of Amer.[1,4,9]	4.28	3.18	3.26	8.60	4.46	6.14
Teachers Ins. & Annuity[1,3,7,11]	2.89	1.92	2.01	7.23	3.26	4.58
USAA Life[2,11]	3.77	2.52	2.58	7.51	3.64	4.91
Union Central Life[1,9]	4.37	3.34	3.42	7.26	4.63	6.31
Union Labor Life[1,3,9]	5.98	3.74	3.82	10.39	4.72	6.47
Union Mutual Life[2,9]	5.38	3.50	3.56	10.26	5.05	6.78
Unity Mutual Life[2,10]	3.95	3.32	3.51	8.56	4.87	6.58
Averages	4.58	3.36	3.43	8.90	4.79	6.34

Footnotes: (1) To calculate the premiums and indexes, company uses age at nearest birthday. (2) To calculate premiums and indexes, company uses age at last birthday. (3) Company issues policies only with disability waiver of premium benefit, which is included in index. (4) Index numbers may be different for policies issued outside New York State. (5) Five-year renewable and convertible policies issued by participating (dividend-paying) companies. (6) Interest figured at 5 per cent for death protection only, without regard to cash values. (7) Company issues only policies to employees of colleges and universities and certain other institutions. (8) This fund handles all life insurance policies for member savings banks in New York State and is not available outside the state. (9) Company sells policies mainly through its own full-time agents. (10) Company sells policies mainly through agents licensed with several companies. (11) Company principally sells by direct mail.
Source: *Consumers Shopping Guide for Life Insurance,* published in 1977 by the New York Insurance Dept., Empire State Plaza, Albany, NY, 12223.

COMPARISON OF $25,000 CASH VALUE
LIFE INSURANCE POLICIES*
For interest-adjusted cost per $1,000 over 10 and 20 years[6]

Company	20-Year-Old Male			35-Year-Old Male		
	Average Premium	10-Year Index	20-Year Index	Average Premium	10-Year Index	20-Year Index
Aetna Life[1,9,10]	$15.66	$14.60	$12.15	$23.55	$21.85	$18.35
Amer. Gen. of NY[1,9,10]	14.40	12.35	11.04	22.47	19.58	17.56
Amer. Republic of NY[2,11]	9.81	9.14	8.45	17.09	15.95	14.79
Bankers Life Co.[2,9]	11.20	9.70	9.09	18.35	15.78	14.70
Berkshire Life[1,4,9]	12.91	12.15	10.68	20.43	18.79	16.83
CUNA Mutual[2,9]	14.78	12.41	10.72	22.76	19.51	17.09
Canada Life of NY[2,9]	12.69	10.23	9.19	20.00	16.70	15.12
Colonial Life of Amer.[1,3,9]	15.43	13.04	11.84	22.81	19.55	17.52
Columbian Mutual[1,10]	14.77	12.29	10.83	22.28	18.35	16.07
Connecticut Gen.[1,9]	13.74	12.56	11.56	21.84	19.88	18.10
Connecticut Mutual[1,4,9]	10.39	9.32	8.73	16.79	15.24	14.24
Continental Amer.[1,9]	10.89	10.12	9.57	18.05	16.81	15.86
Continental Assur.[1,9,10]	14.95	12.94	11.24	23.12	20.03	17.51
Empire State Mutual[1,9]	10.73	9.92	9.66	17.82	16.53	16.00
Equitable Life Assur.[1,4,9]	14.41	10.71	9.12	22.24	17.23	14.86
Equitable Life of Iowa[1,9]	14.24	11.63	10.29	22.21	18.19	16.07
Farm Family Life[1,9]	13.82	11.15	9.95	21.69	17.77	16.07
Farmers & Traders Life[1,9]	11.73	9.94	9.08	19.20	16.61	15.38
Fidelity Mutual Life[1,4,9]	10.12	9.59	9.03	17.24	16.26	15.49
Financial Life[1,9]	13.99	12.26	10.83	22.03	19.03	17.13
First Investors Life[2,9]	14.67	12.03	10.35	23.51	19.49	16.74
Franklin United Life[1,9]	14.48	12.16	10.72	22.51	19.11	16.55
Golden Eagle Mutual[2,9,12]	14.84	14.84	14.84	24.06	24.06	24.06
Gotham Life of NY[1,9]	14.92	11.99	10.36	23.43	19.03	16.21
Guardian Life of Amer.[1,4,9]	12.94	11.37	10.19	20.43	17.98	16.16
Home Life[1,4,9]	14.84	12.15	9.86	22.62	18.86	15.69
INA Life of NY[1,9]	14.93	12.72	11.77	22.90	19.69	18.24
Int'l Life of Buffalo[1,9]	14.98	11.27	10.32	22.85	18.14	16.79
John Hancock Mutual[1,9]	15.00	13.44	11.49	23.51	21.04	18.00
Loyal Protective Life[1,9]	14.31	12.15	10.66	22.61	19.12	16.83
Lutheran Mutual Life[2,9]	13.88	10.89	9.58	22.01	17.76	15.54
Manhattan Life[1,4,9,10]	11.76	11.13	10.25	19.09	18.13	16.59
Massachusetts Mutual[1,4,9]	14.11	11.32	9.86	21.80	17.62	15.49
Metropolitan Life[2,3,4,9]	14.25	12.60	11.24	23.13	20.65	18.37
Monarch Life[1,9]	14.27	12.00	10.80	22.21	19.01	17.25
Mutual Benefit Life[1,4,9]	14.64	11.38	9.68	22.36	18.10	15.58
Mutual Life of NY[1,4,9]	14.40	12.68	11.45	22.70	19.99	18.08
Mutual Trust Life[1,9]	14.77	11.59	10.30	22.80	18.69	16.63
National Life[1,4,9]	14.58	12.40	11.16	22.43	19.27	17.27
Nationwide Life[1,9,11]	13.79	11.24	10.13	22.27	18.04	16.13
New England Mutual[1,4,9]	14.15	11.67	10.37	21.67	18.13	16.17
New York Life[1,4,9]	12.64	11.17	9.65	20.44	18.17	15.58
Northwestern Mutual[1,4,9]	14.42	11.74	10.19	22.35	18.10	15.62
Penn Mutual Life[1,4,9]	13.76	11.85	10.34	21.27	18.24	15.78
Phoenix Mutual Life[1,4,9]	13.45	11.49	9.94	21.14	18.06	16.04
Provident Mutual of Phil.[1,9]	14.47	11.48	10.11	22.46	18.67	16.55
Prudential[2,3,9]	13.24	12.03	10.62	21.04	19.61	16.94
Savings Bank, NY[1,8,11]	10.64	9.31	8.08	17.84	15.45	13.42
Security Mutual[1,9]	14.85	12.99	11.67	22.47	19.49	17.67

COMPARISON OF $25,000 CASH VALUE
LIFE INSURANCE POLICIES*
For interest-adjusted cost per $1,000 over 10 and 20 years[6]

Company	20-Year-Old Male			35-Year-Old Male		
	Average Premium	10-Year Index	20-Year Index	Average Premium	10-Year Index	20-Year Index
State Mutual[1,4,9]	13.31	11.32	9.39	21.09	17.83	15.2
Teachers Ins. & Ann.[1,3,7,11]	10.13	7.34	6.06	17.18	11.89	9.6
Thomas Jefferson[1,9]	13.95	12.03	10.77	22.30	19.27	17.4
Trans World[2,10]	15.16	12.23	10.92	23.78	20.31	18.2
USAA Life[2,11]	11.80	10.42	8.93	19.09	16.26	13.8
Union Central[1,9]	14.47	11.68	10.03	22.09	18.56	16.4
Union Labor[1,3,9]	15.99	13.16	11.95	23.89	20.02	18.1
Union Mutual[2,9]	15.00	12.20	10.42	23.12	19.02	16.3
United Mutual[1,9]	14.48	13.48	13.16	22.78	21.62	21.1
U.S. Life in NY[1,10]	14.51	12.72	11.26	23.83	20.19	17.8
Unity Mutual[2,10]	13.44	12.30	10.50	21.21	19.57	16.8
Averages	13.63	11.62	10.32	21.47	18.47	16.4

*See accompanying term life insurance comparison for footnotes and source.

insurance for the same ages and time periods. The companies are all participating (dividend-paying) ones licensed to sell in New York State. The relative order of companies differs somewhat for other amounts and ages; they also differ for women. Cost indexes might be slightly different in other states because of special regulations in New York, but the relative standings would not differ much in other states because company rates are the same from state to state. Figures are based on 1977 data from the companies.

Residents of some states have especially inexpensive term life insurance available to them. For example, savings banks in New York, Massachusetts and Connecticut sell inexpensive life insurance to residents of those states. The state of Wisconsin also offers inexpensive life insurance to persons who apply for it there even if merely passing through. Life insurance sold in group plans also tends to be cheaper than when sold in individual policies. In addition, a growing number of companies offer special low rates to persons who do not smoke.

The best way to buy life insurance for most people, except those in the highest age brackets, is to buy a low-cost, declining term policy plus an investment in an annuity, mutual fund or other income-producing plan. A low-cost company can be found on the accompanying table produced by the New York State Insurance Department.

SPECIAL VICTIMS OF LIFE INSURANCE: VETERANS

Since 1965, military veterans have been victimized more than any other group by a lack of choices in buying life insurance. A law passed that year ended the custom of allowing veterans to continue low-priced term insurance when they leave government service. The law turned over the insurance role to an industry pool run by the Prudential Insurance Company, the largest insurer, and set up a generous subsidy so the companies in the pool would not lose any money on physically impaired veterans.

The companies developed a program, sanctioned by the Veterans Administration and the Defense Department, that gave the discharged serviceman or woman virtually no choice but to convert to the most expensive (cash value) type of policy after a four-month waiting period or drop life insurance coverage. New veterans were also given a booklet suggesting that they should convert their low-cost term insurance to cash value.

In 1974, the waiting period was extended to five years, after which the policy must still be converted to cash value or dropped. As a result, many veterans have been saddled with unnecessarily expensive life insurance, while others have been forced to drop theirs rather than take out term coverage which they might have afforded.

SPECIAL VICTIMS OF LIFE INSURANCE: STUDENTS

College students are victimized, too, as more and more insurance companies take to the campus with their most expensive and misleading pitches. In the typical deal, a senior is sold "an investment plan," which may not even be identified as life insurance. (The biggest seller in this field is Fidelity Union and its "College Master Plan.") The student is persuaded to sign a note for all but $10 of the first year's premium, which often is around $300 to $400. Yet few college students have any real need for life insurance since they have no dependents and little or no income.

A study of the subject by Joel W. Makower found that many students were not aware they had borrowed the first premium until a bill for the second year's premium arrived 12 months later, and the student still had no job or means of paying the premium. Few students realize that they could get the same amount of life insurance for less than one-fifth the cost and avoid borrowing anything.

SPECIAL VICTIMS OF LIFE INSURANCE: WOMEN

The latest "growth market" is life insurance for women. The increasing number of females earning their own livelihood and supporting children presents a big new target for insurance promoters. But insurance is being pushed also as a status symbol, implying that single women with no dependents, like single men in the same situation, need life insurance when they may not.

Life insurance is cheaper for women than men. That is because women tend to live longer. Premium rates for females are usually pegged at the level of a man three years younger. But for several years, population figures have shown that females live at least eight years more than males on the average. Yet insurance companies continue to cling to the three-year difference.

What has hurt women most has been cash value life insurance for husbands who die prematurely. Because of the prevalence of such policies, widows and children have been left with far less in benefits than they would have had if the policyholder had purchased more term life insurance with the same amount of money spent.

SUGGESTED READINGS IN LIFE INSURANCE

The Consumer's Guide to Life Insurance, Trace Oehlbeck (Pyramid Books, New York) 1975, $1.75; *Life Insurance: A Consumer's Handbook,* Joseph M. Belth (Indiana University, Bloomington, Ind.) 1973, $6.95; *Life Insurance Fact Book 1979* (Institute of Life Insurance, 277 Park Ave., NY, 10017); *The Mortality Merchants,* G. Scott Reynolds (McKay, New York, NY), $4.95.

HEALTH INSURANCE
Easing the Pain of Rising Medical Costs

The soaring cost of health care has become one of life's major problems for millions of Americans. Huge hospital and doctor bills have sent many into bankruptcy or sale of a family homestead. Many others have seen their life's savings wiped out.

Those hit hardest by rising costs are below age 65 with incomes above the poverty level, making them ineligible for either Medicaid or Medicare. The federal government pays virtually all health care costs of the poor through Medicaid and about 38 per cent for those with Medicare.

Approximately one-third of the total bill—$40 billion—is paid by the victims, including those whose expenses are only partially covered by Medicare. According to the Department of Health, Education and Welfare (HEW), costs not covered by government or private insurance total 10 per cent of hospital costs, 40 per cent of physician charges, 86 per cent of dentist bills and 86 per cent of prescription drug costs. As a result, although most people are covered to some extent by health insurance or government programs, there are huge gaps in coverage which cause extreme hardship to many people.

One of the worst problems people face is a sudden, long siege of illness without sufficient insurance benefits to take care of the entire bill. A survey by HEW showed that 84 per cent of such "catastrophic" cases—with costs exceeding $5,000—occurred to people who were not eligible for Medicaid.

REGULATION MOSTLY AT STATE LEVEL

Regulation of health insurance is almost entirely in the hands of state insurance commissions. They attempt to coordinate and standardize laws and enforcement activities through the National Association of Insurance Commissioners (NAIC). But their efforts have been widely criticized as inadequate for the amount of abuses in the industry. They also have been accused of dragging their feet to please industry interests, which have far more resources and tend to dominate the semi-annual conventions of the NAIC.

In recent years, the federal government has been showing an increasing interest in health insurance. However, rather than proposing a comprehensive plan, as promised earlier, the Carter Administration chose instead to focus on hospital costs. It concentrated its efforts on pushing legislation in Congress to set a ceiling on hospital cost increases. Hospital associations joined with other medical groups to oppose these efforts, preferring their own voluntary program to curb rising costs.

The government has also tried to force the health care industry to change many practices deemed too expensive and has pushed development of Health Maintenance Organizations (HMOs) as a promising means of cutting the nation's health bill.

HEALTH MAINTENANCE ORGANIZATIONS

These are pre-paid group practice plans, sometimes called medical supermarkets. A complete, salaried, medical staff, including a variety of specialists provides treatment for a full range of health care needs. HMOs are generally affiliated with hospitals and essentially practice preventive medicine. The aim is to keep costs down by keeping people healthy and out of hospitals. Their records show that the theory works.

Premiums tend to be high but coverage is very broad. All hospitalization and doctor costs are included, leaving few other medical expenses. A subscriber is usually entitled to unlimited use of the medical center. In an emergency, members can go to the nearest hospital emergency room.

Group Health Association of Washington is a typical HMO. GHA's exclusions include: cosmetic and podiatry surgery (except when deemed necessary), chronic psychiatric conditions, institutional care for tuberculosis, eyeglasses, speech therapy and dental treatment. Upon request, Group Health will send a list of HMOs in your area. Address Group Health Associations, Inc., 2121 Pennsylvania Ave., NW, Washington, DC, 20037.

HMOs have shown they can cut administrative costs by 20 per cent because no bills are rendered. Other insurers must include these costs in the price of their policies.

According to an American Medical Association survey, there is no difference in the quality of care provided by HMOs and conventional medical plans, but many doctors have opposed the HMO concept of salaries instead of fees.

MAIN TYPES OF HEALTH INSURANCE

Health insurance comes in more styles and prices than any other type of insurance. For that reason, it is important to know what type you are buying so you can compare coverage and price to other plans. Some plans now cover annual checkups and second opinions before surgery is performed. Some companies even adjust premiums for people who stay healthy.

Following are major types of health insurance:

● **Indemnity Plans** pay specified amounts for various medical services. There is a fixed fee schedule showing the amounts covered for each service. The amounts, however, may not equal the hospital, doctor and surgical fees prevalent in your area. The buyer must pay amounts not covered.

● **Hospital Plans,** as the name implies, help pay expenses incurred only at a hospital. Some pay specified amounts; others have deductible amounts which the buyer must pay.

● **Basic Hospital Plans** pay for room, food, X-rays, laboratory fees, drugs and operating room costs. Some also cover out-patient care. An example of the latter is a diagnostic test outside the hospital. Some plans cover all hospital expenses for a specified number of days, while others pay predetermined amounts per day for each specific service.

● **Major Medical** or "catastrophe" insurance supplements a basic hospitalization plan. It pays for serious or lengthy illnesses when costs exceed the limits of basic coverage. Private insurance companies are the major providers of this type of plan. Generally, there is a deductible amount ranging from $100 to $500. The higher the deductible, the lower the premium. The insurance companh pays a fixed percentage of the remainder. Basic coverage may cover a portion of the deductible. Unlike indemnity plans, major medical plans have no fixed fee schedule. They also cover all eligible expenses within the policy limits.

● **Comprehensive Major Medical** is a combination of hospital, surgical and major medical coverage in a single policy. This type of plan generally has deductible amounts and a percentage of the bill which must be paid by the policyholder. This keeps premiums lower than separate policies offering similar benefits. Coverage usually includes in- and out-patient expenses at a hospital, medication, doctors' fees, nursing care and surgery. The company usually pays 80 per cent above the deductible; the policyholder pays the remaining 20 per cent.

● **Disability** or "loss of income" insurance pays a portion of your salary when you are unable to work because of an illness or accident. But definitions of disability vary considerably. Some policies might define it as being totally incapacitated or unable to do anything. A more reasonable definition is the inability to work at one's regular job or occupation.

Waiting periods before payments begin are usually rather long. The longer the period of time, the lower the premium. Some plans don't pay until a week after you enter the hospital. Yet the average stay is less than eight days. A common clause in the policy says that if another policy covers this loss of income, double payment will not be made.

BLUE CROSS AND BLUE SHIELD

These are non-profit organizations whose tax-exempt status gives them advantages over private carriers. This status enables Blue Cross and Blue Shield to have higher "loss ratios," which reflect the proportion of premiums paid back in benefits.

In many instances, Blue Cross has arrangements with hospitals for stipulated fees but is not always successful in persuading participating physicians to accept its fee schedules as full payment, except for lower-income subscribers.

Blue Cross and Blue Shield plans are generally offered on a "service benefits" basis with payments made directly to the hospital and physicians on the basis of a previously negotiated list of fees. Unlike the Blues, indemnity plans of private carriers reimburse the insured for specific dollar amounts.

Blue Cross and Blue Shield group plans now frequently offer individual subscribers within a group a choice of coverage in a health maintenance organization or the more traditional coverage.

GROUP COVERAGE

As few as two people can qualify for a group. You can be affiliated with a group through your employer, credit union, or professional, fraternal or business association. Most groups offer at least a 6 to 8 per cent savings. Premiums are lower, and coverage is better than individual policies because there usually are fewer exclusions.

INDIVIDUAL PLANS

These offer fairly broad coverage, usually combining basic and major medical coverage. If you are not affiliated with a group, and you must purchase an individual policy, your best place to start is with Blue Cross and Blue Shield. But they are expensive, and you may want to shop around to find a plan that is more suitable for your needs.

Coverage and values vary widely from company to company and from plan to plan. Policies from the same company may also vary in different localities. Some individuals covered by a group plan may desire additional coverage.

With most individual policies, a review of the applicant's health condition is taken before a contract is made. In this way, the company can limit risks and add pre-existing conditions to the policy.

MAIL-ORDER INSURANCE

Mail-order insurance companies tend to be heavy advertisers through television, radio and newspapers. Most individuals are attracted to this type of policy because of the seemingly low rates and endorsements by well-known people, who are paid for their services.

But premiums are relatively high for the benefits offered because of the many exclusions and the cost of advertising. Mail-order policies are usually indemnity plans, with fixed dollar amounts too low to provide worthwhile coverage.

A medical exam or questionnaire is not usually required as a prerequisite to obtaining the policy. Many companies make up for the initial lack of selectivity by cancelling policies when a claim is made. Many mail-order companies have poor reputations for handling claims. Richard Rottman, former director of the National Association of Insurance Commissioners, advises people to avoid mail-order insurance.

But this type of policy can be useful as a supplement to a good basic policy. As with all policies, make sure the company is licensed in your state and read the policy carefully beforehand.

"DREAD DISEASE" PLANS

Insurance experts call the purchasing of "dread disease" policies gambling, not insuring, because coverage is too narrow. Most such policies are for a single disease, such as cancer. However, there are some plans which will cover a variety of diseases.

Some states have outlawed "dread disease" policies. The insurance plan you choose should cover more than one or two types of illnesses. If it does not, then your coverage is inadequate. Most hospital and major medical plans cover expenses for cancer.

Despite the wide criticism of cancer policies, 1979 has been a boom year for cancer insurance. More than 100 companies have convinced the public that a regular insurance policy will not cover them if they are afflicted with a "dread disease."

COMPARING INSURANCE COMPANIES

No matter what a company promises, it may have a poor track record in response to claims. To get some clues as to a company's treatment of claims, check a nearby Better Business Bureau, state insurance commission or consumer protection agency. They may have a record of complaints. Friends and relatives are also good sources of information about insurance companies in your area. State insurance commissioners have lists of all the companies licensed to do business in their states.

A good indicator of performance is a company's loss ratio. This ratio is the percentage of premiums paid back to policyholders in benefits. In general, the higher the loss ratio, the better the value. (See the following table of loss ratios for the 50 largest firms.)

SPECIAL VICTIMS OF HEALTH INSURANCE: THE ELDERLY

As the need for health care increases with age, so does the worry about insurance to cover the costs. Rising prices press especially hard on those who are retired and live on fixed incomes.

HEALTH INSURERS COMPARED
Proportion of Premiums Returned to Policyholders, 1978

Claims Paid as % of Premiums

50 Largest Insurers, in order	On Group and Individual Policies(1)	On Individual Guar. Renew. Policies(2)
Mutual of Omaha Insurance Company	75.9%	60.2%
Combined Insurance Company of America	43.4	66.7
Prudential Insurance of America................	79.9	67.2
Bankers Life and Casualty Co.	60.5	54.5
American Family Life Assurance................	48.9	48.8
U.S. Letter Carriers Mutual....................	94.5	—
Metropolitan Life Insurance Company	72.6	62.8
National Home Life Assurance	53.3	54.5
Continental Assurance Company	79.8	82.4
Physicians Mutual Insurance Company..........	62.2	62.5
United Insurance Company of America..........	45.3	25.2
Pennsylvania Life Insurance Company	48.7	29.9
Paul Revere Life Insurance Company	⁻70.6	139.2
Aetna Casualty and Surety	67.8	59.5
New York Life Insurance Company.............	73.0	56.2
Washington National Insurance	73.7	62.1
Provident Life and Accident	82.6	74.9
State Farm Mutual Auto	58.1	74.8
Colonial Life and Accident	44.3	51.6
Independent Life and Accident	41.8	24.0
Reserve Life Insurance Company	57.4	52.5
Liberty National Life Insurance................	48.1	39.0
National Life and Accident	57.0	33.8
United American Insurance Company...........	62.4	62.9
Travelers Indemnity of Rhode Island...........	84.4	101.6
Union Fidelity Life Insurance	44.8	46.4
Monarch Life Insurance Company	69.6	72.3
Time Insurance Company	65.1	64.5
Equitable Life Assurance Society...............	83.3	57.9
Travelers Insurance Company	88.3	57.8
American Family Mutual......................	68.1	78.3
American Republic Insurance	54.4	52.2
Inter-Ocean Insurance Company...............	52.2	52.2
Guarantee Trust Life Insurance................	59.3	52.6
Bankers Multiple Life Insurance	60.9	60.1
Globe Life and Accident	52.0	48.8
Union Bankers Insurance Company	55.8	53.0
American Health and Life....................	62.1	62.8
Lone Star Life Insurance Company.............	55.1	49.9
Lincoln National Life	85.7	68.9
Alexander Hamilton Insurance Company	72.5	10.7
Massachusetts Indemnity and Life..............	42.4	41.3
American National Insurance Company	72.2	74.6
Occidental Life Insurance, California	90.2	84.4
Certified Life Insurance Company, California.....	49.6	47.5
Ford Life Insurance Company..................	66.7	—
Cudis Insurance Society Incorporated	58.2	—
Beneficial Standard Life	46.6	46.7
Federal Home Life Insurance Company	67.8	50.2
Connecticut General Life.....................	88.5	72.0

(1) Claims paid divided by earned premium for individual and group policies.
(2) Claims paid plus expenses divided by net premium for individual guaranteed renewable policies only.
Source: 1979 Argus Health Chart, National Underwriter Co.

Medicare was designed to provide low cost health insurance for persons 65 and over. But it was never intended to pay all medical bills. Since it began, Medicare has paid an increasingly smaller proportion of the medical bills of the elderly; because of cost increases, it now pays only about 38 per cent.

To make up for the gaps in coverage, many Medicare recipients have found it necessary to buy supplementary insurance from private firms. Some policies cover the gaps effectively, but others are essentially worthless. An investigation by the U.S. House Select Committee on Aging in 1978 revealed widespread abuses in the sale of Medicare supplementary (Medigap) policies. Among the abuses cited by state insurance commissioners were:

● Agents who present themselves as representatives of Medicare or some other government agency to induce confidence in the person they are trying to sell a policy.

● Agents who mislead people into buying a group of different policies, allegedly to get adequate coverage, when in fact they get little additional coverage. Quite often, the purchase of separate policies also leads to overlapping coverage.

● Agents who exploit the fears and apprehensions of the elderly, many of whom live alone and are susceptible to the ploys of a friendly agent who appears to have their best interests at heart.

The Committee compiled a list of loss ratios for Medigap policies from information supplied by individual companies. It found a wide discrepancy in the loss ratios for Medigap policies. (See following table.) The list contains rates only of companies that responded to the Committee's request for information.

LOSS RATIOS FOR MEDIGAP POLICIES

COMPANY	LOSS RATIO	COMPANY	LOSS RATIO
Mutual Protective Ins.	22%	All American Casualty	53%
Medico Life	25%	CNA	55%
New York Life	29%	Bankers Life and Casualty	57%
American United Life	29%	Guarantee Reserve Life	57%
National Casualty Co.	30%	American National	58%
American Progressive	33%	American Variable Annuity	63%
National Security Ins.	35%	Chesapeake Life	65%
Reliable Ins. Co.	36%	Guardian	66%
Constitution Life	37%	Rural Mutual	69%
Old American	38%	Mutual Benefit Life	70%
Pioneer Life of Illinois	39%	Banker's (Iowa)	75%
Pacific Mutual	40%	Home Life	77%
Liberty National Life	40%	Nationwide	78%
Businessmen's Assurance	43%	Durhan Life	79%
American Exchange Life	44%	Life of Virginia	82%
Commercial State Life	47%	Metropolitan	83%
Union Bankers	48%	National Life And Accident	85%
Country Life	49%	Blue Cross/Blue Shield	91%
Aid to Lutherans	50%		

SELECTING A MEDIGAP POLICY

There are basically two types of Medigap policies, service and indemnity. An indemnity policy pays a fixed amount in benefits and this usually does not keep pace with inflation. A service policy pays a fixed percentage of the medical bill and therefore keeps pace with inflation better.

A wide variety of policies is offered in both of these catagories. Some companies offer a string of separate policies which supplement Medicare; others offer single comprehensive policies to which "riders" can be attached. "Riders" are extra benefits provided under the same policy for extra premiums.

Insurance experts recommend that a comprehensive policy is better than a string of separate policies which are likely to provide overlapping coverage. However, even the most comprehensive Medigap policy will not fill all the gaps in Medicare.

Almost every policy has an initial waiting period, during which expenses should be no longer than six months. Some policies also exclude coverage for specific illnesses, while others provide coverage only for certain illnesses. Such policies usually provide few benefits.

In choosing a company it is a good idea to check its loss ratio. However, the Committee on Aging discovered that there is often a wide discrepancy between an insurance company's overall loss ratio and its Medigap loss ratio. Separate loss ratios for Medigap policies are not often disclosed, however. It is important, therefore, to inquire about the general reputation of a company, such as whether it pays claims efficiently and courteously, before buying a policy from it.

AUTOMOBILE INSURANCE

Only health insurance generates more complaints than auto insurance. The present system has been severely criticized in recent years by legislators, motorists and even some insurance companies sensitive about their poor image. Among the most frequent charges are that the present system is hopelessly outdated, far too costly for what it provides, unfair to policyholders and too cumbersome for today's needs.

But proposals to reform the industry by establishing a nationwide system of "no-fault" coverage (to pay accident victims promptly regardless of fault) have been defeated every time they have come before Congress. Principal opponents of reform are trial lawyers (who make $2 billion per year on accident cases) and many insurance companies (who don't want to lose their immunity from federal regulation).

The main point of controversy is the necessity of establishing who is at fault in an accident before liability insurance benefits are paid. Collision and medical payment benefits are already dispensed on a no-fault basis. Problems arise when claims for payment are held up by insurance companies while the question of fault is decided. The average delay for court cases is 16 months, according to a massive study by the U.S. Department of Transportation a few years ago.

BENEFITS NOT DISTRIBUTED EVENLY

Another bone of contention is the inequitable manner in which benefits are distributed. The same study found that 45 per cent of seriously injured accident victims did not receive any benefits at all. And only 15 per cent of those who took their case to court received any award. At the same time, those with small losses receive more than four times their actual losses.

Other studies have shown a low ratio of benefits to premiums. Data uncovered in 1970 by the U.S Senate Antitrust Subcommittee indicated that payments to policyholders for losses amounted to only about half the premiums paid by those policyholders. The rest went to pay for administrative and legal expenses in addition to profit. Much company revenue comes from investments purchased with premiums paid in advance for insurance coverage.

The no-fault system is designed to eliminate much expense by restricting the right to sue. In fact, premiums dropped substantially in states that first adopted no-fault. However, companies opposing no-fault at the federal level contend a national no-fault system would be more costly to motorists than the present system.

Adding to the problems in recent years has been the rapid increase in repair costs. State Farm Insurance Company reported in 1976, that auto parts prices had risen 64 per cent in 1974 and 1975, far faster than other living costs. Premiums inevitably will be raised to reflect these higher costs.

In order to pare down costs, most companies have become very selective in approving customers for coverage. Whole classes of people have been excluded by some companies or put into high-premium categories by others. Persons most often penalized in this way are ones who are young, unmarried or elderly. Even clergymen and physicians have been considered high-risk drivers by some companies. Whole neighborhoods, particularly block sections of large cities, have been "redlined" (excluded) from coverage or required to pay extra high rates. As a result, many good drivers are unfairly penalized because of their neighborhood, occupation, age or sex.

Companies do not routinely tailor their rates to individual driving records or to the relative damageability of cars, even though this information is available. Premiums are set for classes of cars and drivers. Anyone or any car in a particular class must pay the same as any other regardless of individual differences. Some companies offer "safe driver" discounts for motorists who have clean accident slates for a certain number of years, usually three. But these companies are very few and the discounts are small.

NO FAULT AUTO INSURANCE LAWS IN 23 STATES

By October, 1979, there were no-fault auto insurance laws in 23 states representing 53 per cent of the U.S. population, according to a survey by the Alliance of American Insurers, a group of companies that has been pushing no-fault at the state level and opposing it in Congress. (See accompanying list of states and summaries of their laws.) But the laws vary widely, creating a patchwork quilt of legal complications for motorists and companies that cross state borders.

The accompanying list of no-fault laws is divided into two sections: states with restrictions on the right to sue (called tort) and states with no restrictions on the right to sue.

STATE NO-FAULT LAWS

STATES WITH RESTRICTIONS ON THE RIGHT TO SUE

Colorado—Bodily injury only: $25,000 medical, $25,000 rehabilitation, $6,500 loss of income, $5,410 loss of services, and $1,000 death benefits (in lieu of loss of income and loss of service).

Connecticut—Bodily injury only: $5,000 aggregate for various benefits.

Florida—Bodily injury: $10,000 aggregate for various benefits (deductibles of $250 to $8,000).

Georgia—Bodily injury only: $5,000 aggregate for various benefits.

Hawaii—Bodily injury only: $15,000 aggregate for various benefits.

Kansas—Bodily injury only: $2,000 medical, $2,000 rehabilitation and $7,800 loss of income.

Kentucky—Bodily injury only: $10,000 aggregate for various benefits. All owners of registered vehicles must choose whether or not to purchase the minimum of $10,000 of basic no-fault benefits. If benefits are purchased, the owner is exempt from tort actions for special damages by other such purchasers to the extent of such benefits.

Massachusetts—Bodily injury only: $2,000 aggregate for various benefits (optional deductibles up to $2,000).

Michigan—Bodily injury: unlimited medical and $37,000 loss of income (optional deductible of $300); property damage: $1 million for non-vehicular property damage and auto property damage only when vehicle is parked.

Minnesota—Bodily injury only: $20,000 for medical expenses, as well as rehabilitative services, and an aggregate of $10,000 for loss of income, loss of services, survivors benefits, and funeral expenses. (Deductibles of $200 for loss of income benefits and $100 for all medical expense benefits are optional.)

New Jersey—Bodily injury only: unlimited medical expenses and $5,200 loss of income.

New York—Bodily injury only: $50,000 aggregate for various benefits (optional "family" deductible of $200), plus $2,000 for funeral expenses.

North Dakota—Bodily injury only: $15,000 aggregate for various benefits.

Pennsylvania—Bodily injury only: Unlimited medical and rehabilitation expenses (but includes a maximum limit of $1,500 for funeral expenses), $15,000 wage loss benefits, $8,125 loss of service benefits and $5,000 survivors benefits. (A $100 deductible, applicable to all basic loss benefits other than survivors' benefits, and a one-week waiting period, applicable only to wage loss and loss of service benefits, are optional.

Utah—Bodily injury only: $2,000 medical expenses and $7,800 loss of income with a three-day waiting period retroactive after two weeks (optional $500 no-fault deductible).

NO-FAULT STATES WITHOUT RESTRICTIONS ON RIGHT TO SUE

Arkansas—Bodily injury only: $2,000 medical and $7,280 loss of income with a seven-day waiting period. (1)

Delaware—Bodily injury: $10,000 aggregate for various benefits; property damage: $5,000 for non-vehicular damage. (2)

Maryland—Bodily injury only: $2,500 aggregate for various benefits. (2)

Oregon—Bodily injury only: $5,000 medical expenses and $9,000 loss of income with a retroactive 14-day waiting period. (2)

South Carolina—Bodily injury only: $1,000, $1,500, $2,000, $2,500 or $5,000 for medical expenses, loss of income and loss of services. (1)

South Dakota—Bodily injury only: $2,000 medical expenses and $3,120 loss of income with a 14-day waiting period. (1)

Texas—Bodily injury only: $2,500 aggregate for various benefits. (1)

Virginia—Bodily injury only: $2,000 medical expenses and $5,200 loss of income. (1)

(1) Companies must offer these coverages, but motorist has the option of buying or not. (2) Policies must contain these items.

COMPLAINT RATIOS OF AUTO INSURERS

One way to select an auto insurance company is to consider its record on handling complaints from customers. On that basis, the best of the large companies are Amica Mutual and Kemper, according to the latest annual comparison made by the New York State Insurance Department.

Each year, the Department rates auto insurers on the number of complaints per $1 million in premiums in that state. Included are complaints that are adjusted or litigated; not included are unjustified complaints.

Results tend to give higher ratios to companies with low premiums and distort ratios for small companies because of the relatively small numbers involved.

Insurance groups with the 10 highest ratio of complaints in order for 1977, (for which figures were released in 1979) were Nassau, Colonial Penn, Consolidated Mutual, Cosmopolitan Mutual, Eveready, State-Wide, Country Wide, Empire Mutual, Commercial Credit and American Transit.

Companies with the best ratios included the following with premiums of $20 million or more:

Insurance Group*	Total Number of complaints in 1977	Average of 1976-77 premiums (in thousands)	Complaints per $1 million of premiums
Amica Mutual	4 8	$ 24,346	2.0
Kemper Group	213	68,252	3.1
National Grange Mutual	93	26,294	3.5
Continental Insurance Group	252	70,085	3.6
Motors Group	74	20,088	3.7
Utica Mutual Group	166	42,953	3.9
USAA Group	86	20,207	4.3
State Farm Group	602	123,599	4.9
Chubb Group	237	47,770	5.0
Allstate Group	1,711	338,974	5.0
Royal-Globe Group	274	53,378	5.1
Nationwide Group	376	73,518	5.1
Home Group	184	35,366	5.2
Liberty Mutual Group	458	86,573	5.3
Merchants Mutual Group	376	69,558	5.4
Aetna Life & Casualty Group	938	171,044	5.5
Travelers Group	602	105,984	5.7
Commercial Union Assurance Group	145	25,280	5.7
INA Group	310	49,591	6.3
Prudential of America Group	220	34,083	6.5
American Financial Group	141	21,610	6.5
Firemans Fund-American Group	330	49,009	6.7
Crum & Forster Group	171	24,868	6.9
Connecticut General-Aetna Group	173	23,637	7.3
General Accident Group	694	63,423	10.9

*Companies or Groups with $20 million or more in average annual automobile premiums written in New York for 1976 and 1977.

Source: New York State Insurance Department, 1979.

WAYS TO CUT INSURANCE COSTS

Although premiums for auto insurance have been going up, rates continue to vary greatly from company to company and place to place. (See table comparing 50 cities and suburbs.) Surveys have shown rates of some companies two to three times those of others for identical coverage and conditions. Many companies belong to a "rating bureau" such as the Insurance Services Office, but most firms set their rates either above or below those set by bureaus for guideline purposes. Two of the largest non-bureau firms are State Farm and Sears' Allstate. State Farm consistently undersells most other large companies, but some smaller regional firms have even lower rates. If you are not already in an assigned risk pool, it may pay handsome dividends to compare rates of auto insurance firms. Rates for assigned risk drivers are substantially higher than others.

One way to reduce insurance costs is to increase deductible amounts in collision coverage. The industry has encouraged policyholders to take this route. It also now concedes that after four years, the average car loses so much value that any collision insurance may not be worth the cost. Not many motorists realize that they are allowed to deduct uninsured losses above $100 from their income taxes. One place not to scrimp however, is in liability coverage. With jury awards approaching the astronomical in some cases, it is wise to carry as much as you can reasonably afford.

For detailed guidance in shopping for auto insurance, consult the *Consumer Action's Auto Insurance Guide,* an 84-page booklet produced and sold for $3.50 by Consumer Action, 26 Seventh St., San Francisco, CA, 94103. It compares costs of various types of policies and conditions among 14 companies most of which sell in all states.

HOW AUTO INSURANCE COMPANIES COMPARE
For City and Suburban Coverage

The table below shows why it pays to shop around for auto insurance if you can. Rates for some companies are more than three times those of other companies for the same coverage. Many of the lowest rates are from small firms that do business only in a small geographical area. The data below covers only Missouri, but small firms with low rates also abound in other states.

PREMIUMS COMPARED BY COMPANY

"Example One" includes a married male and female driver, aged 36, who drive to work two miles one way, with no traffic violations or accidents in the past three years. Annual mileage is 10,000.

"Example Two" includes married male and female drivers/aged 48, who drive to work six miles one way, with no traffic violations or accidents in the past three years. They have an 18-year-old son who uses the vehicle 25 per cent of the time. Annual mileage is 16,000.

Following are annual rates of individual companies for typical city and suburban drivers in the St. Louis, Missouri area. Rates for the same coverage elsewhere may differ from these (See table of typical rates for 50 major cities). But the relative standing of the companies may not vary much from place to place.

Coverage for both examples includes bodily injury for $25,000 maximum per person and $50,000 maximum for all persons; $10,000 maximum for property damage; $500 in medical payments; $100 deductible on collision; no deductible on comprehensive; maximum of $10,000 for one uninsured motorist and $20,000 for all uninsured motorists. Rates are for April, 1979. Information is taken from the *Consumer Shopping Guide for Automobile Insurance,* published by the Missouri Division of Insurance, Jefferson City, MO, 65101.

Figures in the first column are for a driver living in the 2700 block of Gravois, which the Insurance Division calls "generally representative" of most of the city of St Louis. Figures in the second column are for a driver living in Kirkwood, which is considered typical of St. Louis suburbs.

AUTO INSURANCE RATES BY COMPANY
For City, Suburban Driver

NAME OF COMPANY	EXAMPLE ONE (Annual Rates— 12 month coverage)	EXAMPLE TWO	EXAMPLE ONE (Annual Rates— 12 month coverage)	EXAMPLE TWO
Aetna Casualty & Surety Ins. Co. (f)	$426	$1048	$324	$802
Aetna Insurance Company.	696	1389	453	924
Allstate Insurance Company (o).	419	809	257	505
American Continental Ins. Co. (k)	916	1184	864	1108
American Economy Insurance Co.	502	1241	326	823
American Family Mutual Ins. Co. (c).	393	902	262	613
American Insurance Company (o)	480	1234	306	800
American Motorists Ins. Co.	552	1418	330	862
Amer. Nat'l Property & Casualty Ins. Co. .	644	1384	256	554
American Standard Ins. Co. of WI	822	1584	679	1272
American States Ins. Co.	558	1379	363	917
Associated Indemnity Corp. (o)	408	1052	258	680
Auto Club Inter-Ins. Exchange (e)	370	830	236	528
Auto Owners (Mutual) Ins. Co.	515	854	338	574
Bituminous Casualty Corp.	557	1377	362	912
Cameron Mutual Ins. Co. (h).	624	1216	624	1216
Casualty Reciprocal Exchange	415	1030	273	684
Colonial Penn Ins. Co. (m)(o)	379	908	271	650
Commercial Union Ins. Co. (d)	536	1361	340	868
Continental Casualty Co. (d)	519	1186	342	794
Continental Ins. Co.	594	975	419	705
Continental Western Ins. Co.	456	1241	297	820
Country Insurance Co.	821	2084	289	725
Countryside Casualty Co. (d)	639	997	410	834
Dairyland Ins. Co. (k)	994	1844	888	1706
Economy Fire & Casualty	503	1210	320	769
Employer's Fire Ins. Co. (d).	468	1171	300	758
Employers Mutual Casualty Co.	761	1592	501	1064
Employers Mutual Liability Ins. Co.	557	1377	362	912
Equity Mutual Insurance Co.	415	1030	273	684
Farm Bureau Town & Country Ins. Co. (g)			318	654
Farmers Alliance Mutual Ins. Co.	557	1377	362	912
Farmers and Merchants Ins. Co.	320	740	252	566
Farmers Ins. Co., Inc. (b).	570	1209	359	769
Federal Insurance Company	556	1380	362	909
Federal Kemper Ins. Co.	575	1456	322	812
Federated Mutual Ins. Co.	465	1156	304	770
Fireman's Fund Ins. Co. (o)	480	1234	306	800
Gen. Accid., Fire & Life Assurance Corp. (o)	559	1258	364	837
General Casualty Co. of WI.	396	892	274	613
Gov't Employees Ins. Co. (o).	490	1138	322	740

NAME OF COMPANY	EXAMPLE ONE (Annual Rates— 12 month coverage)	EXAMPLE TWO	EXAMPLE ONE (Annual Rates— 12 month coverage)	EXAMPLE TWO
Grinnell Mutual Reinsurance Co. (l)	457	817	293	551
Hanover Ins. Co. (f) (i) (n).............	434	1127	272	716
Hartford Accident & Indemnity Ins. Co. (f)	548	1342	330	828
Home Indemnity Co..................	741	1779	464	1118
Home Insurance Co. (n)...............	467	1140	284	707
Home Mutual Ins. Co.................	405	879	289	634
Horace Mann Ins. Co. (n)	705	1811	407	1035
Insurance Co. of North America (l) (n) ...	552	1568	290	824
Iowa National Mutual Ins. Co. (i) (n).....	462	1156	294	751
J.C. Penney Casualty Ins. Co...........	483	905	297	557
Kenilworth Ins. Co. (k)	1080	1502	789	1090
Liberty Mutual Fire Ins. (i) (o)	527	1051	275	575
Lumbermens Mutual Casualty Co.	552	1418	330	862
Maryland Casualty Co. (f) (o)	354	900	292	746
MFA Mutual Ins. Co.	409	886	198	526
Michigan Mutual Ins. Co.	503	1247	328	822
Mid-Century Ins. Co. (b) (d)	932	1727	642	1182
Miller's Mutual Ins. Assn. of IL (i) (n)....	462	1282	274	754
National Indemnity Co. (k)	990	1964	739	1477
National Surety Corp. (o).............	620	1600	392	1038
Penna. General Ins. Co. (o)	454	1022	296	676
Penna Nat'l Mutual Casualty Ins.	583	1093	364	691
Preferred Risk Mutual Ins.	545	1099	366	748
Progressive Casualty Ins. (k) ((d)	1139	2726	878	2072
Prudential Property & Casualty Ins. Co. ...	628	1260	346	714
Ranger Ins. Co. (k)	828	1020	756	948
Reliance Ins. Co.....................	522	1412	356	922
Riverside Ins. Co. of America	480	1064	340	752
Royal Globe Ins. Co..................	679	1320	423	824
Safeco Nat'l Ins.	430	980	313	722
St Paul Fire & Marine Ins. Co...........	732	1941	445	1193
St Paul Mercury Ins. Co.	575	1533	355	957
Sentry Insurance, A Mutual Co. (i) (n)....	643	1433	331	743
State Auto & Casualty Underwriters	559	1387	339	923
State Farm Fire & Casualty Ins. Co. (o) ...	703	1670	362	853
State Farm Mutual Auto Ins. Co. (a) (o) ..	425	1110	211	549
State Security Ins. Co. (k) (l)	890	1180	668	876
Transamerica Inc. Co.................	550	1222	392	870
Travelers Indemnity Co.	562	1258	350	721
United Security Ins. Co...............	438	1139	274	716
United Services Auto Assn (j) (o) (p)	377	943	250	634
U.S. Fidelity & Guaranty (d) (f)	432	1112	294	754
United States Fire Ins. Co. (o) (d)........	518	1319	328	838
Universal Underwriters Inc. Co.	557	1263	362	840
Western Casualty & Surety Co.	579	1493	403	1040
Western Fire Ins. Co.................	435	1127	301	778
Mo. Joint Underwriting Assn. (JUA) (r)	721	1334	471	915

(a) A one-time, not yearly, membership fee of approximately $15.00 is not included in the rates. (b) A $15.00 one-time additional charge for new customers is not included in the rates shown. (c) A $10.00 one-time additional charge for new customers is not included in the rates shown. (d) These rates are for coverage that requires you to pay a $50.00 deductible on comprehensive. All other rate examples are for no deductible required. (e) Must be a member of the Automobile Club of Missouri in order to be eligible for insurance, with $25.00 yearly dues. Dues are not included in the rates shown. (f) The company offers two different rates based upon the type of coverage selected. Check with your agent. (g) Must be a member of the Missouri Farm Bureau in order to be eligible for insurance, with $30.00 yearly membership. Membership is not included in the rates shown. (h) This company is organized under the farmers mutual insurance laws of Missouri. (i) Special auto policy, $50,000 liability limit, higher amount of medical payments coverage, some provisions differ from family policies, check with your agent. (j) Membership is limited to commissioned officers on active duty, retired regular officers, retired reserve officers of all branches of the military service. (k) Writes coverage primarily for non-standard "high-risk" drivers and has higher deductibles for comprehensive and collision coverage and liability coverage amounts are less than example calls for. (l) Accident-free discount available on renewal. (m) Writes coverage principally for older drivers. (n) $2,000 medical payments coverage. (o) $1,000 medical payments coverage. (p) Offers a 10% dividend at this time, not included in rates shown. (r) The Missouri Joint Underwriting Association (JUA), made up of all companies selling auto insurance in Missouri, provides insurance to those who need it.

Source: Missouri Dept. of Consumer Affairs, May, 1979.

HOMEOWNER AND TENANT INSURANCE

Not many years ago, it was necessary for a homeowner to take out a number of insurance policies for complete protection. One policy would cover fire, another theft, still another personal liability. Today, the standard homeowner package policy wraps all these items together at a substantial saving in cost over separate policies and with considerable reduction in paperwork.

There are now six standard policy forms. Numbers 1, 2, 3 and 5 are for conventional home protection. Each covers financial protection against loss or damage to the house, garage and furnishings, plus comprehensive personal liability. Contents are usually covered at half the total policy coverage. Most policies now also provide for additional living expenses if occupants are forced to live temporarily in a motel or apartment. Form 1 provides basic coverage; forms 2, 3 and 5 provide progressively broader protection. Form 2 is the most popular.

Form 4 is for tenants who want protection for personal property and emergency living expenses. Form 6, the latest product, is for condominium owners. It is patterned after homeowners' policies but also includes protection for an owner's interest in common property such as recreational facilities.

The most confusing aspect of homeowner insurance is the "80 per cent cut-off" clause. This standard clause says that the owner must carry protection equal to 80 per cent of the replacement cost of the house in order to collect the full amount of a loss. For example, if your house cost $20,000 when new but would cost $40,000 to replace at today's costs, you would have to carry at least $32,000 in fire insurance in order to collect $32,000 or the full replacement costs of partial losses if your house were completely destroyed. It is assumed that 20 per cent of the value would be left in the foundation even if a house burns to the ground, which is a rare occurrence. If you had less than $32,000 of insurance, the company might pay only the "actual cash value," which is the replacement cost minus depreciation due to wear, tear and obsolescence. Depending on how close your insurance coverage is to the 80 per cent figure, you would receive a portion of your replacement cost, but it would never be less than "actual cash value."

DEDUCTIBLES CAN SAVE MONEY

About the only way to save money on homeowner insurance is to take full advantage of deductibles. Since most claims are for relatively small amounts to cover thefts of bicycles and personal possessions, insurance companies are willing to cut premiums substantially in return for relief from covering relatively small losses which the average homeowner may be able to handle without trouble. By doubling the deductible, from $50 to $100, premiums can often be reduced by at least 10 per cent. A $500 deductible can reduce premiums by 25 per cent or more.

A concerted industry move to simplify policy language has reached six states: Colorado, Georgia, Illinois, Nevada, Ohio and Vermont. They were chosen because their laws permitted such revamping of policy terminology. The new model policy comes in the form of a booklet instead of the usual lengthy folded document. Its type is about 25 per cent larger, and the wording is simplified and shortened.

Policy coverage also has been expanded. For example, coverage for theft of personal property away from home has been increased from the usual 10 per cent to 100 per cent of the limit of liability set in the policy, but the 10 per cent limit still applies to property at a second, or vacation, home. Credit card coverage has been increased to $500; the new limit also for loss of a tree or shrub. Theft coverage now includes personal property of students living at school.

At the same time, some coverages have been restricted. For example, losses from theft of silverware or guns are now limited to $1,000 unless covered by a special endorsement. And if part of the property is rented, theft must be covered by a special endorsement to the policy.

Rates for homeowner and tenant insurance vary considerably by locality, depending on the incidence of crime and fire, also the quality of police and fire protection. Rates also vary substantially among some companies for coverage in the same neighborhood. It is not unusual to find rates of one company as much as twice those of another company for the same amount of coverage on the same street.

MISSOURI SURVEY SHOWS RATES VARY BY 300%

A survey released in 1979 by the State of Missouri showed that prices for the same coverage varied by as much as 300 per cent from one company to another. (See table.) Rates were compared for 100 companies on standard policies: Homeowners Basic Form (HO-1), Homeowners Broad Form (HO-2) and Special Homeowners Policy for Renters, Contents Broad Form (HO-4).

Form HO-1 includes damage from fire, lightning, windstorm, hail, explosion, riot, aircraft, smoke, vandalism, glass breakage, theft, limited damage to trees and shrubs, damage to property of others, personal liability insurance and medical payments. HO-2 includes all the above plus damage from falling objects, ice, snow, sleet, building colapse, hot water system failure, accidental water damage, freezing of plumbing and damage from sudden electrical currents. The renters policy covers all items covered by Policy HO-2.

Results of the survey have been published in *The Consumer Shopping Guide for Homeowners and Renters Insurance,* which is available free from the Missouri Dept. of Consumer Affairs, P.O. Box 1157, Jefferson City, MO, 65102. Rates may vary in other parts of Missouri and the U.S., but differences among companies are similar in other states.

Following are results for the three policies in St. Louis and a typical suburb, Kirkwood:

HOMEOWNER/TENANT INSURANCE COSTS
Annually By Company for St. Louis City and Suburb

	—CITY—			—SUBURB—		
	Example No. 1	Example No. 2	Example No. 3	Example No. 1	Example No. 2	Example No. 3
Aetna Casualty and Surety Company..	141	256	54	116	206	54
Aetna Fire Underwriters Ins. Co......	129	235	DNW	106	197	DNW
Aetna Insurance Company..........	161	281	66	133	246	66
Allstate Indemnity Company (j)......	100	258	96	179	233	86
Allstate Insurance Company (j)	133	172	64	119	155	57
American Economy Insurance Co.....	128	214	57	104	174	59
American Family Mutual Ins. Co. (d) .	95	130	52	95	130	52
American Indemnity Company	161	294	69	133	246	69
American Insurance Company (b)	147	226	53	126	194	53
American Motorists Ins. Co.	151	252	63	122	205	66
American National Fire Ins. Co. (a)...	112	163	62	94	136	62
Amer. Nat'l Prop. & Casualty Ins. Co. (c) (g).......................	88	137	55	87	123	55
American States Ins. Co............	151	252	63	122	205	66
Associated Indemnity Corp. (b)......	124	192	DNW	107	165	DNW
Auto-Owners (Mutual) Ins. Co.......	126	210	57	130	218	57
Blue Ridge Ins. Co.	98	151	37	82	125	37
Casualty Reciprocal Exchange.......	109	172	59	97	154	59
Centennial Insurance Company......	165	264	66	137	221	66
Charter Oak Fire Ins. Co. (h).......	223	DNW	57	232	DNW	59
Commercial Union Ins. Co..........	211	329	71	174	272	71
Continental Ins. Co.	162	236	55	122	175	46
Continental Western Ins. Co. (n) (l)...	98	165	53	82	136	53
Economy Fire & Casualty Co.	100	157	78	76	119	74
Employers' Fire Ins. Co.	179	278	71	148	231	71
Employers Mutual Casualty Co. (k)...	125	230	81	104	190	81
Equity Mutual Ins. Co.	109	172	59	97	154	59
Farmers and Merchants Ins. Co.	98	136	35	79	111	36
Farmers Ins. Exchange.............	161	294	66	133	246	66
Federal Kemper Ins. Co. (a)........	145	146	66	121	122	66
Federated Mutual Ins. Co...........	128	181	53	106	151	53
Fidelity and Casualty Co. of NY	162	236	55	122	175	46
Fidelity and Guaranty Ins. Underwriters	126	230	DNW	104	192	DNW
Fire Ins. Exchange (e) (k)	108	157	68	105	140	68
Fireman's Fund Ins. Co. (b).........	147	226	53	126	194	53
Firemen's Ins. Co. of Newark, NJ	162	236	55	122	175	46
First National Ins. Co. of America....	198	287	64	201	265	64
First of Georgia Ins. Co.	90	165	50	74	135	50
General Accident Fire & Life Assurance	147	270	62	122	224	62
Grain Dealers Mutual Ins. Co........	128	214	54	104	174	56
Gulf Ins. Co.	144	240	63	116	194	66
Hanover Ins. Co. (e)	133	211	66	103	171	66
Hartford Accident & Indemnity Co. ..	134	224	82	129	216	79
Hartford Fire Ins. Co.	158	263	82	152	254	79
Hawkeye-Security Ins. Co.	121	223	51	101	185	51
Home Indemnity Co................	161	294	66	100	162	56
Home Insurance Co................	161	294	66	133	246	66
Home Mutual Ins. Co..............	107	180	50	89	149	50
Horace Mann Ins. Co. (a)	103	172	50	106	172	50
Ins. Co. of North America..........	120	193	75	108	173	78
Iowa Kemper Ins. Co. (a)...........	118	160	66	97	134	66
Iowa National Mutual Ins. Co.	126	236	62	104	192	62
Liberty Mutual Fire Ins. Co.	139	187	59	114	156	59
Lititz Mutual Ins. Co.	151	252	78	111	185	59

| | —CITY— | | | —SUBURB— | | |
	Example No. 1	Example No. 2	Example No. 3	Example No. 1	Example No. 2	Example No. 3
Maryland Casualty Co.	151	252	63	122	205	66
MFA Mutual Ins. Co.	83	120	39	85	123	39
Michigan Mutual Ins. Co.	147	270	62	122	224	62
Mid-America Fire and Marine Ins. Co.	145	175	53	121	146	53
Mid-Century Ins. Co. (e) (k)	108	157	68	105	140	68
Millers Mutual Fire Ins. Co. of Texas .	116	182	58	118	189	58
Millers Mutual Ins. Assn. of IL	79	118	32	82	122	32
National American Ins. Co. (i).......	110	203	44	92	168	44
National American Ins. Co. of CA (i) .	147	270	58	122	224	58
New Hampshire Ins. Co.	151	252	63	122	205	66
Northern Ins. Co. of NY	128	214	54	104	174	56
North River Ins. Co.	104	168	DNW	95	151	DNW
Northwestern National Casualty Co...	125	230	62	104	190	62
Pennsylvania General Ins. Co........	118	216	50	98	179	50
Penna. Nat'l Mutual Casualty Ins. Co. (e).........................	126	204	53	128	213	53
Potomac Ins. Co..................	147	270	62	122	224	62
Prudential Property & Casualty Ins. Co...........................	102	139	54	97	133	54
Reliance Ins. Co.	161	294	62	133	246	66
Republic Ins. Co..................	164	251	62	136	209	62
Reserve Ins. Co. (c)	403	DNW	DNW	416	DNW	DNW
Riverside Ins. Co. of America (a).....	118	175	66	98	145	66
Royal Globe Ins. Co.	125	200	50	112	181	50
Royal Indemnity Co.	100	160	40	90	145	40
Safeco Ins. Co. of America (f) (g)	125	181	48	127	167	48
St. Paul Fire and Marine Ins. Co. (a) ..	138	241	66	127	220	66
Sentry Ins. Mutual Co. (a)	129	176	59	103	140	59
Standard Fire Ins. Co.	113	204	43	93	164	43
State Automobile Mutual Ins. Co.....	119	197	45	99	163	45
State Farm Fire and Casualty Co. (e) ..	115	144	50	107	135	50
State Farm General Ins. Co. (e)	141	222	85	132	208	85
Transamerica Ins. Co.	146	229	61	121	190	61
Travelers Indemnity Co.	164	312	66	133	248	66
United Fire & Casualty Co.	93	149	62	96	156	62
United Services Automobile Assn. (m).	78	114	50	80	117	50
United States Fidelity & Guaranty	161	294	66	133	246	66
United States Fire Ins. Co...........	139	224	50	125	204	51
Valley Forge Ins. Co. (e)	97	173	43	81	143	43
Vanguard Ins. Co.	136	208	51	113	173	51
Western Casualty and Surety Co......	111	170	66	103	159	67
Western Fire Ins. Co...............	162	257	66	134	215	67
Western Indemnity Co., Inc.	94	145	66	88	135	67
Zurich Ins. Co.	147	270	62	122	224	62

(a) Discount given on newer homes; discount included in premium for Example 2. (b) Examples 1 and 2 provide coverage for a structural loss to a building on replacement cost basis, regardless of amount of insurance carried. (c) Mandatory $250.00 deductible on theft. (d) New home discount for homes 1-6 years old; discount does not apply to example 1 or 2. (e) Discount given on newer homes; discount does not apply to Example 1 or 2. (f) Requires insurance coverage equal to full replacement cost. (g) Minimum amount of coverage for Example 3 is $7,000. (h) For Example 1; writes a special form of dwelling owners coverage based on actual cash value rather than replacement cost. (i) Mandatory $250.00 deductible for Example 3. (j) This company does not offer Broad Form (HO-2) homeowners coverage; rates quoted for Rating Example 1 are for more coverage. (k) Minimum amount of coverage for Example 3 is $8,000. (l) Company offers two rates; policyholders without claims in the past 3 years receive the lower rate. (m) Membership or eligibility is limited to the military. (n) The company offers two different rates based upon the age of the home or the amount of insurance carried, check with your agent. DNW company does not write homeowners insurance at present.

Example No. 1—(Form HO-2) $100 deductible, all perils, $25,000 coverage on one-family brick dwelling with approved roof, a 30-year-old home. Example No. 2—(Form HO-3) $100 deductible, all perils, $40,000 coverage, on one-family brick dwelling with approved roof, an 8-year-old home. Example No. 3—(Form HO-4) $100 deductible, all perils, $6,000.00 coverage, three to four-family brick apartment with approved roof.

Source: Missouri Dept. of Consumer Affairs, 1979.

COMPARING INSURANCE RATES
Some People Pay a Premium Premium

The following table offers two benefits. It shows how insurance rates as of April 1, 1978, vary among 50 large metropolitan areas for three types of insurance: homeowner, tenant and automobile. It also can serve as a guideline against which to compare an individual's policy costs. The rates are ones set by "bureaus," to which many insurance companies belong. Member companies do not all charge "bureau" rates, but a study by a task force of the U.S. Department of Justice found that "bureau" rates tend to fall at about the median point of rates for all companies, including non-bureau ones in California. Policy coverages are explained in the footnotes.

TYPICAL INSURANCE RATES IN 50 CITIES

State	City	Homeowners Policy [1]	Tenant Insurance [2]	Auto Insurance [3] City	Auto Insurance [3] Suburb
Alabama	Birmingham	$336	$ 97	274	246
Arizona	Phoenix	261	100	382	293
California	Los Angeles	228	100	562	315
	Sacramento	250	92	343	269
	San Diego	177	68	266	266
	San Francisco	215	105	562	562
Colorado	Denver	296	85	276	283
District of Columbia				374	374
Florida	Jacksonville	222	50	222	194
	Miami	239	60	727	565
Georgia	Atlanta	401	135	296	265
Hawaii	Honolulu	138	113	317	317
Illinois	Chicago	280	98	470	246
Indiana	Indianapolis	292	85	335	304
Kentucky	Louisville	334	74	270	239
Louisiana	New Orleans	552*	310	419	294
Maryland	Baltimore	147	50	412	282
Massachusetts	Boston	286	107	651	401
Michigan	Detroit	296	55	466	408
Minnesota	Minneapolis	292	74	316	295
Missouri	Kansas City	292	83	385	277
	St Louis	304	72	443	299

State	City	Homeowners Policy [1]	Tenant Insurance [2]	Auto Insurance [3] City	Auto Insurance [3] Suburb
Nebraska	Omaha	340	52	292	203
New Jersey	Newark	186	55	651	472
New York	Buffalo	243	46	349	268
	Rochester	231	46	251	251
	Syracuse	243	46	277	281
	New York City:				
	Bronx	256	53		
	North			526	
	South			636	
	Brooklyn	313	65	698	
	Manhattan	448	55	488	
	Queens	235	60	532	
	Staten Island	263	53	452	
North Carolina	Charlotte	207	53	181	173
Ohio	Cincinnati	221	72	347	261
	Cleveland	259	72	648	392
	Columbus	224	73	323	262
	Toledo	224	73	357	261
Oklahoma	Oklahoma City	364	88	262	249
	Tulsa	364	88	272	251
Oregon	Portland	184	70	408	353
Pennsylvania	Philadelphia	228	93	589	489
	Pittsburgh	147	72	327	300
Rhode Island	Providence	336	77	462	351
Tennessee	Memphis	371	72	346	247
	Nashville	287	72	239	238
Texas	Dallas	541	75	266	266
	Houston	733	95	353	353
Utah	Salt Lake City	200	68	314	231
Virginia	Norfolk	191	72	255	238
	Richmond	173	68	300	238
Washington	Seattle	182	55	232	288
Wisconsin	Milwaukee	186	53	284	244

FOOTNOTES

(1) Homeowners rates are for "standard" package (form 2) for a $50,000 policy for a frame house with a $100 deductible.

(2) Tenants Insurance rates are for a "standard" package (form 4) for a $7,000 policy for a city apartment (brick, over 4 families) with a $100 deductible, including off-premise theft.

(3) Auto Insurance rates are for a 1978 Chevy Malibu with a 30 year old male operator for pleasure use, with no accidents in the last 3 years. Coverage includes liability (financial responsibility law of area), personal injury protection (no-fault) if required or an available option in the area, comprehensive ($200 deductible), collision ($200 deductible) and uninsured motorists.

Source: Alliance of American Insurers and Insurance Services Offices, 1979.

GOVERNMENT INSURANCE PROGRAMS

FEDERAL CRIME INSURANCE

Federal Crime Insurance offers low-cost, con-cancellable protection against loss from burglary and robbery for small businessmen and property owners and tenants in certain areas where such insurance is impossible to get at reasonable costs. Crime insurance is subsidized completely by the federal government. It is available in the District of Columbia and the following states:

Alabama, Arkansas, Colorado, Connecticut, Delaware, Florida, Georgia, Illinois, Iowa, Kansas, Maryland, Massachusetts, Minnesota, Missouri, New Jersey, New Mexico, New York, North Carolina, Ohio, Pennsylvania, Rhode Island, Tennessee, Virginia and Wisconsin.

You don't have to live in a high crime neighborhood to be eligible to buy federal crime insurance. Any resident of a state in the program is eligible. Business losses from $1,000 to $15,000 and residential losses from $1,000 to $10,000 are covered. Residential coverage not only includes burglary and robbery but loss of $500 in contents from a locked car trunk and loss of securities worth $500.

On residential losses there is a deductible of $75 or 5 per cent of the gross loss, whichever is larger. Premiums vary from $20 to $80 per year in residential burglary and robbery coverage, depending on the amount desired and the area involved. Premiums on commercial coverage range from $35 per $1,000 of burglary insurance to a maximum of $748 for burglary and robbery insurance for $15,000 coverage.

To apply for crime insurance, contact any licensed broker or agent or write to Federal Crime Insurance, P.O. Box 41003, Washington, DC, 20014. The toll-free number is 800/638-8780. (In Maryland, 301/652-2637.)

THE "FAIR" PLAN

If obtaining fire and vandalism insurance is your problem, you may be eligible for government subsidized protection under the FAIR (Fair Access to Insurance Requirements) Plan. It is operated by the industry to provide insurance for fire, riots, windstorms and vandalism at a reasonable cost. It is intended for residents of areas who may not be able to obtain such insurance because of disorders or unusual hazards such as forest fires. The government re-insures policies sold by the companies.

FAIR Plans are available in Puerto Rico, the District of Columbia and 26 states: California, Connecticut, Delaware, Georgia, Illinois, Indiana, Iowa, Kansas, Kentucky, Louisiana, Maryland, Massachusetts, Michigan, Minnesota, Missouri, New Jersey, New Mexico, New York, North Carolina, Ohio, Oregon, Pennsylvania, Rhode Island, Virginia, Wisconsin and Washington.

For the name and address of the placement facility of any state or jurisdiction on the above list, contact the Federal Insurance Administration, HUD, Washington, DC, 20410, 202/755-6580, any regional HUD office, or any insurance agent. HUD has a free folder describing the plan entitled *The FAIR Plan.*

FLOOD INSURANCE

The National Flood Insurance Program enables individual property owners in flood-prone areas to get insurance coverage that would not otherwise to available and to get it at reasonable (subsidized) rates. At the same time, it requires communities with flood-prone areas to adopt measures to prevent future flooding.

To be eligible for this federally subsidized protection, a community must apply to the Federal Insurance Administration (FIA) of the U.S. Department of Housing and Urban Development (HUD). Once an area is accepted in the program, local insurance agents sell the policies directly to those who want them.

FIA has notified more than 17,000 communities that they are flood prone and should apply for this special coverage. Each has been provided a map tentatively identifying hazardous areas. To be accepted in the program, a community must submit an application, part of which requires the adoption of minimum flood plain management regulations, such as a simple building permit system if one does not exist.

By January, 1978, there were 1.2 million policies in force for a total coverage of about $36 billion. About 16,000 out of some 20,000 flood-prone communities were participating in the program. Between 1968, when the program began, and 1978, more than 266 million claims were paid with an average payment of $3,600.

Once a community is accepted in the program, individual property owners throughout the entire community can immediately purchase subsidized insurance to cover losses. Insurance is available up to $35,000 on a single dwelling; $100,000 on multi-unit dwellings, and $10,000 on the contents of each unit; and $100,000 on non-residential buildings and $100,000 on their contents. The rate for residential coverage is only 25 cents per $100 of value. Thus, insurance protection for a residence valued at $20,000, for example, would cost only $50 per year.

Following acceptance in the program, FIA will contract with a federal agency or private engineering firm to provide the community with the data necessary to develop adequate measures to minimize flood damage. The technical information will include an actuarial rate map enabling property owners to purchase an equal additional amount of non-subsidized insurance at actuarial rates once the additional flood plain management measures are adopted for their area.

In flood prone areas, flood insurance is required whenever property is involved in federally financed or federally guaranteed mortgages, such as those of the FHA and VA.

For further information, contact community officials, local insurance agents or the FIA. The FIA toll-free number is 800/424-8872. FIA's insurance servicing contractor, Electronic Data Services Federal Corporation, may be consulted through its toll-free number, 800/638-6620.

In addition, the National Flood Insurance Program has publications explaining how it works, how much it costs and other details. The program's address is P.O. Box 34294, Bethesda, MD, 20034. Several state insurance commissions also have brochures explaining the program.

INFORMATION ON OTHER TYPES OF INSURANCE

For information about credit insurance, see the chapter on Banking and Borrowing.

For information about real estate title insurance, see the chapter on Housing and Land.

RETIREMENT INCOME INSURANCE
Large Variances Among Plans

Will you have enough money to live comfortably when you retire?

That is a question that worries many people throughout their working career. Even social security provides only enough income for minimum living expenses. But, many people will not qualify for social security payments because their jobs were not covered or they may not have met all the eligibility requirements. People who belong to formal pension programs where they work also may not be secure in view of the many cases where people found out too late that their benefits had been mismanaged, misappropriated or simply misunderstood.

(Information about **Social Security** benefits and requirements is described in the chapter on Financial Assistance.)

In 1974, Congress passed a law designed to correct many of these inequities, the Employee Retirement Income Security Act (ERISA). Its purpose is to strengthen existing pension programs for employees of private business and to set up Individual Retirement Accounts (IRAs) for those who do not have a pension program where they work. The IRA, sometimes called an Individual Retirement Annuity when sold by an insurance company, is similar to the older and better known Keogh Plan, which is designed for self-employed people.

The main idea of both Keogh and IRA is to allow individuals to set aside part of their earned income each year in a tax-deferred retirement fund. Under the Keogh Plan, self-employed people can set aside up to $7,500 or 15 per cent of annual income without paying current taxes on it. Under both plans, the interest earned on the money over the years is also not taxed. The investor pays taxes only when he withdraws the money upon retirement.

There are many requirements, however. In the first place, the plan must have been approved by the IRS. Official approval has already been given to almost all savings and investment institutions to offer such plans. There are five principal types of organizations eligible: banks, savings and loan associations, mutual funds, insurance companies and the government itself through its Individual Retirement Bonds. The Bonds are available in $50, $100 and $500 denominations and provide interest at six per cent per year. No interest is paid if they are redeemed in the first year.

DEFERRED TAXES MEAN BIG SAVINGS

Over a period of years, either one of these tax-deferral plans can mean thousands of dollars extra for retirement purposes over what might otherwise be available. For example, a person who set aside $1,500 yearly from age 30 to 65 would have $52,500 in an IRA account but only $44,030 if he put it in a non-IRA account and paid taxes on $10,000 income. If his income was $20,000, the amount after taxes in a non-IRA account would be only $39,150 compared to the $52,500 in the tax-deferred IRA account.

But that is not all. If his money earned six per cent compound interest as it accumulated during those years, the IRA account would total $177,181 compared with $113,482 on the amount taxed on the $10,000 salary bracket and only $92,662 taxed at the $20,000 level. The latter two amounts are after taxes have been deducted on the earnings.

But that is not the entire difference either. If the money is withdrawn gradually for 16 years after retirement, part of it would continue to earn interest while the rest is withdrawn. The net result after 16 years of retirement would be benefits totaling $242,224 for the IRA account, compared with $177,970 and $146,132 for the two non-IRA situations. That amounts to a net advantage of more than $96,000 for the IRA account over the non-IRA account for a person with $20,000 income. These savings are all because of the tax advantage.

They are also based on earning six per cent per year, far from the highest rate available for serious investors these days.

YIELDS OF 20 COMPANIES COMPARED

A survey in 1976 by Joe A. Mintz, a Dallas insurance agent, showed wide variances in both guaranteed and expected yields among 20 of the largest insurance companies. He compared the 25-year returns that would result from a yearly investment of $1,000 by a 45-year-old man. He found that one company, Bankers Life of Iowa, estimated benefits of $78,744, compared to an estimate of only $44,462 by Provident Mutual Insurance Co., a difference of more than $34,000 in 25 years. The company with the highest guaranteed return over the same period was $40,395 from Provident Life and Accident Co. The lowest guaranteed return was $33,442 from Northwestern Mutual.

It should be pointed out that although insurance companies almost always pay what they estimate, sometimes even more, the amounts they guarantee are considerably less. By the same token, banks and savings and loan associations cannot guarantee the present high rates over an extended period of time. The most they will guarantee is for the length of a certificate of deposit.

In comparing yields among competing investment vehicles, the first few years' performance may be the most important because of the strong chance that plans may change or an emergency may cause a person to withdraw retirement funds prematurely.

If you withdraw invested funds from an insurance company annuity plan in the early years, you may be surprised to find that you won't even get back what you put in. If you invested $1,000 at the beginning of the year, for example, in Pacific Mutual, and had to withdraw your money at the end of the year, you would get back only $750. After three years, you would get back $2,981 of the $3,000 you put in. The differences went to pay sales expenses. During the same three years, your money could have accumulated to $3,456 at seven per cent interest in a savings and loan association.

For a comprehensive description of what an IRA is, consult *IRA's*, a booklet from the Pension Benefit Guaranty Corporation, which sells for 35 cents from the Government Printing Office. The Federal Trade Commission has a four-page booklet of general advice on IRAs which is free from the agency.

PENSIONS AND PROMISES
New Studies of Deficiencies Get Underway

Many Americans are unprepared to meet their retirement needs. Despite Social Security and private pension funds, the United States does not have a comprehensive, dependable retirement income policy. "While the fortunate few have their retirement estate planners," says Washington University Professor Merton C. Bernstein, author of *The Future of Private Pensions*, the great bulk.

of the population depends on fickle fate. . . Private pensions, unfortunately, cover only a minority of the private work force, pay off only a minority of them, and yield surprisingly paltry benefits. . . Longer life is turning out to be one of modern society's major hazards."

In 1974, Congress passed the Pension Reform Law or ERISA to correct many of the abuses in pension programs and extend coverage to more people. However, the act has corrected only a few of the problems and has left hugh gaps in coverage. Many workers lose pension benefits when they change jobs. Women are likely to suffer the most, since their time in the labor force is often broken up.

Those who have contributed to pension programs may also lose out if their employer's business plummets or if benefit projections were unrealistically high. In 1974, Congress established a guarantee program for private pension systems, designed to take over monthly benefit payments when a pension becomes insolvent. While most pension funds are in good shape, a number of multi-employer plans (set up by one union and a number of employers) are in danger of collapse. Their collapse would lead to more payout obligations than the government program can meet.

The President's Commission on Pension Policy, established to review existing retirement programs and develop national policies as guidelines for private and public plans, began work in March, 1979, 21 months after it was first announced.

To serve as a prod to the government group, Ralph Nader's Pension Rights Center established a Citizens Commission on Pension Policy. The Pension Rights Center has two publications of interest to people concerned about retirement problems. *Pension Facts 1* focuses on "myths and facts;" and *Pension Facts 2* focuses on problems relating to women. Each can be obtained for 25 cents plus a stamped and addressed envelope from the Pension Rights Center, 1346 Connecticut Ave., NW, Suite 1019, Washington, DC, 20036

INVESTMENTS WORTH INVESTIGATING

As anxiety about inflation increases, so does the conpulsion to invest. Living within a tight budget makes people think seriously about taking steps to insure that they won't be worse off in the future when the economy may be even less stable.

But while a well-planned investment program can be good insurance against rising costs, one that is impulsively executed or based on insufficient information may prove unwise in the long run.

Many people are unfamiliar with the complexities of stocks and bonds, commodity futures and options and limited partnerships in oil, gas and land. They are therefore easy prey for slick salesmen who promise quick profit on "no-risk" propositions. Deception is rampant in the sale of such investments, as boiler-rooms outfitted with WATS lines pressuring unwary consumers nationwide into paying large amounts of cash for questionable or non-existent products.

FEDERAL AGENCIES INVOLVED

The Commodities Futures Trading Commission (CFTC), the Securities and Exchange Commission (SEC), the Department of Housing and Urban Development (HUD) and the Federal Trade Commission (FTC) are among the federal agencies which try to eliminate unscrupulous investment practices. Their efforts are reinforced on the national level by a number of self-regulatory industry associations such as the Securities Investor Protection Corporation (SIPC) and the National Association of Securities Dealers (NASD).

But although each of these organizations has been able to eliminate some of the glaring problems, an endless supply of more shady promoters continues to take advantage of a highly vulnerable public.

Before investing money, some time should be invested in determining one's current financial status and ability to absorb a loss. Following are some types of transactions which should not be approach blindly, plus sources of further information.

COMMODITIES—THE FUTURE IS YOUR OPTION

Commodities trading can allow investors to pay a relatively small amount for the opportunity to double or triple their cash in a short period of time by speculating on the future prices of products ranging from corn and soy beans to gold and foreign currencies. Prices are negotiated on the floor of 11 U.S. exchanges. Investors profit by accurately predicting whether prices will rise or fall during a certain month.

The two basic contracts in commodities trading are futures and options. A futures contract is an agreement to buy or sell a product at some later date at a price negotiated on the floor of the exchange by open bids and offers. Options, on the other hand, entitle a buyer to purchase or sell a commodities futures contract or a commodity at a fixed price within a certain period of time. The buyer pays the option seller a fixed sum (premium) and has the right to buy or sell the commodity before the contract is up. If it is unprofitable for the option holder to exercise his purchase or sales right, he might simply let the option expire and lose only the premium paid plus commission.

Commodities trading is a highly risky business. Only about 25 per cent of those who speculate can expect to make a profit. An additional risk is the chance of being hood-winked by a disreputable salesperson. Fraudulent and unsound sales practices in the sale of commodity options, for example, seem to be "the rule rather than the exception," according to the Commodity Futures Trading Commission, which was established in 1975 to regulate the industry.

Questionable practices include charging outrageously high commissions on options contracts, guaranteeing a profit based on false market conditions and collecting premiums for an option but failing to take action if prices increase or decrease in the buyer's favor.

The CFTC has established a toll-free hotline to provide information on salespeople offering futures, options and other commodity transactions. The number for the continental states is 800/424-9838 and for Alaska and Hawaii, 800/424-9707.

The Commission recommends that people be especially wary of unsolicited phone calls offering commodities and suggests that people who receive them ask the following questions:

● How did you get my name?
● Are you and your company registered with the CFTC?
● Is there a well-known bank or brokerage firm I can call that will recommend your firm?

● Will you send me a current financial statement and a summary of your recent recommendations?

● What is the total cost, including commissions, fees and other charges? When and how often will I have to pay? Will there be margin or storage charges?

● How much of my money is actually used to purchase the commodity?

● What is the current price of the commodity on the open market? How can I verify that?

● Exactly how much does the market price have to move in my favor for me to start making a profit?

● What kind of written confirmation do I get?

● Does your firm keep customer money separate from company money to protect my funds?

● How do I trade out of my position? And how long before I get money?

If a firm is registered, the CFTC can confirm registration and report whether it has taken any action against the firm.

Investors who become victims of deceptive practices which may be covered under the Commodity Exchange Act (call the CFTC hotline for details) may be able to receive compensation by filing a claim with the CFTC within two years of the violation. The complaint procedure is called "reparation" and can only be used if no arbitration or court action has been initiated. To file such a complaint, contact the Reparations Unit, CFTC, 2033 K Street, Washington, DC, 20581

OIL, GAS AND COAL—CASH IN THE GROUND

Investments in energy resources such as oil, gas and coal are becoming popular not only for their potential high profits but for their tax advantages. In addition to common stock, companies are offering fractional undivided interests in leases, limited partnerships and other complex securities.

A limited partner has no control over the management of the venture and liability is limited to the amount of the investment. A fractional undivided interest gives the owner a voice in the management and a responsibility for any debts and obligations.

While many legitimate firms offer such arrangements, the infamous "boiler room" selling technique is prevalent here as well. Unscrupulous promoters have shown prospective investors maps of non-existent wells, claimed that a phychic selected sites for drilling and represented that they had developed new equipment to improve the "risk/reward ratio 400 per cent." Over $1.4 million was paid to one promoter for shares in wells which had been capped and abandoned.

The U.S. Securities and Exchange Commission (SEC) has published a free booklet called "Investing in Oil, Gas and Coal" which outlines some of the problems and gives suggestions for evaluating such offers. It recommends being skeptical of promoters who cite prior success in drilling wells and suggests asking any caller the following questions:

● Is the offering filed with the SEC or the state securities commission? (If so, it has information on file)

● May I have a copy of any geological reports which have been prepared? (Review the report with a geologist or petroleum engineer.)

● How long has your company been in existence and what are the backgrounds of your principal officers?

● Will my funds be kept separate from company funds?

A copy of the booklet is available from the Consumer Information Center, Pueblo, CO, 81009.

For information about registered companies, contact the SEC Public Reference Section, 500 N. Capitol Street, Washington, DC, 20549; 202/523-5506. Complaints should be sent to the Office of Consumers Affairs at the same address.

CORPORATE STOCKS—NOT ALL BLUE CHIPS

The stock market can provide investors with the thrills of high-risk speculation or the security of long-term savings. It is no longer the payground of the idle rich. Stockholders are just as likely to be young, middle-income professionals, wealthy corporate vice-presidents or widows depending of dividends for grocery money.

While deception in the stock market may be less obvious than some of the practices documented in the sale of commodities or oil and gas leases, many problems exist. The Securities and Exchange Commission (SEC) released a report in 1979 outlining numerous abuses in the sale of stock options. Like commodity options, stock options give people the right to buy a certain number of shares of stock at a specified price within a certain period of time.

The report revealed that many salespeople and their supervisors don't understand options and have no idea whether the strategies they suggest make sense. Lax supervision, ignorance and greed have resulted in many sales to investors who don't understand the risks and are in no position to take losses.

In October, 1978, the Commission also issued a warning to the securities industry to stop unfair practices, such as:

● Increasing commissions without telling customers;

● Writing checks on distant banks to prolong the firm's use of customers' money;

● Retaining interest and dividend payments on securities held by the firm for the customer;

● Charging custodial fees on inactive accounts without telling customers they should close or transfer their accounts; and

---

DIGGING GOVERNMENT LAND

One prevalent get-rich-quick scheme invites people to pay a promoter a small fee to take advantage of a chance to lease valuable government land containing oil and gas deposits. Promoters offer to enter contestants' names in the Bureau of Land Management's oil and gas lottery. If chosen in the lottery, people pay $1 an acre to lease government land for a year and may collect a portion of any profits in the event of a successful drill. For an additional fee, some promoters offer to recommend the best lot to bid on.

What the promoters fail to mention is that anyone can enter the lottery on his or her own through the state offices of the BLM for a $10 filing fee. Promoters also omit the fact that the land has been recognized as virtually worthless, that 90 per cent of the lots are never drilled and that chances of winning the lottery are slim. The lots range from 40 acres to 2,560 acres. Lists are available from BLM offices for a few dollars.

For more information, ask for "Can You Really Strike It Rich in the Government Oil and Gas Lottery?" from the Consumer Information Center, Pueblo, CO, 81009.

● Delaying transfers of accounts to another firm.

The Commission claimed that none of the practices were specifically illegal but were "inconsistent with just and equitable practices of the trade."

Persons with complaints about securities should contact the state securities commission or the SEC, Consumer Affairs Office, Washington, DC, 20549. Such offices will also provide information about registered firms.

Another source of redress is the National Association of Securities Dealers (NASD). This industry group has an arbitration department to mediate disputes between its broker-dealer members and investors. It does not have the authority to direct its members to remit funds, reverse securities transactions or require specific performance of any kind, however. Contact NASD, 1735 K St, NW, Washington, DC, 20006.

COLLECTIBLES—THE NEWEST FAD

People who feel a need to invest but are not anxious to get rich quick are turning increasingly to "collectibles." They are buying up everything from beer cans to Braques in hopes that items they appreciate will appreciate in value.

But the value of art, antiques, stamps and other collectibles is subject to changing tastes, and most items must be kept off the market for 15 to 20 years before showing a profit. Many people find that their treasures do not increase in value even after a long period of time and that their money would have earned more in a regular savings account.

Whether buying collectibles for pleasure or profit, experts recommend the following precautions:

● Before buying or selling, consult an independent appraiser. The American Society of Appraisers (PO Box 17265, Washington, DC, 20041) and the Appraisers Association of America (541 Lexington Ave., New York, NY 10022) will provide members' names on request.

● Watch out for fakes; ask for written verification of any claims of value or authenticity.

● Ask friends to recommend a reputable dealer. Good dealers will suggest reading materials and allow independent appraisals of their items.

IF YOUR BROKER GOES BANKRUPT

In 1970, Congress established the non-profit Securities Investor Protection Corporation (SIPC) to insure stock investments if brokers go bankrupt. And now, due to a 1979 amendment, all members display the SIPC symbol in their offices and in ads. By shopping for a SIPC broker, investors can be sure that any major losses will be due to a poor choice of securities, not securities dealers.

If a member experiences financial problems, SIPC begins court proceedings to liquidate and sends its customers claim forms. It then either transfers accounts to another member firm or sends customers any secutities registered in their names.

Outstanding claims are paid out of SIPC funds to a maximum of $100,000. The broker's remaining assets are liquidated and funds not used are applied on a pro-rata basis to creditors' claims.

Brokerage failures have decreased due to a number of factors, including improved regulation, better management and more stringent requirements for entry into the business. Since SIPC was instituted, failures have dropped.

Financial Assistance

In This Chapter
- **New Social Security Laws**
- **Medicare and Medicaid**
- **Federal Food Programs**
- **Disaster Aid**
- **Veterans Benefits**

Being poor, in debt or broke is not a crime in America. Long gone are the days of debtor's prisons that isolated the indigent from the rest of society. Yet there is still a stigma attached to needing financial help. The same society which induces Americans through advertising to "buy now, pay later" frowns upon individuals who go financially overboard in their monthly payments. Corporate executives, who would not think twice about taking advantage of federal bankruptcy laws if they thought it would be to their advantage, point to the disastrous effects of bankruptcy on an individual and the rising cost of welfare payments.

This chapter provides information about programs designed to help individuals in financial trouble. In addition to assistance programs offered by the federal government there is also information about where to get free counseling on credit problems from a non-governmental, non-profit service, and details about how bankruptcy may help ease personal financial difficulties.

SOCIAL SECURITY

Social Security is a government insurance system to provide continuing income when family earnings are reduced or discontinued because of retirement, disability or death.

During working years employees, their employers and self-employed people pay into special trust funds. When earnings stop or are reduced because the worker retires, becomes disabled or dies, monthly cash benefits are paid to replace part of the earnings the family has lost.

Part of the contributions go into a separate hospital insurance trust fund so workers and their dependents will have help in paying their hospital bills when they become eligible for Medicare. The medical insurance part of Medicare is financed by premiums paid by the people who have enrolled for this protection and amounts contributed by the federal government.

If you are employed, you and your employer each pay an equal share of social security contributions. If you are self-employed, you pay contributions for retirement, survivors, and disability insurance at a somewhat lower rate than the combined rate for an employee and his employer. The hospital insurance contribution rate is the same for the employer, the employee, and the self-employed peson.

Your wages and self-employment income are entered on your social security record throughout your working years. This record of your earnings is used to determine your eligibility for benefits and the amount of cash you and your dependents will receive.

SOCIAL SECURITY AMENDMENTS OF 1977

In order to control the system's soaring costs and cut down on its massive debt, Congress passed the Social Security Amendments in 1977.

The amendments sharply increased the amount of payroll taxes workers contribute as well as the amount of a worker's salary that is subject to the tax. Both changes went into effect in 1979.

When the new law went into effect, the rate paid by both employers and employees increased from 6.05 per cent to 6.13 per cent and the self-employed rate remained at 8.10 per cent. In 1981, the rate will climb to 6.65 per cent, with self-employed persons paying 9.30 per cent (see chart for additional rate increases).

In addition, the amendments eased rules on eligibility and added to the overall benefits paid out of the system. Among the major changes are:

● Higher benefits for 65-71-year old workers. Under the old law, the benefits of recipients under the age of 72 were reduced if they earned more than $3,000 a year. The new law raised the earnings limit to $4,500 in 1979 and pushes up the limit in $500-a-year amounts, to a maximum of $6,000 in 1982. Beginning in 1982, there will be no limit on earnings for people 70 and older.

● Retention of benefits when beneficiaries remarry. The old law cut benefits back when two recipients over 60 married. Many older couples were living together rather than getting married in order to retain both sets of benefits. Under the new law, they will retain their total benefits upon remarriage.

● Simpler reporting of payrolls for employers. Employers now report wages on an annual, not quarterly basis.

SCHEDULE OF SOCIAL SECURITY RATES

Year	Retirement, Survivors, and Disability Insurance	Hospital Insurance	Total
Employer-Employee, each			
1979-80	5.08%	1.05%	6.13%
1981	5.35	1.30	6.65
1982-84	5.40	1.30	6.70
1985	5.70	1.35	7.05
1986-89	5.70	1.45	7.15
1990 and later	6.20	1.45	7.65
Self-Employed			
1979-80	7.05%	1.05%	8.10%
1981	8.00	1.30	9.30
1982-84	8.05	1.30	9.35
1985	8.55	1.35	9.90
1986-89	8.55	1.45	10.00
1990 and later	9.30	1.45	10.75

WHO GETS CHECKS?

Monthly social security checks may go to workers and their dependents when the worker retires, becomes severely disabled, or dies. Medicare helps pay the cost of health care for eligible people who are 65 or over or disabled.

Monthly benefits social security pays include:

- **Retirement checks**—You can start getting retirement checks as early as 62.
- **Disability checks**—A worker who becomes severely disabled before 65 can get disability checks.

Under social security, you're considered disabled if you have a severe physical or mental condition which prevents you from working, and is expected to last (or has lasted) for at least 12 months, or is expected to result in death. Your checks can start for the sixth full month of your disability. Once checks start, they'll continue as long as you are disabled. If you are severely disabled, you can get benefits even though you manage to work a little.

- **Survivors checks**—If a worker dies, survivors checks can go to certain members of the worker's family. This payment usually goes to the widow or widower.
- **Retirement or disability**—Monthly payments can be made to a retired or disabled worker's unmarried children under 18 (or 22 if full-time students); unmarried children 18 or over who were severely disabled before 22 and who continue to be disabled; wife or dependent husband 62 or over; wife under 62 if she's caring for worker's child under 18 (or disabled) who's getting a benefit based on the retired or disabled worker's earnings.
- **Survivors**—Monthly payments can be made to a deceased worker's unmarried children under 18 (or 22 if full-time students); unmarried son or daughter 18 or over who was severely disabled before 22 and who continues to be disabled; widow or dependent widower 60 or older; widow, widowed father, or surviving divorced mother if caring for worker's child under 18 (or disabled) who is getting a benefit based on the earnings of the deceased worker; widow or dependent widower 50 or older who becomes disabled not later than seven years after worker's death, or in case of a widow, within seven years after she stops getting checks as a widow caring for worker's children; and dependent parents 62 or older.

WORK CREDIT FOR DISABILITY

If you become disabled before age 24, you need credit for 1½ years of work in the 3 years before you become disabled. If you are between 24 and 31, you must have credit for half the time between your 21st birthday and the time you become disabled. If you become disabled at 31 or later, you need as much credit as you would need if you reached retirement age in the year you are disabled; and five years of your work must be in the 10-year period just before you become disabled. The work requirement is different if you are disabled by blindness.

SPECIAL RULES APPLY TO SOME WORK

Although almost all jobs are covered by social security, there are special rules which apply to some. You should check with a social security office about these special rules if you work in or about someone's home doing housecleaning, gardening, or babysitting; if you are a student and also are employed by your school or college; if you own, operate, or work on a farm; if you are a member of a religious order; if you have a job where you get cash tips; or if you are an employee of a state or local government, a non-profit or international organization.

WHEN TO RETIRE

You can retire as early as age 62 or continue working past age 65, but when you retire will determine to a large extent, how much you'll get each month. If you retire on Social Security at age 62, your basic benefit will be reduced by 20 per cent to make up for the extra three years of payments you will be receiving. The closer you are to age 65 at retirement, however, the smaller the reduction in your payments.

If you don't collect any benefits before age 65 and postpone retirement past that age, you will get a special bonus. This bonus, called the "delayed retirement credit" increases the benefit by one per cent for each year between the ages of 65 and 72 in which you do not get benefits because of work.

Under the 1977 amendments, if you reach 65 after 1981 and decide to delay retirement, your benefit will increase three per cent for each year you were eligible for benefits but did not receive them.

CHECKING YOUR RECORDS

The Social Security Administrator has said that your Social Security investment is "as sound as the United States government." If those words are more foreboding than encouraging, you may want to check your Social Security account regularly.

Ask your local Social Security office for Form 7004, "Request for a Statement of Earnings." When you have completed the form and mailed it in, you will receive a statement that includes your total earnings in each of the last three years for which the posting has been completed; total earnings reported since 1950; total earnings in the period 1937-1950; and total earnings reported since 1936.

Only earnings on which you have paid Social Security tax will be shown. Because there is a time lag in processing information on earnings, your most recent wages probably will not appear on the statement.

Earnings records should be checked at least every three years. Errors in reporting earnings are more easily corrected if caught within three years, three months and 15 days of the time the wages were paid or self-employment income derived.

If you suspect that there is an error in your records or want a more detailed breakdown, contact your local Social Security office.

MEDICARE

There are two parts to Medicare: hospital insurance (Part A) and medical insurance (Part B). Both help protect people 65 and over from the high costs of health care.

Also eligible for Medicare are disabled people under 65 who have been entitled to social security disability benefits for 24 or more consecutive months. Insured workers and their dependents who need dialysis treatment or a kidney transplant because of chronic kidney disease also have Medicare protection.

MEDICAID SERVICES
Furnished by States, 1979

Additional Services

State	BASIC MEDICAID SERVICES*	Clinic services	Prescribed drugs	Dental services	Prosthetic devices	Eyeglasses	Private duty nursing	Physical therapy services	Other diagnostic, screening, preventive & rehabilitative services	Emergency hospital services	Skilled nursing facility services for patients under 21	Optometrists' services	Podiatrists' services	Chiropractors' services	Care for patients 65 or older in institutions for mental diseases	Care for patients 65 or older in institutions for tuberculosis	Care for patients under 21 in psychiatric hospitals
Alabama	•		•		•	•			•	•	•				•	•	•
Alaska	•	•			•	•			•	•	•				•		•
Arizona																	
Arkansas	+	+	+	+	+	+		+	+	+	+	+	+	+	+	+	+
California	+	+	•	+	•	+		•	•	•	•	•	•	+	•	+	•
Colorado	•		+		+	+		+	+	+	+	+	+	+	+		+
Connecticut	+	+	•	+	•	+	+	•	•	•	•	•	+		•	+	+
Delaware	•	•	+		+					+	+	+	+		+	+	•
D.C.	+	+	•							•	•	•	•		•	•	•
Florida	•		•							•	•	•			•	•	
Georgia	•	•	•	+	•					•	•	•	•	•	•	•	
Hawaii	+	•	•		+					•	•	•	•	+	•		
Idaho	•	+	•	+	•	+	+	+	+	•	•	•	•	+	+	+	+
Illinois	+	+	+	•	•	•	•	•	•	•	•	•	•	•	•		•
Indiana	•	•	•	•	•	•	•	•	•	•	•	•	•	•	•	+	•
Iowa	•	•	•	•	•	+		•	•	•	•	•	•	•	•	•	
Kansas	+	+	+	+	+	+	+	+	+	+	+	+	+	+	+	+	+
Kentucky	+	+	+	+				+		+	+		+	+	+	+	+
Louisiana	•	+	+		+					•	•				•		•
Maine	+	•	+		+		+	+	+	+	+				+		
Maryland	+	+	+	+	+	+	+	+	+	+	+	+	+		+	+	+
Massachusetts	+	+	+	+	+	+		+	+	+	+	+	+	+	+	+	
Michigan	+	+	+	+	+	+		+	+	+	+	+	+	+	+		+

State														
Mississippi	●	●	●	●	●					●				●
Missouri	●	●	●	●	●	●	+	●	+	●			●	●
Montana	+	+	+	+	+	+	+			+				
Nebraska	+	+	+	+	+	+	+	+	+	+				
Nevada	●	●	●	+	●	●	●		●	●				
New Hampshire	+		+	+	+		+	+		●		+	●	+
New Jersey	●	●	●	●	●	●	●	●	●	●		●	+	●
New Mexico	●	●	●	●	●	●	●	●	●	●	+	●	●	●
New York	+	+	+	+	+	+	+	+	+	+	+	+	+	+
North Carolina	+	+	+	+	+	+	+	+	+	+	+	+	+	+
North Dakota	+	+	+	+	+	+	+	+	+	+	+	+	+	+
Ohio	●	●	●	●	●	●	+	+	●	●	+	●	●	●
Oklahoma	+	+	●	●	+	●			+	+		+	+	+
Oregon	●	●	●	●	●	●	●		●	●		●	●	●
Pennsylvania	+	+	+	+	+	+	●		●	●		+	+	+
Rhode Island	+	+	+	+	+	+	●							
South Carolina	●	●	●	●	●	●	●	●	●	●	●	●	●	●
South Dakota	●	●	●	●	●	●	●	●	●	●	●	+	●	●
Tennessee	+	+	+	+	+	+	+		+	+		●	●	+
Texas	●	●	●	●	●		●	●				+	●	
Utah	+	+	+	+	+	+	+	+	+	+	+	+	+	+
Vermont	+	+	+	+	+	+	+		+	+		+	+	+
Virginia	+	+	+	+	+	+	+	+	+	+	+	+	+	+
Washington	+	+	+	+	+	+	+	+	+	+	+	+	+	+
West Virginia	+	+	+	+	+	+	+	+	+	+	+	●	+	+
Wisconsin	+	+	+	+	+	+	+	+	+	+	+	+	+	+
Wyoming	●	●	●	●	●	●	●	●	●	●		+	+	+

*BASIC REQUIRED MEDICAID SERVICES: Every Medicaid program must cover these services for everyone receiving federally supported financial assistance: inpatient hospital care; outpatient hospital services; other laboratory and X-ray services; skilled nursing facility services and home health services for individuals 21 and older; early and periodic screening, diagnosis, and treatment for individuals under 21; family planning; and physician services.

● Services offered for people receiving federally supported financial assistance.

+ Additional services offered for people in state public assistance and federal supplemental security income (SSI) programs who are eligible for finanical but not medical assistance.

Source: U.S. Department of Health, Education and Welfare.

The hospital insurance part of Medicare helps pay the cost of inpatient hospital care and certain kinds of followup care. The medical insurance part of Medicare helps pay the costs of physicians' services, outpatient hospital services, and ror certain other medical items and services not covered by hospital insurance. People who have medical insurance pay a monthly premium covering part of the cost. The other part is paid from general Federal revenues. The premium is $8.70 monthly.

If you are eligible for a social security or railroad retirement check either as a worker, dependent, or survivor, you automatically have hospital insurance protection when you are 65. If you are not eligible for a check, you need credit for some work under social security to get hospital insurance protection without paying any monthly premium.

When you apply for hospital insurance, you will be enrolled automatically for the medical insurance part of Medicare unless you don't want it.

People 65 and over who have not worked long enough to be eligible for hospital insurance can get this protection by enrolling and paying a monthly premium just as they would for other health insurance. The premium is $69 a month. People who buy Medicare hospital insurance also must enroll in medical insurance.

For more information about Medicare, ask at any Social Security office for a copy of the leaflet, *A Brief Explanation of Medicare.*

FOR MORE INFORMATION

The Social Security Administration has about 1,300 offices throughout the country. Representatives of these offices also make regular stops in neighboring communities.

Before you or your family can get any social security checks, you must apply for them. Get in touch with any social security office if you are unable to work because of an illness of injury that is expected to last a year or longer); you are 62 or older and plan to retire; you are within two or three months of 65 even if you don't plan to retire; someone in your family dies.

FEDERAL FOOD ASSISTANCE PROGRAMS

More than 45 million people receive some kind of food aid from the U.S. Department of Agriculture (USDA). As of December, 1978, the total includes about 16.1 million people receiving food stamps and 29.7 children receiving school breakfasts or lunches (up from 28.3 million a year earlier). Here is a summary of the federal food programs:

SUPPLEMENTAL FOOD PROGRAM

The SUPPLEMENTAL FOOD PROGRAM FOR WOMEN, INFANTS, AND CHILDREN (WIC) provides nutritious food supplements to pregnant and nursing women as well as to children up to their fifth birthday. All mothers and children who participate are certified as "nutritional risks" because of inadequate nutrition and income.

The WIC Program provides money to participating state health departments or comparable state agencies. Indian tribes recognized by the Department of Interior or by the Indian Health Service of the Department of Health, Education and Welfare may also act as state agencies.

CHILD NUTRITION PROGRAMS

The NATIONAL SCHOOL LUNCH PROGRAM provides nutritious lunches every day to school children. All public and nonprofit private schools of high school grade and under—as well as public and licensed nonprofit private residential child care institutions— may participate in the program.

To be eligible to receive federal aid, schools and institutions must: operate the lunch program on a nonprofit basis to all children; serve nutritious lunches according to the requirements established by USDA; provide lunches free or at a reduced price to children who are unable to pay the full price of the lunch; and insure that such children are not overtly identified.

The SCHOOL BREAKFAST PROGRAM started as a pilot project aimed only at schools with large numbers of needy children or students who traveled long distances to school. The program is now available to all public and nonprofit private schools of high school grade and under, and to public and licensed nonprofit private residential child care institutions.

The CHILD CARE FOOD PROGRAM provides nutritional benefits similar to those of the school food programs. It operates year-round in nonresidential institutions such as day care centers, Head Start Centers and family day care homes.

The SUMMER FOOD SERVICE PROGRAM FOR CHILDREN provides meals to children during extended vacation periods. It operates during the summer and vacations of more than three weeks for schools with continuous school-year calendar. Any public, nonprofit private, nonresidential institution or residential summer camp may sponsor the program in areas where at least one-third of the children are eligible for free or reduced-price school meals. Meals are served without charge.

The SPECIAL MILK PROGRAM makes it possible for children attending a school or institution to purchase milk at a reduced price, or, if they are needy, to receive it free. Schools and institutions which participate in other federal-state child nutrition programs may also participate in the Special Milk Program.

The FOOD SERVICE EQUIPMENT ASSISTANCE PROGRAM provides funds for eligible schools and residential child care institutions to help them acquire food service equipment. These funds are used primarily to reimburse schools and residential child care institutions which serve needy children and which have either no equipment or grossly inadequate equipment. In order to receive assistance, eligible schools and residential child care institutions must participate in either the National School Lunch Program or the School Breakfast Program.

FOOD STAMPS

The Food Stamp Program enables low-income individuals to buy more food of greater variety in order to improve their diets. In the past, participants have been required to pay a sum of money each month in order to receive food stamps of a larger value than the amount paid.

In October, 1977, Congress changed the program. Effective in January, 1979, participants are no longer required to pay money in order to receive stamps. Instead, they are given a smaller number of stamps each month free. Another change lowers the eligibility requirements in order to conform to revised federal poverty limits.

How does a household get food stamps? The head of the household must go to the local welfare office with documentation to show: where the household is; how many people reside in it; how much money the household members receive each month; and what the household's monthly expenses are. If no one in the household is able to go to the office, a friend or relative may go instead. An elderly or disabled person can arrange to be interviewed at home or by telephone.

How do participants use food stamps? Stamps are used as money to buy food at authorized stores. Nearly all grocery stores are authorized to accept the stamps. They may be used to buy almost any food, or seeds and plants to grow food for personal use. They cannot be used to buy liquor, beer, cigarettes, soap, pet food or other non-food items. They also may not be sold in exchange for cash or other goods.

Who is eligible for food stamps? Anyone who meets nationwide standards for income and resources. Supplemental Security Income (SSI) recipients residing in Massachusetts and Wisconsin are not eligible. With certain exceptions, a household consists of individuals or groups of individuals, provided that they are not residents of an institution, who purchase and prepare meals for home consumption. Able-bodied household members 18 and over must register for employment.

What are the income standards for a household? The monthly set income for all households is based on its size. The maximum monthly income standards are revised twice yearly (in January and July). As of January, 1979, maximum income levels were:

1 person	$227	5 persons	$630
2 persons	365	6 persons	719
3 persons	454	7 persons	807
4 persons	542	8 persons	895

For each additional household member over 8, add $89.

VETERANS' BENEFITS
Inflation Brings Increases

Veterans' benefits went up with inflation in 1979. Benefits were expanded in guaranteed loans, work study programs, disability compensation and pension and retirement compensation. Also increased were benefits for automobiles, mobile homes and burial costs.

Compensation rates for disability were increased for all degrees of disability by an average of $20. Also, eligibility for an additional allowance of $89 per month was extended to those with 30 percent disability. Severely disabled veterans can collect up to $2,308 in additional payments.

Dependency and indemnity compensation, for a surviving spouse and children was increased. A spouse can now receive from $297 to $814 monthly, which is increased $35 for each child. If there is no surviving spouse, children can receive from $150 to $278, depending on number of survivors. Payment to dependent parents was also increased.

Death pensions were also raised: for a surviving spouse alone, $2,379; with one child, $3116; in need of aid and attendance, $3,806; in need of aid and attendance with one child, $4,543; spouse homebound, $2,908; spouse homebound with one child, $3,645. For each additional child there is an additional monthly payment of $600.

Under the improved pension system, veterans living alone can receive $3,550; with one dependent, $4,561; plus $600 annually for each additional child. A homebound veteran under the new plan with one dependent can receive $5,441 annually.

Work study and loan guaranty eligibility was shortened from 181 days of active service to 90 days. The minimum work study wage was also raised to $2.90 with the total work study allotment up from $17,500 to $25,000.

VA may now also guarantee home loans made by a private lender up to $25,000 or 60 per cent of the loan, whichever is less. Mobile home loans may be guaranteed up to 50 per cent of the total or $17,500, whichever is less. Specially adapted housing loans are up from $25,000 to $30,000.

Compensation for burial services was increased from $250 to $300 and from $800 to $1,100 for service connected deaths.

For information or assistance in applying for veterans benefits write, call, or visit a VA Center or Hospital. Most states have a toll-free number for VA offices.

For more information: see free booklets: *Summary of Educational Benefits Under the Post-Vietnam Era Veterans Educational Assistance Program* (VA Pamphlet 22-79-1) and *Benefits for Veterans and Service Personnel with Service Since January 31, 1955, and Their Dependents* (VA 20-67-1). Both revised in January, 1979, and distributed free by the VA, Washington D.C., 20420.

AID FOR DISASTER VICTIMS
From Government Programs

Since 1947, the federal government has had a growing set of programs to provide assistance to victims of disasters. The aid ranges from cash payment to clearing of debris and providing temporary housing. In 1974, a new law greatly broadened government assistance now handled by the Federal Disaster Assistance Administration.

Government programs include search and rescue by the Coast Guard, flood protection by the Army Corps of Engineers, aid to states for emergency health and welfare work, emergency loans from the Farmers Home Administration, loans from the Small Business Administration, repairs to federal roads by the Federal Highway Administration and tax refunds by the Internal Revenue Service.

Help for individuals can involve:

● Temporary housing in which no rental may be charged for 12 months when homes are made uninhabitable;

● Minimum essential repairs to owner-occupied residences so families can return home;

● Temporary assistance with mortgage or rental payments for people facing loss of residences for as long as 12 months;

● Employment assistance;

● Loans for refinancing, repair, rehabilitation and replacement of damaged property not fully covered by insurance;

● Payments to farmers of up to 80 per cent of the cost of emergency con-

servation measures and donation of federally owned feed grain;
- Distribution of food coupons to eligible victims;
- Individual and family grants of up to $5,000 to meet necessary expenses or serious needs not met in other ways;
- Legal services to low-income families and individuals;
- Crisis counselling for mental problems caused by disasters; and
- Aid through regular problems of Social Security and Veterans Administration.

The FDAA maintains regional offices and headquarters at 451 Seventh St. SW, Washington, DC, 20410. The telephone number is 202/634-7800. Among publications available from FDAA are a "Program Guide," "When You Return to a Storm Damaged Home," and "Tips on Repairing Your Disaster Damaged Home."

MONEY FOR FUEL BILLS

For three years, Congress has appropriated $200 million to help low-income people to meet the high cost of heating their homes. The program is administered by the Community Services Administration (CSA) with the money actually paid through state agencies, mostly to fuel dealers.

To be eligible, according to CSA criteria, household income must be no higher than 125 per cent of the poverty level and there must be a real inability to obtain heating fuel or pay fuel bills. Proof of income is required.

In case of dire need, as much as $50 can be paid in cash directly to an eligible household which is hardpressed because of paying large winter fuel bills, with up to $250 more paid directly to fuel suppliers.

But a review of the program in 1979 by the General Accounting Office showed considerable variance in the way the states implement the program. The elderly are given priority in many states but not all. More than 1 million families received such funds last year, but some $37 million of the funds was not spent and was transferred to the CSA's program to help weatherize the homes of the poor.

Taxes

In This Chapter

Taxes are more controversial than ever. They became a big issue in 1978 as Californians passed Proposition 13, designed to slash property taxes in the state. Similar taxpayer revolts quickly spread to other states. They symbolized Americans' resentment towards a tax system they often don't understand and can't seem to justify.

A study by the Roper Organization before Proposition 13 was passed concluded that Americans have "a sense that the income tax system is not equitable, that 'others' aren't paying their fair share, that taxes are too high, and, to a lesser degree, that tax revenues are being wasted."

"Reforms" such as Proposition 13 fail to address what most critics see as the basic unfairness of the current tax system, whereby the wealthy pay the lowest rates. Before Proposition 13, California homeowners paid 35 per cent of the state's property taxes and businesses paid 65 per cent. When the change becomes fully effective, these figures will be reversed.

INEQUITIES BRING REFORM EFFORTS

Like tax rates, tax fairness varies from state to state. A study by the Coalition of American Public Employees on sales tax, property tax, personal income tax, business tax and tax administration policies, found Oregon had the fairest tax policies. Michigan came in second, while Alabama and Mississippi were the worst.

Taxes tend to fall most heavily on middle- and lower-income groups, causing increasing debate and reform efforts. Philip M. Stern, himself a millionaire, stated the case for income tax reform in a popular paperback book, *The Rape of the Taxpayer* (Vintage Books, 1974). He found that a family with less than $2,000 in annual income paid more than seven times the Social Security tax rate paid by a family with an income of $50,000, six times the rate in state income taxes and eight times the rate paid by the higher-income family in property taxes. The total taxes a person pays varies from state to state.

Income tax breaks also tend to favor the rich. Business meals and expenses are deductible, and the tax code provides breaks to those who fly first class or hire a maid. A variety of special interests also receive tax relief.

INFLATION WIPES OUT TAX CUTS

Recent changes in tax laws mean cuts for some people, but mostly for those with incomes over $30,000. Potential savings for many Americans will fade away as continuing inflation and payroll tax hikes are felt. Wage increases to meet rising prices will push most taxpayers into higher tax brackets, while leaving their purchasing power intact. Maintaining the current standard of living will become more difficult, as a larger portion of wage gains are taxed away.

Increased Social Security taxes further limit potential savings. In January, 1979, the tax rate paid by employees rose from 6.05 to 6.13 per cent, and the base on which taxes are paid increased from $17,700 to $22,900. Every income group below $50,000, except for those earning $5,000 to $10,000, is worse off in 1979 as a result of the changes. Those above the $50,000 range, the top 2 per cent of taxpayers, are better off because of the changes.

Other proposed reforms would leave most taxpayers in better shape. In place of across the board cuts, the Tax Reform Research Group suggests: that property tax exemptions be reviewed carefully, intangible property be taxed, uniform assessment standards be established, tax abatements to businesses be eliminated, sales taxes be less regressive, sales tax administration be improved, business taxes be more carefully administered, and tax relief be based on need.

RECENT CHANGES IN U.S. INCOME TAX LAWS

Recent changes in tax laws include:

Personal Exemptions: $1000 for each taxpayer and dependent, up from $750 in 1978. A family of four or a couple, both of whom are 65 or older, will not have to pay taxes on the first $4000 of income.

Tax Credits: The general tax credit of $35 for each personal exemption or 2 per cent of the first $9000 of taxable income has expired.

Income Tax Brackets: Reduced and widened. The minimum standard deduction is $3400 on joint returns, $2300 on single returns, and $1700 on separate returns for married persons.

Energy Tax Credits: 15 per cent of up to $2,000 spent on certain energy saving measures; up to $2200 for expenditures on solar, wind, or geothermal energy equipment. The limit applies to total expenditures between April 20, 1977 and 1985, when the credit expires.

Political Contributions: No longer deductible. Maximum tax credit is $50 on individual returns and $100 on joint returns.

Capital Gains: 60 per cent of new, long-term gains are excluded from taxable income, up from 50 per cent. 40 per cent of the gains are taxable at the individual's normal rates.

Housing: For those 55 and older, the first $100,000 of profit from the sale of a house is tax free.

Individual Retirement Accounts: Rules governing programs established by individuals not covered by company pension plan have been simplified.

Taxpayer Appeals: Taxpayers can ask the U.S. Tax Court to act as a referee in disputes with the IRS of up to $5000. The limit had been $1500.

PROPERTY TAXES—WHO PAYS AND WHO DOESN'T

Property taxes, the primary source of revenue for cities and states, do not fall on people equally. According to a study by the Advisory Commission on Intergovernmental Relations, American taxpayers are paying $15 billion a year extra in property taxes (about $300 per family) because of the breaks given to tax-exempt organizations. Over $800 billion, about one-third of all U.S. real estate, is tax exempt. Those who pay taxes must make up for revenues lost because some people pay no taxes at all.

Exemptions vary from state to state. In all 50 states churches, cemeteries and federal, state and municipal property are tax exempt. In many states, universities and colleges, parsonages, YMCAs, YWCAs, YMHAs, veterans organizations, and fraternal organizations are exempt, too. Labor and professional groups, property-owning senior citizens, veterans, welfare recipients, hospitals, and literary, historic and charitable organizations also receive breaks.

Another vast source of tax revenue is "intangible property." When property taxes were devised in the early 19th Century, the codes called for uniform taxes to be imposed on all property. A century later, investment began to shift from physical property—such as real estate or jewels—to intangible property—such as stocks, bonds and bank accounts. Yet tax laws continue to ignore these types of properties, imposing taxes only on physical property.

According to the Tax Reform Research Group, there is about $3.9 trillion worth of intangible property, most of which remains untaxed. Taxing it at one-fifth of the real estate tax rate could add $10 billion in revenues, enough to cut property taxes in some states by one-third.

PREPARING YOUR INCOME TAX RETURN

If you are a person of average intelligence and your tax problems are not unduly complicated, you can probably save money as well as trouble by preparing your own income tax return. Yet, as many as 70 per cent of the 80 million individual returns filed are prepared by someone other than the taxpayers. The cost for these services exceeds $1 billion a year.

Even the experts can be wrong. Studies reveal that in about three out of four cases, your return will be filled out incorrectly if done by anyone other than yourself. The studies show that there is virtually no difference in error rates between professional preparers and commercial and professional tax services. Even the Internal Revenue Service's own tax preparers erred in 79 per cent of the returns surveyed by the IRS.

In deciding who should do your tax return, here are three basic options:

DO IT YOURSELF. If your annual income is under $30,000 and comes only from wages, tips, dividends and interest, there is little reason why you should not be able to prepare your own return. Even with income from other sources such as rental property or other investments, you may still be able to wind your way through the complexities of the tax laws. To do this, you will probably need some good reference materials. A wide number are available. See "Rating the Tax Guides," on an accompanying page.

The IRS has free services that may help you solve some of the problems you encounter in doing your own taxes. In all 58 IRS districts, toll-free telephone lines are available for advice on computation problems as well as such problems as lost refund checks. Or you may visit one of the 1,000 or so IRS offices for assistance in filling out your return.

LET THE IRS DO IT. If you elect, the IRS will do all the figuring for you. This service is offered to those filling the "short form," 1040A, and only those using form 1040 whose adjusted gross income is under $20,000, derived solely from wages, salary, tips, dividends, interest, pensions and annuities and who take the standard deduction.

To have the government figure out your tax, fill in the basic information on the form and mail it to the IRS by April 15.

HIRE SOMEONE TO DO IT. There are four basic types of commercial or professional tax preparers. The most widely used are the **national tax services,** such as H&R Block, Tax Corporation of America, Beneficial's Income Tax Service or Mr. Tax of America. Each company has its own training standards and testing procedures; since tax preparing is a seasonal occupation, many of the employees moonlight from other jobs.

There is one big advantage to these agencies: Most are open year-round in the event you need to return to an agency for complaints or other problems.

In choosing an agency, it is advisable to ask about the education experience of the preparers, whether the business is open year-round and how long the agency keeps copies of returns it prepares. Three years is the legal statute of limitations in most cases.

In the Internal Revenue Service survey of tax preparer accuracy, the national tax services had an error rate of 74 per cent.

Local tax services and small local chains may give you more personal attention for a reasonable fee, but there are serious drawbacks. As with the national services, there is a wide variation in the qualifications and experience of the preparers. But there is also a higher chance that the company may not be around after April 15 to handle any questions or problems you may have. Under federal law, if you are requested to appear before the IRS about your return, any other preparer must also appear as a witness. In the case of the national companies, there is little problem in getting the preparer to accompany you. If the preparer is no longer in business, however, your problems may be more complex.

In the IRS accuracy survey, local tax services had a 78 per cent error rate.

One can easily become confused about the difference between **public accountants** and **Certified Public Accountants.** A public accountant can be anyone who has taken an accounting course. Licensing requirements vary widely and don't exist at all in most states. Public accountants give personal service but cost slightly more than the national and local chains. It is important to find out what the qualifications of a public accountant are.

You can get a list of members of the National Society of Public Accountants by writing to the Society, 1717 Pennsylvania Ave. NW, Washington, DC, 20006. Public accountants had a error rate of 75 per cent in the IRS survey.

Certified Public Accountants are the professionals of the tax preparers. To become a CPA, one must usually be a college graduate and pass stiff entrance examinations. Most states also require a certain amount of work experience before the test can be taken. CPAs are primarily for people with complex economic situations and who are in the higher income brackets. However, you may also need the services of a CPA if you have had a major change in your life, such as a divorce, death in the family or retirement.

The error rate for CPAs in the IRS survey was 72 per cent.

CHOOSING A TAX PREPARER

The IRS may provide all the help you need. But if not, and you decide to have your taxes done by a professional tax preparer, consider these suggestions from the Tax Reform Research Group:

Choose your preparer carefully. If you pay someone to prepare your return the preparer is required under the law to sign the return and fill in the other blanks in the "Paid Preparer's Information" area of your return. However, you are still responsible for the accuracy of every item entered on your return.

Avoid tax preparers who:

- Suggest that you lie about the information on the return.
- Suggest that you sign the return before it is completely filled out.
- Fail to provide you with a copy of the return.
- Refuse to sign the return as the preparer.
- Offer to pay an "instant" tax refund (it is usually a loan, with high interest rates).

RATING THE TAX GUIDES

Each year the Tax Reform Research Group rates the most popular tax guides in its monthly publication, *People & Taxes.* The following reviews of top guides were excerpted with permission from its 1979 study. For more details, write: Tax Reform Research Group, P.O. Box 14198, Washington, DC, 20004.

YOUR INCOME TAX, by J.K. Lasser, Simon & Schuster, NY.

This is not a book for the run-of-the mill, middle- or low-income taxpayer. Of all the books reviewed, this is the only one that does not have a special section on how to use it, and judging from its somewhat confusing organization, it may be the one that needs it most. A complex numbering system and the book's small print are enough to put off all but the most patient taxpayer looking for above-average technical advice.

EVERYONE'S INCOME TAX GUIDE, by S. Jay Lasser, Harcourt Brace Jovanich, Inc., NY.

This is a more basic guide than *Your Income Tax* above but manages to hide one piece of very useful information: the fact that the IRS will compute some people's tax for them. The table of contents is also hidden, but the organization of the chapters is logical.

INCOME TAX GUIDE, by Sylvia Porter, CBS Publications, NY.

Conspicuously absent from this guide is an index. To find an answer to a specific question one has to locate the appropriate chapter and sub-chapter in the contents and then skim pages for it. But as a line-by-line guide to filling out the forms, the guide is well organized.

H & R BLOCK INCOME TAX WORKBOOK, Macmillan Publishing Co., NY.

Compared to the other guides, this book is a visual delight. The type is large and easy to read, and the pages are neat and not jammed with columns of print. Chapters are well organized, and specific topics can be found either in the table of contents or in the index.

YOUR FEDERAL INCOME TAX, IRS Publication 17, free.

Perhaps because it has to be, the IRS tax guide is probably the most thorough of all the guides. But considering the volume of information covered, it is straightforward and clear. The basic organization is easy to follow. Throughout the guide, readers wishing more information on specific issues are referred to other free publications available from the IRS.

IRS publications are available from local IRS offices or from the Internal Revenue Service, Publications Division, 1111 Constitution Ave., NW, Washington, DC, 20224.

STATE AND LOCAL TAX BURDENS, BY CITY
1979 Taxes for Family of Four

City	$7,500 Amount	Pct.	$15,000 Amount	Pct.	$22,500 Amount	Pct.	$30,000 Amount	Pct.	$40,000 Amount	Pct.	$50,000 Amount	Pct.
Atlanta	$ 571	7.6	$1,291	8.6	$2,032	9.0	$2,865	9.6	$3,805	9.5	$4,690	9.4
Baltimore	937	12.5	1,922	12.8	2,855	12.7	3,847	12.8	4,956	12.4	5,815	11.6
Boston	1,783	23.8	3,535	23.6	5,012	22.3	6,804	22.7	8,575	21.4	10,306	20.6
Chicago	603	8.0	1,098	7.3	1,542	6.9	1,995	6.7	2,591	6.5	2,987	6.0
Cleveland	551	7.4	1,048	7.0	1,563	7.0	2,132	7.1	2,782	7.0	3,321	6.6
Columbus	465	6.2	895	6.0	1,370	6.1	1,882	6.3	2,492	6.2	3,010	6.0
Dallas	505	6.7	1,116	7.4	1,518	6.8	2,270	7.6	3,222	8.1	4,132	8.3
Denver	546	7.3	1,208	8.1	1,742	7.7	2,374	7.9	3,174	7.9	3,744	7.5
Detroit	748	10.0	1,685	11.2	2,488	11.1	3,366	11.2	4,384	11.0	5,196	10.4
Honolulu	331	4.4	1,106	7.4	1,912	8.5	2,713	9.0	3,748	9.4	4,644	9.3
Houston	493	6.6	1,072	7.2	1,457	6.5	2,162	7.2	3,049	7.6	3,889	7.8
Indianapolis	742	9.9	1,409	9.4	1,984	8.8	2,644	8.8	3,378	8.5	4,145	8.3
Jacksonville	348	4.6	652	4.4	915	4.1	1,183	3.9	1,485	3.7	1,639	3.3
Kansas City	518	6.9	1,063	7.1	1,628	7.2	2,214	7.4	2,907	7.3	3,554	7.1
Los Angeles	569	7.6	1,382	9.2	2,436	10.8	3,306	11.0	4,555	11.4	5,905	11.8
Milwaukee	769	10.3	1,869	12.5	2,975	13.2	4,132	13.8	5,516	13.8	6,737	13.5
Memphis	604	8.1	993	6.6	1,307	5.8	1,642	5.5	2,014	5.0	2,257	4.5
Nashville	462	6.2	733	4.9	953	4.2	1,168	3.9	1,446	3.7	1,619	3.2
New Orleans	331	4.4	736	4.9	972	4.3	1,281	4.3	1,726	4.3	2,036	4.1
New York City	932	12.4	1,983	13.2	3,131	13.9	4,575	15.3	6,620	16.6	8,412	16.8
Philadelphia	1,140	15.2	2,098	14.0	2,982	13.3	3,871	12.9	4,866	12.2	5,684	11.4
Phoenix	653	8.7	1,221	8.1	1,857	8.3	2,569	8.6	3,355	8.4	4,086	8.2
Pittsburgh	794	10.6	1,447	9.7	2,049	9.1	2,650	8.8	3,346	8.4	3,854	7.7
St. Louis	670	8.9	1,337	8.9	1,996	8.9	2,696	9.0	3,479	8.7	4,163	8.3
San Antonio	510	6.8	1,107	7.4	1,504	6.7	2,229	7.4	3,137	7.8	3,995	8.0
San Diego	587	7.8	1,369	9.1	2,397	10.7	3,235	10.8	4,458	11.2	5,791	11.6
San Francisco	657	8.8	1,534	10.2	2,638	11.7	3,566	11.9	4,864	12.2	6,249	12.5
San Jose	474	6.3	1,178	7.9	2,144	9.5	2,899	9.7	4,059	10.2	5,352	10.7
Seattle	566	7.6	926	6.2	1,229	5.5	1,557	5.2	1,920	4.8	2,260	4.5
Washington, D.C.	647	8.6	1,425	9.5	2,296	10.2	3,266	10.9	4,584	11.5	5,609	11.2
30-City Average	650	8.7	1,348	9.0	2,029	9.0	2,770	9.2	3,683	9.2	4,503	9.0

Source: District of Columbia, Department of Finance and Revenue.

COMPARISON OF STATE TAXES
Where the Bite's the Biggest

States	Income Tax as Pct. of Personal Income	Sales Tax (cents)	Beer Tax (dollars)[1]	Cigarette Tax (cents)[2]	Gasoline Tax (cents)[3]	Motor Vehicle Registration Fee[4]	Real Estate Deed Tax[5]	Per Capita Tax Burden
Alabama	1.26%	4¢	$16.53	12¢	7¢	$13.75	.50	$ 506.97
Alaska	4.88	0	7.75	8	8	30.00	0	2,295.71
Arizona	1.28	4	2.48	13	8	13.00	2.00	826.58
Arkansas	1.38	3	7.44	17.75	8.5	26.00	.55	494.08
California	2.09	4.75	1.24	10	7	11.00	0	1,088.92
Colorado	1.81	3	2.48	10	7	15.20	.05	823.82
Connecticut	0.24	7	2.50	21	11	21.00	.55	885.10
Delaware	3.75	0	2.00	14	9	20.00	10.00	829.36
D.C.	3.23	5	2.25	13	10	79.00	5.00	1,070.58
Florida	0	4	12.40	21	8	32.00	2.05	628.16
Georgia	1.63	3	10.00	12	7.5	8.00	.50	609.10
Hawaii	3.00	4	(6)	(7)	8.5	22.06	.25	974.39
Idaho	2.19	3	4.65	9.1	9.5	30.15	0	639.36
Illinois	1.62	4	2.17	12	7.5	30.00	.25	860.29
Indiana	1.30	4	2.94	10.5	8	12.25	0	652.45
Iowa	2.26	3	4.34	13	8.5	68.97	.55	748.60
Kansas	1.26	3	5.58	11	8	26.00	0	727.56
Kentucky	1.64	5	2.50	3	9	12.50	.50	601.25
Louisiana	0.58	3	10.00	11	8	3.00	0	636.07
Maine	1.21	5	7.75	16	9	15.00	.55	658.12
Maryland	2.57	5	2.79	10	9	30.00	3.05	891.97
Massachusetts	2.84	5	3.30	21	8.5	7.00	1.14	1,001.87
Michigan	2.05	4	6.30	11	10	34.00	.55	878.17
Minnesota	3.38	4	4.00	18	9	68.00	1.10	906.10
Mississippi	1.09	5	13.23	11	9	23.25	0	527.46
Missouri	1.22	3.125	1.86	9	7	25.50	0	608.93
Montana	2.40	0	4.00	12	8	11.00	0	765.66
Nebraska	1.63	3	3.41	13	9.5	15.50	.55	773.90
Nevada	0	3	1.86	10	6	8.50	.55	892.24
New Hampshire	0.13	0	4.65	12	10	25.00	1.25	618.36
New Jersey	1.21	5	1.03	19	8	51.00	1.75	931.45
New Mexico	0.38	3.75	2.48	12	7	36.00	0	624.58
New York	3.35	4	1.38	15	8	39.75	.55	1,252.22
North Carolina	2.39	3	15.00	2	9	15.00	.50	592.79
North Dakota	1.36	3	2.48	11	8	72.00	0	681.69
Ohio	0.81	4	2.50	15	7	10.00	0	640.74
Oklahoma	1.22	3	10.00	13	6.58	79.00	.75	598.30
Oregon	3.37	0	2.60	9	7	21.00	0	793.13
Pennsylvania	1.43	6	2.48	18	9	24.00	5.00	770.01
Rhode Island	1.64	6	2.00	18	10	21.00	1.10	792.82
South Carolina	1.79	4	25.95	7	9	9.00	1.00	548.90
South Dakota	0	4	8.30	12	8	40.00	.50	629.35
Tennessee	0.09	4.5	3.40	13	8	18.75	1.30	564.09
Texas	0	4	5.00	18.5	5	30.30	0	637.44
Utah	2.11	4	3.10	8	9	6.00	0	652.18
Vermont	2.50	3	7.75	12	9	32.00	2.50	810.10
Virginia	2.03	3	7.95	2.5	9	20.00	1.25	674.39
Washington	0	4.6	1.00	16	10	14.40	.50	821.22
West Virginia	1.48	3	5.50	17	10.5	36.00	1.10	622.40
Wisconsin	3.57	4	2.00	16	7	18.00	.50	870.43
Wyoming	0	3	.62	8	8	15.00	0	988.43

[1]31-gallon barrel; alcoholic content of 4.5%. [2]per pack of 20. [3]per gallon. [4]one-year old, 4-door, 6-passenger, 8-cylinder, 59.2-hp automobile costing $5,000 new and weighing 4,680 pounds. [5]state real estate deed recordation and transfer tax, per $500 of consideration. [6]20% of whole sale price. [7]40% of whole sale price.
Source: District of Columbia, Department of Finance and Revenue

A TAXPAYER'S GUIDE TO THE IRS

Congress keeps making the tax law more complex—by inventing tax breaks for the not-so-ordinary taxpayer. But the IRS has been prodded into trying to make it easier for ordinary taxpayers to file their own returns.

Services provided by the IRS include much simpler instructions and forms, a variety of free booklets and taxpayer assistance by telephone and at local IRS offices. In addition, the IRS cooperates with community groups in setting up free fax clinics for elderly and low-income people.

Some clinics will even send volunteers out to help shut-ins with their tax forms; other clinics in urban areas have been set up to help Spanish, Chinese, and Vietnamese-speaking taxpayers.

Plain English is replacing some of the gobbledygook that used to prevail in most tax material. In fact, many of the questions you may have about filling out a form are probably answered right in the instruction book—and in understandable terms.

IRS WILL COMPUTE YOUR TAX

One thing the instructions point out is that if you qualify, the IRS will figures your taxes for you. If you file the 1040A form—about half the taxpayers do—you need only fill in the part of the form up to line 11a that applies to you, sign the form, attach your W-2, and mail it in.

Even if you file on the 1040 form, you may qualify to have the IRS figure your taxes. See the instructions on page four. However, the IRS does not guarantee the accuracy of its own representatives' advice. If he or she makes a mistake, you will be liable for any extra tax due.

If the instructions don't answer your questions, you can call the toll-free, taxpayer service number for your area, listed on the inside back pages of the instruction tax booklet.

In the IRS office, a "taxpayer service representative" (TSR) will answer your questions, give you any forms you need, and, if you qualify, help fill out your form.

IRS HAS 10,000 COLLECTORS

The IRS has over 10,000 collection employees in its offices across the nation. A local IRS collection division is divided into office and field branches. If the office branch does not resolve a collection case, it is transferred to the field branch for further action. IRS Revenue Representatives work in the office branches handling relatively minor matters, like seizure of salaries.

IRS Revenue Officers, who are more experienced and better paid, work in the field branches and deal with complex collection cases.

If you do not respond to an IRS notice, your account may be turned over to the collection division. The IRS trains collectors to secure payment as rapidly as possible. It encourages them to seize salaries or property if a taxpayer does not settle a debt promptly.

While the IRS recognizes that people experiencing financial hardship may deserve special treatment, it has not defined what "hardship" means. Instead, it allows individual revenue officers to decide when hardship exists and how to handle such cases.

WHAT TO DO ABOUT TAX BILLS

The IRS ordinarily does not use forcible collection methods until it has mailed four notices to the taxpayer and received no answer. The taxpayer should respond immediately upon receipt of a bill from the IRS, even if he or she believes the bill is erroneous. Any delay in response works against the taxpayer. (Penalties and interest also mount up.)

The first IRS notice (or bill) explains how much is owed and most important, the reason it is owed. The notice also includes a return envelope for payment and instructions on how to correct any IRS errors. None of the next three notices explains why the taxpayer owes the money. Each one assumes the first notice was received, even if it was not. Each becomes increasingly threatening.

When an IRS notice is received, the directions should be carefully read. The taxpayer should also read the general explanation of IRS procedures in *The Collection Process,* a free brochure which the IRS includes with the second notice. Those who do not have a copy can call the toll-free IRS telephone number to receive one.

CONTACTING THE IRS ABOUT A BILL

The first three notices direct the taxpayer to respond to the IRS Service Center which issued it. However, if he or she finds the notice confusing or frightening, or receives the notice after the deadline for response has passed, the taxpayer should take the following steps:

1. Secure a copy of the tax return in question. A copy can be obtained by writing to the Service Center. The taxpayer's Social Security number, name and address as it appeared on the return and the tax year should be included. There is generally a $1 charge for the first page and 10 cents for each succeeding page. The taxpayer should also contact the local IRS office and let a taxpayer service employee know that he or she is working on the problem since the process may take several weeks.

2. With the return and the tax bill in hand, the taxpayer should call the local IRS toll-free number. A TSR will answer the telephone. He or she will be the go-between with the Service Center or the contact with the local IRS office.

3. The taxpayer should discuss the notice with the TSR, explaining the problem clearly and taking notes during the conversation. If the TSR believes the bill is a mistake, he or she will suggest that the taxpayer go to the local office or mail in copies of the documents supporting the claim, so that a request for adjustment can be filed.

4. A taxpayer who owes money but needs time to pay can ask the TSR to explain how he or she can help and to describe assistance available in the collection division. A TSR can grant an extension of 60 days for payment on an individual account to those whose debt does not exceed a certain dollar limit and who have never owed a tax bill before. If a taxpayer needs more than 60 days to pay, and is a first-time "tax delinquent," TSRs can help arrange for regular monthly payments. The collection division must approve any agreement made.

5. The TSR can also stop the Service Center computer from issuing bills while your account is reviewed.

HOW THE IRS CAN HELP THOSE WITH A TAX BILL

A "Final Notice Before Seizure" signifies that the IRS has declared an account delinquent and has sent it to the district office for forcible collection. A taxpayer who cannot pay the tax, or who believes the bill is a mistake, should call the IRS office listed in the notice and ask to speak to a revenue officer. This official can correct errors and help those in financial trouble. A taxpayer who needs assistance must ask for it.

(The above material is excerpted from *People & Taxes,* a monthly publication of the Public Citizen Tax Reform Research Group. For a sample copy, write Tax Reform Research Group, P.O. Box 14198, Washington, DC 20004.

CORPORATE TAXES
Everyone's Running for Shelter

Uncle Sam is generous to large corporations. While individuals who have an annual income over $50,000 might pay 50 to 70 per cent of it in income taxes, corporations which make billions of dollars a year may pay as little as 5 per cent or less in taxes.

The reason for this is a series of complicated tax loopholes that corporations are able to take advantage of. To do this, many corporations keep two sets of books. One set, which glorifies profits to their fullest extent, is shown to company shareholders and determines shareholder dividents. The other, which deducts an endless number of items from profits, is shown to the Internal Revenue for purposes of computing taxes.

As Philip Stern points out in *The Rape of the Taxpayer,* the favors given to corporations by the government are getting larger each year. In 1960, for example, corporate taxes contributed one-fourth of all federal taxes; today they con-

---

WHERE TO COMPLAIN ABOUT IRS PROCEDURES

If the Complaint Involves:	Write to:
Threats, harassment, extortion	Assistant Regional Commissioner, Inspection. Call local IRS office for address.
Audit problems	Chief, Audit Division, IRS District Office. Call local IRS office for address.
Collection problems	Chief, Collections, IRS District Office. Call local IRS office for address.
Wrong tax advice, computer billing errors	Chief, Taxpayer Services (IRS District Office). Call local IRS office for address.

For refund problems: Call a local IRS office; if your problem is not solved call the Problem Resolution Officer at the local IRS office. If this also fails, write to District Director, IRS District Office. Call the local office for address.

In case of an emergency, go directly to the office of the District Director and make the complaint. Send copies of all correspondence to: (1) IRS District Director, your district; (2) Commissioner, Internal Revenue Service, Washington, DC 20224; (3) Your Congressman; (4) Rep. Sam Gibbons, Chairman, House Ways and Means Oversight Subcommittee, U.S. House of Representatives, Washington, DC 20515; and (5) Sen. Max Baucus, Chairman, Senate Subcommittee on Oversight of the Internal Revenue Service, Washington, DC 20510.

tribute about one-seventh. In 1960, corporate taxes were the second largest source of federal revenue; now they are third. Payroll taxes paid by the nation's wage earners are now second on the list.

And, says Stern, the larger corporations are granted more favors than the smaller ones. The 100 largest corporations generally pay a considerably smaller per cent of their income in taxes than do the smaller corporations.

HOW BIG BUSINESS CUTS DOWN ON TAXES

Here are descriptions of some of the more lucrative tax breaks available to corporations:

● **Deferral:** Since the beginning of our income tax system, U.S. corporations operating through overseas subsidiaries have been allowed to put off paying U.S. taxes on their foreign income until the earnings are brought home. So long as the profits and tax savings are reinvested in foreign countries, this deferral amounts to a permanent forgiveness of U.S. taxes.

The deferral privilege is an incentive for firms to invest abroad rather than in the U.S. As a result, U.S. business has invested more than $160 billion of job-creating capital overseas in the past decade. A study prepared for the State Department showed that Americans would have had one million more jobs if U.S. corporations had served its foreign customers from a U.S. base rather than from a foreign one.

The largest, fastest-growing and most profitable and sophisticated companies benefit from deferral. Between 80 and 90 per cent of the multinational subsidiaries involved in deferral are controlled by "Fortune 500" corporations, with firms such as IBM, Kodak, Polaroid and Dupont heading the list. A recent Treasury Department study showed that the largest 30 U.S.-based multinationals—all with assests of more than $250 million—picked up over half their benefits from deferral.

● **DISC (Domestic International Sales Corporation):** DISC gives U.S. companies exporting their products overseas a tax advantage similar to that enjoyed by companies producing through foreign subsidiaries. DISC, say tax reformers, pays a small number of companies to do what they would do anyway—export overseas. Currently, American taxpayers pay $1 billion a year for special tax subsidies to a few thousand firms engaged in export activities. Two-thirds of these DISC benefits go to companies with assets of more than $250 million—the top 0.1 per cent of U.S. businesses.

● **Investment Tax Credit:** The ITC is designed to encourage capital investments resulting in more jobs. It gives a corporation a credit against taxes on 10 per cent of the purchase of new machines or other investments.

Critics say that the ITC "encourages" businesses to make investments they would have made anyway, making the ITC a multi-billion-dollar tax giveaway. In 1975, just five corporate giants collected more than $1 billion from ITCs. The largest, American Telephone and Telegraph, saved $750 million. In 1977, the ITC cost $11 billion overall, with close to 80 per cent going to the top 0.1 per cent of corporations.

Another example of ITC savings is through "phantom taxes" collected by electric utilities from customers, but not paid to the government in taxes. In 1976, electric companies charged their customers for $3 billion in federal taxes, but paid only $562 million to the treasury.

THE BIGGEST WELFARE CASES
How Loopholes Save Corporate Taxpayers $31 Billion

"It seems as if old loopholes never die, they just get bigger," said Congressman Charles Vanik (D-Ohio) in presenting his seventh annual study of U.S. taxes paid by America's top corporations in June, 1979. The study, based on payments for 1977, showed a continued downward trend in the average corporate tax rate paid during the 1970s. According to Vanik, "This trend line makes hash of the argument—for large corporations at least—that federal taxes take too much venture capital and that additional general corporate tax relief is needed."

The study, prepared for the Joint Committee on Taxation, found that for many major profitable US corporations, the 48 per cent effective corporate tax rate "is a myth." Seventeen top corporations, with pretax worldwide earnings of nearly $2.6 billion paid no federal income taxes in 1977. As a result of corporate tax subsidies, the effective rate for those companies Vanik studied was only 17.2 per cent. This rate is the same rate paid by an average family of four with an income of $26,150.

Corporate tax breaks for these firms cost other American taxpayers $31.8 billion. While these top corporations should have paid $42.1 billion in taxes on incomes of $87.8 billion, actual payments totaled only $10.3 billion. The amount of taxes paid in the future will be cut further by special benefits in the Revenue Act of 1978, including the reduction of the corporate tax rate from 48 to 46 per cent. This alone will cost Americans another $5 billion, said Vanik.

The large oil companies paid an average of 11 per cent in taxes on $30.1 billion in income. By treating foreign royalties as taxes, they avoided paying $24.8 billion in taxes in 1977, according to Vanik.

As a result of the 1976 Tax Act, airlines and railroads also paid little federal corporate income tax, and the largest banks paid an average income tax rate of only 7.1 per cent on over $2.5 billion in worldwide income. Utilities generally pay little or no federal income tax.

AT&T, which had $7.1 billion in before-tax income in 1977, paid only .8 per cent of that in U.S. taxes.

(See next page for data from Vanik's 1979 study.)

REDUCING YOUR CHANCES OF A TAX AUDIT

It is impossible to avoid the chance of having your income tax return selected at random for audit under IRS's TCMP (Taxpayer Compliance Measurement Program). But it is possible to reduce your chances of being audited for other reasons.

The surest way to prevent the computer from bouncing your return is to stick to the IRS limits on various types of deductions, such as for sales taxes and gasoline taxes, and, of course, to comply strictly and correctly with the various tax schedules.

According to one confidential source within the IRS, the agency has set up special categories of red flags that will automatically cause an audit. Such items are:

● deductions for child care;
● credit for purchasing a new home;
● claims for casualty and theft losses, except for those who live in an area which was declared by the President as an official disaster area.

CORPORATIONS PAYING LESS THAN 10%
FEDERAL INCOME TAXES, 1977

	Thousands of Dollars	Percent
Company	Worldwide income before tax	Effective U.S. tax rate on worldwide income
United States Steel	$ 87,200	0 %
Rockwell International	266,700	0
Bethlehem Steel	(895,200)	0
Esmark	97,999	0
LTV	(57,380)	0
National Steel	45,806	0
Republic Steel	33,848	0
Inland Steel	88,507	0
United Brands	17,714	0
American Motors	5,616	0
American Airlines	83,089	0
Eastern Airlines	34,737	0
Pan American World Airways	33,489	0
Seaboard Coastline Industries	97,263	0
American Electric Power	333,403	0
Commonwealth Edison	361,589	0
Southern California Edison	317,174	0
A & P	5,046	0
First Chicago Corp.	152,113	0
Exxon	7,664,453	7.4
Mobil	4,349,431	2.5
Texaco	1,645,713	6.3
Gulf Oil	2,198,000	6.3
I.T. & T.	656,102	6.9
Atlantic Richfield	908,578	1.3
Union Carbide	587,100	0.1
Occidental Petroleum	887,142	0.9
Union Oil of California	550,088	8.1
Marathon Oil	754,899	6.6
W. R. Grace	253,920	7.7
Colgate Palmolive	290,065	6.6
International Paper	316,200	4.7
Continental Group	238,600	5.4
Gulf & Western	205,458	0.5
Standard Oil (Ohio)	235,906	0.6
Lockheed	115,800	0.1
Allied Chemical	233,312	2.3
General Dynamics	178,796	1.7
Uniroyal	59,833	7.0
NCR	265,934	9.0
Trans World Airlines	80,754	1.1
United Airlines	140,102	0.5
Union Pacific	337,989	8.2
Burlington Northern	76,979	1.4
Southern Pacific	166,637	1.9
Santa Fe Industries	218,479	4.9
AT & T	7,117,146	0.8
Southern Co.	601,353	2.9
Pacific Gas & Electric	406,471	1.9
Public Service Electric & Gas	325,164	2.7
Virginia Electric & Power	249,887	3.8
Citicorp	576,845	3.3
Chase Manhattan Corp.	151,606	0.1
Manufacturers Hanover Corp.	231,945	6.8
J. P. Morgan & Co.	297,450	8.1
Chemical New York Corp.	113,544	1.0
Bankers Trust New York Corp.	76,433	6.0

Charities

In This Chapter
- Lack of Regulation
- Ratings of Charities
- Ethical Standards
- How to Evaluate a Charity

Americans continue to give money to charities in record amounts. The total reported in 1979 for the previous year was $38.3 billion, according to the American Association of Fund-Raising Counsel. That was 8.8 per cent more than the year before. Nearly 90 per cent came from individuals, the rest from corporations and foundations.

The healthy increase occured despite a continuing series of news reports about questionable organizations and practices. The sources of greatest controversy continued to be religious groups, which have led a surge of fund-raising efforts via television. For the first time, many of these groups began complying with the standards of practice set by the two leading monitoring organizations which operate nationally: the National Information Bureau Inc. (NIB) of New York City and the Philanthropic Advisory Service (PAS) of the Council of Better Business Bureaus in Washington, D.C. Both provide free information to the public about hundreds of charitable organizations. (See following pages for 1979 ratings of groups by both NIB and PAS.)

PRIEST PUT ON PROBATION

One of the biggest scandals involving charities came to an end in 1978 when a Roman Catholic priest pleaded guilty in Baltimore to charges of misusing millions of dollars donated by the public for the poor. Rev. Guido John Carcich of the Pallottine Fathers religious order received 18 months probation. He also was ordered to minister to the needs of state penitentiary prisoners for one year. Over a 20-year period, Carcich had raised over $170 million by direct mail.

Another controversy involved the Billy Graham Evangelistic Association of Minneapolis. In response to growing reports that the well known evangelist had built up a secret fund of many millions, his organization disclosed financial details in 1978 showing total income of $38,429,855 in the previous year, and total expenditures of $41,630,570 and assets of $17,378,769. But the Association refused to disclose the compensation of its 25 board members and whether any board or staff members or their families had any financial interest in the organization. The Philanthropic Advisory Service of the CBBB concluded that the Association did not meet its standards for charitable solicitations (See description of these standards on the following pages.) The group also failed to supply copies of its articles of incorporation, by-laws and IRS rulings as requested by PAS.

Another well known evangelistic group, the Oral Roberts Evangelistic Association, also failed to meet PAS standards. In response to a request for financial data, the Association called such information confidential. Still another religious group, the internationally televised PTL Club, did not meet the PAS standards of disclosure, according to the CBBB organization. NIB does not evaluate many religious groups.

REGULATION OF ABUSES SPOTTY

Until recent years, there was little regulation of charity solicitations. Some 42 states now have some rules that apply, mostly requiring registration and some reporting of financial information. But few states have restrictions deemed sufficient by Helen O'Rourke, who heads the PAS service in Washington. She says New York State has the best control, with Pennsylvania and North Carolina also with good laws and enforcement. (See comparison of state charity laws in first chapter.)

On the national front, Congress has shown little interest in investigating questionable practices in this field. One of the few exceptions has been Rep. Bob Wilson, Calfornia Republican. He has pushed legislation that would require charities to provide full financial disclosure with each solicitation. He points to similar requirements in his home territory of San Diego as evidence that such a law is needed nationally.

Meanwhile, the Internal Revenue Service has begun to revise its Form 990, which is required of such organizations. The IRS is trying to make the information on the form more useful to the general public, which theoretically is free to inspect the form at IRS regional offices where a charity is headquartered. In practice, the few people who have managed to track down a 990 form invariably have found that the information is many years old and lacking in sufficient detail to permit drawing any conclusions as to an organization's worthiness.

FUND-RAISING EXPENSES DIFFER GREATLY

One of the key factors in evaluating a supposedly charitable organization is the proportion of money spent on raising money. This proportion varies considerably from one organization to another. Expenses tend to be relatively low for older, established groups that raise funds largely through volunteers from door-to-door. Newer groups and ones that use the telephone or the mail tend to have higher expenses per dollar raised. Some groups, such as the Greenpeace Foundation, pay commissions to solicitors. Others, such as the National Foundation for Cancer Research, run sweepstakes with hundreds of prizes, including a $1,000 prize "just for promptness." (See the accompanying table showing expense ratios for leading charities.)

NON-TRADITIONAL GROUPS BECOME MORE AGGRESSIVE

As the stakes grow higher, many organizations not in the traditional mold are raising their voices and demanding a bigger piece of the action. One of the main targets is the United Way, the nationwide federation of local community funds, which raised more than $1.2 billion last year.

Most of the opposition is coming from the National Committee for Responsive Philanthropy (NCRP), which represents a number of non-traditional organizations and interests. They claim that the United Way has a virtual monopoly on fund-raising at places of work, and they feel that too much of the money raised goes to established organizations such as the Boy Scouts, Girl Scouts, YMCA and YWCA. They dispute the theme: "United Way. Thanks to you, it works for all of us."

NCRP members include the National Black United Fund, Environmental Policy Center, National Congress of American Indians, Native American Rights Fund, Center for Community Change, National Council of Negro Women, National Association of Neighborhoods, The Grey Panthers, Fund for Women's Rights, National Council of LaRaza and the Institute for Local Self-Reliance.

FOUNDATIONS ALSO CRITICIZED
These groups contend that foundations also tend to ignore them. They point to several studies completed in 1979 to prove their point. One in Colorado found

---

FUND RAISING DATA FOR NATIONAL CHARITIES
Percentage of Income Spent on Administration

Agency (for year ending)	Total Income	Fund Raising (%)	Other Adm. Expenses (%)	Total Adm. Costs (%)
American Cancer Society (8/77)	$126,767,460	12.1	10.0	22.1
National Easter Seal Soc. (8/76)	81,634,934	10.9	11.5	22.4
National Foundation/ March of Dimes (5/78)	68,490,121	17.2	6.6	23.8
Muscular Dystrophy Assoc. (12/77)	59,216,238	10.9	2.7	13.6
United Cerebral Palsy Assoc. (9/77)	50,476,000	6.9	11.9	18.8
American Lung Association (3/77)	49,985,877	24.4	6.8	31.2
National Multiple Sclerosis Society (12/77)	18,052,559	13.1	8.7	21.8
Arthritis Foundation (12/76)	15,684,566	12.3	11.4	23.7
Cystic Fibrosis Foundation (2/78)	11,316,578	11.9	11.7	23.6
American Diabetes Assoc. (12/77)	10,495,779	8.5	11.3	19.8
Epilepsy Foundation of America (12/77)	7,904,974	18.4	15.1	33.5
National Kidney Foundation (6/77)	6,919,016	10.4	11.8	22.2
National Hemophilia Foundation (6/77)	4,458,000	7.7	13.1	20.8
National Society for the Prevention of Blindness (3/78)	4,326,536	14.7	4.5	19.2
National Council on Alcoholism (12/77)	3,378,210	3.4	8.8	12.2
National Foundation for Ileitis and Colitis (6/78)	1,112,097	13.7	11.3	25.0
American Social Health Assoc. (12/77)	609,262	7.3	10.3	17.3
National Society for Autistic Children (12/76)	447,840	1.7	8.9	10.6
Committee to Combat Huntingon's Disease (9/78)	235,963	14.7	6.7	21.4
Asthma and Allergy Foundation* of America (12/77)	219,328	7.3	10.4	17.7

*National office only.

Source: National Health Council Inc., 1979

that only 2.7 per cent of foundation money went to groups representing minorities, women, the poor and others advocating rights of the elderly, youth, consumers, children and the environment. A study in San Francisco said the figure was 5 per cent, and one in Washington, D.D., indicated that less than 2 per cent went to such groups.

"The bulk of foundation money goes to things that interest wealthy people, health, the arts and higher education," says Mary Jean Tully, an NCRP board member. "Foundations are meeting public needs that existed 30 or 40 years ago," says another NCRP member, Pable Eisenberg of the Center for Community Change.

Officials of the United Way deny that there is any substantial unfairness in the disbursement of funds raised. They point out that each community United Way sets its own policies within certain broad guidelines laid down by the national organization. They also claim that United Ways have been responding well to social change by adding new recipients steadily. Nearly 37,000 agencies serving some 34 million American families are funded by the 2,330 local United Ways, according to George A. Shea, executive of United Way of America, the national office.

FOR MORE INFORMATION

The principal sources of detailed information about charitable organizations in the United States are:

● **The Philanthropic Advisory Service,** Council of Better Business Bureaus, 1150 17th St. NW, Washington, DC, 20036;

● **The National Information Bureau,** 419 Park Ave. South, New York, NY, 10016;

● **United Way of America,** 801 North Fairfax St., Alexandria, VA, 22314; and

● **National Committee for Responsive Philanthropy,** 1028 Connecticut Ave. NW, Suite 822, Washington, DC, 20036.

RATINGS OF CHARITIES
By Two Private Agencies

Two national organizations presently rate charities, based on information disclosures (or lack of disclosure) on a wide range of criteria, including administrative practices, staff expenses and solicitation procedures. The organizations are the Council of Better Business Bureaus (CBBB) Philanthropic Advisory Service, 1150 17th St. NW, Washington, DC, 20036 and the National Information Bureau (NIB), 419 Park Avenue South, New York, NY, 10016. Both organizations publish brochures with ratings of charitable organizations as well as tips on giving to charities.

Below is a summary of 1979 ratings of the two organizations. Omission from either list should not be interpreted as either approval or disapproval by CBBB and NIB. Both lists are continually updated. A copy of the latest lists can be obtained for $1 from CBBB and at no charge from NIB.

A description of the code letters can be found at the end of the ratings.

Charity	NIB	CBBB	Charity	NIB	CBBB
A Better Chance	—	OK	American Heart Association	D	OK
Accion Int'l/AITEC	A	—	American Horse Protection	D	B,C
Accuracy in Media	C	—	American Host Foundation	A	—
Action for Children's TV	OK	—	American Humane Association	C	—
Action on Smoking & Health	OK	OK	American Indian Dev. Assn.	C	B
Addiction Research Council	—	OK	American Institute of Mgt.	C	—
Advertising Council	—	OK	American Jewish Committee	—	OK
Africa Emergency Mission	—	A	American Judicature Society	—	OK
Africa Fund	A	OK	American Kidney Fund	A	OK
African Fund for Endangered			American Leprosy Foundation	—	OK
Wildlife/Phelps Stokes	—	OK	American Leprosy Missions	OK	OK
African Wildlife Leadership			American Lung Association	A	OK
Foundation	—	OK	American Med. Ctr., Denver	—	OK
Africare	OK	OK	American Nat'l Red Cross	OK	OK
AFS International	—	OK	American Near East Refugee		
AISOM Foundation	A	—	Aid	A	OK
AMC Cancer Research	D	—	American ORT Federation	—	OK
Amateur Athletic Union	A	—	American Parkinson Disease		
Alliance to Save Energy	—	OK	Assn.	C	C
			American Printing House for		
America the Beautiful Fund	D	—	the Blind	A	OK
American Arbitration Assn.	D	—	American Productivity Center	—	B
American Athletic Union	A	—	American Red Cross	OK	OK
American Bible Society	—	OK	American Rescue Workers	—	B,C
American Blood Commission	—	OK	American Security Council	C	—
American Brotherhood for			American Social Health Assn.	OK	OK
Blind	B	B,C	American Symphony Orchestra		
American Bureau for Medical			League	OK	—
Aid to China	OK	—	American Trauma Society	D	—
American Cancer Society	A	OK	American Viewpoint/Ethics		
American Cause	C	B,C	Resource Center	—	B
American Civil Liberties Union	A	—	Americans for Effective Law		
American Committee on			Enforcement	D	OK
Africa	A	—			
American Council of Blind	C	—	Americans for Indian		
American Council for			Opportunity	C	OK
Nationalities Service	C	—	America's Future	C	—
American Crafts Council	—	OK	Amigos de las Americas	—	A
American Diabetes Foundation	OK	OK	Amnesty International USA	D	C
American Economic			AMVETS	D	C
Foundation	B	OK	Amyotrophic Lateral Sclerosis		
American Enterprise Institute	OK	—	Society of America	D	OK
American Field Service	D	—	Animal Protection Institute	C	B,C
American Forestry Assn.	D	—	Animal Welfare Institute	C	—
American Found. for Blind	D	—	Anti-Defamation League of		
American Freedom from			B.B.	—	OK
Hunger	D	—	Appeal of Conscience Found.	—	C
American Friends Serivce			Arrow/Inc.	OK	OK
Com.	OK	OK	Arthritis Foundation	A	OK
American Fund for Dental			Asia Society	OK	OK
Health	OK	OK	Aspira of America	OK	—
American Health Assistance			Associated Humane Societies	—	B
Foundation/Arthero-			Assn. of Governing Boards of		
sclerosis Research	C	A	Universities & Colleges	—	A
American Health Foundation	—	B,C	Assn. for Integration in Mgt.	—	OK

STANDARDS FOR CHARITABLE ORGANIZATIONS

These standards were developed by the Council of Better Business Bureaus in order to help individuals make informed decisions about donating to charities. Organizations which do and do not meet CBBB's standards are listed in this chapter.

To meet the CBBB standards for charitable solicitations, organizations are required to:

GENERAL
● Disclose upon request current information about activities, finances, voting trusteeship and accomplishments.

RESPONSIBLE GOVERNING BODY
● Disclose upon request information about the decision-making structure.
● Meet with reasonable frequency and attendance.
● Avoid business transactions in which any board or staff member has a substantial financial interest.
● Limit compensated board members to a minority in any decision of the voting trusteeship.

FINANCIAL ACCOUNTABILITY
● Provide upon request an annual, externally audited financial statement and the auditor's report.
● Employ generally accepted accounting principles in preparing the annual financial statement, which shall be audited independently in accordance with generally accepted auditing standards. Disclose in the statement all income and accrued expenses, including all fund raising costs.
● Spend a reasonable percentage of total income directly for program services, as distinct from fund raising and administration.

ETHICAL FUND RAISING
● Pay no commissions or percentages for any fund raising activity.
● Inform recipients of unordered items that they are under no obligation to pay for or return them.
● Maintain adequate systems of control over contributions.

TRUTHFUL ADVERTISING AND INFORMATIONAL MATERIAL
● Ensure that information distributed by any means is not untrue, misleading, or deceptive in whole or in part.
● Ensure that photographs, films, and illustrations of programs, services, or recipients of aid are accurate and typical representations.

Charity	NIB	CBBB	Charity	NIB	CBBB
Assn. for Voluntary			Black Women's Community		
Sterilization	OK	—	Development Found.	C	—
Assn. of American Colleges	—	OK	Blinded Veterans Assn.	D	C
Assn on American Indian			Boy Scouts of America	OK	OK
Affairs	OK	OK	Boys Clubs of America	OK	OK
Asthma and Allergy Found.	OK	—	Braille Bible Foundation	—	A
Asthmatic Children's Found.	—	B,C	Business Committee for Arts	—	OK
Atlantic Council of U.S.	A	B	Business Council for		
Bach Mai Hosp. Relief Fund	C	—	International Understanding	—	B
Bibles for the World	—	B,C	CA1 Farley's Boys Ranch	A	B,C
Big Brothers/Big Sisters	B	OK	Camp Fire Girls	OK	OK
Billy Graham Evang. Assn.	—	B	Camps for the Blind	B	—
Black Christian Nat. Church	—	C	Campus Crusade for Christ	—	OK

Charity	NIB	CBBB
Campus Studies Institute	B	—
Cancer Care/Inc./National Cancer Found.	A	OK
Cancer Research Institute	D	—
CARE	OK	OK
Catalyst	OK	OK
Cathedral of Tomorrow/Rex Humbard Foundation	—	A
Catholic Near East Welfare Assn.	—	C
Cedars Home for Children Found.	D	C
Center for Constitutional Rights	C	—
Center for Environmental Educ.	C	C
Center for Science in the Public Interest	—	B,C
Center for Study of Presidency	—	OK
Center on Nat. Labor Policy	C	—
Child Study Assn. of America	A	—
Child Welfare League of America	OK	—
Children of God	—	A
Children/Inc.	OK	OK
Children's Aid International	C	—
Children's Asthma Research Institute and Hospital	B	—
Children's Defense Fund	OK	OK
Children's Rehabilitation Institute/John F. Kennedy Institute	—	OK
Children's Village USA/101	—	OK
Christian Appalachian Project	B	B,C
Christian Broadcasting Network	—	B,C
Christian Children's Fund	OK	OK
Christian Record Braille Found	D	OK
Citizen's Research Found.	—	B,C
Christian Youth Corps	C	—
Church League of America	C	—
Citizens for Decency Through Law	B	OK
Citizen's Scholarship Found.	D	OK
City of Hope	—	OK
Close Up Foundation	—	OK
College Placement Services	OK	—
Committee for Economic Dev.	OK	B
Committee to Combat Huntington's Disease	D	OK
Community Churches of America	C	B,C

Charity	NIB	CBBB
Compassion	C	OK
Congress of Racial Equality (CORE)	B	—
CORE Special Purpose Fund	—	B,C,D
Conservation Foundation	OK	OK
Consortium for Graduate Study in Management	OK	—
Coro Foundation	—	OK
Council for Basic Education	OK	B,C
Council for Financial Aid to Education	OK	OK
Council for Opportunity in Graduate Mgt. Education	D	—
Council on Economic Priorities	OK	—
Council on Financial Aid to Educ.	OK	—
Council on Foreign Relations	OK	—
Council on Municipal Performance	D	—
Council on Social Work Education	OK	OK
Cousteau Society	B	B
Cyprus Children's Fund	—	OK
Cystic Fibrosis Foundation	OK	OK
Dakota Indian Foundation	B	A
Damon Runyon-Walter Winchell Cancer Fund	OK	—
David Livingston Missionary Foundation	B	A,B,C
Day Care and Child Development Council of America	C	B,C,D
Deafness Research Foundation	A	—
Defenders of Wildlife	A	OK
Direct Relief Foundation	D	OK
Disabled American Veterans	B	C
Ducks Unlimited	OK	—
Dysautonomia Foundation	OK	—
Ear Research Institute	—	OK
Easter Seals	B	OK
Eastern Paralyzed Veterans	—	C
Economic Education Foundation for Clergy	OK	OK
Eisenhower Exch. Fellowships	A	—
Entrepeneurship Institute	C	—
Environmental Action Foundation	D	—
Environmental Defense Fund	A	OK
Epilepsy Foundation	B	OK
Ewing W. Mays Mission for the Handicapped	B	B,C
Experiment in Int'l Living	OK	—

Charity	NIB	CBBB	Charity	NIB	CBBB
Fair Campaign Practices Com.	C	—	Fund for Peace	OK	—
Fair Chance	A	—	Futures for Children	D	OK
Family Service Assn. of			Girl Scouts of the USA	OK	OK
America	D	—	Girls Clubs of the USA	D	OK
Father Close/Mercy Mission	—	A	Gompers Memorial Rehab.		
Father Flanagan's Boys Home	D	OK	Center	—	OK
Father Kelley's Home for			Good Smaritan Children's		
Homeless Boys	B	—	Foundation	C	A
Federation of Handicapped	—	OK	Goodwill Industries	D	OK
Fifty-Two (52) Association	OK	OK	Good Smaritan Children's		
Food for the Hungry	C	OK	Found.	—	A
Food for Work/Institute for			Guide Dogs Found. for Blind	A	OK
International Development	C	C	Guiding Eyes for Blind	B	A
Foreign Policy Association	D	—	Handi-Shop	B	—
Fortune Society	B	—	Heart Disease Research Found.	—	A
Foster Parents Plan	OK	OK	Heart Fund (American Heart		
Foundation for American			Assn.)	OK	—
Communications	—	B,C	Helen Keller International	D	B
Foundation for Econ. Educ.	C	—	Help Hospitalized Veterans	B	B
Foundation for National			Heritage Foundation	B	—
Progress/Mother Jones	—	B,C,	Holt Int'l Children's Services	—	OK
Franklin Book Program	A	—	Holy Land Christian Mission	OK	OK
Freedom House	OK	—	Hope School	D	C
Freedoms Found., Valley			Hospital Audiences	A	—
Forge	D	—	Hospitalized Veterans Writing		
Friends of Animals	—	B	Project	OK	—
Friends of Earth Found.	D	—	Hugh O'Brian Youth Found.	OK	—
Friends of the FBI	—	A	Human Growth Foundation	OK	OK
Fund for Animals	D	C	Human Resources Network	—	C
Fund for an Open Society	D	—	Humane Society of the US	OK	OK
Fund for Overseas Research			Hunger Project	C	—
Grants and Education	C	—	Huxley Institute	C	—

SOLICITATIONS IN THE FORM OF INVOICES

One of the most common ploys is to send solicitations in the form of bills or invoices. They may be disguised solicitations for advertising services, or purchase of a periodical or other publication. Many are paid in the mistaken belief that money is actually owed when it is not.

Federal law prohibits solicitations in the form of bills unless they bear either of two disclaimers in large type saying:

*"THIS IS A SOLICITATION FOR THE ORDER OF GOODS OR SERVICES, OR BOTH, AND NOT A BILL, INVOICE, OR STATEMENT OF ACCOUNT DUE. YOU ARE UNDER NO OBLIGATION TO MAKE ANY PAYMENTS ON ACCOUNT OF THIS OFFER UNLESS YOU ACCEPT THIS OFFER."

*"THIS IS NOT A BILL. THIS IS A SOLICITATION. YOU ARE UNDER NO OBLIGATION TO PAY UNLESS YOU ACCEPT THIS OFFER."

The Council of Better Business Bureaus suggests that anyone receiving a solicitation not meeting these requirements promptly report it to a post office or the Chief Postal Inspector, Fraud Branch, U.S. Postal Service, Washington, DC, 20260.

Charity	NIB	CBBB
ICD Rehab. & Research Ctr.	—	OK
Independent College Funds	OK	—
Indian Rights Association	D	—
Inner Peace Movement	—	B
Institute for Contemp. Studies	—	C
Institute of Cultural Affairs	C	OK
Institute of Fiscal & Political Educ.	C	—
Institute for Humane Studies	D	—
Institute for Int'l Development/Food for Work	C	C
Institute of Int'l Education	OK	—
Institute of Judicial Admin	C	B
Institute for World Order	D	OK
Inst. of Religion & Health	B	B
Institutional Development Corp.	—	B
International Christian Misistries/Mission to Children	—	A,B,C,
Internal Christian Relief	—	B,C,
International Church Relief Fund/Guatemala	C	A,E
International Exec. Service Corps	OK	B
Int'l Eye Foundation	C	—
Int'l Found. for Art Research	—	C
Int'l Fund for Animal Welfare	C	—
Int'l Human Assistance Programs	OK	OK
Int'l Insititute of Rural Reconstruction	D	—
Int'l Oceanographic Found.	—	B
Int'l Peace Academy	OK	—
Int'l Rescue Committee	OK	OK
Int'l Social Service, American Branch	OK	—
Society for Krishna Consciousness	—	B,C
Interracial Council for Business Opportunity	OK	OK
Island of Lepers	—	A
Izaak Walton League	C	—
Jesus to the Communist World	—	OK
Jewish Braille Institute	—	OK
Jewish National Fund	—	A
Jimmy Swaggart Evangelistic Assn.	—	B
Joint Council on Econ. Educ.	OK	OK
Jonas Partridge/World Changers	—	A,B
Joslin Diabetes Found.	—	B,C

Charity	NIB	CBBB
Junior Achievement	A	OK
Junior Engineering Technical Society	D	—
Juvenile Diabetes Found.	OK	OK
Keep America Beautiful	D	OK
King's Garden/World Concern	OK	—
Korean Cultural & Freedom Found.	C	B,C,D
Korean Relief	B	A,D
Lake Placid 1980 Olympic Games	—	B
Laubach Literacy Int'l	OK	—
Law Students Civil Rights Research Council	C	—
Lawyers' Committee for Civil Rights under Law	—	OK
Laymen's National Bible Comm.	—	OK
League of Women Voters	OK	OK
Legis 50	B	—
Leukemia Society of America	A	OK
Linus Pauling Institute of Science & Medicine	C	—
Little League Baseball	D	—
Little Sioux/St. Francis Mission	—	C
Living Bible Int'l	—	A
Mainstream	—	OK
MAP International	—	B
March of Dimes	OK	OK
Martin Luther King Center for Non-Violent Social Change	C	A
Maryknoll Fathers	—	C
Maternity Center Assn.	OK	—
Meals for Millions	OK	OK
Medgar Evans Fund	A	—
Medic Alert Found. Int'l	OK	OK
Medical Assistance Programs	D	—
Memorial Sloan-Kettering Cancer Center	—	A,B
Menninger Foundation	—	B
Mental Health Association	OK	OK
Mercy Mission/Father Close	—	A
Mexican American Legal Defense & Education Fund	OK	A
Military Order, Purple Heart	—	A
Mission to Children	—	A,B,C
Missionaries of Africa/White Fathers	—	C
Missionhurst	A	OK
Morality in Media	OK	OK
Muscular Dystrophy Assn.	B	OK

Charity	NIB	CBBB	Charity	NIB	CBBB
Myasthenia Gravis Found.	D	C	Nat'l Council of Jewish Women	—	OK
NAACP	A	—	Nat'l Council of Negro Women	OK	OK
NAACP Legal Defense and Educational Fund	D	C	Nat'l Council of Women of US	OK	—
NAACP Special Contrib. Fund	OK	OK	Nat'l Development Council	C	—
National Accreditation Council for Agencies Serving Blind, Handicapped	—	OK	Nat'l Education Program	C	—
National Alliance of Business	C	OK	Nat'l Federation of Settlements and Neighborhood Ctrs.	A	—
National Alliance for Optional Parenthood	OK	—	Nat'l Federation of Blind	B	—
Nat'l ALS Foundation	—	OK	Nat'l Fire Protection Assn.	A	—
Nat'l Antivivisection Soc.	—	C	Nat'l Found. for Cancer Research	B	—
Nat'l Assembly of Vol. Health & Social Welfare Org.	A	OK	Nat'l Found. for Ileitis and Colitis	C	OK
Nat'l Assn. for Hearing & Speech Action	B	—	Nat'l 4-H Council	D	B
Nat'l Assn. for Pract. Nurse Ed.	D	—	Nat'l Fund for Med. Educ.	OK	OK
Nat'l Assn. for Retarded Citizens	OK	—	Nat'l Fund for Minority Engineering Students	A	OK
Naa'l Assn. for Sickle Cell Disease	—	A	Nat'l Genetics Found.	OK	OK
Nat'l Assn. for Visually Handicapped	D	OK	Nat'l Glaucoma Research Program	C	—
Nat'l Audubon Society	OK	X	Na0'l Health Council	OK	OK
Nat'l Black United Fund	—	OK	Nat'l Health Federation	—	A
Nat'l Bureau of Ec. Research	D	B	Nat'l Hearing Assn.	—	OK
Nat'l Camp for the Blind	D	OK	Nat'l Hemophilia Found.	OK	OK
Nat'l Cancer Cytology Ctr.	B	B	Nat'l Indian Youth Council	C	—
Nat'l Cat Protection Soc.	—	OK	Nat'l Kidney Found.	OK	OK
Nat'l Center for State Courts	—	OK	Nat'l League for Nursing	OK	—
Nat'l Center for Vol. Action	A	OK	Nat'l Legal Aid & Defender Assn.	D	OK
Nat'l Child Labor Comm.	C	—	Nat'l Legal Center for the Public Interest	C	—
Nat'l Child Safety Council	—	OK	Nat'l Leukemia Assn.	B	B,C,D
Nat'l Citizens Comm. for Broadcasting	D	—	Nat'l Manpower Inst.	—	OK
Nat'l Comm. for Labor Israel	—	A	Nat'l Medical Fellowships	OK	OK
Nat'l Comm. for Prevention of Child Abuse	OK	C	Nat'l Merit Scholarships Corp.	OK	—
Nat'l Conference of Christians and Jews	OK	OK	Nat'l Multiple Sclerosis	A	OK
Nat'l Conf on Citizenship	B	—	Nat'l Municipal League	A	OK
Nat'l Consumer Inf. Ctr.	—	C	Nat'l Org. for Non-Parents	A	—
Nat'l Corporate Fund for Dance	OK	OK	Nat'l Paraplegia Found.	C	OK
Nat'l Council on the Aging	A	OK	Nat'l Parkinson Found.	C	—
Nat'l Council on Alcoholism	OK	OK	Nat'l Parks & Conservation Assn	D	OK
Nat'l Council to Combat Blindness	OK	—	Nat'l Recreation & Park Assn	C	B
Nat'l Council on Crime and Delinquency	OK	OK	Nat'l Retinitis Pigmentosa Found.	A	OK
Nat'l Council for Homemaker-Home Health Aid Services	OK	OK	Nat'l Right to Work Comm.	C	—
			Nat'l Right to Work-Legal Defense Found.	—	OK
			Nat'l Scholarship Service & Fund for Negro Students	C	—
			Nat'l Schools Committee for Economic Education	D	—
			Nat'l Sharecroppers Fund	D	—

Charity	NIB	CBBB
Nat'l Society for Autistic Children	OK	OK
Nat'l Society for Prevention of Blindness	A	OK
Nat'l Strategy In. Center	—	A
Nat'l Sudden Infant Death Syndrome Found.	OK	OK
Nat'l Trust for Historic Preservation in US	D	—
Nat'l Urban Coalition	A	OK
Nat'l Urban League	OK	—
Nat'l Wildlife Federation	B	—
Native American Rights Fund	OK	OK
Natural Resources Defense Council	OK	OK
Nature Conservancy	OK	OK
Navaho Nat'l Health Found.	C	—
Near East Foundation	OK	OK
Negative Population Growth	A	—
New Eyes for the Needy	OK	OK
Newsweek Talking Magazine Fund	D	—
North Shore Animal League	D	C
Oblates of Mary Immaculate	—	A
Omaha Home for Boys	—	C
Open Doors with Brother Andrew	—	B,C
Operation Happy Child	—	C
Operation Crossroads Africa	C	OK
Operation Help	B	B,C
Operation PUSH	—	A
Opportunities Industrialization Centers of America	D	OK
Oral Roberts Evangelistic Assn.	D	OK
Osborn Foundation	—	A
Our Little Brothers & Sisters	D	C
Outward Bound	—	B
Overseas Devel. Council	D	—
Oxfam-America	B	—
Pacific Legal Found.	OK	OK
Pallotine Missions	A	A,B
Pan American Dev. Found.	OK	OK
Paralyzed Veterans of America	B	C
Parents Without Partners	—	C
Parkinson's Disease Found.	B	—
Partners of the Americas	D	—
Pearl S. Buck Foundation	OK	OK
Piney Woods Country Life School	—	B,C
Planned Parenthood Federation	OK	OK
Population Council	OK	—

Charity	NIB	CBBB
Population Crisis Comm.	OK	—
Population Institute	A	—
Population Reference Bureau	D	—
Project Reference Bureau	D	—
Project Concern	B	OK
Project Hope/People-to-People Health Foundation	D	OK
PTL Television Network	—	B,C
Public Affairs Council	OK	—
Public Citizen	C	—
Puerto Rican Legal Defense & Education Fund	OK	OK
PUSH for Excellence/PUSH Foundation	C	A
Readers Digest Fund for the Blind	D	—
Reading is Fundamental	OK	OK
Recording for the Blind	D	OK
Red Cloud Indian School	D	—
Rehabilitation Center	—	B,C,D
Religion in American Life	OK	—
Research to Prevent Blindness	A	—
Resources for the Future	B	—
Rev. Al/United Faith Found.	—	A
Rev. Ile/United Christian Evangelical Assn.	—	A
Robert A. Taft Inst. of Gov't	—	OK
Rural Advance Fund	—	OK
St. Anthony's Zuni Indian Mission	—	A,B,C
St Christopher's Inn	—	B,C
St. Francis Mission	—	C
St. John's Missions	—	A
St. Joseph's Indian School	—	B,C
St. Jude Children's Research Hospital (ALSAC)	B	OK
St. Labre Indian School	D	OK
St. Stephen's Indian Mission	—	OK
Salesian Missions	B	B,C
Salvation Army	C	OK
Save the Children Fed.	OK	OK*
Save the Redwoods League	A	—
Scholarship, Education & Defense Fund for Racial Equality	A	—
Second Amendment Found.	—	B,C
Seeing Eye	B	C
SER-Jobs for Progress	C	C
Sex Information and Education Council of the U.S.	OK	—
Share/Inc.	C	A
Shrines of the Black Madonna	—	

Charity	NIB	CBBB	Charity	NIB	CBBB
Sierra Club and Found.	OK	—	USO/United Service Organizations	OK	OK
Solar Action	—	A	Veterans of Foreign Wars	C	—
SOS Children's Villages, Friends of	—	B,C	Veterans Hospital Radio & TV Guild	A	—
Southern Christian Leadership Conference	C	—	VITA (Volunteers in Technical Assistance)	OK	—
Southern Poverty Law Ctr.	B	A,C	Volunteers of America	C	—
Southwest Indian Found.	B	A,B,C	Way International	—	A
Spanish Refugee Aid	OK	—	Weal Fund/Women's Equity Action League	—	OK
Starr Commonwealth for Boys	OK	OK	Whale Protection Fund	—	C
Synanon Foundation	C	B	Wider Opportunities for Women	—	OK
Tax Foundation	D	OK	Wilderness Society	D	OK
Teen Missions Int'l	—	B,C	Wildlife Society	D	—
Teenage American Freedom Fund	—	B,C	Women's Action Alliance	—	B,C
Thomas A. Dooley Found.	A	—	Woodrow Wilson National Fellowship Foundation	—	B
Thomas Alva Edison Found.	A	—	World Changers Int'l	B	A,B
Tolstoy Foundation	D	—	World Concern	—	OK
Travelers Aid Association	A	—	World Education	—	OK
Twenty First Century Found.	—	C	World Evangelism	—	A
UN We Believe	D	—	World Literature Crusade	—	OK
Underground Evangelism	—	B	World Mercy Fund	B	E
Unification Church	—	B,C	World Missionary Evangelism	C	B
Union of Concerned Scientists	C	B,C	World Neighbors	OK	OK
United Action for Animals	C	B	World Rehabilitation Fund	A	—
United Cerebral Palsy Assns.	A	OK	World Research	B	B
United Jewish Appeal	—	A	World Vision International	C	—
United Nations Assn. of USA	OK	OK	World Wildlife Fund	D	OK
United Negro College Fund	OK	OK	Xavier Society for Blind	—	A
United Seamen's Service	OK	—	YMCA National Board	—	OK
United Student Aid Fund	A	—	Young America's Found.	—	A
United Way of America	OK	OK	Young Americans for Responsible Action	C	—
Universal Life Church	—	A	Young Audiences	D	OK
Universal Truth of Life Church	—	A	Youth Development	—	OK
Up With People	D	OK	Youth for Christ Int'l	—	B
Urban Environment Found.	—	B,C	Youth for Understanding	D	OK
Urban Institute	—	OK	YWCA of the USA	OK	—
U.S. Committee for Refugees	D	—	Zero Population Growth	OK	—
U.S. Committee for UNICEF	OK	OK			
U.S. Industrial Council Education Found.	—	B,C			
U.S. Olympic Committee	OK	C			

RATING CODES

NIB (National Information Bureau): **OK:** Meets NIB standards; **A:** Questions make charity impossible to rate. But questions are not so substantial as to assume that the charity does not meet standards; **B:** Does not meet one or more standards; **C:** Has not provided adequate information.

CBBB (Council of Better Business Bureaus): **OK:** Meets CBBB standards; **A:** Will not disclose general information; **B:** Questions about nature of governing body; **C:** Questions about financial accountability; **D:** Questions about ethical fund-raising practices; **E:** Questions about truthful advertising and informational materials.

Ratings current as of March, 1979, and are subject to change on a continuing basis. Agencies not on lists may be undergoing new evaluation.

HOW TO EVALUATE A CHARITY

Below are some questions that the Council of Better Business Bureaus suggest you consider when deciding whether to give to a charity:

MAIL APPEALS
- Does it make a clear statement of purpose and need?
- Is the appeal deceptive or disguised as a bill or invoice?
- Does it make clear you are not obligated to pay for or return any enclosed unordered items, such as stamps or key rings?
- Does it include an address where you can write for more information?
- Does it state whether donations are tax-deductible?
- Is the appeal overly emotional in trying to pressure you to give?

TELEPHONE SOLICITATIONS
- Does the solicitor state clearly at the outset the identity of the sponsoring organization and purpose of the call?
- Does the appeal have overtones of intimidation or harassment?
- Is the solicitor willing to answer all reasonable questions and to put the request in writing?
- If soliciting for a special event, what percentage of donations is tax-deductible?
- Does the solicitor try to pressure you into a decision by insisting on the need for immediate collection?

DOOR-TO-DOOR AND STREET APPEALS
- Does the solicitor carry identification specifying the benefiting organization and solicitor's name?
- Does the solicitor make clear, if selling merchandise such as candy or magazine subscriptions, how much goes to the benefiting organization?
- If children are soliciting, are they supervised by an adult?
- Is the solicitor willing to accept your check payable to the organization instead of to an individual?
- Will the solicitor provide you with a source for obtaining more information?
- Are donations tax-deductible?

Death and Burial

In This Chapter

- **Common Deceptions**
- **Proposed Government Regulations**
- **Ways to Save Money with Dignity**
- **Hospice Movement**
- **Memorial Societies**

Revolutionary changes are occuring in the $6.4 billion business of giving Americans their last rites. Most important to people faced with arranging a funeral or burial is a new set of government regulations designed to reduce deceptive practices in a field where little consumer protection has existed in the past.

The funeral industry fought hard and long against any attempt by the government to impose restrictions. It succeeded in obtaining some sympathy from members of Congress who helped get proposed rules of the Federal Trade Commission (FTC) watered down before they were acted on in 1979.

But news reports of the continuing controversy over the years had its effect, along with the new rules. Before final FTC action, many funeral directors began voluntarily to disclose more information to consumers and improve practices that had been criticized most widely.

FTC FINDS WIDE RANGE OF PRICES

In 1972, the Federal Trade Commission began a preliminary investigation of the funeral industry in response to complaints received from consumer groups and the general public. Lack of price disclosure was one of the most frequent complaints.

A full investigation began the following year. It featured a pilot survey of funeral prices in the District of Columbia. Funeral directors were asked to submit average prices for their three lowest-priced, complete adult funerals. A complete funeral was defined as including a casket; removal of remains to the funeral home; arranging for church services; procurement of burial permit; arranging for collection of life insurance proceeds and Social Security, veterans', fraternal, and labor union death benefits; arranging for obituary notices and transcripts of death certificates (but not including cost in quoted price); arranging flowers; providing guestbook and acknowledgement cards; use of hearse and one limousine; arranging for but not the cost of pallbearers and extension of credit.

The lowest price submitted was $210 for the complete funeral. Most were between $700 and $1,000, with one mortuary admitting a price of $1,830. The "typical" funeral was found to cost $1,137 for basic charges.

But additional charges brought the total price of the "typical" funeral to $1,886, according to the FTC survey data. Additional charges included interment receptacle (concrete liner for $85 or burial vault for $411, averaged for cost and frequency) $136; newspaper death notice, $20; clergyman fee, $15; transcript of death certificate, $5; flower wagon, $25; organist, $15; single gravesite, $160; opening and closing grave, $150; marker or monument, $178; sales tax, $45.

Each mortuary was also asked for the average price for two types of cremation services: an immediate cremation and a cremation after viewing. An immediate cremation includes: picking up the deceased; preparing and filing permits and forms; transporting the body to the crematory; crematory charge; and delivery of remains to the family or place of internment. Receptacles were considered extra. A cremation after viewing includes all of the above plus embalming and preparation, a casket and use of room for viewing. Among 11 funeral directors responding, the lowest price for immediate cremation was $80, and the highest was $485. Ten firms were under $200. Prices for cremation after viewing ranged from $350 to $890.

GOVERNMENT TRYING TO STOP EXPLOITATION OF PUBLIC

The FTC concluded that although prices varied greatly from one funeral home to another, the lack of price information given to the public was "a sign of a feeble competitive environment." In August, 1975, the agency proposed a set of rules designed primarily to require more disclosure of prices and other information and prohibit certain "exploitative, unfair and deceptive practices."

The FTC said it "had reason to believe" that bereaved friends and relatives are put in an especially vulnerable position when forced to arrange for a funeral, and this vulnerability is often exploited by undertakers through a variety of misrepresentations, improper sales techniques, non-disclosure of vital information and interferences with the market. The results, said the FTC, are "substantial economic and emotional injuries on large numbers of consumers." It noted that some state laws are designed to prevent disclosure of vital facts.

After the rules were proposed, protests arose from the funeral industry. The FTC became flooded with critical letters and phone calls, and some Members of Congress took sides with funeral directors in their states and districts. The National Funeral Directors Association, headquartered in Milwaukee, tried unsuccessfully to block scheduled public hearings with a court suit. And members of the Association sought to flood the oral and written record with objections.

But the FTC pushed ahead and completed 55 days of public hearings in six cities during 1976. A total of 325 witnesses were heard, mostly from the funeral industry. When the record was closed, it contained 30,000 pages of written comments and 15,000 pages of transcripts of oral testimony.

REPORT FINDS BUYER IGNORANCE WIDESPREAD

In June, 1978, the FTC staff issued a 526-page final report which accused the industry of taking unfair advantage of public ignorance and emotional trauma that usually grip buyers of funeral services. Among the worst misrepresentations alleged by the agency staff were:

● Claims that a casket is required by law for all funerals, even for cremation. A survey cited in the report indicated that 92 per cent of consumers did not know the law: that no state requires a casket for funerals or cremations. Most states require only a "suitable container," meaning firm (fibreboard) and combustible, for cremations.

● Claims that embalming is required by law, although no state requires it under normal circumstances. Exceptions in some states are death from a communicable disease and when interstate transportation is necessary. Many consumers also were found to believe falsely that embalming is designed to preserve the body beyond the funeral period.

● Claims that embalming is a vital health measure. The FTC said many funeral directors themselves have been misled into believing this, which they repeat in ignorance to consumers. Such claims, said the FTC, are "at best dubious."

● Claims that burial vaults or grave liners are required by law although no state requires a vault or liner and not all cemeteries require a liner.

● Claims that "sealer" caskets preserve the body for long periods; neither embalming nor a special casket can prevent decomposition. Fifty-five per cent of people surveyed did not know these facts.

ABSENCE OF PRICE DATA

The most serious problem faced by consumers was found to be the absence of itemized price information in advance. The FTC said price advertising, although increasing, is considered unethical by leading associations of funeral directors.

The agency also found that funeral directors dominate state boards and that the boards rarely penalize unscrupulous activity. Many of the state regulations, said the FTC, were passed at the behest of the funeral industry and thus are not designed to protect the public from major abuses.

REGULATIONS APPROVED BY THE FTC

In March, 1979, the FTC tentatively approved rules calling the following practices unfair and deceptive:

● **Embalming without permission of a family member or representative** unless such a person cannot be contacted or state law allows such a practice.

● **Requiring purchase of a casket for cremation** or claiming that such a purchase is required.

● **Charging more than a service cost** when a funeral director pays in advance for such things as pallbearers, flowers, singers, clergy, public transportation, obituary notices, death certificates and gratuities.

● **Stating inaccurate prices over the telephone** or failing to disclose price information over the phone when requested.

● **Failing to disclose upon request a printed list of casket prices** from the least to most expensive, and failing to state that no law requires purchase of a sealer or casket except in special circumstances.

● **Failing to disclose a statement** that no law requires purchase of a burial vault or grave liner although many cemeteries require the latter.

● **Failing to disclose prices of other funeral merchandise and services** including charges for minimum and full services, embalming, transportation, use of viewing facilities, funeral ceremony, hearse, limousine and a statement saying:

"You may choose only the items you desire. You will be charged only for those you use. If you have to pay for any items you did not specifically ask for, we will explain the reason in writing on the agreement form. Also note that there may be extra charges for items we do not provide, such as cemetery fees, flowers and newspaper notices. These are not included on this list."

● **Failing to give each customer making funeral arrangements a written agreement** listing the major services and other items and any cash advances already made. (However, package prices are allowed despite the contention of consumer groups that this practice leads to frequent abuses by making consumers buy services they don't need.)

PLANNING AHEAD CAN SAVE MONEY

When death occurs, survivors are faced with two basic decisions: what arrangements should be made for disposition of the body and what ceremony should be planned to commemorate the person and comfort the family and friends. Arrangements for body disposition can be done in advance with substantial savings and greater peace of mind. Pre-arrangements also makes comparison of alternatives possible.

One alternative is membership in a memorial society or association. The cost of joining ranges from $10 to $20. For this fee, members are able to have an entire funeral and burial or cremation for only $250 to $500. Most memorial societies have contracts with one or more local funeral homes which agree to offer low prices to members. The usual arrangements are simple and dignified. A list of memorial societies is in this chapter. Since the list is constantly changing, you may want to contact the Continental Association of Funeral and Memorial Societies, 1828 L St. NW, Washington, DC, 20036, for the latest information. A 64-page book, *A Manual of Death Education and Simple Burial,* is available at the above address for $2.00.

Veterans and their families are eligible to receive $300 toward financial costs and free burial in a national cemetery. If a private cemetery is preferred, the Veterans Administration will pay an additional $150 and supply a headstone or monument at no charge. Social Security benefits currently total $225 for those eligible.

Arrangements by funeral homes are usually sold on a package basis, keyed to the price of the casket. The standard adult funeral includes removal of the deceased from the place of death to the funeral home, embalming, casket, arranging for obituary notices and burial permits, use of viewing room and other facilities and transportation to the cemetery. These services are usually provided for all funerals regardless of the price of the casket, which may vary from $100 to $2,000.

LOW-PRICED CASKETS NOT ALWAYS SHOWN

Caskets are usually displayed in a room or by means of photographs. The lowest-priced ones may not be on display or may be shown in colors or materials which are less desirable than others. Some funeral homes may reduce costs for services not desired, but not many are willing to cut the package price for items not wanted. Whatever is chosen, buyers should request a total price in writing in advance.

Cremation can be arranged through a funeral home, a memorial society, or, in some areas, a company which handles only cremations. It can occur after a funeral service or instead of a service. Purchase of a casket for cremation is not usually required by law. But some type of container may be required by the funeral home, cemetery or crematory. A plain fibre or wooden box may be adequate.

Most economical is to choose an immediate cremation. This can avoid standard funeral items such as embalming or viewing and can avoid purchase of an elaborate casket.

CEMETERIES MAY REQUIRE GRAVE LINER

Cemeteries, like funeral homes, offer a wide variety of services and prices.

The cost of grave space may include a charge for care of cemetery property if that cost is not included in an endowment fund. Most cemeteries require purchase of a grave liner, a concrete container into which the casket is placed, to prevent the earth from caving in. Vaults are more expensive than grave liners but serve the same purpose. There may be a charge for disposition of cremated remains in what may be called an "urn garden." All cemetery costs should be listed in advance. They also can be completely avoided. In some states, the casket can be buried on the individual's private property. Most states allow private burial or scattering of ashes on land or sea.

The grave marker is another expense that can be avoided. Most markers are purchased from the cemetery where the burial is to take place. But they are also sold by monument dealers at lower prices. Here, too, it is possible to save substantial sums by shopping around and asking for all costs to be listed in advance in writing.

HOW TO SAVE MONEY AND BENEFIT HUMANITY

Even more economical is donating the body to a medical school. Most schools need bodies for training future doctors and will pay for transportation within the same state. But the body must be accepted in advance before being sent. The procedure is simple. When death occurs, a phone call to the school can complete transportation arrangements. A death certificate is essential. It must be made out by the attending physician and taken to the city or county health department. Embalming is not necessary unless the body is shipped by common carrier, such as an airline or trucking company.

Donations of other parts of the body can help the living, especially where there is urgent need. Eyes are in very short supply, largely because of the increase in corneal transplant operations. If you are interested in donating your eyes to help other people regain their eyesight, contact the nearest Eye Bank and notify your physician of your intentions. Lions Clubs International, the social organization, runs a nationwide eye donating program and can provide information. An eye bank is usually listed in the telephone book as "Lions Eye Bank." Or contact the Eye-Bank Association of America, 1111 Tulane Ave., New Orleans, LA, 70112.

Other parts of the human body needed for medical or research purposes include ear bones, kidneys, skin tissue, pituitary glands and blood. Inner ears are needed for research by the Deafness Research Foundation, 366 Madison Ave., New York, NY, 21205. Kidney donations are coordinated by the National Kidney Foundation, 116 East 27th St., New York, NY, 10010. Skin tissue is wanted by the Naval Medical Research Institute, Wisconsin Ave., Bethesda, MD, 20014. Information about pituitary glands—for transplant to children with serious growth problems—can be obtained from the National Pituitary Agency, Suite 503, 210 West Fayette St., Baltimore, MD, 21202. The Red Cross or the nearest hospital will accept almost any kind of blood for transfusion purposes. They particularly want blood from voluntary donors because of the greater risk of hepatitis from commercial donors. For general information about body donations, there are two non-profit organizations to contact: Living Bank, P.O. Box 6725, Houston, TX, 77025, 713/528-2971 and Medic Alert, Turlock, CA, 95380, 209/632-2371.

For a free, standard wallet-size donor card, which is recognized as a legal document in most states and Canadian provinces, contact any of the above organizations or the American Medical Association, 535 North Dearborn, Chicago, IL, 60605.

Meanwhile, the Seattle regional office of the FTC has published a 55-page booklet containing much of the above information, plus suggestions for the general public. The booklet also includes instructions and questionnaires for use in conducting a local survey of funeral prices. The handbook, *The Price of Death,* is available without charge from the FTC Regional Office, 2480 Federal Building, Seattle, WA, 98174.

FOR MORE INFORMATION
   The American Funeral, by Leroy Bowman, Public Affairs Press, Washington, DC, 1959.
   The Cost of Dying, by Paavo Arvio, Harper & Row, New York, 1974.
   The High Cost of Dying, by Ruth Mulvey Harmer, Collier-Macmillan, New York, 1963.
   The American Way of Death, by Jessica Mitford, Simon and Schuster, New York, 1978, $2.50 (reprint of 1963 edition, with a "Post Mortem" updated section).

MAKING A WILL

There are many reasons why people put off making a will. Not to do so, however, means that the federal and state governments will make disposition of your property for you. Making a will involves estate planning; even people of moderate means have an estate. Most consumer experts recommend that making a will is tricky enough to require professional advice. They say people need advice on joint ownership of property, planning for children's guardianship should both parents die together and life insurance and retirement funds.

You should be able to find a lawyer to draw up a simple will and estate plan for $50 to $100. Consult lawyers' ads in newspapers or ask a bank or the local bar association for a referral. Many unions now offer group legal services, similar to group health insurance. If you belong to such a plan, use it to have your will drawn up. You can do it yourself, but a technical slip-up may invalidate it. If you have a good idea of what constitutes your estate and how you want to distribute your assets before seeing a lawyer, the cost will be greatly reduced.

Even if your estate is modest you might look into setting up a trust, particularly if young children are involved, to provide for your family's support. If after taking stock of your assets, you realize you do not have enough to leave for your family's protection, consider taking out additional life insurance.

If you set up a trust, the trustee can handle your estate properly, protect it from hasty or unwise use by your family, give you maximum flexibility in planning and possibly diminish the amount of estate taxes due—all for a fee, of course.

If you are elderly, you can avoid some estate taxes and any gift taxes by giving away up to $3,000 per year to any number of people or $6,000 to couples. Or you can give up to $100,000 to your spouse. Any gift made within three years of death can be presumed to have been made "in contemplation of death," however, and thus still subject to estate taxes.

In addition, make sure that someone in your family knows the whereabouts of your will, your life insurance policy, pension plan, deeds to any property you might own and any other information pertaining to your estate. Some people keep originals in a safe deposit box, with copies at home and at a lawyer's office.

HOSPICES
Easing the Pain for the Terminally Ill

The concept of caring for terminally ill patients in a hospice, which started in the Middle Ages, is suddenly gaining a foothold in this country. As of 1979, there were 59 such institutions in operation and another 73 in the planning stages, according to a study by the U.S. General Accounting Office (GAO).

Hospices vary in their methods of providing care. Some offer care in the home, while others operate a special facility or unit in a hospital. All, however, share the principle that pain be alleviated but no attempt be made to cure its causes and that the patient's family have a role in the care.

Some hospice services are covered by existing government programs such as Medicare and Medicaid, but the GAO study concluded that amendments to federal law would be necessary to provide sufficient supervision and assistance for such services. It said costs would not add significantly to federal expenditures. Some private health insurors already cover certain hospice services.

The first national conference on hospices was held in June, 1979, by the Department of Health, Education and Welfare (HEW) in Washington, DC. Topics of discussion included cost reimbursements and patients' rights. For more information, contact the conference coordinator, James Hamner, Office of the Secretary, HEW, 300 Independence Ave, SW, Washington, DC, 20023. The telephone number is 202/245-1753.

MEMORIAL SOCIETIES

ALABAMA: MOBILE: Baldwin-Mobile Funeral & Memorial Society, P.O. Box U1178, University P.O. 36688, 205/344-0122.

ALASKA: ANCHORAGE: Cook Inlet Memorial Society, P.O. Box 2414, 99510, 907/277-6001, 907/272-7801.

ARIZONA: PHOENIX: Valley Memorial Society, P.O. Box 15813, 85060, 602/956-2919.

PRESCOTT: Memorial Society of Prescott Inc., P.O. Box 190, 86302, 602/445-7794.

TUSCON: Tuscon Mem. Soc., P.O. Box 12661, 85732, 602/323-1121.

YUMA: Mem. Soc. of Yuma, P.O. Box 4314, 85364, 602/783-2339.

ARKANSAS: FAYETTEVILLE: Northwest Arkansas Memorial Society, 1227 S. Maxwell, 72701, 501/442-5580.

LITTLE ROCK: Memorial Society of Central Arkansas, 12213 Rivercrest Dr., 72207, 501/225-7276.

CALIFORNIA: ARCATA: Humboldt Funeral Society, 666 11th St., 95521, 707/822-1321.

BERKELEY: Bay Area Funeral Soc., P.O. Box 264, 94701, 415/841-6653.

FRESNO: Valley Mem. Soc., P.O. Box 101, 93707, 209/224-9580.

LOS ANGELES: Los Angeles Funeral Society Inc., P.O. Box 44188, Panorama City, 91412, 213/786-6845.

MODESTO: Stanislaus Memorial Society, P.O. Box 4252, 95352, 209/523-0316.

PALO ALTO: Peninsula Funeral Society, 168 S. California Avenue, 94306, 415/321-2109.

RIDGECREST: Kern Memorial Society, P.O. Box 2122, 93555.

SACRAMENTO: Sacramento Valley Memorial Society Inc., P.O. Box 161688, 3720 Folsom Blvd., 95816, 916/451-4651.

SAN DIEGO: San Diego Memorial Society, P.O. Box 16336, 92116, 714/284-1465.

SAN LUIS OBISPO: Central Coast Memorial Society, P.O. Box 679, 93406, 805/543-6133.

SANTA BARBARA: Channel Cities Memorial Society, P.O. Box 424, 93102, 805/962-4794.

SANTA CRUZ: Funeral & Memorial Society of Monterey Bay Inc., P.O. Box 2900, 95063, 408/462-1333.

STOCKTON: San Joaquin Memorial Society, P.O. Box 4832, 95204, 209/462-8739.

COLORADO: DENVER: Rocky Mountain Memorial Society, 4101 East Hampden, 80222, 303/759-2800.

CONNECTICUT: GROTON: Southeastern Branch of Greater New Haven Memorial Society, Box 825, 06340, 203/445-8348.

HARTFORD: Memorial Society of Greater Hartford, 2609 Albany Ave., West Hartford, 06117, 203/523-8700.

NEW HAVEN: Greater New Haven Memorial Society, 60 Connelly Parkway, c/o Co-op, Hamden 06514, 203/288-6436, 203/865-2015.

SOUTHBURY: Southbury Branch of Greater New Haven Memorial Society, 514A Heritage Village 06488, 203/264-7564.

STAMFORD: Council Mem. Soc., 628 Main St., 06901, 203/348-2800.

WESTPORT: Memorial Society of SW Conn., 71 Hillendale Rd., 06880, 203/227-8705.

D.C. WASHINGTON: Memorial Society of Metropolitan Washington, 16th & Harvard Sts., NW, 20009, 202/234-7777.

FLORIDA: COCOA: Brevard Memorial Society, P.O. Box 276, 32922, 305/783-8699.

DeBARY: Funeral Soc. of Mid-Fla., P.O. Box 262, 32713, 305/668-6587.

FT. MYERS: Memorial Society of Southwest Florida, P.O. Box 1953, 33902, 813/936-1590.

GAINESVILLE: Memorial Society of Alachua County, Box 13195, 32604, 904/376-7073.

JACKSONVILLE: Jacksonville Memorial Society, 6915 Holiday Rd., North, 32216, 904/724-3766.

MIAMI: Community Funeral Society, P.O. Box 7422, Ludlam Branch, 33255, 305/667-3697.

ORLANDO: Orange County Memorial Society, 1815 E. Robinson St., 32803, 305/898-3621.

ST. PETERSBURG: Suncoast-Tampa Bay Memorial Society, 719 Arlington Avenue North, 33701, 813/898-3294.

SARASOTA: Memorial Society of Sarasota, P.O. Box 5683, 33579, 813/953-3740.

TALLAHASSEE: Funeral & Memorial Society of Leon County, P.O. Box 20189, 32304.
TAMPA: Tampa Mem. Soc., 3915 N. "A" St. 33609, 813/877-4604.
WEST PALM BEACH: Palm Beach Funeral Society, P.O. Box 2065, 33402, 305/833-8936.
GEORGIA: ATLANTA: Memorial Society of Georgia, 1911 Cliff Valley Way, NE, 30329, 404/634-2896.
HAWAII: HONOLULU: Funeral and Memorial Society of Hawaii, 200 N. Vineyard Blvd., Suite 403, 96817, 808/538-1282.
ILLINOIS: BLOOMINGTON: McLean County Branch of Chicago Memorial Society, 1613 E. Emerson, 61701, 309/828-0235.
CARBONDALE: Memorial Society of Carbondale Area, 1214 W. Hill St., 62901, 618/549-7816.
CHICAGO: Chicago Memorial Association, 59 E. Van Buren St., 60605, 312/939-0678.
ELGIN: Fox Valley Funeral Association, 783 Highland Ave., 60120, 312/695-5265.
PEORIA: Memorial Society of Greater Peoria, 908 Hamilton Blvd., 61603, 309/673-5391.
ROCKFORD: Memorial Society of Northern Illinois, P.O. Box 6131, 61125, 815/964-7697.
URBANA: Champaign County Memorial Society, 309 W. Green St., 61801, 217/328-3337.
INDIANA: BLOOMINGTON: Bloomington Memorial Society, 2120 North Fee Lane, 47401, 812/332-3695.
FT. WAYNE: Northeastern Indiana Memorial Society, 306 W. Rudisill Blvd., 46807, 219/745-4756.
INDIANAPOLIS: Indianapolis Memorial Society, 5805 E. 56th St., 46226, 317/545-6005.
MUNCIE: Memorial Society of Muncie Area, 1900 N. Morrison Rd., 47304, 317/288-9561, (evenings) 317/289-1500.
VALPARAISO: Memorial Society of N.W. Indiana, 356 McIntyre Ct., 46383, 219/462-5701.
WEST LAFAYETTE: Greater Lafayette Memorial Society, Box 2155, 47906, 317/463-9645.
IOWA: AMES: Central Iowa Memorial Society, 1015 Hyland Ave., 50010, 515/239-2421.
CEDAR RAPIDS: Memorial Option Service of Cedar Rapids, 600 3rd Ave., S.E., 52403, 319/398-3955.
DAVENPORT: Blackhawk Memorial Society, 3707 Eastern Ave., 52807, 319/326-0479.
IOWA CITY: Memorial Society of Iowa River Valley, 120 N. Dubuque St., 52240, 319/338-1179.
KANSAS: HUTCHINSON: Mid-Kansas Mem. Soc., Box 2142, 67501.
KENTUCKY: LOUISVILLE: Memorial Society of Greater Louisville, 322 York Street, 40203, 502/585-5119.
LOUISIANA: BATON ROUGE: Memorial Society of Greater Baton Rouge, 8470 Goodwood Ave., 70806, 504/926-2291.
MAINE: PORTLAND: Memorial Society of Maine, 425 Congress St., 04111, 207/773-5747.

MARYLAND: BALTIMORE: Memorial Society of Greater Baltimore, 3 Rux-view Ct., Apt. 101, 21204, 301/486-6532, 301/296-4657.

COLUMBIA: Howard County Memorial Foundation, c/o Suite 100, Wilde Lake Willage Green, 21044, 301/730-7920, 301/997-1188.

GREENBELT: Maryland Suburban Memorial Society, c/o Bruce Bowman, 14Z3 Laurel Hill, 20770, 301/474-6468.

MASSACHUSETTS: BROOKLINE: Memorial Society of New England, 24 Monmouth Street, 02146, 617/731-2073.

ORLEANS: Mem. Soc. of Cape Cod, Box 1346, 02653, 617/255-3841.

NEW BEDFORD: Memorial Society of Greater New Bedford Inc., 71 Eighth St., 02740, 616/994-9686.

SPRINGFIELD: Springfield Memorial Society, P.O. Box 2821, 01101, (evenings) 413/567-5715.

MICHIGAN: ANN ARBOR: Memorial Advisory & Planning Service, P.O. Box 7325, 48107, 313/663-2697.

BATTLE CREEK: Memorial Society of Battle Creek, c/o Art Center, 265 E. Emmett St., 49017, 616/962-5362.

DETROIT: Greater Detroit Memorial Society, 4605 Cass Ave., 48201, 313/833-9107.

EAST LANSING: Lansing Area Memorial Planning Society, 855 Grove St., 48823, 517/351-4081.

FLINT: Memorial Society of Flint, G-2474 S. Ballenger Hwy, 48507, 313-232-4023.

GRAND RAPIDS: Memorial Society of Greater Grand Valley, P.O. Box 1436, 49501, 616/458-4032.

KALAMAZOO: Memorial Society of Greater Kalamazoo, 315 West Michigan, 49006.

MT. PLEASANT: Memorial Society of Mid Michigan, P.O. Box 313, 48858, 517/772-0220.

MINNESOTA: MINNEAPOLIS: Minnesota Memorial Society 900 Mt. Curve Ave., 55403, 612/824-2440.

MISSISSIPPI: GULFPORT: Funeral and Memorial Society of the Mississippi Gulf Coast, P.O. Box 265, 39501, 601/435-2284.

MISSOURI: KANSAS CITY: Greater Kansas City Memorial Society, 4500 Warwick Blvd., 64111, 816/561-6322.

ST LOUIS: Memorial and Planned Funeral Society, 5007 Waterman Blvd., 63108, 314/361-0595.

MONTANA: BILLINGS: Memorial Society of Montana, 1024 Princeton Avenue, 59102, 406/252-5065.

MISSOULA: Five Valleys Burial-Memorial Assn., 401 University Ave., 59801, 406/543-6952.

NEBRASKA: OMAHA: Midland Memorial Society, 3114 Harney St., 68131, 402/345-3039.

NEVADA: RENO: Memorial Society of Western Nevada, Box 8413, University Station, 89507, 702/322-0688.

NEW HAMPSHIRE: CONCORD: Memorial Society of New Hampshire, 274 Pleasant St., 03301, 603/224-0291.

NEW JERSEY: CAPE MAY: Memorial Society of South Jersey, P.O. Box 592, 08204, 609/884-8852.

EAST BRUNSWICK: Raritan Valley Memorial Society, 176 Tices Lane, 08816, 201/246-9620, 201/572-1470.
LANOKA HARBOR: Memorial Association of Ocean County, P.O. Box 173, 08734.
LINCROFT: Memorial Assn. of Monmouth County, 1475 West Front St., 07738, 201/741-8092.
MADISON: Morris Mem. Soc., Box 156, 07940, 201/540-1177.
MONTCLAIR: Mem. Soc. of Essex, 67 Church St., 07042, 201/746-9352.
PARAMUS: Central Mem. Soc., 156 Forest Ave., 07652, 201/265-5910.
PLAINFIELD: Mem. Soc. of Plainfield, P.O. Box 307, 07061.
PRINCETON: Princeton Mem. Assn., Box 1154, 08540, 609/924-1604.
NEW MEXICO: ALBUQUERQUE: Memorial Association of Central New Mexico, P.O. Box 3251, 87190, 505/299-5384.
LOS ALAMOS: Memorial & Funeral Society of N. New Mexico, P.O. Box 178, 87544, 505/662-2346.
NEW YORK: ALBANY: Albany Area Memorial Society, 405 Washington Avenue, 12206, 518/465-9664.
BINGHAMTON: Southern Tier Memorial Society, 183 Riverside Dr., 13905, 606/729-1641.
BUFFALO: Greater Buffalo Memorial Society, 695 Elmwood Ave., 14222, 716/885-2136.
ITHACA: Ithaca Me. Soc., P.O. Box 134, 14850, 607/272-5476.
NEW HARTFORD: Mohawk Valley Memorial Society, 28 Oxford Rd., 13413, 315/797-1955.
N.Y.C. Community Funeral Soc., 40 E. 35th St., 10016, 212/683-4988.
N.Y.C. Consumers Mem. Soc., 309 W. 23rd St., 10111, 212/691-8400.
N.Y.C. Memorial Society of Riverside Church, 490 Riverside Dr., 10027, 212/749-7000.
ONEONTA: Memorial Society of Greater Oneonta, 12 Ford Ave., 13820, 607/432-3491.
POMONA: Rockland C. Mem. Soc., Box 461, 10970, 914/354-2917.
PORT WASHINGTON: Memorial Society of Long Island, Box 303, 10050, 516/627-6590.
POUGHKEEPSIE: Mid-Hudson Memorial Society, 249 Hooker Ave., 12603, 914/454-4164.
ROCHESTER: Rochester Memorial Society, 220 Winton Rd. S., 14610, 716/461-1620.
SYRACUSE: Syracuse Mem. Soc., P.O. Box 67, 13214, 315/474-4580.
WELLSVILLE: Upper Genesee Memorial Society, 4604 Bolivar Rd., 14895, (in process of joining) 716/593-1060.
WHITE PLAINS: Funeral Planning Assn. of Westchester, Rosedale Avenue & Sycamore Lane, 10605, 914/946-1660.
NORTH CAROLINA: ASHEVILLE: The Blue Ridge Memorial Society, P.O. Box 2601, 28801.
CHAPEL HILL: Triangle Mem. & Funeral Soc., Box 1223, 27514, 919/942-4427.
CHARLOTTE: Charlotte Memorial Society, 234 N. Sharon Amity Rd., 28211, 704/597-2346.
GREENSBORO: Piedmont Memorial & Funeral Society, Box 16192, 27406, 919/674-5501.

LAURINBURG: Scotland Co. Funeral & Mem. Soc., Box 192, 28352.

OHIO: AKRON: Canton-Akron Memorial Society, 3300 Morewood Rd., 44313, 216/836-8094.

CAMPBELL: Mem. Soc of Greater Youngstown, 75 Jackson Dr., Campbell, 44405, 216/755-8696.

CINCINNATI: Memorial Society of Greater Cincinnati Inc., 536 Linton St., 45219, 513/281-1564.

CLEVELAND: Cleveland Memorial Society, 21600 Shaker Blvd., 44122, 216/751-5515.

COLUMBUS: Memorial Society of the Columbus Area, P.O. Box 14103, 43214, 614/267-4696.

DAYTON: Dayton Mem. Soc., 665 Salem Ave., 45406, 513/274-5890.

ELYRIA: Memorial Society of Lorain County (branch of Cleveland Memorial Society) 226 Middle Ave., 44035, 216/323-5776 ext. 441.

TOLEDO: Mem. Soc. of Northwestern Ohio, 2210, Collingwood Blvd., 43620, 419/475-4812.

WILMINGTON: Funeral & Memorial Society of Southwest Ohio, 66 North Mulberry St., 45177, 513/382-2349.

YELLOW SPRINGS: Yellow Springs Branch of Memorial Society of Columbus Area, 317 Dayton St., 45387, 513/767-2011.

OKLAHOMA: OKLAHOMA CITY: Mem. Soc. of Central Oklahoma, 600 NW 13th St., 73103, 405/232-9224.

TULSA: Mem. Soc. of E. Okla., 2952 S. Peoria, 74114, 918/743-2363.

OREGON: PORTLAND: Oregon Memorial Association, 5255 Southwest Dosch Rd., 97201, 503/283-5500.

PENNSYLVANIA: BETHLEHEM: Lehigh Valley Memorial Society, 701 Lechauweki Ave., 18015, 215/866-7652.

ERIE: Thanatopsis Soc. of Erie, P.O. Box 3495, 16508, 814/864-9300.

HARRISBURG: Memorial Society of Greater Harrisburg, 1280 Clover Lane 17113, 717/564-4761.

PHILADELPHIA: Memorial Society of Greater Philadelphia, 2125 Chestnut St., 19103, 215/567-1065.

PITTSBURGH: Pittsburgh Memorial Society, 605 Morewood Ave., 15213, 412/-621-8008.

POTTSTOWN: Pottstown Branch of Phila. Memorial Society, 1409 N. State St., 19464, 215/323-5561.

SCRANTON: Memorial Society of Scranton-Wilkes-Barre Area, 303 Main Ave., Clark's Summit 18411, 717/587-5255.

RHODE ISLAND: See Massachusetts for New England Me. Soc.

SOUTH CAROLINA: CHARLESTON: Mem. Soc. of Charleston, 2319 Bluefish Circle, 29412.

CLEMSON: Clemson Funeral Society, P.O. Box 1132, 29631.

MYRTLE BEACH: Memorial Society of Eastern Carolina, P.O. Box 712, 29577, 803/449-6526, 803/449-3064.

TENNESSEE: CHATTANOOGA: Memorial Society of Chattanooga, 1108 N. Concord Rd., 37421, 615/267-4685.

KNOXVILLE: East Tennessee Memorial Society, P.O. Box 10507, 37919, 615/523-4176.

NASHVILLE: Middle Tennessee Memorial Society, 1808 Woodmont Blvd., 37215, 615/383-5760.
PLEASANT HILL: Cumberland Branch of E. Tennessee Mem. Soc., P.O. Box 246, 38578, 615/277-3795.
TEXAS: AUSTIN: Austin Memorial & Burial Information Society, P.O. Box 4382, 78765.
BEAUMONT: Golden Triangle Memorial Society, Box 6136, 77705, 713/833-6883.
COLLEGE STATION: Memorial Society of Bryan-College Station, P.O. Box 9078, 77840, 713/696-6944.
DALLAS: Dallas Area Mem. Soc. 4015 Normandy, 75205, 214/528-3990.
HOUSTON: Houston Area Memorial Society, 5210 Fannin St., 77004, 214/526-1571.
LUBBOCK: Lubbock Area Memorial Society, P.O. Box 6562, 79413, 806/792-0367.
SAN ANTONIO: San Antonio Memorial Society, 777 S.A. Bank & Trust Bldg, 771 Navarro, 78205.
UTAH: SALT LAKE CITY: Utah Memorial Association, 569 South 13th East, 84102, 801/582-8687.
VERMONT: BURLINGTON: Vermont Memorial Society, P.O. Box 67, 05401, 802/863-4701.
VIRGINIA: ALEXANDRIA: Mt. Vernon Memorial Society, 1909 Windmill Lane, 22307, 703/765-5950.
ARLINGTON: Memorial Society of Arlington, 4444 Arlington Blvd., 22204, 703/892-2565.
CHARLOTTESVILLE: Memorial Planning Society of the Piedmont, 717 Rugby Road, 22903, 703/293-3323.
OAKTON: Fairfax Mem. Soc., P.O. Box 130, 22124, 703/281-4230.
RICHMOND: Memorial Society of Greater Richmond Area, Box 180, 23202, 804/355-0777.
ROANOKE: Memorial Society of Roanoke Valley Inc., P.O. Box 8001, 24014, 703/774-9314.
VIRGINIA BEACH: Memorial Society of Tidewater Virginia, 2238 Oak St., 23451, 804/428-1804.
WASHINGTON: SEATTLE: People's Memorial Association, 2366 Eastlake Avenue East, 98102, 206/325-0489.
SPOKANE: Spokane Mem. Assn., Box 14701, 99214, 509/926-2933.
WISCONSIN: RACINE: Funeral & Mem. Soc. of Racine & Kenosha, 625 College Ave., 53403, 414/634-0659.
RIVER FALLS: Western Wisconsin Funeral Society, 110 N. 3rd, 54022, 715/425-2052.
STURGEON BAY: Memorial Society of Door County, c/o Hope United Church of Christ, 54235, 414/743-2701.

Source: Continental Association of Funeral and Memorial Societies Inc., 1979.

Communications

In This Chapter

- Media Concentration
- TV Program Ratings
- Truth and Advertising
- Postal Consumer Protection
- Package Delivery Rates
- Telephone and Telegraph Rates

"Explosive" is the word to describe the expansion of information and the business of transmitting it in this country. Communications have become so rapid and so available that news events are often witnessed by millions before they are reported as news. Electronic and printer matter have reached flood stage. Among the major news media, only newspapers have fallen behind the pace.

Americans have become hooked on television. They spend an average of more than six hours a day watching the flickering screen—much like people who watch a good fire—with glazed eyes. The average child spends more time before the set than in the classroom. TV has become even more essential—at least more prevalent in homes—than indoor plumbing and telephones.

Television has become so much a part of our lives that we may not know how much effect it has. On the plus side, television has provided a broader view of the world than many people would otherwise get. It has helped many people learn the English language. And it has helped the country focus, at least temporarily, on the major events of importance such as Presidential press conferences, Congressional hearings and national elections. It also has brightened the waking hours of millions confined to a room or otherwise living lonely lives.

TV also has come in for considerable criticism. It has been blamed for almost everything wrong with society although, in many ways, it merely reflects life as it is. One young murderer even blamed a televised serial for his own horrible act. Parents blame television for their children's poor grades in school. Others blame TV for a breakdown in moral standards, lowering of personal tastes and lessening of sensitivity of people to each other. The screen is also filled with deceptive advertisements.

One of the biggest controversies concerning television is the extent of sex and violence on prime time, roughly from 7 to 11 o'clock in the evening. In the past two years, much public opposition has confronted the networks, which control this segment of daily programming. Critical studies and threats to boycott advertisers of such shows have helped force the rate of violence down. But sex-oriented programming—often featuring near-nudity and simulated sexual acts—has increased.

Resistance to TV advertising has also grown over the years, particularly as it affects children. In response to demands from various citizen groups, the Federal Trade Commission took an unprecedented step in March, 1978, when it proposed banning all TV ads aimed at children under age 8 and banning ads for sugary products beamed at children from 8 to 12.

COMMERCIAL TIME INCREASES

Meanwhile, the number of commercials aimed at general audiences has been growing steadily without any announcement or notice, according to a report in the *Wall Street Journal.* It said the networks have expanded the usual six minutes per hour to seven and increased the number by shortening the average commercial time. A voluntary code of the National Association of Broadcasters allows up to 9½ minutes of "non-program material" per hour of prime time and 16 minutes per hour most other times.

The increase in offensive programming and commercial time may have helped cause the shock wave that hit the broadcasting industry in late 1977 when the A.C. Nielsen Co. reported an 8 per cent drop in the number of homes watching daytime TV and 3 per cent drop in homes turned to prime-time TV.

In February, 1979, a poll by the *Washington Post* reported that 53 per cent of people interviewed said they were watching less television than they had five years before, while only 32 per cent were watching more.

One of the most important roles of television is journalistic. It is now generally conceded to be the prime source of news for two out of every three people in this country. Yet it is essentially little more than a headline service. The limitations of camera coverage tend to capsulize reporting of major issue to only a few seconds while emphasizing others of less importance but with more dramatic qualities.

INFLUENCE OF ADVERTISING ON THE NEWS

One of the biggest limitations on the news is advertising. Although television journalists and executives consistently deny any connection, the fact is that many issues of extreme sensitivity to large advertisers are touched on only lightly, if at all, by most stations and networks. A glance at the country's largest advertisers in the major media including television shows the industries and companies with the biggest economic clout.

The key topics are soap, cars, cigarettes, drugs, liquor and food. Other large advertisers produce soft drinks, fast food, cosmetics and beer. Although few of these products are essential to daily survival, they represent many important national problems, from pollution to inflationary pricing. Yet numerous studies of news coverage shows a paucity of time devoted to problems affecting large advertisers.

Other news media are also vulnerable to pressures, both actual and imagined, from large economic interests. Women's magazines are notorious for their unwillingness to tackle subjects that might displease advertisers. Daily newspapers tend to be more objective on the whole but have also shown on occasion that they, too, are not insensitive to the feelings of advertisers in making journalistic judgments.

Many people had hoped that public television would make up for at least some of the defects and drawbacks of commercial programming. Congress has shared that hope with steadily increasing funds. But there is general agreement even among public broadcasting executives that these efforts have failed to match public television's programming to its potential. The most popular serials have been imported from Great Britain, and the major contribution to news and public affairs in recent years has been the McNeil-Lehrer Report, essentially an interview show, that has been highly praised.

CARNEGIE REPORT CRITICIZES PUBLIC TV

In 1979, a second Carnegie Commission issued a critical report saying that non-commercial television and radio should be restructured and given substantially more funds, both private and governmental. Some $200 million would be raised through a system of fees from major users of the airwaves. And although the government would be called on for nearly $600 million, new protections would be installed to insulate programming from political interference such as occurred in the Nixon Administration.

Another bright hope that has failed to live up to its early promise is cable television. For many years, the Federal Communications Commission (FCC) has discouraged cable network arrangements in line with the wishes of major commercial broadcasting interests. Gradually, however, with changes in membership of the FCC, these impediments have been disappearing.

MEDIA CONCENTRATION
More Chains Mean Less Diversity

Independent voices among the nation's news media are steadily being squeezed out by the drive for higher profit. They are being gobbled up by newspaper and broadcasting chains as well as conglomerates with no primary interest in journalism. Conglomerate firms also are taking over book and magazine publishing houses. News has become a big, growing business in America.

Time Inc., which publishes magazines and books, sold its broadcasting outlets to McGraw Hill and purchased the *Washington Star* and the Book-of-the-Month Club. CBS, which owns magazine publishing firms as well as its extensive broadcasting holdings, now owns two paperback book publishing firms plus manufacturers of toys and tools. Capital Cities Communication Inc., which owns several television stations and trade journals, now owns the *Kansas City Star*. The New York Times Company, which owns several newspapers and broadcasting outlets, also now owns two book publishing companies and several specialty magazines. NBC is owned by RCA, which also owns Random House book publishers as well as Hertz Rent-a-Car and Banquet frozen foods. ABC owns more than 250 movie theaters, plus amusement parks, ABC Records, several magazines and a book publishing company. One of the biggest conglomerates is the Times Mirrow Company, which publishes the *Los Angeles Times* and owns a book publishing company, paper mills, map makers, forests, and the *Dallas Times Herald*.

FOUR FIRMS CONTROL 25% OF CIRCULATION
By 1979, chains owned 72 per cent of the daily newspaper circulation in the country. Only four chains owned 25 per cent of total daily circulation. They were Newhouse, Knight-Ridder, Chicago Tribune Company and Gannett Corp. The last named swallowed Combined Communications Corp. in June, 1979, giving Gannett 80 daily papers, seven television stations, 12 radio stations, plus weekly papers, newsprint production facilities and other allied businesses. It was the largest merger of media interests in history, creating a corporation with nearly $1 billion in annual sales.

As a result, only 2.5 per cent of American cities have daily papers actually competing with each other. The trend toward increased concentration of ownership of both print and broadcast media caused the Federal Trade Commission to hold a symposium in November, 1978, to determine what, if anything, could be done to preserve what was left to diversity of opinion. It also caused a Senate hearing on media concentration. But no new government actions were contemplated, and the merger trend continued at a steady rate.

DOES OWNERSHIP AFFECT NEWS COVERAGE?

Still another problem of chain and conglomerate ownership is the homogenizing effect it can have on news coverage. For many years, only two national news services have supplied the bulk of all daily news consumer in this country. Broadcasting networks and stations, as well as newspapers and other media depend heavily on these services. Of special concern is the now common situation where a local newspaper owns a local television station, or vice vera.

A survey by William T. Gormley, Jr. of the University of North Carolina, entitled "The Effects of Television-Newspaper Cross-Ownership on News Homogeneity," indicated that cross-ownership tends to restrict the variety of news available to the public. It also tends to increase story duplication because of "pack journalism," the tendency of reports to cover the same stories because other reporters are.

The likelihood of television stations and newspaper exchanging carbon copies of news stories also increases, as does the likelihood of a television station hiring a reporter or editor who has worked for the paper which owns the station. Gormley also found that the flow of opinion material is reduced by cross-ownership. Twenty-five per cent of non-newspaper owned stations in his survey never editorialized, as opposed to 52 per cent of the newspaper-owned stations studied.

For many years, the Federal Communications Commission (FCC) has limited ownership of broadcasting facilities by any individual or company to five television stations, seven AM radio stations and seven FM radio stations, a total of no more than 19 stations. An owner in one market is limited to one TV station and one AM and FM station. But these limits are sometimes waived by the FCC.

The FCC has done little to curb cross ownership of news media in one community. When finally issuing a rule in 1975, it decided against cross ownership of newspapers and broadcasting stations in one community but limited the rule to future transfers and to existing combinations in only 16 small communities. Not satisfied with the change, the National Citizens Committee for Broadcasting (NCCB), a public interest group headed by former FCC Commissioner Nicholas Johnson, filed suit to force the FCC to broaden its prohibition to all existing joint ownerships between local TV stations and newspapers.

In March, 1977, an appeals court in Washington ruled in favor of the NCCB and ordered the FCC to break up all such cross ownerships except those that could be shown to be in the public interest. The FCC, broadcasters and newspapers appealed this decision to the Supreme Court, which supported the FCC position.

SEX AND VIOLENCE ON TV
Broadcasters Forced to Change Their Tunes

Citizen groups have begun to wield considerable influence on television program content. Their principal weapons are publicized lists of shows deemed offensive and advertisers who spounsor such shows.

After the National citizens Committee for Broadcasting (NCCB) began to list violent shows in 1976, nine of the 12 sponsors reduced their purchases of such programs. The networks also reduced the overall number of violent acts. At the same time, they increased the number of sexual references.

But "sexploitation" has fallen off, along with violence, since the National Parent-Teacher Association (NPTA) started to rate programs in 1978. Its ratings, now made twice a year, are based on evaluations of citizen review groups in every state. Criteria include the degree of "positive contribution to the quality of life in America, lack of offensive content and high program quality."

In 1979, both PTA and NCCB reported that violence continued to drop, with most of it occurring in prime time, network movies, especially ABC movies. NBC had the best rating at last count.

Shows with sex themes suffered poor ratings in general, and some were cancelled. Ads that bothered PTA viewers the most were network promos with "titillatingly violent or sexual material" injected into programs watched by children and ads for feminine hygiene products shown in prime time.

MOST COMMENDABLE PROGRAMS LISTED

"Most commendable" programs, according to NPTA's July, 1979, ratings were Jesus of Nazareth (NBC), Little House on the Prairie (NBC), Friends (ABC), 60 Minutes (CBS), Paper Chase (CBS), World of Disney (NBC), Family (ABC), NBC Specials (NBC), Eight is Enough (ABC), and Weekend (NBC).

Programs of least overall quality on NPTA's list were Cliffhangers (NBC), Highcliffe Manor (NBC), Dukes of Hazzard (CBS), Delta House (ABC), Just Friends (CBS), Three's Company (ABC), Brothers and Sisters (NBC), The Ropers (ABC), Supertrain (NBC), and Carter Country (ABC).

Most violent programs in order, according to NCCB, were Young Guy Christian (ABC), The Duke (NBC), Cliff Hangers (NBC), Buffalo Soldiers (NBC), Charlie's Angels (ABC), Greatest Heroes of the Bible (NBC), Rockford Files (NBC), Dukes of Hazzard (CBS), Walt Disney (NBC), and Incredible Hulk (CBS).

Least violent programs, according to NCCB, included: All in the Family (CBS), Angie (ABC), Bad News Bears (CBS), Barney Miller (ABC), Beanes of Boston (CBS), Car Wash (NBS), Carter Country (ABC), CHIPS (NBC), Different Strokes (NBC) and Eight is Enough (ABC).

SPONSORS OF MOST VIOLENCE LISTED

NCCB listed the following as sponsors of the least violence: Nikon Cameras, Alberto Culver Products, Perrier Mineral Water, Timex Watches, Shulton Old Spice, Beneficial Finance, Ace Hardware, Lincoln-Mercury Motors, Fruit of the Loom and Breck Products.

NPTA listed the following as the most distinguished advertisers for program quality: Campbell Soup, General Electric, Oscar Mayer, Bristol-Myers, Ford Motor, Hallmark Cards, Kellogg, Mars, Nabisco, Nestle and Ralston Purina.

NCCB's list of sponsors of the most violence included Chrysler, HiC Fruit Drinks, Budweiser, Duracell Batteries, Mennen Products, Borden Food Products, Wrangler Jeans, General Mills, Sealy Mattress and Miller Products (beer).

NPTA's list of most offensive advertisers included Esmark, Heublein, Miles Laboratories, American Home Products, Anheuser-Busch, Coca-Cola, Colgate-Palmolive, Consolidated Foods, J.C. Penney and Pepsi.

NPTA's Program Review Guide can be obtained for 50 cents from NPTA

TV Action Center, 700 N. Rush St., Chicago, IL, 60611. A copy of NCCB's Media Watch newsletter listing program details may be obtained free from NCCB, 1530 P St. NW, Washington, DC, 20005.

TV ADVERTISING AND CHILDREN

Although the Federal Trade Commission (FTC) draws comments from industry, Congress, public interest groups and consumers concerning nearly every proposal it develops, it was probably unprepared for the heated controversy sparked by its investigation of children's advertising.

Affected industries accused the agency of being a "National Nanny" meddling with their first amendment rights. In November, 1978, several groups asked a court to disqualify Chairman Michael Pertschuk from the proceedings because he was an advocate of more regulation. Attempts were made in Congress to keep agency funds from being used for such a purpose. On the other hand, some citizen groups accused the Commission of being too slow to take action.

AUDIENCE CALLED TOO YOUNG TO UNDERSTAND

At issue are ads directed to young children. Action for Children's Television and the Center for Science in the Public Interest, two citizen groups, petitioned the Commission to stop the "manipulation of children for private gain." The groups contended that children do not understand advertising claims, making such ads by their nature deceptive.

The FTC Bureau of Consumer Protection in March, 1978, issued a number of proposals for comment. Among them were to:

● Ban all television advertising for any product directed to, or seen by, children under 8, considered too young to understand the selling purpose of or evaluate the ad;

● Ban ads directed to children under 12 for sugary products which pose serious dental health risks; and

● Require other televised ads aimed at children under 12 for sugary products to be balanced by nutritional information funded by advertisers.

The Commission held hearings on the proposals and received comments from the public. Final action has yet to be taken.

QUESTIONS ABOUT CHILDREN'S ADVERTISING

In 1974, the National Advertising Review Board established a separate division to evaluate ads directed to children under 12. Since that time, a major portion of its inquiries have concerned ads aimed at this special market.

Consultants in child psychology, behavioral sciences and nutrition counsel the Children's Advertising Review Unit to ensure that ads are fair to children's "still developing perceptions." The Children's Unit monitors ads which appear in print, television and radio and responds to complaints from the public. Its address is CARU, National Advertising division, 845 Third Avenue, New York, NY, 10022.

Following are questions which the Children's Unit recommends asking to determine if a children's ad is unfair or deceptive:

● Is the size of the product made clear?
● Does the ad clearly indicate what is included in the purchase?
● Are separate purchase requirements clearly indicated?
● If batteries are needed, is this clearly stated?
● Are other essential disclosures clearly voiced or worded, legible, prominent and in language understandable by the child audience?
● In ads featuring premiums, is the premium offer clearly secondary?
● If fantasy elements are used, are they clearly "just pretend?"
● Are children shown using a product in a way that the average child could not?
● Is the child or adult shown doing something unsafe?
● Is the child or adult shown using a product not intended for children?
● Is a child-directed advertising appeal being used for vitamins or medication?
● Does the ad suggest that a child will be superior to friends or more popular if the childs owns a given product?
● Does the ad employ any demeaning or derogatory social stereotypes?
● Does the ad suggest that an adult who buys a product for a child is better or more caring than one who does not?
● Does the ad reflect unfavorably on parental judgment and other generally recognized sources of child guidance?
● Does the ad show bad manners or use offensive language?
● Does the ad imply that one food provides all the nutrients contained in a well-balanced food plan?
● Does the ad suggest over-consumption of a particular food product?
● Does the ad urge children to ask parents or others to buy a product?
● Does the ad use words such as "only" or "just" to describe a product?
● Do program hosts or characters appear in commercials within their own program?
● Is there anyting misleading about the product's benefits?

If the answer to any of the first seven questions is "no" or the answer to any of the subsequent questions is "yes," the ad may be questionable under the guidelines.

BE YOUR OWN TV CRITIC

The "Program Evaluation Worksheet" on the next page was designed by the National PTA TV Action Center to help you analyze the programs your family watches. The PTA suggests that you make the worksheet a part of your regular TV viewing for a month or two, keeping on-going records of programs you watch regularly.

The PTA also suggests that you send copies of the complete worksheets to the local TV station; advertisers on the program; the network; the FCC; and the TV Action Center (700 North Rush St., Chicago, IL, 60611).

PROGRAM EVALUATION WORKSHEET

Program:_____ Date/Time:_____

		NEVER		RARELY		OFTEN
I.	**QUALITY OF LIFE:**					
	—Conflict Resolution through Negotiation/Discussion	1	2	3	4	5
	—Broadens human awareness	1	2	3	4	5
	—Reinforces positive social or humane values	1	2	3	4	5
	—Exemplary Role Models	1	2	3	4	5
	—Wholesome entertainment	1	2	3	4	5
	—Educational value	1	2	3	4	5
	Other or comment:_____	1	2	3	4	5

		OFTEN		RARELY		NEVER
II.	**OFFENSIVE CONTENT:**					
	—Gratuitous Violence: (violence to maintain interest, violence not necessary for plot development, glorified violence)	1	2	3	4	5
	—violence to persons	1	2	3	4	5
	—violence to property	1	2	3	4	5
	—violence to laws	1	2	3	4	5
	—Sex - double entendre, casual or illicit sex, innuendo	1	2	3	4	5
	—Stereotyping					
	—racial	1	2	3	4	5
	—ethnic	1	2	3	4	5
	—sexual	1	2	3	4	5
	—age	1	2	3	4	5
	Other or comment: _____	1	2	3	4	5

		CRUDE	INFER-IOR	TASTE-FUL		SUPER-IOR
III.	**PROGRAM QUALITIES:**					
	1. Consider the plot, plot development, character portrayals, dialogue. Were you able to anticipate the dialogue or next scene, or was there a skillful development of characterizations and actions?	1	2	3	4	5
	2. Consider the music, the photography, the costuming, special effects.	1	2	3	4	5
	3. In all, would you consider the program crude or superior?	1	2	3	4	5
	Other or comment:_____	1	2	3	4	5

I would recommend this program for:

Children 6-10   Early Teen 11-14   Teen   14-18   Adults   No One

Comments: _____

_____

Advertisers: _____

_____

TRUTH AND ADVERTISING

Celebrity Pat Boone may not be an expert on acne but he became an expert on advertising practices following a 1978 Federal Trade Commission (FTC) investigation of claims for Acne-Statin, a product he endorsed.

The Commission found the product would not cure acne nor eliminate its cause, as ads featuring Boone and his family claimed. Boone agreed to pay a percentage of the penalty ordered against the manufacturer, Karr Preventive Medical Practices Inc., and to make a reasonable inquiry into the basis for ad claims before endorsing any more products.

The FTC said a person who was not an expert on a particular subject should not endorse a product unless he or she had consulted reliable sources to verify claims made by the advertiser. It was the first time an endorser agreed to be personally accountable for ad claims. The agreement clarified and expanded the Commission's stance on advertised product endorsements, one of the many areas it monitors for deceptive claims.

FEDERAL AD MONITORS

The FTC and the U.S. Postal Service are the chief agencies policing truth in advertising. Neither has the power to prohibit an ad from appearing initially, but both can see that it is eventually discontinued or modified if statements are determined to be misleading or false.

Among the factors considered in evaluating an ad are whether:

● the ad creates misleading impressions, although the statements in it may be factually correct;

● important facts about the product or service are concealed or omitted;

● attention is diverted from the actual terms and conditions of the offer; and

● false and misleading comparisons with other products are included.

Even in cases where there is no evidence of intent to deceive, an ad can be judged deceptive if it has a tendency to deceive.

MISLEADING AND DECEPTIVE PRACTICES

Following are some of the practices which have been found misleading or deceptive by federal regulators:

Bait and Switch: Ads entice people to go to a certain store to purchase a special item. Once they arrive, the item is said to be not available or less desirable than represented in the ad. The salesperson then pushes a similar item at a higher price.

Sale Prices: Ads claim that a product is available at a reduced price ("Was $10, now $5.99") when the old price quoted is higher than normally charged. Other ads suggest "Two for the price of one" when, actually, the original price has been raised or doubled.

Free Gifts: Ads offer a free gift with purchase of a certain product and fail to disclose that the usual price of the product has been inflated to cover the cost of the gift or that there are conditions or prerequisites which must be met before receiving it.

List Prices: Terms such as "suggested retail price," and "manufacturer's list price" are mentioned in ads to show that the retailer's price is a bargain. But the prevailing retail price in a particular area is found to be substantially lower than that mentioned in the ad, making the savings substantially less.

"Easy Credit": This term implies that people may purchase an item regardless of their ability to pay or their credit rating. Often, however, finance charges are higher for people with poor ratings, and the cost of the item is exaggerated.

Trade Status: Ads claim that a seller is a "factory outlet" or sells products "direct from maker" when the seller neither owns nor controls the factory. "Wholesale price" and "at cost" are used to indicate a good buy, but the prices listed are higher than the prices normally paid by retailers when buying the product for resale.

Extra Charges: Ads fail to state that there is an additional charge for shipping, installation, assembly, tax, delivery, etc., thereby misrepresenting the total cost of the item.

Distress Sales: "Going-out-of-Business" and "Fire" sales are among those advertised to lure customers into believing that they should act fast to get discount merchandise. In many cases, such sales are interminable, and cheap merchandise is shipped in for the sale.

Product Comparisons: Ads comparing products concentrate on the areas in which the advertiser's product excels and ignores areas in which the competitor's product excels. Performance claims are sometimes based on outdated or subjective data.

Specials: Ads list products available for a special price and when the customer arrives, the retailer claims to be sold-out. Grocery stores must now disclose limited availability, and many other retailers have begun to do so voluntarily, provide customers with "rain checks."

While some practices have been documented as clearly deceptive, others are decided on a case-by-case basis. In addition to federal law, there are laws in many states and local communities to regulate advertising practices, on the theory that truthful advertising is the key to a fair and competitive marketplace.

HOW TO COMPLAIN ABOUT ADVERTISING

There are a number of ways to fight back when misled by advertising. In most successful cases, the deceptive ad or practice is discontinued; seldom are refunds provided for people who are coaxed into making an unwise purchase on the basis of advertised claims.

All complaints should be made in writing and a copy of the ad included if possible. They should include the following information:
- The name of the product and manufacturer,
- When and where the advertisement appeared, and the
- Reason for complaint and any substantiation.

The complaint should first be brought to the attention of the newspaper, magazine or television or radio station which carried the ad. In some cases, they will take action to help readers or viewers or consider dropping the ad. Complaints about ads placed by local firms may also be sent to the Better Business Bureau or postmaster in the community.

Complaints about ads for national products or firms should be directed to the following agencies.

National Advertising Division (NAD): This organization of industry and private representatives was established by the industry and the Council of Better Business Bureaus in 1971 to "sustain high standards of truth and accuracy in national advertising."

As the industry's self-regulatory mechanism, NAD monitors ads and investigates complaints received from the public. If it feels that a complaint has merit, it will submit it to the advertiser for substantiation of claims in question.

With the help of independent consultants, NAD will then evaluate the evidence and recommend that the advertiser discontinue or change the ad if unsubstantiated. Cases that are not settled to the satisfaction of the complainant may be appealed to the National Advertising Review Board, a panel of private citizens.

In many cases, advertisers will cease using an ad which has come under question even if the board rules in the company's favor. Complaints should be mailed to NAD, 845 Third Ave., New York, NY, 10022. (NAD also operates a Children's Unit—see elsewhere in this chapter.)

Federal Trade Commission: The FTC also monitors ads for deceptive practices. Complaints should be sent to the nearest FTC regional office or to the FTC, Division of Advertising Practices, Washington, DC, 20580.

If the Commission determines that a complaint is within its jurisdiction, it will forward it to a committee which then assigns an investigator. The investigator reports back to the committee with recommendations. If the Commission determines that a practice is clearly deceptive or false, it notifies the advertiser of its intent to file a complaint and usually negotiates a consent agreement. This is a legal arrangement in which the advertiser modifies or discontinues a practice without admitting that it violated the law.

The investigation and negotiation process is usually long and complaints may take months to be resolved.

U.S. Postal Service: Ads for products which are sold through the mail or which are promoted by direct mail are monitored by the Postal Service. Complaints should be sent to the nearest Postal Inspection Service, or to the U.S. Postal Inspection Service, Washington, DC, 20260.

The Postal Service also negotiates consent agreements with companies which it determines have made false representations. If there is a clear violation of the law, it may return all mail received at the advertised address and stamp it "Return to sender; order issued against addressee for violation of the false representation law."

A number of public interest organizations solicit information about ads that maybe unfair or deceptive. Among them are:

Action for Children's Television, 46 Austin St., Newton, MA, 02159; **AD-monitor,** Hearthside Studio, Box 425, Pleasantville, NJ, 08232; and **Council on Children, Media and Merchandising,** 1346 Connecticut Ave. NW, Washington, DC, 20036.

A CITIZEN'S GUIDE TO BETTER PROGRAMMING
Ways to Sound Off About TV and Radio Stations

In 1934, when Congress created the Federal Communications Commission to oversee electronic communications in the U.S., it deemed that broadcasters were public trustees of the nation's airwaves. Programming, it said, must be "in the public interest."

To guarantee those promises, the FCC requires each radio and television station to renew its broadcast license every three years. All stations in the same state must renew at the same time. A list of states and upcoming renewal deadlines can be found on an accompanying page.

As a member of a community served by a station, you have a legal right to participate in the license renewal process. Your written comments must be kept on file at the station for public viewing, and must be presented for inspection by the FCC at the time of renewal. In addition, you may petition the FCC to deny a station renewal of its license — or require it to amend its practices before the license is renewed — by notifying the FCC of the station's failure to broadcast "in the public interest."

WHAT THE FCC WANTS TO KNOW

Not every complaint against a station may be regarded as relevant to the "public interest." Here are some issues that are considered by the FCC when renewing station licenses. They indicate what you could check to monitor a station's performance:

● **Ascertainment.** Stations must interview community leaders in all "major segments" of the community (labor, business, women, agriculture, education, etc.) to ascertain the "problems, needs and interests" of the community. Stations must also survey members of the general public.

● **Responsive Programming.** The station must propose and present programming designed to respond to the "problems, needs and interests" that emerge from the ascertainment.

● **Public Affairs Programs.** Stations are required to present *some* public affairs programming, although the FCC has never said how much and has even renewed licenses to stations that present none. Look into whether the amount and quality are sufficient for service to your local community.

● **News.** Stations are required to present news programming, although the FCC has never said how much and has even renewed licensees who present none.

● **Local Programs.** Stations are required to present some locally originated programming (although the FCC has never said how much).

● **Special Programs.** Stations are required to present some programming on religion, education, agriculture, weather, market, sports and minority groups if there is a need in its service area for programming of this type.

● **Children's Programs.** Television stations are required to present some programming especially designed for children. The FCC suggests that different programs may be needed by pre-school and school age children. A "reasonable amount" of such programming must be "designed to educate and inform—and not simply to entertain."

● **Overcommercialization.** The FCC has no standards on quantity of commercials but will recognize repeated violations of the industry's own code. Those maximums are: 9½ minutes per hour in prime time, 12 minutes per hour in other time periods for network affiliates, 14 minutes per hour in other time periods for independent stations. The standards for radio are slightly more liberal.

● **Public Service Announcements.** Stations are required to present some public service announcements—non-commercial educational messages for the public good.

● **Fairness Doctrine.** Each station is required to: discuss controversial issues of public importance in the community and afford reasonable opportunity for contrasting views on those issues. Fairness doctrine complaints may be filed if a station fails to do either of these two things.

● **Equal Time/Editiorialization/Reasonable Access.** Each station must provide "reasonable access" to all candidates running for federal office. Once a station permits an appearance by one legally qualified candidate for any public office in an election, it must provide the same opportunity to all opposing candidates in that election. If a station endorses one candidate in an election, it must provide comparable access for response to all other candidates for that office.

● **Violence.** The FCC has no standards on violent content in programs; it relies on station "self-regulation." The NAB TV code says that "violence...may only be projected in responsibly handled contexts, not used exploitatively... Presentation of details of violence should avoid the excessive, the gratuitous and the instructional. The use of violence for its own sake and the detailed dwelling upon brutality or physical agony, by sight or by sound, are not permissible." Not all stations live up to this code. Check elsewhere in this chapter for listings of the most violent TV shows.

● **Obscenity and Indecent Language.** In program content, obscenity is that material "taken as a whole, that appeals to the prurient interest and is patently offensive by contemporary community standards, and lacks serious scientific, literary, artistic, or political value." The rule applies more stringently depending on the time of day, i.e., whether children are likely to be watching.

● **Format Change [Radio Stations Only].** Generally, radio stations can choose any format they desire. However, if one station wants to drop a format unique to a community and there is a great "hue and cry" over the change from listeners, the FCC must conduct an inquiry on the reasons for the change. If the reason is economic, the station will be required to prove that the old format was not profitable.

● **Deceptive Advertising.** The Federal Trade Commission prohibits "false, misleading or deceptive advertising." The FCC requires stations not only to be aware of FTC activities but to independently take responsibility for guarding against this kind of advertising.

● **Advertising for Children.** The FCC has no standards for ads to children, but it does take stock of stations' adherence to the industry code: no more than 9½ minutes of commercials per hour during children's weekend programming; no program host can sell products (because that might confuse children); vitamins cannot be advertised as candy on children's programs.

● **Equal Employment Opportunity.** No station may discriminate in hiring, promotion or other employment practices according to race, religion, national origin or sex. Each licensee with 10 or more full-time employees must have a written "affirmative action" program describing its procedures for assuring that minority and female applicants are recruited for all jobs, and that salaries of such employees are comparable with other employees with similar jobs.

● **Other Considerations.** These include a wide range of areas, such as concentration of control (limiting station owners to a certain number of stations within a geographical area); "promise versus performance" (on a license renewal application, a station is required to propose program service for the next license term); failure to negotiate in good faith (stations must meet periodically with members of the community to attempt to deal with suggestions and criticisms).

HOW TO FILE A COMPLAINT

A complaint against a station may be based simply on a belief that, in general, the station could do a better job. Or it may be based on a complaint about a specific problem.

There are four legal remedies that are handled by FCC:

● **Complaint.** Anyone may file a complaint at any time against any station. Action taken by the FCC will depend upon how much the complaint relates to any of the specific standards of performance mentioned above, and what evidence is submitted with the complaint. Usually, a complainant seeks a specific remedy, such as correcting employment practices or airing response time for a candidate or community representative.

● **Petition to Revoke.** This may be filed at any time and is the equivalent of a petition to deny, except that the burden is not on the station to prove that continued operation is in the public interest. The burden is on the petitioner to show that continued operation is not in the public interest. The petition to revoke should be used primarily for strategic purposes (e.g. to accelerate the bargaining process between the station and members of the community).

● **Informal Objection.** This is the equivalent of a petition to deny, except that it is not procedurally correct. For example, if a petition to deny is filed late, or with the wrong number of copies, it is treated as an informal objection. Generally, the FCC treats it with the same weight as a petition to deny, but it is not required to do so.

● **Petition to Deny.** This asks the FCC to deny a license renewal because the station is not serving the public interest. It should be the culmination of a lengthy analysis of the station's performance. Such a petition should include all information you know about the station's performance, even if the information does not relate strictly to your principle complaint.

Your complaint should be typed, double-spaced, with an original and nine copies. The original must be signed. Send by registered mail to the FCC, Washington, DC, 20554. A copy must be sent to the station involved by first-class mail on the date of filing. You must send the FCC a separate affidavit affirming that you have done this.

The following books may be of help:

FCC Procedure Manual: The Public and Broadcasting (1974 edition), free from the FCC, Washington, DC, 20554. It gives the official rules and procedures about filings.

How to Protect Your Rights in Television and Radio, $5.50 from the Office of Communication of the United Church of Christ, 289 Park Ave. South, New York, NY, 10010. The book provides basic information on the regulatory process and gives simplified versions of the FCC rules.

Excerpted from access magazine, *issue 40, a publication of the National Citizens Committee for Broadcasting. Copies may be obtained from NCCB, 1028 Connecticut Ave. NW, Washington, DC, 20036.*

POSTAL CONSUMER PROTECTION
Ways to Lick Problems With Mail

1. **MAIL FRAUD.** The U.S. Postal Service has been protecting the rights of mail users since 1872, when Congress enacted the Mail Fraud Statute providing criminal penalties for fradulent use of the mails. Although the statute makes no provision for restitution, millions of dollars have been returned to victims.

Common mail fraud schemes include: Chain-referral plans, fake contests, investment schemes, home improvements, debt consolidation, job opportunities, retirement homes, missing heirs, charity rackets, business franchises, distributorships, work-at-home, business directories, membership offers and correspondence schools.

2. **FALSE REPRESENTATIONS.** In 1890, the False Representations Statute gave the Postmaster General the power to stop mail in false advertising schemes. Under this statute, mail-stop orders are issued, causing the return of all subsequent mail to senders except that which clearly is not related to the mail-order scheme. Payment of outstanding postal money orders is also forbidden.

Examples of misrepresentation cases in which action has been taken by the Postal Service:

● **Diet plans** in which grapefruit juice, vitamins and other harmless but ineffective ingredients are falsely alleged to have the ability to cause a person to lose weight.

● Firms sending what appear to be bills or invoices for subscriptions to "Telex"—and other business directories or services—but are mere **solicitations for advertising services,** often in publications which do not currently exist.

● Persons offering various worthless **methods of obtaining loans** without regard to credit standing or ability to repay.

● Promoters of **work-at-home** schemes falsely promising that the purchaser will be able to earn a substantial sum for stuffing or addressing envelopes.

● Sellers of a variety of **nostrums** falsely described as having the ability to cure such diseases or disabilities as cancer, cataracts and arthritis. Such promotions are regarded as particularly dangerous in that the user may, to his or her detriment, rely upon the seller's false promise to cure instead of seeking competent medical assistance.

REMOVING YOUR NAME FROM MAILING LISTS

Under federal law, you may have your name removed from mailing lists for sexually oriented material by filling out Postal Service form #2201, which is available from local post offices. Your name will be sent to mailers of sexually oriented advertising, who will be required to remove your name from their lists.

You may remove your name from a specific advertiser's list by filing a Prohibitory Order, Postal Service form #2150, also available from post offices.

You may also have your name removed from dozens of mailing lists by filling out a "Name Removal" form, available from the Direct Mail/Marketing Association, 6 East 43rd St., New York, NY, 10017. DMMA is a trade organization representing about 65 companies. DMMA also has an "add-on" form for people who want to be placed on mailing lists.

3. MAIL-ORDER PROBLEMS. Mail-order problems are handled by the Postal Inspection Service, the Consumer Advocate's Office and the Consumer Protection Office. Through one or all of these departments, the Postal Service works to resolve mail-order complaints about unsatisfactory transactions: when postal customers fail to receive merchandise ordered, refunds promised, or find that the service or product purchased is not as advertised.

This program provides a means of notifying mail-order firms of complaints against them. When a complaint is received by the Postal Service, a decision is made to investigate for commercial deception or to resolve it informally under the consumer protection program. Many times the problem is found to be only poor business practices. Whatever the case, the customer will be notified of the action taken.

4. MAIL PROTECTION. The Postal Service is mandated to protect the mail from the time it is deposited in a postal receptacle until the recipient has removed it from the mail box. These laws, many of which incorporate strong criminal penalties, make crimes against the Postal Service federal offenses.

Postal Inspectors investigate theft of mail and work with other law enforcement groups and local officials to insure coordination. Inspectors also investigate burglaries and holdups of postal facilities, mail theft, narcotics, mail bombs, embezzlements, etc.

5. CONSUMER SERVICE COMPLAINTS. In 1975, the Postal Service launched a nationwide Consumer Service Card Program to handle individual problems about mail service.

The Consumer Service Card is available at post offices and from most letter carriers. The card has two parts and is designed so that after being filled out, one copy goes to the postmaster for resolving the problem and the other goes to Postal Service Headquarters in Washington for cataloging and analysis.

PUBLICATIONS FOR FURTHER HELP

A Consumer's Guide to Postal Services and Products (publication No. 201), available free from post offices or from Consumer Information, Pueblo, CO, 81009.

Mail Fraud Laws (publication No. PI-10), available free from post offices or from Consumer Information, Pueblo, CO, 81009.

Shopping by Mail? You're Protected!, available free from the Federal Trade Commission, Washington, DC, 20580.

Tips on. . .Work at Home Schemes and *Tips on Mail Order Profit Mirages,* both available free from the Council of Better Business Bureaus, 1150 17th St., NW, Washington, DC, 20036.

MAIL SIZE LIMITS

Since July 15, 1979, the U.S. Postal Service has imposed limits on the size of mail so it does not get lost among other items.

Envelopes and cards measuring less than 3½ inches high or 5 inches long are prohibited.

So are flimsy cards less than seven-thousandths of an inch thick. An official post card is nine-thousandths of an inch.

DOMESTIC POSTAL RATES

FIRST CLASS: 15¢ for first ounce, 13¢ each additional ounce, up to 12 ounces; over 12 ounces, Priority Mail rates apply. Consult post office for rates. Post cards: 10¢.

SECOND CLASS (Newspapers and periodicals mailed by the public): 10¢ for first two ounces, 6¢ each additional ounce, or the fourth-class book rate, whichever is lower.

THIRD CLASS (Circulars, catalogs, and other printed matter or merchandise weighing less than 16 ounces): 20¢ up to two ounces, 40¢ up to four ounces; add 14¢ per two ounces over four ounces. Over 14 ounces, use the 4th class zone if lower.

FOURTH CLASS (Book rate): 59¢ up to first pound, plus 22¢ per pound up to seven pounds, plus 13¢ per pound over seven pounds. For other four class rates, contact post office.

SPECIAL HANDLING (Third and fourth class only): add 70¢ up to ten pounds, $1.25 over ten pounds.

SPECIAL DELIVERY: For first class and priority mail, $2.00 up to two pounds, $2.25 for two to ten pounds, $2.85 over ten pounds. All other classes: $2.25, $2.85 and $3.25, respectively.

MONEY ORDERS:	Amount of Money Order	Fee
	$ 0.01 to $10	$ .55
	10.01 to 50	.80
	50.01 to 400	1.10

INSURANCE:	Liability	Fee
	$ 0.01 to $15	$ .50
	15.01 to 50	.85
	50.01 to 100	1.10
	100.01 to 150	1.40
	150.01 to 200	1.75
	200.01 to 300	2.25
	300.01 to 400	2.75

CERTIFIED MAIL: Add 80¢ to postage

REGISTERED MAIL:	Declared value	Fee
	$ 0.01 to $ 100	$3.00
	100.01 to 200	3.30
	200.01 to 400	3.70
	400.01 to 600	4.10
	600.01 to 800	4.50
	800.01 to 1,000	4.90

RETURN RECEIPT: Requested at time of mailing: 45¢; if requested after mailing: $2.10.

INTERNATIONAL POSTAL RATES

SURFACE RATES: Canada: 15¢ for first ounce, 13¢ each additional ounce up to 12 ounces, decreasing thereafter, 60 pounds maximum weight. Mexico: 15¢ for first ounce, 13¢ each additional ounce, up to 12 ounces, decreasing thereafter, 4 pounds maximum weight. All other countries: 20¢ for one ounce, 36¢ up to 2 ounces, 48¢ up to 4 ounces, 96¢ up to 8 ounces, $1.84 up to one pound, $3.20 up to 2 pounds, $5.20 up to 4 pounds, the maximum weight.

AIR MAIL RATES: Canada and Mexico: 15¢ for first ounce, 13¢ each additional ounce. Central America, Columbia, Venezuela, Caribbean Islands, Bahamas, Bermuda, St. Pierre and Miquelon: 25¢ for each half ounce up to 2 ounces; after 2 ounces, 21¢ for each additional half ounce. All other countries: 31¢ for each half ounce up to 2 ounces; after 2 ounces, 26¢ for each additional half ounce.

YOUR MAIL-ORDER RIGHTS

When purchasing merchandise by mail order, federal law ensures you of the following rights:

● **To know when you can expect your merchandise to be shipped.** Unless stated otherwise, you have the right to receive your order within 30 days.

● **To get a full refund for shipping delays.** If the seller does not ship your merchandise with 30 days—or within any other period of time promised—you have the right to cancel your order and receive a full refund. If the shipping delay is 30 days or less, the shipper must notify you and give you some free means (such as a postage-paid card or toll-free phone number) to request a refund. If you don't answer, you are assumed to have agreed to the new shipping date.

If the delay is more than 30 days, you must give your express consent to the delay. Otherwise, the seller must return your money within 30 days.

● **To keep any unordered merchandise you receive by mail.** If you receive in the mail merchandise you did not order, federal law says you may consider it a gift and keep it without paying for it.

SENDING A PARCEL
How To Get The Best Package Deal

Competition between the Postal Service and private carriers—and between private carriers themselves—has increased tremendously in recent years. The wide variety of services and prices has made it especially difficult for consumers to find the cheapest and most reliable company.

Each company must file tariffs with its regulatory agency (the Civil Aeronautics Board for air freight companies, Interstate Commerce Commission for ground freight companies). A tariff is a schedule of rates and conditions under which a freight forwarder will accept and transport merchandise.

Included in a tariff are conditions of acceptance and delivery, packing requirements, rules covering when to file claims, what the carrier will and won't pay on claims and many other shipping regulations established by the carrier. You can usually obtain such information with a simple telephone inquiry. Should a difficulty arise, it is the tariff that is the final legal authority, no matter what the company may tell you verbally.

Rates charged by one carrier may be higher or lower than the rates charged by others. Each carrier sets its own rate schedule, subject to approval by the appropriate regulatory agency. But rate structures are confusing: a low rate on one route by a particular company does not necessarily indicate an inexpensive company. Often, a company that does a considerable amount of business between a few cities will have low rates for packages going to and from those cities, but rates on other routes may be substantially higher.

FACTORS WHICH DETERMINE RATES

Extent of Delivery: Rates may include pick-up and delivery, pick-up or delivery, or depot-to-depot transportation only. Often, extra charges are required for packages going to or from small towns. Carriers that make deliveries also differ in the number of delivery attempts that will be made before the recipient is required to pick-up the package from the carrier. Some carriers may assess storage charges for packages not picked up in 48 or 72 hours.

Characteristic of Commodity: What you are sending often has as much to do with determining the rate as the package's weight and destination. Special rates may be available from many carriers on shipments of books and other commodities. You can save a considerable sum by finding out about them in advance.

The package's size can also determine the rate. If the package is lightweight and bulky (less than 10 pounds per cubic foot), a higher rate may be charged based on "dimensional weight" rather than on actual shipping weight. Be prepared to furnish the exact dimensions of a package to the carrier when asking for a rate quotation.

Carrier's Liability: The limit on a carrier's liability for most domestic shipments is typically 50 cents per pound, but not less than $50 per shipment, although some carriers maintain lower limits on certain commodities. On international routes, the carrrier's liability is limited to $8.16 per pound on the weight of the goods lost, damaged or delayed.

For an additional charge, you may purchase excess liability coverage. The domestic charge is usually 10 to 15 cents per $100 (40 to 50 cents on international routes) of coverage over the carrier's liability. Such insurance covers only actual damages sustained on the shipment, not any consequential damages (such as the loss of business resulting from a late delivery).

FILING CLAIMS

If your shipment is damaged, lost or delayed, you should file a claim with the carrier that accepted or delivered the shipment. File the claim as soon as you discover that something is wrong with your shipment. Make sure the claim is submitted in writing within the time limit specified in the carrier's tariff. It is best to send any claims by registered mail, return receipt requested.

If you discover damage or shortage at the time the shipment is delivered, ask the carrier's agent to acknowledge the problem on the delivery receipt. In case of damage, get a general notation on the delivery receipt and ask that a damage inspection report be made immediately. If the carrier's agent delivering the shipment will not give you a proper notation, *do not accept the shipment.*

COMPARING FREIGHT RATES

The tables that follow compare the cost of sending packages between Washington, D.C., and twelve large U.S. cities for major companies and the U.S. Postal Service. The 12 distances are a representative sample of distances between most cities. By comparing the approximate distance your package is going with a similar distance in the table, you can find your approximate cost per company.

The companies and services included in the tables are:

Bus Service. Interstate bus companies, such as Greyhound and Continental Trailways, transport parcels on most regularly scheduled passenger routes. Buses travel between nearly all U.S. cities, although parcels are delivered only to the bus station nearest the addressee, where they must be picked up. Due to limited cargo space on buses, there are strict limits on size and weight. Bus service is generally slower than other freight carriers; on long-distance routes, a package may take a week or more, especially to smaller towns. For more information, contact your local bus station.

United Parcel. United Parcel Service is the largest nationwide small package carrier. UPS ground service is relatively fast and efficient. Packages will be picked up at private addresses in most areas for a once-a-week charge of $2. There is a weight limit of 50 pounds and a size limit of 108 inches in length and girth combined. Three delivery attempts are usually made. Rates include up to $100 liability per package.

UPS's Blue Label Air Service provides combined ground and air service between selected cities on the East and West coasts (see air freight chart for cities served). For more information, contact UPS.

Emery Air Freight. The largest air freight carrier in the country, Emery has a relatively efficient ground and air freight service. Emery charters space on major commercial flights and has an extensive ground service. Emery's rates include pick-up and delivery and instant tracking via computer. Emery has other carrier services, including combined air-rail-truck service for bulky materials. For more information call toll-free 800/621-2222 (in Illinois, 800/972-2666).

Airborne. Airborne, the second largest domestic air freight carrier, has airport-to-airport and door-to-door service. Rates quoted in the comparison chart are door-to-door. Minimum charge for any door-to-door delivery is $16.83. Airborne also has a plan in conjunction with Greyhound Bus Lines to provide combination air-bus service between large and small cities. For more information, call toll-free 800/426-2827.

United States Postal Service. USPS, commonly known as the U.S. Mail, has a variety of services:

● **Parcel Post** is the slowest and cheapest of the three methods. Mail is processed by machine in bulk mail centers and trucked to its destination. While USPS's goal is to deliver packages within eight days to the most extreme distances, officials admit the schedule is not always met. On distances up to 300 miles, the goal is three days. Packages must be delivered to post offices. Insurance is extra.

● **Priority Mail** gives packages the same status as first class mail. Packages are hand-processed, which is faster than machine processing, and sent on first available transportation. Packages are automatically sent by air to destinations greater than 100 miles away. As with parcel post, there is no pick-up, and insurance is extra.

● **Express Mail** is considerably more expensive but is fast. Available only in selected locations, this service requires packages to be brought to a post office by 5 p.m. for guaranteed delivery at the destination post office by 10 a.m. the following day. For an extra charge, delivery to the addressee can be guaranteed by 3 p.m. The USPS claims 95 per cent success with this system and promises a full refund if the schedule is not met.

COMPARISON OF DELIVERY RATES
For Leading Ground Freight Carriers*

Washington, DC, to:	Hwy. Miles	5-Pound Package				10-Pound Package				20-Pound Package			
		Parcel Post	United Parcel	Grey-hound Bus	Trail-ways Bus	Parcel Post	United Parcel	Grey-hound Bus	Trail-ways Bus	Parcel Post	United Parcel	Grey-hound Bus	Trail-ways Bus
Baltimore	39	$1.66	$1.21	$ 3.45	$ 3.80	$1.89	$1.60	$ 3.45	$ 3.80	$2.27	$2.38	$ 4.25	$ 4.20
Philadelphia	136	1.66	1.21	4.60	5.10	1.89	1.60	4.60	5.10	2.27	2.38	5.05	5.60
New York	226	1.77	1.31	5.40	5.95	2.10	1.79	5.40	5.95	2.58	2.76	5.70	6.30
Boston	440	1.92	1.46	6.45	7.10	2.39	2.09	7.35	7.10	3.01	3.36	7.35	8.10
Detroit	516	1.92	1.46	7.30	8.05	2.39	2.09	8.85	8.05	3.01	3.36	8.85	9.75
Chicago	687	1.92	1.46	7.30	8.05	2.39	2.09	7.30	8.05	3.01	3.36	8.85	9.75
St. Louis	804	2.14	1.62	7.30	7.55	2.83	2.42	7.30	7.55	3.67	4.02	8.85	9.75
Miami	1,105	2.14	1.62	7.65	7.35	2.83	2.42	7.65	7.35	3.67	4.02	9.55	9.20
Dallas	1,385	2.43	1.86	9.25	8.95	3.41	2.89	9.25	8.95	4.54	4.96	12.90	12.45
Denver	1,667	2.77	2.10	9.20	9.20	4.08	3.38	9.20	9.20	5.55	5.94	12.65	12.65
Salt Lake City	2,185	3.39	2.39	9.75	9.75	5.34	3.95	9.75	9.75	7.62	7.08	14.10	14.10
Los Angeles	2,666	3.39	2.39	11.55	11.55	5.34	3.95	11.55	11.55	7.62	7.08	17.40	17.40
Average	———	2.25	1.67	7.43	7.70	3.07	2.52	7.63	7.70	4.06	4.22	9.63	9.94

*See text for details on service. Rates effective May, 1979.

COMPARISON OF DELIVERY RATES
For Leading Air Freight Carriers*

Washington, DC, to:	Air Miles	5-Pound Package					10-Pound Package					20-Pound Package				
		Emery	Airborne	(1) United Parcel	(2) USPS Priority	(3) USPS Express	Emery	Airborne	(1) United Parcel	(2) USPS Priority	(3) USPS Express	Emery	Airborne	(1) United Parcel	(2) USPS Priority	(3) USPS Express
Baltimore	30	$17.95	$18.89	----	$2.72	$ 9.10	$28.05	$28.42	----	$3.93	$11.10	$35.90	$35.01	----	$ 6.36	$15.10
Philadelphia	119	17.65	18.89	----	2.72	9.10	27.50	28.42	----	3.93	11.10	35.20	35.01	----	6.36	15.10
New York	215	17.65	19.27	----	2.72	9.10	27.50	28.99	----	3.93	11.10	35.20	36.09	----	6.36	15.10
Boston	406	18.30	19.27	----	3.04	9.30	27.70	28.99	----	4.58	11.45	35.30	35.37	----	7.66	15.75
Detroit	391	18.30	18.89	----	3.04	9.30	27.70	28.42	----	4.58	11.45	35.30	35.01	----	7.66	15.75
Chicago	591	18.30	19.27	----	3.04	9.30	27.70	28.99	----	4.58	11.45	35.30	36.45	----	7.66	15.75
St. Louis	719	18.65	19.65	----	3.42	9.50	28.25	29.56	----	5.33	11.85	36.00	35.73	----	9.16	16.55
Miami	920	19.50	19.27	3.71	3.42	9.50	28.70	28.99	6.58	5.33	11.85	36.45	36.45	12.43	9.16	16.55
Dallas	1,192	20.15	19.65	3.71	3.85	9.75	29.05	29.56	6.58	6.20	12.30	38.15	37.17	12.33	10.90	17.40
Denver	1,488	20.55	19.65	----	4.29	10.00	29.60	29.56	----	7.07	12.75	38.90	37.53	----	12.64	18.25
Salt Lake City	1,851	21.80	19.65	----	4.83	10.30	30.80	29.56	----	8.16	13.30	41.80	37.90	----	14.82	19.30
Los Angeles	2,299	21.40	19.65	4.41	4.83	10.30	30.25	29.56	7.98	8.16	13.30	41.00	38.62	15.38	14.82	19.30
Average	----	19.18	19.33	3.94	3.49	9.55	28.57	29.08	7.04	5.48	11.92	37.04	36.36	13.34	9.21	16.66

*See text for details on delivery service of each carrier. Rates effective May, 1979.

(1) United Parcel's "Blue Label" air service serves only limited markets between the East and West Coasts, the Southeast and parts of Texas, Hawaii and Alaska.

(2) Priority Mail sent to destinations less than 100 miles away will be shipped via ground transportation.

(3) Rates are for post office-to-addressee service. Slightly lower rates for post-office-to-post office service; call local post office for details.

TELEGRAPH SERVICE GUARANTEED

Although it is not highly publicized, Western Union offers money-back guarantees on delivery time for all types of domestic services.

Telegrams, for example, are supposed to be delivered within 1½ to 2 hours by phone, or within 5 hours if delivered by hand.

Night letters are supposed to be delivered between 9 am and 2 pm the following business day.

Mailgrams are supposed to arrive in the first business mail delivery the day after it is sent.

If you do not get service within these time limits, you are entitled to a full refund or you may have your message resent at no charge. Contact your local Western Union customer service operator to file a claim.

DETERMINING LONG-DISTANCE TELEPHONE RATES

The charts below and on the following page enable you to determine the cost of any long-distance call within the Continental U.S. The cost, however, will be based on four factors: the class of the call, such as station-to-station, operator-assisted station-to-station or person-to-person; the distance of the call; the length of time you talk; and the time of day you place the call.

To use the chart, first match the city you are calling from and the city you are calling to on Chart A. You'll find a letter code where the two columns intersect.

Then find the same letter code in the Rate Key column on Chart B.

For example, if you want to call from New York City to Los Angeles, you would obtain the letter code "N" from Chart A. The entire "N" line applies to your call. You can then see from Chart B that the rate for an unassisted call during a weekday would be 54 cents (plus tax).

Chart A

	BOSTON	CHICAGO	CLEVELAND	DETROIT	LOS ANGELES	NEW YORK	PHILADELPHIA	PITTSBURGH	SAN FRANCISCO	ST. LOUIS	WASHINGTON
ALBUQUERQUE	N	M	M	M	L	M	M	M	L	M	M
ATLANTA	M	L	L	L	N	L	L	L	N	L	L
BALTIMORE	K	L	K	K	N	I	H	J	N	L	E
BIRMINGHAM	M	L	L	L	M	L	L	L	N	K	L
BOISE	N	M	M	M	L	N	N	M	L	M	N
BOSTON		L	L	L	N	I	J	L	N	M	K
BUFFALO	K	L	I	J	N	°	J	I	N	L	K
CHARLESTON, W VA	L	K	J	J	N	K	K	I	N	L	J
CHARLOTTE	L	L	K	L	N	L	L	K	N	L	K
CHEYENNE	M	L	M	M	L	M	M	M	L	M	M
CHICAGO	L		K	J	M	L	L	K	M	J	L
CINCINNATI	L	J	°	J	M	L	J	J	N	K	K
CLEVELAND	L	K		H	N	K	K	H	N	L	K
COLUMBIA, S.C.	L	L	L	L	N	L	L	L	N	L	K
CONCORD, N.H.	G	L	L	N	J	J	L	N	M	K	
DALLAS	M	L	M	M	M	M	M	M	M	L	M
DENVER	M	M	M	M	L	M	M	M	M	L	M
DES MOINES	M	K	L	L	M	M	M	L	M	J	L
DETROIT	L	J	H		N	L	L	J	N	M	K
FARGO	M	L	L	L	M	M	M	M	L	M	L
HARTFORD	H	L	L	L	N	H	I	K	N	M	K
HELENA	N	M	M	M	M	M	M	M	L	M	M
HOUSTON	M	L	M	M	M	M	M	M	M	L	M
INDIANAPOLIS	L	I	J	J	M	L	L	K	N	J	L
JACKSON, MISS.	M	L	L	L	M	M	M	L	M	K	L

	BOSTON	CHICAGO	CLEVELAND	DETROIT	LOS ANGELES	NEW YORK	PHILADELPHIA	PITTSBURGH	SAN FRANCISCO	ST. LOUIS	WASHINGTON
LAS VEGAS	N	M	M	M	J	N	N	N	K	M	N
LITTLE ROCK	M	L	L	L	M	M	M	L	M	J	L
LOS ANGELES	N	M	N	N		N	N	N	°	M	N
LOUISVILLE	L	J	K	K	L	L	K	L	N	J	L
MEMPHIS	M	L	L	L	M	M	L	L	M	J	L
MIAMI	M	M	M	M	N	M	M	M	N	M	K
MILWAUKEE	L	H	K	J	M	L	L	L	M	K	L
MINNEAPOLIS	M	K	L	L	M	M	M	M	L	M	L
NEWARK	J	L	K	L	N	A	H	K	N	L	I
NEW ORLEANS	M	L	L	L	M	M	M	L	N	L	M
NEW YORK	I	L	K	L	N		H	K	N	L	J
OMAHA	M	K	L	L	M	M	M	L	M	J	L
PHILADELPHIA	J	L	K	L	N	H		°	N	L	I
PHOENIX	N	M	M	M	K	N	N	N	M	L	M
PITTSBURGH	L	K	H	J	N	K	°		N	L	I
PORTLAND, ME.	H	L	L	L	N	J	K	L	N	M	L
PORTLAND, ORE.	N	M	N	N	L	N	N	N	M	M	N
RICHMOND	L	L	K	L	N	J	J	J	N	L	H
ST. LOUIS	M	J	L	L	M	L	L	L	M		L
SALT LAKE CITY	N	M	M	M	L	N	N	M	L	M	M
SAN FRANCISCO	N	M	N	N	N	N	N		°	M	N
SEATTLE	N	M	N	N	M	N	N	N	L	M	N
TULSA	M	L	L	L	M	M	M	L	M	K	M
WASHINGTON	K	L	K	K	N	J	J	I	N	L	
WICHITA	M	L	L	L	M	M	M	M	M	K	M

°INTRASTATE RATES APPLY

Chart B

RATE TABLE FOR
OUT-OF-STATE SERVICE BETWEEN POINTS IN THE UNITED STATES
(except Alaska & Hawaii)*

MILEAGE		DIAL-DIRECT						OPERATOR-ASSISTED	
		WEEKDAY FULL RATE		EVENING 35% DISCOUNT		NIGHT & WEEKEND 60% DISCOUNT		STATION-TO-STATION Full Rate All Days All Hours	PERSON-TO-PERSON Full Rate All Days All Hours
		First Minute	Each Add'l Minute	First Minute	Each Add'l Minute†	First Minute	Each Add'l Minute†	First 3 Minutes =	First 3 Minutes =
1-10	A	$.19	$.09	$.12	$.06	$.07	$.04	$ .45	$1.45
11-16	B	.23	.12	.14	.08	.09	.05	.60	1.60
17-22	C	.27	.14	.17	.10	.10	.06	.80	1.80
23-30	D	.31	.18	20	.12	.12	.08	1.00	2.00
31-40	E	.35	.21	.22	.14	.14	.09	1.10	2.10
41-55	F	.39	.25	.25	.17	.15	.10	1.35	2.35
56-70	G	.41	.27	.26	.18	.16	.11	1.60	2.60
71-124	H	.43	.29	.27	.19	.17	.12	1.75	2.75
125-196	I	.44	.30	.28	.20	.17	.12	1.85	2.85
197-292	J	.46	.32	.29	.21	.18	.13·	1.95	2.95
293-430	K	.48	.34	.31	.23	.19	.14	2.00	3.05
431-925	L	.50	.34	.32	.23	.20	.14	2.05	3.15
926-1910	M	.52	.36	.33	.24	.20	.15	2.15	3.30
1911-3000	N	.54	.38	.35	.25	.21	.16	2.25	3.55

* For direct dial rates to Alaska & Hawaii, contact your local telephone company business office
† Total charge may be less than the sum of the initial minute(s) plus additional minute(s) charges shown, due to rounding. Charges are based upon rates in effect at the time of connection at the calling point, including calls beginning in one rate period and ending in another
■ For each additional minute, see dial-direct tables under time period that applies (Weekday, Evening or Night & Weekend)

FOR MAP OF AREA CODES AND TIME ZONES SEE THE CALL GUIDE PAGES OF YOUR TELEPHONE DIRECTORY.

RATES SHOWN DO NOT INCLUDE TAX

HOLIDAY RATES

New Year's Day/July 4th/Labor Day/ Thanksgiving/Christmas Day.

On these legal holidays, the Evening rate applies all day on dial-direct calls unless a lower rate would normally apply (Nights & Weekends). On operator-assisted calls, the dial-direct discount rate applies only on additional minutes.

HIGHEST RATES
Operator-Assisted
Three-Minute Rates

Operator-assisted calls are those requiring the assistance of an operator to complete the call. These include person-to-person, coin, collect, credit card, billed to a third number, hotel-guest, and time and charge calls. The initial period for all operator-assisted calls is three minutes.

STATION-TO-STATION	PERSON-TO-PERSON
FULL RATE	FULL RATE
ALL DAYS, ALL HOURS	ALL DAYS, ALL HOURS
Minimum charge: 3 minutes	Minimum charge: 3 minutes

Additional minutes are charged at dial-direct rates, and include the same discount applicable to the time period when you call.

LOWEST RATES
Dial-Direct One-Minute Rates

Dial-direct calls are those interstate calls (excluding Alaska and Hawaii) completed from a residence or business phone without operator assistance.
Dial-direct rates also apply on calls placed with an operator from a residence or business phone where dial-direct facilities are not available.
On dial-direct calls, you pay only for the minutes you talk. The initial rate period is one minute, any time of day or night.
Additional savings apply if you dial direct during the "discount" time periods indicated on the chart below.

	MON. TUES. WED. THURS. FRI. SAT. SUN.	
8 A.M. to 5 P.M.*	WEEKDAY FULL RATE Minimum charge: 1 minute	
to 11 P.M.*	EVENING 35% DISCOUNT from Full Rate. Minimum charge: 1 minute	EVE. 35% DIS.
to 8 A.M.*	NIGHT & WEEKEND 60% DISCOUNT from Full Rate. Minimum charge: 1 minute	

*To, but not including.

STATES PERMITTING CHARGES FOR DIRECTORY ASSISTANCE CALLS

States	Calls Free Per Month	Charge for Excess Calls (A)	Standard Exemptions Additions & Exceptions (B)
Alabama	5	20/40¢	
Arizona	5	20/40	Reading Disability
Arkansas	3	10/10	Except Hotel/Hospital
California	3	20/40	
Colorado	5	20/40	Reading Disability
Connecticut	5	20/45	Mobile
Delaware	3	20/40	
D.C.	3	20/40	
Florida	6	15	
Georgia	5	20	
Idaho	5	20/40	Except Hotel/Motel
Illinois	8	20/	Operator Surcharge
Indiana	5	20/40 (E)	Except Hotel/Motel
Iowa	3	20/40	
Kansas	5	10/20	Illiterates
Kentucky	5	20/40	
Louisiana	5	20	
Maine	10	20	
Maryland	3/12 (F)	20/40	Mobile
Michigan	5	(G)	
Minnesota	5	20/40	
Mississippi	3	20/40	
Missouri	5	20	Except Hotel/Hospital
Montana	3	20/40	
Nebraska	3	20/40	
Nevada	3	25	
New Jersey	3	20/40	
New Mexico	3	10/20	
New York	3	10	Request for non-pub
North Carolina	5	20	Except Hotel/Hospital
North Dakota	3	20/40	
Ohio	3	20/40	Except Hotel
Oklahoma	3	20/40 (E)	
Oregon	5	20/40	Reading Disability (D)
Pennsylvania	3	10/20	
Rhode Island	3	20/40	
South Carolina	5	20	
Tennessee	3	20/40	
Texas	10	20/40	Except Hotel/Motel (D)
Utah	5	20/40	
Vermont	3	20/40 (D)	
Virginia	6	10/20	Reading Disability
Washington	6	15	Reading Disability (D)
West Virginia	3	20/40	
Wisconsin	5	(G)	Except Hotel/Motel
Wyoming	5	20	

(A) Amount charged per call after free allowance. "10/20" means customer pays 10¢ for first 10 calls, 20¢ for others. (B) standard exemptions are coin, handicapped, hotel/ motel, hospital. (C) 10 call allowance applies to single line subscribers. Multi-line subscribers get a 10-call allowance for first line, 1 call allowance for each additional line up to 25 lines and 1/2 call for each line above 25. (D) Credit cards will be issued to handicapped subscribers to allow exemptions on all calls made by them whether from their own phone or elsewhere. (E) Effective January, 1980. (F) 3 call allowance for residence, 12 call for business. (G) 10¢ for the first 5 calls, 20¢ thereafter.

Source: American Telephone and Telegraph Co., General Telephone and Electronics and others.

WESTERN UNION RATES

TELEGRAM . . . . $ 4.95 for up to 15 words
  (message phoned to   .15 per word for next 35 words
  recipient, then mailed)   .09 per word over 50 words
  For physical delivery
  add 3.00

NIGHT LETTER. . . . . $ 4.20 for up to 100 words
                      .08 per word over 100 words

MONEY ORDER . . . . $ 5.70 for amounts of $50 or less
                     6.65 for amounts over $50 to $100
                     8.90 for amounts over $100 to $300
                 13.25 for amounts over $300 to $500
                 17.70 for amounts over $500 to $1,000
           For amounts over $1,000, call Western Union

NIGHT MONEY ORDER . . . $ 4.95 for amounts of $50 or less
                     5.90 for amounts over $50 to $100
                     8.50 for amounts over $100 to $300
                 12.50 for amounts over $300 to $500
                 16.95 for amounts over $500 to $1,000
           For amounts over $1,000, call Western Union

MAILGRAM. . . . . $ 2.95 for up to 100 words
                     1.50 for each additional 100 words

PUBLIC OPINION
MESSAGES . . . . $ 2.00 maximum 15 words

WHERE TO COMPLAIN

Telephone: For problems that cannot be resolved by your local telephone service representative, contact the Federal Communications Commission, Office of Consumer Complaints, 1919 M St., NW, Washington, DC, 20554, (202/632-6917), or your local FCC field office.

Mail: Your local postmaster is the first place to file complaints. If your problem cannot be resolved by the postmaster, write to the Consumer Advocate, U.S. Postal Service, 475 L'Enfant Plaza West, SW, Washington, DC, 20460 (202/245-4514).

Telegraph: All areas of the U.S. are served by a toll-free phone number to Western Union, listed in your telephone directory. Each office has a customer service representative and a supervisor on duty at all times. If you cannot resolve your complaint at that number write Western Union, One Lake St., Upper Saddle River, NJ, 07458, or contact the Federal Communications Commission.

Air and Ground Freight Carriers: See previous section entitled "Sending a Parcel" for complaint procedures.

HELP WITH BOOKS

This section tells about a number of ways in which books can help with personal problems, hobbies, education and other interests. Some books you may want to buy; others are available in libraries.

Readers in the United States are served by a vast network of local libraries. Small rural ones often are open only a few hours a week. However, arrangements can usually be made to pick up or leave books at a store, church or school.

Most public libraries have arrangements with neighboring libraries permitting them to borrow books they do not have for short periods of time. State libraries and the federal Library of Congress finance this service through regional libraries. A special library postal rate permits inexpensive mailing of such books. Rural libraries are increasing their use of the mail through "Books By Mail" programs.

The local library can help identify books or magazines that may interest you. You may also get help at a larger library in a neighboring city. As a non-resident, you might not be able to borrow books, but in most cases, you will get courteous, thoughtful help.

PRINCIPAL REFERENCE BOOKS

Some important reference books to help you at many libraries:

Books in Print is a reference set listing all books known to be available currently through bookstores or directly from publishers. Many bookstores selling new books and most large and middle-sized libraries have it. It lists publishers, authors and prices.

Paperbound Books in Print is also available in most libraries.

Subject Guide to Books in Print lists books such as hobby books and how-to-do-it books in convenient groups.

Out of Print Books lists older books that are no longer available through book stores but may be available through out-of-print book dealers. Some of these dealers have large, varied stocks of used books; others specialize in limited subjects. They are listed in the yellow pages of the telephone directory and in hobby magazines. The *New York Times Book Review* lists out-of-print dealers that operate by mail. Most dealers use a weekly search magazine called *A.B. Bookman's Weekly,* originally *Antiquarian Bookman,* whose directory lists hundreds of specialty dealers.

HOBBY PUBLICATIONS

Many larger libraries have two useful directories:

Encyclopedia of Associations (Gale Research Co., Detroit) lists 13,063 organizations, including trade, agriculture, legal, scientific, cultural, ethnic, health, fraternal, religious, hobby, athletic, labor, business and Greek letter. Through them, you can find people who share your interest, where the organization is located and how many members it has. (When writing to such an association, it is a courtesy to send a self-addressed, stamped envelope; many have limited funds for extensive correspondence.)

Ulrich's International Periodical Directory (R. R. Bowker, NY) is a comprehensive listing of magazines with publishers' addresses, frequency of publication and price.

DICTIONARIES

The most popular American-English dictionaries come in families that include large, unabridged editions, medium-sized college or desk editions and the small, paperbound editions. They include:

● *Webster's Third New International Dictionary of the English Language,* Unabridged (G. and C. Merriam Co., 47 Federal St., Springfield, MA, 01101, $59.95). Published in 1961 to take the place of the Second Edition of 1934, it caused much controversy by accepting popular usage more indiscriminately than critics felt necessary. Thus: "Biweekly. 1. every two weeks. 2. twice a week." Since this left openly ambiguous whether there are 26 or 104 issues in an annual subscription to a biweekly magazine, other dictionaries took care to indicate that every two weeks was the generally accepted definition. But Webster's Third and the (no-longer-available) Second Edition are the most popular among the larger works.

Webster's New Collegiate Dictionary (8th ed., 1973, $9.95) is the most popular college or desk dictionary. By careful elimination of obsolete or obscure words and meanings, this dictionary provides everything needed for most office, home and general college use.

The Merriam-Webster Dictionary for Large Print Users (G. K. Hall & Co., 70 Lincoln St., Boston, MA, 02111, $27.50) is highly abridged but gives access not elsewhere available to people who can't read small type.

Merriam-Webster also has a paperbound dictionary at $1.95.

● *Random House Dictionary of the English Language,* Unabridged, (201 E. 50th St., New York, NY, 10022, $25) is an excellent buy. Its acknowledgement of usage, giving its degree of acceptability, is often more sensitive than Merriam-Webster's. Thus: "Irregardless is considered nonstandard because it is redundant: once the negative idea is expressed by the *-less* ending, it is poor style to add the negative *ir-* prefix to express the same idea. Nevertheless, it does creep into the speech of good English speakers, perhaps as a result of attempting greater emphasis."

Random House Dictionary of the English Language: College Edition ($9.95) finds many users. It puts proper names within the same alphabet, whereas in Merriam-Webster, place names and names of individuals are in separate alphabets.

● *American Heritage Dictionary of the English Language* (10 Rockefeller Plaza, New York, NY, 10020, $9.95) is a third challenger to Merriam-Webster. This one is larger than the usual desk dictionary. Like Random, the attention to usage is strong. Thus, the definition of "Chutzpah: Brazenness, gall" is better than Merriam-Webster's "supreme self-confidence." American Heritage is thoroughly illustrated, and the single alphabet includes place names and personal names.

American Heritage also has a paperbound edition at $3.95, more durably bound than most paperbacks.

● *The Compact Edition of the Oxford English Dictionary* (200 Madison Ave., New York, NY, 10016, $95). For word buffs, this is the most complete and scholarly dictionary of the English language. This edition, in two volumes of microprint, can be read easily with a magnifier which is included in the $95 price.

ENCYCLOPEDIAS

If you have no children in school and only occasionally consult an encyclopedia, the nearest library might supply all your family's needs. However, if you have school-age youngsters, and the library is not convenient, an encyclopedia set might be worth the investment.

Finding the right set, though, may be more difficult and expensive than you think. Here's why.

● **It is virtually impossible to shop around.** The only place to make a ready comparison is in a library that has competing sets in use. However, a useful source of guidance is Kenneth Kister's *Encyclopedia Buying Guide* (R. R. Bowker, New York, $15.50). This book is stocked in many libraries, which use it themselves in purchasing reference works.

● **The matter of buying an encyclopedia usually is brought up by a door-to-door salesman for a particular company.** His well-honed, often deceptive sales pitch is designed to create pressure on the potential buyer to sign up immediately in order to take advantage of a "special" deal or discount. In such situations, the choice suddenly becomes either buying a particular encyclopedia or none at all. No time is available to shop around, check sales claims or consult a library or expert on encyclopedias. Encyclopedia selling practices have frequently brought government charges of deception. (If you do buy a set from a salesman, by law you have three days in which to reconsider your purchase.)

● Encyclopedias are complex products that are not easy even for the experts to evaluate. Even after studying Kister's 282-page reference book on reference books, the final choice may not be apparent. For example, Kister discusses the various qualities of some three dozen major works in detail, but he chooses not to continue a point-scoring system used by preceding authors of the biennial Bowker series of encyclopedia buying guides.

FOUR RATED ABOVE REST

He narrows down the field of encyclopedias for adult readers to three: *Encyclopedia Britannica, Collier's Encyclopedia* and *Encyclopedia Americana.* Kister goes on to explain the distinctive qualities of each, but he does not say which is the best overall value. He says the *Britannica* is the most authoritative and the largest; *Collier's* is the most readable and the lowest in price; and the *Americana* is the most practical, has the most special features and the best coverage of American topics.

Among seven sets aimed at young people from age 9 to 18, Kister calls the *World Book Encyclopedia* the best overall, followed by *Compton's, Merit Students* and *Encyclopedia International.* "Pound for pound," Kister says, the *World Book* is "the best encyclopedia on the market today."

Automobiles

In This Chapter

- **Operating Costs**
- **1980 Car Prices**
- **1980 Gas Mileage Ratings**
- **Repair Ripoffs**
- **Safety and Pollution Recalls**
- **Tire Grading Begins**

America's love affair with the automobile ran into an increasing number of obstructions in 1979, including soaring prices for gasoline, shortages of small cars, a rash of safety defects and near-bankruptcy for the Chrysler Corporation. But there were signs that auto manufacturers were responding to consumer demands for improved safety features, better warranties and more fuel-efficient vehicles.

Among the developments:

● The Ford Motor Company finally agreed to recall some 1.5 million Pintos for safety defects in the fuel tank design. The cars were said to be responsible for dozens of deaths and hundreds of serious injuries resulting from low-speed rear-end collisions in which the fuel tanks were punctured and the leaking fuel caused a blazing fire. Ford was accused of being aware of the defect for years and refusing to add a simple plastic sleeve that cost less than one dollar and could have substantially lessened the fire risk. The company was the subject of law suits totaling hundreds of millions of dollars for damages resulting from the defect.

● Demand for fuel-efficient small cars gained new impetus in 1979, because of the Iranian oil crisis and lower domestic energy supplies. Buyers of the diesel-powered Volkswagen Rabbit faced waits of up to a year for delivery due to increased demand. Some buyers were willing to pay hundreds of dollars above sticker prices and accept cars loaded with options by dealers wanting to cash in on the new trend.

● The federal government finally got tough on labeling of octane at gasoline pumps. Gas stations were required to post labels using the average of the two most common rating systems, the "research" and "motor" ratings. The required labels now use the average figures, which is abbreviated as "R plus M over 2." Octane numbers indicate anti-knocking quality; the higher the number the better that gasoline quality. Most cars built since 1971 are designed to operate efficiently on an average octane of 87, which is about 4 points below the former rating.

● General Motors introduced a major new 1980 line of cars in the spring of 1979, including front-wheel-drive compact "X-body" autos with relatively high fuel efficiency. Even before they were introduced, consumer groups said they had some serious defects, and GM later recalled 225,000 of them.

● The big three American auto makers began offering extended auto warranties as new car options. Ford's "Extended Service Plan" and General Motor's "Continuous Protection Plan" both extended warranty coverage from the standard 12 months or 12,000 miles to 36 months or 36,000 miles. Chrysler later topped the others with a five-year, 50,000-mile "5/50 Protection Plan." American Motors had been offering an additional 12-month, 12,000-mile extended warranty for about three years.

● American Motors Corporation began a three-year warranty against rusting-through of body parts. The warranty, which does not cover exhaust systems, requires owners only to maintain their cars in accordance with the owner's manual—"reasonable washing and touching up of nicks in the paint. There is no mileage limitation and the warranty applies to subsequent owners if the car is sold before it is three years old. Other manufacturers have had secret warranties to cover rust in order to resolve cases where car owners showed persistence with their complaints. For example, Chrysler has replaced rusty front fenders on some 1976 and 1977 Dodge Aspens and Plymouth Volares without charge but has not announced the policy publicly. In August, 1979, General Motors announced a formal warranty against rust after the Federal Trade Commission began a probe of warranties offered by auto rust-proofing companies.

● The Federal Trade Commission came to the rescue of people whose cars are repossessed and resold without proper recompense. In October, 1978, it ordered the Ford Motor Credit Company to refund all money not needed to cover the amount owed by the defaulting owner and reasonable expenses of the resale. The average surplus was said to be $200 and could amount to $1 million a year in refunds.

● Under threat of other legal action by the Federal Trade Commission, Ford voluntarily agreed to replace prematurely worn engine parts in 1974-77 and early 1978 models with 2.3-liter four-cylinder engines. The company agreed to notify some 1.8 million owners that it would replace camshafts and rocker arms worn out before 36 months or 36,000 miles of use. The FTC staff claimed that the company was secretly reimbursing dealers for such repairs but that dealers were not doing the repairs because costs were too high.

● The quality of auto repairs came under renewed attack in May, 1979, when Transportation Secretary Brock Adams released a survey of repair shops showing that consumers had "only about a 50-50 chance of getting a car fixed right and for the right price." Adams concluded that most of the $50 billion spent by Americans on auto repairs each year was wasted on unnecessary work.

CONFUSING DRIVING LAWS

Driving across state lines usually means encountering an entire new set of laws for motor vehicles, pedestrians and bicycles. For the unprepared motorist, the result can sometimes be an accident or an unneeded brush with the law. For years, numerous groups have sought more uniformity in traffic laws. Some states do follow an unofficial Uniform Traffic Code, but it may be years until national unification of laws takes place.

If you travel frequently to certain states, you may want to write to those states' departments of motor vehicles and request a digest of traffic laws. For information on the Uniform Traffic Code, write to the National Committee on Uniform Traffic Laws, 1776 Massachusetts Ave NW, Washington, D.C., 20036.

THE COST OF RUNNING AN AUTOMOBILE
Prices Climb a Steep Grade

Increasing gasoline and repair costs added to soaring sales prices to send the cost of owning and running an automobile skyrocketing during 1979. According to the American Automobile Association (AAA), the "average" intermediate sized 1979 car costs $2,690 a year to own and operate. That is 17.9 cents per mile if driven 15,000 miles annually.

The annual AAA study breaks down auto costs into "fixed" and "variable" costs. Examples of fixed costs are insurance, license and registration fees, depreciation and taxes—expenditures made regardless of how much the car is driven. Variable costs include gas and oil, maintenance and tires. AAA computed the "national average costs" for a 1979 Chevrolet, 8-cylinder (305 cu. in.) Malibu Classic four-door sedan with standard accessories, automatic transmission, power steering, power disc brakes and radio, driven 15,000 miles as follows:

Variable Costs	Av. per mile
Gasoline (unleaded) and oil	4.11 cents
Maintenance	1.10 cents
Tires	.65 cents
Total	5.86 cents

Fixed Costs	Annually
Comprehensive insurance ($100 ded.)	$ 74.00
$250 ded. collision insurance	168.00
Property damage and liability ($100,000/$300,000/$25,000)	241.00
License, registration, taxes	90.00
Depreciation	942.00
Finance Charge	296.00
Total	$1,811.00
	(or $4.96 per day)

Based on the above figures, a motorist driving 15,000 miles a year would pay:

15,000 miles @ 5.86 cents	$ 879.00
365 days @ $4.96	1,811.00
Total	$2,690.00
	(or 17.9 cents per mile)

The same person driving 10,000 miles a year would pay:

10,000 miles @ 5.86 cents	$ 586.00
365 days @ $4.96	1,811.00
Total	$2,397.00
	(or 24 cents per mile)

WHAT IT COSTS TO RUN *YOUR* CAR*

1. Actual price paid, including
   trade-in allowance: $ _____

2. Interest on car loan (three years' total ÷ 3) . . . . $ _____

3. Taxes and fees:
   Sales tax ÷ 3 $ _____
   Excise/Property tax
     (average bill) $ _____
   Registration $ _____
   Title fee ÷ 3 $ _____
   License (divide total fee
     by number of years valid) $ _____
   Inspections $ _____

   TOTAL. . . . . $ _____

4. Depreciation (Take the following percentage of item 1:
   full-size car 20%; intermediate 18%; compact 17%; sub-
   compact 15%) . . . . $ _____

5. Insurance (total annual premium). . . . . $ _____

6. Total gasoline cost (Determine miles per gallon, divide
   into total annual miles, then multiply by the average
   per gallon cost) . . . . $ _____

7. Maintenance:
   Tuneups $ _____
   Oil, filters, lubes $ _____
   Tires $ _____
   Other $ _____

   TOTAL. . . . . $ _____

YEARLY TOTAL . . . . $ _____

COST PER MILE (Divide yearly total by annual number
   of miles driven) . . . . $ _____

---

*Average annual cost based on the first three years of ownership.
 Source: ALA Travel and Auto Club

PUBLICATIONS ON DRIVING COSTS

Two publications give more detailed information on how to figure auto costs. An 8-page booklet, *Your Driving Costs,* of the American Automobile Association (AAA) is helpful in figuring itemized car expenses for taxes or other business calculations. Write to AAA, Falls Church, VA, 22042.

Another booklet, *Cost of Owning and Operating an Automobile, 1976,* published by the U.S. Department of Transportation, breaks down the cost on an annual basis over ten years. Write to the Federal Highway Administration, Washington, DC, 20590.

HOW INFLATION BOOSTS CAR PRICES

How much of the annual price increases by auto manufacturers go to pay for actual quality changes?

For 1979 models, the answer was only 15.4 per cent of the $300.30 average price increase, according to the Bureau of Labor Statistics (BLS) in the Department of Labor. That included $12.10 for redesign of emission controls, $5.75 for safety changes and $28.50 for other quality changes.

For 1978 models, said BLS, quality improvements accounted for only 11.8 per cent of the average increase in price of $424.49.

But the operating costs would not be the same for everyone. For example, gas prices differ around the country, due to levels of competition and state and local taxes; insurance costs vary widely (see comparison for 50 cities in Insurance chapter); and finance charges differ among financial institutions.

Following is a comparison of driving costs for 20 places compiled by the ALA Travel and Auto Club of Wellesley, Massachusetts. The figures show average costs for the first three years of operation. They assume that the car was purchased new, is driven 48,000 miles during the first three years, and has average maintenance needs.

Neither the ALA nor any other study is meant to be definitive. Many variables and frequent changes affect car operation costs. Following the ALA study is a table that can help determine your own car operating costs.

NEW PROTECTION FROM ODOMETER FRAUD
There Can Be No Turning Back

In March, 1978, the Department of Transportation issued new rules to combat "the billion dollar fraud of rolling back odometers." The new rules strengthen existing federal laws that require a disclosure statement with used cars to indicate the number of miles a car has been driven.

The disclosure statement must include the odometer reading at the time of transfer; the date of transfer; the seller's name, address and signature; make, body type, year, model, vehicle identification number and license plate number; a statement certifying that the odometer has not been altered in any way, and whether the seller has reason to believe that the mileage reading on the odometer is incorrect or that the actual mileage is unknown.

The new law requires car dealers and distributors to retain the disclosure statements for four years. This requirement will provide consumers and enforcement agencies with the necessary documents to prove a violation of the law.

Penalties for altering an odometer, or selling a car with knowledge that the odometer has been altered, are $1,500, or three times the amount of damages suffered, paid to the car's buyer, plus court and attorney costs.

The new DOT law also requires that odometers be tamper resistant and indicate whether a vehicle's cumulative mileage exceeds 100,000 miles.

The new law also sets accuracy requirements for speedometers and odometers and limits the speedometer reading to a maximum of 85 miles per hour beginning with the 1980 model year.

For more information, write the Chief Counsel, National Highway Traffic Safety Administration, Washington, DC, 20590.

COST OF OPERATING A CAR

SUBCOMPACT CAR:

AREA	PRICE PAID	TAXES & FEES	DEPRECIATION	INSURANCE	GAS COST/GAL.	GAS EXPENSE	MAINTENANCE	TOTAL COST	COST PER MILE[1]
Boston, MA	$4381.88	$273.48	$525.83	$584.00	81.10¢	$519.04	$362.32	$2264.67	14.15¢
Springfield, MA	4381.88	273.48	525.83	482.00	81.90	524.16	333.66	2139.13	13.36
Worcester, MA	4381.88	273.48	525.83	526.00	80.90	517.76	333.66	2176.73	13.60
Rural Massachusetts	4381.88	273.48	523.83	417.00	81.90	524.16	333.66	2074.13	12.96
Hartford, CT	4391.88	274.90	527.03	466.00	85.00	544.00	363.31	2175.24	13.59
Rural Connecticut	4391.88	196.32	527.03	332.00	85.00	544.00	363.31	1962.66	12.27
Providence, RI	4391.88	249.93	527.03	419.00	85.90	549.76	376.94	2122.60	13.26
Rural Rhode Island	4391.88	213.21	527.03	315.00	75.90	485.76	319.61	1860.61	11.63
Portland, ME	4381.88	180.27	525.83	318.00	80.00	512.00	347.99	1884.09	11.78
Rural Maine	4381.88	180.27	525.83	230.00	80.90	517.76	340.82	1794.68	11.22
Manchester, NH	4381.84	72.93	525.83	315.00	81.80	523.52	338.36	1775.64	11.10
Rural New Hampshire	4381.88	72.93	525.83	245.00	80.00	512.00	338.36	1694.12	10.59
Rutland, VT	4360.88	102.49	523.31	214.00	82.50	528.00	347.50	1715.30	10.72
Rural Vermont	4360.88	102.49	523.31	206.00	81.90	524.16	338.36	1694.32	10.59
Chicago, IL	4336.88	121.62	520.43	469.00	94.90	607.36	394.08	2112.49	13.38
Dallas, TX	4445.88	108.85	533.51	312.00	72.90	466.56	401.25	1822.17	11.38
Los Angeles, CA	4518.26	164.08	542.19	508.00	90.90	581.76	394.44	2194.47	13.72
Miami, FL	4435.88	79.82	532.31	606.00	82.00	524.80	365.41	2108.34	13.17
New York, NY	4399.88	140.76	527.99	748.00	86.90	556.16	433.50	2406.41	15.04
Washington, DC	4391.88	125.86	527.03	378.00	87.90	562.50	405.57	1999.02	12.49
20-AREA AVERAGE	$4393.65	$173.98	$527.24	$404.50	83.01¢	$531.26	$360.83	$2000.81	12.51¢

FULL-SIZE CAR:

Boston, MA	$6642.81	$406.95	$1082.78	$741.00	$81.10¢	$811.00	$383.72	$3425.45	21.41¢
Springfield, MA	6642.81	406.95	1082.78	616.00	81.90	819.00	363.72	3288.45	20.55
Worcester, MA	6642.81	406.95	1082.78	670.00	80.90	809.00	363.72	3332.45	20.83
Rural Massachusetts	6642.81	406.95	1082.78	534.00	81.90	819.00	363.72	3206.45	20.04
Hartford, CT	6614.81	399.56	1078.21	624.00	85.00	850.00	385.66	3337.43	20.86
Rural Connecticut	6614.81	281.43	1082.13	444.00	85.00	850.00	385.66	3039.30	18.99
Providence, RI	6638.81	379.69	1082.13	625.00	85.90	859.00	344.69	3340.51	20.88
Rural Rhode Island	6638.81	312.10	1082.13	445.00	75.90	759.00	354.69	2952.92	18.46
Portland, ME	6653.81	275.68	1084.57	432.00	80.00	800.00	373.72	2965.97	18.54
Rural Maine	6653.81	275.68	1084.57	322.00	80.90	809.00	368.72	2859.97	17.87
Manchester, NH	6653.81	136.54	1081.31	435.00	81.80	818.00	363.87	2834.72	17.71
Rural New Hampshire	6633.81	136.54	1081.31	355.00	80.00	800.00	363.87	2736.72	17.10
Rutland, VT	6544.81	132.33	1066.80	292.00	82.50	825.00	372.75	2688.88	16.81
Rural Vermont	6544.81	132.33	1066.80	284.00	81.90	819.00	352.75	2654.88	16.59
Chicago, IL	6493.81	164.77	1058.38	667.00	94.90	949.00	405.25	3244.40	20.28
Dallas, TX	6766.81	119.62	1102.99	338.00	72.90	729.00	410.25	2749.86	17.19
Los Angeles, CA	6837.13	240.56	1112.82	638.00	90.90	909.00	409.69	3310.07	20.69
Miami, Fla	6766.81	119.62	1102.49	746.00	82.00	820.00	385.25	3173.86	19.84
New York, NY	6652.35	211.78	1084.34	1060.00	86.90	869.00	432.50	3657.62	22.86
Washington, DC	6585.81	173.80	1073.49	502.00	87.90	879.00	414.20	3042.49	19.02
20-AREA AVERAGE	**$6640.30**	**$255.99**	**$1082.61**	**$541.00**	**83.01¢**	**$830.10**	**$382.40**	**$3092.10**	**19.33¢**

¹Computed on the basis of 16,00 miles drive per year. See text for additional details.

Source: ALA Auto & Travel Club, Wellesley, MA, 1979

GASOLINE OCTANE

Chances are that you are paying more than necessary for gasoline if you do not closely observe gasoline octane ratings. One authority estimates that American motorists pay $1 billion more than they need to annually because of confusion built into the rating system.

Due to changes in engine design a few years ago, some automobile engines began to be rated by the "Motor" method, rather than the traditional "Research" method. A Research number is usually about eight points higher than the Motor number for the same engine. In order to settle the confusion, government agencies ordered octane ratings to be listed as an average of the Motor and Research numbers.

The confusion continues, and it works to the disadvantage of motorists. Almost all cars made since 1971 require only 91 octane. That is equivalent to economy or sub-regular grade gasoline under the traditional Research method. But since many gasoline pumps are marked with the averaging method, 91 octane appears to require premium gasoline when it does not.

EFFECTS OF SPEED, AIR CONDITIONING AND TUNE-UP ON GASOLINE MILEAGE

	30 MPH	40 MPH	50 MPH	60 MPH	70 MPH
EFFECT OF TURNING A/C OFF:					
MPG WITH A/C ON	18.14	17.51	16.42	15.00	13.17
MPG WITH A/C OFF	20.05	19.71	18.29	16.23	14.18
INCREASE IN MPG WITH A/C OFF	10.53%	12.56%	11.39%	8.33%	7.67%
EFFECT OF TUNE-UP:					
MPG BEFORE TUNE-UP	19.30	18.89	17.29	15.67	13.32
MPG AFTER TUNE-UP	21.33	21.33	18.94	17.40	15.36
INCREASE IN MPG AFTER TUNE-UP	10.52%	12.92%	9.54%	11.04%	15.32%

Source: Department of Transportation.

HOW TO FIGURE *YOUR* GAS MILEAGE

1. Fill tank until it is exactly full at the filler neck. At the same time, record the mileage reading on the dashboard odometer.	Odometer reading _____
2. Drive until the tank is almost empty; a calculation based on fewer miles is less accurate. Then, fill the tank to the same level on the filler neck. Write down the number of gallons needed to fill the tank and the new odometer reading.	Gallons of gas _____ New odometer reading _____
3. Subtract the original odometer reading from the new one to obtain the number of miles traveled between fill-ups.	New odometer reading _____ ÷ Original reading _____ = Miles traveled _____
4. Divide the miles traveled by the gallons required to refill the tank. The result is the number of miles traveled per gallon of gas.	Miles traveled _____ ÷ Gallons of gas _____ = Miles per gallon _____

ANNUAL CARPOOL SAVINGS

Daily Commute (one way)	Item	SUBCOMPACT (Pinto, Datsun, Vega, VW, Colt)	COMPACT (Nova, Dart, Maverick, Pacer)	STANDARD (Matador, Cutlass, LTD, Caprice)
	Cost of driving to work alone			
	Gasoline and oil	$ 163	$ 224	$ 299
	Maintenance and repair	130	145	163
	Parking	191	191	191
	Insurance	280	297	319
10	Depreciation	144	188	327
MILES	Total	$ 908	$1045	$1299
	Savings per person in a:			
	2-person carpool	$ 381	$ 439	$ 646
	3-person carpool	490	564	701
	4-person carpool	544	627	779
	5-person carpool	572	658	784
	Cost of driving to work alone			
	Gasoline and oil	$ 245	$ 336	$ 448
	Maintenance and repair	194	218	260
	Parking	191	191	191
	Insurance	280	297	319
15	Depreciation	217	282	490
MILES	Total	$1127	$1324	$1208
	Savings per person in a:			
	2-person carpool	$ 496	$ 583	$ 752
	3-person carpool	620	728	939
	4-person carpool	721	847	1093
	5-person carpool	755	887	1144
	Cost of driving to work alone			
	Gasoline and oil	$ 328	$ 448	$ 595
	Maintenance and repair	257	290	347
	Parking	191	191	191
	Insurance	280	297	319
20	Depreciation	289	374	664
MILES	Total	$1345	$1600	$2116
	Savings per person in a:			
	2-person carpool	$ 605	$ 720	$ 952
	3-person carpool	753	896	1185
	4-person carpool	874	1072	1375
	5-person carpool	928	1104	1460
	Cost of driving to work alone			
	Gasoline and oil	$ 409	$ 560	$ 746
	Maintenance and repair	321	363	433
	Parking	191	191	191
	Insurance	280	297	319
25	Depreciation	361	468	817
MILES	Total	$1562	$1879	$2506
	Savings per person in a:			
	2-person carpool	$ 719	$ 864	$1153
	3-person carpool	890	1071	1428
	4-person carpool	1047	1259	1679
	5-person carpool	1093	1315	1254

Source: Department of Transportation's 1975 study, updated to reflect price increases as of March, 1979.

WHOLESALE AND RETAIL CAR PRICES
To Help You Drive a Bargain

In the wheel-and-deal jungle of new-car shopping, it is difficult to determine when you are getting a bargain and when you are being fleeced. Car dealers' claims of "$250 over cost" and "$500 below sticker price" do not always hold up to the light of truth. A big problem, as with many other major products, is lack of useful buying information.

One of the best ways of driving a bargain in a new car is to know what the dealer pays and what the list price is for the model of your choice with the desired options. With such information in hand, you will find it easier to tell which dealer is offering the best deal. Your decision, of course, should also be based on other factors, such as a dealer's reputation for service, the trade-in value of your old car and the type of financing offered. What you save in price can be wiped out by interest charges.

In the price arena, the following figures relating to 1980 wholesale and list price may be helpful. They were estimated by Car/Puter on the basis of advance company announcements. Actual prices may vary somewhat from those shown; they also are subject, of course, to price changes which are frequent in the automobile business.

Car/Puter itself sells cars directly to consumers and advertises that it can save up to $1,000 or more off the retail price. For $11, it will furnish a printout of exact wholesale and retail prices for almost any car and set of optional equipment. Car/Puter's address is 1603 Bushwick Ave., Brooklyn, NY, 11207.

DEALER VS. LIST PRICES OF 1980 CARS
Estimated for Selected Domestic Models

Make and Model	Description	Estimated 1980 Dealer Cost	Estimated 1980 List Price
AMERICAN MOTORS			
AMX	2 Dr liftback, 6 cyl.	5,506	6,228
Concord	2 Dr hatchback, 6	3,994	4,509
	2 Dr sedan, 6	3,900	4,403
	4 Dr sedan, 6	3,994	4,509
	4 Dr wagon, 6	4,176	4,716
	DL 4 Dr hatchback, 6	4,266	4,819
	DL 4 Dr sedan, 6	4,266	4,819
	DL 4 Dr wagon, 6	4,450	5,028
Pacer	DL 2 Dr hatchback, 6	4,497	5,081
	DL 2 Dr wagon, 6	4,634	5,237
Spirit	2 Dr liftback, 4	3,625	4,003
	2 Dr sedan, 4	3,532	3,899
	DL 2 Dr liftback, 4	3,848	4,251
	DL 2 Dr sedan, 4	3,754	4,146
BUICK			
Riviera	2 Dr coupe, 8	8,705	11,053
Skylark	4 Dr sedan, 6	4,333	4,591
	2 Dr coupe, 6	4,182	4,779
Skyhawk	Hatchback coupe, 4	4,343	4,962
Century	Custom 4 Dr sedan, 6	4,587	5,485
	Custom 2 Dr coupe, 6	4,328	5,355
	Custom wagon, 6	5,034	6,019

Make and Model	Description	Estimated 1980 Dealer Cost	Estimated 1980 List Price
Regal	2 Dr coupe, 6	4,689	5,606
	Sport 2 Dr coupe, 6	5,634	6,737
Le Sabre	4 Dr sedan, 6	5,064	6,273
	2 Dr coupe, 6	4,980	6,169
	Estate wagon, 6	5,994	7,424
Electra	4 Dr sedan, 8	7,235	9,185
	2 Dr coupe, 8	7,093	9,004
	Park Ave. 4 Dr sedan, 8	8,115	10,303
	Park Ave. 2 Dr coupe, 8	7,974	10,123
CADILLAC			
Cadillac	Coupe Deville, 8	9,434	12,128
	Fleetwood Brougham, 8	11,344	14,584
	Eldorado Coupe, 8	11,799	15,169
	Seville Sedan, 8	17,590	22,616
CHEVROLET			
Corvette	2 Dr coupe, 8	9,400	11,935
Monza	2 + 2 hatchback, 4	3,669	4,193
	Station wagon, 4	3,787	4,328
Chevette	Hatchback 2 Dr coupe, 4	3,843	3,980
	Hatchback, 4 Dr sedan, 4	3,591	4,104
	Scooter hatchback coupe, 4	3,137	3,470
Malibu	4 Dr sedan, 6	4,170	4,986
	Classic 4 Dr sedan, 6	4,425	5,291
	Wagon 4 Dr, 6	4,309	5,152
Monte Carlo	Sport coupe, 6	4,599	5,498
	Landau coupe, 6	5,334	6,378
Camaro	Rally Sport coupe, 6	4,911	5,611
	Berlinetta coupe, 6	5,214	5,958
Citation	2 Dr hatchback, 4	4,072	4,653
	4 Dr hatchback, 4	4,162	4,757
	2 Dr coupe, 4	3,745	4,142
Impala	2 Dr coupe, 6		6,035
	4 Dr sedan, 6	4,956	6,139
	3 Seat wagon, 8	5,548	6,872
Caprice	2 Dr coupe, 6	5,181	6,418
	4 Dr sedan, 6	5,296	6,548
	3 Seat wagon, 8	5,818	7,207
CHRYSLER			
Le Baron	2 Dr coupe, 6	4,665	5,504
	4 Dr sedan, 6	4,751	5,606
	Salon 2 Dr coupe, 6	4,878	5,756
	Salon 4 Dr sedan, 6	5,080	5,995
	Town & Country wagon, 6	5,505	6,496
	Medallion 4 Dr, 6	5,503	6,494
Cordoba	2 Dr hardtop, 8	5,584	6,590
Newport	4 Dr hardtop, 6	5,470	6,683
New Yorker	4 Dr hardtop, 8	7,617	9,533
DODGE			
Colt	2 Dr coupe, 4	3,640	3,998
	2 Dr custom hatchback, 4	4,239	4,735
	4 Dr sedan, 4	4,045	4,517
	4 Dr wagon, 4	4,980	5,563
St. Regis	4 Dr hardtop, 6	5,579	6,816

Make and Model	Description	Estimated 1980 Dealer Cost	Estimated 1980 List Price
Omni	2 + 2 hatchback, 4	4,432	4,923
	4 Dr hatchback, 4	4,077	4,533
Aspen	4 Dr sedan, 6	4,138	4,659
	2 Seat wagon, 6	4,331	4,890
Diplomat	2 Dr coupe, 6	4,545	5,363
	4 Dr sedan, 6	4,632	5,466
	Salon 4 Dr sedan, 6	4,962	5,855
	Salon wagon, 6	5,330	6,290
	Medallion 4 Dr sedan, 6	5,384	6,354
FORD			
Fairmont	2 Dr sedan, 4	3,570	4,078
	4 Dr sedan, 4	3,661	4,182
	Wagon, 4	3,974	4,539
Fiesta	3 Dr hatchback, 4	4,002	4,379
Pinto	Pony 2 Dr sedan, 4	3,144	3,476
	2 Dr sedan, 4	3,485	3,981
	2 Dr wagon, 4	3,848	4,396
Granada	2 Dr sedan, 6	4,067	4,761
	4 Dr sedan, 6	4,168	4,866
	Chia 4 Dr sedan, 6	4,501	5,256
Mustang	2 Dr sedan, 4	3,963	4,527
	3 Dr sedan, 4	4,274	4,882
	Chia 2 Dr sedan, 4	4,483	5,121
LTD II	S 2 Dr hardtop, 8	4,837	5,780
	S 4 Dr hardtop, 8	4,924	5,884
	4 Dr hardtop, 8	5,152	6,157
LTD	2 Dr sedan, 8	5,184	6,418
	4 Dr sedan, 8	5,268	6,502
	Landau 4 Dr sedan, 8	5,709	7,069
	Wagon, 8	5,492	6,799
Thunderbird	2 Dr hardtop, 8	5,503	6,077
	Town Landau, 8	7,756	9,590
	Heritage, 8	9,271	11,480
LINCOLN			
Versailles	4 Dr sedan, 8	9,576	12,302
Lincoln Mark V	2 Dr coupe, 8	9,576	12,302
	4 Dr sedan, 8	9,758	12,535
MERCURY			
Bobcat	3 Dr runabout, 4	3,636	4,163
	2 Dr wagon, 4	3,914	4,471
	Villager wagon, 4	4,017	4,589
Cougar	2 Dr hardtop, 8	4,679	5,591
	4 Dr hardtop, 8	4,804	5,741
Marquis	2 Dr coupe, 8	5,274	6,530
	4 Dr hardtop, 8	5,354	6,629
	Brougham 4 Dr sedan, 8	6,015	7,448
	Grand Marquis 4 Dr hardtop, 8	6,630	8,209
Monarch	2 Dr sedan, 6	4,128	4,822
	4 Dr sedan, 6	4,220	4,928
Zephyr	2 Dr sedan, 4	3,707	4,235
	4 Dr sedan, 4	3,798	4,359

Make and Model	Description	Estimated 1980 Dealer Cost	Estimated 1980 List Price
OLDSMOBILE			
Cutlass	Salon 2 Dr coupe, 6	4,282	5,120
	Salon 4 Dr sedan, 6	4,369	5,223
	Salon Brougham, 2 Dr, 6	4,532	5,419
	Salon Brougham, 4 Dr, 6	4,641	5,549
	Supreme 2 Dr coupe, 6	4,674	5,588
Delta 88	4 Dr sedan, 6	5,150	6,379
	Royale 4 Dr sedan, 6	5,410	6,702
Omega	4 Dr sedan, 6	4,301	4,915
	Brougham sedan, 6	4,542	5,190
Starfire	2 Dr coupe, 4	3,885	4,440
	SX 2 Dr coupe, 4	4,068	4,648
PLYMOUTH			
Horizon	2 + 2 hatchback, 4	4,227	4,697
	4 Dr hatchback, 4	3,888	4,320
Volare	2 Dr coupe, 6	3,715	4,195
	4 Dr sedan, 6	3,819	4,301
	2 Seat wagon, 6	4,158	4,695
PONTIAC			
Catalina	2 Dr coupe, 6	4,989	6,180
	4 Dr sedan, 6	5,036	6,238
Bonneville	2 Dr coupe, 8	5,511	6,827
	4 Dr sedan, 8	5,615	6,956
Firebird	Coupe, 6	4,614	5,272
	Esprit, 6	4,957	5,664
	Formula, 8	5,800	6,627
	Trans Am, 8	6,089	6,958
Grand Prix	2 Dr coupe, 6	4,704	5,624
	LJ 2 Dr coupe, 8	5,654	6,760
	SJ 2 Dr coupe, 8	5,878	7,028
LeMans	2 Dr coupe, 6	4,273	5,109
	4 Dr sedan, 6	4,360	5,213
	Grand Am 4 Dr sedan, 6	4,794	5,732
Phoenix	2 Dr coupe, 6	4,133	4,633
	5 Dr hatchback, 6	4,293	4,906
	LJ 5 Dr hatchback, 6	4,662	5,327
Sunbird	Coupe, 4	3,545	4,049
	Sport coupe, 4	3,770	4,308
	Sport hatch, 4	3,861	4,412

AIR BAGS READIED AS OPTIONS

The big three car makers are planning to offer air bags in some 1981-model cars, a full year before automobile crash protection becomes mandatory in full-sized cars.

GM will provide air bags as an option on its "full-sized" Chevrolets, Pontiacs, Buicks, Oldsmobiles and Cadillacs. Ford will do the same on its 1981 Lincoln and Mark lines, and will offer an optional automatic belt system on its 1980 Mustang and Mercury Capri. Chrysler plans to introduce air bags as an option in its 1981 LeBaron and Dodge Diplomat but has no plans for automatic seat belts.

Air bags are required on cars with wheelbases greater than 114 inches by the 1982 model year and on all models two years later.

GASOLINE MILEAGE RATINGS

Car buyers began to get more accurate miles per gallon information with 1980-model autos. This development came as a result of complaints by consumers that fuel-efficiency stickers were substantially inaccurate. Government regulations now require that the estimated miles-per-gallon figure be four times larger than any other printing on the new-car sticker. It must also emphasize that the numbers are for comparison purposes only and are not actual figures obtained from road experience.

The problem of accuracy remains, however. In 1978, a study by the Environmental Protection Agency—the agency responsible for gas-mileage figures—concluded that the figures were significantly inflated over real-life experience. One reason is the use of machines instead of humans to test the cars. Another reason is that the cars tested are carefully prepared by manufactures; they are not random models selected from the assembly line. The EPA study found that the mileage ratings overstated a car's performance from two to five miles per gallon. On the whole, the difference is greater for smaller cars, with subcompacts getting about 7 miles per gallon less than the EPA estimates say.

The EPA estimates, which begin on the following page for 1980 models, are still useful because they are done uniformly. Although the ratings may be overstated, they can still determine the relative performance of one car to another.

DRIVER EDUCATION
Are Young People Getting a Bum Steer?

Evidence is growing that driver education programs in high schools are not succeeding in their main aim: to reduce the incidence of serious automobile accidents. In fact, a study by the Insurance Institute for Highway Safety indicates that such programs may be doing more harm than good.

The Institute looked at fatal-crash figures in 27 states. It found "much higher death involvement rates per 10,000 population, on average, in states with greater proportions of 16- and 17-year-olds receiving driver education." At least 2,000 fatal crashes per year that would not otherwise occur were attributed to increased licensure of 16- and 17-year-olds because of driver education.

Critics of driver education programs have maintained all along that one of the main reasons for the cooperation of auto companies in the driver ed programs has been to encourage driving and automobile buying at the earliest possible ages.

Research results similar to the Institute study were reported in England. A large-scale controlled study there found no difference in crashes per mile between youngsters who had classroom instruction and ones who had not. But total crash involvement per person was actually higher among those who had 30 classroom hours and five hours of behind-the-wheel training. The increase was attributed to a higher rate of licensing for this group.

The Institute concluded that programs tending to increase confidence that the risk of accident is reduced by the program itself are "far worse than no programs at all."

FUEL EFFICIENCY OF 1980 CARS

Here are the EPA ratings. The lists show, from left, model, type of transmission (a-automatic, m-manual), engine size in cubic inches, number of cylinders, 49-state mileage, California mileage and estimated annual fuel cost for 49-state mileage. Numbers after model names indicate two-or four-wheel drive.

MINICOMPACTS

Model	Trans	Engine	49	CA	Cost
Honda Civic	m5	91-4	36	na	$375
Honda Civic	m	91-4	35	na	386
Renlt LeCar	m	85-4	30	na	450
Ddge Celeste	a	98-4	29	na	466
Ddge Celeste	m5	98-4	29	na	466
Honda Civic	s	91-4	29	na	466
Plym Arrow	m5	98-4	29	27	466
Plym Arrow	a	98-4	29	27	466
Ford Pinto	m	140-4	24	21	563
Merc Bobcat	m	140-4	24	21	563
Ddge Celeste	a	156-4	23	na	587
Ply Arrow	a	156-4	23	22	587
Ddge Celeste	m5	156-4	22	na	614
Ford Pinto	a	140-4	22	21	614
Merc Bobcat	a	140-4	22	21	614
Ply Arrow	m5	154-4	22	22	614

SUBCOMPACT CARS

Model	Trans	Engine	49	CA	Cost
VW Rabbit	d-m5	90-4	42	na	286
VW Rabbit	d-m	90-4	40	na	300
Ddge Colt	m	86-4	37	na	364
Ply Champ	m	86-4	37	na	364
VW Dasher	d-m	90-4	36	na	334
Ddge Colt	m	86-4	35	31	386
Ply Champ	m	86-4	35	31	386
Ddge Colt	m	98-4	33	31	409
Ply Champ	m	98-4	33	31	409
Toy Tercel	m	89-4	33	30	409
Datsun 210	m	75-4	31	na	436
Datsun 210	m	85-4	31	na	436
Datsun 310	m5	85-4	31	na	436
Datsun 310	m	85-4	31	na	436
Datsun 510	m5	119-4	31	29	436
Toy Tercel	m5	89-4	31	30	436
Datsun 510	m5	119-4	30	30	450
Datsun 510	m	119-4	30	na	450
Ddge Colt	a	98-4	30	29	450
Mazda GLC	m5	86-4	30	30	450
Ply Champ	a	98-4	30	29	450
Datsun 210	m	75-4	29	29	466
Datsun 210	m5	85-4	29	29	466
Datsun 210	m	85-4	29	29	466
Datsun 310	m5	85-4	29	29	466
Datsun 310	m	85-4	29	29	466
Datsun 510	m	119-4	29	29	466
Mazda GLC	m	86-4	29	29	466
Toy Tercel	a	89-4	29	na	466
Datsun 200SX	m5	119-4	28	27	466
Datsun 210	a	91-4	28	na	482
Datsun 510	a	119-4	28	27	482
Toy Corolla I	m	108-4	28	23	482
Datsun 200SX	m5	119-4	27	27	500
Datsun 510	a	119-4	27	27	500
Mazda GLC	a	86-4	27	25	500
Toy Corolla	m5	108-4	27	23	500
Chevelle	m	98-4	26	na	520
Datsun 200SX	a	119-4	26	na	520
Datsun 210	a	91-4	26	26	520
Toy Corolla	a	108-4	26	23	520
Chevelle	a	98-4	25	na	540
Datsun 200SX	a	119-4	25	25	540
VW Rabbit	m5	97-4	25	26	540
VW Scirocco	m5	97-4	25	26	540
Chev Monza	a	151-4	24	na	563
Ddge Omni	a	105-4	24	23	563
Mazda 626	a	120-4	24	24	563
Mazda 626	m5	120-4	24	24	563
Mazda 626	m	120-4	24	24	563
Olds Starfire	a	151-4	24	22	563
Ply Horizon	a	105-4	24	23	563
Pont Sunbird	a	151-4	24	22	563

Model	Trans	Engine	49	CA	Cost
VW Rabbit	m	97-4	24	26	563
VW Scirocco	m	97-4	24	26	563
Ddge Omni	m	105-4	23	24	587
Ford Mustang	m	140-4	23	21	587
Merc Capri	m	140-4	23	21	587
Ply Horizon	m	105-4	23	24	587
Toy Celica	m	134-4	23	na	587
Toy Corona	m	134-4	23	na	587
VW Dasher	m	97-4	23	24	587
VW Rabbit	a	97-4	23	24	587
VW Scirocco	a	97-4	23	24	587
AMC Spirit	m	151-4	22	23	614
Audi 4000	m	97-4	22	24	614
Chev Monza	m	151-4	22	21	614
Datsun 810	m5	146-6	22	22	614
Ddge Challenger	a	156-4	22	20	614
Fiat Brava	m5	122-4	22	na	614
Ford Mustang	a	140-4	22	21	614
Merc Capri	a	140-4	22	21	614
Olds Starfire	m	151-4	22	21	614
Ply Sapporo I	a	156-4	22	20	614
Pont Sunbird	m	151-4	22	21	614
VW Dasher	a	97-4	22	24	614
Datsun 280ZX	m5	168-6	21	20	643
Datsun 810 I	m	146-6	21	21	643
Datsun 810	m	146-6	21	na	643
Datsun 810	a	146-6	21	21	643
Datsun 810	a	146-6	21	na	643
Datsun 810	m5	146-6	21	22	643
Ddge Challenger	m5	156-4	21	21	643
Ford Mustang	m	200-6	21	na	643
Merc Capri	m	200-6	21	na	643
Ply Sapporo	m5	156-4	21	21	643
Toy Celica	m5	134-4	21	19	643
Toy Supra	a	156-6	21	21	643
Toy Corona	m5	134-4	21	19	643
Toy Cressida	a	156-6	21	21	643
AMC Spirit	a	151-4	20	20	675
Chev Camaro	m	229-6	20	na	675
Datsun 280ZX	m5	168-6	20	20	675
Datsun 280ZX	a	168-6	20	20	675
Fiat Brava	a	122-4	20	na	675
Ford Mustang	a	200-6	20	na	675
IMerc Capri	a	200-6	20	na	675
Pont Firebird	a	231-6	20	na	675
Pont Sunbird	a	231-6	20	na	675
Toy Celica	a	134-4	20	18	675
Toy Corona	a	134-4	20	18	675
Buick Skyhawk	a	231-6	19	na	710
Chev Camaro	a	229-6	19	na	710
Chev Monza	a	231-6	19	na	710
Datsun 280ZX	a	168-6	19	20	710
Olds Starfire	a	231-6	19	na	710
Toy Supra	m5	156-6	19	19	710
AMC Spirit	m	258-6	18	17	751
AMC Spirit	a	258-6	18	18	751
Ford Mustang	a	255-8	18	na	751
Merc Capri	a	255-8	18	na	751
Chev Camaro	a	305-8	17	14	794
Pont Firebird	a	301-8	16	na	844
Buick Skyhawk	m	231-6	15	na	900
Chev Monza	m	231-6	15	na	900
Olys Starfire	m	231-6	15	na	900
Pont Sunbird	m	231-6	15	na	900
Chev Camaro	a	350-8	14	na	964
Pont Firebird	a	301-8	14	na	964

COMPACT CARS

Model	Trans	Engine	49	CA	Cost
Fiat Strada	m	91-4	25	na	540
Bulc., Skylark	m	151-4	24	24	563
Fiat Strada	a	91-4	24	na	563
Olds Omega	m	151-4	24	24	563
AMC Concord	m	151-4	22	23	614
Buick Skylark	a	151-4	22	22	614
Olds Omega	a	151-4	22	22	614
AMC Concord	a	151-4	20	20	675
Buick Skylark I	a	173-6	20	18	675
Buick Skylark	m	173-6	20	na	675
Olds Omega	a	173-6	20	18	675
Olds Omega	m	173-6	20	na	675
Ford Granada	m	250-6	19	na	710
L-M Monarch	m	250-6	19	na	710

AMC Concord	a	258-6	18	16	751
AMC Pacer	a	258-6	18	na	751
AMC Concord	m	258-6	17	16	794
AMC Pacer	m	258-6	17	na	794
Audi 5000	a	131-5	17	na	794
Audi 5000	m	131-5	17	na	794
Ford Granada	a	302-8	17	16	794
Ford Granada	a	250-6	17	na	794
L-M Monarch	a	302-8	17	16	794
L-M Monarch	a	250-6	17	na	794
L-M Verslts	a	392-8	15	15	900
Rolls Camargue	a	412-8	10	na	1,350
Rolls Bentley	a	412-8	10	na	1,350

MID-SIZE CARS

Chev Citation	m	151-4	24	24	563
Pont Phoenix	m	151-4	24	24	563
Ford Fairmont	m	140-4	23	21	589
L-M Zephyr	m	140-4	23	na	587
Chev Citation	a	151-4	22	22	614
Ford Fairmont	a	140-4	22	21	614
L-M Zephyr	a	140-4	22	21	614
Ford Fairmont	m	200-6	21	na	643
L-M Zephyr	m	200-6	21	21	643
Pont Phoenix	a	151-4	21	22	643
Buick Century	a	231-6	20	na	675
Buick Regal	a	231-6	20	na	675
Chev Citation	a	173-6	20	18	675
Chev Citation	m	173-6	20	na	675
Chev Malibu	m	229-6	20	na	675
Ford Fairmont	a	200-6	20	na	675
L-M Zephyr	a	200-6	20	na	675
Olds Cutlass	a	231-6	20	na	675
Olds CutSupr	a	231-6	20	na	675
Pont GrPrix	a	231-6	20	na	675
Pont GrandAM	m	229-6	20	na	675
Pont Phoenix	a	173-6	20	18	675
Pont Phoenix	m	173-6	20	na	675
Chev Malibu	a	229-6	19	na	710
Chev MCarlo	a	229-6	19	na	710
Olds Cutlass	a	260-8	19	na	710
Olds CutSupr	a	260-8	19	na	710
Pont GrandAM	a	229-6	19	na	710
Buick Century	a	231-6	18	na	751
Buick Regal	a	231-6	18	na	751
Chev MCarlo	a	231-6	18	na	751
Ford Fairmont	a	255-8	18	na	751
Ford T-bird	a	255-8	18	na	751
L-M Cougar	a	255-8	18	na	751
L-M Zephyr	a	255-8	18	na	751
Buick Century	a	301-8	17	na	794
Buick Regal	a	301-8	17	na	794
Chev Malibu	a	305-8	17	15	794
Chev Malibu	a	267-8	17	na	794
Chev MCarlo	a	305-8	17	15	794
Chev MCarlo	a	267-8	17	na	794
Chry Icordoba	a	225-6	17	na	794
Chry LeBaron	a	225-6	17	na	794
Ddge Aspen	m	225-6	17	na	794
Ddge Aspen	a	225-6	17	16	794
Ddge Aspen	m	225-6	17	na	794
Ddge Diplomat	a	225-6	17	na	794
Ddge Mirada	a	225-6	17	na	794
Ford T-bird	a	302-8	17	17	794
L-M Cougar	a	302-8	17	17	794
Olds Cutlass	a	305-8	17	14	794
Olds CutSupr	a	305-8	17	14	794
Olds Toronado	a	307-8	17	na	794
Ply Volare	m	225-6	17	na	794
Ply Volare	a	225-6	17	16	794
Pont GrPrix	a	301-8	17	na	794
Pont GrandAM	a	301-8	17	na	794
Buick Riviera	a	231-6	16	na	884
Buick Riviera	a	350-8	15	15	900
Chry Crdba 300	a	318-8	15	16	900
Chry LeBaron	a	318-8	15	16	900
Ddge Aspen	a	318-8	15	16	900
Ddge Diplomat	a	318-8	15	16	900
Ddge Mirada	a	318-8	15	16	900
Olds CutSupr	a	350-8	15	na	900
Olds Toronado	a	350-8	15	15	900
Ply Volare	a	318-8	15	16	900

Buick Century	a	305-8	na	15	900
Buick Regal	a	305-8	na	15	900
Pont GrPrix	a	305-8	na	15	900
Pont GrandAM	a	305-8	na	15	900
Cdlc ElDorado	a	350-8	na	14	964
Cdlc ElDorado	a	368-8	14	na	964
Cdlc Seville	a	350-8	na	14	964
Cdlc Seville	a	368-8	14	na	964
Chev Malibu	a	350-8	14	na	964

LARGE CARS

Buick LeSabre	a	231-6	18	na	751
Chev Caprice	a	229-6	18	na	751
Olds Delta 88	a	231-6	18	na	751
Pont CatBonne	a	231-6	18	na	751
Buick Electra	a	252-6	17	na	794
Buick LeSabre	a	252-6	17	na	794
Chev Caprice	a	267-8	17	na	794
Chev Caprice	a	305-8	17	14	794
Ford LTD	a	302-8	17	15	794
L-M Marquis	a	302-8	17	na	794
Olds Delta 88	a	307-8	17	na	794
Olds 98	a	307-8	17	na	794
Buick LeSabre	a	301-8	16	na	844
Buick LeSabre	a	231-6	16	na	884
Chry Newport	a	225-6	16	na	884
Ddge St.Regis	a	225-6	16	na	884
Ford LTD	a	351-8	16	16	884
L-M Marquis	a	351-8	16	16	884
Ply Gran Fury	a	225-6	16	na	884
Pont CatBonne	a	301-8	16	na	884
Buick Electra	a	350-8	15	15	900
Buick LeSabre	a	350-8	na	15	900
Cdlc Brougham	a	368-8	15	14	900
Chry Newport	a	318-8	15	16	900
Ddge St.Regis	a	318-8	15	16	900
Linc Cont	a	351-8	15	15	900
Cont Mark VI	a	351-8	15	15	900
Pont CatBonne	a	350-8	na	15	900
Olds Delta 88	a	350-8	15	15	900
Olds 98	a	350-8	15	15	900
Ply Gran Fury	a	318-8	15	16	900
Chev Caprice	a	350-8	14	na	964
Chry Newport	a	360-8	14	na	964
Ddge St.Regis	a	360-8	14	na	964
Ply Gran Fury	a	360-8	14	na	964

SMALL STATION WAGONS

VW Dasher	d-m	90-4	36	na	334
Datsun 210	m	85-4	31	29	436
Datsun 210	m5	85-4	31	29	436
Honda Civic	m5	91-4	31	na	436
Datsun 510	m	119-4	30	29	450
Mazda GLC	m	86-4	30	30	450
Datsun 210	m	85-4	29	29	466
Datsun 210	m5	85-4	29	29	466
Datsun 510	m	119-4	29	29	466
Mazda GLC	m	86-4	29	29	466
Datsun 210	a	91-4	28	26	482
Datsun 510	a	119-4	28	27	482
Honda Civic	s	91-4	28	na	482
Toy Corolla	m	108-4	28	23	482
Datsun 510	a	119-4	27	27	500
Toy Corolla	m5	108-4	27	23	500
Datsun 210	a	91-4	26	26	520
Mazda GLC	a	86-4	26	24	520
Toy Corolla	a	108-4..26	23		520
Ford Pinto	m	140-4	23	21	587
Merc Bobcat	m	140-4	23	21	587
VW Dasher	a	97-4	23	24	587
AMC Concord	m	151-4	22	21	614
Ddge Colt	a	156-4	22	20	614
Ford Pinto	a	140-4	22	21	614
Merc Bobcat	a	140-4	22	21	614
Ply Lancer	a	156-4	22	na	614
VW Dasher	a	97-4	22	23	614
Datsun 810	a	146-6	21	21	643
Datsun 810	m.	146-6	21	21	643
Ddge Colt	m5	156-4	21	21	643
Fiat Brava	m5	122-4	21	na	643
Ply Lancer	m5	156-4	21	na	643
Toy Corona	m5	134-4	21	19	643

Toy Cressida	a	156-6	21	21	643
AMC Concord	a	151-4	20	20	675
Fiat Brava	a	122-4	20	na	675
Toy Corona	a	134-4	20	18	675
AMC Concord	a	258-6	18	16	751
AMC Pacer	a	258-6	18	na	751
AMC Concord	m	258-6	17	16	794
AMC Pacer	m	258-6	17	na	794

MID-SIZE STATION WAGONS

Ford Fairmont	m	140-4	23	21	587
Merc Zephyr	m	140-4	23	21	587
Ford Fairmont	m	200-6	21	na	643
Merc Zephyr	m	200-6	21	na	643
Buick Century	a	231-6	20	na	675
Chev Malibu	m	229-6	20	na	675
Ford Fairmont	a	200-6	20	na	675
Merc Zephyr	a	200-6	20	na	675
Olds Cutlass	a	231-6	20	na	675
Chev Malibu	a	229-6	19	na	710
Pont LeMans	a	229-6	19	na	710
Chev Malibu	a	305-8	17	14	794
Chev Malibu	a	267-8	17	na	794
Olds Cutlass	a	260-8	17	na	794
Olds Cutlass	a	305-8	17	14	794
Buick Century	a	301-8	16	na	844
Chry LeBaron	a	225-6	16	na	844
Ddge Aspen	m3	225-6	16	na	844
Ddge Aspen	a	225-6	16	16	844
Ddge Aspen	m	225-6	16	na	844
Ddge Diplomat	a	225-6	16	na	844
Ply Volare	m3	225-6	16	na	844
Ply Volare	a	225-6	16	16	844
Ply Volare	m	225-6	16	na	844
Pont LeMans	a	301-8	16	na	844
Chry LeBaron	a	318-8	15	16	900
Ddge Aspen	a	318-8	15	16	900
Ddge Diplomat	a	318-8	15	16	900
Ply Volare	a	318-8	15	16	900
Buick Century	a	305-8	na	14	964
Pont LeMans	a	305-8	na	14	964

LARGE STATION WAGONS

Ford LTD	a	302-8	17	15	794
Merc Marquis	a	302-8	17	15	794
Chev Impala	a	267-8	16	na	844
Buick Estate	a	350-8	15	15	900
Chev Impala	a	305-8	15	na	900
Ford LTD	a4	351-8	15	15	900
Ford LTL	a3	351-8	15	na	900
Merc Marquis	a4	351-8	15	15	900
Merc Marquis	a3	351-8	15	na	900
Olds CusCruiser	a	307-8	15	na	900
Olds CusCruiser	a	350-8	15	15	900
Pont Catalina	a	350-8	15	15	900

SMALL PICKUP TRUCKS

Ford Courier	m	120-4	27	26	500
Mazda B2000	m	120-4	27	26	500
Chev Luv	m	111-4	25	24	540
Datsun	m	119-4	25	23	540
Datsun	a	119-4	24	22	563
Volkswagen	m	97-4	23	23	587
Chev Luv	a	111-4	22	22	614
Dodge D50	m	122-4	22	22	614
Dodge D50	a	122-4	22	22	614
Dodge D50	m	156-4	22	21	614
Dodge D50	a	156-4	22	22	614
Ford Courier	m	140-4	22	20	614
Ply Arrow	m	156-4	22	21	614
Ply Arrow	a	122-4	22	22	614
Ply Arrow	a	156-4	22	22	614
Toyota	a	134-4	21	19	643
Toyota	m	134-4	21	18	643
Volkswagen	a	97-4	21	21	643
Ford Courier	a	140-4	20	20	675

STANDARD PICKUP TRUCKS

Toyota	m	134-4	21	18	643
Chev ElCamino	m	229-6	20	na	675
GMC Caballero	m	229-8	20	na	675
Ford F100	m	300-6	19	17	710
Chev C10	m	250-6	18	15	751
Chev ElCamino	a	229-6	18	na	751
Ford F100	a	300-6	18	17	751
Ford F250	m	300-6	18	na	751
GMC Caballero	a	229-6	18	na	751
GMC C15	m	250-6	18	15	751
Chev ElCamino	a	267-8	17	na	794
Dodge D150	a	225-6	17	na	794
Dodge D150	a	225-6	17	na	794
Dodge D200	m	225-6	17	na	794
Dodge D200	a	225-6	17	na	794
Ford F250	a	300-6	17	16	794
GMC Caballero	a	267-8	17	na	794
Chev C10	a	305-8	16	na	844
Chev C10	a	250-6	16	14	844
Chev C10	m	305-8	16	na	844
Chev ElCamino	a	305-8	16	na	844
Chev K10	m	250-6	16	na	844
Dodge D150	m	225-6	16	na	844
Dodge W150	m	225-6	16	na	844
Ford F100	m	302-8	16	15	844
Ford F100	a	302-8	16	14	844
Ford F250	m	302-8	16	na	844
GMC Caballero	a	305-8	16	na	844
GMC C15	a	305-8	16	na	844
GMC C15	a	250-6	16	14	844
GMC C15	m	305-8	16	na	844
GMC K15	m	250-6	16	na	844
Intl Harv Terra	m	196-4	16	16	844
Chev C10	m	350-8	15	14	900
Chev C20	a	250-6	15	15	900
Chev K10	a	250-6	15	na	900
Ford F150	a	300-6	15	na	900
Ford F150	m	302-8	15	14	900
Ford F150	a	302-8	15	13	900
Ford F250	a	302-8	15	13	900
Ford F250	a	300-6	15	na	900
GMC C15	m	350-8	15	14	900
GMC C25	m	250-6	15	15	900
GMC K15	a	250-6	15	na	900
Jeep J10	m	258-6	15	na	900
Chev C10	a	350-8	14	14	964
Chev C20	a	250-6	14	15	964
Chev C20	a	350-8	14	13	964
Chev K10	m	350-8	14	13	964
Ford F250	m	302-8	14	na	964
GMC C15	a	350-8	14	na	964
GMC C25	a	250-6	14	15	964
GMC C25	a	350-8	14	13	964
GMC K15	m	350-8	14	13	964
Jeep J10	a	258-6	14	na	964
Chev C20	a	350-8	13	14	1,038
Chev K10	a	350-8	13	12	1,038
Chev K20	m	350-8	13	na	1,038
Dodge W150	a	318-8	13	na	1,038
Dodge W150	m	318-8	13	na	1,038
Dodge W200	a	318-8	13	na	1,038
Dodge W200	a	318-8	13	na	1,038
Ford F100	a	351-8	13	na	1,038
Ford F150	a	351-8	13	12	1,038
Ford F250	a	351-8	13	12	1,038
GMC C25	a	350-8	13	na	1,038
GMC K15	a	350-8	13	12	1,038
GMC K25	m	350-8	13	na	1,038
Intl Harv Terra	m	304-8	13	13	1,038
Intl Harv Terra	a	345-8	13	13	1,038
Intl Harv Terra	m	345-8	13	13	1,038
Chev K20	a	350-8	12	11	1,125
Dodge W150 I	a	360-8	12	11	1,125
Dodge W150	m	360-8	12	11	1,125
Dodge W200	a	360-8	12	na	1,125
Ford F100	m	351-8	12	11	1,125
Ford F150	a	351-8	12	11	1,125
Ford F250	m	351-8	12	12	1,125
Ford F250	a	351-8	12	12	1,125
Ford F250	a	400-8	12	12	1,125
GMC K25	a	350-8	12	1i	1,125
Jeep J10	a	360-8	12	12	1,125
Jeep J20	a	)60-8	12	na	1,125
Dodge W200	a	360-8	11	na	1,227
Jeep J10	m	360-8	11	na	1,227

| Jeep J20 | m | 360-8 | 11 | na | 1,227 |

VANS

Ford	m	300-6	18	16	751
Chevrolet	m	250-6	17	17	794
Ddge Sportsman	a	225-6	17	12	794
Dodge Van	a	225-6	17	11	794
Ford	m	300-6	17	16	794
GMC	m	250-6	17	17	794
Plymouth	a	225-6	17	11	794
Chevrolet	a	305-8	16	14	844
Chevrolet	a	250-6	16	16	844
Chevrolet	a	305-8	16	16	844
Chevrolet	m	305-8	16	16	844
Ddge Sportsman	m	225-6	16	16	844
Dodge	m	225-6	16	16	844
Ford (2)	a	300-6	16	16	844
GMC Sportvan (2)	a	305-8	16	16	844
GMC Sportvan (2)	m	305-8	16	16	844
GMC (2)	a	250-6	16	16	844
GMC (2)	a	305-8	16	16	844
Ply Voyager	m	225-6	16	16	844
Chev Sportvan	m	250-6	15	15	900
Chevrolet	m	350-8	15	14	900
Chevrolet)2)	m	305-8	15	15	900
Ford	m	302-8	15	13	900
GMC Sportvan (2)	m	250-6	15	15	900
GMC (2)	m	350-8	15	14	900
GMC (2)	m	305-8	15	15	900
Chev Sportvan	a	250-6	14	14	964
Chev Sportvan	m	350-8q	14	14	964
Chev (2)	a	350-8	14	14	964
Ford (2)	a	302-8	14	13	964
Ford (2)	a	302-8	14	14	964
GMC Sportvan (2)	a	250-6	14	14	964
GMC Sportvan (2)	m	350-8	14	14	964
GMC (2)	a	350-8	14	14	964
Chev Sportvan	a	350-8	13	14	1,038
Ford (2)	a	351-8	13	11	1,038
GMC Sportvan (2)	a	350-8	14	13	1,038
Chev Sportvan	a	400-8	12	12	1,125
Chevrolet (2)	a	400-8	12	12	1,125
Ford (2)	a	351-8	12	11	1,125
GMC Sportvan (2)	a	400-8	12	12	1,125
Ford (2)	a	400-8	11	11	1,227

SPECIAL PURPOSE VEHICLES

Jeep (4)	m	151-4	21	21	643
Chevrolet Luv	m	111-4	20	20	675
Chevrolet Luv	a	111-4	19	20	710
Dodge 8100 (2)	a	225-6	17	17	794
Ford Courier	m	140-4	17	17	794
Plymouth PD100	a	225-6	17	17	794
AMC Eagle	a	258-6	16	14	0844
Chevrolet C10	a	305-8	16	16	844
Chevrolet C10	m	305-8	16	16	844
GMC C15	a	305-8	16	16	844
GMC C15	m	305-8	16	16	844
I-H Scout (2)	m	196-4	16	16	844
I-H Scout (4)	m	196-4	16	16	844
I-H SS (4) I	m	196-4	16	16	844
Jeep	a	258-6	16	16	844
Toyota P-U	m	134-4	16	16	844
Chevrolet C10	m	250-6	15	15	900
Datsun P-U	m	119-4	15	15	900
Ford Bronco (4)	m	300-6	15	15	900
Ford Bronco	a	302-8	15	13	900
GMC C15	m	250-6	15	15	900
I-H Scout (2)	m	196-4	15	15	900
I-H Scout (4)	m	196-4	15	15	900
Intl Harv SS-II	m	196-4	15	15	900
Jeep Cherokee	a	258-6	15	15	900
Jeep Cherokee	m	258-6	15	15	900
Jeep CJ (4)	m	258-6	15	15	900
Chev C10 Blazer	a	250-6	14	14	964
Chev C10 Blazer	m	350-8	14	13	964
Chev K10 Blazer	a	250-6	14	14	964
Chev K10 Blazer	m	250-6	14	14	964
Ford Bronco (4)	m	302-8	14	13	964
GMC C15	m	350-8	14	14	964
GMC C15	a	250-6	14	14	964
GMC K15	a	250-6	14	12	964
GMC K15	m	250-6	14	12	964
I-H Scout II	a	345-8	14	14	964
I-H SS-II	a	345-8	14	14	964
Jeep	m	304-8	14	11	964
Jeep	a	304-8	14	12	954
Chev C10	a	350-8	13	13	1,038
Chev C10	m	350-8	13	14	1,038
Chev K10	a	350-8	13	13	1,038
Chev K10	m	350-8	13	13	1,038
Dodge AW100	a	318-8	13	13	1,038
Dodge AW100	m	318-8	13	13	1,034
GMC C15	a	350-8	13	14	1,038
GMC C15	m	350-8	13	13	1,038
GMC K15	m	350-8	13	13	1,038
GMC K15	a	350-8	13	13	1,038
I-H Scout II	a	304-8	13	13	1,038
I-H Scout	m	345-8	13	13	1,038
I-H Scout II	m	304-8	13	13	1,038
I-H Scout (4)	m	345-8	13	13	1,038
I-H Scout (2)	m	345-8	13	13	1,038
I-H Scout (4)	m	304-8	13	13	1,038
I-H Scout	a	345-8	13	13	1,038
I-H Scout	m	345-8	13	13	1,038
I-H SS-II	m	345-8	13	13	1,038
I-H SS-II	a	304-8	13	13	1,038
I-H SS-II	m	345-8	13	13	1,038
I-H SS-II	m	304-8	13	13	1,038
I-H Traveler	a	304-8	13	13	1,038
I-H Trav (2)	m	345-8	13	13	1,038
I-H Trav (2)	a	345-8	13	13	1,038
I-H Trav (4)	a	345-8	13	13	1,038
I-H Trav (4)	m	345-8	13	13	1,038
Plymouth PW100	a	318-8	13	13	1,038
Plymouth PW100	m	318-8	13	13	1,038
Chev C10 (2)	a	350-8	12	12	1,125
Plymouth PW100	m	315-8	13	13	1,125
Chev C20 (2)	a	350-8	12	12	1,125
Chev C20	a	350-8	12	12	1,125
Chev K10	a	350-8	12	12	1,125
Dodge AW100	m	360-8	12	12	1,125
Ford Bronco	a	351-8	12	12	1,125
Ford Bronco	m	351-8	12	12	1,125
GMC C15	a	350-8	12	12	1,125
GMC C25	a	350-8	12	12	1,125
GMC K15	a	350-8	12	12	1,125
I-H Scout (2)	m	304-8	12	12	1,125
I-H Scout (4)	m	304-8	12	12	1,125
I-H Scout (4)	a	304-8	12	12	1,125
I-H SS-II	m	304-8	12	12	1,125
I-H Trav (2)	m	304-8	12	12	1,125
I-H Trav (4)	a0	304-8	12	12	1,125
I-H Trav (4)	m	304-8	12	12	1,125
Jeep	a	360-8	12	12	1,125
Plymouth PW100	m	360-8	12	12	1,125
Toyota Wzgon	m	258-6	12	12	1,125
Toyota	m	258-6	12	12	1,125
Chevrolet	a	350-8	11	11	1,227
Dodge	a	360-8	11	11	1,227
Ford	m	351-8	11	11	1,227
GMC	a	350-8	11	11	1,227
Jeep	m	360-8	11	11	1,227
Plymouth	a	360-8	11	11	1,227
Chevrolet	m	350-8	10	10	1,350
GMC	m	350-8	10	10	1,350
Chevrolet	m	111-4	na	20	675
Ford	m	140-4	na	17	794
Intl Harvester	m	196-4	na	16	844
Toyota	m	134-4	na	16	844
Datsun	m	119-4	na	15	900
AMC	a	258-6	na	14	964
GMC C15	a	350-8	na	14	964
Intl Harvester	m	345-8	na	14	964
Chevrolet	m	350-8	na	13	1,038
Ford	a	302-8	na	13	1,038
GMC	m	350-8	na	13	1,038
Intl Harvester	m	345-8	na	13	1,038
Intl Harvester	a	304-8	na	13	1,038
Chevrolet	a	350-8	na	12	1,125
Ford	a	351-8	na	12	1,125
GMC C25	a	350-8	na	12	1,125
Jeep	a	360-8	na	12	1,125
GMC	a	350-8	na	9	1,500

AUTOMOBILE REPAIR
50-50 Chance of Getting Money's Worth

The federal government put its official seal on estimates of how much consumers waste on unneeded, incompetent, or downright fraudulent repairs in May, 1979, when then Transportation Secretary Brock Adams announced the results of a government survey on auto repair shops. The survey involved 62 repair shops in Atlanta, Philadelphia, Miami, Nashville, Houston, Brooklyn and White Plains, N.Y. Typical used cars were obtained by local district attorneys and checked out before being driven to repair shops. Some were rigged with a simple problem; others were left untampered with. Drivers were given prepared scripts so as not to entrap shops into doing needless work.

The results were not encouraging. The chances of getting a needless repair were found to be 25 per cent in the case of brakes, 19 per cent in the case of suspensions, 78 per cent in the case of engines, and 39 per cent overall.

The chances of not getting needed repairs were found to be 11 per cent for brakes, 31 per cent for suspensions, 28 per cent for engines and 21 per cent overall. The chances that the shop would either fix something that did not need fixing or fail to fix the real problem or both were 32 per cent for brakes, 44 per cent for suspensions, 89 per cent for engines and 51 per cent overall.

In total, Adams concluded that more than half of the $50 billion spent by Americans on auto repairs each year is wasted on unnecessary work. He didn't say how much was fraudulent and how much was merely incompetent work.

Although the results were similar to other undercover studies, industry spokesmen called on President Carter to have Adams apologize for an unfair attack. The request was rejected.

IMPROVED WARRANTIES MAY EASE SOME PROBLEMS

Better news for consumers came when the major auto makers announced extended warranty coverage as an option on new cars. The most comprehensive plan was from Chrysler, which offered a five-year, 50,000-mile coverage on the components of the car's drive train. The plan, which buyers pay extra for as they would any other option, becomes effective upon the expiration of the regular 12-month, 12,000-mile warranty that comes with most new cars.

Ford Motor Company announced an "Extended Service Plan" for three years or 36,000 miles. A similar "Continuous Protection Plan" was offered by General Motors. The other major American auto maker, AMC, has been offering an additional 12-month, 12,000-mile extended warranty for about three years.

The new service policies have a deductible—usually $25 per repair—and provide a rental allowance in case a car is out of service for more than a day. Ford's plan even covers used cars, but coverage is not available beyond 60,000 miles.

NATIONAL AUTO REPAIR LAW CONSIDERED

Although auto repair problems are rampant nationwide, the vast majority of repair shops are local or regional. Yet, few states have enacted effective laws regulating repair shops, and only a handful of states require licensing of shops or mechanics.

As a result, legislation to regulate repairs on a national level is being considered both in Congress and the Department of Transportation. An outline of one possible law was drafted by DOT. It would:

● Establish a "Federal Center for Automotive Repairs" within DOT. The center would provide technical assistance to states in strengthening auto repair laws; help develop diagnostic facilities; provide consumer information; and establish standards on specific repair practices which tend to mislead or deceive consumers.

● Set standards for DOT-approved auto repair programs, which might include a state office of auto repairs, laws requiring disclosure about repair transactions—such as written estimates, consumer authorization of repairs, etc.—registration of repair facilities, mediation of consumer complaints, and enforcement of fraudulent and incompetent practices.

'APPROVED' MECHANICS AND GARAGES

Most of the progress has come through independent organizations which have set up programs for approving mechanics and repair facilities. The two largest programs are:

● National Institute for Automotive Service Excellence (NIASE), a nonprofit, Washington, D.C.-based organization. NAISE conducts a voluntary nationwide program to test and certify auto mechanics in eight areas of diagnosis and repair, as well as bus and truck repair and body repair, paint and refinishing. In order to obtain NAISE certification, a mechanic must have at least two years' working experience and must pass the NAISE tests and have at least two years' job-related working experience. Mechanics must take requalification tests every five years to maintain certified status.

NAISE-certified mechanics wear special patches attesting to their certification in each of eight fields in which they have qualified.

NAISE publishes an annual directory of its certified mechanics. For a copy of *Where to Find Certified Mechanics for Your Car,* send $1.95 to: NIASE, 1825 K. St. NW, Washington, DC, 20006. An individual listing for a particular state will be provided free for a self-addressed stamped envelope.

● American Automobile Association's "Approved Auto Repair Services" program, currently underway in pilot projects in Washington, DC and parts of Florida, Minnesota and California. Under the program, local repair shops are approved by the local AAA affiliate by meeting a wide range of standards, including manpower and training, equipment, range of services, community reputation, customer satisfaction, even facility appearance. After a facility has passed inspection, a list of the shop's previous customers is drawn at random from the shop's files and a letter of inquiry is sent to each. Shops receiving a favorable response are "approved."

The approved status means that AAA members get a limited guarantee of 90 days or 4,000 miles, whichever comes first, for all repairs done by an approved facility. AAA also assists in resolving disputes between its members and an approved shop.

For more information about the Approved Auto Repair Services program, contact your local AAA-affiliated office, or write to AAA, 8111 Gatehouse Rd., Falls Church, VA, 22042.

AUTO SAFETY RECALLS
Down From Record Set in 1977

More than 9 million motor vehicles were recalled for safety defects in 1978, according to the National Highway Traffic Safety Administration of the Department of Transportation.

The figure represented a drop from the record 12.9 million recalled in 1977 but was still one of the largest in the history of auto safety. Domestic manufacturers recalled 8.1 million, and foreign manufacturers recalled the rest. Total campaigns were 270, including 199 by domestic producers.

The largest single recall was by Ford Motor Co. It involved 1.5 million 1971-76 Pintos and Bobcats with potentially unsafe fuel tanks that could explode or burn in a rear-end collision.

General Motors recalled 320,000 subcompact Chevettes also for gas tank problems, plus 265 Chevrolet, Pontiac, Oldsmobile and Buick models for defective rear axles. Chyrsler Corp. recalled 1.1 million Aspen and Volare models to correct steering defects.

During the year, Consumers Union, the product testing organization, alleged that Chrysler's Omni and Horizon cars were unsafe if the steering wheel were suddenly turned at high speeds. But government officials determined after tests that the cars did not behave significantly differently than others. Later, Consumers Union reported that the cars had been improved by the company.

Recalls continued to be a problem in 1979. General Motors voluntarily recalled 172,000 1977 and 1978 Chevrolet Monza, Pontiac Sunbird and Oldsmobile Starfire models with L-4, 151 CID engines to correct a steering problem. And Subaru of America Inc. recalled about 170,000 of its 1977 and 1978 models because of unsatisfactory engine operation and the possibility that the throttle valve might stick in cold weather.

Following are major recalls, involving more than 100,000 vehicles during 1978, listed alphabetically by company:

AMERICAN MOTORS

Gremlin, 1974; Hornet, 1975; Pacer and Matador, 1976;—411,333 cars. Electrical system failure.

CJ-5, CJ-6, and CJ-7, 1975; Cherokee and Wagoneer, 1976;—102,398. Electrical system failure.

Gremlin, 1975; Hornet, 1976;—133,593. Power steering hose too close to exhaust manifold.

CHRYSLER CORPORATION

Plymouth Fury 1975, Grand Fury 1976-77; Dodge Cornet 1975, Charger 1976, Monaco and Royal Monaco 1977; Chrysler Cordoba 1975-76, 77;—370,000. Carburetor accelerator pump seal distortion, caused by contact with certain types of gasoline.

Plymouth Volare 1976-77; Dodge Aspen 1978;—1,100,000. Front suspension pivot bar support plate may experience fatigue.

FORD MOTOR COMPANY

Ford Fairmont 1978; Mercury Zephyr 1978;—185,000. Loss of total electrical power control could occur without warning.

Ford Pinto 1976; Mercury Bobcat 1976;—284,000. Leakage may occur in engine compartment.

Ford Thunderbird 1978, Ford 4-Dr 1978, Station Wagon 1978; Mercury Cougar 1978;—110,000. Shoulder harness retractors do not lock.

Ford Pinto 1971-1976; Mercury Bobcat 1975-76;—1,400,000. Fuel leakage may cause fire.

Ford F, B, LN 1975-1978; Ford L-800 1970-1977;—335,000. Cooling fan may crack, causing personal injury.

Ford Fairmont 1978; Mercury Zephyr 1978;—400,000. Windshield wiper system may become inoperative without warning.

Mercury Capri 1971-1973;—187,000. Windshield wiper system may become inoperative without warning.

Ford Fairmont 1978; Mercury Zephyr 1978;—218,000. Possible stalling or overheating due to defect in emissions control system.   .

Ford Granada 1976-77; Mercury Monarch 1976-77;—120,000. Cooling fan may crack causing personal injury.

GENERAL MOTORS

Chevrolet Monte Carlo and Malibu 1977; Pontiac LeMans and Grand Prix 1977; Oldsmobile Cutlass 1977; Buick Century and Regal 1977;—265,068. Rear

---

HOW TO CHECK RECALL RECORD

You can check to see if your car—or a used car you are interested in purchasing—has ever been recalled.

The National Highway Traffic Safety Administration has a toll-free "hot-line" to provide such information. The number—800/424-9393 (202/426-0123 for residents of Washington, DC)—is open 9:30 a.m. to 5 p.m. eastern time.

Automatic equipment will take your message during off-hours, and an operator will call you back. You must be able to give the operator your Vehicle Identification Number (serial number), which can be found on your automobile registration.

axle shaft may break, causing tire and wheel assembly to separate from vehicle.

Chevrolet Malibu and Monte Carlo 1978; Pontiac Catalina, Bonneville, LeMans, Firebird and Phoenix 1978; Oldsmobile 88, Cutlass and Omega 1978; Buick LeSabre, Electra, Century, Regal and Skylark 1978; GMC Sprint 1978;—333,619. Fan blade spider may break apart, allowing blade segments to be thrown off.

Chevrolet CK 10/20/30 1978; GMC CK 15/25/31 1978;—237,693. Nut on carrier support bolt may break, causing a crash.

Cadillac Seville 1977, Limousine and Brougham 1978;—388,867. Fire caused by combustible materials in ashtray may reach interior of instrument panel and become difficult to extinguish.

Oldsmobile Starfire 1975; Chevrolet Monza 1975; Buick Skyhawk 1975;—130,965. Under certain driving conditions, wheel bearing could decrease viscosity of grease, causing failure and possible damage to spindle.

Chevrolet Chevette 1976-77;—320,000. Fuel tank does not comply with requirements of federal safety standard.

AMERICAN HONDA MOTOR
Honda CB750F 1975, GL1000 1976-77, GL1000 LTD 1976;—118,544. Rear disc brake applied during heavy rain may reduce effectiveness. If pedal force is increased to compensate for reduction in effectiveness, skidding may occur.

BRITISH LEYLAND MOTORS
Triumph GT6 1969-1973, TR6 1973-1976, Spitfire 1969-1974;—107,950. Master headlamps may fail.

TOYOTA MOTOR SALES
Corona 1969; Mark II 1970; Sedan and Coupe 1971;—131,046. Road salt combined with water could cause corrosion in luggage compartment, allowing in extreme cases pinhole perforation of fuel tank, allowing fuel to leak into spare tire well.

IMPROVING VAN SAFETY
When Refrigerators, Stereos Prove Fatal

The craze for customized vans has resulted in such a large increase in van-related accidents that the National Transportation Safety Board undertook a special study in 1979. NTSB became concerned about the 740 van-related deaths in 1977, more than the number of deaths in air carrier or rail accidents.

Part of the problem is that interior furnishings—chairs, couches, beds, cabinets and appliances, for example—come loose during most accidents. In one head-on crash studied by the board, two occupants seated in the rear of the van were killed by the refrigerator, stereo components, paneling, and an unsecured couch and chair inside the van.

The Board recommended that the Recreation Vehicle Industry Association determine the best methods of securing appliances in the vans. While RVIA has published guidelines, they have not yet been adopted as voluntary standards.

For more information, contact NTSB, Washington, DC, 20594.

MAJOR AUTO EMISSIONS RECALLS, 1978-79

Nearly 10 million domestic and foreign automobiles were recalled for emissions problems by the U.S. Environmental Protection Agency during 1978 and the first half of 1979. The recalls came as the result of orders by EPA, voluntarily by the auto makers, or those "influenced" by the EPA, in the agency's terminology.

Following are summaries of recalls involving 10,000 cars or more. If your car is included in the list, or you want more information on any emissions recall, contact the EPA, Mobile Source Enforcement Division, Washington, DC, 20460, 202/426-9434, or any EPA field office.

AMERICAN MOTORS: 330,330 1976 cars sold to the federal government, for defective EGR valves; 122,377 Jeeps, 1974-76, for defective EGR valves.

CHRYSLER: 198,454 1976-77 Dodge Colts and Plymouth Arrows with 1.6 or 2.0 liter engines, for defective reed valve in air injection system; 66,000 1978 Plymouth Furys, Dodge Monacos, Chargers, Magnums, and Chrysler Cordobas with 318 CID engines, for excessive CO emissions.

FORD: 640,000 1975-76 Fords, Torinos, Rancheros, Elites, Montegos, Marquis and Cougars with 351M and 400 CID engines and 2 bbl carburetors, for defective EGR valves; 1,000,000 1975-76 Granadas, Mavericks, Monarchs, Comets, Mustangs, Lincolns, T-Birds, Mark IV, Ford, Marquis, Torinos, Elites, Montegos, Cougars, F-100s, E-100s, and Broncos, with defective EGR valves; 16,140 1977 F-Series trucks with dual fuel tanks, for kink in fuel vapor inlet hose; 1,500,000 1978 LDW models (except Fiestas and Couriers), for defective canister purge valve; 218,000 1978 Fairmonts and Zephyrs equipped with 3.3L (200 CID) engines and automatic transmission, for defective valve in air injection system.

GENERAL MOTORS: 16,103 1977 Chevrolets and GMC vehicles with L-6 250 CID engines, for clogged EGR passages; 95,000 1975 Cadillac 500 CID engines with 4 bbl carburetor, for defective carburetor design; 107,000 1979 Chevettes with 1.6 liter "high output" engine and automatic transmission, for defective EGR system; 40,000 1975-78 Pontiac Catalinas, Bonnevilles, Firebirds, Le Mans and Grand Prix with 350, 400 and 455 CID engines, for defective EGR systems.

AMERICAN HONDA: 422,610 1975-77 Civic CVCC sedans and wagons, 1976-77 Accords, and 1973 and 1977 Civics, for defective thermosensor in vacuum advance system.

BRITISH LEYLAND MOTORS: 53,096 1976-78 MGB's with 110 CID engines, for defective catalytic converters.

FIAT: 10,223 1978 128 sedans, hatchbacks, 124 Spyders, and 131 station wagons, for defective vapor-liquid seperator.

NISSAN (DATSUN): All 1977 Datsuns, except pickups, for defective EGR valves.

WARRANTIES FOR EMISSION DEVICES

Under 1979 proposals of the Environmental Protection Agency, (EPA), auto manufacturers will have to warranty and pay for repairs necessary to make pollution control devices meet federal standards.

The first cars to be affected are 1980 models in places where cars are tested for emission levels. These places include the states of New Jersey and Rhode Island; the metropolitan areas of Portland, Oregon; Los Angeles and Cincinnati. Similar programs are being planned in Philadelphia, Pittsburgh, several counties in Colorado and the state of Connecticut. Most urban areas are expected to have such requirements by 1982.

The warranty will cover cars for five years or 50,000 miles, whichever comes first. For the first 24 months or 24,000 miles, the manufacturer must repair any portion of the vehicle necessary to bring it into compliance with applicable emission standards. After that, the manufacturer need only pay for repairs to pollution-control equipment. Owners would have to follow manufacturer's maintenance instructions.

RECREATIONAL VEHICLES
Many Loaded Unsafely

Forty per cent of pickup trucks carrying slide-in campers are overloaded beyond safe limits, according to a 1977 survey by the National Highway Traffic Safety Administration (NHTSA). That fact represents an improvement over 1971 conditions, when a similar survey found 62 per cent of such campers to be loaded beyond safe capacity.

The figures are for rear axles. Campers with front axles overloaded dropped from 56 to 22 per cent of those checked between the two surveys. Some campers checked in 1971 became overloaded as soon as one adult got into the truck. Motor homes were also found hazardous but to a less extent. Of those checked in 1977, 19 per cent had overloaded front axles, and 10 per cent had overloaded rear axles. In 1971, the comparable figures were 54 and 27 per cent. Travel trailers were found still less hazardous, with 8 per cent of those tested recently carrying unsafe loads, against 34 per cent in 1971. The findings are based on inspections of

---

GAS CANS CAN BE 'DYNAMITE' IN THE TRUNK

Carrying or storing gasoline in a portable container in the trunk of a car is like "riding around with dynamite that can explode at any time," the National Highway Traffic Safety Administration (NHTSA) has warned.

The explosive power of one gallon has been compared to that of 14 sticks of dynamite, NHTSA said in an advisory to consumers.

"We have an extremely dangerous situation developing," NHTSA Administrator Joan Claybrook said. "Concern over the availability of gasoline is prompting an increasing number of people to store fuel in their homes and cars.

"Even a minor rear-end collision or a spark from a short in a tail light or brake light could set off an inferno resulting in injury or death," Claybrook said. The advisory explained that gasoline vapors "expand and can split the seams of an unvented can or plastic container," and that the expansion can even "cause vapor leakage from a vented 'safety' can."

NHTSA said motorists should consider transporting fuel "only in the most extreme emergencies." The container "should be rugged, securely closed but vented, and protected against accidental spillage or damage." The agency cautioned that glass and plastic containers are especially hazardous.

1,000 travel trailers, 196 motor homes and 176 trucks carrying slide-in campers in South Carolina, Michigan and Florida.

NHTSA claimed partial credit for the improved figures. After the 1971 study, the agency took major steps to give buyers of such vehicles more information about loading limits. Manufacturers were required to provide specific loading information and guidance in an owner's manual, plus an affixed label on each vehicle providing weight ratings for each axle. In addition, manufacturers of trucks capable of accommodating slide-in campers were required to provide cargo weight ratings and longitudinal limits for the center of gravity. NHTSA issued a warning to drivers of recreational vehicles along with the new report, saying that overloading can result in suspension system failures, stability and control problems and difficulty in stopping vehicles quickly in emergencies, all of which could result in serious accidents. Many fatalities have been linked to overloaded recreational vehicles.

The 1977 survey also found that cars and trucks towing travel trailers were more frequently overloaded than in 1971. The proportion of cars with unsafe loads on rear axles increased from 37 to 38 per cent, and the proportion of trucks with unsafe loads on rear axles rose from 27 to 30 per cent.

To check your own vehicle's safety, look for the metal plate stating load capacity, then have the vehicle weighed both unloaded and loaded before embarking on a trip. If you have specific questions about your vehicle's weight limits, call NHTSA's toll-free hotline, 800/424-9393 (in Washington, DC, 202/426-0123).

AUTOMOBILE TIRES
Massive Recall Deflates Firestone

Uncle Sam flexed his muscle against faulty performance of tires in 1978 by ordering the largest tire recall in history. It involved about 14 million Firestone "500" tires. The recall came after the National Highway Transportation Safety Administration (NHTSA) received reports from tire buyers and from the Center for Auto Safety, a public interest group, that Firestone 500 steel-belted radials were failing in unusually high numbers and causing accidents. A NHTSA questionaire of over 5,000 consumers showed that Firestone had the highest percentage problems—46.4 per cent, while Michelin had the lowest at only 1.7 per cent.

Firestone's handling of the recall, however, ran into frequent complaints from the beginning when many customers could not obtain replacements, and the company said it was producing them as fast as it could. By May, 1979, NHTSA Administrator Joan Claybrook said only about 15 per cent of the required free replacement tires had been provided to customers. She said also that the vast majority of customers had not even received their notification letter. As a result, she said, millions of people were still riding on defective, potentially dangerous tires.

For the latest information on Firestone and other tire recalls, call the NHTSA toll-free hot-line, 800/424-9393 (in Washington, DC, 202/426-0123).

IMPORTANCE OF TIRE CARE
Tires are vital to both safety and economy of automobile travel. Proper in-

flation, for example, can increase gas mileage as much as 2 per cent. It also can increase the life of tires and improve overall performance. The chance of a highway blowout and other hazards are greatly reduced by proper care of tires. In fact, tires are wrongly blamed for many problems actually due to improper care.

Proper wheel alignment is crucial to tire longevity. Unaligned wheels can lead to uneven tire wear and greatly reduce traction and tire life. Loss of traction reduces braking effectiveness and increases the chance of skidding.

The vast majority of accidents attributable to vehicle failures involve cars with bald or underinflated tires, according to the Tire Industry Safety Council. Ironically, the government requires all tires to meet certain minimum safety standards. But standards imposed on the states no longer require mandatory vehicle inspections that helped identify cars with potentially dangerous tires. In early 1977, 41 states had minimum tread laws that were enforced through annual vehicle inspections. One year later, only 38 states had such laws. By mid 1979, at least four other states were considering repealing such laws. Most state laws prohibit tires with less than 1/16th of an inch of tread.

Hopes for implementation of a uniform tire-grading system diminished with continued litigation over government proposals. The grading system, explained elsewhere in this chapter, would enable tire buyers to make more intelligent purchasing decisions.

A good source of information about tire care is a free booklet by the Tire Industry Safety Council, *Consumer Tire Guide.* The booklet is available from the Tire Council, Box 1801, Washington, DC, 20013. Enclose a stamped, self-addressed envelope.

HOW TO READ A TIRE'S MARKINGS

Federal law requires all passenger car tires to have imprinted on the sidewall information listing the tire's size, name and location of manufacturer, date of manufacture, load range, tire type and maximum inflation pressure. Unfortunately, most of this information is listed in coded language not easily understood by the average consumer. The accompanying picture illustrates the markings on a typical tire.

This tire contains the following information:

1. **Tire Identification Number.** A typical number may look like this: DOT WYL9 ABC498.

"DOT" means the tire meets or exceeds U.S. Department of Transportation safety standards. "WY" is the code number assigned by DOT to the manufacturing plant. A complete list of the manufacturer codes is included in this chapter. "L9" is the tire size (for example, F78-14). "ABC" is a group of up to four symbols, optional with the manufacturer, to identify the brand or other significant characteristics of the tire. "498" means the tire was made during the 49th week of 1978.

A tire retailer is required by law to record the name and address of the person who buys each tire, along with the identification number, and return that information to the manufacturer. The manufacturer must keep the information and use it as a ready reference in the event of a safety recall campaign.

2. **Tire Size.** On the above tire, the size is "F78-14." "F" refers to the width of a cross section of the tire. The letters used, A through N, have numerical equivalents (the letter "F" equals 7.75 inches). Use of the letter "R" indicates the

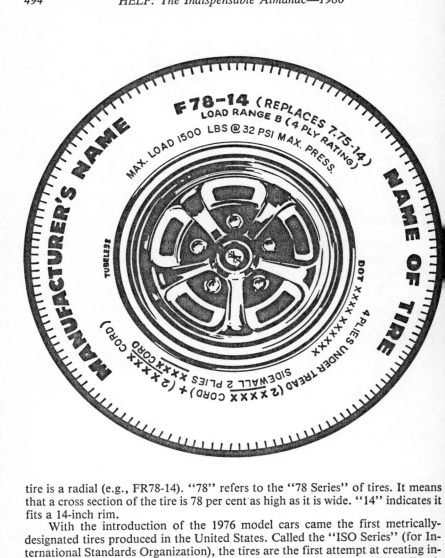

tire is a radial (e.g., FR78-14). "78" refers to the "78 Series" of tires. It means that a cross section of the tire is 78 per cent as high as it is wide. "14" indicates it fits a 14-inch rim.

With the introduction of the 1976 model cars came the first metrically-designated tires produced in the United States. Called the "ISO Series" (for International Standards Organization), the tires are the first attempt at creating international uniformity in tire sizes. A typical ISO Series tire size will be listed: P155/80R13. The "P" stands for passenger car. The "155" is the cross section width in millimeters. The "80" means the tire is 80 per cent as high as it is wide. The letters "R," "B" or "D" stand for radial, bias-belted and bias-ply, respectively. "13" is the rim size in inches.

3. **Load Range** refers to the tire's particular load and inflation limits and service requirements. Load ranges are generally listed as B, C or D. The load range identifies the maximum weight the tires can hold.

4. **Tire Type.** The tire must be marked either "tubeless" or "tube-type." If it is a radial tire, the word "radial" must also appear.

TIRE IDENTIFICATION CODES

You can identify any tire's manufacturer by the first two code letters or numbers of the tire identification number. The manufacturers' code numbers are listed below:

CODE	MANUFACTURER	CODE	MANUFACTURER
AA,AB,AC, AD,AE,AF, AH	General Tire	DX	N.V. Bataafsche Rubber
		DY	Denman Rubber
		D1	Viking Askim
AJ,AK,AL, AM,AN,AP	Uniroyal	D2	Dayton Tire
		D3	United Tire
AT	Avon Rubber	D4,D5	Dunlop
AU	Unitroyal		
AV	Seiberling Tire	EA,EB,EC	Metzler, A.G.
AW	Samson Tire	ED	Okamato Riken Gomu
AX,AY	Phoenix Gummiwerke		
A1	Michalin	EE	Nitto Tire
A2	Lee	EF	Hung Ah Tire
A3	General Tire	EH,EJ,EK, EL,EM,EN, EP	Bridgestone Tire
A4	Hung-A Industrial Co.		
A5	Debickie Zaklady Opon Samochodowych		
		ET,EU	Sumitomo Rubber
		EV,EW,EX, EY	Kleber Colombes
BA,BB,BC, BD,BE,BF, BH,BJ,BK, BL,BM,BN, BP	Goodrich	E1	Chung Hsing
		E2	Firestone
		E3	Seiberling
		E4	Firestone
BT,BU	Semperit	FA,FB,FC, FD,FE	Yokohama Rubber
BV	International Rubber		
BW,BX,BY	Gates	FF,FH,FJ, FK,FL,FM, FN	Michelin
B1	Michelin		
B2	Dunlop		
B3	Michelin	FP	Ste. d' Applications Techniques
B4	Taurus Rubber Works		
B5	Olsztynskie Zaklady Opon Samochodowych	FT,FU,FV, FW,FX,FY, F1	Michelin
		F2	Firestone
CA,CB,CC	Mohawk Rubber	F3	Michelin
CD	Alliance Tire	F4	Fabrica de Pneus-Fapabol
CE,CF,CH	Armstrong Rubber		
CJ	Inque Rubber	HA,HV,HC, HD,HE,HF, HH,HJ,HK, HL,HM,HN, HP	Michelin
CK	Armstrong Rubber		
CL,CM	Continental		
CN	Usine Francaise des Pneumatics		
CP,CT,CU	Continental	HT,HU,HV	Ceat
CV	Armstrong Rubber	HW	Rudy Rijen, Narodui Podnik
CW,CX	Toyo Rubber	HX,HY	Dayton
CY	McCreary Tire	H1	Michelin
C1	Michelin	H2	Sam Yang
C2	Kelly-Springfield	H3	Sava Industrije Gumijevin
C3	McCreary Tire	H4	Bridgestone
C4	Armstrong		
C5	Poznanskie Zaklady Opon Samochodowych	JA,JB,JC, JD,JE,JF, JH,JJ,JK, JL,JM,JN, NT,JU,JP, JV,JX,JW, JY	Lee Tire
DA,DB,DC, DD,DE,DF, DH,DJ,DK, DL,DM,DN, DP,DT,DU	Dunlop Tire		
DV	N.V. Nederlandsch-Amerikaansche	J1	Phillips Petroleum
		J2	Bridgestone
DW	Rubberfabriek Vredestein	J3	Gumarne l Maja

CODE	MANUFACTURER	CODE	MANUFACTURER
J4	Rubena,n.p.	T2,T3	Uniroyal
J5,KA,KB,	Lee Tire	T4	S.A. Carideng
KC,KD,KE,	Lee Tire	UA,UB,UC,	Kelly-Springfield
KF,KH,KJ,		UD,UE,UF,	
KK,KL,KM,		UH,UJ,UK,	
KN,KP,KT,		UL,UM,UN	
KU,KV,KW,		UP,UT	Cooper Tire
KX,KY		UU	Carlisle Tire
K1	Phillips Petroleum	UV	Kzowa Rubber
K2	Lee Tire	UW	Okada Tire
K3	Kenda Rubber	UX	Tay Feng Tire
		UY	Cheng Shin Rubber
LA,LB,LC,	Lee Tire	U1	Lien Shin Tire
LD,LE,LF		U2	Sumitomo
LH,LJ,LK,	Uniroyal	U3	Miloje Zakic, FAG
LL,LM,LN,		U4	Geo. Byers Sons
LP,LT,LU			
LV	Mansfield-Denman	VA,VB,VC,	Firestone
LW	Trelleborg Gummifariks	VD,VE,VF,	
	Aktiebolag	VH,VJ,VK,	
LX,LY	Mitsuboshi Belting	VL,VM,VN,	
L1	Goodyear Tire	VP,VT	
L2	Wuon Poong Industrial	VV	Universal Tire
L3	Tong Shin Chemical	VV	Firestone
L4	Centrala Ind. Rumania	VW	Ohtsu Tire
		VX,VY	Firestone
MA,MB,MC,	Goodyear	V1	Livinston's Tire Shop
MD,ME,MF,		V3	V.A. Hsin Tire
MH,MJ,MK,		V4	Ohtsu Tire
ML,MM,MN,	Goodyear		
MP,MT,MU,		WA,WB,WC,	Firestone
MV,MW,MX,		WD	
MY,M1,M2		WE	Nankang Tire
M3	Michelin	WF,WH	Firestone
M4	Goodyear	WK	Pennsylvania Tire
		WL	Mansfield Tire
NA,NB,NC,	Goodyear	WM,WN	Olympic Tire
ND,NE,NF,		WP	Schneuit Industries
NH,NJ,NK,		WT	Madras Rubber
NL,NM,NN,		WU	Ceat
NP,NT,NU,		WV	General Rubber
NV,NW,NX,		WW,WX,WY	Euzkadi
NY		W1,W2	Firestone
N1	Maloja AG, Pneu-Und	W3	Vredestein Doetinchem
N2	Hurtubsle Nutread	W4	Olympic
N3	Nitto Tire	W5,W6	Firestone
N4	Centrala Ind. Rumania		
		XA,XB,XC,	Pirelli
PA,PB,PC,	Goodyear	XD,XE,XF,	
PD,PE,PF		XU	Sam Yang Tire
PH,PJ,PK,	Kelly-Springfield	XV,XW	Dayton
PL,PM,PN,		XX	Bandag
PP,PT,PU,		XY	Dayton
PV,PW,PX,		X1	Tong Shin Chemical
PY		X2	Hwa Fong Rubber
P1	Gummifabriken Gislaved		
P2	Kelly-Springfield	YA,YB,YC,	Dayton
P3	Skepplanda Gummi, AB	YD,YE,YF,	
P4,TA,TB,	Kelly-Springfield	YH,YJ,YK,	
TC,TD,TE,		YL	Oy Nokia
TF,TH,TJ,		YM,YN,YP	Seiberling
TK,TL,TM,		TY,YU,YV,	
TN,TP,TT,		YW,YX,YY	
TU,TV,TW,		Y1	Goodyear
TX,TY		Y2	Dayton
T1	Hankook Tire	Y3	Seiberling
		Y4	Dayton

Source: Department of Transportation.

AUTO TIRES NOW GRADED
To Make It Easier to Compare Quality

Grading of bias-ply tires started on April 1, 1979, at manufacturing plants. Grading of bias-belted tires began October 1, 1979; grading of radials is set for April 1, 1980.

There are three grade categories: treadwear, traction and temperature resistance.

Treadwear grades are in numbers, with the higher numbers meaning longer tire life. Grades for traction and temperature resistance are in letters A, B and C, from best to worst. Treadwear numbers are comparative ratings certified by manufacturers on the basis of their own testing and experience.

Traction grades represent a tire's ability to stop straight ahead on wet pavement; Grade C represents poor traction, but it does not mean the tire is unsafe.

Temperature grades represent a tire's resistance to the generation of heat and its ability to dissipate heat in controlled tests. Sustained high temperatures can reduce tire life and cause sudden tire failure.

A poor grade does not mean a tire fails to meet minimum federal standards of safety. All tires sold must meet these standards. But, as with treadwear, the way a tire is used makes a big difference. For example, excessive speed, underinflation and excessive loads can cause a tire to heat up too much and increase the risk of tire failure.

Grades for all bias-ply tires are listed in the accompanying table. Grades are as certified by manufacturers to the National Highway Traffic Safety Administration.

OFFICIAL TIRE GRADES
For Bias Ply by Company and Brand

Company	Line	Tread-wear	Traction	Temperature
ARMSTRONG (Sears)	Guardsman	60	B	C
	Silent Guard 78	110	B	C
	Dynasport	60	A	B
	Dynaply 24	80	A	C
	Dynaply 20 and Dynaply 18	70	B	C
	Present Antique and Proposed Antique	50	B	C
ATLAS	All Brands	80	B	C
COOPER	Poly-Mark IV, Falls Allstar and Cushion Ride	120	B	C
	Trendsetter, Falls Persuader, Starfire-	100	B	C
	Poly IV and Giant Roadmaster	90	A	C
	Sportsmaster II and Starfire Poly Sport			
DAYTON	Sport Premium, Allroad, Premium Heavy-Duty, Road Runner, Delux 78 and Road King Performance 78	80	B	C
	Duralon D.S. Premium, (560-15 Tread 90)	130	B	C
	Thorobred Premium 78 Poly	110	B	C
	Road King Premium Plus 78	110	B	C
	Thorobred Premium	90	B	C
DELTA	XP78, Premium 125 and Road Max	80	B	C
	Victorian 478 and 784	100	C	C
DUNLOP	Gold Seal Poly Sport, Gold-C-60	100	A	C
	Gold-RS Patrol	100	A	A
	Gold Cup	90	A	B

OFFICIAL TIRE GRADES
For Bias Ply by Company and Brand

Company	Line	Tread-wear	Traction	Temper-ature
FIRESTONE	Delux Champion, Super Sports, Triumph-Ride 78, Triumph Foreign and Compact, Emblem, Big Boss and Imperial Falcon	80	B	C
	Courier	40	B	C
	Regency 30	50	B	C
	Golden Falcon	70	B	C
GENERAL	All Brands	80	B	C
GOODRICH	Premium Poly	110	A	C
	78 Poly	80	A	C
	Sport King	80	A	C
GOODYEAR	Rally GT and Cruiser and Mini Custom G8	80	B	C
	Power Streak	70	B	C
HERCULES	Premium 478	120	B	C
	Sportspreme	90	A	C
	Saftipreme 78 and Superior Poly Four	100	B	C
K MART (Uniroyal)	KM 50	50	B	C
	KM 78	80	B	C
	KM 100	100	B	C
KELLY-SPRINGFIELD	Super Star 50 and Super Charger 50	90	B	C
	Sky Trac 78, Road Mark and Super Comet	80	B	C
	Deluxaire and Delux 78	70	B	C
MULTI-MILE	Jet Star 120, Grand Prix Broadway, Nova and Bonneville Superwide 70	80	B	C
	Grand Prix Superwide GT/50, and Bonneville Superwide 60	90	B	C
	Power King Custom Poly and Power King-Custom Poly IV	70	B	C
PENNEY'S	Premium Poly	110	A	C
	Mileagemaker, Mileagemaker Sport and Sport King GT	80	B	C
	78 Poly	80	A	C
REMINGTON	Cushion-Aire Poly Four and Centennial 78	100	A	C
	Taxi and Flash Cad Taxi	100	B	C
SEARS ROEBUCK	(See Armstrong)			
UNIROYAL	Fisk Premier II, Peerless-Ambassador, Gillette-Ambassador and Tiger Paw Polyester	80	B	C
	Ambassador, Peerless PT 78, Golden Bear Tiger Paw (LR 8-15) and Fastrack (B78-13/2)	100	B	B
	Peerless-Sport Special	80	B	B
	Tiger Paw Nylon and Sport Special	70	B	B
WARDS	Wide Track Oval (50/60/70 series), Super Sport (50 series) and Highway Handler II	70	B	C
	Runabout	40	B	C
	Poly Sport	80	B	C

Source: Letters sent by companies to the National Highway Traffic and Safety Administration, 1979. Data compiled by Kurt Bacci.

TREADWEAR—Treadwear grade is a comparative rating based on the wear rate of the tire when tested under controlled conditions on a specified government test course. For example, a tire graded 150 would wear one and a half (1½) times as well on the government course as a tire graded 100. The relative performance of tires depends upon the actual conditions of their use, however, and may depart significantly from the norm due to variations in driving habits, service practices and differences in road characteristics and climate.

TRACTION A, B, C—Traction grades, from highest to lowest, are A, B and C, and they represent the tire's ability to stop on wet pavement as measured under controlled conditions on specified government test surfaces of asphalt and concrete. A tire marked C may have poor traction performance. Warning: The traction grade assigned to this tire is based on braking (straight ahead) traction and does not include cornering (turning) traction.

TEMPERATURE A, B, C—Temperature grades are A (the highest), B, C, representing the tire's resistance to the generation of heat and its ability to dissipate heat when tested under controlled conditions on a specified indoor laboratory test wheel. Sustained high temperature can cause the materials of the tire to degenerate and reduce tire life, and excessive temperature can lead to sudden tire failure. Grade C corresponds to a level of performance which all passenger car tires must meet under the Federal Motor Vehicle Safety Standard No. 109. Grades B and A represent higher levels of performance on the laboratory test wheel than the minimum required by law. Warning: The temperature grade for this tire is established for the tire that is properly inflated and not overloaded. Excessive speed, underinflation, or excessive loading either separately or in combination, can cause heat buildup and possible tire failure.

Travel and Transportation

In This Chapter

- **Travel Fraud**
- **Passenger Rights**
- **Air Charters**
- **Complaints Against Airlines**
- **Household Movers Compared**

Gasoline shortages and high prices are making Americans change their travel patterns in a big way. Buses, trains and airplanes, which had been struggling to stay alive financially, have become attractive and economical alternatives to travel by car. Big increases in patronage have occurred in all forms of public transportation.

Ridership on Amtrak, the nation's federally funded passenger railroad lines, switched upward in 1979, even while cutbacks were being planned because of poor patronage. Large financial losses in 1978 had brought proposals to eliminate two dozen trains, reducing passenger service 43 per cent. In the spring of 1979, new records were set for the number of passengers carried on some lines, spurring efforts by supporters of passenger rail transportation to block the cuts. During May the dollar volume of ticket sales rose 72.5 per cent, reservations increased 90 per cent over year-ago levels. On some trains, only standing room was available. The increased demand forced Amtrak to suspend sales of its USA Rail Pass, good for unlimited travel during a specified period of time, because pass holders were unable to find seats on some routes. However, many new passengers switched back to cars later.

PLANE AND BUS PATRONAGE ALSO UP

Air travel was also growing fast. Over 30 million more people traveled by plane between March 1, 1978, and February 28, 1979, than in the same period a year earlier. U.S. airlines carried 13 per cent more passengers in 1978 than in 1977, largely because of fare cuts.

Bus and subway travel got a big boost when the gasoline shortages hit much of the nation in May, 1979. In several cities, bus patronage was up from 10 to 15 per cent over the previous year's levels, increasing a trend that began after the Arab boycotts in 1973. Buses have become so crowded in most cities that there is only standing room now on vehicles that were less than full before the gasoline crunch.

The Department of Energy considers buses to be the most energy efficient form of transportation available. Intercity bus lines averaged 1,010 British Thermal Units (BTUs) per passenger per mile in 1976. Intercity trains averaged 3,230 BTUs, domestic airlines averaged 6,620 BTUs, and autos averaged 4,320 BTUs. The figure for autos includes both intra- and inter-city travel; if only intercity travel was considered, the figure would be substantially lower.

Bus companies have been slow to respond with discounts and have suffered as a result of stiff airline competition. Greyhound, the nation's largest bus line, carried 91.6 million passengers in 1969 but only 56.4 million in 1978. Many routes remain unprofitable, but increased ridership in 1979 led Greyhound to add buses steadily to its routes.

BUS PASSENGERS GET 'BILL OF RIGHTS'

In June, 1977, the Interstate Commerce Commission announced regulations that amounted to a bus users' bill of rights. They are designed for long-distance travelers, not for commuters on municipal bus lines or charter services. Among the new rules:

● Carriers shall reimburse passengers, to the extent possible, for the inconvenience suffered by those whose travel plans are disrupted at the fault of the bus line. This includes bridging a missed connection or providing food, shelter or alternate transportation.

● Bus lines are required to send all baggage checked up to 30 minutes before departure "on the same schedule as the ticketed passenger." If the baggage is not checked within 30 minutes of departure, passengers must be notified that it may not travel "on the same schedule." But it must be sent on the next available bus to the same destination.

● If a carrier does not make baggage available to a passenger within 30 minutes of arriving at the destination, it must deliver the bags to the passenger's local address at the carrier's expense.

● Checked baggage that cannot be located within one hour of arrival will be designated as "lost." The passenger must be notified and provided appropriate forms for submitting a tracer and claim. If the bags cannot be located within 15 days, the company must process the matter as a claim and settle or deny it within 60 days. These rules do not apply to unchecked baggage.

● Bus companies must post any changes in schedules at bus stations and in each bus.

● Carriers cannot deny transportation to a person with a physical disability. A dog traveling as a guide to a blind person must be given free passage.

DEREGULATION SHATTERS AIR FARES

Deregulation of commercial airlines has led to an increased and often confusing number of airfare discounts for both domestic and international flights. Among the biggest bargains was World Airways' $99.99 transcontinental fare. In addition, United Airlines, in an attempt to recover passengers lost during a two-month strike in 1979, offered a "Half-Fare Coupon" good for a 50 per cent discount on one-way flights. American Airlines also offered half-fare coupons. Some airlines began offering budget fares on international flights at lower-than-standby rates.

However, new doubts about the safety of air travel rose in May, 1979, when 278 people were killed in the crash of an American Airlines DC-10 shortly after take-off from Chicago's O'Hare International Airport. An investigation following the crash led to the temporary grounding of all DC-10s and inspection of all wide-bodied aircraft after structural defects were discovered. The news raised more questions than answers about airline inspection programs and the safety of other aircraft in use.

There were six fatal airline accidents in the U.S. in 1978. One hundred forty two of the 163 deaths in 1978 were the result of the mid-air collision of a Pacific Southwest Airlines B-727 and a Cessna 172 over San Diego, California. There were also 19 non-fatal accidents during this time.

SAFETY RECORDS COMPARED

When compared to other forms of transportation, commercial air travel remains relatively safe. In 1978, U.S. air carriers reported a passenger fatality rate of .006 per 100 million passenger miles flown, the second lowest rate ever.

Non-airline air travel (general aviation) has the worst safety record. A National Transportation Safety Board study of over 17,000 accidents in 1978 involving single-engine, propeller-driven, fixed wing planes found the following rates of fatal accidents per 100,000 hours: Cessna, 1.65; Piper, 2.48; Mooney, 2.50; Beech, 2.54; Grumman, 4.13; and Bellanca, 4.84. Because of a variety of factors, including pilots, weather and maintenance, the safety rates for different manufacturers cannot be directly compared.

Following is a comparison of the relative safety of alternative forms of transportation:

Type of Transportation	Passenger Fatalities Per 100 Million Passenger Miles.	
	1977	1976
Domestic Scheduled Flights[1]	0.04[2]	0.003[3]
All Buses	0.13	0.17
Railroad	0.04	0.05
Local Transit	0.05	0.09
Automobile	1.35	1.34
Motorcycle	17.00	16.00
Private Planes	30.00	29.49
Class I Buses	0.04	0.01

[1]Does not include fatalities on charter flights or intrastate carriers which do not have a certificate from the Civil Aeronautics Board.

[2]Does not include the collision of a Pan American Airlines charter flight and a KLM plane at the Canary Islands in which 321 passengers and six crew members on the Pan Am plane were killed and 246 more were killed on the KLM plane. The figure also does not include three crew members killed on a Fleming International Airlines cargo plane.

[3]Does not include three crew members killed on a Mercer Airlines DC-6.

Source: Transportation Association of America.

FRAUD IN TRAVEL INDUSTRY
Regulation Called Inadequate

Consumer fraud in the travel industry is becoming rampant, and federal agencies are doing little to stop it, according to testimony given to a subcommittee of the House Government Operations Committee in April, 1979.

Subcommittee Chairman Benjamin S. Rosenthal (D-N.Y.) said the main problems are misrepresentation, overbooking, bait-and-switch tactics and refusal to provide refunds. He reported "a lack of adequate federal regulatory response." He said help for the traveling consumer "has fallen between the regulatory cracks, and we want to know why fraudulent practices are allowed to continue when at least two federal agencies have authority to stop it."

His complaints were echoed by Henry Eschwege of the General Accounting Office, an investigative arm of Congress. He asked for a law requiring the Federal Trade Commission to enforce rules against unfair and deceptive practices concerning package tours.

Thomas Dickerson, a private lawyer specializing in class actions involving airlines, hotels, tour operators and travel agents, said, "Agencies are either incapable or unwilling to do more than write a threatening letter." He found "an astonishingly high level of consumer dissatisfaction" after a two-year investigation by the FTC's Boston regional office. But the agency "ceased activity" in this area, according to Rodney E. Gould, a New York attorney who supervised the investigation.

The FTC promptly denied losing interest in the matter. Chairman Michael Pertschuk claimed that his agency did not issue new rules because of higher priorities and because sufficient regulation was being done by the Civil Aeronautics Board (CAB). The two main areas of complaints to the FTC, according to Pertschuk, were (1) hotels, particularly overbooking, and (2) deficiencies in package tours, such as itinerary and carrier changes and failure to receive advertised items ranging from welcome cocktail parties to tickets to the Super Bowl.

CAB rules that took effect May 1, 1979, include requirements that advertising disclose the possibility of hotel substitutions, naming possible substitute in the contract. Ads must also disclose alternative departure or destination cities and alternative flight dates. Exact information must be given at least 10 days prior to departure and passengers given the choice to accept or reject major changes, including dates, cities, hotels and price increases, in favor of a refund.

Two industry groups offer to help resolve travel complaints: The American Hotel and Motel Association, 888 7th Ave., New York, N.Y., 10019, and the American Society of Travel Agents, 711 Fifth Ave., New York, N.Y., 10022.

HEALTH TIPS FOR TRAVELERS

Health conditions vary from country to country, and they change frequently, making life especially difficult for travelers. To help protect their health, the Center for Disease Control annually publishes *Health Information for International Travelers,* a booklet containing information on vaccinations and other health measures. Information in the publication is updated weekly in the Center's *Blue Sheet.* Both are available from the Center for Disease Control, Bureau of Epidemiology, Atlanta, GA, 30333.

Among the Center's recommendations are the following:

● The traveler should take an extra pair of glasses or lens prescriptions, and a card, tag, or bracelet identifying any physical condition that may require emergency care.

● If a physician is needed while abroad, travel agents or the American Embassy or Consulate can usually provide names of physicians or hospitals.

● Prescription medications should be accompanied by a letter from the traveler's physician, stating major health problems and dosages of the prescribed medications. The traveler should carry an adequate supply of these drugs.

● Water may be safe in hotels in large cities, but only chlorinated water sources afford significant protection against bacterial and waterborne diseases. Yet chlorine, at the levels used to disinfect water, may not kill all harmful organisms. In areas where chlorinated water is not available and where hygiene and sanitation are poor, only the following may be safe to drink: beverages made with boiled water; canned or bottled carbonated beverages; beer and wine.

Where water is contaminated, ice should also be considered contaminated and may contaminate containers used for drinking.

Food should be selected with care to avoid illness. Where hygiene and sanitation is poor, travelers should avoid unpasteurized milk and milk products, and eat only what can be peeled or has been cooked and is still hot.

AIR PASSENGER RIGHTS

Passengers on commercial airlines have gained many new rights in recent years, largely because of pressure from consumer groups and assertive passengers. Improvement has been speeded by the appointment of consumer-oriented officials to the Civil Aeronautics Board (CAB), the federal agency in charge of all but the safety aspects of air travel.

Regulations have been improved in regard to baggage liability, "bumping" of confirmed passengers because of overbooking of flights and other problems. But the new rules can help only if known by passengers. The following tips and regulations are excerpted from material produced by the CAB in 1979.

CHOOSING THE BEST DEAL

Because of the new emphasis on deregulation, airlines no longer charge the same rates. Some are trying a "back to basics" approach—offering rides at bargain basement prices with few, if any, extras.

One way to shop for the lowest possible air fares is to call or write each airline and ask for a copy of their fare summaries to places you want to visit. These booklets list the air fares between most major cities and any conditions attached to them.

An easier way is to ask a travel agent to determine the best route, airline and price. Agents get commission from airlines for such service, so the service should not cost you anything above the actual ticket price.

DELAYED AND CANCELLED FLIGHTS

Airlines don't guarantee their schedules, but they generally will help stranded passengers find alternate flights and may provide food and other basic amenities during long waits at the airport.

If a flight is cancelled, the airline will rebook you on the first available flight to your destination, usually at no additional charge, even if you must ride first class.

Each airline has its own policies about what it will do for delayed passengers. If the delay is expected to last longer than four hours, most airlines will:

● Pay for a telephone call or telegram to your destination, to let people there know your flight will be late.

● Arrange and pay for a hotel room if you are stranded overnight away from home.

● Pay cab or limousine fare between the airport and hotel.

● Give you a voucher to buy food at an airport restaurant.

If you are stranded by a long delay and the airline's staff can't or won't help you, keep track of these kinds of out-of-pocket expenses and write to the airline's consumer office for reimbursement when you get home.

OVERBOOKING (BUMPING) OF PASSENGERS

Most airlines overbook their flights to a certain extent, and passengers are sometimes left behind or "bumped" as a result. CAB rules encourage people who are not in a hurry to give up their seats voluntarily in exchange for money and a later flight. Passengers bumped against their will are, with few exceptions, entitled to compensation. CAB rules require airlines to seek out people who are willing to give up their seats for some compensation before bumping anyone involuntarily.

Since the CAB does not say how much money the airline has to pay you to volunteer, airlines may negotiate for a mutually acceptable sum. Airlines give employees suggested guidelines to follow, allowing them to select volunteers offering to sell back their tickets for the lowest price.

The CAB also requires airlines to give every passenger who is bumped involuntarily a written statement explaining how the carrier decides who gets on an oversold flight and who does not. Travellers who do not get to fly are almost always entitled to an on-the-spot payment of denied boarding compensation. The amount depends on the price of the ticket and the length of the delay.

PENALTY FOR BUMPING: $37.50 to $200

If you are bumped, the airline must pay you the fare to your destination, with a $37.50 minimum and a $200 maximum. If it cannot arrange another flight to your destination within two hours of the original flight (four hours on international flights), the amount of compensation doubles. In addition, you get to keep your original ticket, so you can use it on another flight or refund it. The denied boarding compensation is essentially a payment for your inconvenience.

There are some exceptions, however:

● To qualify for compensation, you must have a confirmed reservation, and you must meet the airline's deadline for buying your ticket.

● Most airlines require passengers to arrive at the boarding gate 10 minutes or more before scheduled departure. If you do not, you may lose your reservation and your right to compensation.

● If the airline substitutes a smaller plane for the one originally planned, the airline is not required to pay people who are bumped.

● If you are bumped to accommodate government travelers on emergency official business, you are not entitled to denied boarding compensation.

● If being bumped costs you more money than the airline will pay you at the airport, you can try to negotiate a higher settlement with the carrier's complaint department, or take the airline to court.

CHECKING BAGGAGE

Items that should not be put into a bag checked into the cargo compartment include money, jewelry, medicine, liquids, glass, negotiable securities, or other things that are valuable, irreplaceable, breakable, or have sentimental value. These should be packed in a carry-on bag that will fit under the seat.

If you plan to check electrical equipment, small appliances, typewriters, pottery, glasswear, musical instruments, or other fragile items, they should be packed in a container specifically designed to survive rough handling, preferably a factory-sealed carton or a padded hard-shell carrying case.

If your bags are delayed, lost, or damaged on a domestic flight, the airline need pay no more than $750. When your luggage is worth more than that, you may buy "excess valuation" as you check in. This will increase the carrier's potential liability. Excess valuation costs about 10 cents for each additional $100 worth of coverage. There is no charge for the first $750, and excess value is sold in units of $100. The airline can refuse to sell excess valuation on items that are especially valuable or breakable, such as antiques, musical instruments, jewelry, manuscripts, negotiable securities and cash.

If your suitcase arrives smashed or torn, the airline will usually pay for repairs. If it cannot be fixed, the airline will negotiate a settlement to pay you its depreciated value. The same holds true for clothing packed inside.

Airlines do not have to pay for damage caused by the fragile nature of the item or by your carelessness in packing rather than the airline's rough handling. Airlines may also refuse to give money for damaged items inside the bag when there is no evidence of external damage to the suitcase. But they must not disclaim liability for fragile merchandise packed in its original factory-sealed carton, a cardboard mailing tube, or other container designed for shipping and packed with protective padding material.

When you check in, the airline must let you know if it thinks your suitcase or package may not survive the trip intact. Before accepting a questionable item, it will ask you to sign a statement in which you agree to check it in at your own risk. Even if you do sign this form, the airline must pay for damage if it is caused by its own negligence shown by external injury to the suitcase or package.

DELAYED OR LOST BAGS

If you and your suitcase do not connect at your destination, don't panic. The airlines have sophisticated systems that can track down about 98 per cent of the bags they misplace and return them to their owners within hours. They will also generally absorb reasonable expenses you incur while they look for your missing belongings. You and the airline may have different ideas of what is reasonable, however, and the amount may be subject to negotiation.

If your bags don't come off the conveyor belt, report this to the airline and fill out the required forms. Most carriers disburse money at the airport for emergency purchases. The amount depends on whether or not you are away from home and how long it takes to track down your bags.

If the airline misplaces sporting equipment, it will pay for rental of replacements. For replacement clothing, the carrier might offer to absorb half its purchase cost, arguing that you will be able to use the new clothes in the future. If this is not acceptable to you, the airline will probably agree to pay the full replacement costs, but you will be asked to return the new clothing to the airline.

When you have checked fresh foods or other perishable goods which are ruined because their delivery is delayed, don't expect the airline to reimburse you. Airlines are liable only if they lose or damage perishable items.

Airlines are liable for consequential damages up to the $750 in connection with a delay.

COMPLAINING ABOUT AIRLINES

Airlines have trouble shooters at airports (customer service representatives) to take care of most problems on the spot. They can arrange meals and hotel rooms for stranded passengers, write checks for denied boarding compensation, arrange luggage repairs, and settle other routine claims or complaints that involve relatively small amounts of money.

If you cannot resolve the problem at the airport and want to file a complaint, send a letter to the airline's consumer office. Take notes at the time the incident occurs, and jot down the names of the carrier employees with whom you dealt. Keep all ticket receipts, baggage check stubs, boarding passes, etc., as well as receipts for any out-of-pocket expenses incurred as a result of the mishandling.

If your letter to the airline does not produce the desired results and if you still want to pursue the complaint, you may write to the Civil Aeronautics Board, Bureau of Consumer Protection, Washington, DC 20428. The CAB will forward your letter to the airline for handling and review your complaint along with the airline's response. The CAB may ask the carrier to reconsider the way it handled the complaint. The agency uses its complaint files to identify possible violations of consumer protection regulations.

If your complaint is about safety, write to the Federal Aviation Administration, 800 Independence Ave SW, Washington, DC 20591.

You might also complain to the Aviation Consumer Action Panel (ACAP), a Ralph Nader group that has helped get many improvements for airline passengers. Its address is P.O. Box 19029, Washington, DC 20036.

As a last resort you may turn to a small claims court.

For further details, consult a pocket-size pamphlet of the CAB entitled "Fly-Rights: A Guide to Air Travel in the U.S." It is available from Consumer Information, Pueblo, CO 81009.

GUIDE TO CHARTER FLIGHTS
How to Land a Low-Cost Trip

Rules affecting charter air travel have been changed substantially by the Civil Aeronautics Board (CAB), the federal agency that regulates commercial air travel. Recent changes include:

● Granting commercial airlines the right to sell charter transportation directly to the public or through their own tour operators, effective since September 28, 1979; and

● New rules to increase passenger protection on almost all charter trips by air, effective since July 1, 1979.

Although some fares on scheduled airlines have come down dramatically, it is still possible to save a lot by traveling in a charter group. That is because fares on most regular flights have increased while fares only for certain situations and places have dropped.

The new rules to protect passengers apply specifically to Public Charters, a type set up by the CAB in 1978 to replace a number of others, including ABCs

---

TOLL-FREE TRAVEL ARRANGEMENTS

You can make travel arrangements by dialing toll-free "800" telephone numbers. Most airlines, hotels, motels, rent-a-cars, ski resorts and railroads have such numbers. You can obtain the numbers by calling 800/555-1212 for information. If a particular hotel or airline is not listed, ask the operator for phone numbers of reservation systems serving many companies.

COMPARISON OF AIRLINE PERFORMANCE

Total Complaints Made to the Civil Aeronautics Board in 1978 about commercial passenger airlines

Airline	Flights (delayed, cancelled, etc)	Reservations	Baggage (lost, damaged, delayed)	Fares/Refunds	General Customer Service	Discrimination (Racial/psngr.)	Other Complaints (1)	Total Complaints 1978	12-Month Enplanements (000's) (2)	Complaints[1] per 100,000 Enplanements
American	205	363	267	262	253	9	192	1,551	27,835	5.6
Braniff	141	104	137	134	116	4	102	738	11,406	6.5
Continental	89	82	54	141	83	1	83	533	9,357	5.7
Delta	99	145	70	165	112	6	108	686	36,983	1.9
Eastern	454	498	267	233	389	13	261	2,114	36,924	5.7
National	108	72	86	95	117	1	93	572	6,904	8.3
Northwest	357	47	65	69	100	0	88	736	6,776	10.9*
TransWorld	178	266	307	297	455	18	436	1,957	20,021	9.8
United	317	233	208	323	162	2	213	1,528	40,677	3.8
Western	102	100	62	76	81	1	61	483	11,005	4.4
Pan American	186	202	193	159	194	7	221	1,162	9,365	12.4
Airwest	84	84	43	47	52	1	40	351	6,334	5.5
Allegheny	223	124	96	89	126	2	66	737	14,565	5.0
Frontier	110	69	50	76	45	1	42	393	5,391	7.3
North Central	64	50	52	90	46	1	17	320	6,710	4.8
Ozark	49	47	28	54	66	3	30	277	4,634	6.0
Piedmont	90	38	21	25	49	1	16	240	4,520	5.3
Southern	113	40	25	19	42	2	30	271	4,150	6.5
Texas Int'l.	75	37	66	21	35	5	29	268	4,063	6.6
Aloha	8	12	22	3	3	0	4	52	2,696	1.9
Hawaiian	12	31	9	4	19	0	7	82	3,603	2.3

(1) Includes complaints relating to equipment, facilities, tariff rules, tours, charters, smoking, schedules, advertising and cargo. (2) Charter flights are not included.　*Northwest Airline figures are distorted by a strike.

These statistics reflect alleged problems with airline service as stated in complaint letters. The Civil Aeronautics Board has made no determination as to the validity of the complaints, and the statistics should not be considered ratings of airline service by the CAB. These figures do not include complaints made directly to the airlines. Figure compiled by Kurt Bacci from monthly reports.

(Advance Booking Charters), TGCs (Travel Group Charters), OTCs (One-Stop-Inclusive Tour Charters), ITCs (Inclusive Tour Charters) and SGCs (Study Group Charters).

PUBLIC AND AFFINITY CHARTERS

Some of the above types continue to operate because of extended authorizations prior to the new rules, but they are being phased out. Remaining are two principal types: Public Charters and Affinity Charters. The new rules are being extended eventually to all types of charters.

Public Charter, the term to describe almost every type of air charter except Affinity, refers to a trip organized by a commercial operator who buys most or all of the seats on a plane and sells them to anyone wishing to participate. Affinity refers to a trip planned by a private group with prior connections, such as an Elks Club, which essentially buys seats directly from the airline or agent involved.

Most of the abuses occur in connection with charters run by commercial operators. Problems include changes in hotels and tours without notifying passengers, sudden changes in times and dates and failure to return advance payments when a tour is cancelled. It is to reduce these problems that the new rules were adopted by the CAB.

RIGHTS TO RECEIVE REFUNDS

Under the new rules affecting Public Charters, participants can cancel and get a refund if:
- The departure or return date or city is altered (unless the change results merely from a permissible flight delay);
- A hotel is used other than one named in the contract—the contract must list all possible hotels to be used—and
- The tour price increases 10 per cent or more, whether all at once or in several smaller increases. The operator must have reserved the right in the contract to increase the price. No increase is allowed after the tenth day before departure.

Charter operators also must notify participants of any major change within seven days after learning of it. The participant then has seven days to cancel and must receive the refund 14 days later. The CAB decided not to prohibit charter operators from naming alternative original or destination cities as long as participants are adequately informed of the risks involved.

OPERATOR OPTION PLANS

Contracts that allow changes are called Operator Option Plans (OOPs), said the CAB with a straight face. The contracts must name all alternative cities and dates, state that the final selection is at the charter operator's option and will not entitle the participant to a refund and state that the operator will notify the participant of the actual cities and dates at least 10 days in advance of departure.

Advertising that states a price must identify the plan, name all alternative cities and dates and state that the selection of the actual cities and dates are at the operator's option. If a change involves a city or date not on the list, the participant is eligible for a refund.

Operators are not allowed to collect money until contracts are signed, in order to give buyers a chance to inspect the terms of the deal before paying.

MOVING HOUSEHOLD GOODS
Problems by the Truckload

The household moving industry is in a state of turmoil, largely because of an invigorated Interstate Commerce Commission (ICC), which nearly everyone is trying to put out of existence. Emerging from its traditional doldrums in 1978, the ICC demanded $4.5 million in civil forfeitures from 45 moving companies, including the largest in the business, for alleged violations of federal regulations governing household moves.

The Commission reported receiving more than 20,000 individual customer complaints in 1978, double the number received only two years earlier. The three main problem areas are inaccurate estimates of charges, late pickups and deliveries and loss and damage claims. Partly in response, the American Movers Conference announced it was installing a hotline for complaints: 800/336-3094.

For the first time in history, a Congressional hearing was held in 1979 on problems encountered by moving van customers. The Senate Commerce Committee heard testimony that consumer protection rules were not being enforced properly and that ICC rules allowed a few large firms to block smaller ones from entering the business.

Among newly proposed rules of the ICC is one which would make advance estimates of charges binding. Customers would be allowed to pay the lower of the estimate or the actual charge. In June, 1979, the ICC proposed a rule to prohibit companies from charging a full month's storage for one day or more of storage, which was allowed under existing rules. Earlier, the ICC authorized use of credit cards by customers, a move designed to ease the pain of having to pay cash at the end of the line, especially when charges are above original estimates.

Following are key data from company performance reports for 1978. The data were supplied by the companies themselves and were released by the ICC.

ILLEGAL CARGO ON AIRPLANES

It is illegal and extremely dangerous to carry on board, or check in your luggage, any of the following hazardous materials:

Aerosols—polishes, waxes, degreasers, cleaners, etc.

Corrosives—acids, cleaners, wet cell batteries, etc.

Flammables—paints, thinners, lighter fluid, liquid reservoir lighters, cleaners, adhesives, etc.

Explosives—fireworks, flares, signal devices, loaded firearms, etc. (Small arms ammunition for personal use may be transported in checked luggage if it is securely packed in fiberboard, wood, or metal boxes. These may not be placed in carry-on baggage.)

Radioactives—betascopes, radiopharmaceuticals, uninstalled pacemakers, etc.

Compressed gases—tear gas or protective type sprays, oxygen cylinders, divers' tanks (unless they're empty), etc.

Loose book matches or safety matches—may only be carried on your person.

You may, however, carry up to 75 ounces of medicine or toilet articles, which are exempt from these regulations. For details, check with the airline.

A violation can result in a civil penalty of up to $10,000 or a criminal penalty of up to $25,000 and/or up to five years in jail to an individual and the employer of an individual travelling on business.

COMPARATIVE PERFORMANCE REPORTED BY 20 LARGEST MOVERS FOR 1978

PERCENT OF HOUSEHOLD SHIPMENTS

Moving Company	Over-estimated by 10% or more	Under-estimated by 10% or more	Picked up at least 1 day late	Delivered at least 1 day late	With $50 or more loss or damage claim	With claim for expenses caused by delay	Average no. of days to settle a claim	% claims taking 60 days or more to to settle
Aero Mayflower Transit	33.2	25.4	2.7	9.8	22.8	1.3	33	21.9
Allied Van Lines	26.5	21.4	6.4	9.5	12.9	1.1	15	8.4
Allstates Van Lines	16.8	29.5	8.0	9.7	15.7	0.4	41	21.7
American Red Ball	28.8	24.3	2.6	22.4	20.3	3.3	39	19.9
Atlas Van Lines	26.1	32.6	3.7	26.1	22.6	2.7	24	15.8
Bekins Van Lines	35.8	23.8	3.5	17.7	18.2	3.4	23	9.8
Burnham Van Service	35.5	24.9	0.5	21.0	20.5	2.4	14	0.5
Engel Van Lines	13.5	18.1	0.8	15.7	9.3	1.5	40	34.5
Fogarty Van Lines	26.9	24.6	2.0	5.3	27.6	0.3	31	14.5
Global Van Lines	18.7	14.5	1.1	24.4	10.5	1.9	29	12.8
Ivory Van Lines	29.9	21.9	3.3	9.4	18.1	1.1	13	8.2
King Van Lines	16.1	17.9	10.8	27.7	16.2	0.8	55	43.4
Lyon Moving & Storage	20.7	20.4	1.1	12.7	18.5	0.6	27	6.4
National Van Lines	26.0	31.5	2.0	19.3	22.8	4.8	51	31.4
North American Van Lines	27.2	18.2	6.1	10.5	20.8	2.1	24	12.9
Pan American Van Lines	29.0	23.0	2.3	10.5	14.0	0.2	23	6.0
Republic Van Lines	20.5	20.4	3.4	14.8	20.8	3.7	39	15.4
Smyth Van Lines	24.4	26.7	3.3	15.7	17.5	2.0	106	69.0
United Van Lines	25.6	21.4	4.5	15.6	15.0	1.4	21	9.0
Wheaton Van Lines	32.7	16.7	1.2	9.6	13.1	2.6	44	33.0
AVERAGE	28.1	22.4	4.4	13.6	17.7	2.0	26	15.1

Source: Interstate Commerce Commission, 1979

Energy for the Home

In This Chapter

- New Aid From Utilities
- Ways to Save Fuel
- Solar Energy Systems
- Solar Tax Incentives
- Appliance Efficiency
- Guide to Utility Regulators

The supply and cost of energy have become the Number One domestic issue in the United States, and they are certain to remain there for many years to come.

Americans have become so accustomed to cheap, freely available fuel that they are having a difficult time coping with tightening supplies and soaring prices. Although most people have cut down on their use of gasoline, heating oil and electricity to help save energy and money, some have done little or nothing.

During 1979, gasoline prices skyrocketed in many areas past $1 per gallon. Supplies began to become scarce allegedly because of the temporary shutdown of supplies from Iran. But most people were skeptical of the reasons offered by the oil industry and the Carter Administration for the rapidly escalating prices and shortened supplies. Many people suspected that the oil companies were deliberately cutting back on refinery imports and operations in order to keep prices going up at a fast rate.

Profits of the eight largest firms leaped upward in 1979, well above the level of a year earlier. Formal accusations of overcharging by the federal government against both producers and retailers in 1979 fanned suspicions that much of the scenario was being engineered by the oil companies. Industry officials, however, insisted that they were doing their best to increase production and keep prices down.

A FEW LARGE FIRMS IN CONTROL

Public skepticism was further fueled by a study showing a high degree of economic concentration in the energy field, giving petroleum companies greater leverage than ever to control prices of alternate fuels as well as oil. The study, by the Tennessee Valley Authority in 1979, warned that giant energy companies were continuing to corner fuel markets in an effort to cut supplies and raise prices.

"The lifeblood of the country," said the TVA report, "is in the hands of a few people who have more power than the government." The report contended that the price of coal and uranium, the chief fuels used to produce electricity, is now set by a small group of large energy conglomerates." The report added that "prices are higher than the cost of production plus a reasonable profit."

Concentration had increased to a "startling" degree in the past 18 months, said the TVA. It cited the takeover of six coal producing firms by oil-related ones and attempts to take over seven other firms in coal and uranium production. The report disagreed with an earlier study by the Justic Department showing less concentration in the coal industry than claimed by TVA.

FTC OFFICIALS ALSO CONCERNED

Officials of the Federal Trade Commission also showed concern about growing concentration in the energy field and launched investigations into a number of mergers. But top officials in the agency have contended for years that they lack sufficient legislative authority to take effective legal action.

Congress also has become worried about concentration in energy industries. Numerous bills have been introduced to break up the big oil companies by requiring them to get rid of some operations between producing and selling operations. In 1979, Senator Edward Kennedy (D-MA), chairman of the Senate Antitrust and Monopoly Subcommittee, sought to restrict oil companies that want to buy into other industries.

The aim was to force oil companies to put their increased profits into exploration of more oil rather than acquisition of other large companies. Throughout the public debate about decontrolling oil prices, oil companies argued that freeing up prices would provide greater incentives for drilling. But Mobil used its inflated profits from the 1973 crisis to purchase Montgomery Ward, the large retail chain, and Arco purchased a British newspaper.

DECONTROL OF PRICES ORDERED BY CARTER

On June 1, 1979, President Carter began gradual elimination of controls on oil prices despite growing opposition among members of his own party in Congress and from numerous citizen groups. At the same time, he repeated his request to Congress for a windfall profits tax for oil companies. But few people were satisfied with his tax proposal. Most said it was too small.

The Administration also aroused a furor with its offer to give oil companies a $5-per-barrel subsidy for all heating oil they could import on the open world market. The additional cost, estimated to be at least $70 million, will be added to home heating bills. The move was designed to guarantee sufficient supplies of heating oil in the winter of 1979-1980.

An unexpected addition to the nation's fuel bills in 1980 will be the cost of the Three Mile Island accident. Despite consumer sentiment for making stockholders and insurers shoulder the entire burden, it became clear in the following months that taxpayers and customers would eventually pay for the estimated $1 billion cost of the nuclear accident as well as other nuclear shutdowns.

PUBLIC VS. PRIVATE UTILITY

Electricity costs even became a city election issue in February, 1979, after Mayor Dennis Kucinich charged that Cleveland Electric Illuminating Co., a private firm, had tried to force the city to sell its publicly owned Municipal Light Company. When the issue was put to a referendum, the voters chose to raise their own taxes in order to keep the public plant and its lower electric rates.

In many parts of the country, citizen groups were beginning to change the complexion of utility rates and practices. Among their major goals are: reversing the practice of offering discounts to large users, lowering rates during off-peak hours, prohibiting cutoffs under certain hardship conditions and easing company requirements for deposits. There is also a growing move to prohibit power companies from adding the costs of advertising and charitable contributions to customer rate bases.

SOME 'PHANTOM TAXES' ELIMINATED

One of the biggest bones of contention between citizen groups and utilities—and one of the least known to the general public—has been the collection of so-called "phantom taxes." Utility companies are allowed to charge customers for taxes expected to be paid to the federal government but are in fact not paid.

Environmental Action Foundation (EAF), a national citizen group, estimated that in one year, 1976, the total amount of taxes collected but never paid was over $2 billion. The same practice has gone on for years with very little public attention given to the matter.

A court decision in February, 1979, however, struck a blow for taxpayers and ratepayers. The U.S. Court of Appeals for the District of Columbia ruled against a decision of the Federal Power Commission (later absorbed into the Department of Energy) allowing private companies to keep the overcharges rather than returning them to publicly owned utilities. Millions of dollars in refunds may eventually flow to consumers if state public utility commissions follow the court lead.

N.H. GOVERNOR "CWIPPED"

Another major controversy is "CWIP," construction work in progress. At issue is whether utilities may add costs of such work to customer bills. EAF and other groups have argued that it is unfair to require customers to pay for a plant not yet in production. They contend that such costs should be borrowed or obtained through stock sale from private investors.

This issue became a major factor in the 1978 gubernatorial election in New Hampshire. Governor Meldrim Thompson went down to defeat when his Democratic opponent, a relative unknown, accused the governor of "taxing" utility customers unfairly by approving CWIP. The CWIP issue later went to Washington for a decision by the Federal Energy Regulatory Commission.

WAYS TO SAVE FUEL AT HOME
New Law Requires Utilities to Help

A massive fuel conservation program involving utilities and homeowners was launched in 1979 by the Department of Energy (DOE), as required by the 1978 National Energy Conservation Policy Act. The purpose is to get the utility companies to help homeowners save fuel. DOE estimates that the various steps suggested may cost consumers as much as $6.7 billion but could save $30 billion and 8.2 quads of energy over the lifetime of the improvements. However utility rate hikes may offset some of the money saved by fuel users.

Under the program, large utilities are required to furnish fuel-saving information and other assistance to homeowners. Firms involved have annual sales in excess of 10 billion cubic feet of natural gas or 750 million kilowatt hours of electricity. These utilities are required to perform energy audits on request and evaluate whether the residence making the request meets conservation criteria and, if so, what can be done at what cost to improve energy savings. Audits are expected to cost $25 to $50.

In addition, utilities are authorized to make arrangements for the purchase, installation, financing and billing of energy conservation and renewable resource measures. The firms cannot actually do the installation but can lend up to $300 to homeowners.

Conservation measures under the program include:

- Caulking and weatherstripping of doors and windows;
- Furnace efficiency changes;
- Clock thermostats;
- Ceiling, attic, wall and floor insulation;
- Water heater insulation;
- Storm windows and doors;
- Heat-absorbing or heat-reflective glazed windows and door materials; and
- Load management devices.

Additional conservation measures made eligible earlier for tax credits include: duct insulation, pipe insulation, thermal windows, thermal doors and meters that show energy usage. Renewable resource measures covered include:

- Solar domestic hot water systems;
- Active solar space heating systems;
- Combined active solar space heating and solar domestic hot water systems;
- Passive solar space heating and cooling systems;
- Wind energy devices; and
- Replacement solar swimming pool heaters.

Utilities are also required to provide information on measures that have little or no cost and can be installed by homeowners independently. These include: changing furnace and air conditioning filters; installing low-flow shower heads and faucets; sealing leaks in pipes and ducts; raising thermostat settings in summer; reducing thermostat settings on water heaters; and closing vents, valves and doors in infrequently used rooms.

States are to administer the voluntary program. But they have to submit their proposals to DOE for approval. State plans vary according to climate, but they all must include on-site inspection audits, arrangements for installation and financing and lists of contractors and suppliers supplied by the utilities.

TYPES OF INSULATION

Three basic types of products are most commonly used. All have high insulating value if properly manufactured and installed. They are:

- **Mineral wool,** which includes rock wool and fibrous glass. Both of these products can be blown in place or purchased in blankets or batts with a foil or paper vapor barrier. Rock wool can also be purchased in bagged form.

- **Plastic foam or resin,** which is made of polystyrene, polyurethane or urea formaldehyde, can be purchased in pre-formed sheets or bolts or foamed in place by a contractor. Foam insulation can vary considerably in its final properties depending on the operator's skill, how various reactants are mixed and the time allowed for "curing."

- **Cellulosic insulation,** which is made of any finely-ground cellulose product such as recycled newspaper and can be poured or blown into place.

HAZARDS OF INSULATION

Because insulation can vary widely in quality, it can present several hazards:

FLAMMABILITY. Flammability standards include flame spread, fuel contribution and smoke development rates. Although many manufacturers' insulation products meet these criteria, an "acceptable" product may still be flammable and should not be installed near heat.

Mineral wools themselves pose no flammability problem, but some of their paper vapor barriers are flammable.

Since cellulose is inherently flammable, flame-retardant chemicals are usually added to cellulosic insulation to reduce flammability. Negative side effects of such chemicals include a possible reduction in the insulation's thermal resistance and, if too many sulfate chemicals have been added, a potential for corroding pipes and other metal.

Polyurethane and polystyrene come in flame-resistant and nontreated rigid forms. But even the flame-proofed products may pose a risk. Once the high temperature of a fire is reached, these products emit high levels of smoke and toxic gases which can be as lethal as fire itself.

Urea formaldehyde products can be made flame-resistant but are not as safe as claimed. Their biggest hazard is toxic fumes that are given off if mixing and curing has not been done properly. Flame-resistance can be improved for all these products if they are enclosed in a flame- and heat-retardant structure such as gypsum board.

Questions have been raised about the cancer-causing potential of fibers inhaled from fibrous glass insulation. The federal government is studying these questions to determine whether regulatory action is needed.

HOW TO READ YOUR METER

Electric meters measure the amount of electricity you use. The unit of measurement is in a killowatt hour (KWH). One KWH is the equivalent of 1,000 watts of electricity used for one hour; an example is ten 100-watt light bulbs burning for one hour.

Most electric meters have a set of dials which are read in multiples of 10. The dial on the far right indicates tens of KWHs; the next one, hundreds of KWHs; the next, thousands of KWHs, and so on. Reading the dials can be tricky because some of the dials read clockwise, some counterclockwise. When the pointer is between two numbers, read the lower of the two numbers.

The set of dials below show a typical reading of an electric meter. This meter is showing a reading of 79,420 kilowatt-hours.

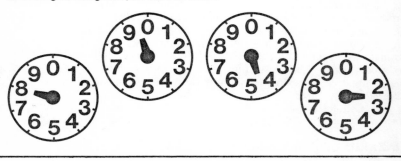

INADEQUATE MATERIALS. Deception is most likely to occur: 1) in claims about a product's flammability—either by misrepresentation or by no reference to its unacceptable flammability; or 2) in claims about the product's thermal resistance—either through generalizations without providing "R" values or exaggerations of the "R" values. An "R" value is a number indicating how much resistance insulation presents to heat flowing through it. Generally, the higher the "R" value, the more effective the insulation.

To help guard against dishonest contractors or salespeople who overstate the "R" value of an insulation product, here are the generally accepted maximum-design-standard "R" values for commonly used insulating materials:

Product	"R" Value Per Square Inch of Insulation
Mineral wool batts and blankets	3.1
Cellulose loose fill	3.1—3.7
Urea formaldehyde	4.1
Polystyrene (expanded)	6.25
Polyurethane	6.25
Perlite	2.7
Aluminum foil	2.0

ON CHOOSING A CONTRACTOR

● Under the new government program, large utilities are supposed to supply all the information you need to choose a qualified contractor to do home insulation. But you can protect yourself by checking into the reputations of all names suggested by a utility, friend or other source.

● One good way of checking is to ask for references, including previous customers. The Better Business Bureau also may have information to double check what you get from other sources.

● Talk with a contractor in terms of "R" values. If a contractor won't deal with you in "R" value language, don't deal with him.

● Bags of insulation should be marked with "R" values and figures indicating the area the contents will cover to achieve the desired "R" value. Federal law requires that each bag of loose fill be labeled as shown below. If a contractor uses insulation packed in bags that aren't labeled, don't hire him; the quality of his material may be unknown.

R-value	Minimum Thickness	Maximum net coverage per bag
R-22	10"	45 sq. ft.
R-19	8—3/4"	51 sq. ft.
R-11	5"	90 sq. ft.

● After selecting a contractor, have a specific contract drawn up for the job; sign it only when you are fully satisfied that it details everything you want done.

● Any warranty for the insulation should be in writing and a part of the contract. Seek a warranty giving enough time after installation to judge whether the insulation actually reduced your home energy costs.

TIPS FOR DO-IT-YOURSELFERS

If you decide to do your own installation, you should take the following safety precautions:

● Wear protective clothing, preferably long sleeves, long trousers, gloves, a hard hat to protect your head and a disposable respirator marked for "dust" to avoid breathing small fibers.

● Avoid direct contact with insulation dust since flame-retardant chemicals may be absorbed through the skin.

● Don't place insulation near electrical light fixtures, furnances or similar heat-producing devices; extreme heat, even without a flame, can ignite some insulation.

● Don't place insulation over attic vents.

● Be sure that there is good ventilation when installing insulation to help remove water vapors.

● To avoid locking in noisture and causing wall or ceiling rot, install insulation so that the vapor barrier is placed toward the living space.

● If adding new insulation over old, either purchase a product that has no vapor barrier, or slash the barrier at frequent intervals to allow moisture to escape.

ENERGY-SAVING HOME IMPROVEMENTS
How to keep your money from going up the chimney

Following are some simple ways to cut home heating and cooling bills. Most of the work can be done without measuring or counting a thing. A few minutes' work will give you a rough idea of what home improvements you need, how much they will cost and how much the improvements will save in energy costs per year.

The figures below are for a single-story, 1250-square-foot home. For purposes of comparison, these cities fall at about the midpoint of cost ranges:

DOING YOUR OWN APPLIANCE ENERGY AUDIT

You can run an energy audit of appliances in your home simply by operating one appliance at a time and reading your meter. First, unplug all appliances and turn off the lights and heat. Then operate one appliance at a time for 15 minutes. Read your meter when you turn on the appliance and again in 15 minutes. The difference between the first reading and the second is the amount of energy that appliance consumes in 15 minutes. To get an hourly rate, multiply that figure by four.

Do this for all appliances and for heating and lights. Then, estimate how many hours a week you use each appliance and multiply that times the hourly consumption rate. That should be an approximation of the monthly consumption of electricity for each appliance.

An energy audit may help you find ways to reduce energy use and use your appliances more efficiently.

● Packages 1 and 2 (Natural Gas Heat); Washington, DC, Youngstown, OH, Shreveport, LA, Eureka, CA;

● Package 3 (Electric Air-Conditioning): Washington, DC, Cairo, IL, Atlanta, GA, Oklahoma City, OK, Bakersfield, CA.

SAVING ON HEATING COSTS

There are two possible packages of energy-saving measures;

—Package 1 is cheap and easy, and it can pay for itself every year;

—Package 2 can save even more each year. It requires a modest investment,

---

ENERGY-EFFICIENT NEW HOMES
A Checklist for Buyers

The price of a new home is high enough without having to pay excessive energy costs. Studies have found some new homes—particularly those in developments—have little or no insulation, lots of windows and no caulking. Energy savings from a well-insulated home could pay a significant portion of monthly mortgage payments.

Below is a list of items to inspect or ask about when considering the purchase of a new home. The information was excerpted from a free booklet, *Energy Conservation and You,* available from the United States League of Savings Associations, 111 E. Wacker Dr., Chicago, IL, 60601.

WHAT TO LOOK FOR IN A NEW HOME

Attics, walls and floors insulated to R values recommended for that part of the country.

Window area limited to 12 per cent of living area unless the windows are designed as passive solar collectors.

Windows of insulated glass or single-pane windows equipped with storm windows in the northern part of the U.S.

Weatherstripping on all windows and thermal break on metal windows.

Insulated metal doors with weatherstripping, or conventional wood doors with weatherstripping and storm doors in the northern U.S.

Vapor barrier on the room side of walls, floors or ceilings. (In hot, humid parts of the country where air conditioning is common, a vapor barrier may be required on the outside face of construction.)

Attic ventilation equal to any of the following standards:

● 1 sq.ft. of vent area for each 150 sq.ft. of ceiling if no vapor barrier is provided.

● 1 sq.ft. of vent area for each 300 sq.ft. of ceiling with a vapor barrier, or if one half of the required vent area is located high in the roof and the other half at the eaves.

Tightly caulked and sealed windows, door frames, sillplates and other places where air can leak through exterior walls, floors and ceilings.

Heating and air conditioning equipment sized so that:

● Heaters are large enough to heat the house but do not exceed the area for which they were intended by more than 15 per cent.

● Air conditioners large enough to cool the area but no more than 5 per cent below or 12 per cent above the area for which intended.

Water heater insulated to R-9 or above.

Ductwork for heating and cooling insulated to R-7 or above if it passes through unheated or uncooled spaces.

Energy Efficiency Ratio (EER) of at least 7.0 for air conditioners and heat pumps.

but it can cut your heating bills by as much as one-half, and could pay for itself within five years.

Here is an idea of what the two packages cost and how much they can save in the typical home:

PACKAGE ONE	Your Annual Cost	Your Annual Savings
1. Turn down thermostat 6 degrees in the winter	$0	$27 − 87
2. Put on plastic storm windows	$6 − 8	$27 − 73
3. Have oil furnace serviced	$28	$33 − 87
TOTAL	$30 − 32	$87 − 247

PACKAGE TWO	Your Initial Cost	Your Annual Savings*
1. Turn down thermostat 6 degrees in the winter	$0	$13 − 53
2. Put on plastic storm windows	$6 − 8	$20 − 60
3. Have oil furnace serviced	$28	$20 − 53
4. Caulk and weather strip doors and windows	$83 − 116	$40 − 100
5. Insulate attic	$176 − 320	$47 − 160
TOTAL	$293 − 472	$140 − 426

*In Package 2, items 4 and 5 reduce the savings effects of items 1, 2, and 3, so that those items create less savings than in Package 1. "Initial Cost" for items 4 and 5 are do-it-yourself costs. If you hired a contractor, these items could cost twice as much.

SAVINGS ON AIR CONDITIONING COSTS

You can use Package 3 to cut air conditioning costs if you live in the shaded portion of the map below:

Here is an idea of how much Package 3 can save:

PACKAGE THREE	Your Initial Cost*	Your Annual Savings
1. Turn up thermostat 6 degrees in the summer	$0	$7 — 20
2. Insulate attic	$176 — 320	$33 — 67
3. Caulk and weatherstrip doors and windows	$83 — 116	$27 — 67
TOTAL	$259 — 436	$67 — 154

*These are do-it-yourself costs. If you hired a contractor, these items could cost twice as much.

SAVING ON BOTH HEATING AND AIR CONDITIONING

If you have whole-house air conditioning, and you live in the part of the country shaded on the map, some of the energy-saving steps can cut costs of both heating and cooling, but you need only pay for them once:

PACKAGE ONE PLUS RAISING THERMOSTAT IN SUMMER	Your Annual Cost	Your Annual Savings
Turn down thermostat in winter	$0	$27 — 87
Turn up thermostat in summer	$0	$7 — 20
Install storm windows	$6 — 8	$27 — 73
Service oil furnace	$28	$33 — 87
TOTAL	$34 — 36	$94 — 267

PACKAGE TWO AND THREE	Your Initial Cost	Your Annual Savings
Turn down thermostat in winter	$0	$27 — 87
Turn up thermostat in summer	$0	$7 — 20
Install storm windows	$6 — 8	$27 — 73
Caulk and weather strip	$83 — 116	$67 — 167
Insulate attic	$176 — 320	$80 — 227
TOTAL	$265 — 444	$208 — 574

WHICH ITEMS DO YOU NEED?

Unless you live in the southernmost portion of the U.S., you will profit from:

● Putting in storm windows;

● Servicing your oil furnace once a year; if you have a gas furnace, service it once every three years;

● Installing weatherstripping and caulking or attic insulation where needed. Here is how to determine your needs:

How to tell if you need caulking or putty: Look around the edges of your windows and doors. There should be some filler in all of the cracks. If not, it is needed. If existing caulking or putty is brittle or broken you should put some in.

How to tell if you need weatherstripping: Look for the strips of vinyl, metal or foam rubber around the edges of your windows and doors. If it is missing or deteriorated you need to install new weatherstripping.

How to tell if you need attic insulation: Three or four inches of insulation properly placed in the air space can reduce heat transfer through the walls by as much as two-thirds. If you have less than that amount you probably need to add insulation.

The above cost information is excerpted from *In the Bank....Or Up the Chimney?,* a publication of the U.S. Department of Housing and Urban Development. Complete copies are available for $1.70 from the Government Printing Office, Washington, DC, 20202. A more detailed examination of home insulation needs can be found in the National Bureau of Standards' booklet, *Making the Most of Your Energy Dollars,* available for 70¢ from Consumer Information, Pueblo, CO, 81009. For a free 30-page booklet, *Tips for Energy Savers,* write to the Department of Energy Technical Information Center, P.O. Box 62, Oak Ridge, TN, 37820.

SOLAR ENERGY IN YOUR HOME
Saving Money While the Sun Shines

Installing a solar energy system requires a modest investment, but it can return substantial financial rewards. The most economically feasible system is for hot water; space-heating systems require a substantially larger investment, and take longer to pay for themselves in most parts of the U.S. Hot water, on the other hand, is already affordable in much of the country.

A 1976 study by the Mitre Corporation found solar energy to be competitive with electricity in 12 of the cities studied: Atlanta; Bismarck, ND; Boston; Charleston, WV; Columbia, MO; Dallas/Ft. Worth; Grand Junction, CO; Los Angeles; Madison, WI; Miami; New York City; Seattle; and Washington, DC. A

UNDERSTANDING LIGHTING

There is probably as much confusion surrounding energy used by electric lighting in the home as there is with any other energy form.

For example, you may be surprised to learn the following:

● One 100-watt bulb *gives off more light* than two 60-watt bulbs and uses 20 per cent less energy;

● One 100-watt bulb *equals the same light* as six 25-watt bulbs;

● One 75-watt blub *gives off 68 per cent more light* than three 25-watt bulbs.

In general, the higher the bulb's wattage, the more efficient the bulb in energy use. The reason is that they produce more light per watt than lower wattage bulbs. But note that "long life" bulbs, although they last longer, give off less light per watt and cost more than a standard bulb. They are best for "hard-to-reach" areas.

Finally, there is no truth to the premise that switching a light on and off shortens bulb life.

solar system was deemed "economic" if the savings on fuel costs became more than the annual payments on a loan to install the equipment within five years after the system was installed, or if the entire system were paid off in 15 years or less. The Mitre study assumed that fuel costs would increase at an annual rate of 10 per cent.

An economical system is one designed to meet between 50 and 80 per cent of the space and hot water needs of a house. The reason a larger system would not be economical is this: building a system designed to meet 100 per cent of space and hot water needs would require a much larger investment, and a large portion of the solar collectors would be idle during the warmer months of the year. Thus, the investment would take considerably longer to pay for itself through savings in fuel costs.

HOW TO CHOOSE A HOT WATER SYSTEM

Two important factors are initial cost and collector efficiency. Both must be considered when comparing collectors. Thus a relatively inexpensive collector with a low efficiency may be a poor choice when compared to a more expensive one that captures and delivers the sun's energy more efficiently. All other things being equal, the collector that delivers more *heat per dollar* should be selected.

There are other considerations besides cost and efficiency.

● **Warranties.** What is specifically covered and for what period of time? Warranties on equipment now available are generally limited. That is, they cover only certain features.

● **Durability.** How long is it expected to last? Is it weatherproof and does it shed water?

● **Ease of Repair.** If something goes wrong, who will fix it, how long will it take to fix it and are repair parts easily obtainable? How much will repairs cost?

● **Susceptibility to Freezing or Overheating.** There are adequate solutions to both problems, and the collector must have protection against both extremes.

ENERGY EQUIVALENTS

1 Barrel (bbl) = 42 Gallons
1 Kilowatt (KW) = 1,000 Watts or about 1⅓ Horsepower (hp)
1 Kilowatt Hour (Kwh) = 1,000 Watt-hours (i.e. one 100-watt light bulb burning for 10 hours)
500 Kilowatt Hours (Kwh) = 1 Barrel of Oil

BTU Equivalent Comparisons

1 Btu = the amount of heat produced from one wooden match
1 cf of natural gas = 1,024 Btu's
1 Kwh = 3,413 Btu's
1 Therm = 100,000 Btu's
1 Gallon of gasoline = 125,000 Btu's
1 Gallon of no. 2 fuel oil = 139,000 Btu's
1000 cf natural gas = 1,024,000 Btu's
1 Barrel of crude oil = 5,800,000 Btu's
1 Ton of bituminous coal = 23,730,000 Btu's

In addition, if antifreeze fluid is used in the collector, it must not mix with water for domestic use.

● **Protection Against Corrosion.** Metal corrosion can cause irreparable damage to a solar system and shorten a system's life span. More importantly, corrosion can cause serious health problems if the water is consumed. The three metals commonly used in collectors are copper, steel and aluminum. Inhibitors are usually added to prevent corrosion in most systems. Copper will function over a long period without inhibitors, while steel and aluminum may fail quickly without special protection. With inhibited water, all three will last indefinitely as long as inhibition is maintained.

● **Protection Against Leaks.** The greater the number of joints, the greater the possibility of leakage. Some liquid collectors using channel systems have reduced the need for soldered joints considerably without affecting efficiency. Know what happens if a leak occurs, how it will be fixed, who will fix it and how much it will cost.

● **Consumer Protection.** Try to obtain the names of other buyers, and learn whether they are satisfied with its performance and whether the collector has lived up to the claims of the seller.

● **Insulation.** The pipes, ducts, and back parts of collectors, and storage tank should be insulated to prevent heat loss. This is true of inside and outside pipes and ducts. Avoid use of heating tapes to prevent freezing. They may use more energy than the solar system saves.

● **Fans and Pumps.** These items use electricity and hence should not be any bigger than necessary to perform. If they are too big then they will reduce the total energy savings.

HOW TO PROTECT YOURSELF

Ask for proof that the product will perform as advertised. The proof could come from an independent laboratory or a university. You should have the report itself, not what the manufacturer states the report claims.

Solar components are like stereo components—some work well together, others don't. If the system you are purchasing is not sold as a single package by one manufacturer, be certain that the seller has strong experience in choosing compatible components.

Ask whether the collector will meet the Intermediate Minimum Property Standards for Solar Heating and Domestic Hot Water Systems. If the manufacturer claims such standards are met, get that in writing. These standards provide a degree of assurance for the consumer, and if a seller claims that such standards are met, he is legally accountable for that claim. A copy of the Standards is available from the Government Printing Office, Washington, DC, 20402.

The amount you save in energy costs with solar depends in part on the type of fuel you now use. Solar energy is competitive with electric and oil heating in many parts of the country, but relatively low prices of natural gas do not make solar an economically feasible alternative for natural gas consumers.

The tables that follow illustrate how solar energy systems can pay for themselves through reduced fuel bills. Calculations are made for seven representative parts of the U.S., and are based on "typical" hot water usage by a family of four. Energy prices cover the ranges encountered in each area. They assume that electricity prices will escalate at 7.5 per cent annually, and gas and oil prices will escalate at 10 per cent annually.

SOLAR VS. NATURAL GAS HOT-WATER HEATING

Region/ system size	Solar, pct of hot water	Solar system cost ($)	Pay out time, years (gas)			
			12.5¢/ Therm	15¢/ Therm	17.5¢/ Therm	20¢/ Therm
East Coast						
(N.Y., Boston, Washington)						
50 ft² system	47	900	19.0	17.4	16.1	15.0
75	60	1,200	19.4	17.8	16.5	15.4
100	72	1,500	19.7	18.1	16.8	15.7
South Florida						
(Miami)						
50 ft² system	69	900	15.7	14.3	13.1	12.1
Upper Midwest						
(Chicago - Omaha)						
50 ft² system	54	900	17.8	16.2	15.0	13.9
75	69	1,200	18.1	16.6	15.3	14.3
100	84	1,500	18.4	16.8	15.5	14.5
Lower Midwest						
(St. Louis - Nashville)						
50 ft² system	51	900	18.3	16.7	15.4	14.4
75	65	1,200	18.7	17.1	15.8	14.7
100	79	1,500	18.9	17.3	16.0	15.0
Southwest						
(Dallas)						
50 ft² system	62	900	16.6	15.1	13.9	12.9
75	84	1,200	;6.5	15.0	13.8	12.8
Desert Southwest						
50 ft system	80	900	14.5	13.1	12.0	11.1
Southern California						
(Los Angeles)						
50 ft system	62	900	16.6	15.1	13.9	12.9
75	84	1,200	16.5	15.0	13.8	12.8

SOLAR VS. ELECTRIC HOT-WATER HEATING

Region/ system size	Solar, pct of hot water	Solar system cost ($)	Pay out time, years (electricity)		
			3¢/kWh	3½¢/kWh	4¢/kWh
East Coast					
(N.Y., Boston, Washington)					
50 ft² system	47	900	8.9	8.0	7.2
75	60	1,200	9.2	8.2	7.4
100	72	1,500	9.5	8.5	7.7
South Florida					
(Miami)					
50 ft² system	69	900	6.7	5.8	5.3
Upper Midwest					
(Chicago - Omaha)					
50 ft² system	54	900	8.1	7.1	6.4
75	69	1,200	8.3	7.4	6.7
100	84	1,500	8.5	7.5	6.8
Lower Midwest					
(St. Louis - Nashville)					
50 ft² system	51	900	8.4	7.5	6.7
75	65	1,200	8.7	7.7	7.0
100	79	1,500	8.9	7.9	7.1
Southwest					
(Dallas)					
50 ft² system	62	900	7.4	6.4	5.7
75	84	1,200	7.1	6.3	5.7
Desert Southwest					
50 ft² system	80	900	7.1	6.3	5.7
Southern California					
(Los Angeles)					
50 ft² system	62	900	7.4	6.4	5.7
75	84	1,200	7.1	6.3	5.7

The "pay out time," is the amount of time required for the cumulative savings (reduced fuel costs) to equal the initial cost of the solar energy system. But this is not the amount of time it takes to make a solar system economically feasible. Another factor, called "positive savings," indicates the number of years it takes for your annual fuel savings to be larger than your annual payments on the solar system, assuming you borrowed the money to build it. This, of course, depends on numerous variables, such as the price of your system, how much of your energy needs it supplies and your present energy costs. Typical systems provide "positive savings" in two to four years for solar hot water systems, and 6 to 10 years for space heating systems.

STATE SOLAR ENERGY INCENTIVE LAWS
To Save Both Fuel and Taxes

The following summary reflects state solar laws as of January, 1979. For further information contact the agency listed or the National Solar Heating and Cooling Information Center, through its toll-free telephone service. (See box following this section).

ALASKA: allows a 10% residential fuel conservation credit up to $200 per individual or married couple for solar energy systems installed between 1/1/77 and 12/31/82. Contact: Revenue Dept., Income Tax Division, Pouch SA, State Office Bldg., Juneau, AK, 99811; 907/465-2326.

ARIZONA: allows taxpayers to choose one of three: depreciation, amortization over 36 months, or a 30% tax credit on the cost of a solar energy system added to business or investment property. This credit decreases by 5% each year until the law expires on 12/31/84. The maximum claim allowed is $1,000. Solar energy equipment is exempt from property tax through 12/31/84 and from Transaction Privilege & Use Tax indefinitely. Contact: State Dept. of Revenue, Box 29002, Phoenix, AZ, 85038, 602/225-3381.

ARKANSAS: allows taxpayers to deduct the entire cost of solar equipment from taxible income. Contact: State Dept. of Revenue, Income Tax Section, 7th & Wolfe Streets, Little Rock, AR, 72201, 501/371-2193.

CALIFORNIA: allows both individual and corporate taxpayers a tax credit equal to 55% of solar energy system cost, maximum value $3,000. In a multi-family residence, tax credit equals 25% of system cost or $3,000, whichever is greater. State credit is reduced by the amount of federal credit claimed. Attorney's fees and recording fees associated with obtaining a solar easement are considered eligible expenses for credit. Credit expires 12/31/80. Contact: Franchise Tax Board, Attn: Correspondence, Sacramento, CA, 95807, 917/355-0370.

COLORADO: assesses solar heating and cooling equipment at 5% of its value for property tax. Contact: Local Board of Assessors. Individual taxpayers may deduct cost of solar equipment from taxible income. Corporate taxpayers may use the deduction in lieu of depreciation. Contact: State Dept. of Revenue, Income Tax Division, 1375 Sherman St., Denver, CO, 80261, 303/839-3781.

CONNECTICUT: exempts solar collectors from sales tax through 10/1/82. Contact: State Tax Dept., Audit Division, 92 Farmington Ave., Hartford, CT, 06115, 203/566-2501. Municipalities are authorized to exempt solar heating and cooling or solar electrical systems from property tax for 15 years. Systems must be installed before 10/1/91 and meet the standards of the Commission of Planning and Energy. Contact: Local Board of Assessors.

DELAWARE: provides a $200 income tax credit for solar domestic hot water heating systems, which meet criteria set in *HUD Intermediate Minimum Property Standards Supplement for Solar Heating & Domestic Hot Water Systems.* System warranties must meet criteria set in law. Contact: Division of Revenue, State Office Bldg., 820 French St., Wilmington, DE, 19801, 302/571-3380.

GEORGIA: allows real estate owners to claim refund of sales tax paid on solar equipment until 7/1/86. Contact: State Dept. of Revenue, Sales Tax Division, 309 Trinity-Washington Bldg., Atlanta, GA, 30334, 404/656-4065. Counties and municipalities may exempt solar heating and cooling equipment and machinery used to manufacture solar energy equipment from property taxes until 7/1/86. Contact: Local City Council or County Board of Supervisors.

HAWAII: provides a 10% income tax credit to individuals & corporations that install solar energy equipment before 12/31/81. Solar energy equipment is

YOUR HOME'S SOLAR POTENTIAL

Each day, the sun delivers anywhere between 500 and 2,000 BTU's of energy per square foot—depending on the season and location. This is enough energy to heat one gallon of water from 50 degrees Farenheit to boiling. Where you live is one important factor that will determine the size of the solar system that you will need. The latitude of your city is another factor.

The map below shows the average percentage of daily sunshine for all parts of the U.S. The higher the per cent of sunshine, the more the savings from installing solar energy.

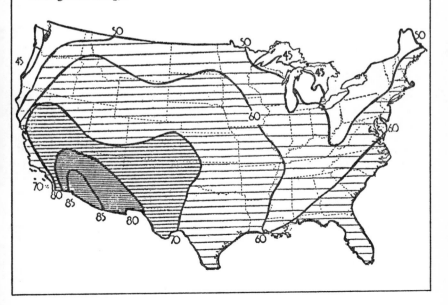

exempt from property tax through 12/31/81. Contact: State Tax Dept., P.O. Box 259, Honolulu, HI, 96809, 808/548-3270.

IDAHO: allows taxpayers an income tax deduction on solar residential installations. The deduction equals 40% of the first year's cost and 20% of the next 3 years' cost. The maximum deduction for any year is $5,000. Contact: State Tax Commission, 5257 Fairview, Boise, ID, 83722, 208/384-3290.

ILLINOIS: allows property owner who installs solar or wind energy equipment to claim an alternate valuation for property taxes. The property is assessed twice: with solar or wind equipment and as if equipped with a conventional energy system. The owner pays tax on the lesser assessment. Systems must meet standards of the Division of Energy of the Dept. of Business and Economic Development. Contact: Local Board of Assessors.

INDIANA: permits property owner who installs a solar heating and cooling system to have property assessment reduced by the difference between property assessment with system and property assessment without system. Contact: Local Board of Assessors.

IOWA: Installation of solar energy system will not increase assessed, actual, or taxable value of property between 1979-1985. Contact: Local Board of Assessors.

KANSAS: allows individual taxpayer an income tax credit equal to 25% of residential solar energy system cost, maximum $1,000. A business or investment property installation is eligible for a credit equal to 25% of system cost, $3,000 or that year's tax bill, whichever amount is least. Business or investment property cost may be amortized over 60 months. Contact: State Dept. of Revenue, P.O. Box 692, Topeka, KS, 66601, 913/296-3909.

LOUISIANA: exempts solar energy equipment installed in owner-occupied residential buildings or swimming pools from property tax. Contact: Local Parish Tax Assessor.

MAINE: exempts solar space or water heating systems from property tax for 5 years after installation. Contact: Local Board of Assessors. Solar energy system buyers may receive a sales tax rebate from: Office of Energy Resources, 55 Capitol St., Augusta, ME, 04330, 207/289-2196.

MARYLAND: assesses solar energy system at value equal to that of conventional system needed for building. Contact: Local Board of Assessors. Baltimore City and any other city or county may offer property tax credits for solar energy systems used in any type of building. Credit may be applied over a 3-year period. Contact: Local City or County Dept. of Revenue.

MASSACHUSETTS: exempts solar energy systems from property tax for 20 years from the date of installation. Contact: Local Board of Assessors. Residential solar energy systems, wind power systems, and heat pumps are exempt from sales tax. Corporations may deduct the cost of a solar or wind energy system from income; these systems are exempt from property tax. Contact: State Dept. of Corporations & Taxation, 100 Cambridge St., Boston, MA, 02204, 617/727-4201.

MICHIGAN: will exclude proceeds from sale of solar, wind, or water energy conversion devices for heating, cooling or electrical generation in new or existing residential or commercial buildings from business activities tax until 1/1/85. Solar, wind, or water energy devices used to heat, cool, or electrify a new or existing commercial or residential building are exempt from excise tax until 1/1/85. Income tax credit may be claimed for residential solar, wind, or water energy devices used for heating, cooling, or electricity. Swimming pool heaters are eligible if 25% or more of heating capacity is used for residential purposes. Credit may be claimed from year to year until expended. Equipment must be bought by 12/31/83. Contact: State Dept. of Treasury, State Tax Commission, State Capitol Bldg., Lansing, MI, 48922, 517/373-2910. Solar, wind, or water energy conversion devices are exempt from real and personal property tax until 7/1/85. Contact: Local Government Services, Treasury Bldg., Lansing, MI, 48922 517/373-3232.

MINNESOTA: excludes the market value of agriculturally derived methane gas, solar, or wind systems used for heating, cooling, or electricity in a building or structure. Installation must be done before 1/1/84. Contact: Local Assessor or Board of Assessors.

MONTANA: allows taxpayer a credit of 10% for the first $1,000 and 5% of next $3,000 spent on residential energy system—solar, wind, or decomposition of organic wastes—installed before 12/31/82. If federal tax credit is claimed, state credit is reduced by half. Contact: State Dept. of Revenue, Income Tax Section, Mitchell Bldg., Helena, MT, 59601, 406/449-2837.

NEVADA: establishes a property tax allowance on solar, wind, geothermal, water-powered, or solid waste energy systems in residences, equal to the difference in tax on the property with the energy system, and the tax on the property without the energy system. The allowance may not exceed tax accrued or $2,000, whichever is less. Contact: Local County Assessor.

NEW HAMPSHIRE: permits cities and towns to grant property tax exemptions to owners of solar heating, cooling, or hot water systems. Contact: Local Board of Assessors.

NEW JERSEY: exempts solar heating and cooling systems from property tax until 12/31/82. Systems must be certified under the State Uniform Construction Act and meet State Energy Office standards. Contact: Local Board of Assessors. Solar energy devices for heating, cooling, electric, or mechanical power are exempt from sales tax. Contact: State Division of Taxation, Tax Counselors, P.O. Box 999, Trenton, NJ, 80646, 609/292-6400.

NEW MEXICO: provides an income tax credit of 24% of solar energy system cost, or a maximum of $1,000, for residential heating and cooling and swimming pool heating systems. Credit in excess of tax due will be refunded, but state credit will not be given if federal credit is claimed. Tax credit is allowed for a solar irrigation pumping system, if system is approved by energy resources board before installation and if it reduces fossil fuel use by 75%. Credit in excess of tax due will be refunded, but will not be given if claimed under other state or federal laws. Contact: State Dept. of Taxation & Revenue, Income Tax Division, P.O. Box 630, Santa Fe, NM, 87503, 505/827-3221.

NEW YORK: provides property tax reductions for solar or wind energy systems. Assessment reduction equals the difference between assessment of the property with the energy system and assessment without it. System must conform to state energy office guidelines and be installed before 7/1/88. The exemption is good for 15 years after it is granted. Contact: Local Board of Assessors.

NORTH CAROLINA: provides corporate and individual income tax credit of 25% of the cost of a solar heating, cooling, or hot water system, maximum $1,000 per unit or building. Although this credit may be taken only once, it may be spread over 3 years. Contact: State Dept. of Revenue, Income Tax Division, P.O. Box 25000, Raleigh, NC, 27640, 919/733-3991.

NORTH DAKOTA: provides income tax credit for solar or wind energy systems that produce heating, cooling, electrical, or mechanical power. The credit is 5% per year for 2 years. Contact: State Tax Commission, Income Tax Division, Capitol Building, Bismarck, ND, 58505, 701/224-3450. Solar heating and cooling systems in any building are exempt from property tax for 5 years after installation. Contact: Local Board of Assessors.

OKLAHOMA: allows taxpayer an income tax credit for solar energy devices used to heat, cool, or furnish electrical or mechanical power at principal's residence. Credit equals 25% of system cost to maximum of $2,000. Although this credit may be taken only once, the amount may be spread over 3 years. Credit expires 1/1/88. Contact: State Tax Commission, Income Tax Division, 2501 Lincoln Blvd., Oklahoma City, OK, 73194, 405/521-3125.

OREGON: provides an income tax credit for the installation of solar, wind, or geothermal energy systems that produce heating, cooling, hot water, or electrical power for a residence. Credit equals 25% of system cost, maximum $1,000. Although this credit may be taken only once, the amount may be spread over 3 years. Credit expires 1/1/85. Contact: State Dept. of Revenue, State Office Bldg., Salem, OR, 97310, 503/378-3366. A property tax exemption is allowed on property equipped with solar energy systems. The exemption equals the property value with solar energy systems minus property value without it. Credit expires 1/1/98. Contact: Local Board of Assessors.

RHODE ISLAND: assesses solar heating or cooling systems at no more than the value of a conventional system needed to serve the building. Contact: Local Board of Assessors.

SOUTH DAKOTA: provides property tax assessment credit for renewable resource energy systems (solar, wind, geothermal and biomass). For residences, credit equals assessed value of property with system minus assessed value without it, but not less than actual installation cost of system. Credit for commercial buildings equals 50% of installation cost. For residential buildings full credit is given for 5 years and 75%, 50%, and 25% of full credit for next 3 years. Commercial buildings receive full credit for 3 years and 75%, 50%, and 25% of credit for next 3 years. Taxpayers must apply to the county auditor. Contact: Local County Assessor.

TENNESSEE: exempts solar and wind energy systems for heating, cooling, and electrical power from property tax until 1/1/88. Contact: Local Board of Assessors.

TEXAS: allows legislature to exempt solar or wind energy systems from property tax. Solar energy systems used for heating, cooling, or electrical power are exempt from sales tax. Corporations may deduct from taxable capital the amortized cost of a solar energy system over a period of 60 months or more. A franchise tax exemption is provided for corporations exclusively engaged in manufacturing, selling, or installing solar energy devices for heating, cooling, or electrical power. Contact: Comptroller of Public Accounts, Capitol Station, Drawer SS, Austin, TX, 78775, 512/475-2206.

VERMONT: permits towns to enact property tax exemptions on grist mills, windmills, solar energy systems, and methane systems. All system components are exempt, including up to 1/2 acre of land on which system is located. Contact:

Local Board of Assessors. Wood fired central heating, solar and wind energy systems for heating, cooling, or electrical power are eligible for income tax credit, if installed in taxpayer's residence before 7/1/83. Credit equals 25% of system cost or $1,000, whichever is less. Businesses may deduct 25% of system cost or $3,000, whichever is less. Contact: State Tax Dept., Income Tax Division, State St., Montpelier, VT, 05602, 802/828-2517.

VIRGINIA: permits any county, city, or town to exempt solar energy equipment from property tax, for not less than 5 years. System must be certified by State Board of Housing to qualify. Contact: Local Tax Governing Body.

WASHINGTON: exempts solar water and space heating or solar power systems from property tax for 7 years. Claims must be filed by 12/31/81. Contact: Local Board of Assessors.

WISCONSIN: allows businesses to use alternate energy systems as a tax deduction in the year paid for, to depreciate it, or amortize it over 5 years. The system must be certified by the Dept. of Industry, Labor, and Human Relations. Individuals may claim income tax credit on systems costing $500 or more. Credit may not exceed $10,000. Credit in excess of tax due may be refunded. Expenses must be incurred before 12/31/84.

SOLAR INFORMATION CENTER

The National Solar Heating and Cooling Information Center—established by the U.S. Department of Housing and Urban Development and the U.S. Department of Energy—answers public inquiries about solar heating and cooling of buildings, both commercial and residential.

The Center prepares and distributes free solar publications for the Department of Housing and Urban Development and the Department of Energy. Among its most frequently requested titles are : *Solar Energy and Your Home, Solar Hot Water and Your Home,* and *Reading List for Solar Energy.*

Inquiries and publication requests may be made by calling the Center's toll-free numbers: 800/523-2929; in Pennsylvania, 800/462-4983; in Alaska and Hawaii, 800/523-4700, between 9 a.m. and 8 p.m., or by writing to: National Solar Heating and Cooling Information Center, P.O. Box 1607, Rockville, MD, 20850.

ENERGY EFFICIENCY OF APPLIANCES
Government Prepares to Require Data on Labels

The long campaign to get appliance manufacturers to label their products with information about energy efficiency was coming to a climax in late 1979, four years after a law requiring such action.

The Federal Trade Commission (FTC) proposed such a rule in 1978 and held public hearings the same year. One purpose was to give buyers an indication of relative costs of operating various types of major home appliances. For a number of products, fuel costs have become bigger factors than original prices in total lifetime costs. Another purpose of the rule is to help the nation conserve energy.

Originally, the FTC wanted to cover 13 types of products: refrigerator-freezers, freezers, dishwashers, clothes washers, furnaces, room air conditioners, water heaters, television sets, clothes dryers, ranges and ovens, humidifiers, dehumidifiers and heating equipment other than furnaces. But the agency later decided to exclude all products in the above list after water heaters because such labeling was neither technologically nor economically feasible.

For most other types of appliances, the FTC proposed an "Energy Guide" label in yellow indicating the annual range of energy costs and the estimated an-

ENERGY COST OF 48 HOUSEHOLD APPLIANCES

Appliance	Average Wattage	Av. Hours Per Year	KWH Hours Per Year	Av. Cost (1) Per Year
Air Cleaner	50	4320	216	$ 12.96
Air Conditioner	566	887	1398	83.34
Blanket	177	831	147	8.42
Blender	386	39	15	.90
Broiler	1436	69	100	6.00
Clock	2	8500	17	1.02
Clothes Dryer	4856	204	993	59.58
Coffeemaker	894	119	106	6.36
Dehumidifier	257	1467	377	22.62
Dishwasher (2)	1201	302	363	21.78
Fan, Attic	370	786	291	17.46
Fan, Circulating	88	489	43	2.58
Fan, Window	200	850	170	10.20
Freezer, 15 cu. ft.	440	4002	1761	105.66
Freezer, Frostless, 15 cu. ft.	440	4002	1761	105.66
Frying pan	1196	157	188	11.28
Hair dryer	381	37	14	1.04
Heater, Portable	1322	133	176	10.56
Heating pad	65	154	10	.60
Hot plate	1257	72	90	5.40
Humidifier	177	921	163	9.78
Iron, Hand	1008	143	144	8.64
Mixer	127	102	13	.78
Oven, Microwave	1500	200	300	18.00
Oven, Self-Cleaning	4800	239	1146	68.76
Radio	71	1211	86	5.16
Radio/Record player	109	1000	109	6.54
Range	8200	128	1175	70.50
Refrigerator, 12 cu. ft.	241	3021	728	43.68
Refrigerator, Frostless, 12 cu. ft.	321	31	1217	73.02
Refrigerator/Freezer, 14 cu. ft.	326	3488	1137	68.22
Refrigerator/Freezer, frostless, 14 cu. ft.	615	2974	1829	109.74
Roaster	1333	154	205	12.30
Sewing machine	75	147	11	.66
Shaver	14	129	2	.12
Sun lamp	279	57	16	.96
Toaster	1146	34	39	2.34
Toothbrush	7	7	1	.06
Trash compacter	400	125	50	3.00
TV, B&W	237	1527	362	21.72
TV, Color	332	1512	502	30.12
Vacuum cleaner	630	73	46	2.76
Waffle iron	1116	20	22	1.32
Washing Machine, automatic (2)	521	198	103	6.18
Washing Machine, nonautomatic (2)	286	266	76	4.58
Waste disposer	445	67	30	1.80
Water heater	2475	1705	4219	253.14
Water heater, quick recovery	4474	1075	4811	288.66

(1) At 6 cents per KWH (kilowatts per hour). (2) Does not include hot-water heating.

nual cost for each model. It would also show estimated costs at different costs per unit of fuel.

For air conditioners, furnaces and other home heating or cooling equipment, the FTC would allow an alternate system indicating only energy efficiency ratings, not costs, largely because efficiency varies so much by geography and climate. Air conditioners already are labeled according to energy efficiency ratings.

The FTC is expected to make the rules apply to appliances manufactured in 1980 and beyond.

WHERE TO COMPLAIN

Here are some sources for action on complaints regarding appliances:

—**Major Appliance Consumer Action Panel (MACAP)**, 20 North Wacker Drive, Chicago, IL, 60606, 312/236-3165. A panel of non-industry individuals helps settle disputes in cases where the consumer has already contacted the manufacturer and is dissatisfied with the result.

—**Whirlpool Corporation**, 800/253-1301; in Michigan, 800/632-2243. This 24-hour, toll-free number provides consumer assistance on all Whirlpool products, including complaints, locations of nearby service centers and questions on warranties and product operation.

—**Westinghouse Appliance Service**, 800/245-0600, in Pennsylvania 800/242-0580. This 24-hour toll-free number handles consumer complaints not satisfactorily resolved through local dealers and service centers. Local authorized service centers can be located through this number.

—**Maytag Corporation**, in Iowa, Missouri, Oklahoma, South Dakota and Wyoming only: 800/228-9445. Handles complaints and questions regarding parts and service for Maytag appliances. In other states, contact your nearest Maytag service representative, or company headquarters: 403 West 4th St. N., Newton, Iowa 50208, 515/792-7000.

—**Admiral Corporation**, 309/827-0002. This number handles basic consumer complaints for major appliances and questions regarding authorized service centers.

—**General Electric Company**, Major Appliance Group, Appliance Park, Louisville, KY, 40225, 502/452-3248. For problems not solvable by local GE service centers, write to the customer relations director at the above address. The phone number listed is not toll-free.

—**Sears Roebuck**, According to company policy, the customer service department of the nearest store is responsible for customer satisfaction, regardless of where the appliance was originally purchased. The nearest store policy also applies to purchases made through the catalogue.

YOUR PUBLIC UTILITY COMMISSION
How to Make it Work for You

What a PUC does. A state public utility commission is charged with the regulation of electric companies, gas companies, water companies, phone companies, taxis, trucking lines, railroads, airlines that fly only within a state, and other carriers that transport people or property. In some states a public utility commission may also regulate firms transporting gas, oil, petroleum or other fluids by pipeline; sewage collection, treatment and disposal; and other businesses.

There are exceptions. For example, in Pennsylvania, cooperative associations which furnish utility services only to their own members or stockholders are not under PUC regulation. Nor are rates charged by municipally owned utilities, except those to customers served beyond their corporate limits.

Your state may have similar exceptions. If you are in doubt about the responsibility of your state PUC, write for a copy of its laws and its most recent publications and annual report.

Letters of complaint can help. You can often get action with an informal complaint to your state PUC or to the utility itself. An informal complaint is nothing more than a letter or phone call setting out your problem and suggesting what you want done.

One way to get action from a utility is to go over the head of those you believe are treating you unfairly. For example, if you can't get a utility employee to properly explain your bill, ask for his supervisor or write directly to the president of the utility.

Another possibility on a major problem is to write to your state senator or representative or your U.S. Senator or Congressman. They may only forward your letter to the utility but they can also ride herd on those responsible for replying to you. Some bureaucrats pay more attention to complaints coming from elected officials than from ordinary consumers.

You may also write your state PUC for help. You may want to find out the names of those on the PUC or just send to the PUC itself or the Counsel of the PUC. (In some states the PUC is an independent commission with three or five members, for example. In other states it may have a single head and be a part of the Executive Branch.)

In writing a complaint letter on almost any subject, the same rules apply. Include full details in your letter and attach any supporting documents that will be useful in understanding your problem. Then indicate what action you want. Keep carbons of all correspondence. A good record will make it easier to follow up on your complaint and force action if you do not get an acceptable response.

Consider a formal complaint on rates when you feel unfairly treated. Any good public utility law gives you the right to file a complaint about the rates you are being charged by a utility. Typically, if the PUC finds the rates charged are unjust, unreasonable or in any way in violation of the law, it may order new rates. You may complain about individual treatment or about a rate schedule in general. You can usually file a formal complaint anytime a utility asks for a rate increase. When you file a formal complaint, you probably will then be entitled to participate in the rate hearing by calling your own witnesses and cross-examining those of the utilities. Even without filing a formal complaint, you can attend hearings and testify on a rate increase.

How to get your utility to do some free work for you. If you think your utility bill is too high, don't hesitate to ask the utility for a recheck. You may want your meter checked in the case of an electric or gas utility. You can also ask the utility to analyze your usage. The utility may then be able to identify the appliances or other uses that makes your bill so high. For example, the utility may check your wiring or equipment to see if they are wasting electricity. The utility can also check your meter. Many utilities charge for inspecting a meter, unless it proves to be defective. Some services, such as an analysis of usage, may be rendered without a charge. Check with your utility and see what service it offers.

Don't forget other agencies and organizations that can help. There are many other government agencies that can help you with a problem related to utilities. The U.S. Department of Energy in Washington has responsibilities relating to such things as transportation of natural gas and interstate electrical matters. If a utility is suspected of polluting, you may want to complain to the environmental protection agency of your state or the nearest office of the U.S. Environmental Protection Agency.

County and city consumer affairs agencies can also help, as well as non-government consumer organizations. Other organizations that can help are listed in chapters in this book on government sources of help and non-government sources of help.

Learn the kinds of problems other consumers have with utilities. Here are some examples of consumer complaints about utilities and possible remedies:

● A utility shuts off or threatens the shut-off of service. Customers can often work these disputes out by agreeing to pay past due accumulations of bills in installments. If there is a good reason for not paying the bill, you should file an informal or formal complaint with the PUC. A formal complaint can request a stay order pending completion of hearings on the matter. Many low-income customers go to groups such as Legal Aid and Community Legal Services to get help on this and other types of complaints.

● Customers frequently complain because they simply do not understand their bills. One major source of misunderstanding is the fuel-adjustment clause which allows utilities to raise their rates to reflect the increasing cost of fuel. Most utilities have done a poor job of explaining it to the public, and some may have abused it. The fuel-adjustment clause is under examination on a number of grounds.

● Customers complain when they suspect their bill is excessive or mistaken. There are many sources of possible error such as defective meters, other faulty equipment, misreading of a meter and outright error in billing. Insist on a good explanation from the company and then consider a formal or informal complaint to the PUC.

● A utility may force property owners to sell property needed for construction of new facilities or right-of-ways. When this power of condemnation is exercised, it is subject to supervision and review by the PUC and the courts. A property owner may feel he is not properly compensated or that the utility is being arbitrary in condemning his property rather than using some alternative possibility.

One way to learn about utilities is to read a 112-page book published by the Environmental Action Foundation called "How to Challenge Your Local Electric Utility." It is written by Richard Morgan and Sandra Jerabek, sells for $3.50 and can be obtained from EAF, 724 Dupont Circle Building, Washington, DC 20036.

Excerpted from a publication by Herbert S. Denenberg, former consumer advisor to the Governor of Pennsylvania.

Environmental Hazards

In This Chapter
- **Index of Pollutants**
- **Industrial Waste**
- **Ratings of Nuclear Plants**
- **Radiation Hazards**
- **Water, Air and Noise Pollution**
- **Most Dangerous Products**
- **Pesticides, Plants and Flowers**

Since "Earth Day" in 1970, Americans have become increasingly concerned about pollution and other hazards that threaten all forms of life to some extent here and abroad. Some have called it an "Environmental Revolution" because of the vast changes in public attitudes and values. Suddenly, many Americans are beginning to have doubts about the technology and material growth that they have always taken for granted.

The biggest event of the decade was passage of the National Environmental Policy Act in 1969 with its requirement for environmental impact statements before major projects of the government are begun. As a result, many policies have been altered and some programs and projects dropped altogether because of their adverse effects on nature.

But many decisions regarding the environment are still being debated. Although important progress has been attained in almost all fields, those who must pay the initial costs are continuing to resist on nearly every front. Continued growth of the population and economy have added to the problems of pollution and hazardous products.

NEW WORRIES ABOUT RADIATION AND CANCER
A serious accident at a nuclear power plant near Harrisburg, PA, in 1979 suddenly put nuclear radiation high on the list of concerns. Although a core meltdown was narrowly averted, the uncontrolled release of radioactive gases and the resulting evacuation of many people raised new doubts about nuclear power and the safety standards for it. Public polls showed a substantial drop in public approval of nuclear power and deep fears where virtually none had existed before.

While effects of the accidental radiation may not be known for decades, evidence disclosed in 1979 indicated especially high rates of cancer among residents of Utah who had been exposed to fallout from numerous bomb tests there in the 1950s. In addition, studies of workers at nuclear facilities showed excessive rates of cancer, particularly leukemia, from relatively low levels of exposure. The new data suggested that long-standing exposure limits were much too high.

MEASURING ENVIRONMENTAL PROGRESS
Looking at all the changes in the past 10 years, does the record show substantial progress against pollution and other assaults on the natural habitat? Ac-

cording to the National Wildlife Federation, which issues a yearly report on such things, little has changed for the better. Of the seven areas assessed in 1979, only air quality was higher than it was ten years earlier. The status of land, minerals, wildlife, living space and water were all reported lower, while the forestry situation was unchanged.

The following includes some excerpts from the Federation's 1979 Environmental Quality Index:

WILDLIFE INDEX: Down From 55 to 43

Inadequacy of wildlife protection is reflected in the rise in number of endangered species, from 89 in 1969 to 192 in 1979.

Major steps in preserving wildlife have been the setting aside of some 30 million acres by the Wildlife Refuge System. This amount could double after adding the 2 million acres of wetlands acquired by the government and the new park lands in Alaska.

AIR INDEX: Up From 35 to 36

The nation's air may be cleaner by a few puffs of smoke than a decade ago, but it is still unfit to breathe in many places, according to the Wildlife Federation. New York City, Chicago, Philadelphia, Los Angeles, Cleveland and Pittsburgh head the list of such places. Among the nation's largest 105 urban areas, only Honolulu has what the Environmental Protection Agency calls "clean air."

Almost 90 per cent of major factories now comply with anti-pollution laws regarding air. But in 1979, EPA eased its smog (ozone) limit from .08 parts per million to .12 ppm because of pressure from industry groups.

SOIL INDEX: Down From 80 to 70

As the nation's demand for agriculture steadily increased over the past decade, the total amount of harvestable land decreased substantially due to soil erosion.

The U.S. Soil Conservation Service estimates that 180 million acres of cropland are affected by wind and water erosion at a cost of $1 billion each year despite extensive conservation programs.

In 10 years, 17 million rural areas were lost to highways, shopping centers and parking lots.

MINERALS INDEX: From 50 to 37

As resources dwindle, prices rise. The effect of dwindling minerals was felt sharply with the Arab oil embargo in 1973 and also in 1979, with new increases in oil prices by producing nations. While skyrocketing fuel prices are having a profound effect on society, many people are continuing to use fuel as if nothing has changed.

The day of reckoning is fast approaching when many more people will be buying fuel-efficient cars, cutting back on driving, using mass transportation more and turning home thermostats down even further.

Americans continue to throw away about two-thirds of everything they produce.

FORESTS INDEX: No Change in 10 Years

Most of the conflicts over use of the nation's forests have not been resolved.

But new laws ensure better balance between logging and recreation. Clear cutting is being more closely regulated, and restrictions on logging are likely to produce cleaner waterways and better fishing in many areas.

LIVING SPACE INDEX: Down From 60 to 46

In the last 10 years, millions of acres have been taken over for factories, houses and schools without effective planning for land use. Only nine states have adopted comprehensive land-use plans, and six states have developed plans for zoning and managing fragile coastal areas. Two dozen others have similar plans.

Highway construction has dropped and roadside litter and solid waste have been reduced significantly in seven states which have banned throwaway beverage containers. Meanwhile, concern is growing about the rising mounds of solid waste.

WATER INDEX: From 40 to 33

Water pollution remains the largest environmental problem. Virtually every stream, river, lake and estuary in the country is polluted. Progress has been limited, especially on the state level where the principal confrontations exist. Some standards are set too high to be practical, while others are only voluntary.

Approximately 50,000 industrial plants still flush their wastes directly into municipal sewers, and 2,600 towns and cities still dump raw sewage into lakes and streams.

Although some improvements have been made, most notably in the Delaware and Susquehanna Rivers and 50 other major bodies of water, almost half of the lakes above 2,000 feet in the Adirondack Mountains no longer have any fish because of "acid rain" borne by air from polluted urban areas hundreds of miles away.

By 1979, many people were growing alarmed by the amount of toxic wastes, which can enter public water supplies through seepage from burial sites. Much of the new attention stemmed from discovery of serious health effects among residents of the Love Canal area of Niagara Falls, NY, leading to mass evacuation of the area, largely at government expense.

The danger of getting cancer from drinking water also appears to be growing, as more and more carcinogens are found in public water supplies.

INDUSTRIAL WASTES
Serious Health Problems Come to the Surface

For almost two decades, officials of the Hooker Chemical Company approved of the dumping of highly toxic wastes at Love Canal in Niagara Falls, NY, but did nothing to notify residents of the dangers. In 1953, homes and a school playground were built on the land, still with no warning given.

Then in the spring of 1978, the whole mess bubbled to the surface. In response to inquiries and complaints of toxic funes and exploding rocks, the New York State Health Department found numerous serious health problems. They included high rates of birth defects, miscarriages, leukemia and other ailments, such as red blisters known as the "Hooker Bumps." Authorities identified more than 100 toxic chemicals—including mercury, chlorine and pesticides—oozing from the ground.

News stories drew nationwide attention to the bizarre scene and dramatized a problem that few had considered to be so widespread before. Eventually, residents of Love Canal were ordered to move away at the expense of the state. President Carter declared an official emergency so that federal funds would also be used to help clean up the area and assist in the resettling of 235 families. Later, another dump three times larger with similar wastes from Hooker was found near the city's water treatment plant. And it was learned that still other areas in Niagara County were contaminated by waste materials from Hooker.

32,000 WASTE DUMPS IN U.S.

When asked why the company had not notified residents and workers of the dangers, executives said they had feared "substantial legal liability." When a Congressional committee requested copies of a 1968 study of ground water contamination in Michigan by the company, executives at first said they did not know what was in the study, then refused to hand over a copy. Hooker, now a subsidiary of Occidental Petroleum, was not unusual in its disposal practices or efforts to keep them secret.

Love Canal is only one of some 32,000 industrial waste dumps in the United States, including 1,200 which are considered substantial threats to public health. Even more serious than the danger of direct human contact with industrial poisons is the danger of water contamination. This hazard is greatest when heavy rains cause a polluted liquid called leachate to flow from such sites into sources of drinking water. One dump near Islip, New York, polluted a billion gallons of ground water.

Yet Hooker and other companies violated no laws and may not have to pay a very large share of the costs of evacuation, cleanup and medical bills, despite an influx of damage suits. Most of the cost will be borne by state and federal taxpayers. That is because few companies have the funds to foot the entire bill and responsibility may not be easy to establish in all cases.

The fact is that it has been, and still is, cheaper for a company to bury its dangerous waste materials or dump them into public waterways than to have them treated or shipped away for proper disposal. That is also why toxic wastes will continue to turn up in sewers, swamps, playgrounds, backyards and drinking water supplies. EPA estimates that 90 per cent of hazardous wastes is currently being handled in ways that do not meet minimum health standards.

400 EXAMPLES OF DAMAGE REPORTED

The agency has listed over 400 cases of damage to health or the environment due to improper hazardous waste management. Among the more recently discovered are:

● In Coventry, Rhode Island, officials found an illegal and highly toxic dump on a pig farm. Wastes included carbon tetrachloride—known to cause cancer—and another toxic compound that could ignite at only 80 degrees Fahrenheit.

● A disposal site used by a chemical company was found about 400 feet from a residential area in Elkton, Maryland. Reports from residents included complaints of sore throats, respiratory problems and headaches.

● In 1964, Velsicol—a Chicago-based chemical company—built a pesticide disposal facility in Meldon, Tennessee. Neighbors' well water became contaminated three years later, but it wasn't until 1972 that the dump was closed. When EPA investigators tested the water in 1978, they found that it contained 2,400 times the amount of carbon tetrachloride considered "safe."

● The owner of a New York company pleaded guilty in 1978 to federal charges of spilling polychlorinated biphenyls (PCBs) along 211 miles of roads in eastern and central North Carolina. PCBs, which are commonly used in electrical insulation, cause skin and internal disorders in humans and have been linked to birth defects and cancer in laboratory animals.

● EPA found a 93-acre industrial landfill site in a residential area of Jacksonville, Arkansas, where deadly pesticide waste had been dumped for 30 years. The landfill, which was part of a pesticide plant complex owned by the Vertac Corporation, contained high levels of dioxin, a highly lethal compound that causes severe reproductive defects in laboratory animals and is suspected of causing human miscarriages. The chemical was used by the United States in the Vietnam War in the manufacturing of a defoliant known as "Agent Orange." It has been linked to a high incidence of liver cancer in South Vietnam.

GOVERNMENT SLOW TO IMPLEMENT LAW

Despite mounting reports of serious waste disposal hazards, the government has not formed a clear-cut policy to deal with the problem. The Resource Conservation Act of 1976, which was set up to control the disposal of hazardous solid wastes not covered under the Federal Water Pollution Control Act or the Atomic Energy Act of 1954, was to be promulgated by April, 1978. Due to various delays and industry opposition, EPA does not expect to carry out its goals until 1980 or later. Under the 1976 Act, EPA is authorized to test and identify hazardous materials, regulate hazardous substances from point of generation through disposal, take inventories of disposal sites, and provide financial and technical assistance to state and local governments to set up solid waste management programs.

One criticism of EPA's testing procedures has been that they are too broad, leading to too stringent requirements for even low-hazard materials. In May, 1979, for example, the Senate Environment and Public Works Committee voted to exempt the crude oil industry from proposed EPA regulations because materials from oil drilling, such as mud and brine, were said to be nonhazardous.

INDUSTRY CLEAN-UP FUND PROPOSED

Money for cleanup purposes is small compared to the size of the problem. In 1979, only $71.9 million was appropriated to carry out the Resource Conservation and Recovery Act. Yet EPA estimates the cost of cleaning up abandoned hazardous waste dumps could total $5 billion. To try to solve the problem, President Carter and several Congressmen introduced legislation that would establish a special fund from oil and chemical producers for cleaning up hazardous waste dumps and oil spills. Under the administration's bill, companies would be required to contribute up to $600 million annually, with half of the money for correcting abandoned sites and half for operating new sites.

The best ways to lessen the environmental damage from waste disposal, according to the Council on Environmental Quality, are to generate less waste and to recover and reuse valuable resources from wastes. Through the establishment of information exchanges or clearinghouses on wastes available from industrial firms, companies can buy and trade wastes for reuse. Examples of such tradings are clean acid wastes to be used for pickling, fertilizer manufacturing, and electroplating; alkali wastes for scrubbing and acid neutralization; and specialty wastes containing valuable metals. Since 1977, when the model St. Louis Industrial Waste Exchanged opened, about 15 more exchanges have been set up.

Another future strategy set by EPA is to require the 40,000 industrial plants across the country to "pretreat" their wastes to remove chemicals that cannot be treated adequately by municipal treatment plants. During 1979, EPA set pretreatment standards for 21 industries, including chemical plants and petroleum refining companies.

ENFORCEMENT EFFORTS CRITICIZED

Success in cleaning up hazardous waste dumps and waterways depends to a large extent on EPA's enforcement capabilities. But in 1978, the General Accounting Office said the agency has not been very successful in enforcing permits issued to industrial facilities to discharge wastewater into rivers and streams. "About 55 per cent of the 165 permittees failed to comply with one or more discharge limits during a 15-month period," the report said. The GAO added that EPA's enforcement procedures are lacking in timeliness and strength. Previous enforcement methods included referring violators to the Justice Department and/or barring them from receiving Federal contracts, grants or loans. A more efficient method, according to the GAO, would consist of warning letters, telephone calls, administrative orders and notices of violations.

EPA also needs tougher enforcement investigators, said James W. Moorman, assistant attorney general. He said EPA has only about 30 to 50 enforcement people working nationwide on hazardous wastes. "These investigators are needed not only to identify sites and their contents, and owners and operators and former owners and operators; they are also needed to ferret out the elements of organized crime that are alleged to be involved with hazardous waste pollution." Moorman said the FBI will help EPA investigate hard-to-document chemical dumping cases.

CITIZEN GROUPS BECOME INTERESTED

In an effort to increase public awareness of the waste disposal problem, various environmental organizations have joined in a Waste Alert campaign. They include the American Public Health Association, Environmental Action Foundation, National Wildlife Federation, League of Women Voters Education Fund and Izaak Walton League of America. They plan to alert citizens to solid and hazardous waste issues through regional conferences, state and local workshops and public information activities.

A similar program is Waste Watch of the Technical Information Project, a national citizens organizing group specializing in resource conservation. The organization arranges and conducts workshops, seminars and strategy sessions for citizen leaders concerned with national and regional waste problems.

Environmental groups have brought some progress in the battle against hazardous dumping procedures. In Poughkeepsie, New York, for example, an educational campaign prompted by the New York Public Interest Research Group led to public support for removing toxic chemicals from the city water supply with the help of a $200,000 activated carbon filtration system.

TRANSPORTING HAZARDOUS MATERIALS
No Place Safe From Sudden Disaster

Public concern about the transportation of hazardous materials increased dramatically in 1979 as a result of the nuclear accident at Three Mile Island on March 28 and the train wreck near Crestview, FL, on April 8.

Routine shipment of nuclear wastes suddenly became a national controversy when the governor of South Carolina, the principal dumping ground for the nation's radioactive wastes, refused to accept a shipment from Three Mile Island. When trucks carrying the materials started moving to another site, in Washington state, across midwestern states, several state officials protested publicly. They complained that no permission to transport the dangerous cargo had been asked or given. But transportation was not interrupted, because state officials found they had no authority to stop it. Only a few places have sought to block such shipments or have them rerouted around heavily populated areas. One is New York City, which passed an ordinance in 1976 prohibiting shipments of radioactive materials through the main part of the city. In May, 1979, the Illinois Senate banned the importation of used nuclear fuel from other states.

In Florida, many of the 116 cars were derailed on a curve, causing cars containing anhydrous ammonia to explode, cars with acetone, alcohol and liquid sulfur to burn and other cars to leak dangerous substances. Approximately 4,500 people were evacuated from the area but few were injured. Damage was estimated at more than $1 million.

INCREASING NUMBER OF DANGEROUS SHIPMENTS

The wreck was typical of accidents becoming more frequent because of increasing shipments of hazardous cargoes over antiquated track. Truck transport also often involves deadly materials. Another worry is liquified petroleum gas.

Increased amounts of hazardous substances are also shipped via planes. Radioactive metals such as uranium ore and plutonium were once carried in cargo compartments of regularly scheduled passenger flights, but that practice was recently stopped, due largely to the efforts of the Air Line Pilots Association.

Shipments of uranium have also been halted by a number of airports, including O'Hare Airport at Chicago, which became the center of uranium shipments between the U.S. and Europe after New York City banned transport of nuclear materials through that city's streets in 1975.

But the largest problems on the basis of number of tons and miles involved are gasoline and fuel oil. They account for more than half of the 218,000 million ton-miles of hazardous materials transported each year in this country. In 1978, there were 18,022 accidents reported with such materials, a 19 per cent increase over the year before. The number of incidents has increased steadily in recent years, along with deaths, injuries and property damage.

Congress has also become concerned. In April, 1979, the Senate Commerce Committee held hearings to consider a report done by the Library of Congress at the Committee's request. The report cited the growing degree of hazards and questioned whether the government or industries involved were doing enough to protect the public. It noted that the Materials Transportation Bureau in the Department of Transportation had only six full-time inspectors to oversee 20,000 container manufacturers and 100,000 shippers of hazardous goods.

Government agencies also "do not take vigorous enforcement action," said the study. Average penalties, it said, ranged from only $304 for the Coast Guard to $2,541 for the Federal Aviation Administration for violations of regulations. The maximum allowed is $10,000. "Small penalities," the report continued, "are unlikely to have much effect on industry activities."

Testimony at a 1978 Senate investigation revealed that some of the worst accidents could have been avoided if tank cars met safety standards established in September, 1977.

FEW TANK CARS HAVE SAFETY COUPLERS

Philip Hogue, a member of the National Transportation Safety Board (NTSB), told a Senate subcommittee that although NTSB had been pushing for safety measures on tank cars for eight years, little had been accomplished. He said only a few of the 18,000 cars had been fitted with safety shelf couplers and headshields that could protect tank cars from being punctured during derailments. Pressurized tank cars with extra-size capacity of 33,000 gallons are susceptible to overriding during derailment or collision when the coupler of the adjacent car punctures the end of the tank, releasing the contents.

Rail-car owners were sharply criticized at the hearings for not spending the $2,000 per car necessary to add safety equipment. Ninety-eight per cent of tank cars are owned not by financially hard-pressed railroads but by large corporations and wealthy individuals who purchased the cars for investment and tax advantages. The 11 largest tank car operators had more than $50 billion in revenues in 1977.

Tank car owners asked for a four-year schedule for fitting cars with the safety equipment, saying it would take from 45 to 60 days to refit each of the older cars. But NTSB found that it took only 7 1/2 minutes to remove an old coupler and install a new shelf coupler and about 93 minutes to weld on a head shield.

Nearly all other forms of transportation have run into problems with hazardous materials. Tanker ships have become sources of massive oil spills. Such problems intensified in 1977 with the wreck of the Liberian freighter Argo Merchant off the coast of Nantucket—the worst oil spill off an American coast—and the largest oil spill in history, the wreck of the Amoco Cadiz off the French Brittany coast in 1978. About 10,000 oil spills occur off the U.S. coast annually, but 80 per cent involve less than 100 gallons. Not counted are leaks from improperly cared-for pipelines, valves and storage tanks that lose millions of gallons of oil and chemicals over the course of a year.

RECYCLING SOLID WASTE

Solid waste is becoming an increasing problem in the United States, especially because of the hugh volume of beverage bottles and cans as well as plastic containers. Many communities are running out of space to dump the growing pile of non-biodegradable materials, adding to the pressure to ban "throwaway" containers. An increasing number of states have approved of such bans, but industry forces have slowed down the move, which began auspiciously in Oregon.

Business opposition has succeeded in bottling up such legislation every time it has popped up in Congress.

To date, Oregon, Vermont, Michigan, South Dakota and Maine have adopted mandatory deposit laws. Washington, California, Colorado, Virginia and Maine have instituted statutes against litter. A mandatory deposit law passed by the Connecticut legislature in March, 1978, will go into effect in 1980.

At the same time, Congress began in 1978 to debate a national mandatory deposit system, although passage of such a bill is considered unlikely at this time. The bill came on the wake of a General Accounting Office study that found that a national system of mandatory deposits would substantially reduce litter and solid waste as well as reduce industry packaging costs.

Not mentioned in the GAO report are reduced energy costs resulting from the increased use of refillable containers. In the first two years after a mandatory deposit system took effect in Oregon, some 1.4 trillion BTUs were reported saved each year, enough to provide the home heating needs for 50,000 Oregonians or generate 130 million kilowatt hours of electricity worth $2.8 million annually.

Recycling of glass, metals and paper is increasing, and recycling centers are growing in number, as individuals realize the potential profits from recycling.

SEWAGE RECYCLING GIVEN BOOST

Provisions included in the Clean Water Act of 1977 made federal funds available to cities for turning sewage into valuable resources and cleansing the local water supply in the process. Such a system now operates in Muskegon, Michigan, where partially treated waste water is sprayed over 10,000 acres of corn crop. The water irrigates the crop. The "pollutants" in the water, nitrogen and phosphorus, fertilize it. The soil and corn in turn cleanse the water, which is captured in drains beneath the soil and returned to its source, clean and fresh.

In some recycling systems, revenues received from crop sales (or, in the case of Muskegon, for animal feed), have reduced operating costs, leading to lower sewer bills for residential consumers. Such systems also reduce the amount of sludge—consisting of pollution cleaned from treated waters—that must be somehow disposed of. Another advantage of alternative systems is that they use less water and energy.

HAZARDS OF NUCLEAR POWER
Chain Reactions Raise Public Fears

The year 1979 was a turning point for nuclear power, as a series of dramatic events suddenly sent public concern soaring like a mushroom cloud.

The biggest event was one that industry and government officials had repeatedly said would never happen, the accidental loss of control of a nuclear power reactor at Three Mile Island near Harrisburg, PA, on March 28. No one knows exactly how much radiation was released to the surrounding countryside, because there were few monitors to measure levels. Several days later, pregnant women and children were asked to leave the area indefinitely by Governor Richard Thornburgh when it became apparent that the core of the reactor had been badly damaged and many people had been exposed unknowingly to escaping radiation.

The accident became especially newsworthy because of a new movie, "The China Syndrome," which portrayed a fictional accident of the same kind. The movie aroused controversy even before it was released on March 16 to public theaters. Weeks before, Columbia Pictures was accused of making a "ridiculous" film with "no scientific credibility," in the words of one utility executive. The movie was released just after the Nuclear Regulatory Commission (NRC) had ordered the shutdown of five nuclear plants because of defects that might be dangerous in case of an earthquake.

ACCIDENT CHANGED PUBLIC ATTITUDES

The accident at Three Mile Island and the daily headlined mystery about whether the core would melt completely or a hydrogen bubble would explode became one of the biggest news stories of the year. It created doubts in the minds of many people who had previously either been neutral or supportive of nuclear power. Tapes of NRC meetings revealed that neither NRC members nor utility executives knew exactly what was going on or what to do about it for several days after a combination of human errors and mechanical malfunctions had created the crisis.

The accident also helped turn the nuclear issue from a local one to a national one. So did a massive rally of some 100,000 nuclear critics in Washington, DC, on May 6. The rally represented the first organized effort to reverse the nation's commitment to nuclear power. Although demands for a shutdown of all nuclear plants fell on deaf ears at the White House and Department of Energy, rally leaders managed to get President Carter to express new concern and Senator Edward M. Kennedy to urge new safeguards before opening any more plants. Governor Jerry Brown of California, an outspoken critic of nuclear power, used the rally to increase the political pressure on Carter to reverse the U.S. policy of continuing to expand the nation's reliance on nuclear.

Adding further to the negative publicity was a court award of $10.5 million to the family of Karen Silkwood on May 17 in Oklahoma City. Relatives of the young nuclear worker at the Kerr-McGee Co. had sued the company on the grounds that it had been negligent in allowing her to become extremely radioactive. She had died mysteriously in a one-car crash while allegedly on her way to give information to reporters about plant conditions. The jury decision was seen widely as a major blow to the nuclear industry and a rejection of federal radiation standards of safety.

DEBATE GROWS AROUND NUCLEAR HAZARDS

These events increased public discussion of nuclear issues, particularly:

● Radiation exposure to workers at nuclear plants and to people residing and working near such plants. Until Three Mile Island, serious incidents of exposure had been infrequent within nuclear plants and rare outside them. But evidence collected over many years and surfacing in 1979 for the first time indicated that the risk of getting cancer eventually from small amounts of radiation were far greater than previously assumed by government and industry standards. (See section on radiation hazards elsewhere in this chapter.)

● Radiation exposure because of transportation accidents involving nuclear materials. An example of this problem occurred in May, 1979, when a tractor-trailer loaded with radioactive wastes caught fire at Beatty, NV, 110 miles northwest of Las Vegas. Eighteen people, including 12 volunteer firemen, became exposed to radiation from the smoking materials.

● Radiation from exposure to nuclear wastes. For 30 years, the government has been trying unsuccessfully to find a safe and economical means of disposing of atomic waste materials. Meanwhile, radioactive wastes continue to pile up in hugh amounts, some in makeshift burial grounds that have contaminated nearby land and ground water. Some wastes will be radioactive hazards to health for 50,000 years.

● Risk of terrorism and sabotage. Security at nuclear plants has not been sufficient to prevent some incidents of sabotage, but it has prevented any serious attempt to commit nuclear blackmail. As long as the possibility remains, however, safeguards must be taken to prevent it, and people will consider this one of the major hazards of nuclear power.

EVACUATION PLANS DUSTED OFF

The Pennsylvania accident stirred up new interest in plans for evacuating people living or working near nuclear plants. For many years, the NRC and its predecessor agencies tried to get nuclear licensees to develop such plans with little success. It set up detailed requirements which no plant was willing or able to meet. So the agency whittled them down to the bare minimum but still found few takers. Pennsylvania had typical reactions. It submitted an evacuation plan in 1975, but it was not approved. The state never returned with an improved plan and indicated that it was not interested in conforming to federal standards, according to Harold Collins, NRC's director of emergency preparedness.

The NRC itself was prodded the same year by the Public Interest Research Group (PIRG) to require an approved evacuation plan before granting an operating license for a nuclear plant. PIRG also recommended that regular tests be conducted and the public be informed fully. PIRG's petition was rejected by the Commission.

In May, 1979, PIRG renewed its petition. Along with 14 other citizen groups, it said recent events had made the matter more urgent. It asked the NRC not only to impose new standards for evacuating people but to require regular monitoring of radiation at intervals as far as 50 miles from nuclear plants. The groups also asked the NRC to evaluate plant design and performance on a formal basis and require deficient plants to be brought up to standard or be shut down. Public disclosure of radiation hazards as well as complete instructions as to what to do in case of an emergency was emphasized by the petitioners.

ONLY 10 STATES HAVE APPROVED PLANS

The most timely study of the subject was released by the General Accounting Office two days after the Three Mile Island affair. Entitled, *Areas Around Nuclear Facilities Should Be Better Prepared for Radiological Emergencies,* the report recommended that the NRC prohibit nuclear operations where state and local emergency plans did not meet all requirements. It also recommended public drills. "We believe it is better to identify problems in an emergency drill rather than wait until the actual event occurs," said the GAO.

Only 10 of the 43 states with nuclear plants had emergency plans approved by the NRC as of May, 1979, two months after Harrisburg. And only one state,

Oregon, had actually conducted a limited evacuation drill for emergency personnel. The other nine states were Alabama, Arkansas, California, Connecticut, Florida, Iowa, New Jersey, New York, South Carolina and Washington.

INSURANCE PROTECTION ALSO LIMITED

Insurance protection also drew new attention because of the Pennsylvania mishap. Damage suits began to pile up in the billions as if there were no limit on what could be collected. But the Price-Anderson Act imposes a limit of $560 million that can be collected by all victims of a nuclear accident in the country. Insurance companies would have to come up with only $140 million, and nuclear firms would share the next $325, while the federal government would supply the remaining $95 million.

These limits mean that individual victims of even a relatively minor nuclear accident would collect only a small proportion of their losses.

Ralph Nader's Litigation Group has estimated that a homeowner with a $40,000 house would collect only $10,000 in case of total damages of $2.24 billion in a nuclear accident. Claims involving the Harrisburg incident already exceed that figure. In a more serious accident, losses could be nearly 30 times that figure, according to the conservative risk assessment in the so-called *Rasmussen Report*. If losses totaled $22.4 billion, the homeowner would collect only 2.5 per cent of the $50,000 value, not to mention the personal losses.

At present, individuals cannot buy nuclear insurance on their property or life. Not even Lloyds of London will sell insurance against nuclear disaster. The reason: the odds are too great that a disaster will happen. That is why the insurance and nuclear industries lobbied for passage of the Price-Anderson Act. In addition to limiting claims, the act puts a 20-year cutoff on claims, a period far short of what it takes for some cancers to become apparent.

EVALUATING NUCLEAR POWER PLANTS
How Safe Is the Nearest One to You?

More than 20 million Americans now live within 30 miles of a nuclear plant, well within the area that could suffer damaging radiation in case of a serious accident. The safety and performance of these facilities thus can be important to these people.

Until recently, however, such information was virtually impossible to obtain from the government agencies charged with monitoring the industry. In fact, the agencies themselves have done little over the years to evaluate plant performance and design. Thus, when the Three Mile Island accident aroused public interest in such matters, not much information was available.

At a Nuclear Regulatory Commission in Washington, the only public data on plant performance was contained in a thick volume entitled only *Board Notification* dated February, 1979. And the only formal scoring was for the year 1977, when each plant was given a "Z" score on the basis of infractions and deficiencies. The following year, there were no such scores, only informal comments by inspectors. For example, the 1978 evaluation of Three Mile Island's Unit 2, which failed in 1979, said:

"Station and unit superintendents are new. Security has improved. This the first Babcock & Wilcox plant of current generation. Management control during construction was deficient. Management control in operations is strong. Overall site safety may decrease because staff has become diluted with licensing of Unit 2."

Following are performance evaluations done in 1977 and 1978 by the NRC for the 70 privately owned nuclear reactors licensed in the U.S. They are grouped alphabetically by state and within each state. After each plant's name is a figure in parentheses indicating how many reactors the plant has. Also given is the name of the nearest community, the number of people living within 50 miles and the name of the company holding the license to operate. Also shown is the percentage of workers exposed in 1977 to 500 millirems or more of radiation, according to data collected by the Health Research Group. The federal limit is 5 rems per year. The 1977 "Z" score is summarized as either average, below average or above average, as indicated by the NRC. The 1978 performance evaluation is quoted in full from the report. The status of each state's emergency evacuation plan as of May, 1979, is given after the name of each state. The NRC has set minimum standards for such plans but does not require approval before granting a license to operate. Plans "concurred in" by the NRC are in effect approved.

NUCLEAR PLANT RATINGS

ALABAMA (Evacuation plans approved by NRC)

Brown's Ferry (3), Decatur. Population, 50 miles: 630,000; Licensee: Tennessee Valley Authority; Exposure: 12 per cent; 1977 Performance Rating: Out of commission because of fire; 1978 Evaluation: "Attention to quality assurance details has decreased slightly. Greater experience of plant personnel has contributed to improved safety and operations. More NRC inspections and plant management changes have also helped. Response to alarms has improved as a result of an enforcement (meeting). Greater safety awareness. Fire protection improved."

Joseph M. Farley (1), Dothan. Population, 50 miles: 320,000; Licensee: Alabama Power; Exposure: Plant not open; 1977 Performance Rating: Plant not open; 1978 Evaluation: Plant not open.

ARKANSAS (Evacuation plans approved by NRC)

Arkansas One (2), Russellville. Population, 50 miles: 150,000; Licensee: Arkansas Power & Light; Exposure: Unit 1—18 per cent, Unit 2—Plant not open; 1977 Performance Rating: Unit 1—below average, Unit 2—Plant not open; 1978 Performance Rating: "Management control of plant may be diluted when Unit 2 becomes operational. Safety slightly improved by upgrading of cable penetration barriers, fire protection and procedural controls. Technical Specifications should be upgraded to standard levels."

CALIFORNIA (Evacuation plans approved by NRC)

Humboldt Bay (1), Eureka. Population, 50 miles: 100,000; Licensee: Pacific Gas & Electric; Exposure: Not Available; 1977 Performance Rating: below average; 1978 Evaluation: "Safety is substantially improved due to seismic modifications. Other safety-relevent matters are being pursued by nuclear reactor regulation. The plant would be hard pressed to meet current safety criteria."

Rancho Seco (1), Clay Station. Population, 50 miles: 1,382,000; Licensee: Sacramento Municipal Utility; Exposure: 30 per cent; 1977 Performance Rating: average; 1978 Evaluation: "Safety is slightly improved due to increasing operation experience and quality of plant management."

San Onofre (1), San Clemente. Population, 50 miles: 3,600,000; Licensee: Southern California Edison and San Diego Gas & Electric; Exposure: 26 per cent; 1977 Performance Rating: below average; 1978 Evaluation: "Safety is slightly improved because of quality assurance program improvements. Safety is substantially improved because of upgrading of the emergency power system. Utility management has been successful in instilling good safety attitudes and habits uniformly throughout the organization. Extensive emergency core coolant system and seismic modes have been completed."

COLORADO (Evacuation plans not approved by NRC)

Fort St. Vrain (1), Platteville. Population, 50 miles: 1,400,000; Licensee: Public Service of Colorado; Exposure: Plant not open; 1977 Performance Rating: Not rated by statistical method; 1978 Evaluation: "Safety substantially improved due to upgrading of cable separation, fire prevention, training program and operation experience. (There) have been instrumentation improvements. This high temperature gas reactor could be categorized as a demonstration plant. Plant safety characteristics are unique. Existing Tech Specs need revision."

CONNECTICUT (Evacuation plans approved by NRC)

Haddam Neck (1), Haddam Neck. Population, 50 miles: 3,200,000; Licensee: Connecticut Yankee Atomic Power; Exposure: 35 per cent; 1977 Performance Rating: Below average; 1978 Evaluation: "Overall safety should be improved at the completion of ongoing design requirement and license condition upgrading."

Millstone (2), Waterford. Population, 50 miles: 2,500,000; Licensee: Northeast Nuclear Energy; Exposure: Unit 1—13 per cent, Unit 2—13 per cent; 1977 Performance Rating: Unit 1—below average, Unit 2—above average; 1978 Evaluation: "Unit 1, a boiling water reactor, is rated lower than Unit 2. Awareness of safety has increased. The different units operate relatively independently and each has a different vendor. Improved security arrangements. Plant lacks full separation and fire protection systems. Radioactive waste system undersized. New quality assurance organization seems slightly better."

FLORIDA (Evacuation plans approved by NRC)

Crystal River (1), Red Level. Population, 50 miles: 170,000; Licensee: Florida Power; Exposure: Plant not open; 1977 Performance Rating: Not rated by statistical method; 1978 Evaluation: "Safety slightly improved because of more safety awareness. Operations and administrative controls improved."

St Lucie (1), Fort Pierce. Population, 50 miles: 320,000; Licensee: Florida Power & Light; Exposure: 6 per cent; 1977 Performance Rating: Not rated by statistical method; 1978 Evaluation: "Safety has improved due to increased experience of plant personnel. Plant's greater than average of Licensee Event Reports is probably due to conscientiousness in reporting."

Turkey Point (2), Florida City. Population, 50 miles: 1,700,000; Licensee: Florida Power & Light; Exposure: 22 per cent; 1977 Performance Rating: above average; 1978 Evaluation: "Safety may be slightly worse due to steam generator degradation."

GEORGIA (Evacuation plans not approved by NRC)

Edwin I. Hatch (2), Baxley. Population, 50 miles: 250,000; Licensee: Georgia Power; Exposure: Unit 1—17 per cent, Unit 2—Plant not open; 1977 Performance Rating: Unit 1—above average, Unit 2—Plant not open; 1978 Evaluation: "Upgrading of administrative and quality assurance controls is continuing."

ILLINOIS (Evacuation plans not approved by NRC)

Dresden (3), Morris. Population, 50 miles: 6,300,000; Licensee: Commonwealth Edison; Exposure: 29½ per cent; 1977 Performance Rating: above average; 1978 Evaluation: "Training and quality assurance programs have improved. Unit 1, a smaller plant, does not receive the priority attention of Units 2 and 3. Manpower availability is a concern. Safety has improved due to better housekeeping and attention to detail. Safety is substantially worse due to poor operations and instrumentation problems."

Quad Cities (2), Cordova. Population, 50 miles: 670,000; Licensee: Commonwealth Edison and Iowa-Illinois Gas & Electric; Exposure: 23 per cent; 1977 Performance Rating: average; 1978 Evaluation: "Licensee has been "overinspected" by NRC and the state for several years. Plant not permitted by state to operate at design load; this affects operator attitudes. Safety slightly improved because of improvements in the training program, the quality assurance program, and the radiological program."

Zion (2), Zion. Population, 50 miles: 7,000,000; Licensee: Commonwealth Edison; Exposure: 32 percent; 1977 Performance Rating: Unit 1—below average, Unit 2—above average; 1978 Evaluation: "Safety is substantially worse because of poor attitude and marginal management. Inadequate management controls. Management lacks ability to discipline employees for operator errors and carelessness. Personnel selection and discipline may be adversely affected by union relations. Poor management attitude and followups. Size of Commonwealth Edison creates special management problems. Stability of staff a problem. Safety is substantially worse because of failures to conform to Tech Specs and administrative, operating, emergency, and test procedures. Attitude regarding safety is poor. Some improvements in procedures and training."

IOWA (Evacuation plans approved by NRC)

Duane Arnold (1), Palo. Population, 50 miles: 560,000; Licensee: Iowa Electric Light and Power; Exposure: 18 per cent, 1977 Performance Rating: above average; 1978 Evaluation: "Safety slightly improved due to improvements in quality assurance and administrative controls, new plant superintendent, enforcement action and increased inspection effort. Staff is more aware of significance of personnel error. Steady improvements in management controls, competence of staff and attention from corporate office."

MAINE (Evacuation plans not approved by NRC)

Maine Yankee (1), Wiscasset. Population, 50 miles: 360,000; Licensee: Maine Yankee Atomic Power; Exposure: 16 per cent; 1977 Performance Rating:

average; 1978 Evaluation: "The cleanliness of this plant reflects a pride of ownership and indicates happy people working at a good plant. Quality assurance was recently upgraded."

MARYLAND (Evacuation plans not approved by NRC)

Calvert Cliffs (2), Lusby. Population, 50 miles: 2,400,000; Licensee: Baltimore Gas and Electric; Exposure: Unit 1—11 per cent, Unit 2—Plant not open; 1977 Performance Rating: Unit 1—average, Unit 2—Plant not open; 1978 Evaluation: "Management more attentive as a result of enforcement conference. An important staff member is anti-NRC and anti-quality assurance. Security is improved. This site doesn't do more for safety than meet minimum requirements. Emphasis is upon commercial operation; attitude toward safety is that meeting NRC requirements literally is sufficient."

MASSACHUSETTS (Evacuation plans not approved by NRC)

Pilgrim (1), Plymouth. Population, 50 miles: 4,300,000; Licensee: Boston Edison: Exposure: 52 per cent; 1977 Performance Rating: average; 1978 Evaluation: "The generation of its design may be an overriding factor for this early boiling water reactor. Corporate management improved. Radiation management improved. Frequent station manager changes. Significant reductions in effluents and worker exposures expected. Plant management has not been stable. This is the cleanest B.W.R. in the country."

Yankee (1), Rowe. Population, 50 miles: 1,500,000; Licensee: Yankee Atomic Electric; Exposure: 12 per cent; 1977 Performance Rating: average; 1978 Evaluation: "Plant is very small and very isolated. It presents virtually no health hazard to the public. Has old Tech Specs. Upgraded quality assurance program in 1977."

MICHIGAN (Evacuation plans not approved by NRC)

Big Rock Point (1), Big Rock Point. Population, 50 miles: 130,000; Licensee: Consumers Power; Exposure: 33 per cent; 1977 Performance Rating: average; 1978 Evaluation: "Design and operation of this early boiling water reactor are relatively uncomplicated. Plant safety improving due to continuing implementation of quality assurance program and improving technical capability of staff."

Donald C. Cook (2), Bridgman. Population, 50 miles: 1,100,000; Licensee: Indiana & Michigan Electric; Exposure; Unit 1—10 per cent, Unit 2—plant not open; 1977 Performance Rating: Unit 1—below average, Unit 2—Plant not open; 1978 Evaluation: "Plant has standardized Technical Specifications. Resident inspector stationed at site for some time. Plant has had increased personnel and procedural errors in 1977. Safety at Unit 1 is slightly worse because plant personnel and management have diverted attention to Unit 2 startup, fire protection and security. Events are occuring that would not have a year ago."

Palisades (1), South Haven. Population, 50 miles: 1,000,000; Licensee: Consumers Power; Exposure 10 per cent; 1977 Performance Rating: below average; 1978 Evaluation: "Safety is improved as a result of continuing quality assurance program implementation. Management has been more attentive to timely correction of problems. Resident inspector was assigned to site.

MINNESOTA (Evacuation plans not approved by NRC)

Monticello (1), Monticello. Population, 50 miles: 2,000,000; Licensee: Northern States Power; Exposure: 33 per cent; 1977 Performance Rating: below average; 1978 Evaluation; No narrative comments.

Prairie Island (2), Red Wing. Population, 50 miles: 2,100,000; Licensee: Northern States Power; Exposure: 19 per cent; 1977 Performance Rating: Unit 1—below average, Unit 2—average; 1978 Evaluation: "The technical staff is closely integrated with operations and maintenance; this helps prevent safety problems and provides good information."

NEBRASKA (Evacuation plans not approved by NRC)

Cooper (1), Brownville. Population, 50 miles: 170,000; Licensee: Nebraska Public Power and Iowa Power & Light; Exposure: 11 per cent; 1977 Performance Rating: average; 1978 Evaluation: No narrative comments.

Fort Calhoun (1), Fort Calhoun. Population, 50 miles: 710,000; Licensee: Omaha Public Power; Exposure: 31 per cent; 1977 Performance Rating: average; 1978 Evaluation: "Safety at this plant is improving as management matures. Management recognizes its safety responsibilities. Employee morale could be affected by top utility attitudes about nuclear power."

NEW JERSEY (Evacuation plans approved by NRC)

Oyster Creek (1), Toms River. Population, 50 miles: 3,300,000; Licensee: Jersey Central Power & Light; Exposure: 50 percent; 1977 Performance Rating: below average; 1978 Evaluation: "Security should be upgraded (guard force and surviellance). New operating procedures and maintenance systems have improved safety. Quality assurance program has been more fully implemented. As an early boiling water reactor, plant has inherently different safety characteristics. Facility management has not endorsed in principle a comprehensive management control system. They tend to just meet the minimum requirements. Design review of this plant was deficient. Plant was built at minimum cost. Rad waste, fire protection and system separation are inadequate. Corporate management has firsthand knowledge of plant."

Salem (1), Salem. Population, 50 miles: 4,800,000; Licensee: Public Service Electric and Gas; Exposure: Not Available; 1977 Performance Rating: Not rated by statistical method; 1978 Evaluation: "The plant control room is very poorly designed. This is a relatively new plant with growing pains. It needs close inspection attention to assure that appropriate improvements are made. Have had a number of problems in startup phase, which were corrected by management. Problems with operator controls."

NEW YORK (Evacuation plans approved by NRC)

James A. FitzPatrick (1), Scriba. Population, 50 miles: 840,000; Licensee: Power Authority of the State of New York; Exposure: 32 per cent; 1977 Performance Rating: average; 1978 Evaluation: "Plant has a new operator (P.A.S.N.Y.) that appears to have made improvements. (The reason) is increased management attention to operations. New security procedures are in effect. New management has improved technical competence and management and administrative controls. Design has been modified to add safety systems. Excellent fire protection and security system. Management improvements noted."

R.E. Ginna (1), Ontario. Population, 50 miles: 1,200,000; Licensee: Rochester Gas & Electric; Exposure: 40 per cent; 1977 Performance Rating: above average; 1978 Evaluation: "The plant is old, small and run safely."

Indian Point (3), Buchanan. Population, 50 miles: 17,200,000; Licensee: Units 1 and 2—Consolidated Edison, Unit 3—Power Authority of the State of New York; Exposure: Unit 1—Plant not open, Units 2 and 3—28 per cent; 1977 Performance Rating: Unit 1—Plant not open, Unit 2—average, Unit 3—Plant opened too recently; 1978 Evaluation: "Indian Point Unit 3 is superior in all respects to Unit 2, primarily because of its management control and personnel. Considerable recent attention to health physics, safeguards and other areas of Unit 2 operations has resulted in considerable upgrading. Radiation health controls have improved. Recent problem with instrumentation. Does not have a quality assurance plan meeting current requirements. Unit 3 rated higher than Unit 2 because P.A.S.N.Y. management better than that of Con Ed. Significant recent improvements in management control. Corporate management attitude continues to limit effectiveness of site management. Need to continue more frequent inspections by our best inspectors."

Nine Mile Point (1), Scriba. Population, 50 miles: 840,000; Licensee: Niagara Mohawk Power; Exposure: 35 per cent; 1977 Performance Rating: average; 1978 Evaluation: "Plant was operated by former fossil plant people; they have not yet become nuclear people. This is an old plant, but its engineering, layout and construction are good. Do not have enough on-site plant support except in operations. Security program excellent. Plant deficient in system separation and high pressure inspection systems. Conservative approach to operations. Plant staff has been stable. Plant has experienced boiling water reactor operators."

NORTH CAROLINA (Evacuation plans not approved by NRC)

Brunswick (2), Southport. Population, 50 miles: 170,000; Licensee: Carolina Power and Light; Exposure: Unit 1—Plant opened too recently, Unit 2—16 per cent; 1977 Performance Rating: Unit 1—Plant opened too recently, Unit 2—average; 1978 Evaluation: "Site has reorganized and has new people in key positions. Some improvement in administrative controls. Management seems to become more aware of events at plant. None of the top site management have had senior reactor operator training in boiling water reactors. High personnel turnover rate. Plant management seems to believe that they are 'overregulated.' "

OHIO (Evacuation plans not approved by NRC)

Davis-Besse (1), Oak Harbor. Population, 50 miles: 1,800,000; Licensee: Toledo Edison and Cleveland Electric Illumination; Exposure: Plant opened too recently; 1977 Performance Rating: Plant opened too recently; 1978 Evaluation: Plant opened too recently.

OREGON (Evacuation plans not approved by NRC)

Trojan (1), Prescott. Population, 50 miles: 1,100,000; Licensee: Portland General Electric; Exposure: 11 per cent; 1977 Performance Rating: below average; 1978 Evaluation: "Safety slightly improved by equipment upgrading and accumulation of operation experience. Active state regulation could affect safety through conflicting requirements. On site quality assurance program implementation has improved. Fire protection program is being implemented. Attitude toward quality assurance and prevention of recurring problems has improved."

PENNSYLVANIA (Evacuation plans not approved by NRC)

Beaver Valley (1), Shippingport. Population, 50 miles: 3,600,000; Licensee: Duquesne Light and Ohio Edison; Exposure: 3 per cent; 1977 Performance Rating: Not rated by statistical method; 1978 Evaluation: "Staff is experienced, quality assurance controls improved. Staff is improving. Bugs are being worked out of equipment and administrative controls. Plant management has improved. Security has improved with increased requirements. Staff still learning."

Peach Bottom (2), Peach Bottom. Population, 50 miles: 4,000,000; Licensee: Philadelphia Electric; Exposure: 30 per cent; 1977 Performance Rating: Unit 2—average, Unit 3—above average; 1978 Evaluation: "This is the least safe site in Region 1 and has the poorest management. Quality assurance and security are not upgraded to current standards. Many repeat items of noncompliance. Plant staff has appeared incapable of correcting increased plant radiation levels. Management is slow responding to (the NRC) regional office. Expect improvements as a result of management meeting with company president. Operating staff presently error-prone due to back-to-back overhaul periods for Units 2 and 3. General attitude of plant appears to be compliance only as required. Careless operations and poor maintenance."

Three Mile Island (2), Middletown. Population, 50 miles: 1,800,000; Licensee: Metropolitan Edison and Jersey Central Power & Light; Exposure: 18 per cent; 1977 Performance Rating: Unit 1—average, Unit 2—Plant opened too recently; 1978 Evaluation: "Station and unit superintendent are new. Security has improved. This the first Babcock & Wilcox plant of current generation. Management control during construction was deficient. Management control in operations is strong. Overall site safety may decrease because staff has become diluted with the licensing of Unit 2."

SOUTH CAROLINA (Evacuation plans approved by NRC)

Oconee (3), Seneca. Population, 50 miles: 730,000; Licensee: Duke Power; Exposure: 40 per cent; 1977 Performance Rating: average; 1978 Evaluation: "A change in the operating superintendent is expected to result in improvements."

H.B. Robinson (1), Hartsville. Population, 50 miles: 530,000; Licensee: Carolina Power and Light; Exposure: 17½ per cent; 1977 Performance Rating; average; 1978 Evaluation: "Licensee has made increased commitment to quality assurance and quality control. Licensee reports only those items that are conspicuously reportable. Licensee impedes inspector access and freedom of movement at site. No information freely given. Does only what is required."

VERMONT (Evacuation plans not approved by NRC)

Vermont Yankee (1), Vernon. Population, 50 miles: 1,200,000; Licensee: Vermont Yankee Nuclear Power; Exposure: 16 per cent; 1977 Performance Rating: below average; 1978 Evaluation: "Quality assurance plan has been upgraded. Management controls somewhat degraded by frequent changes in plant superintendent. Very clean plant. Management experience and depth is increasing."

VIRGINIA (Evacuation plans not approved by NRC)

North Anna (1), Mineral. Population, 50 miles: 860,000; Licensee: Virginia Electric & Power; Exposure: Plant opened too recently; 1977 Performance Rating: Plant opened too recently; 1978 Evaluation: Plant opened too recently.

Surry (2), Gravel Neck. Population, 50 miles: 1,600,000; Licensee: Virginia Electric & Power; Exposure: 50 per cent; 1977 Performance Rating: Unit 1—below average, Unit 2—average; 1978 Evaluation: "Safety slightly worse due to degradation of steam generator."

WISCONSIN (Evacuation plans not approved by NRC)

Kewaunee (1), Carlton. Population, 50 miles: 560,000; Licensee: Wisconsin Public Service; Exposure: 24 per cent; 1977 Performance Rating: average; 1978 Evaluation: "Resident inspector was assigned at this site. Plant management very stable and (competent). Good (attitude) toward safety. Overall, the site has good operating performance."

LaCrosse (Genoa) (1), LaCrosse. Population, 50 miles: 320,000; Licensee: Dairyland Power; Exposure: 38 per cent; 1977 Performance Rating: above average; 1978 Evaluation: "Safety slightly worse because of fuel degradation. Safety slightly better because of improved quality assurance program. This plant is an Atomic Energy Commission Developmental Reactor with a limited technical staff and minimal corporate backup. This small utility has difficulty absorbing the costs of NRC regulation."

Point Beach (2), Two Creeks. Population, 50 miles: 560,000; Licensee: Wisconsin Michigan Power; Exposure: 29 per cent; 1977 Performance Rating: above average; 1978 Evaluation: "Plant is an older design. (Attitude) of plant management is extremely good. Staff is disciplined, well motivated, and proud of work. Staff offers constructive criticism of NRC. Plant management is strong in all areas, and has a total team effort from staff. Attitude on safety matters is excellent."

WASHINGTON (Evacuation plans approved by NRC, but plants were not evaluated in the NRC report.)

RADIATION HAZARDS
New Data Indicate No Safe Level

Several events in 1978 and 1979 raised public concern about the dangers of radiation. They included the accident at the Three Mile Island nuclear plant, discovery of numerous "hot spots" under Denver properties caused by radioactive waste and a number of studies indicating that cancer rates among nuclear workers and residents near bomb test sites were abnormally high.

Perhaps the most significant study was one by Thomas Mancuso of the University of Pittsburgh on employees of the Hanford (Wash.) nuclear facility. Results indicated that at exposure levels not previously considered significant, cancer rates were higher than normal. Mancuso and fellow researchers concluded that no level of radiation exposure was without some health risk and that the risk increased steadily with exposure. He found that cancer rates among 35,000 workers exposed to 1.8 to 12 rads a year for 30 years were twice the number experienced by people not so exposed. He said the government's yearly limit of 5

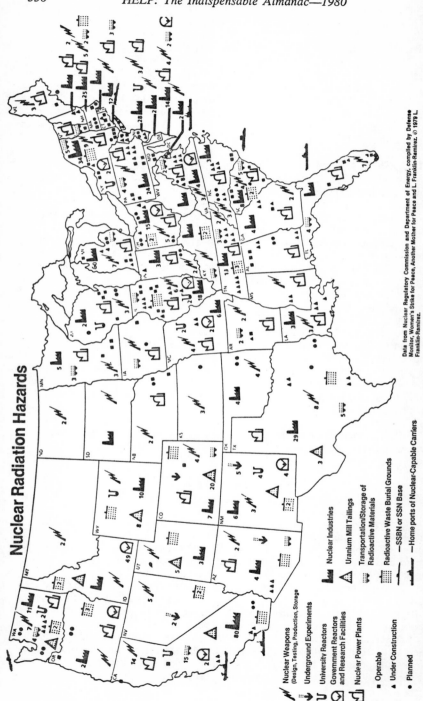

Nuclear Radiation Hazards

Nuclear Weapons
(Design, Testing, Production, Storage)

Underground Experiments

University Reactors

Government Reactors and Research Facilities

Nuclear Power Plants

■ Operable

▲ Under Construction

● Planned

Nuclear Industries

Uranium Mill Tailings

Transportation/Storage of Radioactive Materials

Radioactive Waste Burial Grounds

—SSBN or SSN Base

—Home ports of Nuclear-Capable Carriers

Data from Nuclear Regulatory Commission and Department of Energy, compiled by Defense Monitor, Women's Strike for Peace, Another Mother for Peace and L. Franklin-Ramirez. © 1979 L. Franklin-Ramirez.

rads (a unit of measure sometimes referred to as a rem) for nuclear workers was ten times higher than it should be. At 5 rads, he said, the cancer rate doubles. His was the first massive study linking cancer rates to relatively low levels of exposure.

MEDICAL X-RAYS COULD ADD TO CANCER

Mancuso's work, although based on nuclear workers because of the detailed records available, had considerable significance for the general population. Many people experience the same levels of exposure from medical radiation. For example, a barium or back X-ray series could expose a patient to 5,000 to 8,000 millirems (a millirem is one-thousandth of a rem or rad). And a set of whole-mouth dental X-rays could add 1,000 more.

According to Mancuso's data, people between the ages of 18 and 40 are more resistant to the effects of ionizing radiation than people of other ages, and men are more resistant than women.

A review of research by Irwin D. Bross and others (published in the *American Journal of Public Health* for February, 1979) indicated that leukemia and heart disease can be related to diagnostic X-ray doses of less than one rad. A long-suppressed study of people who were exposed to radioactive fallout from bomb tests in Utah in the 1950s showed a strong association between amount of fallout received and incidence of leukemia. In the areas of highest exposure, it said, leukemia rates were three times above normal. Government data, also withheld for many years, showed leukemia among soldiers exposed to low-level radiation during a 1957 nuclear test called "Smoky" was twice normal. A review by advisers to the National Academy of Sciences agreed that all radiation poses some health risk.

40 PER CENT OF X-RAYS HELD NEEDLESS

For the general population, however, the main sources of radiation are medical and dental X-rays. A survey done in 1977 by the government's Bureau of Radiological Health found that as much as 40 per cent of all medical and dental X-rays are unnecessary. Some 5 per cent of the population (11 million people) suffers adverse effects from medical X-rays, according to data from the Rosewell Park Memorial Cancer Research Institute in Buffalo.

People who had X-ray treatment for acne and other minor ailments have a high risk of acquiring cancer 10 to 40 years later. After more than 100 studies provided evidence of this, the National Cancer Institute decided in 1977 to alert the public to the risks. An estimated one-third of such irradiated people develop tumors of the thyroid, and as much as a third of the tumors become cancerous, said the Institute at a press conference.

The Institute also withdrew its endorsement of routine mammography exams for women below the age of 50. It concluded that the risk of cancer was greater than the benefit of detecting a dangerous tumor. Analysis of medical records had indicated that such X-rays had been erroneously interpreted, resulting in needless surgery in a significant number of cases.

GOVERNMENT ISSUES WARNING

Despite these studies and calls by some scientists and health experts for reduced federal radiation standards, the Carter Administration decided not to make any changes. In a formal announcement, HEW Secretary Joseph A.

Califano Jr. said data were not sufficient "to justify further reductions" in the standards. But he warned people against unnecessary exposure to radiation. And he said the government was expanding research on health effects from nuclear testing and medical X-rays.

A year earlier, President Carter had called for substantial reductions in X-ray use by government personnel. He urged that medical radiation be "reduced considerably by limiting its use to clinically indicated procedures utilizing efficient exposure techniques and optimal operation of radiation equipment." He said reduced exposure could be accomplished by minimizing such prescriptions and minimizing the number of views required. In addition, he urged an upgrading in the quality of X-ray equipment, much of which is antiquated and improperly used, according to previous surveys.

PRESIDENT URGES FEWER X-RAYS

Among the President's recommendations were that:

● Routine or screening examinations in which no prior clinical evaluation of the patient is made should not be performed. Examples of such X-rays which should not be done, with few exceptions are of the chest and lower back in routine physical exams or as a requirement for employment, TB screening by chest X-ray, chest X-rays for routine hospital admission, chest X-rays for routine prenatal care and mammography exams of women under age 50.

● The number, sequence and types of standard views should be clinically oriented and kept to a minimum.

● Equipment used in federal facilities must meet federal standards of performance (established in 1974).

● Facilities should have quality assurance programs designed to produce radiographs that satisfy diagnostic requirements with minimal patient exposure.

● Operation of X-ray equipment should be by individuals who have demonstrated proficiency by formal training or certification.

● Equipment should be focused to restrict the X-ray beam as much as practicable, with shielding of fetus and gonads of patients.

● Neither full-mouth nor bitewing X-rays should be used as a routine screening tool in the absence of clinical evaluation in preventive dental care.

MANY X-RAY MACHINES FOUND FAULTY

Carter's action was based on surveys in several states showing that substantial numbers of X-ray machines in dentist offices were emitting excessive radiation. Out of 420 machines checked in 1977 in Virginia, 251 were found faulty. Some machines were giving off five times the accepted amount, while one machine was emitting ten times the allowed amount. Similar findings were reported in other states checked under the supervision of the U.S. Food and Drug Administration's Bureau of Radiological Health.

The survey also found untrained and unlicensed operators handling many X-ray machines. As of 1979, only nine states had laws requiring licensing of X-ray operators.

A 1974 study by Ralph Nader's Health Research Group concluded that nearly one-third of all X-rays ordered by doctors were not medically justified but that many were done to protect doctors from malpractice suits. The study reported that more than half of all diagnostic X-rays expose patients to excessive radiation with X-ray beams larger than the film area. It found 90 per cent of all medical X-rays being performed without protective shielding of patients.

The author of the report, Priscilla W. Laws, said routine dental X-rays of the entire mouth on a six-month or one-year basis are unnecessary for a normal, healthy individual. She said such X-rays would not be needed normally more often then every ten years.

WATER POLLUTION

Many of the recent changes in pollution laws have been in the area of regulatory reform, modifying or relaxing current regulatory practices. In early 1979, the Environmental Protection Agency proposed regulations designed to consolidate, shorten and simplify existing regulations dealing with environmental discharges. These regulations would simplify the paperwork facing polluters applying for permits, make the process less of a burden for them.

Other new regulations call for cheaper and more realistic planning of sewage plant construction. Grants to municipalities for wastewater treatment plants represent the EPAs largest activity, with $4.2 billion appropriated for this purpose in 1979.

The EPA has also become more specific in its efforts to deal with water pollution. In February, 1979, the Agency issued new regulations dealing with chemical spills. Anyone spilling one of the 271 designated chemicals is responsible for cleaning up the spill. Liability for chemical spills was also established. In March, the EPA proposed water quality criteria for 27 of the 65 pollutants listed as toxic under the Clean Water Act. Proposed controls on suspected carcinogens in drinking water issued in February, 1978, are still pending.

MAJOR CHANGE IN POLICY

The Clean Water Act, passed by Congress in December, 1977, represents a major change in U.S. environmental policy. The act sets out a comprehensive plan for cleaning up the nation's water supplies, and amends the Federal Water Pollution Control Act of 1972.

The 1972 law set up a special procedure to control dumping of dangerous substances that end up in drinking water. But the procedures did not work, due partially to Environmental Protection Agency (EPA) timidity and industry resistance, often with the tacit support of Presidents Nixon and Ford.

The new law strengthens procedures. The law gives the EPA a free hand in adding to and removing toxic substances from the list of controlled substances. In March, 1978, the EPA issued a list of 271 hazardous chemicals for which heavy fines may be imposed if spilled into waterways, accidentally or otherwise. Under the EPA rules, civil penalties of up to $5 million can be levied for a spill, plus clean-up costs of up to $50 million. In cases of "willful negligence," there is no limit on the liability for clean-up costs. Failure to report a spill could result in additional criminal penalties of up to $10,000 and a year in jail.

The measure is intended to reduce the more than 700 damaging chemical spills occurring each year from tank cars, trains, ships, storage tanks and pipes that break, derail, run aground, rust or otherwise malfunction. Among the worst incidents include a massive amount of carbon tetrachloride spilled into the Ohio River in February, 1978, temporarily disrupting drinking water supplies used by millions of people downstream. Effects from discharges of Kepone into Virginia's James River in 1975 are still being felt both on the natural habitat and by residents over a wide area.

INCREASED OIL SPILLS

Results from oil spills from tanker ships have increased in proportion to the amount of oil being transported. Estimates for 1977 are that 4,000 ships carried 11 billion gallons of crude oil across open seas. Most of the spills involve ships not registered in the U.S., frustrating government officials as to what deterrents to take. Most efforts have been aimed at finding efficient methods of cleaning up spilled oil.

For industries, the 1977 Clean Water Act extends to July, 1984, the deadline for applying the "best available technology (BAT) economically achievable" to reduce pollution of substances controlled by the EPA, one year later than the deadline imposed in the 1972 law.

But for all other pollutants — the vast majority — the deadline was pushed back even further. For those pollutants, BAT must be applied no earlier than 1984 and no later than 1987.

Industries can escape controls for these pollutants altogether or apply weaker controls if they can demonstrate to the EPA that their pollution will not prevent recreational activities, decimate fish populations or cause "unacceptable" health risk. Thus, say environmentalists, the 1977 law is a step backward for the 1972 law that called for fishable and swimmable waters through the nation by 1983.

MUNICIPAL SEWAGE TREATMENT

Municipal sewage, the waste-carrying water which communities send down the drain, is one of the primary causes of water pollution. The new law contains many provisions to encourage cleaning up cities' wastes, including:

● Allocating $25 billion in federal money to be spent over five years to design and construct municipal sewage treatment facilities, matched by up to $8 billion in state and local money.

● Incentives to encourage cities to try alternative methods of waste control that conserve water and convert pollutants into useful resources. Communities that choose these technologies are entitled to a higher percentage of federal funding.

● Relaxing the 1972 law to allow large coastal cities — Miami, Los Angeles, Anchorage, Honolulu and Seattle among them — to discharge partially treated sewage into the ocean, which many believe causes no ecological harm. This provision is highly controversial.

The new law gives the EPA authority to enforce pollution laws against federal government installations the same as against private companies. Civil servants, however, are immune from civil penalties, and federal agencies are exempt from criminal penalties. Since passage of the law, the EPA set deadlines for some of the worst federal polluters, primarily military bases.

SUING MAY BE THE MOST EFFECTIVE ENFORCEMENT

Under federal law, citizens may bring suit against any party (corporation, association, state, municipality, etc.) which appears to be in violation of water

DRINKING WATER POLLUTANTS IN 100 CITIES

Data shows micrograms of trihalomethanes (suspected carcinogens) per liter of water sampled.

City	Micrograms per liter	City	Micrograms per liter
Albuquerque, NM	15	Lincoln, NE	28
Amarillo, TX	130	Little Rock, AR	42
Annandale, VA	200	Los Angeles, CA	49
Atlanta, GA	75	Las Vegas, NV	76
Baltimore, MD	65	Louisville, KY	150
Baton Rouge, LA	1.6	Madison, WI	0.02
Billings, MT	13	Manchester, NH	60
Birmingham, AL	75	Memphis, TN	17
Bismarck, ND	100	Milwaukee, WI	16
Boise, ID	16	Montgomery, AL	110
Boston, MA	5.0	Nashville, TN	24
Brownsville, TX	450	New Haven, CT	49
Buffalo, NY	23	Newport, RI	160
Burlington, VT	91	Norfolk, VA	150
Camden, AR	120	Oklahoma City, OK	200
Casper, WY	41	Oakland, CA	45
Cheyenne, WY	130	Omaha, NE	120
Charleston, SC	200	Phoenix, AZ	130
Charlotte, NC	71	Portland, ME	7.4
Chattanooga, TN	98	Portland, OR	20
Chicago, IL	50	Poughkeepsie, NY	78
Cleveland, OH	49	Providence, RI	8.0
Columbus, OH	210	Provo, UT	12
Concord, CA	110	Pueblo, CO	9.6
Dallas, TX	79	Richmond, VA	34
Davenport, IA	100	Rockford, IL	7.9
Dayton, OH	40	Sacramento, CA	29
Denver, CO	39	Salt Lake City, UT	43
Des Moines, IA	15	San Antonio, TX	13
Detroit, MI	34	San Diego, CA	97
Duluth, MN	12	San Francisco, CA	78
Elizabeth, NJ	86	Sante Fe, NM	180
Erie, PA	31	Sioux Falls, SD	79
Eugene, OR	25	South Pittsburg, PA	43
Fort Worth, TX	61	Spokane, WA	1.9
Fort Wayne, IN	59	Springfield, MA	20
Fresno, CA	0.37	St. Croix, VI	23
Greenville, MS	2.4	St. Louis, MO	51
Grand Rapids, MI	69	St. Paul, MN	90
Hackensack, NJ	110	Syracuse, NY	18
Hagerstown, MD	100	Tacoma, WA	8.9
Hartford, CT	36	Tampa, FL	230
Houston, TX	250	Toledo, OH	38
Huntington, WV	110	Topeka, KS	180
Huron, SD	300	Tulsa, OK	50
Indianapolis, IN	82	Washington, DC	110
Jackson, MS	240	Waterbury, CT	110
Jacksonville, FL	8.7	Wheeling, WV	160
Jersey City, NJ	64	Wichita, KS	27
Kansas City, MO	34	Wilmington, DE	64

Source: Environmental Protection Agency

purity standards or government order. As exemplified by suits already brought against corporations and the EPA by environmental organizations, such suits may be the most effective means of halting polluters until final rules are passed on a national level.

In bringing suit, you must give 60 days notice to both the state and the violator to allow voluntary compliance or the initiation of enforcement action by the state. In the interim, you can seek a temporary restraining order to halt serious pollution. In seeking immediate relief, you may have to post substantial bond as proof of interest and urgency. The 60-day waiting period may be waived in cases of a clear danger to public health and welfare.

Citizens filing suit should also notify the Environment Protection Agency by formal notice. It is usually more effective to bring suits through an established organization, such as the Clean Water Action Project, Sierra Club, Environmental Defense Foundation or other group actively involved in environmental-oriented litigation.

HOW TO EVALUATE YOUR WATER SYSTEM

The average citizen has little means of analyzing the quality of water. Such an assessment requires complicated chemical and physical procedures and access to water utility facilities generally available only to government regulators.

However, there are some questions you can ask your local water utility based on the survey cited above. If you are not satisfied with the answers, you may wish to ask a local, state or federal authority to investigate further. Merely asking questions of proper authorities may bring improvements.

DRINKING WATER HAZARDS
Can They Be Avoided?

Following is an analysis of four alternatives to water company water, as compiled by the Clean Water Action Project, a Washington, DC-based public interest group:

Water Filters: While tap-water filters containing activated carbon may remove some tastes, odors or color from the water, this cure may be worse than the disease. These filters trap material in the water and this in turn feeds disease-causing bacteria that get caught in the filter, enabling them to grow. Turning on the tap, especially after a night or period of disuse of the water, may then release a dangerous level of these bacteria. For this reason *Consumer Reports* has not found any home water filters it can recommend. Unfortunately, no government agencies regulate the claims that tap water filter makers commonly make about their products or test their efficiency.

Bottled Water: Both the Environmental Protection Agency and the General Accounting Office looked into the quality of bottled water several years ago. They found that the bacteriological and chemical purity of some of these products was deficient and sanitary conditions at bottling plants were not capable of assuring a pure product. After these reports were released, the Food and Drug Administration wrote standards for bottling plants and their products, but the agency does not frequently check conditions at the plants or test the product to make sure that standards are met. If you still want to buy bottled water, check with an FDA office or a state health office to see if they have information on the bottled water you want to buy.

Water Distillers: These are effective at killing bacteria that may occur in your water. They also remove most of the natural minerals, but not necessarily the carcinogenic materials. In addition, distilled water is rather flat and tasteless.

Spring or Well Water: If these are uncontaminated, they will probably be the cleanest and least "risky" sources of drinking water. The problem is that it can be very inconvenient to obtain spring or well water directly from its original source.

AIR POLLUTION
Deadlines Set Back to Please Detroit

Clean air was supposed to exist nationwide by 1975, but it is taking a little longer to arrive. Amendments to the 1970 Clean Air Act passed by Congress in August, 1977, delayed until 1981 final reductions in auto exhaust that were originally supposed to take effect in 1976. Auto manufacturers had requested the delay.

But clean air won't come in 1981 either. While the amendments require pollution controls on cars by that date, it takes about a decade for a complete turnover of the automobile population, making it at least 1991 until most cars on the roads will be low-polluting.

The 1977 amendments also moved the original deadline for states to comply with air quality standards up to the end of 1982 and allowed some cities until 1987 to clean up auto exhaust pollution. Industries are given until 1980 to meet pollution control standards.

It is unlikely that even these reduced goals will be reached. According to a 1978 study by the GAO, current air quality standards are not likely to be achieved by 1982, or even 1987.

STANDARDS FOR LEAD SET BACK

Inflation and shortages of gasoline are creating further pressures to relax or set aside some pollution control standards. In June, 1979, the government relaxed air quality standards to increase the production of unleaded gas, deferring regulations that would have reduced the maximum amount of lead in leaded gasoline for a year.

In May, 1979, the EPA decided to relax proposed air pollution standards for new coal-fired power plants. Three months earlier, the levels of air pollution permitted in cities were increased. The standard for ozone, a major part of smog, was raised 50 per cent from .08 parts per million to .12 parts per million.

The EPA also agreed to give the Tennessee Valley Authority additional time to bring 10 of its coal-fired power plants into compliance with pollution standards. The plants, in Kentucky, Alabama and Tennessee, are supposed to be in compliance by 1982. The state standards for monitoring air quality were also revised.

Although air quality improvements have taken place in some areas, the biggest problems remain in urban areas, due mostly to automobile pollution.

Tests conducted in New Jersey, Arizona and Oregon found that most cars exceeding federal emissions tests needed only carburetor adjustments and motor tune-ups in order to comply. In Oregon, 90 per cent of cars failing emissions tests required less than $50 in repairs in order to comply. Most repairs were much cheaper: 70 per cent would have cost less than $10, and the average was below $20. As a result, numerous states are considering implementing some form of mandatory vehicle inspection.

Automobile pollutants have been associated with a wide variety of diseases and ailments ranging from headaches to cancer. Not all the effects are known, but some have been defined:

Carbon Monoxide, a colorless, odorless, tasteless gas, hinders the blood from carrying oxygen to the body tissues when inhaled. This, in turn, diminishes reflexes, visual sharpness and muscle coordination; causes headaches; impairs judgment; damages arteries and heart tissues; and may hinder development of the fetus. Carbon monoxide has the same effect on a heart patient as strenuous exercise and has been associated with fatal heart attacks.

Hydrocarbons, produced by the incomplete burning of gasoline, are a complex mixture of different compounds. Although some hydrocarbons may have carcinogenic (cancer-causing) effects, evidence is inconclusive. Of primary concern is their indirect effect through interaction with nitrogen oxides under sunlight to form photochemical smog which causes irritation to eyes and lungs and damage to vegetation.

Nitrogen oxides are major participants in photochemical smog and, when inhaled deeply, can cause bronchial and lung damage.

Lead, a component of much of the gasoline sold in the U.S., is another hazardous pollutant resulting from automobile emissions. Lead particles have proven to be a serious irritant to lungs and a suspected cause of cancer as well as neurological impairments such as mental retardation and cerebral palsy. Ethylene dibromide, an additive in gasoline used to prevent excessive lead deposits in engines, is another cancer-causing pollutant in auto exhaust. Lead from gasoline may also contribute to the high levels of lead in the blood of children in urban areas.

Some pollutants are hazardous even in minute amounts. Each has its own particular adverse characteristics which place stress on humans.

Three major ones are:

Asbestos fibers, when inhaled, can cause asbestosis, bronchogenic cancer, mesothelioma and other malignant diseases. Symptoms of mesothelioma develop about 30 years after the initial exposure to asbestos, and some physicians expect an increase in the disease among persons who worked in shipyards during World War II. Asbestos is used mainly in industrial operations and in road paving.

Beryllium is a metal commonly used in rocket fuels, missile guidance systems, nuclear reactors and atomic weapons. The most serious effect of inhaled beryllium is a progressive lung disease.

Mercury is commonly used in batteries, mildew-proofing and the manufacture of paint, pulp and paper. Airborne mercury can affect the central nervous system and can lead to weight loss, insomnia, tremors and psychological disturbances.

AIR POLLUTION IN 105 LARGEST CITIES

("X" indicates city does not meet federal standards for pollutants shown. See text for details on individual pollutants.)

Metropolitan Area	1970 Population	TSP	SO$_2$	OX	CO	NO$_2$
New York, Northeastern NJ	16,206,841			X	X	
Los Angeles-Long Beach, CA	8,351,266	X	X	X	X	X
Chicago, IL-Northwestern, IN	6,714,578	X		X	X	X
Philadelphia, PA-NJ	4,021,066		X	X	X	
Detroit, MI	3,970,584			X	X	
San Francisco-Oakland, CA	2,987,850	X		X	X	
Boston, MA	2,652,575	X		X	X	
Washington, DC-MD-VA	2,481,489	X		X	X	
Cleveland, OH	1,959,880	X	X	X	X	
St. Louis, MO-IL	1,882,944	X	X	X	X	
Pittsburgh, PA	1,846,042	X	X	X	X	
Minneapolis-St. Paul, MN	1,704,423	X	X	X	X	
Houston, TX	1,677,863	X		X		
Baltimore, MD	1,579,781	X		X	X	
Dallas, TX	1,338,684	X		X		
Milwaukee, WI	1,252,457	X		X	X	
Seattle-Everett, WA	1,238,107	X		X	X	
Miami, FL	1,219,661			X		
San Diego, CA	1,198,323	X		X	X	X
Atlanta, GA	1,172,778	X		X	X	
Cincinnati, OH-KY	1,110,514	X	X	X	X	
Kansas City, MO-KS	1,101,787	X		X	X	
Buffalo, NY	1,086,594			X	X	
Denver, CO	1,047,311	X		X	X	X
San Jose, CA	1,025,273			X	X	
New Orleans, LA	961,728			X		
Phoenix, AZ	863,357	X		X	X	
Portland, OR-WA	824,926	X		X	X	
Indianapolis, IN	820,259	X	X	X	X	
Providence-Warwick, RI-MA	795,311	X		X	X	
Columbus, OH	790,019	X	X	X	X	
San Antonio, TX	772,513	X		X		
Louisville, KY-IN	739,396	X	X	X	X	
Dayton, OH	685,942	X	X	X	X	
Fort Worth, TX	676,944	X		X		
Norfolk-Portsmouth, VA	668,259			X		
Memphis, TN-MS	663,976	X		X	X	
Sacramento, CA	633,732			X	X	
Ft. Lauderdale-Hollywood, FL	613,797			X	X	
Rochester, NY	601,361			X	X	
San Bernardino-Riverside, CA	583,597	X		X	X	X
Oklahoma City, OK	579,788	X		X		
Birmingham, AL	558,099	X		X		
Akron, OH	542,775	X	X	X	X	
Jacksonville, FL	529,585			X		
Springfield-Holyoke, MA-CT	514,308	X		X	X	
St. Petersburg, FL	495,159		X	X		
Omaha, NE-IA	491,776	X		X	X	
Toledo, OH-MI	487,789	X	X	X	X	
Albany-Schenectady-Troy, NY	486,525			X	X	
Salt Lake City, UT	479,342	X	X	X	X	

Metropolitan Area	1970 Population	TSP	SO$_2$	OX	CO	NO$_2$
Hartford, CT	465,001	X		X	X	
Nashville-Davidson, TN	448,444	X		X	X	
Honolulu, HI	442,397					
Richmond, VA	416,563			X		
Bridgeport, CT	413,366			X	X	
Youngstown-Warren, OH	395,540	X	X	X	X	
Syracuse, NY	376,169	X		X	X	
Tulsa, OK	371,499	X		X	X	
Wilmington, DE-NJ	371,267			X		
Tampa, FL	368,742			X		
Allentown-Bethlehem, PA-NJ	363,517	X		X		
Grand Rapids, MI	352,703			X		
New Haven, CT	348,341	X		X	X	
El Paso, TX	337,471	X		X	X	
Tacoma, WA	332,521	X	X	X	X	
Flint, MI	330,128	X		X		
Orlando, FL	305,479			X		
Wichita, KS	302,334				X	
Albuquerque, NM	297,451	X			X	
Tucson, AZ	294,184	X	X	X	X	
South Bend, IN-MI	288,572	X	X	X		
West Palm Beach, FL	287,561			X		
Charlotte, NC	279,530			X	X	
Trenton, NJ-PA	274,148			X	X	
Newport News-Hampton, VA	268,263			X		
Davenport-Moline, IA-IL	266,119	X		X		
Austin, TX	264,499			X		
Fresno, CA	262,908	X		X	X	
Mobile, AL	257,816	X		X		
Des Moines, IA	255,824	X			X	
Baton Rouge, LA	249,463			X		
Worcester, MA	247,416	X		X	X	
Peoria, IL	247,121	X	X	X	X	
Oxnard-Ventura-Thousand Oaks, CA	244,653	X		X		
Canton, OH	244,279	X	X	X		
Columbia, SC	241,781			X	X	
Harrisburg, PA	240,751	X		X		
Las Vegas, NV	236,681	X		X	X	
Shreveport, LA	234,564			X		
Aurora-Elgin, IL	232,917			X		
Spokane, WA	229,620	X			X	
Lansing, MI	229,518		X	X		
Charleston, SC	228,399	X		X		
Fort Wayne, IN	225,184			X		
Chattanooga, TN-GA	223,580	X		X		
Wilkes-Barre, PA	222,830	X		X		
Little Rock, AR	222,616			X		
Corpus Christi, TX	208,616	X		X		
Columbus, GA-AL	208,616			X		
Rockford, IL	206,084					
Madison, WI	205,457		X			
Colorado Springs, CO	204,766	X		X	X	X
Scranton, PA	204,205	X		X		
Lawrence-Haverhill, MA-NH	200,280			X		

*TSP: Total Suspended Particulates (dust, sand, soot, smoke, etc.); SO$_2$: Sulfur Dioxide; OX: Photochemical Oxidant (smog); CO: Carbon Monoxide; NO$_2$: Nitrogen Dioxide. Source: U.S. Environmental Protection Agency.

MEASURING AIR QUALITY
And Its Effect on Health

To provide clear and consistent information to the public on air quality, the U.S. Environmental Protection Agency (EPA) and other agencies developed the Pollutant Standards Index (PSI).

PSI reports pollutant concentrations on a scale of 0 to 500. Intervals on the PSI scale are related to the potential health effects of the measured concentration of five major pollutants: carbon monoxide, photochemical oxidants, nitrogen dioxide, sulfur dioxide and particulate matter. PSI places maximum emphasis on acute health effects for three stages of air pollution: Alert, Warning and Emergency. PSI values of 200-400, correspond to the Alert, Warning, and Emergency levels. (See table.)

POLLUTANT STANDARDS INDEX

Index	PSI Descriptor	General Health Effects	Cautionary Statements
500		Premature death of ill and elderly. Healthy people will experience adverse symptoms that affect their normal activity.	All persons should remain indoors, keeping windows and doors closed. All persons should minimize physical exertion and avoid traffic.
400	Hazardous	Premature onset of certain diseases in addition to significant aggravation of symptoms and decreased exercise tolerance in healthy persons.	Elderly and persons with existing diseases should stay indoors and avoid physical exertion. General population should avoid outdoor activity.
300			
	Very Unhealthful	Significant aggravation of symptoms and a decrease of exercise tolerance in persons with heart or lung disease with widespread symptoms in the healthy population.	Elderly and persons with existing heart or lung disease should stay indoors and reduce physical activity.
200			
	Unhealthful	Mild aggravation of symptoms in susceptible persons, with irritation symptoms in the healthy population.	Persons with existing heart or respiratory ailments should reduce physical exertion and outdoor activity.
100			
50	Moderate		
0	Good		

Source: Environmental Protection Agency, 1979.

NOISE POLLUTION
Trying to Get the Ear of Lawmakers and Police

Just when the fight against noise pollution was beginning to make some headway, the Senate approved the Aircraft Noise Abatement Bill (S413) in May, 1979. The measure would allow airlines to fly noisy aircraft for up to three years past the federal 1985 deadline if quieter replacements have been ordered.

Senator John Culver (D-Iowa) blamed approval of this bill on the lack of commitment by environmentalists and consumers to influence members of Congress. "The progress we started in 1976," he said, "has been waived away by these votes." The House is expected to follow the Senate lead.

On the brighter side was passage of the Quiet Communities Act in November, 1978. This law directed the Environmental Protection Agency to increase its assistance to states and communities for noise pollution programs. Under EPA's Quiet Communities Program, Allentown, PA became the first community to receive EPA funds and technical assistance to start a two-year noise control program. After completing acoustic monitoring and attitudinal surveys, Allentown passed an ordinance to assist the community in dealing with its traffic, industrial and airport noise problems.

But, according to EPA, an anti-noise law is meaningless without active, well-trained enforcement. The agency praised a pioneer program in Salt Lake City where policemen are paid time and a half for extra hours spent on noise control. On the other hand, said EPA, some cities have good noise ordinances, but crime takes precedence over noise problems in police department priorities.

MANY INJURED BY EXCESSIVE NOISE

According to EPA's 1977 Urban Noise Survey, about half the U.S. population is exposed to levels of noise that bother and annoy as well as interrupt normal activities. More than 20 million Americans have some degree of irreversible hearing loss because of excessive noise. And researchers now suggest that noise plays a large role in the development of physical and psychological stress, leading to heart disease, high blood pressure, ulcers and other physical and mental disorders. One study found that steel workers and machine shop operators working under high noise levels had a higher incidence of circulatory problems than did workers in quiet industries.

Air raid siren — 130
Jet takeoff (100 ft.) — 120
Rock music (amplified) — 110
Chainsaws — 100
Motorcycles (modified) — 95
— 90
Lawnmower — 80
Heavy traffic — 75
Vacuum cleaner
Conversation (normal) — 60
Moderate rainfall — 50
Library — 40
— 30
Soft Whisper — 20
— 10

Another study found that grade school children exposed to aircraft noise in school and at home exhibited higher blood pressure than children in quieter areas.

There also is evidence that noise-related stress can aggravate emotional problems and strain relations between individuals. One experiment found that while a loud lawnmower was running nearby, people were less willing to help a passerby with a broken arm pick up a load of dropped books. Research in the United States and England indicates a higher rate of admission to psychiatric hospitals among people living close to airports.

TRAFFIC CALLED BIGGEST PROBLEM

EPA studies estimate that continuous exposure to sound exceeding 70 decibels— including highway traffic, street noise and jet takeoffs—can cause hearing loss and other health problems. The biggest contributor to everyday noise is traffic. Of respondents classifying their neighborhoods as noisy in answer to an EPA survey, 55 per cent identified automobiles as the primary source. Fifteen per cent identified aircraft, 12 per cent cited voices, with the remaining 18 per cent divided among five other categories.

Street motorcycles are a major source of public noise complaints. The problem is aggravated by motorcycle owners who modify their muffler systems—creating more noise—under the false assumption that they can achieve better performance by tampering with their mufflers. In answer to the motorcycle problem, EPA has proposed a regulation to require cycles to be quieted gradually over a six-year period.

EPA also has proposed noise standards for new buses, trucks, bulldozers, pavement breakers and power lawn mowers. In addition, the agency has proposed a noise labeling program requiring certain products to disclose the number of decibels emitted along with the range of decibels in competing products of the same type.

Eventually, EPA plans to have decibel labels on all noisy consumer products. The first products to have rating labels are hearing protectors; their labels indicate relative effectiveness in reducing noise. For example, a Noise Reduction Rating (NRR) of 20 means that noise entering the ear is reduced by about 20 decibels.

FOR MORE INFORMATION

The National Information Center for Quiet, a federally-funded clearinghouse for information on noise abatement, provides information on the effects of noise and possible solutions to the problem. Typical free publications include:

- *Noise: A Health Problem,* a pamphlet on the impact of noise on hearing and health;
- *Noise—It Hurts,* a pamphlet on noise control and abatement programs;
- *Noise at Work,* a pamphlet on noise on the job and what can be done to lessen the problem;
- *Quieting in the Home,* a book on the physics of sound, sources of noise and a guide to reducing noise in the home;
- *Noise: A Challenge to the Cities,* a pamphlet on noise in cities.

They can be obtained from the Center, P.O. Box 57171, Washington, DC, 20037.

MOST DANGEROUS PRODUCTS
Ranked As to Number and Severity of Injuries

Product	Estimated Annual Injuries	Rank of Severity
Stairs, Steps, Ramps and Landings	572,000	2
Bicycles and Bicycle Accessories	430,000	1
Football and Related Equipment	403,000	3
Baseball and Related Equipment	401,000	4
Basketball and Related Equipment	349,000	13
Nails, Carpet Tacks, Screws and Thumbtacks	265,000	12
Glass Doors, Windows and Panels	186,000	18
Non-Glass Tables	171,000	6
Chairs, Sofas and Sofa Beds	162,000	8
Playground Equipment	151,000	5
Beds, Including Springs and Frames	135,000	7
Snow Skiing and Related Equipment	108,000	26
Glass Bottles and Jars	106,000	30
Unpowered Cutlery and Knives	102,000	43
Floors and Flooring Materials	101,000	17
Skateboards	101,000	17
Skates	92,000	28
Desks, Storage Cabinets, Glass Shelves, Bookshelves	89,000	21
Drinking Glasses	88,000	53
Ladders and Stools	83,000	22
Cans	79,000	35
Soccer and Related Equipment	73,000	40
Volleyball and Related Equipment	72,000	65
Fences, Non-Electric	70,000	32
Power Lawn Mowers and Other Mowers	69,000	10
Power Home Workshop Saws	68,000	25
Swimming Pools and Related Equipment	68,000	11
Bathtubs, Non-Glass Shower Enclosures and Showers	67,000	16
Tennis, Badminton and Squash Equipment	60,000	70
Tableware and Flatware, Excluding Cutlery	59,000	56
Toboggans, Sleds, Snow Discs and Snow Tubing	58,000	20
Fishing Equipment	53,000	37
Walls, Not Otherwise Specified	52,000	47
Gymnastics and Associated Equipment	52,000	47
Lumber	48,000	49
Porches, Balconies, Open side Floors, and Floor Openings	48,000	27
Chain Saws	48,000	96
Wrestling and Related Equipment	46,000	58
Non-Glass Doors	45,000	46
Pins and Needles	40,000	73
Bleaches, Dyes and Cleaning Agents	40,000	14
Hammers	40,000	86
Hockey, Incl. Field Hockey and Related Equipment	39,000	63
Razors and Shavers	39,000	97
Pencils, Pens and Other Desk Supplies	36,000	42
Ice Skates	35,000	50
Hand Garden Tools	34,000	55
Miscellaneous Household Chemicals	29,000	19
Bricks, Concrete Blocks, Not Part of Structure	29,000	61
Water Skiing, Surfboarding and Equipment	28,000	54

Source: Consumer Product Safety Commission, 1979 Annual Report.

MAJOR HAZARDS

The U.S. Consumer Product Safety Commission (CPSC) decided in 1979 that it can best reduce the annual toll of 650,000 deaths and injuries from unsafe products by doing a more effective job on fewer products and problems. Topics singled out for priority attention were:

Aluminum Wiring—CPSC has asked a federal court to declare that aluminum wiring presents an imminent hazard in the approximately 1.5 million American homes where it was installed between 1965 and 1973. Wiring could overheat, causing fire.

Asbestos—CPSC has banned consumer patching compounds and artificial emberizing fireplace materials containing asbestos that can be inhaled. Asbestos in the lungs can cause cancer. CPSC is considering the need for mandatory safety rules regarding other products containing inhalable asbestos fibers. (See section on asbestos.)

Antennas—CPSC has received reports that 494 persons were electrocuted in 1975 and 1976 when CB and TV antennas they were servicing touched overhead power lines. CPSC has issued a regulation for safety labeling of CB and TV antennas and is presently studying the feasibility of a design standard for reducing accidents.

Bathtub and Shower Enclosures—The Commission is developing safety standards for these products. (In 1977, bathtub, shower enclosures and ladders together caused 144,000 injuries.)

Benzene—this chemical, used in paint strippers and rubber cements, has been suspected of causing leukemia, other blood disorders, and genetic abnormalities. The Commission is considering a ban on all products containing benzene.

Carpets and Rugs—The Commission presently requires carpets and rugs to meet certain flammability standards. The Commission will also develop requirements for testing random samples of carpets and rugs for flammability during the manufacturing process.

Cellulose Insulation—As a result of a law enacted by Congress, CPSC recently issued an interim standard for cellulose insulation, limiting flammability and corrosiveness. The Commission is considering labeling that tells consumers how to install cellulose insulation to avoid fires.

Chain Saws—CPSC is working with the Chain Saw Manufacturers Association on voluntary standards to deal with the hazard of chain saw kickback. Almost 40,000 persons received chain saw-related injuries in 1977 that were treated in hospital emergency rooms.

Children's Sleepwear. The Commission currently requires children's sleepwear to be flame-resistant. It will clarify the definitions of children's sleepwear covered in its existing standards because of confusion as to what garments are included.

Christmas Tree Lights. Miniature Christmas tree lights can cause fires and electric shock. The Commission has proposed a safety standard to reduce this risk and will review comments from the public.

Formaldehyde. CPSC will investigate the need for mandatory safety rules to help protect those who suffer allergic reactions and respiratory problems when exposed to formaldehyde vapors in consumer products such as certain construction materials.

Gas-Fired Space Heaters. Unvented space heaters have led to at least 165 deaths from carbon monoxide poisoning since 1973. CPSC recently proposed a ban on these products which is now before the public for comment.

Glass Doors and Windows. Approximately 62,000 people were treated in hospital emergency rooms in 1977 for injuries associated with glass doors and panels, according to CPSC. A new regulation will soon be final on tests that manufacturers must perform.

Ladders. The Commission is currently providing technical assistance to development of voluntary standards for these products.

Playground Equipment. Approximately 75,000 children received hospital treatment in 1977 for fractures and other injuries from using public playground equipment. CPSC is considering a standard.

Power Mowers. An estimated 62,000 people suffered power mower-related injuries, including amputations, lacerations and burns in 1977, CPSC reports. A mandatory standard has been proposed.

Skateboards. The Commission estimates 140,000 people required hospital treatment in 1977 for injuries from skateboarding. It is conducting a publicity campaign urging that protective equipment be used and that skateboarding not be done in the streets.

Smoke Detectors. CPSC is conducting an evaluation of smoke detectors to see if action is needed to assure consumer safety since the installation of smoke detectors is now required in many locations.

Toys. Over 7,000 children received treatment in hospital emergency rooms in 1976 for injuries from small parts found in children's products. The CPSC is proposing safety regulations on such easy-to-reach small parts and for propelled toys (such as dart guns, flying discs, and planes and toys which are shot out of a device) that can cause eye injuries. Over 1,000 people were treated in emergency rooms in 1977 from projectile toys. Another 68,000 people were treated in 1977 for injuries from sharp edges and points in toys intended for children under eight years of age.

Upholstered Furniture. Most fires in upholstered furniture are started by smoldering cigarettes. CPSC is considering the development of a mandatory standard with a test method to reduce the hazard.

GAS PUMPS ARE BIG POLLUTERS

Although most gasoline pumps automatically cut off the flow of gas into the car's tank when the tank is filled, most gas attendants "top off" the tank, putting in enough extra gas to bring the level to the very edge.

In many cases, the gasoline spills out when the tank is filled too much. After a few minutes of driving, the rising temperature may cause the gasoline to expand and spill even more.

It has been estimated that this practice wastes as much as 40 million gallons of gasoline each year. The fumes emitted from the raw gasoline are as dangerous as the emissions after it has been burned.

The American Automobile Association, the American Lung Association and federal agencies urge that drivers discourage attendants from topping off gas tanks.

ASBESTOS HAZARDS EVERYWHERE
More Than 100 Products Involved

Asbestos has long been known to cause a fatal lung disease called asbestosis as well as cancer. Yet little has been done to remove the hazard from common products ranging from toothbrushes to blackboards.

In fact, little was heard about the pervasiveness of this natural mineral with tiny fibers until a television reporter linked it to hair dryers in 1979. Lea Thompson of WRC, an NBC affiliate in Washington, D.C., caused a sensation when she told of tests that asbestos fibers were released by numerous brands of hair dryers. An estimated 10 million such devices are in use in this country.

She said the level of fibers given off by some models surpassed the level found in the homes of workers in asbestos plants. Many workers have come down with cancer 15 to 30 years after being exposed to high levels of asbestos dust. Recent research, however, indicates that the risk of cancer is increased at much lower exposure over shorter periods of time than those experienced by asbestos workers.

Asbestos does not pose a hazard with every product containing it. When it is completely sealed with an adhesive, there is no health risk. Even when it is not sealed, the degree of exposure may not be significant unless the product is used frequently.

Thompson's revelations caused intense activity at the Consumer Product Safety Commission, which has jurisdiction over most products containing it. In 1977, the agency had banned synthetic fireplace ash with breathable asbestos. After Thompson's report, the agency quickly got manufacturers to voluntarily recall hair dryers containing the substance and refund the purchase price. A complete list of more than 100 dryers with it can be obtained from the agency.

A year earlier, the Commission had received a report it had requested from Kearney Management Consultants listing more than 100 products containing asbestos, including hair dryers. The list included the following products:

Abrasive wheels, pipe joint sealant, acoustical ceiling tile, glue and epoxy adhesives, air conditioners, airduct joint sealing cement, aluminized cloth, aluminum roof coating, ammunition shell wadding, appliance wiring, aprons, arm protectors, cement pipe for water and sewer use, cement pipe airducts, ash trays, auto mufflers, auto undercoating, awnings, window display backgrounds, baking sheets, barbecue firebed materials, bearings, berets, blackboards, blankets, brake linings, buffing and polishing compounds, candle wicks, carpet underlays, catalytic heater mantles, ceramic and quarry floor tile cement, chalk boards, Christmas decorative snow, cigarette filters, cigarette lighter wicks, asbestos cloths and clothing, composition for lighting campfires and patching plywood, conveyor belts, electrical cord, corrugated roofing, curling irons, theater curtains, dehumidifying apparatus, diaphragms, dish towels, draperies, electric blankets, fiberglass polishing cloths, filler for shoe soles, auto emission filters, fireplace ash and logs, flashing cement, flower pots, garbage incinerators, gaskets, gloves, graphic paper, grinding wheels, hats, hair dryers, heating pads, ironing board pads and covers, potters kilns, lamp mantles, lamp sockets, latex paints, radiator covers, mailbags, metallic cloths, mittens, molded plastics, motion picture screens, packaging film, packing, padding for prisons, patching compounds, phenolic laminates, phonograph records, pipe coverings, plastic coverings, plastic shingles, plywood patch, polishing cloths, pot holders, pressure cooker gaskets, putty, radiator insulation, radiator sealant, ranges, resins, roof cement, roof coatings, roof patch, rope, sealants, siding, spackling, stains, stove linings for gas and electric, stove mats, tape joint cement, thermal insulation, vinyl tile, toasters, tooth brushes, television sets, twine, umbrellas, varnish, wallpaper, wicks, felt wipers and woven asbestos tape.

TOBACCO AND HEALTH

Fifteen years after its historic report describing the harmful effects of smoking, the U.S. Surgeon General released a new report which "overwhelmingly" supports many of his original findings. The 1979 report, *Smoking and Health,* provides new information dramatizing the dangers of cigarette smoking.

It calls smoking an expensive form of "slow-motion suicide," costing the American public $12 to $18 billion each year in health care expenses, lost productivity, wages and absenteeism due to smoking-related illnesses. Among the new findings are the following:

● The percentage of male smokers declined from 53 to 38 per cent between 1964 and 1978. During the same period, the number of female smokers remained almost constant at 30 per cent. Smoking among young women, especially teenagers, increased.

● The death rate from lung cancer for women nearly tripled since 1964. The ratio of male to female deaths from lung cancer declined by almost one-half.

● Cigarette smoking greatly increases the risk of heart attacks, strokes and circulatory problems for women using birth control pills. It is a major factor in heart attacks and sudden death for both men and women.

● Smoking during pregnancy slows the rate of fetal growth and increases the possibility of death of the fetus or newborn baby. It may lead to deficiencies in physical growth and intellectual and emotional development.

● Cigarette smoking causes lung damage even in the very young.

● The effects of smoking may be worse for minorities.

● The health risks of smoking increase for those exposed to toxic industrial substances.

● Smoking increases the risk of heart disease among those with hypertension and high levels of choesterol.

● Low tar and nicotine cigarettes appear safer, but other factors, including the number of cigarettes smoked per day and whether a smoker inhales, are important.

TAR AND NICOTINE IN CIGARETTES

Since 1967, the Federal Trade Commission (FTC) has been testing cigarettes for tar and nicotine content and publishing results for the benefit of smokers who wish to find brands with small amounts of these harmful ingredients.

Following are results of FTC testing for 167 brands as of May, 1978, the latest figures available. In 1979, the agency was preparing to test for carbon monoxide and did not publish its usual report. Figures are milligrams per cigarette.

TAR AND NICOTINE IN CIGARETTES

BRAND	TYPE	Tar (mg/cig)	Nicotine (mg/cig)
Alpine	king size, filter, menthol	14	0.8
Marlboro	king size, filter, menthol	14	0.8
Belair	king size, filter, menthol	15	0.9
Saratoga	120 mm, filter, (hard pack)	15	1.0
Eve 120's	120 mm, filter, menthol, (hard pack)	15	1.1
Kent	king size, filter, (hard pack)	15	1.0
Saratoga	120 mm, filter, menthol, (hard pack)	16	1.0
Pall Mall	100 mm, filter, menthol	16	1.2
Sano	reg. size, non-filter	16	0.5
Eve	100 mm, filter, menthol	16	1.0
Galaxy	king size, filter	16	1.0
DuMaurier	king size, filter, (hard pack)	16	1.1
Silva Thins	100 mm, filter, menthol	16	1.1
Raleigh	king size, filter	16	1.0
Virginia Slims	100 mm, filter, menthol	16	0.9
Virginia Slims	100 mm, filter	16	0.9
Tall	120 mm, filter, menthol	16	1.3
Eve	100 mm, filter	16	1.0
Long Johns	120 mm, filter, menthol	16	1.3
Silva Thins	100 mm, filter	16	1.2
Philip Morris International	100 mm, filter, menthol, (hard pack)	16	1.0
Viceroy	king size, filter	16	1.1
Salem	king size, filter, menthol	16	1.1
Kent	king size, filter	16	1.1
Old Gold Filters	king size, filter, (hard pack)	16	1.1
Belair	100 mm, filter, menthol	16	1.1
Tareyton	100 mm, filter	16	1.2
St. Moritz	100 mm, filter	16	1.1
Twist	100 mm, filter, lemon/menthol	17	1.3
L & M	king size, filter, (hard pack)	17	1.0
Tareyton	king size, filter	17	1.2
L & M	king size, filter	17	1.0
L & M	100 mm, filter	17	1.1
St. Moritz	100 mm, filter, menthol	17	1.1
Long Johns	120 mm, filter	17	1.3
Philip Morris International	100 mm, filter, (hard pack)	17	1.1
Kent	100 mm, filter, menthol	17	1.1
Max	120 mm, filter	17	1.3
Marlboro	king size, filter, (hard pack)	17	1.0
Benson & Hedges	king size, filter, (hard pack)	17	1.2
Marlboro	100 mm, filter, (hard pack)	17	1.1
Benson & Hedges 100's	100 mm, filter, menthol, (hard pack)	17	1.1
Kool	king size, filter, menthol	17	1.4
Raleigh	100 mm, filter	17	1.2
Newport	king size, filter, menthol, (hard pack)	17	1.2
Lark	king size, filter	17	1.1
Chesterfield	king size, filter	17	1.1
Chesterfield	101 mm, filter	17	1.2
Pall Mall	king size, filter	17	1.0
Benson & Hedges 100's	100 mm, filter, menthol	17	1.1
Benson & Hedges 100's	100 mm, filter, (hard pack)	17	1.0
Marlboro	king size, filter		

BRAND	TYPE	Tar (mg/cig)	Nicotine (mg/cig)
Max	120 mm, filter, menthol	17	1.3
Benson & Hedges 100's	100 mm, filter	17	1.1
Montclair	king size, filter, menthol	17	1.3
Tall	120 mm, filter	17	1.4
Salem	king size, filter, menthol, (hard pack)	18	1.2
Kool	king size, filter, menthol, (hard pack)	18	1.4
Marlboro	100 mm, filter	18	1.1
Viceroy	100 mm, filter	18	1.2
Newport	king size, filter, menthol	18	1.3
Kool	100 mm, filter, menthol	18	1.3
L & M	100 mm, filter, menthol	18	1.1
Old Gold Filters	king size, filter	18	1.2
Oasis	king size, filter, menthol	18	1.1
Kent	100 mm, filter	18	1.3
Pall Mall	100 mm, filter	19	1.4
Salem	100 mm, filter, menthol	19	1.3
Winston	100 mm, filter, menthol	19	1.3
Camel	king size, filter	19	1.3
Lark	100 mm, filter	19	1.2
L.T. Brown	120 mm, filter, menthol	19	1.4
Winston	king size, filter, (hard pack)	19	1.3
Newport	100 mm, filter, menthol	19	1.4
Winston	100 mm, filter	19	1.3
Spring 100's	100 mm, filter, menthol	20	1.1
Winston	king size, filter	20	1.3
Old Gold Straights	reg. size, non-filter	20	1.2
Phillip Morris	reg. size, non-filter	20	1.1
L.T. Brown	120 mm, filter	20	1.5
Kool	reg. size, non-filter	20	1.3
Home Run	reg. size, non-filter	21	1.5
Old Gold 100's	100 mm, filter	21	1.4
Chesterfield	reg. size, non-filter	23	1.3
Picayune	reg. size, non-filter	23	1.6
English Ovals	reg. size, non-filter, (hard pack)	23	1.6
More	120 mm, filter	23	1.7
More	120 mm, filter, menthol	23	1.7
Lucky Strike	reg. size, non-filter	24	1.4
Mapleton	king size, filter	24	1.4
Piedmont	reg. size, non-filter	24	1.4
Raleigh	king size, non-filter	24	1.4
Half & Half	king size, filter	24	1.5
Stratford	king size, filter	25	1.4
Old Gold Straights	king size, non-filter	25	1.5
Philip Morris Commander	king size, non-filter	25	1.4
Camel	reg. size, non-filter	25	1.6
Pall Mall	king size, non-filter	26	1.6
Mapleton	reg. size, non-filter	27	1.2
Stratford	king size, non-filter	28	1.1
Fatima	king size, non-filter	28	1.7
Chesterfield	king size, non-filter	28	1.7
Herbert Tareyton	king size, non-filter	29	1.8
Bull Durham	king size, filter	30	2.0
English Ovals	king size, non-filter, (hard pack)	30	2.1
Players	reg. size, non-filter, (hard pack)	35	2.5

Source: Federal Trade Commission

PEOPLE AND PESTICIDES
Are We Killing Ourselves With Protection?

Since man began farming land, he has used more and more powerful pesticides to control crop-destroying pests such as bugs, worms, birds, animals and fungi. As farms expanded in size and technology demanded greater efficiency, use of pesticides grew tremendously. More potent chemicals were developed every time a particular pest became resistant to previous deterrents.

Today, some of the most deadly poisons ever created are routinely sprayed on foods, forests, inner-city parks and gardens of millions of American homes. The United States has become the world's largest exporter of poisons, sending millions of pounds of highly sophisticated and deadly chemicals abroad, especially to underdeveloped, poorly educated Third World nations.

GOVERNMENT FAILS TO ENFORCE PESTICIDE LAWS

Meanwhile, regulation of pesticides by federal and state government has lagged. For many products, there is no enforcement at all. Proposed laws to keep pace with the changing needs have fallen by the wayside.

Federal regulation of pesticides started in earnest in 1972 with enactment of the Federal Environmental Pesticide Control Act. It mandated that the nation's giant pesticide industry be firmly in control by 1976.

But since enactment of the law, the following has happened:

● The number of pesticides known to cause cancer in humans has climbed to more than 100, with new disasters occurring more frequently.

● The number of pesticides that the Environmental Protection Agency (EPA) has been able to identify as killers and remove from the market totals only one: kepone, which received massive publicity about its effects on workers and residents in the town where it was manufactured.

● EPA officials admit they won't be able to finish testing the more than 30,000 existing pesticides for another decade or more, not counting the hundreds of new products that appear on the market without prior approval by the EPA.

But such facts pale in comparison to the findings released in February, 1978, by the General Accounting Office (GAO) in testimony before Congress. The GAO announced that harmful pesticides may be a larger part of our diet than most people ever thought — and that little can be done to reduce the hazards even by washing produce before eating, because the chemicals often penetrate far beyond the outer skin.

The GAO originally studied the EPA's pesticide control programs in 1975, when it released a study showing the agency's deficiencies in keeping points out of human food. In its 1978 testimony, the GAO revealed that few improvements had been made in the interim. By the time foods with excessive amounts of poisons have been identified, there is no way that the contaminated products can be located and removed from sale, since the products have usually been purchased and consumed.

Part of the problem is that agencies responsible for detecting illegal amounts of pesticides on consumer products — primarily the EPA and the Food and Drug Administration — do not even test foods for a substantial number of pesticides on a regular basis. When the EPA establishes safe human tolerance levels for pesticide residues, according to the GAO, it does so without sufficient test data. And the agencies fail to tell many pesticide manufacturers to submit missing or better data in order to establish their products' safety.

The latest survey of pesticide residues in food (*Total Diet Studies* for Fiscal 1974, published in 1977 by the Food and Drug Administration) shows a wide variety of highly toxic substances present in increasing quantities of the American diet. However, amounts average below Acceptable Daily Intake (ADI) levels where such standards exists. ADIs have been established only for aldrin and dieldrin, DDT compounds, heptachlor, diazinon, malathion, lindane, parathion and carbaryl. No one knows whether the ADIs have been set at proper levels to protect human health in the long term.

The diet studies sample 117 food items for a typical "market basket" in various regions of the country. Foods are washed and cooked, where appropriate, before being tested, so that many harmful substances are removed before analysis.

Figures for fiscal 1974 show a continued decline in DDT-related compounds due to the 1970 ban. Dieldrin was the most frequently occuring pesticide, appearing especially in dairy and meat products. Levels increased by 10 per cent in one year. Amounts of heptachlor epoxide, also found mostly in dairy and meat products, doubled. Other pesticides that increased in food in one year included BHC, methoxychlor, ronnel, parthane, thiodane, lead, zinc, arsenic, selenium, toxaphene, carbaryl, aldrin and phosalane.

U.S. MAJOR EXPORTER OF CARCINOGENS

In light of such findings, it became apparent that the U.S. has become a major exporter of cancer and other diseases through its $7 billion annual global sales of pesticides. Among manufacturers are some of the country's best-known industrial giants: Dow Chemical, Eli Lilly, DuPont, Monsanto, Shell and Chevron. Many pesticides banned for use in the U.S. are sold freely over seas, including large amounts to underdeveloped countries in South America and Africa.

At the same time, many pesticides are losing their effectiveness as insects and weeds create super strains that are resistant to the poisons. One example is the boll weevil which likes to munch its way through cotton fields in the South. In the 1950s, DDT was found to be an effective eradicater of these pests. Even before DDT was banned, boll weevils had become invincible to DDT. More potent pesticides were found to be effective. In the late 1960s a new strain of the budworm — a caterpillar which feeds on the buds of plants — was found to resist every known pesticide. Some farmers began spraying their fields more than 35 times in attempts to eradicate them. Farmers lost up to 25 per cent of their crops.

"Pesticide" is a general term for any material used to kill "pests." Pesticides include insecticides (to kill insects), herbicides (to kill weeds), fungicides (to kill fungi, such as molds, rust, etc.), and rodenticides (to kill mice, rats, etc.).

The objective of pesticide use should be to reduce the population of the organism below the threshold at which it achieves pest status, not just to kill bugs. The same rule applies to weeds, which are plants that grow where they are not wanted.

All pesticides damage wildlife. All pesticides have a broad spectrum of activity and can affect beneficial plants and animals as well as pests. Insecticides reduce the food supply for insect-eating birds and mammals. They also kill predators and parasites which form part of natural control systems. Their use often promotes resurgence of the target pest or outbreaks of new pests. Herbicides eliminate plants on which beneficial animals may depend. They also kill nontarget plants, and weeds are often the first plants to regrow on the treated site.

GENERAL RECOMMENDATIONS

● Do not use combinations of pesticides. Do not buy insecticide mixtures, insecticides in herbicides or fertilizers containing either insecticides or herbicides.

● **Be aware of unsafe products.** The following pesticides are not illegal for use in home and gardens: aldrin, dieldrin, DDT, DDD, heptachlor, chlordane (except when used underground against termites), 2,4,5-T (liquid and powder), Compound 1080 (fluoroacetate) and thallium sulfate.

Other pesticides still registered for home and garden use but posing health hazards include lindane, amitrol, captan, zineb, maneb, pentachlorophenol and DDVP (Vapona).

Pesticides whose labels display the word "danger" and a skull and crossbones are too hazardous to handle without special equipment.

If you have stocks of any of the above, dispose of them carefully. Bury them deep in the ground or send them to a well operated landfill. *Do not discard them in open dumps, burn them or pour them down the toilet.* If you have no safe way to dispose of them, return them to the store where you bought them.

● **Pregnant women should avoid contact with all chemicals.** They may be harmful or deadly to both the fetus and mother. Particularly dangerous chemicals include 2,4,5-T, silvex, 2,4-D, captan, folpet, carbaryl (Sevin) and fungicides containing mercury compounds.

● **Pesticides remain harmful for years after use.** Chlordane, heptachlor, DDT, aldrin and dieldrin persist for many years in soil. Do not grow vegetables near buildings or in plots previously used as lawns, unless you know these chemicals have not been used in the preceding decade.

● **Herbicides** — Use sparingly. Apply to target plants only and do not broadcast over lawns. For poison ivy, cut the stems close to the ground and apply Ammate or 2,4-D on and around the cut stems. Crabgrass can be controlled by managing the height of the surrounding plants and by building a tight turf. Picloram (Tordon) is effective in controlling woody plants but is long-lasting and must be used with great care. Never use 2,4,5-T or silvex.

● **Rodenticides** — Use warfarin. Baits containing arsenic, phosphorus or zinc phosphide pose a hazard to children and should never be used (except, perhaps, in locked bait boxes).

● **Fungicides** — Do not use compounds of mercury or cadmium. The commonest fungicide on hardware store shelves, captan, poses a health hazard and should be used only with extreme caution. Some of the oldest fungicides, such as Bordeaux mixture, are still among the best.

● **Systemics** — Almost nothing is known of the secondary poisoning effects of chemicals injected or absorbed into plants to protect against insect attacks. For some trees and shrubs, however, it is probably acceptable to use Meta-Systox or dimethoate (Cygon), but handle with great care.

SAFE WAYS TO ELIMINATE PESTS

Household Pests. Cleanliness is the best safeguard against household pests.

Ants rarely need controlling. Do not use "ant traps" or chlordane. If **ants** or **silverfish** pose a genuine problem, try desiccant powders (Dri-Die, SG-67, or Perma-Guard). **Weevils** in food cannot be controlled safely, so keep flour, cereals, etc., in sealed containers or in a refrigerator. **Cockroaches** are often resistant to pesticides. Try boric acid or borax powder and pyrethrin sprays. For **houseflies** use window screens, flypaper and a flyswatter. Pyrethrins are the safest pesticides for general indoor use, but frequent use of sprays should be avoided.

Do not use DDVP (Vapona, No-Pest-Strip, etc.). Use of No-Pest-Strips is illegal in sickrooms and places where food is prepared. Do not patronize restaurants, delicatessens or meat counters where they are used. Report such illegal use to the regional office of the U.S. Environmental Protection Agency.

For **moths,** use mothballs only inside closed garment bags; naphthalene is preferable to paradichlorobenzene. Do not wear commercially mothproofed garments.

TOXIC PLANTS
Poison for Toddlers and Health Food Buyers

The craze for household plants has caused an "alarming" growth of poisonings, especially to small children, according to the National Poison Center Network. Dr. Richard Moriarty, a pediatrician who directs the Network, says the problem arises mostly with infants who are prone to put everything in their mouths. Few parents apparently realize the number of plants that can cause everyday health problems if ingested.

"So far," says Moriarty, "plant ingestions by infants have caused few serious health problems." But he sees a dangerous trend. In six months, he says, there were over 3,500 cases of plant exposures in children five years old and younger. Nearly one-half of these cases involved children under the age of one. In nearly 100 per cent of the cases, the child had eaten the leaf of the plant.

Moriarty suggests that people with young children keep plants out of their reach. He urges parents also to learn the names of plants and mark the containers; then, if an accident happens, call the nearest Poison Center.

FREE LIST OF HAZARDS AVAILABLE

To help plant owners learn which plants are poisonous, the Network has prepared a bulletin which is available for 50 cents from NPON, 125 De Soto St., Pittsburgh, PA., 15213. The bulletin lists 38 cultivated plants, from caladium, which can cause intense irritation to mucous membranes, to rhubarb leaves, which can erode the gastrointestinal tract.

It also lists 12 wild plants, from jack-in-the-pulpit, which can cause similar problems, to altropa belladonna (deadly nightshade) which can cause fever, visual disturbances, burning of the mouth, headache, dry skin, thirst and confusion.

Other cultivated plants that are toxic if certain parts are taken into the mouth, include the castor bean plant, lantana, hens-and-chicks, bunchberry, English ivy, foxglove, rhododendron, azalea, crowfoot, delphinium, hydrangea, lily of the valley, sweet pea, morning glory, hyacinth, iris, ligustrum, narcissus, daffodil, jonquil, bird-of-paradise, wisteria, oleander, japanese yew, choke cherry and daphne.

PESTICIDE RESIDUES ON FLOWERS

High levels of pesticides have been found on cut flowers imported to this country, according to a report in the American Journal of Public Health for January, 1979. Tests made on carnations, pompon chrysanthemums and standard chrysanthemums showed concentrations of organophospate pesticides of as much as 4,750 parts per million, enough to cause illness from skin contact.

Eighty-five per cent of samples tested had at least some pesticide residues. The pesticides found most frequently were endosulfan, a chlorinated hydrocarbon, and diazinon and phosphamidon, both organophosphates. The highest concentrations were recorded for monochrotophos.

The poisonous substances include alkaloids, glycosides, oxalates, resins and phytotoxins. They may be in root, stem, leaf or fruit. Details about what symptoms to look for and the recommended treatment are contained in the bulletin.

HEALTH FOOD PLANTS ALSO CAN BE DANGEROUS

Many plants and plant products sold in health food stores can also be dangerous, according to a report in the April 6, 1979, Medical Letter, which evaluates drugs and therapeutics for physicians.

Examples of hazards cited by the letter include:

● Licorice root. In large amounts, it can cause salt and water retention, hypokalemia, hypertension, heart failure and cardiac arrest.

● Sassafras root bark. It contains sassafras oil that is at least 70 per cent safrole, which is toxic to the liver and is carcinogenic to animals.

● Indian tobacco. When smoked or used in tea, its lobeline stimulant in large doses can cause sweating, vomiting, paralysis, coma and death.

● Seeds or pits, bark and leaves of apricot, bitter almond, cassava beans, cherry, choke cherry, peach, pear, apple and plum contain cyanogenetic glycoside amygdalin, which after ingestion can liberate hydrogen cyanide sometimes in sufficient quantity to cause death.

● Nutmeg. In very high doses, this hallucinogen can cause liver damage and death; in fairly small amounts, it can cause severe headache, cramps and nausea.

● Diuretic teas made from juniper berries can irritate the stomach and intestines.

● Herbal teas from buckthorn bark and senna leaves can cause severe diarrhea; also teas made from dock roots and aloe leaves.

● Ginseng, a popular remedy, which contains estrogens in small amounts can cause swollen and painful breasts.

GETTING YOUR MONEY BACK
For Hazardous Products

If you have purchased a product that has been banned as a hazardous product by the Consumer Product Safety Commission, you can return it to the retailer and get your money back.

Federal regulations require the retailer not only to buy it back but to pay for any "reasonable and necessary" expenses incurred in returning it.

Index